IT

As well as editing a number of dictionaries – of slang, jargon and quotations – and assembling two previous oral histories – on the Sixties 'underground' and on immigrants to the UK – Jonathon Green has posed as 'Simon Viridian' to edit the letters page of *Fiesta* magazine and as 'Angie Heath' for the composition of his sole work of fiction: *Diary of a Masseuse.*

by the same author

The Dictionary of Jargon
The Slang Thesaurus
The Cynic's Lexicon
The Dictionary of Contemporary Slang
The Dictionary of Contemporary Quotations

Days in the Life: Voices from the English Underground
      1961–1971
Them: Voices from the Immigrant Community
      in Contemporary Britain

IT

Sex Since The Sixties

JONATHON GREEN

Secker & Warburg
London

First published in Great Britain 1993
by Martin Secker & Warburg Limited,
an imprint of Reed Consumer Books Limited,
Michelin House, 81 Fulham Road, London SW3 6RB
and Auckland, Melbourne, Singapore and Toronto

A CIP catalogue record for this book is
available from the British Library
Hardback edition ISBN 0 436 20046 5
Paperback edition ISBN 0 436 20156 9

Typeset by Saxon Graphics Ltd, Derby.
Printed in England by Clays Ltd, St Ives plc

Life can little more supply
Than just a few good fucks, and then we die.

Thomas Potter, attrib., John Wilkes MP
'The Essay on Woman' (1763)

Contents

Acknowledgements

As well as all those who with great generosity gave me their time and allowed me to ask them questions which they might not normally choose to address, I must thank a number of those who, as it were, pandered to my needs with research, introductions and tables across which to converse. Notably Sarah Oliver, Simon Prosser and Katie Owen, and Sarah West. Many of those interviewed also offered what turned out to be useful suggestions for new contacts, and to them too I am duly grateful.

Thanks also to Heather Laughton, who transcribed a number of tapes, to Lesley Bryce, copy-editor at Secker and Warburg, and as ever to my editor Dan Franklin.

JG

Introduction

I.

There has been, as innumerable media pundits, outrageds of Chigwell and a wide range of self-proclaimed experts will attest, a vast revolution in our experience and our perception of sex in the last three or four decades. Sexual intercourse, as Philip Larkin put it, began in 1963, somewhere, he added, between the freeing for public consumption of D. H. Lawrence's once-risqué novel *Lady Chatterley's Lover* and the release of the first album by The Beatles, icons of a quite different brand of rebellion. Thirty years after 'the Chatterley ban' (and coincidentally thirty years since the introduction of the contraceptive pill) one may argue with the chronology of Larkin's lines but his point remains. In 1963 or at some other date the sexual landscape did change, and has continued to change ever since.

As we move through the Nineties, and the year 2000 beckons all too close beyond, it seems valid enough to wonder as to the future. Are we looking at a reprise of the final decade of the nineteenth century – a mix of 'naughty Nineties' chauvinist masculinity and *fin de siècle Yellow Book* decadence? Or will the millenarianism such decades inspire, grimly underlined by the unavoidable presence of AIDS, lead us in a different direction; to celibacy, the very epitome of 'safe sex'. The answer seems to be that the new decade sees us confused, open to suggestion. The old battles may seem to have been won, but we live by progress, and turning back is equivalent to defeat. History, despite the proclamations of some utopian illusionists, has not ended. The calendar is an arbitrary thing, and the end of a century does not provide some neatly finite punctuation. If it's true of history, then it's true of sex – as essential an aspect as any of the forces that drive events along.

Up till now the obvious changes have been dramatic, 'sexy' in not just the literal but in the media sense. As successive recreations of the

1

prevailing and lovingly publicised 'youth culture' follow each other, the tabloids and television documentaries have been close to hand, charting the lurid frissons of the 'love generation' of the Sixties, the bisexual chic of the glitzy Seventies, and the hard edge of punk coupling, all torn fishnets and bondage accessories. The Eighties, when sexual freedoms were supposedly suffering the limitations of a new and terrifying sexually transmitted disease, offered some restraint, though 'safe sex' too is good for its own especial mileage.

The revolution has not, of course, been restricted to the ephemeral, if alluring posturings of the young and the trendy. The changes in sexual life have permeated every area of society. World War II, like its predecessor, loosened up moral attitudes. The immediate post-war years produced a corrective backlash to what some saw as moral laxity, but austerity was an economic phenomenon, not a sexual one. Still, the Fifties remain a shrouded era, somewhat ambivalent with their mix of 'Never had it so good' / 'Live now pay later' vulgarity on the one hand, and a determined effort by 'society' and by what in 1955 had been christened the 'Establishment' to maintain the status quo. Certainly that same status quo condoned a good deal of sexual fun and games among that same Establishment, but, as laid down by the rulers of the nanny state, such pleasures were definitely listed as *pas devant les enfants*. The masses, reproduce though they might, were considered overly delicate for too great a knowledge of their masters' (and mistresses') vices.

Larkin's 'Annus Mirabilis' is as good a turning point as any although his verses fail to mention the truly pivotal event of that year: the Profumo Affair. The Tory grandee Quintin Hogg may have dismissed it as a squalid affair 'between a woman of easy virtue and a proven liar', but this was Establishment bluster. Some chroniclers might, of course, prefer 1959, when Parliament passed the first Obscene Publications Act since 1857, an event that heralded the 'end of the Chatterley ban' (after a trial that paraded a great deal more bluster, from both conservative and liberal establishments) and much more besides. The point of both dates, or any other moment in the period to which one might attach the onset of more open sexuality, is that what was happening was that sex (heterosexual first, gay somewhat later) was entering public life. It was something to do with rock 'n' roll, something to do with pop (both art and culture), something to do with the pill, with a spate of liberal new laws – on abortion, on homosexuality, on capital punishment – and something above all to do with the cult of youth. A good deal was illusory, but that didn't matter. The media defined the era and the media said London (and the rest of the country) was swinging. That was sufficient.

2

Sex in the Sixties was almost wholly a male phenomenon. The women's movement, apostrophised as 'bra-burners', was emerging, but that was later. 'Do it to me now,' murmured girls called Pussy, and a million James Bond clones breathed a little more heavily. The so-called counter-culture was as macho as the James Bond fantasists. 'The only position for women in the revolution,' said black power activist Stokeley Carmichael, 'is prone.' In the end the much touted 'sexual revolution' was shorthand for male self-indulgence.

If the advent of feminism and, shortly afterwards, the parallel movement for gay liberation didn't completely destroy the macho merry-go-round, it certainly concentrated minds – both male and female – on radical new attitudes to sex. The Seventies saw separatist lesbians, unclosetted homosexuals, bisexual chic, every variety of what Norman Mailer had termed the 'polymorphous perverse'. Sexual politics, a concept unknown before the late Sixties, took centre stage and has remained there ever since. Whether through feminism or gay liberation, traditional attitudes to sexual roles have been, if by no means completely jettisoned, then put under the microscope of re-analysis. The first of the great modern 'isms' – sexism – permeates our daily discourse.

All of which, for all that it bears substantially on the present, essentially reflects the past. In many ways the twentieth century has echoed its predecessor. As author Peter Gay put it in *The Bourgeois Experience* (1984) there was 'a broad band of far-reaching cultural shifts between, for the most part, the 1850s and 1890s. In those decades, patterns of courtship and ideals of education, fears about masturbation and notions about corporal punishment, portrayals of women and tastes in architecture, and many other cultural traits were transformed, sometimes imperceptibly and sometimes out of all recognition.'

Looking back on the past four decades, substituting '19' for '18', the picture seems very familiar. As we move into the Nineties all the options seem to be open, although whether our Nineties will produce a pioneer of sexual knowledge to rival Freud, the dominant figure of Gay's massive work, remains to be seen. In the meantime, we can consider what is going on. The inevitable millenarianism, epitomised by the current concerns with the environment, is bound to extend into sex. If one looks back at the turn of the last century, one can see this same mix of decadence and puritanism. Our Nineties are already producing much the same emotions in the sexual arena. As we approach the year 2000 the precise role of sex remains fluid and capable of contradictory assumptions. It's quite possible to state that many if not all of the changes listed above have, if not exactly failed

3

to deliver, then proved less simplistic, less black and white, less 'goodies vs. baddies' than their original champions might have hoped.

Feminism, in its mass market version, led to the power-dressed career girl of the Eighties – as much a fashion statement as sociological one. Her counterpart, the 'New Man', with his tears, his Fair Isle sweaters and his hands full of Pampers, is more a staple of bad sitcom than of real life. Hardcore feminism remains a niche interest, as reviled and mocked as ever it was, its devotees still determined on separate development. The facts may proclaim otherwise, and AIDS may be spreading inexorably into the heterosexual population, but what the tabloids mischievously corralled as a 'gay plague' is still seen by a majority of the 'straight' population as a strictly homosexual problem, and, as those same tabloids are happy to imply, the logical progression of all that vaunted 'liberation'. Indeed, the subtext is clear: the wretched queers deserve everything that's happened.

In the same way we're giving and receiving contradictory messages when it comes to the discussion and display of sex. Censorship as such is primarily a cultural rather than a sexual issue, but its shifting role is germane to this discussion. Certainly some of the constraints that hedged our attitudes to sex have been cast off. The puritan tradition that has informed the British treatment of sex has been, if not vanquished, then certainly eroded. Censorship, that standby of any authority that seeks to mask its self-interested repression as concern for the supposedly 'innocent', was for a while placed under as radical a siege as once it levelled at allegedly 'dangerous' works of art and literature. It's more than twenty years since Kenneth Tynan asked rhetorically of a BBC2 audience whether 'any intelligent person' would really find the public use of the word 'fuck' that terrifying, and if the 'f-word' still raises more timorous hackles, the language, and its users are a little less easily bruised – for all that Mrs Whitehouse and her supporters can (and enthusiastically will) draw a direct line from the odd obscenity to the decline and fall of the British, if not the Roman Empire.

Yet the moral high ground is once more under siege from the censorious. The BBC can transmit the once notorious *Lady Chatterley's Lover* as a 'book at a bedtime', as it has also broadcast Radcliffe Hall's lesbian novel *The Well of Loneliness*, with nary a complaint, but the Broadcasting Standards Council lurks in the background, alert for anything it considers excessive. The Obscene Publications Act is to be extended to cover television, even if satellite TV will prove no respecter of local puritanism. Scotland Yard's Obscene Publications Squad, a unit formerly best known for its

4

obeisance to the lucrative kickbacks of those same villains whom it pretended to pursue, has now laid its favours unashamedly at the feet of another interest group: the fundamentalists of the pro-censorship lobby. And once more, under the guise of 'morality', authority, typified by the prosecution of the gay sado-masochists in the 'Operation Spanner' trial, is seeking to interfere not just in public but in private sexuality.

On the other hand, the 'bonking bimbo', who might once have been seen as the personification of moral decline, has become in her way, a culture heroine, albeit on or around Page 3. Her predecessors in the Profumo scandal of 1963 brought down a government; the best she can expect these days is a guest spot in the *Sun* or perhaps in a libel court, where her exploits will be merely one more verse of a prurient litany that includes the schoolboy seductions of noted members of the Establishment, the 'fragrance' of their wives and the frequency of their nightly potency. Though even she, nipples pert and suspenders taut, is strangely, safely asexual. Her mum has probably forwarded her pictures to the papers. It's all very wholesome cheesecake.

The nineteenth century is celebrated for its uxoriousness, whether accurately or otherwise. Baroness Thatcher's paeans to 'Victorian values', while characteristically notable for their studied rejection of the facts, were never more strident than as regards such bygone sexuality. The family, trumpeted as society's bottom line, still exists, but its mean is neither nuclear nor even in many cases two-parent. Marriage – once the bedrock of legitimate sexual relationships – no longer occupies the central position of biblical injunction. An increasing percentage of couples choose not to sanctify their vows either through religion or even with the secular blessing of the registry office. Those that do are more than ever likely to divorce.

Some Victorian values, however, are on the up. Celibacy, whether chosen through fear of disease or simply through a calculated statement *vis-à-vis* one's need or lack of need for sex, has become, if not yet fashionable, then acceptable to an extent that it could not have been ten or, more so, twenty years ago. In a way that would have been unthinkable in the early Seventies the orgasm has lost its position as the holy grail.

And there is that other Victorian preoccupation: sex crimes. It is not simply a matter of a recurrence of the old cliché of the respectable family man, on the one hand domestic paterfamilias, on the other a regular client of the country's teeming population of underage 'unfortunates'. Even if the 'awayday' girls of the provinces and the prostitutes flocking once more to London's street corners attest to the same kind of economic pressures that drove so many to whoredom a

5

century and more ago. In any case, hypocrisy is not a crime, nor is prostitution what we mean by 'sex crime'. Far more striking is the contemporary recurrence of those crimes of exploitation and sexual violence that provided the underside of the Victorian era. Rape, incest, child abuse are all on regular and distressing display. It cannot simply be that, as meliorists would have it, such crimes are only now being reported rather than covered up. That very willingness to disclose and discuss such topics, repellent and distressing though they may be, in itself attests to a radically changed attitude to sexual topics.

All of which leaves us divided between two poles. At the same time we are infinitely franker and, for all the strictures of the repressive, less easily shocked (or perhaps less automatically hypocritical), while we seem to be running more scared of sex than ever. In this essentially godless age we no longer fear moral retribution (hellfire has few terrors in the age of Auschwitz and 'ethnic cleansing') but physical. AIDS has taken over the devil's role, and become in itself the catalyst for the whole range of prejudices and pretensions through which every interested party can rehearse the arguments of the last thirty years. Abortion, censorship, gay rights, divorce and single parenthood are all up for grabs once more and after fourteen years of right-wing government, the backlash to what is codified as 'the Sixties' mentality' attracts a substantial constituency.

As I assembled the interviews that make up this book we were regaled variously with the misadventures of David Mellor's penis, Frank Bough's bottom and the Duchess of York's breasts. And above them all the progress of the national sex symbol, the hapless Princess of Wales, forever oscillating in the mass consciousness between her archetypal, contradictory roles: the Madonna and the whore. The reactions to all these, and a score of lesser peccadilloes, swung between fascination and fear, prurience and voyeurism. National characteristics are a dubious turf, but in these attitudes to sex Britain does have a certain homegrown style, fundamentally unchanging, perhaps the most genuinely enduring of those otherwise opaque 'Victorian values'.

II.

Sex, as John Lydon, then Johnny Rotten, once suggested, 'is two minutes, fifty-two seconds of squishing noises.' A satisfactorily candid remark, given that the prevailing culture demands a somewhat more impressive staying power from its performers, but more important, a pragmatic one. Nothing, after all, attracts discussion like sex. It's been mythologised half to death, shrouded in contemporary mysteries, girt

6

about with conflicting ideologies. But stripped of such refinements, what you still have in the end is what Anthony Burgess once termed, 'the old in-out'. And in all the interviews that follow, coming as they do from varied and often contradictary standpoints, I find nothing to disabuse me of that thesis. Much gilding of the lily, of course, a wealth of embellishments and obfuscations, theorising and mystification, but in the end: sex remains simply sex.

Nor is this book an ideological tract. As readers will find, a number of axes are duly ground, but there is no party line, there are no declared winners. Nor, again, do I espouse the tiniest vestige of political correctness. PC, that flesh-and-blood embodiment of what in *Nineteen Eighty-four* George Orwell termed 'duckspeak' – the quacking out by the otherwise less-than-articulate of the comforting rhetoric of ideological purity – is possibly the saddest of supposedly intellectual contemporary phenomena. For those who see such impedimenta as vital to their cultural perspective, I can offer only disappointment. This book, I am delighted to attest, has no such credentials. 'The best lack all conviction, while the worst / Are full of passionate intensity,' said Yeats in 'The Second Coming'. I leave such 'passionate intensity' to others.

Not everyone, of course, wishes to talk about sex and, without in any way wishing to criticise those who were happy to face my microphone, those who do are often by nature exhibitionists. Indeed, a number of interviewees admitted to just such a pleasure – albeit verbal rather than physical flashing. My point, therefore, is that in no way would I claim what follows is an exhaustive cross-section of every aspect of sex since the Sixties. I have tried, as it were, to cover the revelatory waterfront, but there are thirty or so million stories in this particular naked city and I have essayed but eighty of them. That said, I would like to feel that most readers can find something here that reflects perhaps a little of their own experience.

One point that will be noted is that in stark contrast to many topics, sex seems to elicit a far more articulate response from women than from men. Thus their preponderance here. It may be, of course, that as some auricular alternative to the traditional voyeur – an *oreilleur* perhaps – I simply enjoy listening to such memoirs: a 'tape freak' as the professionals might term it, but I plead simpler motives. For all the alleged cameraderie of the bar and the changing room, few men seem genuinely comfortable in true confessions mode.

Looking down the list of interviewees, self-defined exhibitionists or otherwise, there is an inescapable paradox here: a large proportion opted for pseudonymity. Of all the revelations up against which I brushed this in many ways was the most surprising. On the whole those concerned pleaded external pressure: family, jobs, partners, children. I've been more than happy to oblige, however much I, and often those concerned, regret the necessity. As for myself, I stand four-square behind the prerogative of the auctorial harlot: overweening power without the slightest personal revelatory responsibility.

When I first proposed this book, the third in an entirely unconnected series that began with *Days In the Life* (on the hippie Sixties) and moved on to *Them* (on first generation immigrants), it was as much intended as a pointer to the sexual future as to a history, however cursory, of its past. As it turned out, the past and the developments it has engendered seem to have taken over. We are still, as one of my younger interviewees pointed out, living in the shadow of the Sixties. The advances of that decade were by no means unique, nor can they be isolated from what preceded them nor what has followed, but where they seem to attain their greater resonance is in their acceleration. However one views the period – as a scapegoat for all that followed, as a tedious refuge for the nostalgic middle-aged, or as a nirvana that has long since been lost – those years were dense with change. The twenty years that have followed have in many represented the unravelling and dilution of the forces that emerged pell-mell.

If *It* reveals anything it is perhaps no more than the fact that in sex there are no absolutes. However much the ideologues of whatever persuasion may prate, sex is the most personal, the most idiosyncratic of phenomena. 'The what should be never did exist, but people keep trying to live up to it. There is no "what should be", there is only what is.' Thus the late American comedian Lenny Bruce. And nowhere is he so apposite: if anything emerges from these interviews it is that in sex there really is no what should be, there is only what is. And it is the infinite variety of those many versions of 'what is' that makes it all so fascinating. In the end, by the standards of those who shelter behind some fantasy of 'normality', we're all warped; but as my final interviewee points out, in a line that should ring universally true: when it comes to sex, that's the only thing that counts.

Jonathon Green
December 1992

The Sixties

'The Sixties', as widely celebrated, is chronology as pure myth. Everything in the myth pertains to sex: the era's landmark legislation, which other than that which ended capital punishment, underpinned newly liberal attitudes to the sexual arena, ranging through divorce, abortion, homosexuality and censorship; the medical advances, notably the contraceptive pill that freed women in a way that was hitherto unimaginable; the twin fantasies of 'swinging London', where rock stars and James Bond wannabees mingled in 'groovy' discos, and the 'alternative society' with its clarion cries of 'love and peace' and 'dope, revolution and fucking in the streets'. Everything turned on sex. The real revolution would not emerge until the Seventies, a harder-edged phenomenon, shorn of the glossiness of the previous decade, but if in Marxist terms the struggles of the Seventies can be seen as the true, proletarian uprising, then the Sixties were their necessary bourgeois front-runner.
The keynote of Sixties' sex is democratisation: there was nothing particularly new – the aristocracy, the rich had always indulged promiscuously in sex and drugs – but for the first time such pleasures were on offer to all comers. Or at least, to those sections of the articulate, and mainly middle-class young, for whom economic security had given freedoms barely conceivable even a decade earlier, and certainly beyond the dreams of their parents' generation.

JEFFREY WEEKS: What happened in the Sixties was very much a cultural burst amongst certain sections of the population. It came at a moment when space was opening up in all sorts of areas because of economic and demographic changes and because of the breakdown of old absolutist traditional ways of doing things. Certain spaces were created, both legal and cultural, which people took advantage of.

There were, essentially, two strands at work: the practical and cultural, and of these the former can be summed up in a single word: the Pill. The contraceptive pill, tradenamed Enovid, had been launched in America in spring 1960; its progress across the Atlantic was swift. Being England, of course, its availability was hedged about with caveats, although few determined girls seemed to have that much problem in getting the necessary prescription.

MARGARET RAMAGE: You couldn't go on the Pill unless you had a wedding date, though about '67 or '68 that changed. The clinics would ask you for the wedding date. You could bypass it by telling lies. But our parents taught us discipline, obedience, to ask no questions – not a healthy way to bring children up. But it did mean you were too intimidated to lie about your wedding arrangements.

TIM WOODWARD: As a kid, you were supposed to ask girls if they'd like to have sex with you, and they were supposed to say, 'No,' and you were supposed to say: 'Oh go on,' and if you really asked nicely they might say: 'Oh well, I suppose I could.' Then the Sixties came along and the Pill and girls came up to you and said: 'Fancy a shag, big boy?' Women came out of the closet and stopped pretending to be little dinky flowers and started being sort of the same as men.

Physiologically at least, the Pill – before its medical downsides began to emerge – was an unrivalled boon for women; psychologically, however, the benefits very much accrued to men.

CLARE CAMPBELL: People felt that they hadn't an excuse for saying no. They hadn't the right any more. They couldn't say, 'I might get pregnant,' because there was the Pill. And everybody else was doing it. So I did sleep with more people in the Sixties than I would have done in the Fifties. There was this feeling that everyone was having sex.

All of which was grist to the mill of hippie ideology. It wasn't just a matter of intoning, 'Make love not war', but doing one's best to live out a life of which the leitmotif was 'I am therefore I fuck'. For the alternative society the Pill gave the old double standards a new twist: it wasn't the 'bad' girls who slept around, it was the repressed, 'straight' ones who didn't. And if Don Juan now threw in the odd reference to smashing the state, then so be it.

10

MATTHEW RUSSELL: What we were doing was what would be called the sexual revolution, but with hindsight it was fantastically naive and innocent. At the time one generally believed that this was changing the world, that if you fucked the girl that you rather fancied with the big tits next door in Kathmandu Valley on Buddha's birthday then that actually was going to make nuclear bombs disintegrate. You really thought that. It was naive but it was an innocent and quite healthy exploration of sexuality. As far as Revolution with a big R goes, I don't think things were any different: there was still the same sort of jealousies and fucked-up-ness and all the rest of it. And for me it was still basically candy-shop stuff, one day you're at public school then suddenly there are all these American chicks who would fuck you. There was a lot of this belief that if you took your knickers off you'd smash the state. I remember going to see Richard Neville, one of the editors of *OZ*, in some film doing it with his girlfriend. I took a girlfriend along in the hope that it might persuade her to sleep with me – it was a useful role model – but she didn't.

NETTIE POLLARD: People like Richard Neville thought one ought to have sex – any woman worth anything should go to bed with him. That may be unfair to him. But the prevailing male attitude certainly was: 'You're not liberated unless you have sex with me.'

HAZEL SLAVIN: There was a sexual revolution for women in terms of the freedom from the fear of pregnancy. It wasn't revolutionary in terms of women's own sexuality, but there was certainly a revolution in sexual behaviour. Women were able to have penetrative sex without fear of getting pregnant, or less fear of it.

LYN PROCTOR: The whole business of free love – most of the people I knew were far too young, far too emotionally involved with all their relationships to be able to detach themselves sufficiently for real 'free love'. Everybody believed it in theory but in practice it wasn't happening. Because for most nineteen- and twenty-year-olds every-thing is emotion and free love doesn't really happen like that. When people get older it does happen. I was involved in a theatre group and the people running it – older men – were very keen on proposing the idea of a free and loving relationship between themselves and all the women in the group. That was very typical of the era. The sexual revolution worked very well for these older men who used it to get young women into bed. Boy, did it work.

11

AVEDON CARROLL: I was sixteen in December '67. I'd been hanging out for a year, going to demos. The long hair, flowered shirts, military jackets – wonderful. Thin guys with long hair have always been my thing. They were beautiful, and there were so many of them – how to choose? Of course monogamy was all we'd ever heard of. You weren't even supposed to get involved with more than one guy in your life. But here were all these beautiful guys, and you didn't know how to pick one. Well, you can't pick one, you have to wait for them to pick you.

Up to when I was twenty-one it seemed I couldn't turn around without a guy hitting on me. They never seemed to get the message, whatever I said. You'd try simple biological analogies: sometimes you've had too much to eat, sometimes you're not hungry, sometimes you're hungry but you don't want fish. They didn't understand why you didn't want to fuck them, and they'd sit there for hours trying to make you. You just didn't say: 'I'd rather fuck an egg.' Why not? Two reasons: (1) women are supposed to be nice to men, and (2) you get them mad, they'll kill you. You know instinctively, you don't get a guy too mad. Making them mad is something *you* do. So you don't do it. All that was enraging, but we didn't become feminists because we were sick of the sexual revolution. It seems like that, but the sexual revolution wasn't the problem – the truth was that we embraced it avidly, we wanted a sexual revolution. The problem wasn't that they were abandoning middle-class hang-ups and making us abandon ours. The problem was they weren't abandoning their hang-ups enough.

> *However much the giddier evangelists might protest, the Sixties, and all that the term implies, are not an isolated phenomenon. Neither are the cultural changes that promoted them. Agitation against censorship, for easier divorce, for a more liberal take on homosexuality, all dated back to the Fifties and sometimes far beyond. The 'sexual revolution' was similarly prefigured.*

JOHN LANKIEWICZ: You had had the Kinsey Reports, the first in 1948, the second five years later. They were very important, in that for the first time relatively objective surveys were being published about sex. Whereas Havelock Ellis and the German sexologists who were writing in the early part of the century had a far more limited impact. Maybe that material was less widely available. If you look at copies of those books now you see 'For the medical profession only'. Whereas the Kinsey Reports, although a bit dry for the general public,

12

were available if people could afford them or be bothered to plough through them.

Then you had Masters and Johnson. That had a big, big impact. They were saying, probably for the first time, that difficulties with sex were not only common but also could be resolved in a quite straightforward and brief way. That was revolutionary. It might also have been a little bit over-optimistic. The psychoanalytic writing at the beginning of the century, which had a big impact culturally throughout the first half of the century, was saying: Look, sexual difficulties are there, are treatable, but they're very difficult to treat, they take a big investment of time, energy, soul-searching and money to overcome. And maybe psychoanalysis was a bit iffy as well. What Masters and Johnson were saying was: No, that's an error; sexual difficulties can be resolved quickly, in say two or three months, and in a fairly superficial way, using techniques that appear – compared to psychoanalytic techniques – superficial, quite straightforward. That had a big impact in the late Sixties/early Seventies first in America and then here, because sexual difficulties were not rare. If you had a population thirty per cent of whom were really quite privately distressed about their sexual functioning, and Masters and Johnson were offering hope – that's got to have a big impact.

Then there was Alex Comfort's *The Joy of Sex*. It was anything but dissident. It was sold in every shop. Since then it's been on the bestseller list for nearly twenty years. He'd written *The Anxiety Makers* in the Sixties and he was talking about the prohibitions and anxieties generated by the medical profession way back, about sexuality. *The Joy of Sex* was like a cookbook, it had 'recipes'. But there was a lot of focus on: if only you could do it in this and that position then somehow you'd be liberated. So with *The Joy of Sex* we are talking sex, openly. I think the book is harmless. It does liberate people, gives them ideas, gives permission, but it's a curious reflection of our culture. It's saying there is a big deal here; as if it was very dramatic, very revolutionary to use this position or that, and to have a name for each position.

CAROLINE STANDISH

'We all felt like superstars'

She sits in an office many storeys high in a mass media tower block. Half the nation's popular reading is churned out amongst these system-built floors. Her magazine targets young women and concentrates on romantic fiction. Softer-core than once-anodyne Mills & Boon, they too can't avoid sexuality. There's pulsing manhood now, and nibbled nipples, condoms and even AIDS.

I was brought up in Liverpool, and was very left wing at school. I'd listen to Trotskyist lectures on the pier. I had had boyfriends before university, but I had incredibly strict parents, which may have something to do with it. For them, education was all, and I had to be a swot. 'Plenty of time for boys when you get to university, dear,' was the line. There was no sex education, though my dad took me aside once and gave me a list of people who wouldn't be suitable as a partner: Irishmen, Jews, Catholics, blacks. There was hardly anybody left. And careers, they had to have a degree. So the first person I brought home was an Irish Catholic dustman.

I wasn't openly rebellious. I would do a Superman change in the phone box at the end of the road, into the stiletto heels, spray-on jeans, loads of make-up. I couldn't wait to get to London. Brian Patten was my first boyfriend. We didn't sleep together. I was seventeen, he was sixteen. We saw a lot of each other, we were both members of the Merseyside Unity Theatre and we'd go to poetry meetings.

I nearly lost my virginity a couple of times, once with Brian on a leather sofa at the theatre, but at the last minute I refused to take my knickers off. I was scared, worried about getting pregnant. This dogged my sex life at university. Even men were shy at asking for a packet of condoms. They'd get them from barber shops but hated chemists. Specially if there was a woman behind the counter. Many a time I had a sexless weekend because my boyfriend had gone to all the local chemists, and each one had a girl behind the counter, and he didn't dare ask for condoms. I went to university in 1963, still a virgin. That ended in my second year. I had a boyfriend in the first year but he turned out to be terribly religious, didn't believe in sex before marriage. Steam was coming out of my ears with frustration. He wouldn't do it! I went out with him the whole of the first year, came back for the holidays, got off with the dustman, but still didn't lose my virginity. Came back for the second year, met another guy and lost it three months later. We went to a party in Liverpool; it was June, the moon was shining, just seemed to be the right occasion. So we lay down in the grass, no precautions, and immediately afterwards I was attacked by a rat which ran out of a bush, nibbling at my feet. I had a hang-up about rats for years after that, and they came to symbolise men who were rats. That guy did dump me. I thought he was wonderful – I think you do fall in love with the first person you sleep with. But he went back to the girlfriend before me. She'd ditched him

14

but wanted him back. The religious guy ended up marrying a vicar's daughter, so he was happy.

With my second boyfriend, we both lived at home with nowhere to do it. It was winter. His parents were in the back room of their little terraced house in Liverpool, watching telly, and we were playing records in the front room. I had my knickers round one ankle when we heard his mother coming down the corridor. Because of the tension, my hip joint locked and I couldn't get my legs back together. I was lying like this, skirt up here, knickers round my ankles. I kicked the knickers under the sofa, he managed to wrap my skirt around me, and with all this cramp going on, we pretended to be looking through record covers. Then I forgot to put the knickers back on and his mother found them the next day when she was hoovering. End of that romance. He was told not to see me any more. I was a bad lot.

1967 was when the fun started for me. I met this amazing hippie character in Liverpool who was working as a spiderman on the Tate & Lyle Tower, at the sugar factory. He had long, long, long blond hair, a flowing beard and always had bare feet. He said he wasn't going to wear shoes or cut his hair until the war in Vietnam was over. When the job came to an end he was going back home to Ipswich, and I decided I'd leave work and go with him. I was working in Lewis' department store – very, very boring, supervisor of the swimwear department, then onto children's wear, a counter of grey socks all day. When I could I would skulk off to the HQ of the Liverpool Anarchists' Society, which is where this bloke was staying. Full of weird and wonderful people. They had a cooker out on the top of the stairs, and I used to create beans on toast messes for everybody.

Three months later I went off to Ipswich with him, which is where I found he hadn't told me the truth. He was living with a bird who had a couple of kids by him. So we tried a ménage à trois. We had sat down, declaring we didn't believe in monogamous relationships, the climate was absolutely against that, and we believed in everybody loving everyone else, and as long as we divided our time equally, and she and I had a loving friendship – not a sexual one because we weren't that way inclined – we believed we could live as a happy family. We had a rota for sex. Within three weeks it had totally broken down – too many jealousies involved. She couldn't stand it when he was in bed with me on Tuesdays, and I couldn't stand it when he was in bed with her on Wednesdays. He was in heaven. But she stopped taking the Pill and got pregnant again – scoring over me. I most certainly did not want to get pregnant.

I got jealous too. You weren't meant to be. But I was seething with it and desperately bottling it up because it wasn't cool to show it. I felt

15

if I showed jealousy, the people I wanted to mix with wouldn't mix with me. A lot of peer-group pressure. I felt I was in charge and directing my life, but of course I wasn't – just a leaf bobbing on the surface. But I did think we were revolutionary, striking a blow for a new generation. Nobody before had ever acted like that. Now I realise they were at it in the Twenties, so it wasn't new at all. But for us it was the first time it was talked about in the press. We all felt like superstars.

I played the guitar and sang, and when that all broke up I came down to London, moved in with friends, and started playing in nightclubs. The Village Club in Chelsea, Manna – the health-food places – the Roundhouse. I went to one of the free festivals at Windsor, and met Sid Rawle, king of the hippies. I lived with him for a while in '67. He was gathering up every redhead at the festival, saying red-haired people would take over the world. He had flaming red hair in those days. A whole crowd of us moved up to Slough with him. Just went back, grabbed my bundle of clothes, my guitar, my tie-dyed T-shirt and off to Slough and shacked up with Sid. It was an amazing house, half full of Sikhs who worked at local factories. Across the road lived this amazing vicar. He had a wife, couple of kids, and he completely believed in the hippie ethic. He'd cook huge vats of curry and stew out on his back lawn and everybody would come in to eat. His little girls used to run around naked with flowers painted on their bodies, and bells and beads. But what his wife didn't like was when he started taking advantage of the girls' free love – he had a go at everybody. Even me. In the commune Sid was the main one for me. Occasionally I'd sleep with somebody else. Sid was having other women, and I wasn't jealous. I knew what he stood for and didn't mind. He was married at the time, and his wife did an interview for the papers. 'To make matters worse,' she said, 'he keeps walking past my window with his red-haired hippie girlfriend.' Which was me. I had very bright red hair then. One day the vicar picked up a hairbrush from the hallstand and started brushing my hair: 'Oh, your hair really shines in the light, come into the study.' And he produced some booze, which he said was holy wine, and the next thing was an attempted grope. I was quite scandalised. I didn't see him as an ordinary man – he was the vicar and father of two kids.

Anything that was going we did. I did a hell of a lot of dope. Not acid though, because I tend to over-react to an aspirin. A few uppers and downers, bennies to get through exams. If you were sitting round smoking a joint in a room full of people and you fancied somebody, you thought nothing of having a bonk in the back room, then back for more dope. It was mutual, all body language. Nobody had to make

16

the moves. Eyes would meet, you'd sit next to them, a conversation would start. At that time if you spent two nights sleeping alone, you were a failure. No day was complete without having been to bed with somebody. And certainly not the same person every night. Sex was fun! We'd go down King's Road to shops like Granny Takes a Trip. One day I bought this purple velvet dress. Later I picked up a bloke in the laundrette. He was putting his things in a machine and I said, 'Come back to my flat and I'll wash them for you.' Of course he had to take them all off, so we ended up in bed. When his clothes were dry he got dressed and I never saw him again.

Looking back on it, the sex wasn't satisfying, but I was more intent on keeping score. I had a girlfriend and we'd keep count: 'Oh, seventy-five now.' 'Oh God, you've beat me by three.' We kept cards and they included height, weight, colour of eyes, of hair, length of cock. We wanted to see if there was a particular type of bloke we fancied more than the others. Being seduced didn't come into it. It was so happy-go-lucky then. I never felt I was being promiscuous, I was just doing what everybody else did. I was doing it out of my own free will, not selling it. My circle consisted of poets, musicians, etc., and they behaved like that. On several occasions I was part of a threesome: 'We all love each other, don't we? Let's get into bed together.' But when a similar situation was presented to me last year, I was appalled. Afterwards I thought: Twenty-five years ago I'd have jumped at that.

To me the Sixties weren't promiscuous, they were fun. I was enjoying myself. By '73 I'd slept with about seventy guys. I slowed down after that. I got married for a couple of years. But in all it can't be more than two hundred. One of my friends had slept with over five hundred by the time she was fifteen, starting at twelve.

Back then we were all very demonstrative. Putting arms round total strangers, giving them a hug, offering them biscuits. I loved that sharing ethic. In the commune, we'd take it in turns to get a job. I thought that was a great way to live – wish I could do it now. I didn't feel exceptional. I acted the way I thought everybody else was. A lot of women were in monogamous relationships, more or less faithful. But I didn't know that. I thought everyone was having it off with everybody else, so I did. I believed the publicity. There was a feeling of liberation, almost a licence to fuck. That's how it felt to me. We were brought up on: 'Save it for marriage; what you do you don't talk about.' It was all right for a man to have had other girlfriends before marriage, but the girl was supposed to be a virgin bride. That was never going to happen to me. My mother had a miserable marriage – she hadn't tried my father out first. She said if only she had, she

17

wouldn't have married him. She told me, 'Whatever you do, sleep with them first.'

I was sexually adventurous in the Sixties and early Seventies, though that didn't mean any of the perversions or dressing up. That all came later on. In the Sixties we'd get *The Perfumed Garden* and it was: 'Let's try this position tonight.' Adventurous in that respect. And it was fun having sex in semi-public places – on the steps of the university, in a bus shelter, in a shop doorway, on a building site.

I think 1976 was when everything changed, when punk music started. A bleakness came in. The light went out in a way. It was three-day-week time, the record companies were laying people off, people went back to three chords and singing out of tune. I felt excluded by the new things starting. Partly it was age, I wasn't into this sort of music. A new rebellion, but I wasn't part of it. Mine had happened. I settled into serial monogamy. Mr Right would give me an orgasm every time, and be creative, sensitive, understanding, with a great sense of humour, wanted to travel to the countries I wanted to see. Never met him. I'm still looking. I don't want to get to sixty and find I'm so hag-ridden and horrible that nobody will have me, that it'll be fifteen cats and a vibrator.

Just occasionally I feel guilty, think: Why did I sell myself so cheap? But I have to remember that when that happened I was enjoying myself. I loved the freedom, loved being on the dole, wandering over Hampstead Heath with my guitar and picking up stray South Americans, getting your leg over behind the bushes. It all seemed like bloody good fun. But I still had the early conditioning that made me feel they ought to come back for more, not just treat me like a one-night stand. Of course I was taken advantage of. But I took advantage too. If I was to go back to the Sixties now, I wouldn't do the same things. I'd be more choosy.

***

TED POLHEMUS: Every generation thinks they are the harbingers of a sexual revolution. To put it in its most blunt terms – and I'm speaking as a member of the baby-boom generation that gained its sexuality in the Sixties – it was absolutely clear to us that we had invented raw sex. Raw sex had never existed before.

The sexual revolution entailed a certain degree of promiscuity. But that certain degree of promiscuity which one experienced as a university student in the second half of the Sixties or that certain degree of promiscuity and petting/necking in the back seat of a car in

18

a drive-in movie in the first half – it seems completely impossible to know whether these things were markers of a change in sexual behaviour, or simply what goes on with every generation.

The first half of the Sixties had this swinging flashness and sharpness – James Bond, that sort of thing. What in Britain would have been called Swinging London and in America was exemplified by *Playboy* magazine. A world apart from the later Sixties' hippie concerns. And it's impossible to reconcile those two. In a way both would have constituted separate sexual revolutions. James Bond, *Barbarella*, those futuristic visions of the early Sixties, their sexuality was promiscuous, fun-based, but it didn't seem to be going to change the world, wasn't done for that reason. Whereas the hippie love-and-peace sexuality – one felt one was making love and not war, and the more one made love, the less war there'd be.

DUNCAN FALLOWELL: Sex wasn't invented in 1963 and Philip Larkin was a bit of an old fart, quite frankly. But because in the last few hundred years permission to talk about sex had not been granted, the British were suddenly very keen to do it. Swinging London kicked out a lot of moribund ethical attitudes, which was very necessary.

TIM WOODWARD: I lived down the King's Road and now I bore my younger friends senseless. They say: 'It can't all have been like that, going about with pop stars in Mini Coopers with black windows, flared strides, having sex.' Well it *was*. I spent the entire Sixties going round in Mini Coopers in flared strides having sex. It was brilliant, absolutely fabulous. But absolutely, there was a revolution. It was a momentary breakdown of the class war. The key to life in Britain is the class system, and in the Sixties that was suspended to a large degree. It was the first time it was fashionable to be working class. Coupled with that, it was the first time it was desirable to be young. Earlier, one always wanted to be older, one aspired to be a grown-up. Whatever class you were you wanted to seem higher caste than you were. In the Sixties that changed totally. It was good to be young, to be working class. You had the Mick Jaggers, middle-class boys furiously trying to be working class. That had a tremendous beneficial effect on British society. It didn't carry on and develop, but it had an effect which hasn't been erased. It was a good thing.

***

19

AVEDON CARROLL: It may have been the peace-and-love Sixties but, ironically, you weren't supposed to express love at that time; and if you did it could be dangerous. If you said you cared particularly about somebody that would devalue the free-loving nature of having had sex. Us girls were confused about sex, what to do. What we didn't realise was that the guys were confused too. We believed a guy had to know you cared about him if you had sex with him, therefore if afterwards they didn't say you were their girl, they were using you. It never occurred to us that we should do anything other than fuck them to show that we liked them.

I didn't know what I wanted. You'd go on dates and you'd been taught a kind of adversarial relationship. Guys were trying to get something which you shouldn't give them. Guys knew it was something they should get, to prove their manhood and it felt good. So no two people could trust each other, and we were raised to think girls didn't like it anyway. Then the idea came along that girls could do it and maybe even like it. That was very confusing because when you did it and didn't like it, you felt: what's wrong with me? I'm frigid. When I was sixteen I had a great sexual experience but didn't remember it because it scared me – it was too weird and kinky. I was really shaken when it happened. What it was, it was a guy I'd never been in the least bit interested in. I knew him vaguely. Joe, my boyfriend, was buying dope from him, and was sniping at me for not being good at anything, and Jim said he would not be as unappreciative of my company as Joe appeared to be. Very sweet. Then Joe said, 'Okay, I'll sell her to you.' I didn't say anything, and they did a deal – me for the dope. Joe took off and I just sat there, really turned on. He was really tender, very sweet. Don't remember much about it. There was a lot of cuddling and kissing – tender. Then he asked me out to dinner. I was freaked out about that and said, 'You'd better take me home.' And he did and that was the end of it. Joe never mentioned it afterwards.

RICHARD WHITFIELD: It appears now that a lot of promiscuous behaviour, even if fun at the time and not leading to medical complications, leaves people feeling a sense of loneliness. Present-day thrills for latter-day loneliness. The more you buzz around like a bee sampling the flowers, you never get enough nectar from one. So yes, the Sixties were an understandable period of change, a quite dangerous phase of behaviour. Increasingly we tended to treat each other sexually rather more as objects than persons. A human being's psychological growth through sexual experience is much more
20

delicate than the Sixties implied. People with strong religious beliefs would say: 'We told you so.'

It was natural with the coming of the contraceptive pill that humans would change their sexual behaviour markedly. That was compounded by the late Sixties' abortion legislation. So the Sixties' revolution was partly predictable. Whether it was a bad thing or not depends on one's ethics, your view of the state of a foetus for example, and your views on sexually-transmitted diseases. Whatever, our social ecology is now in some chaos and many are suffering in consequence.

MARCUS RIGGS: The sexual revolution was almost like the credit society we live in – live now, pay later. Except people couldn't see the 'pay later.' What the Sixties did, in every area of life, was to say: we've taken the lid off our packaged assumptions about ourselves as human beings, Pandora's box you could say. Now, in terms of sexuality, we're trying to shut it again. We haven't used the things from Pandora's box to enrich our lives. You either exploit the contents of Pandora's box willy-nilly or you slam the lid back on again, rather than saying: there are things I've discovered about sexuality, about me as a sexual person which could bring me great fulfilment that I wouldn't have been allowed before.

KAYE WELLINGS: The Sixties were a peak – there was reform of the divorce laws, abortion laws – and it's not yet clear, you can't work out which is the horse and which is the cart, whether the sexual permissiveness provided the impetus for the legal reforms or whether the legal reforms sparked the permissiveness. Something was going on.

JEFFREY WEEKS: The liberal social legislation of the Sixties has been represented by the right wing as the opening of floodgates. That's certainly not how it was intended by those who put it forward. The legislation on all these issues – divorce, abortion, homosexuality – was very much about the limits of what could be allowed, about drawing new boundaries because of a changing perception. Take homosexuality. It wasn't about legalising homosexuality, it was about removing anomalies where people like that weren't supposed to exist, when they transparently did. It was saying: there's a social problem here, we need to find a better way of dealing with this social problem than sticking them in prison. 'Would you lock an alcoholic in a brewery?' as Lord Boothby said. That was the climate that produced the Wolfenden Report and then the change in the law.

The theoretical position on all these issues was identical. Here's a social problem – abortion, marriages breaking up, obscene publications, censorship that didn't work. Let's find a better way of dealing with it than lock-'em-up-and-throw-away-the-key. The old absolutist attitude, rooted in traditional Christian morality. That was crumbling by the Sixties. So what's the best way of dealing with it? Wolfenden looked at a series of ways of dealing with prostitution, with homosexuality. Drug therapies, segregation, etc., were looked at, and found to be impractical. What the law on homosexuality, typically, did was not to say homosexuality is fine, but to say: yes, it's a problem, but it's a problem that should only concern the state when it becomes a matter of public decency. What people do in private we may not like but we cannot control. So we'll create a space for people to do certain things in private that society doesn't approve of. As long as you don't scare the horses it's okay. That legislative change was a little opening of the door, a minor decriminalisation of homosexuality. But what happened then, was that those who were decriminalised acted as if they'd been given more space than they actually had.

Part of the thing about the Sixties was there was a promise of freedom but so little was delivered, and that produced in the Seventies a new urge to realise the promise. So I'm sceptical about seeing the Sixties as a glorious period from which everything else has fallen down. On the contrary, it was a decade bursting with possibilities, some of which were realised, some of which were not. And what we've seen over the last twenty years is an unfolding of some of those possibilities. By and large to good effect. But remember, not only did the Sixties see the emergence of a new progressive democratic spirit, but also of a much more heightened conservatism. Enoch Powell spoke out in '67/'68, for example, just at the moment when the youth revolution came to a head with the Vietnam demonstrations and the Paris revolt. And the Eighties in a sense was a triumph on the political level of what Enoch Powell had opened up. I'd like to see the Nineties as perhaps the moment when the more progressive possibilities of the Sixties achieved their moment.

There definitely *was* a sexual revolution in the Sixties but I'm not sure it's understood properly. I don't think there was an increase in sexual activity, nor a great extension in the range of sexual activities. After all, marriages have always broken up because of adultery – it was the main reason for divorce until the Sixties. There's always been pre- and post-marital sex. There's always been incest, always been homosexuality. All the things that caused such great anxiety in the Sixties have always gone on.

What's started in the Sixties is a democratisation, a greater relaxation of the hidebound class barriers that had kept England rigid since the late nineteenth century. You can see it in the different accents used by broadcasters, a greater openness in the press, a decrease of deference. That took off in the Sixties and has continued, that's the crucial thing. I doubt very much if you could say that because of The Beatles working-class youth had more sex. It's always gone on in telephone boxes, the backs of cars, hay lofts. Otherwise illegitimacy figures wouldn't be as high as they always have been. But people have been more willing to be open about it since the Sixties. It's a greater relaxation of the bounds of acceptability of what you can talk about.

KAYE WELLINGS: Behaviour changes less between generations or decades than does the manner in which it's reported. We start talking, expressing, describing much more quickly than we start changing our behaviour. There was a lot of that going on in the Sixties – a lot of talking about how free we all were, and certainly it seemed as if a lot of the constraints were lifted, certainly on talking about sex, and expressing sexuality in clothes, makeup, in recreational pursuits. That must have had a bearing on behaviour, because behaviour isn't just about basic urges and their expression in practical acts, it's about the opportunity for those practical acts to occur.

JANE MILLS: The Sixties' sexual revolution wasn't a monolithic entity. Like all revolutions, there are different strands. And one particular strand was about democracy inside relationships, about being open and honest between partners. It wasn't about having lots of partners. For some people that was true, and being open and honest in a different way. But it's not helpful to see it as a totally discrete entity.

I began to think that to treat sex like an After Eight mint, which I had been doing – it was something you had after dinner – was to devalue something that could be very good. By that time I'd had the experience, I knew what was very, very good. I had the ability to come to that conclusion from my own experience. I don't think I was harmed in any way by the Sixties' let-it-all-hang-out-fuck-everything ethos. I'm glad I came to that conclusion. And I don't see a lot of promiscuity any more. Then it seemed to be politically necessary. Totally absurd.

Anyway, even those of us who were sexually liberated in the Sixties had some shame and guilt. We'd been encouraged to think of it as a guilty secret. We used that to attack the previous generation, but that

23

came out of a feeling that it shouldn't be something guilty or shameful. But especially in America and here, people still feel guilt and shame over their sexual feelings.

I was very aware of a sexual revolution. Swinging London was a manifestation of that. For older women friends SBM – sex before marriage – was a big issue. For those brought up in the Fifties SBM was absolutely not on. There was no contraception, no abortion. They were rather mushy about it, only going so far, not all the way. Much more romantic. Sex was about desire, wanting it not having it. In the Sixties it was about wanting it and having it – the me generation.

***

'We want the world,' sang The Doors, 'and we want it now!'
Therein, rather than in the essays of the New Left Review or the
pages of Kate Millett and Germaine Greer lay the gospel according
to hippie. Richard Neville might recycle Huizinga's homo ludens as
'Play Power', but for most participants it was the play that counted.
Hedonism decked out in ideological trappings: 'Way to go..!' as the
man undoubtedly said.
In the way that the so-called underground of the period makes
mockery of true contemporary undergrounds, so does the concept of a
'Sixties' sexual revolution' belittle the idea of a real revolution. Like
sexual politics, a topic better considered in the Seventies, the concept of
a sexual revolution in the strictly political sense emerges from the
discourse of late Sixties' feminism and gay liberation. But the wider
term, referring less to ideological quality than to brute quantity, i.e.
more fucking, has few political trappings. King's Road or Portobello,
rock aristocracy or hippie freak, the story was the same: young people
had the chance for more sex. That said, it was very much a male
revolution. Women participated, they had to, but as recipients only.
The miniskirted dolly birds of swinging London were essentially
decorative; they poured the drinks, looked good in the Mini Moke and
dropped their knickers on call. The hippie chicks could roll joints, but
that was where the difference ended. 'Put on the Dead, get on the bed
and spread' ran dialogue from a then-celebrated review of psychedelia's
favourite band, and even such New Left luminaries as Stokely
Carmichael remarked blithely that when it came to participation in the
revolution, 'Women do the licking and the sticking.' It was not
surprising, therefore, that gradually, more and more women began to
question the alternative status quo.

24

JEFFREY WEEKS: Part of the impulse of feminism in the early Seventies was very much a rejection of what women saw as the straight male patriarchalism of the radical movements they'd been involved in – the anti-Vietnam war area for example. Women revolted against radical men, who seemed to think the sexual revolution was about men fucking as many women as they wanted to, but not women doing anything similar. A very limited sexual revolution, the Sixties. There was a sexual revolution for some men, who felt the ideology allowed them to do whatever they wanted to. I'm sure that surrounded the big pop groups as well as certain 'underground' leaders, but for gay people like myself, the Sixties weren't a revolution in any sense at all. It was the Seventies and Eighties which were more of a revolution. Then things began to unbend in relation to homosexuality. Spaces opened up for leading openly gay lives, and new experiments began. It was not a good time to be gay in the Sixties. And not a good time for many women.

AVEDON CARROLL: In the house I shared, a friend of one of the others came into my room in the night, woke me up and demanded that I fuck him and when I said no, he said I was selfish. I said: 'You woke me up, interfered with *my* sleep, and you're calling *me* selfish?' I couldn't get him out of my bed. I couldn't convince him that he was out of line. Finally I grabbed him and said, 'If you can't get laid tonight, is there some other way you can get off?' He looked frightened. I yelled, 'Is it possible you could jerk off?' He allowed that was possible. 'All right, what's the substitute I'm supposed to use for *sleep*?'

KAYE WELLINGS: Women in sound trusting relationships probably had better sex than the women in the Sixties who suddenly found it possible to have sex with more than one man before they were married. People talked about what a good thing experimentation was. I don't think it was. Those relationships didn't last long enough, weren't deep enough, trusting enough, to enable sexual expression to come out. There was a certain exhilaration, but it wasn't sexual satisfaction.

SUZANNE MOORE: One of the things that drove feminism was realising that if the sexual revolution had come along, it hadn't worked for women. It gave men permission to do a lot of things, but not women. But I've heard other women saying other things: it wasn't really so terrible for women after all. I've heard women of that generation say that maybe it wasn't all perfect, but we did grow enormously through those experiences.

25

NETTIE POLLARD: Having people like Janis Joplin around made a difference. I'm not trying to idealise the sexual liberation of the Sixties, but the counter-culture at least showed there was a possibility for other kinds of relationships. And I do feel women got more out of it than some people say. You didn't have to fit into the stereotyped behaviour, even with clothes, and that was important. The idea of sexual experimentation, there was some sexual satisfaction for women coming out of that. It may have been, and was, male oriented, which more than anything else gave rise to the women's movement. It came out of the hippie era, the anti-war movement, children's liberation, etc. They happened at the same time. There was a fabulous time to be had, if you looked right, were the right age and the right sex for that matter. Young boys wouldn't have done half as well. Generally, you were better off if you were a female.

JEFFREY WEEKS: What we saw emerge in the Sixties was sexual politics, which is politics around sex, the relationships between men and women. That was sexual politics. What we see happening from the late Seventies on is what has been called sexual politics – a much greater debate about the nature of sexuality itself, a greater openness about homosexuality, lesbians taking a greater part in the feminist movement, discussions of paedophilia, sado-masochism.

SUZANNE MOORE: The reason that sex was genuinely seen as radical in the late Sixties was this: the proletariat hadn't provided the revolution, so where are we going to look next? Okay, we'll try sex, maybe that'll be what we need. But it was like art – that theory that you only have to see the right art and the system will collapse. But sex isn't separate from the rest of the relationships we live in, therefore it can never on its own be a revolutionary thing. People might feel that it revolutionises parts of their own lives but I don't think you can have a movement based on people's sexual experiences or things like that. The gay movement is based on a sexual identity, but it's based on more than just sex. It's a rejection of a lot of so-called 'normal' relations. Sex is not the whole story. It's not just what you do in the bedroom; it's making the connections between what you do in the bedroom and what you do out of the bedroom. Those connections are political. What people do with each other, which bits of their bodies they rub up against each other is not a political act; what's political is how they connect that up with the kind of relationships they have in the rest of their lives.
26

TED POLHEMUS: The Seventies then tried to come to terms with all of this and quite frankly ended up in an awful jumble. In a very simplistic way, in the Fifties and early Sixties if a man and woman were trying to walk out of a room at the same time, he opened the door and ushered her through. It may have been patronising but it was an efficient way of getting two people out of a room. By the late Seventies nobody knew who was going to open the door, who was supposed to leave first, and in its more infinitely complicated form, in terms of what people were doing in bed, nobody knew how to lead.

***

FRANKIE GODDARD

'An extremely unpleasant experience'

We sit in her flat in West London. There are two daughters – each by a different lover – a pair of dogs, a youthful lodger, a throughput of young men with whom she maintains a bantering relationship, something of the flirty landlady, something of the grande dame 'with a past.' The bottles empty, the joints pass. It's a quarter century since the Sixties, but tonight time, if not perceptions, seems to be on hold.

I was born in 1951, which made me a teenager in the Sixties and not aware of the sexual revolution. No doubt it was a sexual revolution if you were in your twenties. For me I was growing up, and that meant having sexual intercourse with people. Much too young. An extremely unpleasant experience.

My mother talked about nothing else but sex education. My father was rather cynical about it. Home life was very open – I always saw my parents naked. I have an older brother. There's never been any incest between us, though I know loads of people where there has been. But with my brother the thought never crossed my mind – don't know whether it crossed his. We never talked about it. My parents were determined to be liberal, that's how the Sixties affected that generation. They'd had a tough time in their teens and sex was very much under the carpet. They wanted to alter that. Having made stacks of money after the war, they started feeling that now is the time for claret and sex. That rubbed off on us. My mother had given me sex education from a very early age. When I was nine I asked where babies came from. She said, 'Well I was going to tell you when you were older, but I'll tell you now.' She went into a huge biology lesson, much too complicated. She was a teacher so she had to do it accurately. I couldn't take it all in. I then went to school and spread misinformation everywhere. She told me about contraception then. And we had an au pair who had an abortion and she explained that to me. It was all a bit hazy.

My mother thrust Henry Miller at me when I was fourteen: 'That will teach you about sex, darling.' It was her generation's liberation and maybe the literature was not what it would have been later, but it still had 'fuck' in it. Quite a formative experience. Fairly macho. At fourteen it was exciting to read the F word twenty-five times on one page. And *Lady Chatterley's Lover* came out, unexpurgated. Then there was the Christine Keeler affair. So I was surrounded by the new sexual attitude.

I lived in West London. My father was a lawyer. Lawyers are terribly boring. I was at school at St Paul's Girls, frightfully academic, rather dry and crusty. I had a friend who was rather sexy and we'd pick up boys in Carnaby Street and on the boating lake in Regents Park. I was always the wallflower though, standing on the edge never getting anywhere. I was extremely shy, a very late developer. My friend wanted to practise kissing with me, and I wouldn't – I was perhaps a rather inhibited child. I just didn't fancy it. We did a lot of role-playing though, and used to fight a lot. Physical rolling around. Which was very sexy. She would mount me and try and bite my nose off.

My first real sexual experience was with a student of my mother's, an adult – he was fourteen years older than me. I was ten when it started, with piggy-backs up to bed. It gradually became more erotic, until I was fourteen when he didn't penetrate me but we did the business. I lay there, like you do. I can never remember if he came or not. He had an erect penis between my legs, at the vaginal entrance, then he said: 'Do you have periods yet?' 'No.' 'In that case, I won't do what I was going to do.' I still wonder about the logic behind it. My view is, if I didn't have my period I wouldn't get pregnant. But to him it was obviously important I should be 'a woman.' Then he wouldn't be seducing a child. Contorted logic. Extremely outrageous of him. I look back on it now as abuse. But at the time I enjoyed it. The complete submission, with someone I felt very safe with, who was good fun. The day after he did that, I was in love – that's how you look at it as a fourteen-year-old, specially when you're flat-chested, and the other girls have boyfriends and you haven't, so you fixate romantically on this lecherous older man, who's quite keen on feeling you up. What annoyed me was, he went off the next day with a French girl his own age and ignored me completely. That was very

28

emotionally damaging. I was very angry with him for years. I determined never ever to put myself in a position to be rejected again. That really hurt.

A year later I got myself a boyfriend, a nice Westminster boy and we snogged a lot. That was 1966. Before that you'd gone to all the teenage parties, where everyone horned in on the girls with the big tits. I wasn't developed – no period, no tits. I was fourteen/fifteen then. I had very long hair and I'd hang it over me in the hope people wouldn't notice I didn't have any tits. Eventually at the parties the last boy would come up to you, the last girl, and do a slow dance and then he'd start trying to ram his tongue down your throat and it was disgusting, extremely unpleasant. I didn't like it. By this time all the other girls were rolling round on the floor.

We snogged a lot. Lots of fooling around. No coming. He was as repressed as I was. We used to go to Blazes [club] on Saturday if we couldn't find a party to gatecrash. We'd go down to the Chelsea Potter in the King's Road, get a list of parties, see if we could get in. If not, off to Blazes. We always went out in a group – him and me and his mate and girlfriend, a few others. If we went to a party, we lay on the floor and snogged a lot. Boring really. We thought we were being frightfully grown up. We drank a lot – this was before the days of pot, for our age group anyway. I hung onto my virginity until my sixteenth birthday, literally. That must have been to do with my legal upbringing. I had a terribly unhealthy respect for the law. I was shit scared of it. I did think I'd be struck down and incarcerated if I did it before my 16th birthday.

So the birthday came along. Me and my friend Linda went along to a doctor in Barnes, who put us both on the Pill with no hesitation, no examination. I'd only had one period at that time. Now I think that's outrageous. A middle-aged woman doctor giving two sixteen year-old girls the Pill, which they knew fuck all about. And the high oestrogen kind, which was all there was then. I felt awfully grown up, walking out with my prescription.

We both fucked on the same night. She was a virgin as well. She'd done lots of heavy petting but that was all. We rushed off with our boyfriends in different directions, didn't do it in the same room. The boys didn't know we'd arranged to do it on the same night. It was: 'I'll do it tonight if you will.' It was the most awful disappointment. I liked the snogging – there was lots of fingers in vaginas, though I didn't play with him much. It was later I started playing with cocks. I was very passive and submissive – completely frigid. I don't remember getting excited and I certainly never had an orgasm. So the big moment comes. Any foreplay? No. Ram! The thing's up. He comes. Out again

29

in ten seconds. I thought: God, I've been holding out for a year and this is terribly boring. Not what I expected. It made me feel stupid. If this is what it's about, why have I made such a big deal about it, hanging on to my virginity? When actually it's a terribly minor act which has no significance at all. You're expecting the earth will move. That's how you're brought up. It moved a lot less than when I was kissing. I found it terribly boring from then on. Being young, they always want to do it four times a day. And I didn't want to do it at all really. Just a moral obligation. I always felt it was totally artificial. I didn't have any horny feelings whatsoever.

I was with him till I was nineteen. The break up was nobody's fault. We were just very young and didn't have a clue. There was an element of: everybody else is doing it, we'd better. There was another couple we hung around with and they always seemed to be at it. I know the bloke of that couple extremely well – since then I've been to bed with him – and he's as uninterested in sex as I am and always has been. So there was the myth around that everyone else was having fifty orgasms a day. They probably thought we were doing it all the time, really envious of us. And there's the public display side of it too, walking down the street arm in arm, kissing. I'm very suspicious of that these days.

The nearest I got to orgasm was a hot tingling in my feet. Not pleasant, the soles of your feet burning. So you think: Oh, I must be having an orgasm. And if this is an orgasm it's not as good as having a sweet martini – which is what I drank in those days. I was nineteen when I had my first orgasm, lying on my bed reading a very learned book – Tolstoy or something – and I had my hand between my legs and suddenly the earth moved. I didn't have to do anything. The book was not erotic. I thought: This is it, I've been conned for four years. So I get an orgasm and start masturbating. I'd always had my hand between my legs, not consciously trying to come. But after the first time: Christ, let's get into this. So I masturbated several times a day. Smoke some pot, have a wank. It's brilliant. Then I got irritated when my boyfriend was around because I couldn't masturbate. I was doing this secret thing, it was for me, making love to myself was brilliant, I didn't want anyone else around. It was sweet, easy, no worries. You didn't have to relate to another human being either. Or be kind, telling them they'd been wonderful. Then I met Mr Right. He'd walked into my room one day and sold me half an ounce of dope and some acid trips and was incredibly good-looking. I fell in love with him instantly. I then refused to talk to him for a month – that seemed the coolest thing to do if you fell in love. It worked. He was another homosexual. I always pull them – says something about me. My first boyfriend had

had a gay relationship with someone I'd fancied. This one was in the throes of gay relationship too. That made him very desirable. Perhaps the attraction was that a homosexual won't go off with another woman. If you're scared of being rejected by a man because of early sexual experience, you go for a bloke who's not interested in women. You may not get them, but nobody else will either. But if you're flat-chested and look like a boy, you've got a good chance. Specially if you don't mind it up the arse. This guy was much more decadent. That's when I got into sucking cocks. He told me what he liked, so I learnt a lot about sex through him. There's that wonderful book, *Beautiful Losers*, Leonard Cohen. Marvellous bit where they're driving along at eighty miles an hour and one bloke is sucking off another bloke and they crash into a brick wall as the bloke comes. So we did a lot of that on the motorway between London and Oxford. Because you're acting out somebody else's idea, putting fantasy into reality, the thrill lies in that. Later on there was group sex and orgies and that was something to do with that too. The actual thrill is not so much in the sweaty bodies, it's the idea you're playing out a game and you're doing something outrageous. The outrageousness is the thrill.

So we started group sex. Only I never could. Everyone would take a lot of Mandrax then pretend to fuck but fall asleep. I'd take a lot of Mandrax, then when everyone started groping I had to leave the room and totter off down the street for a bottle of whisky to get more stoned, and end up in a gutter. I found group sex utterly repellent. Not where I wanted to be at all. I loved being stoned, and the orgies intruded into that. All these arms, legs, hands everywhere. Not very erotic.

I think straight sex became boring. You had to do something else. By 1969 there was the Pill and that meant it wasn't outrageous to go to bed with a man, or for a sixteen-year-old to be screwing her boyfriend. The only way to be outrageous was to get more deviant. But I crack up, doing things like role-playing. Makes me laugh too much. I know people who do it very successfully, but if you've any sense of humour it's hopeless, you can't get passion going. You've got a sweaty body, you're farting, body fluids all over the place and bouncing up and down in funny positions. Then when you find a really good position, you get cramp in your right foot.

We all took so many drugs, I'm not sure the sex wasn't connected with that. I started smoking dope when I was sixteen, acid when I was seventeen. By the time I was eighteen, anything that came along. I read *The Female Eunuch* and didn't understand a word of it. Sexual politics didn't figure in our set. We were into drugs. Smoking dope was my great act of rebellion. I felt it was very romantic, very right-on to hang round with dope dealers and criminals. They were the ones knocking the state, and these people flashing round being promiscuous and going to orgies weren't doing much for the cause. In the early Seventies all hell broke loose. Heroin had hit the scene for a start. It enabled you to screw people you wouldn't have screwed otherwise. In the Seventies I ended up with a pair of homosexuals, one of whom I later married, the other becoming my lover and still a good friend, and we had a troilistic relationship. It was sustained over an entire summer in France. I've probably had more deviant sexual experiences than most people. I remember being in a field and giving a blow-job to one and being buggered by the other. I was smacked out of my head, didn't feel a thing. My main aim then was to be stoned. It didn't bother me if I was writhing round in a field or not. I don't think the boys were wild about it either. We were all sniffing heroin. We just fooled around in that young animal way, like teenagers, although we were twenty-two at the time.

What I get out of sex does depend on the man. My best affair was with an Irish junkie. That was wonderful. Neither of us had orgasms. We'd sneak into public lavatories – this was on the side, I was married – jack up our heroin and then screw up against the wall. Then sneak out. In the ladies' toilet. There's only two kinds of good sex for me. One's baby-making, which you can't do very often. Then you have a complete sense of abandonment and the animal bit all makes sense. This ridiculous up and down activity which normally makes me crack up, because it's involved in the act of creation is brilliant. The other kind is where you've got a fifty per cent chance of being caught on the job. In Pakistan if you're caught committing adultery, it's the death penalty. That makes adultery a thrilling experience. The element of seediness and naughtiness is an essential requirement. If it's allowable, perfectly all right, with clean sheets – then there are more erotic activities. I did at one point fuck because it makes you look better the next day. You wake up glowing. It took me years to work out you don't need the fucking to have a good skin. You can get that by getting a guy to take you out to dinner. It's the power that gives you a good skin.

I had one very promiscuous period, as a result of a cocaine psychosis in Morocco, where I screwed five men in four days, to see what it was like. It was horrible, unpleasant. This is what feminism did: you thought you were paying men back for all the shit they'd given you. Then you end up feeling a tart. That's why I tried prostitution, and failed miserably. I was trying to get a hotel room for the night, and the hotel boy said: 'Fuck me for a room.' So I did. Then he said: 'Now my friend.' Oh, okay. They were both younger than me, so it was all right. Then *he* said: 'Now my friend.' He was older. I thought

32

I'd end up fucking the whole hotel just to get a room. So I ended up in the street. I was lucky, I got picked up by the police, drunk. Horrendous experience. It's all right with the younger ones because they're still little boys, their little willies are still quite sweet and you feel in control. You're so way ahead of them mentally. I'm like that now. I won't fuck a man my own age or older, ever.

I plead unconsciousness about my own sex life during that period. I would wake up in the mornings to find spunk running out between my legs because my husband had fucked me when I was unconscious. I got heavily into the needle. That's a very sexual experience. It is a substitute for sex. It's self-destructive – seeing your own blood, the plunging in, ramming yourself instead of some bloke ramming you. You're in control. That's why I loved my Irish junkie. There was a lot of love there. He was genuine, really cared about me in his stoned way. I've only been to bed with about twenty men. But none of them talk in bed. If you try to talk they shut you up. I'm interested in what's going on in their heads. We could use our heads to make this act a lot more interesting. Not just through erotic language. The only one who has ever talked to me bed was half my age. The only thing that made him feel safe was me talking. When I stopped talking, he said, 'This is getting like a movie again, could you please go on talking.' One of the nicest fucks I've ever had. We were able to laugh, didn't matter whether you came or not. It's got to be companionable. The seedy element is important, sure, but what's important about *that* is the complicity between you.

It's difficult being a woman. All these people who want to stick awful things up you. Sex with a condom is not sex, why bother? Kissing is really nice, but nobody knows how to do it these days. Now that sex is out of the closet it's all power games, and S&M. It's all rather revolting when it's splattered all over your woman's magazine. If someone can write about it, is there any point in doing it? I don't want to be doing what they're writing about in *Cosmopolitan*. It's all about how to have a good time in bed, how to get sexual satisfaction – so blatant. How the single woman can still have a good time in the days of AIDS, or what happened to the post-feminist woman who can dress like a tiger in high heels and sequined bodice and has got total control. The hippie Sixties chick was probably more real. She was rather a nice creature. She may have been a wimp or fucked up. Post-feminism has given power to the kind of women who've always been around and have always been tarts. Now they can openly use their tartiness and say it's all right. 'Being a tart makes me a powerful woman.' They're expecting their boyfriends to be on their knees buying them diamond earrings, taking them to glamorous

33

restaurants, putting on their coats for them. And at the same time they can stamp on the man's head with a stiletto heel.

If women go round dressing like tarts they deserve to get rammed. There's a lot of young men who've been mauled alive by women and the human animal is only a psychopathic gorilla gone wrong. A man has to be despunked in a civilised way to keep him safe. There could be twenty-five million twenty-two-year-old boys having their heads beaten in with stiletto heels and sooner or later there'll be a backlash. Those women deserve it. Because the male partners of these girls have a very rough time. They come to women like me to have their cocks sucked. Those girls have cut their throats. I know a lot of twenty-twenty-one-year-old boys. That generation has a lot of problems, they're so worried about their performance.

My rule of thumb is never ever let them penetrate you, never let them near you. This is what I say to my children. I say men are good for your skin, they make you look attractive. It's very important to have lots of men in your life. But don't ever fuck them. Don't ever let a horrible smelly dirty willy near you. It's revolting, it smegs all over you, it's disgusting.

All men have got problems. They never come at the right time, they try to do it too quickly, too slowly, they lose their hard-on, or it's so big it hurts. Something's always going wrong with their dick. And they all pretend it's not. If you're going to go to bed with somebody you've got to go the whole hog, to have a nice time mutually. What you get is two very insecure people worried about their performance and not thinking about the person they're with. It's amazing how insensitive people can be to each other in bed. Every time a man hasn't performed for me, I've made sure he did. A blow-job, a cuddle, whatever. One has to face the fact they can't ever do it. The only person who's good at doing it is yourself. The best lover I ever had was the only man who ever sucked me off while I was having a period. I really rated him for that. The trouble with most men is that they're not very interested in sucking off, they're interested in being sucked off. They may do it, but it's a duty, and on a scale of ten, it's number one, number two, number three ... number ten suck her off with a period. And when you meet a man who will do that, then it's really great. It's your dirt coming out, and not only your dirt but your flow, it's you.

I like giving blow-jobs. I started doing that with my husband, in my late teens. I read somewhere that semen was good protein. I don't mind the taste of it. Men like it. They always get a hard-on for a blow-job, never wilt. So it gives them confidence, they feel adored. All men are hung up about their dick, this revolting dangly thing hanging

34

off me. So a blow-job is a nice thing to do. It saves you having to wash too. When it's inside you, you haven't any power at all. You've got a great weight on top of you, and two free hands to stick round your neck. I like being attractive to young boys, looking as though it might be on offer if they behaved themselves: if they read three intellectual books they might get a blow-job. Then you hold out on them. It's educational. I teach maths and you have to work hard to make teaching maths sexy, have to pretend there's a blow-job at the end of the fractions.

Women become very vulnerable as they get older. They need to feel they're still attractive. And men are feeling insecure too. The young boys I know, the ones in their twenties, when they've had a fuck they tell all their mates about it. But I don't think they're getting very much. AIDS hasn't had much effect on my sexual habits. At my age I don't care if I get AIDS – takes ten years to kill you. If I meet someone I really fancy, which is unlikely – and anyway they're likely to be in their twenties so the chance of AIDS is lower. I did do it with a thirty-year-old, my stepbrother, and got very worried. That was two years ago. A one-night stand. He's single, fucked up, taking too many drugs. And our relationship family-wise was the excitant. We drink together a lot too. One day he came round, we got drunk and went to the movies, *Apocalypse Now*. The good thing was going to the cashpoint in Notting Hill Gate, drunk, not being able to get any money out of it, vaulting over the fence in the middle of the road, going to Finches, having a few drinks, then snogging in the movies. He's an overgrown adolescent like me. I'm the one who's fucked up. We should have left it at that point. Up to then it was romantic and wonderful – two people being liberated for the evening. But I said: 'We might as well go to bed now.' I was brought up with: if you kiss somebody you go to bed with them. Ridiculous, isn't it? But that's the Sixties for you, that's what happened. So we did go to bed and that was the bad bit. We were very plastered. Not the point of the exercise. That was vaulting the fence in Notting Hill Gate.

Older women don't get fucked. Intelligent women don't get fucked. Their willies don't work. Or their willies work, but they don't give you an orgasm, and what are you left with: masturbating against a wall. The older woman, and this has nothing to do with chronology, let alone the Sixties, Seventies whatever, the older woman has always been somebody who has maternal control and the filling of the stomach. And as every older man knows, the food is at the centre. If you're doing the rituals of giving food and offering sex, you're going to have a great deal of power over that man. As they say, there are many churches, but only one cathedral.

35

And as you get older, that's the game you play. Your looks won't help you, after all.

SEX EDUCATION: A Little Knowledge

It is, as the old rhyme informs us, 'only human nature after all...'
but in truth, things are not so simple. Hedged about by taboo, by
religious prohibition, by centuries of 'moral' fervour, by ignorance
both involuntary and quite deliberate, even by the tight-lipped
cussedness of our national character, the getting of sexual wisdom is
far from natural; indeed, one might even suggest that so constrained
is our attitude to sex education, that for many the topic seems barely
to fall within the province of humanity. We have progressed from
the days when the mere publication of contraceptive advice led
forthwith to the courts, but the transmission of information on sex
all too often still lies within a hands-off area. Lenny Bruce's
suggestion that 'a knowledge of syphilis is not an injunction to
contract it' appears too hard to swallow. Instead we are in the land
of Hilaire Belloc's Cautionary Verses, where the overly inquisitive
are advised to:

'Always keep a-hold of nurse
For fear of finding something worse.'

Sex education remains a tricky subject: the self-consciously bland
leading the frustratedly blind, a transfer of information in which the
main question is who − the speaker or the audience − is the more
embarrassed. Of course there are experts, there are manuals, today
there are videos too − whether matey, clinical or, for older
consumers, indistinguishable from any other ninety minutes of
softcore, soft-focus body-beautiful writhings − but the subject has
stayed as consistently problematic as ever it was, and simply
framing the words is still for many a screech of chalk on the psychic
blackboard. For boys, solemnly warned of VD and counselled
queasily on contraception, it was at best 'doing what came
naturally' − at least the macho culture expected it of them; for girls,
of whom culture expected something quite the reverse, advice ended
up somewhere between 'cross your legs and say no' and 'lie back and
think of England'. Pleasure was certainly not on the agenda; in any
sense it was quite unsatisfactory.
But 'natural' or not, there was and is always some degree of
information and the primary source for such information, as agreed

36

*by both left and right, are parents. Whether the parents feel the
same is debatable; whether the children seek out information, or
having sought it obtain it, or even having obtained it find it
remotely useful, is another matter.*

*So what did you get, what indeed do you still get? Sex education is
as often indirect as specific. For all the school lectures and the
parental chats – monosyllabic or graphically (and often
confusingly) frank – sex education creeps up rather than appears
all of piece. It's a process of hints and nudges, metaphorical if not
literal nods and winks, all in all a gradual absorption. A condom in
father's drawer, a pamphlet, all mechanics and coy line-drawings,
left promiscuously on the bed, a game of doctors and nurses with
absolutely no qualifications.*

KIM WEST: I started keeping a diary from the age of twelve. I read
it last Christmas for the first time, and I'd written: 'I really want to
have it off with Terry Morgan' – a boy at school. He did speak to me
a couple of times, and I just blushed. I don't think I knew though what
'having it off' entailed. We had sex lessons at school, the biology side
of it. I can't remember where I got my knowledge from, though in fact
I was one of the girls the others came to for information. I think I told
them the right story. I remember asking my mother when I was seven
what belly buttons were for. She said: 'Same reason you've got a big
toe, no reason at all.' I came home from school with some leaflets,
later, and she was frying onions and said: 'Not now, not now and
pushed me away. That was the only time anything was mentioned.

I started periods when I was thirteen. I was at a friend's house, and
her mum had rung and told Mum what had happened. So I came
home and said I'd started and she said: 'It's in the toilet!' Meaning
sanitary towels. My friend Mary's mum had bought me some
Tampax, but Mum was still using sanitary towels and belts, really
grim. And that was never mentioned again.

ISOBEL KAPROWSKI: My mother felt I needn't know the facts of life
until my periods started. She told me a little bit about men, a little bit
about women, but not how they got together. I learnt the facts of life
just before I went to secondary school and I told everybody in my class
the first day, because a lot of girls didn't know. We did have a final
biology lesson from a very embarrassed teacher, but by then we all
knew about it anyway. When we were fourteen the school brought a
woman in to talk about boys and girls and contraception. Quite
interesting. I went to the swimming pool with a girl in a different

37

biology group when I was thirteen – she was the best swimmer in the class but couldn't go because she had her period – and we got talking about sex education and she said: 'Of course, when the man has an erection...' and I thought: an erection?

When I was nine I was sexually assaulted by someone I knew – I was staying at their house in the country for a while – he was eighteen, and I had a little girl's crush on him. I was embarrassed, giggled a lot, but rather liked him. There was a thunderstorm that night, and there was no electric light in this primitive cottage. I went out to the kitchen, which was in the upper part of the house, and was looking out the window, I love thunderstorms. Then I heard him come in – he'd been out with his girlfriend – and he treated me like an adult, very affectionate. He didn't have full sex with me but there was some sexual contact. It was painful, I didn't enjoy it and felt repulsed by it. But he was showing affection and making it 'our secret': 'You mustn't tell anybody about this.' The thing that was really upsetting, next day I thought our relationship had got on to a different footing. Not that I wanted him to touch me again, but I thought we had an emotional link. But he treated me exactly as he always had before – a silly little girl with a crush on him.

I think he did have an orgasm. Of course it put me off sex. It was painful. A betrayal of trust. If we'd carried on having an affectionate relationship I probably would have adjusted to it. But it was doubly painful because of the emotional rejection. My mother said he'd been out with his girlfriend and got randy, but I don't think so. Why would he want a nine-year-old girl? I met him again when I was twenty-six. I thought: He's going to acknowledge it in some way. But he didn't. The interesting thing is, he married that girlfriend and they've never had children. Things like this make it so important that parents tell their children early. They should tell about sex when the child asks. Anyway, when I was thirteen, my mother had a book out of the library about disturbed children. I read this book and then realised I'd been sexually assaulted. That had never occurred to me. So I told her about it. She didn't take it very seriously, yet to me it was very serious. Yet my sister saw a flasher when she was fourteen and my mother called the police, was very upset. And I said: 'But I've been seeing those people for years, from eleven onwards.'

ELLEN SEVERIN: I'm from Northern Ireland, from a small town in County Down. Protestant. There's a really awful joke, about a Mass Observation researcher who goes to Country Antrim, where my family come from. So this interviewer turns up at the door, 'May I ask a few questions, dah dah dah dah, What TV programmes do you

38

watch? What newspapers do you read?' and eventually they work around to the final question: 'What do you do about sex?' 'Oh sex? That's when we have our tea!' Terrible joke, but it is absolutely true. People in Northern Ireland are the most sexless. They're totally addled sexually, they're very unattractive, no one talks about sex at all, certainly no one in my family ever discussed sex. So they were horrified, they simply couldn't believe it when my sister and I finally spilled the beans on our uncle who'd been up to all sorts of wicked tricks.

I think most people have had sex with some member of their family at some point. I didn't exactly have sex but I do remember very spooky incidents with one uncle. We were tiny, really tiny – I was about five, she was twelve. He never actually had sex with us, but there was a lot of sticking his hand into our knickers, and kind of, 'Feel my cock,' and very spooky carrying on. She was a beautiful girl, and he'd be peering at her through the window, watching her change out of her school uniform, that sort of thing. She's never told me, but I think he did something much more serious, because although she's incredibly beautiful – people used to stop her in the street to take pictures of her – she was and still is totally sexually dysfunctional.

Practically every woman I've ever discussed sex with has had some sort of unwanted sexual advances from their family or family friends as a child. It seems to me the norm rather than the aberration. But that was my earliest experience of sex – and I didn't know it was sex at all. Just that it was quite wrong. So it came as a great shock when at twelve or thirteen I finally managed to elicit the facts of life – though not from my parents – that it had been sex. That was all very shocking. The thing is that a lot of people in Ireland are like this: sex is seen as something dirty and if it's not dirty then it's not sex, and I still do see sex as something wicked and naughty.

JOHN LANKIEWICZ: My parents didn't tell me anything, certainly not. When I was little, eight-ish, I remember being summoned by my mother once to look at two dogs copulating in the garden, and she said: 'Look, they're making babies.' That was it. That was the only input on sex education I had from my parents. It was harmless, but a bit limited. The next episode – I would have been about eleven/twelve – and there was an older boy of about sixteen who lived in the house, and he told me and my two brothers the facts of life. Which basically consisted of: women/girls have three holes down there between the legs, and sex meant putting your penis into one of the holes, and that's called the vagina. That was it. As for the rest, playground jokes that were hard to make sense of, and then just life.

39

SARA DALE: My mother was a doctor and I asked her a very embarrassing question when I was about nine. Having heard teenagers talking, I could never understand how a flaccid thing like a cock could possibly go into a woman. So I asked how can babies be caused by a man going into a woman when they have these silly things dangling in front? So I was given my sex education at the age of nine. My mother felt if I was able to ask the question I was old enough to be answered.

KITTY GADDING: I caught my parents, though caught is the wrong word, when I was about eight. I knew about sex, my parents had never ever pretended about anything, Somebody at school had said to me, 'I know what the worst swearword is,' and I said, 'You don't, I bet you don't,' and I went home and I asked my mother and she said, 'Cunt, and it's not a very nice word.' So here I was. I was eight. It was very odd because I was out in the road, during the day, playing, it was a weekend, and I wanted to get in to go to the loo, dreadfully badly, so I rang on the front door and there was no answer and of course I didn't have a key. So I went round to the kitchen and rang on that bell and there was still no answer, and I thought this was very strange because I knew my parents were there and they wouldn't have locked the house and not let me in. So I went round still further to the sitting room where we had french windows and I looked through and they were lying on the sitting room floor and they had their tops on, but not their bottoms and what I thought was that it was funny to see their bottoms naked, that was really what struck me. I knew what they were doing, deep down, and I thought I ought to probably go away, but the need to go to the loo was far greater so I stepped through the window. After that time I did notice that there were times when they would disappear during the afternoon. The effect it had on me was a good, salutary effect – the one area of my life in which I don't have hang-ups is sex.

When I was fourteen I thought I was pregnant – though in fact I was a virgin and couldn't have been. I grew up in Hampstead and there were parties every single Saturday night – lots of parties. Kissing, snogging, getting to third base as we called it – finger-fucking. Lots of fumbling. Anyway, I was very, very upset. What it was was that I'd read *Jackie* or one of these girls' magazines and there was a piece with someone asking: Could you get pregnant from heavy petting – mutual masturbation? And it said, yes, you could. If there was any genital contact at all the sperm could do whatever and so on and I got absolutely sick with worry and obviously my worry delayed my period and I thought, I've got to tell my mother. I was just so upset.
40

I was just fourteen and I was still very religious and was actually considering going to confession – this was my Catholic period.

So there was this girl called Amanda: well known as a naughty girl. In fact it turned out later that she had never done any of the things she was supposed to at all – it was just a myth. Still. So I said to my mother that Amanda's got a problem and thinks she might be pregnant. And my mother actually said, 'Now you're not doing that old thing of saying it's your friend when it's really you?' and I said, 'No, really not,' and she believed me – that was the extraordinary thing. So I carried on with this story and she said again, 'It was you, wasn't it,' – and I burst into tears, floods and floods, just crying with relief. And she was so calm, she just said, 'Can you remember what happened?' and I said, 'No,' and she obviously just put two and two together and she just said, 'Let's wait.' And I said, 'Please don't tell my father, whatever you do.' And as it happened the next day my period arrived and that was that. I wasn't pregnant. And she then said, 'It's better not to have sex until you're ready, but there are lots of other things you can do and enjoy in the meantime.' Though she didn't specify what they were.

If you didn't get it from your parents – and few, especially boys, did – then you got it from your mates. Usually at school, but less often in the classroom than out in the playground. Some hapless teacher might labour their way through an hour's embarrassment, or throw the mechanics into some long-heralded and much-sniggered-over biology lesson, but on the whole it was peer group information. Some peer groups, however, are different to others.

DUNCAN FALLOWELL: The headmaster came in one day and told us that while he was out walking his dog, another male dog had come up behind it and tried to work its haunches as a form of sexual relief. This was known as gross indecency and we were not to do it. The rest was left to the biology teacher, who drew lots of squiggles on the blackboard, with tails, talking about male and female 'factors.'

MATTHEW RUSSELL: My prep school headmaster summoned me in, as he did all the leaving boys, one by one in their last term. He had a banana and an orange for some kind of demonstration as I recall. He was a total pervert. A bachelor who was heavily into beating, very emotionally repressed. His record was beating 110 of the 120 boys in the school on one day. He would supervise naked cold showers in the morning and anyone who had been beaten would be made to stand in the showers and turn round so that he could inspect their buttocks

41

for stripes. Funnily enough at a very late age he married his secretary, who was about six foot three, and they had children. And he stopped beating the boys. Just like that.

From there I went to Eton, where I was a scholar. For some reason College [the scholars' house] had the reputation of being more rampant than the other houses simply because they had what they called Chamber which was basically horse-boxes where you went when you first arrived, which was a complete inversion of logic because obviously where gay sex thrived was where you had rooms to yourself rather than in public. In fact nothing happened in Chamber – it was once you graduated to a room of your own that it all started. There was a lot of sexual exploration, which went in waves, and existed in pockets: certain houses were 'queer' and certain weren't, and there were certain distinctions between whether you were 'queer' or whether you just got up to some hanky-panky. 'Queer' was very distinct: it was what one didn't wish to be. 'Queer' was buggery, effeminacy or anything that implied that you weren't really, actually heterosexual but just doing this because there was nothing else to be done. But, having said that, one then indulged as much as one possibly could. Frightfully innocent, mutual masturbation, corridor creeping type of stuff. Did older boys descend on you? Not as much as one would like to think, the majority of it was very much among one's peer group; it was only when becoming an older boy that one did perhaps develop a little bit of an interest.

JOHN MICHAEL: When I went to big school at thirteen, my father sat me down and gave me a talk about boys and how other boys may approach you, so be careful, they may want to *do* things with you. I was sitting there, saying, 'Oh really?' and sniggering. Then when I was eighteen and leaving big school, he sat me down again and gave me a talk about girls. One thing he said was that if I went to a prostitute I should take some potassium permanganate with me and wash my dick afterwards in the sink. And the other thing was, if ever I got a girl into trouble, he would help me out. Whether it was my own embarrassment or whether it was my parents', I certainly felt deeply embarrassed at having anything to do with me and girls in the house. The idea I might have a girlfriend coming back to the house was unbearably embarrassing.

At public school there was absolutely no sex education. It was off in the bushes with your classmates. Because it was all very much undercover. People might carve on their desks: 'Williams loves Jenkins', whatever, but that was very much among the boys, and the

42

masters behaved as if it didn't happen. Then a new headmaster arrived and he called the entire school in and gave a speech all about things that dared not speak their name. So we had this astounding speech about corruption in the school, how he'd discovered this porn ring, where they took pictures of young boys at the athletics track and sold them off to people. 'This disgusting ring, these vile boys.' He said: 'I've also learned of a group who walk round in the dorms and have bets as to the number of boys they could "jerk off" and they would scurry round the dorm grabbing a slobbering kiss here, a pull of the penis there.' Everyone was sitting there in complete shock – a mixture of horror and hysterics. He went on: 'Boys are carving things: X loves Y, Z is juicy.' He laid out the whole homosexual picture in the school. The upshot was a couple of expulsions and some other punishments, a massive clean-up.

MATTHEW RUSSELL: My own feeling is that what goes on in public school gay sex is very natural, and a healthy sexual thing to have done. I think the people who are fucked up by it are those who didn't, who wanted to do but didn't. There were plenty who didn't want to, and they didn't, but the most fucked up were not the people who did, but the ones who wanted to, but suppressed it. Most of my friends without exception indulged, and all but one are now heterosexual. The one who is gay is the one who didn't indulge in much at Eton. The ones who are fucked up are those who grow into adulthood with that repression.

SUZANNE MOORE: I went to a girls' grammar school and when we were about fifteen we went on holiday to Belgium for about a week and one of the girls went upstairs with supposed period pains and had a baby. She was five months pregnant, nobody knew. One of those girls who was incredibly quiet. There was our teacher: 'Come along girl, don't be so silly.' They decided after this that we should have sex education. It consisted of the deputy head coming into our biology lesson to say, 'I want to talk about procreation. What is the purpose of procreation?' So this girl Anita who always did everything before anyone else, put up her hand and said, 'Pleasure, miss.' 'Get out of this room!' Then she said, 'Girls, I'm going to tell you what the best form of contraception is. The best form of contraception is a brick wall.' This was the late Seventies. Anyway the thing was we were all doing it. By the time they'd decided we should have sex education we were all doing it.

JANE MILLS: Sex education is always clinical – experts in white coats, biology, facts of life. Which means procreation not pleasure. Or it's a problem – the Proopses, the Rayners, etc. Therefore it's dysfunction, not pleasure. Or it's about smut. That could be about pleasure but it's not. It reinforces shame and guilt. It's dirty, furtive, under the counter.

Which for many, is just how it should stay. For the religious, especially those of the evangelical Christian Right, sex education presents no problems. Their ideological opponents, who find few difficulties in defining their terms when it comes to politics, still agonise over sex, betraying an uncharacteristic wishy-washiness, but for those with no such doubts, the Bible is all.

GRAHAM WEBSTER-GARDNER: We at the the Conservative Family Campaign were involved in the framing of the '86 Education Act. What we put in was not having to have sex education on the curriculum. That's where the Campaign made its name and impact. We led a coalition of forty-three groups, mostly family and Christian groups, but also Muslim and Jewish groups. We changed the government's position. Now school governors can decide whether to have sex education or not. The effect is good, some schools don't have it and some of the barmier LEAs can't impose it. So you now can't have the deliberate proselytisation of homosexuality that you had in some far-left councils. We also put in a clause that said that sex education should include mention of the value of family life, but I don't think that's being included. There are no positive views on abstinence. In the States all sex education must have a pro-abstinence programme. That's showing a decline in sexual activity amongst teenagers and in the number of pregnancies. So I'd like to see pro-abstinence incorporated in British law. I'd also like to see something on parenthood and the value of marriage and family life. Even the BBC's educational output talks about partners, not husbands and wives. Marriage doesn't feature.

JEFFREY WEEKS: Sex education is one of the areas the New Right are targeting, specially in the States. But it's tragic, their attitude to sex education in schools, doubly so because of HIV. People's awareness of risk – traditionally, the risk of pregnancy, but now HIV – they're not prepared to face up to it. There's no context, no culture in which responsibility for oneself and others is generated. This isn't an argument for traditional parental values, it's an argument for people being able to talk about their anxieties and desires from quite

44

an early age, being aware of their responsibility to themselves in relation to sexual hygiene, protection, preventing infection and pregnancy. I think it's a tragedy when twelve-year-olds get pregnant and have to have abortions. It can't be good for them and it's not good for the context in which they have to survive. It would be much better if there was proper sex education, proper access to protective devices. But as soon as you say that, you're accused of advocating sex at public expense.

JOHN LANKIEWICZ: Sex education in schools now has to promote a link between sex and love, love and marriage, and family and the law of course. There's a legal restraint in Section 28 of the Education Act. You're not allowed to promote homosexual relations as a supposed equal of heterosexual family life, married life. You can always get round that, but it is a restraint and creates an attitude. If sex education said to kids: sex is great, do it in any way you like, whenever you like, provided there's no coercion, there'd be an uproar. But that's not what happens.

GRAHAM WEBSTER-GARDNER: Ideally sex education is a parental responsibility. We've got five children, from fourteen to eighteen months. They start asking questions from about five years old, and we answer them very directly and clearly. We're not modest around the house. We don't approve of public nudity, but there's nothing wrong with the naked body in one's own home. The two girls who are now teenagers have known for some years how reproduction occurs. We impose our own values on them, of course. I appreciate some parents find sex education difficult, but if it is handed over to the school, they should take a stand on marriage, parenthood, chastity, abstinence, just in the hope it will cut down experimentation.

I don't believe that people whose marital situation is in a mess should be involved in teaching it. Two of our girls had a divorced teacher then living with someone else giving them sex education. We didn't feel she was a suitable person to do that. In that respect she's immoral, although she may be a good teacher in other subjects.

The right wing aside, times have changed. Techniques have improved, leaflets are more graphic, usually more populist and less prescriptive in tone, the media more open to airing the topic, for all that programme after programme seems destined to round up the usual, vociferous subjects. Yet ignorance remains. Embarrassment has not evaporated, the myths are in place. And above all sex

45

*remains a function of human mechanics, of plugs and sockets, of
potential disasters, of dysfunction. The pleasure principle, hymned
so enthusiastically in the Sixties' brief flowering, is still on hold.*

JOHN LANKIEWICZ: Sex education has changed. When I was a kid
we had none at all. Not even in science or biology, nothing. Then
there was a period when kids learnt about rabbits, flowers, etc. And
these days they're getting quite nitty-gritty sex education, in the sense
that they're being shown cartoon films that show the nitty-gritty
anatomy, the whole process of intercourse and the links between that
and reproduction. All of which I think is still under-sold, although
these sort of films do say it's okay to masturbate if it gives you pleasure.
My kid came home the other day, having seen a sex-education
cartoon in which they said if you gently stroke the penis then it gets
hard and it gives you pleasure. Permission-giving.

One of the best sex education books that's been written for young
people is a book by Jane Cousins [Mills] called *Make It Happy*. That
was a very straightforward unemotional book that gave people
information. So there was a small paragraph on bestiality which said
what it was, something on homosexuality, the various 'isms'. There
were questions asked in the House of Commons about it. Why?
Because when it mentioned things like bestiality, it didn't give any
ethical guidance on the subject.

JANE MILLS: The whole subject of sex in my family was very
mysterious. It now seems clear that my parents had a very happy
active sex life. I probably felt jealous and excluded by this. As a
ten-year-old I didn't like seeing my parents holding hands in a
restaurant or kissing in the street, which they did. They were too old,
other people's parents didn't. But the second message coming through
was different. I was lied to about how babies are born and the initial
sex act. Telling the gooseberry bush story to an eight-year-old! When
I discovered at school that that wasn't true, I was very relieved. What
I heard at school was so much better than the version I'd got.

It was in Kingston on Thames on market day, going round by the
clock tower, and I asked my mother how babies were born, was spun
a lie, was totally happy with it. I remember thinking: Even the Queen?
What she said was, 'Daddy pees into a potty, Mummy dips fingers in
pee and puts them into her vagina.' There's no pleasure there, is there?
And it suddenly struck me ten years after I'd written *Make it Happy*,
talking to my analyst, that that's why I'd written a sex education book,
I'm still angry at being lied to. With my stepchild I made absolutely
sure she wasn't lied to, and now I see an extremely relaxed, healthy
46

eleven-year-old. She saw a baby being born on film when she was four – no problem.

People talk about Pandora's box when they're attacking the Sixties, but the thing about Pandora's box was not that it let out all the evils, but it revealed the truth. That's forgotten. Because the truth is painful, it's seen to be only damaging things that are released. But it was Truth she let out. And that's no bad thing. Mine was the first sex education book for young people. There was a gap in the market when I wrote the book – which is why I wrote it. I didn't write it for commercial reasons. I was a stepmother, living with a guy who had three teenage children. They were asking me lots of questions about sex and morality and emotions – things I hadn't given a thought. It was about '78. I would sit in a pub with them every Friday night, talking about what's it like when a girl comes, does she come every time – these were all boys. I thought: this is ridiculous, there must be a book about this. But there wasn't, only the Wardell B. Pomeroy books, *Girls and Sex, Boys and Sex*. I thought, what boy aged fifteen/sixteen would have the courage to go into a bookshop and buy a book called *Girls and Sex*? You'd need an A level in biology to understand it anyway. These were working-class lads who wanted to know what it felt like when their girlfriend came. The answer was not in a book. In *Boys and Sex* there was a chapter on masturbation; in *Girls and Sex*, a paragraph. I thought this was ridiculous. I gave up a snazzy job presenting programmes at Granada TV, took a year off.

The book sold very well, to our surprise. eleven different countries – sold more in Norway than in England. More in Australia. I thought I was writing a book no one would buy, because children don't admit they don't know anything about sex, and they don't buy books, and adults won't let them. So I thought: What the hell am I doing? Because of the banning – it was taken off public library shelves for a while – and the outrage – some housemaster at Eton gave it to every fourteen-year-old in his class, and a Colonel someone wrote and complained. What I was most depressed about was that I'd hoped I was writing something that would provide an education divorced from guilt and shame. Once your book goes under the counter, all that guilt and shame is tied to it. So I was disappointed.

Things have changed, fortunately. The mothers who bought it then would say: 'I just leave it lying around'. Now they can talk about it a bit better. 'Would you like Jane's book?' is more the tendency. I don't know many precocious teenagers. I still find that young people can't talk to their parents about sex. When I was teaching sex education, I was quite useful, because I wasn't a parent or a schoolteacher, so there was no power relationship.

MARGARET RAMAGE: The children of the Sixties' people feel there's something seriously wrong with them if they're still virgins at twenty. People like my children. Their childhood really has been affected by the alleged sexual revolution. Those now in their twenties were the first victims of sex-education programmes. When I say victims, we were very aggressive and assertive in knowing what children needed to know. The general view was that children should be told everything immediately, have all the facts. So there were vigorous sex-education programmes at school, primary and secondary. This was in the Seventies, it was new. Started in about '69, I suppose. That's when it began to take off. For about ten years, non teachers, those called 'sex educators', ran vigorous programmes. The BBC made some excellent programmes for use in schools. There was a mushrooming of such audiovisual material. So those now in their twenties had all that. They got a lot of heavily value-laden educational material about the nuts and bolts of sex – sex is a good thing, this is what mummies and daddies do, everybody enjoys it – but the teachers weren't given enough time to process the impact of that material on the children. So they were left with a lot of quite highly-charged material and a sense that sex is good and you should be doing it. We've now moved beyond that. Teachers now do have time to process the material and they educate the children differently. They have life skill and health skill classes, and the sexuality and human relationships parts of the work go into a big programme of the Humanities. It's taught in a more child-focused way. Instead of saying: This is what you need to know, they're inclined to say: What do you already know, what would you like to know more about, what do you think about these things? The children have more time to process the material and gear it to their own knowledge, own family culture, own lifestyle. In the beginning that wasn't happening.

CLARE CAMPBELL: Sex education is still terrible in this country. Thirteen-to fifteen-year-olds still don't know about parts of their own bodies. Today, in the middle of an AIDS crisis. They still think you can't get pregnant the first time, you can't get pregnant if you do it standing up. I don't understand why these myths are still believed. But the government does seem to believe you shouldn't tell people too much – shove it under the carpet, avoid it. The damage to people's emotional health as a result is incredible. Not to mention when they go on to get VD, AIDS, have abortions. A lot of the letters I had were from graduates in their twenties.

SUZANNE MOORE: Before I went to college I was working with adolescents in a hostel, sixteen-, seventeen-year-olds, mostly black kids, and all these boys were so macho and so tough and they'd all been in trouble since they were eleven and you talk to them about sex and their ignorance was astonishing. One boy, about seventeen, I was talking to him about how he should be careful not to get his girlfriend pregnant. 'She won't get pregnant,' he said, 'she never has an orgasm.'

HAZEL SLAVIN: I spend one day a week talking to men and women, some singly, some couples, who have sexual problems. That's been a very interesting way of reflecting on problems we have in sex education. What I've realised through talking to these people in some quite miserable situations – and of course their relationships are completely locked, tense, and it's not just about sex, it's about talking – is that we don't have any good education in this country about sexuality and lovemaking. What we have is a sex education which is always about birth and pregnancy. If intercourse is mentioned, it's only mentioned as a way of saying this is how babies are made. We don't have sex for sex's sake, no education about the pleasure and the value and the need for sex for its own sake. It's all about reproduction. It's seen as dangerous to go further. If you talked to young people about the pleasures of sex, they might go out – not that they won't anyway – and try it. But there's a notion that if you don't tell them, they won't.

MARGARET RAMAGE: Generally people were and still are woefully ignorant. Not much has changed. It's alleged that behaviour has changed, that there's much more freedom. There's much more explicit material about, educational material – you can read all sorts of things. But still men and women don't know how their bodies are made. They still don't know how sexual response happens, how it works. A lot of women still don't know how a penis is constructed. They don't know the changes that will occur as they get older. People are panicked by these normal changes. There must be an inner prohibition not to pick up on all this information. What the media says and what we say is probably fifty years ahead of what people are actually doing. We always refer back to our parents and grandparents. Most people know their grandparents, they know what Granny would have said and thought. They may not agree with it, but they know. These legacies go on and on and on. It's an evolutionary speed-up, not a revolution. It's a steady movement with an occasional jerk as we get the sex educators in, another jerk as we get the Pill, another jerk with Masters and Johnson's work. It's fairly slow.

49

HAZEL SLAVIN: In papers like the *Sun*, often there's a supplement on sexual techniques. I don't think it's just an excuse to show naked women, but it's about dysfunction again, saying how you can do it better. The ground rules for sex education in schools are that you talk about sex, not in terms of sex for its own sake, and certainly not in terms of pleasure, but in terms of how you make a baby. This kind of teaching goes right through secondary school as well, although there might be a bit more about feelings. But the feelings are about love, not passion or lust. If you love somebody you'll get together with them and there'll be all this scrabbling about, and then there's babies. It's talked about usually in terms of marriage, although that's beginning to change. The new BBC videos do talk about your 'partner' now. But you talk about sex only in terms of how babies are made. When children get a bit older, it's: 'Well, people do do it when they don't want to have babies.' That's the excuse for talking about contraception and venereal disease and now HIV. It's the way in to talk about it. The big things are pregnancy, birth, contraception and these terrible diseases you might get. What underlies all this is sexual pleasure, but that's not talked about. Or very little, in schools. And with homosexuality, if you talk about it you might interest children in it and they might suddenly turn out to be homosexual. It's the same notion that if you talk about sexual pleasure, people will rush out and start doing it. Well they're doing it anyway. There is evidence that shows that the more you talk to children about sexuality, the less likely they are to experiment dangerously. Because you're answering the questions they want answered. When I say 'experiment dangerously', I mean fucking without contraception basically. The other taboo, certainly in primary schools, is any notion of the spectrum of sexual variation and orientation. Everybody is a mummy or a daddy. That changes a bit when kids get to fifteen or sixteen, but it's a very dodgy area in schools. There is no recognition ever that in any classroom of thirty children there are going to be three or four probably, at least, who are concerned about their sexual orientation. One or two will be definitely gay, one or two will be wondering.

KATE HEATH: I saw my sisters having sex with their boyfriends when I was quite young. So I was opened to sex at an early age. Also my sisters used to touch me and masturbate me when I was far too young to know what was going on. Then I was attacked when I was ten. I couldn't talk about that then and I didn't manage to until I was a lot older. Basically the guy told me that if I told anyone he'd come back and kill me. So you don't tell. I was just starting to get pubic hair, my breasts were just starting to develop and it was the first time I
50

became aware of my body. And this was the worst possible way to become aware of your own sexuality, and of course you think that what happened is because of something you've done, that somehow you've caused it to happen, so you carry a lot of guilt. And that coloured a lot of my early sexual experience. I had sexual feelings but I knew that I ought to feel guilty, I shouldn't enjoy them. Some people might have been put off sex after this, but I had a lot of sexual feelings. There was this sexual environment going on around me. But after this attack I felt guilty, dirty or whatever. Which meant that for several years I couldn't enjoy sex, I wouldn't allow myself to participate. I'd cut off my emotions. The physical side was satisfactory, I was able to come, to reach orgasm, but it didn't really touch a core, not an emotional core. I wouldn't let myself be given to another person; I could let my body be taken, but not me myself. On a certain level I have got over it. I'm heterosexual, I enjoy sleeping with men, and I've found that not all men are responsible for what happened to me. There are some nice people and there are a lot of shitty people too.

ANNABEL MERLIN

'Looking for love'

The house in Fulham is large, Edwardian, its furnishings resolutely grown-up. No student throwbacks amidst the sofas and silver frames and the trompe-l'oeil sitting room walls. At thirty-nine she is if anything better looking than in her wedding photos – twenty years old already – but that marriage foundered and a new partner has taken over now.

The first time I felt sexual pleasure was riding my tricycle when I was about six. It was a very bumpy lane and suddenly I got this incredible feeling – to the point where I couldn't control the bike or myself and trundled out onto the main road and nearly got killed. Big fuss at home: 'Why didn't you use the brakes, why didn't you stop?' I couldn't say: 'For God's sake, I've just had my first orgasm.' I sat there absolutely stunned and amazed. Later on I was allowed back on the bike and had another go. Same thing happened. I couldn't believe it, this incredible sensation. I told my friend about it, who was even younger than me, and said: 'You must try it, sit this way.' She thought I was nuts. A few days later I tried it out at home, but it didn't work without the bumpy lane, so I tried to do it myself. That didn't really

51

work. I knew it was something you shouldn't do. I'd been caught in the sandpit much earlier on stuffing pennies up my fanny, and Mummy coming and finding me and saying: 'Darling, what are you doing? Don't do that, that's horrid, nice girls don't do that.' I was very embarrassed.

Sex in the home was very low key – nothing. They were a very devoted couple, seemingly. Dad would often say: 'Your mother is simply wonderful, you're lucky to have a mother like that.' Though they had separate beds. I think that was Dad's idea. But when my mother divorced she had a double bed with my stepfather – she died in it.

I remember vividly being told the facts of life – this was Mummy telling me very grown-up stuff. I was about seven. We were in Scotland and I saw a lamb being born up on the moors. What a horror show for a young child. I thought the animal was dying. The questions came fast and furious after that. So she told me the facts of life.

I used to play Mummies and Daddies with my friend who had a brother. I made him take down his trousers to have a look at his willy. That was odd because I had a brother of my own. I did fool around with him when I was eight. We had a place in Scotland then, and I would creep into bed with him in the morning. We didn't really get on very well, but this time we did. We did all sorts of weird things – watching each other pooing in a pot. He said: 'Right, do one, I'm watching.' Then he went: 'Oh my God, you're going to split.' I got off the pot with the thing jumping back inside me with fright – what's happened? Disgusting. I got into bed with him a couple of times, hanging on to his willy, with him saying: 'I want to go to the loo, don't hold it too tight, it's hurting.' He was three years older than me so he realised it wasn't quite right: 'Don't make a noise, Mummy and Daddy will come in.' 'Why?' 'Because they'll stop us.'

When I was eight or nine I fell in love with a boy called David, blond, blue-eyed. He accosted me in the loo and wanted me to take down my pants. I said not unless he took down his trousers. He duly did and I got rather a shock – don't know why. I didn't think he'd do it. That was the first time I gave anyone a French kiss – anyway, he gave me one. Don't know how he knew that – we were very young, I wasn't quite nine. Julie was like me, she was in the same class, and we fought over David. She won. She was blonde, and a lot prettier. That really hurt when I saw him holding hands with her in assembly. The worst pain I've ever been through. Very funny feelings – too early for those sort of feelings really. Mum used to find notes in my satchel from this boy: 'Kiss-kiss-kiss, I want to marry you badly.' I kept that

52

for years. Mummy said: 'You must keep this, darling. It'll make you laugh so much when you're older, something very special.'

There was another little boy who'd take us behind the shed and show us his willy. He had lots of foreskin. I'd never seen one like that. My brother's was a normal one. I didn't like the look of Jeremy's – liver-red, wet, awful, absolutely revolting.

Our headmistress gave us facts of life at school when we were eleven. My friend and I wanted to know a bit more, so we went to her and she told us a bit more. Then I went on to the next school, where we now had boyfriends. I had fantasies over the boys from the pony club camp, this sort of thing. One I was potty about. But there was one stunning girl who drove me up the wall – she was more mature, had stockings, hair slides etc. I was still wearing bobby socks. I masturbated, but not with boys in mind. Well maybe Paul McCartney. One girl got into bed with me and kissed me goodnight very passionately. I didn't like that. I never had a thing about females. One girl was slightly butch and there was a PE teacher, Miss Corning. I wanted to excel in her eyes, so that was a slight pash.

Then the feelings got more and more intense. I fell for one of the male teachers, and I knew I was being a coquette – I'd deliberately do something outrageous in order to get him to say: 'I need to talk to you about this.' He was bald, at least thirty-six. He arrived every day in his sports car and thought himself quite cool. Wore desert boots. He was very articulate, and he'd amuse me by keeping me back and saying: 'What did you mean by that comment?' I was just attention-seeking. I was quite shy, gauche. I wasn't pretty, just a podgy little schoolgirl.

The thrill of thinking I was a woman came with my first period. Mum was very good, made me feel very womanly about it. I was about eleven. My first real love was someone I went skiing with – absolutely passionate about him. This was 1967, I was thirteen. Mummy would have thought he was perfect. Very nice, well balanced, charming. Passionate letters passed back and forth, but nothing happened. I never even felt his willy. To me sex was pleasurable, enjoyable, but don't talk about it. None of us knew enough, so we were all fishing around, wondering. Sex seemed taboo, naughty, perhaps bad.

Then, in 1969, it happened to me, and I then felt even worse – sullied, ghastly, ugh. I was fifteen and a half. Went on holiday with Mum and new stepfather and my brother Nigel. I'd gone water-skiing and this boy was a cool twenty-eight. He was stunning. I lied and said I was eighteen. He was a Greek Cypriot. Very good-looking. Mum thought he was very nice. She didn't know where this relationship was going and I certainly didn't. He was just very attractive, I enjoyed his

53

company, and he smelt differently. Hipsters. Danced beautifully, was attentive. Very un-English. Dark, suave, debonair.

For three nights we just danced. He kissed me a few times, and then one night he was in for the kill, which I didn't realise at the time. He said: 'We'll give your brother the slip.' – Nigel had been like a ghostly chaperon, chatting up girls at the bar and so on, but basically sent by Mum to keep an eye on me. So we did give him the slip and ran down a lane together, giggling. Nigel shouted over the wall: 'Where are you going?' I shouted, 'We're just going to see a friend of Costas', won't be a minute.' And slipped down some alleyway, where he grabbed me. Then there was fear. He made me touch him, taking his throbbing member out, and said: 'Hold it.' Ugh, I'd never done anything like this before. So I did, yes, now what? He said: 'Come on, you must know!' I said no. 'Kiss it, kiss it.' I dropped it. *What?* Revolting! Then he realised that I hadn't done it before, wasn't eighteen. I think I'd lied and said I wasn't a virgin. Anyway, thank God Nigel had tailed me, and his head popped up over the wall: 'Time we went home!' I was thrilled to see him for the first time in my life. What a relief. I lay in my hotel room thinking how unbelievable. The sight of that thing! It seemed huge. But I still fancied him, felt terrifically in his power.

Needless to say he appeared the next day, we had a picnic on the boat. He didn't push anything for quite a few days, just waited, hung around. Nigel by this time was bored being my minder and chatting up girls. So then it finally happened, on some filthy rocks by the hotel. He'd got fed up by then. I was prick-teasing although I didn't realise it. He walked me down the beach, and then suddenly this thing was being stuffed into me. I screamed: 'Get out, what are you doing, ow this hurts, so painful!' So he stopped. There'd been no foreplay. I don't think he came. But he was gentle and sweet afterwards. I didn't know I'd lost my virginity. I hadn't felt the need to get rid of it – I was too young.

After Costas I was celibate for over a year. It gave me a shock, it was almost like rape. When I went home, he wrote me letters in broken English. He'd given me his ring at the airport, cried and screamed. 'Get your Daddy to get me a job, huh?' I didn't speak to my father; I was very embarrassed and ashamed, so I told nobody. I wasn't even sure what had happened. When I started to bleed after this experience I thought it was my period. But there was a funny sort of pain. The whole thing wasn't enjoyable. So for eighteen months I just kissed boys and danced. I never told anyone. By then I had realised what I'd done.

Then things changed. The flower power hippie era was so cool and wonderful, so different from these people trying to govern you and

54

make you grow up. This was freedom. And I was really keen. I behaved like a complete tart. By then I had no morals and was going for it. It was hippies, filth, dirt, painted jeans, long straggly hair. Loathing one's parents, going to every concert I could. Lying, cheating. Really foul. Trying to slip the leash altogether. Horrible little bitch. That lasted until I was about seventeen/eighteen. Mum would say: 'As soon as drugs came into your life, things went wrong.' But that wasn't true. I'd taken nothing, only pot. I was very into free love. So with my next boyfriend I thought: I'll get this guy, I know how to do this, I can make it fun for him, and presumably this time it wouldn't hurt so much. I didn't even care if Mum found out. I was out for myself, for my own feelings. Anyway, I did it with him. Was mad about him, and it went on for a long time, on and off. Always at steamy parties, stoned out of my brains, falling down stairs. I took mandies with him, acid – I once saw a dog coming out of the carpet. But it was only half a tab. Among my friends, we were all quite quiet about it. It wasn't till much later we talked about it. We felt very renegade, but a bit shocked about what we were doing.

The first time I did it with Gordon, he had me under this tree, and he said: 'Oh Christ, you really want to go all the way! Hang on a minute.' Ran off from the tree, got a johnny from his friend. I was lying there thinking: I'm not going to lie here for much longer. This was in Aylesbury. Somebody's parents' house, lovely big house. Very twee mother, frightfully vague and vapid, hopeless case. That was a bit sordid. Anyway I was under this tree thinking: He might not come back. I remember lying there looking at the stars thinking that. What am I doing here? I didn't think I was being a slag, just a bit over the top.

At this time I had a funny liaison with my stepbrother. He had some mandies, and there was definitely a thing going between us. Both babes at sea, lost, because our parents were both divorced. We were nearly the same age, he's nine months younger. The divorce was grisly in both cases, we both had older siblings, etc. He was quite attractive, warm, considerate, we needed each other to balance the feeling of being abandoned. So there was something there, and we used to tease each other verbally. When he wrote it was always 'Darling Annabel.' And he'd say: 'I do think of you a lot.' He was quite a softie. He actively encouraged his friends to appreciate me, this was in the holidays. They were fifteen, I was sixteen. And I probably had told him I'd done it. We were living in Leicestershire by now, after the divorce and remarriage, then we moved down to Gloucestershire, which is where it happened, in his room, wonderful attic room, very atmospheric. He played guitar quite well, and for only fifteen he was quite cool. It smelt boyish, a very boyish room. One night the joints came out – everyone else was away, I think. We were great friends by then. Anyway, I was stoned, lying on the bed, asking for trouble, probably and I just passed out. I remember a moment when he was on top of me, and then nothing – which has never happened before or since – and then I remember a lot of scuffling and him trying to pull me out of the bed, saying: 'I've got to get you down to your room now.' So there must have been others in the house or he would have worried about that. He was trying to heave me down the stairs. My reaction was to claw like a cat. I was suddenly frightened and cold. 'No, stop it, leave me alone.' I was cross and he then got cross with me – he had a filthy temper – and started to snarl at me: 'Bitch!' I fell asleep sobbing. Next morning I felt ghastly. He came into the room and said: 'Look what you've done!' All these awful marks on his back.

I was kicked out of school for drugs and sent to a Swiss school – nobody else would have me in England. Gordon would write me very cryptic letters. There were one or two scenes with Swiss boys. Nothing happened, I'd bail out. I was foul like that, wouldn't do it unless I felt I was in love. It was a desperate need to be wanted really. I wouldn't have wanted to do it for the sake of doing it.

Then I went to Beechlawn, a sort of finishing school in Oxford. One I left screaming was my first ever date in Oxford. I was entranced with being at Oxford, loved being around those intellectually superior to myself and was thrilled to death when this rather attractive brother of a friend of mine said: 'Come to the debate with me, we'll go back to my rooms afterwards and drink port.' How lovely, can't wait. I'd only been in Oxford a few days then. Heady stuff. I voted opposite to him in the debate, which amused him: wicked girl, ha-ha. It was pouring with rain and he walked beside me, riding my bike. Went back to his rooms, drank port. I was wringing wet. Wonderful chance. He had a lovely gas fire. 'Take these wet things off, you poor girl.' So I did, as much as I could without being totally indecent – down to tights and a shirt. I was steaming, but freezing cold, teeth chattering. He was very amusing and amused. That I wasn't sure I liked. It was slightly spider-and-fly. Then he said, truly, 'I've got some new prints in my bedroom' – we were talking about some artist – so we went in, and I was still shivering. 'Poor you, you're frozen! Let me give you a cuddle.' Cuddle-bang-onto-the-bed. Then he was trying to put his face in my fanny. How revolting, who'd want to do that? More than anything else I felt I must be revoltingly sweaty . Also I didn't want him, didn't like him. I thought we were having a mental thing. So I was horrified, and again the kicking, screaming and shouting.

Anyway he let me off the hook and I sat next to the fire. By then I was nervous. He'd tried it on once and got fairly far, so I knew he was hot and would probably try again. I was very scared. I didn't handle it at all well. He did try a bit more, tried to unpeel a few more layers. I thought: How am I going to get out of this gracefully and with dignity? It ended up in a screaming match – me screaming, him standing against the door saying: 'You don't mean you really want to go?' 'I really do.' 'It's pouring with rain, wait till the morning. I'll get you out through the window.' 'No, I must go now, I must go now. Please let me go.' Then bicycling like a dervish all the way back to my rooms. Where his sister was snoring away. I was freezing cold, absolutely miserable, so disillusioned. My fantasy of Oxford, these wonderful intelligent people, had been ruined. Not only that, he was her brother, he should have had respect for me. He rang up to apologise, sent flowers, and Lucy was saying: 'He thinks you're really wonderful, so different, so special.' Ugh, horrified by it all. The more he rang, the more physically and mentally ill I became.

After that I was unhappy for four, five months, thinking: They're all buggers, only want to screw you. I had expected *Brideshead Revisited* stuff. More cerebral stuff. So I felt let down, humiliated, embarrassed, horrified and very pissed off. After that I'd lead them on then draw back. A nice kittenish person, but then the cat would come out. I've still got that element I think. But I'd rather be thought of for my head than my fanny.

Men don't think about making women happy. They're too worried about getting their own end away. You need someone seven, eight years older who's been through it, done it, and knows how to make a little girl happy. The people I was screwing were the same age as me, perhaps three years older and hadn't done enough themselves. They didn't know what to do for a girl. I did think: Why aren't they doing anything for me, why should I have to accommodate them? There was a bad period where I went through six or seven people in nine months. But I cared for all of them – I just couldn't resist the next one that came along. But by then a lot of them were making an effort and that did make me very happy.

Although there was a one-night stand, which was horrific. It happened in my mother's house, and she walked in just after the thing had occurred. She'd left us the house for the weekend, gone away with my stepfather. My brother was there. We came back from a party with a great friend of my brother's. Nigel was very dismissive of me always, and he said: 'You just be nice to my friend.' I was drunk and stupid and thought: That gives me the okay to bonk this guy – which I felt like doing anyway – and I said: 'But there's nowhere to sleep.' All the spare rooms were full. Nigel pointed to my mother's bedroom and said: 'Go in there.' Again, he'd given me the sanction. I was seventeen/eighteen by then and should have known better, but I was drunk, so I waddled off. The deed was then done, but again I wasn't happy with it. 'Why am I doing this?' I was clawing him, saying: 'Stop, stop,' and crying. He was very sweet and kind, 'Poor you, you're in a state.' I woke up the next morning to hear my mother's voice downstairs in the hall. She was meant to be back at four p.m., not nine a.m. I kicked this guy: 'Get into the bathroom!' Shut the doors and quickly tried to make the bed. Blood all over the sheets from where I'd gouged his back. I thought: She's going to know anyway. Oh fuck. I heard her talking to the dogs, etc. and then she came in: 'Is anybody awake? God, you lot!' I was desperately trying to get the bed straight, make it look like she had it. I got out of the room and pretended to go to my bedroom, 'Oh Mum, hello!' She obviously sensed something – my voice and face gave the whole thing away. She walked off into her room. I followed and said: 'There's somebody using your bath, I'm sorry. I said it was okay.' She said: 'Oh?' Then she looked at the bed and said: 'Oh for God's sake!' and lost her temper and went berserk. He couldn't hear, splashing round in the bath. He then came out, towel around waist, and said: 'I'm so sorry, I'll go back in.' She was standing there, hands on hips, saying: 'I thought I could trust you. What's wrong with your room?' She was appalled, I was appalled. But then as the chap turned to go back into the bathroom, he looked like he'd been done by a gorilla, all these claw marks on his back. Mummy looked at me: 'What the hell did go on here?' She was horrified, made me strip the bed, 'I'll never trust you again. I didn't expect you to do this in my bed!' She was absolutely right, no question. The whole thing was sordid, disgusting and I shook for days after. Why did I do it? Drunk yes, but... I'm sure she wouldn't have cared if I'd come out of my own bedroom and said: 'Don't come in just yet, Mummy.' She would have been cross, but wouldn't have taken such umbrage.

I was just nineteen when I got married. 1973. Not pregnant. No reason. It was far too young. It was very bizarre, considering Rupert's background too, which is significantly important. His family sanctioned us, my family didn't. They were very anti, very upset, wait at least till you're twenty. But I wouldn't wait. He had the intellect, didn't want me all the time, and was very, very low key sexually – very low key. That's where he won. He wasn't mauling me all the time, didn't make me feel like a piece of meat. I was desperately relieved to get that finally. Having said that, going out with him and him not wanting me was ghastly. At eighteen you expect to be bonking all the time with whoever you're going out with. In the early days I'd stay at his parents' house, and some nights he'd come down the corridor and some nights he didn't. I'd wait there and wait there. Nothing fucking happened. Then next morning, frost at breakfast from me. Why did you invite me here for the fucking weekend if you weren't going to screw me!

He'd had a chequered career with all sorts of funny women, some very bright, and he did like my mind. I was very flattered by him, and he's very flattering when he wants to be. When he's seducing he's absolutely fantastic. He was. He knocked me sideways. I'm not saying the way to a woman's heart is through her head. Depends how you've been treated previously, depends on your type. My attitude is: Value me for my company as much as for what I can give you in the sheets. Like me for me.

My first affair was just for sex. Tony opened the door and I went: 'Okayyy!' From nineteen to then there'd been nothing. Now, it's so revolting. I was passionate about him. He is a hot-blooded person. All the things Rupert wasn't. He was fun, reasonable, compassionate, passionate – everything. Now he rings up occasionally: we must have supper etc. I feel sickened. He got too familiar – that was the other thing – in every way. He would do things – if you've got your period you don't like people fishing around down there at all. It was anything goes. And I'm not keen on anal sex. It's been tried and rejected. There was no respect. The only thing my first husband taught me, the one thing you must retain if you're going to continue a relationship is respect. My first affair never had that. He thought I was a coquettish girl who was asking for trouble, then squeaks when she gets it. He started teasing me on a level I didn't care for: 'I understand you, you silly little trollop.' He would tease me on the silly little schoolgirl level. I let him come too close, too intimate.

Yes, I think I'm a sexy woman. In a horrible sense that's exciting. I used to like to make Rupert feel special and I'd flirt and he loved it. I never went that far until the first affair, it was just teasing. It's making people feel they're attractive, and I know I'm attractive. Social finessing of some sort. Nothing nasty or sinister. I admit I find you attractive mentally, physically or whatever, but that's all. It's like pouring a drink and saying: come and sit down, talk to me.

I've always wanted to be loved, respected, not used as a cheap plaything. When I do let myself go, I usually end up with egg on my face. I think sex should be revered, in the sense that it should be honoured and cherished and loved, but not put into a box for high days and holidays. It should be there, thoroughly nice and good, not upsetting to people. And not to be talked about too smuttily. I don't want my children to do what I did. My parents never talked to me about sex, in the way of what you're going to feel, how you're going to

59

approach it. So maybe I'll fill my children in a bit more. If they listen at all, which they probably won't, maybe something might lodge in their heads.

VIRGINITY: A Necessary Sacrifice

Virginity cuts both ways. Purity for women, inexperience for men. Girls were supposed to retain it until the wedding night, men, it was assumed, would rid themselves of it quickly. For those who rejected the stereotypes there were twin, mirrored critiques. The girl who enjoyed sex early was a slut; the boy who failed to find a partner was a wimp. Nor did the Sixties change much of that. The Pill offered opportunity to girls, and the great bugaboo, teenage pregnancy, was much reduced, but the fumbling, the nervousness, the simple lack of sophistication and confidence that goes with youthful experimentation remained the norm. Knowledge did not produce expertise. And the old double standard still held sway, then and now. The 'teenage mum' remains an object of tabloid frisson, for all that statistics prove that our age of consent – sixteen – has become one more area of what might best be termed sexual fantasy. The sexual revolution, assess it as one may, undoubtedly broadened the debate, and put sexual issues forward as never before, but for the young, then and now the progress from grope to grind remains much the same.

KITTY GADDING: There'd be these parties with a general grope room. You snogged a lot of different boys. Then there was a youth club, and you'd go there on Sunday nights and snog some more. There was a lot of very unsophisticated kissing. Just clamping your mouth on people's. A lot of competition about how long you could sustain one kiss. We all kissed in front of everyone else. That was perfectly okay. And you'd get off with one person one week and then a new one the next. That was fine. It was very rare to have a steady boy who you snogged every week. It wasn't particularly physically pleasurable, what made it nice was that you fancied people. It was best for a boy to be tall. Even if you were quite ugly you'd get off with girls if you were tall. Though you couldn't get off with anyone if you had spots.

I remember the very first time I touched a boy's cock. I had this very large boyfriend – not his cock, he was just very, very tall – and there were these gropings going on. I was still very religious – about thirteen or fourteen – and he undid my jeans, they were very, very, very tight

60

and he undid them and I thought, if he's doing that I ought to do something back. So I undid his jeans. I thought I ought to respond, but I was racked with guilt and I went off to confession and felt I'd really sinned. Though what I still don't understand is that these boys with whom I used to engage in all these frenetic fumblings, this 'heavy petting', these boys who presumably thought about sex most of the time, who wanked a lot and who read pornography, I'd get their cock out and they maintained these erections for hours and hours, but they never came.

When I was fifteen I had this affair with a German boy, he was on an exchange and he was seventeen. Bruno. He was also very, very deeply religious. On the last night he was camping in a tent in the garden and I went out to visit him in his tent. It was the first time we'd ever done anything more than kiss. I knew he was a virgin. So we started the usual fumbling, as you do. Then he suddenly stopped, and he produced this towel, which he laid down and then he came. I was amazed – and the most amazing thing was not the sperm, but the fact that he actually knew that he was about to come. Later, when I did start having sex, I couldn't work out why all of these boys hadn't come. Did they wank afterwards, were they very frustrated? Were they too embarrassed to come? Maybe I just didn't do it properly.

The first time I ever had oral sex was underneath a blanket, underneath a table in the sitting room of one of my friends' parents. I remember reading about it earlier when I was about twelve and wanting to say to my mother, do you have to do it, because the whole idea seemed just horrible. But I never got the bottle, I couldn't find the right words, actually to say, 'suck'. But when it did happen I just did it. I was asked to and I did. Game for a laugh. But I didn't boast about it. But I thought it was very, very strange – I thought cocks in general were very, very strange.

When I did come round to having intercourse, which was when I was sixteen, I decided that my mother probably wouldn't want to know. She probably would know, she'd probably guess, but I didn't tell her. She discovered that I was on the Pill a year later, when I was actually sleeping with my second boyfriend, and I said, 'I'm so sorry I didn't tell you.' She said, 'I understand, I'd be having sex if I were your age now. Things are different from when I was young.' I didn't have boyfriends stay over. I never asked if they could – I didn't think it was my place to ask. Maybe that was all part of sex, that it was awkward and fumbling and there was a risk of being found out and you had to do it in a car or whatever. But my parents always went to bed very early – maybe they were having sex – and I absolutely knew for dead certain that they wouldn't come down again.

When it finally happened, I did think that everyone would know that I was no longer a virgin and what really freaked me was that we had a friend called Helen and I'd go and stay with her in the South of France. And off I went this time and her mother met me and immediately announced, 'Kitty's not a virgin any more.' That really freaked me out. I'd lost my bloom, something like that.

ARAMINTA LOCKHEAD: I started getting off with people at parties in the holidays – usually friends of my brother – and messing around with them. I had sex when I was sixteen. That was about average. Lots of girls stayed virginal for longer than that. The ones who had done it were treated with a mixture of contempt and respect. Everyone who'd done it was questioned, but behind their backs they were talked of as real tarts. What annoyed me was the ones who'd done it wouldn't talk about it, became very coy, assuming an air of superiority and grown-up-ness. I didn't feel I had to 'get rid' of my virginity, but didn't feel it was precious either. Didn't care either way. People say it's something you never forget, how important it is. I didn't feel that. I didn't regret sleeping with him, but I didn't think it was great, didn't place much importance on it. I just thought I might as well. I thought that next day I'd feel different, my mother would notice, etc., but it didn't work like that. It was something entertaining to discuss with my friends.

The first time I did it, it was completely horrendous. It was a Tory MP's son. He'd been going on about it for ages. I didn't like him at all, but I felt I might as well get on with it. He had the most enormous dick and didn't really know what he was doing. At the time I had a period, really bad period pains, so it was a complete nightmare. Next morning he put on a blue nylon polo-neck and I decided never to see him again. He got really keen and gave me a gold ring. He became a junkie, then got very religious and is now an estate agent.

After the first time there was no stopping me. I went off with a friend and he taught me how to do blow-jobs. One thing led to another and he said to me: 'Have you ever done a blow-job, would you like to try?' I said, 'Yes'. So he instructed me. He was a very clinical character, something evil about him in a way. It was a completely detached experience – no pretence that he liked me or anything. I did quite enjoy it. I wanted to get really good at it. I realised that a person's desire is a reflection of the other person's. What turned me on was to see him with his eyes glazed, dribbling. It's to do with control as well. Doing it gave me a sense of power. I was still sixteen then.

AVEDON CARROLL: Losing your virginity wasn't spoken of openly. There was all the mythology – you didn't use rubbers because it was like taking a shower in a raincoat; girls say yes to boys who say no; if you told a guy you didn't want to go to bed with him, you were selfish; if you won't fuck me, you don't love me. That went without saying. If a guy made a pass at you and you said no, you got a speech about his version of socialism, which included your body as part of the state property he was entitled to. Trotskyism didn't go down with girls at all. That philosophy probably did work for the guys. Although the main tactic was just wearing them down – we couldn't get rid of them if we didn't fuck them.

When I lost my virginity it was a scheduled event. I wasn't getting into bed with him and screwing because I was hot for it, I was doing it because it's what we're going to do now. It wasn't sex. I didn't get hot, didn't feel good, and all the rest of the time I was with him it was like that – a thing we have to do now. So that was two months of fucking and not liking a minute of it – rather read a comic. When I was with somebody I was getting reciprocal emotion from, when they were feeling passionate about me, it was irrelevant if the fucking itself wasn't that exciting.

My first fuck behaved as if he knew what he was doing but now it's obvious he didn't know some essential things. He didn't get any help from me because I didn't know anything either. I couldn't say: I like *this*, when you do *that*, it's awful.

ISOBEL KAPROWSKI: In my teens I didn't have sex. I took the Catholic faith very seriously, and decided that for me it was sex within marriage – and I didn't want to get married – and that was it. So I'd go out with boys, but not go too far. Then at seventeen, when I was going to be confirmed, I fell in love. He was very keen to have sex and I wouldn't. Then I thought: Which will I regret more, having sex with him or not? I was mad about him. He was very intelligent, not educated but with a very good mind. So I thought: I'll do it.

So here I was, about to lose my virginity. I loved this man very much. There was no question of marriage – it wasn't that sort of relationship but I didn't care about that. I knew the sex would be painful, I thought I wouldn't be large enough to have proper intercourse. But I loved this man. He'd told me he was very good in bed. I thought: Oh come on, all men say that. I thought 'good in bed' meant someone who could give a lot of pleasure to a woman. But I knew even then that it was a line. So we had a drink and went to bed. He'd made his feelings clear: he very much wanted sex with me, he admired me enormously, my mind as well. That's why it was so potent

– it had both. And I believed all this, and still do. He treated me with enormous tenderness. He aroused me as much as he could and tried to penetrate me and he couldn't. He gave up for a while and we did other things, then he tried again and couldn't. This went on for about three hours. How he managed not to lose his erection, give up, get fed up, I don't know.

But I was right to choose him as my first, because when we did finally manage it, I came immediately. I probably did pass out, no joking. I remember thinking: He put something in the drink. Even though I'd had orgasms from an early age, I hadn't realised what sex could be like, and hadn't expected any vaginal pleasure. I'd only had vaginal pain. I felt on top of the world the next day, absolutely feminine. This is what men and women were meant to do together. Wishing I'd had sex many years before. I was a very moody adolescent, and that's one of the reason adolescents do get moody – they've got a lot of sexual energy they don't know what to do with. It's not just careers, school, friends, it's sexual energy. So if I hadn't been sexually assaulted, I would have started earlier. However, after that I absolutely loved it.

JANE MILLS: I was fourteen – very young for those days. It was true love. Same boy from the age of fourteen. I was very fat, went anorexic, got thin, got a boyfriend and we fucked. I got diarrhoea instantly. But it was wonderful. I remember skipping home feeling really excited: (a) that it was illegal; (b) it was lovely being cuddled, made love to, I really liked taking my clothes off, and what was terrific, Mummy and Daddy wouldn't know. Independence from my parents. Contraception? Forget it. From fourteen to eighteen, every month I worried I might be pregnant. Sucking off and coitus interruptus were the two big things. There were only condoms then. No Pill for a fourteen-year-old. I wouldn't have known where to go. And no one my age used contraception that I knew. One girl had an abortion. I had no thoughts of getting rid of my virginity, I just wanted to be loved. Hadn't had time at fourteen to think about it. It was rebelling against my parents and getting love. I then felt I was a misunderstood teenager. One day, I was on the back of my boyfriend's motorbike and we went to a Rolling Stones concert. That meant so many exciting things. I was banned from seeing the Stones – my mother thought they were really dirty, thought they had syphilis. I was not allowed to ride on the back of a motorbike. I was not allowed to make love. And this evening I did all these three things. I'm not sure which was the more exciting.

64

LYN PROCTOR: It was my second term at university. I'd never had a boyfriend before. There were a complicated set of factors behind this, mostly connected with my father being the headmaster of the local boys' school. I saw myself as the skinny kid with the big nose and glasses and so did everybody else. But at university, Keele, things changed. I embarked on my first boyfriend, first love affair, first sexual relationship. I was terrified of losing my virginity, terrified of the idea of pain. But I began to realise after a couple of months of me sleeping in the bed and my boyfriend sleeping on top of the bed that the only reason why I wasn't taking things any further was that I was terrified. So having realised this I thought, This is silly, it's perfectly obvious that the human race has survived this experience, this doesn't make any sense, and other people do seem to quite enjoy it, I've noticed this and the person in question is a person I completely trust. So having established those things in my own mind I went to the doctor's and got myself put on the Pill – all very simple. The sex was good. The first time we were in bed and had been doing that half-and-half not-quite thing that you tend to do before you get to full intercourse and after a certain amount of time I said, 'By the way, I've decided that I do want to have sex with you and I'm on the Pill.' This of course had the obvious effect – he completely lost his erection (as would any normal man in the circumstances). The next night he went out and got so drunk that he couldn't get it up with anxiety. But on the third night things went right. It was my first sexual experience and one of his first; I didn't know what I was doing and I certainly didn't expect him to have an awful lot better idea.

KATE HEATH: Mainly it was curiosity. It wasn't wanting to get rid of my virginity, I was just curious about sex, I wanted to know what the fuss was about. I'd seen my older brothers and sisters, who were all bonking, right left and centre. I knew that and I assumed that sex would be enjoyable. I wanted to try it out for myself.

I'd had sexual fantasies and feelings when I was twelve, thirteen. Even before you've kissed someone you start thinking about what it would be like and the sensations and stuff. So I did. It was a bloody disaster. The guy was a car mechanic, a year or two older than me. He wasn't a virgin. There wasn't any great lust, any great desire, even sexual intensity, it was merely curiosity. I sent him off to get some condoms; which was nothing to do with feminism, just me being bossy: I've decided I want to lose my virginity this afternoon, so off you go. That was the kiss of death, really, by the time he came back I'd really lost interest. He hadn't. So there we were on my living-room floor. No great heady emotional experience and not even particularly

65

pleasurable, though it wasn't particularly painful. The one thing I hadn't learnt was that you had to be active, that you couldn't just lie there and that you'd get all these sensations. I was incredibly naive about the sexual act itself, even though I knew about the mechanics. I just had no idea about what it was really like. I just thought: Is that it? What's all the fuss about?

SUZANNE MOORE: It was the mid-Seventies. Virginity was just something I wanted to get rid of. Teenage girls are very cynical. We'd have long discussions about it. The first time you do it should be with someone you don't really like, so that the next time you do it you'll know how to do it properly. We all had these ideas of technical proficiency – from Erica Jong, *Cosmo*, my friend had this book, which I think was her dad's, called *How To Be a Sensual Woman*. We had this idea that there was definitely a proper way of doing it, a good way of doing it, and we must try to measure up to this, although none of us was actually that sure what 'good' really meant. It preoccupied us a lot. This idea of expertise wasn't really about you enjoying sex, about the woman enjoying sex, but about being able to be very good at it. So something was being imposed upon us. We didn't talk about whether we liked doing it, just that we knew how to do it. Though I don't think the boys appreciated it, that we'd been reading all these books. I was on the Pill. It was easy enough to get. You just went to the clinic. Also condoms. I won't say I didn't take any risks, because I did, but we all thought that girls who didn't use contraception were stupid. There weren't any double standards. It wasn't that girls who did it were bad, because we'd all read Erica Jong and we thought we should all be doing it, all the time. The other thing was that everybody in our town, Ipswich, had the clap, because of the US airforce bases all around there. All these new strains that were coming in from Vietnam. My best friend, the first time she ever had sex she got gonorrhoea. There we were sitting there in the clinic in our nice little grammar-school uniforms.

NICK DAVIES: I was quite late losing my virginity, I was seventeen, at the Reading Rock Festival, with a drunken hippie who dragged me back to her tent. She was about a year younger, but she was much more experienced than I was. She dragged me off, had me, and went to sleep. So I went to sleep and the next morning I was woken up by her best friend who dragged me out into the field by the ankles, stark bollock naked, screaming at me, 'You fucked my best friend when she was drunk!' Meanwhile I was saying, 'That's not really the situation,

66

and can someone throw me some underpants.' And there were all these hippies and punks standing round, screaming and laughing and thinking it was all hilarious. I was quite freaked out about the whole thing, though about four months later I fucked the best friend too.

STUART MORRISON-WALSH: I was eleven. I was in the States. I'd gone to the States for a massive big Jesus festival somewhere in Pennsylvania. 'Jesus 2000' it was called. There was like fucking real raving Christians, except for this one tent of guys who were just into hard rock music – which was ours. I went over on a scheme – taking deprived children from Belfast and giving them some fresh air, you know. So I was staying with this family, and that's where they took me. There was a big complex in the middle of the festival, and in the middle of that was a big store, selling all this Christian stuff, all these bibles, tapes, records, whatever. I bumped into this woman, twice my age, she was a nurse, called Mandy. Literally bumped into her, knocked her over and I picked her up. I walked back to the tent, but later that day I saw her again at an ice-cream stall. It just went on from there. I was the only person at the whole festival with a Northern Irish accent. And I lost my virginity twice. Once with this Mandy, once with another girl, nearer my age, who was working on the ice-cream stall. That stall was covered with fellows. She had on these hot pants and every time she went to scoop out an ice-cream, her arse popped out of these hot pants. So all these fellows were standing there asking for a fucking big double cone that took a long time to pour. So one night I walked up to her and said, 'I think you should invest in a pair of high heels.' She asked me why, so I told her, just to take the piss, and she really loved it. So there was her as well. It was brilliant. But I lost my virginity to a twenty-two-year-old woman and that was scary. I was eleven. I don't know what the fuck she was playing at but I didn't feel abused – I felt fucking fantastic. To be honest I felt a complete vegetable. I was eleven, I didn't know what to do. This was something my mum hadn't told me about.

NICKY SUTHERLAND: I was legal when I first had a screw, it was just after my sixteenth birthday. It was shit. It was like wanking but out of rhythm. I thought, This is wrong, I'd rather be in the bog having one off my right hand. The girl I did it with looked like a boy, and I thought, at least if you're going to break your virginity you should do it with something decent. I did feel you should only do it to the person you love, which I know is a hippie thing to say, but I believe it. So I didn't do that the first time and I didn't really enjoy it, and I don't think she really enjoyed it either – but I don't really give a shit.

ELLEN SEVERIN: After school I went straight to Cambridge. This was 1982. Didn't have a year off. I was as green as grass, straight out of the schoolroom, from this unbelievably prudish, cloistered Irish environment. My mother and sister were fantastically good looking, my brother was good looking, film star good looks and I was the runt of the litter. But when I arrived at Cambridge all the boys started coming on to me. This was not that surprising – there was one woman to every six men at that time – but I thought that this must be a cruel heartless joke on their part. I really couldn't believe that anyone could find me sexually attractive at all. I felt very persecuted by all this, and I was absolutely persecuted for my first term in Cambridge.

I was reading law and there was a group of wild, tearaway young men, ex public-schoolboys, in the third year and apparently they looked over the first year women and targeted two or three and took bets as to who could seduce whom. They made my life an absolute misery for my first term. They came round in a group every night, threw things at my window, shouted at me drunk at three a.m., masturbated outside my door, really... And I had absolutely no idea how to deal with this. I was totally sexually backward. I was horrified and I was still certain that it was all a joke. It got out of all proportion. I went home at Christmas absolutely miserable, didn't want to go back, came back utterly wretched to have it put to me by one of these boys that what I needed was a boyfriend and quite obviously this was what was wrong with me. Everyone else was pairing off and I simply ought to go out with one of their group and everything would be lovely.

So since I was totally terrified and so much at a loss – I didn't know England, I'd never met public schoolboys, didn't know how to deal with that sort of world – and so I thought: Well, he must be right. So I decided, almost at random, to pick one of this group of boys and lose my virginity to him.

I actually managed at this stage to enjoy a reputation simultaneously as an ice maiden and a slut. There was a book in the Law Library, where I spent my time studying, which was supposedly a suggestions book and its purpose was to communicate with the librarian about books and periodicals that were required. These boys lived under the Law Library – which meant I couldn't get to work without running this gauntlet – and they altered it to the 'suggestive' book, and there appeared numerous entries in this book, about other girls but mainly about me. Drawings would appear of me supposedly
68

sucking off one of them, disgusting, revolting. Obscene graffiti. My tutor, who had heard this book had become a source of student humour, went one night to the library, opened this book and read the whole thing – and this was how I acquired the reputation of being a slut – at which time I was in fact still a virgin. It was the most cruel and ghastly persecution. My whole life changed, it became sexualised by this group of bloody hooligans.

But gradually I came to agree with them: there must be something wrong with me, I'm not able to cope with adult college life, and it must be because I don't have a boyfriend. Sex will sort everything out. I still wasn't sure whether they did fancy me, or they were just being cruel to a naive Irish girl, but either way I decided that sex was going to happen. I decided that I would lose my virginity to the one member of the group who lived out of college, at Jesus. Not wholly unattractive, a sort of rugger bugger. So I armed myself with a half bottle of gin and turned up at his door at midnight. He was taken totally by surprise. I turned up with my bottle of gin, my little bag of personal effects, and announced that I'd come to have sex with him. No contraception, but I assumed that he would and indeed he did. I produced my gin and suggested we drink it. He was totally spooked by the whole thing and went into this noble thing of how he wouldn't want me to do anything drunk that I wouldn't do sober... I said, 'No, no, I have decided, I realise I've just been being ridiculous, of course I'd like to go out with you...' So he was obliged to say that he wanted to go out with me and they all fancied me to death and how pleased he was. I was such a child, but I thought I've got to do this and this is how you go about it. I knew I certainly wouldn't be able to do it sober, so I thought I'd better do it drunk.

First we sat on the sofa and we drank and eventually he kissed me and we had a discussion about the ethics of the whole thing and I kept saying, 'Yes, I do want to do this.' Off we went to bed. He put on this condom and stuck his cock into me and because I didn't have a hymen – that had gone horse-riding – and there was no bleeding and shrieking, he immediately said, 'Oh, you've done this before,' and I said, 'Oh, no I haven't.' But he didn't believe me. 'You've been round the block before.' After which it degenerated into the most fiendish, terrifying experience. He made me do all sorts of things, he thought I was much more experienced. Suck him off in this nasty way, that sort of thing. I thought it was utterly ghastly, but I was quite drunk and I just went along with it. I didn't gain the slightest pleasure, but I just did it and thought: Oh, this is what sex is like. After which he started screwing me again, during which he went into this pornographic monologue in the third person. Like reading out some reader's letter to a magazine: 'Then he did this, then she did that,' muttering under his breath in this grotesque monotone. I just thought, Well, that's what sex is like, I always knew it was filthy and dirty and awful – and yes it is. I stayed the night and the next morning it was all terribly embarrassing. I walked back into college the next morning, Sunday, carrying my little bageen, and the first person I met was a boy I'd known since I was eleven or something, who had gone to Cambridge when I did, and he said, 'Oh hello, where have you been then?' and I had to go into this fantastically elaborate story about going out early to do my laundry.

After that I found myself as this man's de facto girlfriend. And I had to have more sex. I hadn't been put off as such, I just thought: Well this is what sex is all about and I suppose I'll get used to it. It wasn't physically pleasurable in the least – it was frightening, but things that are frightening are frequently exciting – and what was really exciting was the idea of this whole new adult world: I've done it now, it's a great relief. I was very glad to lose my virginity, I was expecting all sorts of pain and tears and everything else and now thank goodness I'd done it and that was that. So I carried on sleeping with him, still utterly miserable, for some weeks. The pornographic fantasies wore off, but the sex was still the most perfunctory kind of ritual, utterly grotesque. I got more and more miserable and eventually I told my friend, this older woman. She heard me out and she suggested, the first person who ever did for me, that actually you didn't have to do things you didn't want to do. So I did stop.

The Seventies

ISOBEL KAPROWSKI: Sex was a more intense thing in the Seventies. There was a feeling that every man you met might be a sexual partner, and you didn't have to be committed to people. I remember one man – I feel bad about it now – he came to my flat and we had sex. We'd only met once or twice before. After the sex all I wanted was to get him out, didn't want any more to do with him. He was probably quite hurt. There was no emotion involved, just sexual passion. But I don't think women act like men if they do that. Both sexes are capable of having casual sex and enjoying it. The difference is, it's easier for men to enjoy it than women.

The Sixties retain the image, but if the sexual revolution, in whatever form it took, may be seen actually to have taken place, then it's the Seventies, that much maligned and somewhat tawdry decade, that have the substance. Almost everything that is seen today as quintessentially 'Sixties' took off in the years that followed, and nothing more so than sex – which became simultaneously both a battleground and a hotbed of experimentation. In terms of what would follow, the gender politics of the future, the revolution of the '60s was irrelevant – a self-indulgent love-in for youthful patriarchs for whom 'Let's smash the state' was just one more variation on 'Get your knickers off'.
The 'counter-culture' of the Sixties had never been much more than the preserve of a cultural élite, staffed by bright middle-class boys and girls parlaying the fruits of the 'never had it so good' boom into a vocal denunciation of the mores of that same excursion into materialism. For that élite even the sedulously pursued hedonism of the period had its ideological trappings. For most the hedonism dropped away, but the ideology, any ideology, became even more important. It was that group, the liberal to left offspring of the

71

bourgeoisie, who pioneered the sexual politics of the Seventies – feminism, gay liberation, even the nascent, earnest and much-derided 'New Man'.

Across the tracks, as it were, lay the preserves of the mass market, those for whom the chronological Sixties had been pretty much business as usual, and for whom the mythologised Sixties were something you enjoyed at second hand, lovingly doled out through the hyped-up lubricity of the media. Come the new decade, they too wanted a piece of the action. The ideology certainly wasn't that exciting - the bra-burning 'libber' was a lineal descendant of that other sitcom stock-in-trade, the mother-in-law, and her gay peers still 'queers' to be bashed - but the sex looked like fun, and whether purveyed through the pages of Cosmopolitan or, for the more determined, through the swingers' ads in the contact magazines, it seemed to be there for the taking. The hippie philosophy had always been presented as a thinly-veiled licence for promiscuity; now the subtler trappings of the alternative lifestyle - 'peace', environmentalism, exploration of the inner self (whether psychedelic or spiritual) - all that was stripped away. What remained was the sex, and you didn't need LSD, long hair or the remotest desire to change the world to enjoy that.

Thus the Seventies can be seen as two strands of sexual progress. The self-obsessed and the self-indulgent, as it were. And as the decade moved along, both strands became ever more intense, the politicos in their endless fissiparous wranglings, the swingers in their polymorphous perversity. Sometimes paths could even cross - the intensity of late-Seventies gay sex, typified by the hardcore S/M clubs and the bath houses of New York and San Francisco, might have seemed purely hedonistic, but in an era when, as the slogan had it 'the personal was political', even fist-fucking could be invested with political overtones.

SWINGING: All Together Now

For all its protestations of equality, the hippie scene, let alone that of the gilded élite who pranced their way across 'Swinging London', was an exclusive playground. The very nature of that world, call it alternative society, counter-culture or underground, was that it stood in opposition to the mainstream. To enjoy the delights of dope, sex and rock 'n' roll, one needed to cross certain lines, abandon certain habits and substitute for them a whole new set; to do it properly it was necessary, in short, to abjure the Establishment world. If the alternative society was indeed to be 'alternative', the 'straights' simply didn't count. The mainstream, on the other hand, was far less keen to ignore the hippies. The media loved them, trivialising their beliefs and regurgitating them as simplistic slogans. None more so than 'Make Love Not War'. And it was 'love', instantly decoded by the mass market as 'sex', that really piqued the readers and watchers. That hippie boys and, even more excitingly, hippie girls spent their waking hours locked in polymorphous perversity, their writhing limbs wreathed in druggy vapours, their minds careering madly in psychedelic spirals, was axiomatic to readers of the tabloid press. And reading about such frolicking was not enough. Bluntly, the mainstream wanted a piece of the action. They didn't want the philosophy, they certainly didn't want the drugs and rock 'n' roll, but they did want the sex.

It is in the nature of revolutions to thin out as they spread. The real sexual revolution, the women's and gay liberation movements, which were gathering ever-greater strength as the Seventies progressed, held little appeal for the unconverted; it was all those supposedly rutting longhairs that attracted attention. It wasn't a matter of beating the freaks, and not that many particularly wished to join them, but why should the weirdos have all the fun? As the Sixties moved into the Seventies, the essential hippie lifestyle first diluted, then seeped into everyday life. Various tenets of hippiedom – environmentalism, alternative medicine, the varieties of religious philosophy that would become known as 'New Age' – gradually infiltrated the mainstream. These would take time, but one thing was easily suborned: sex. It required no ideology, no politics, merely a propensity for self-indulgence. If this mass market sexual revolution had an image, it was far from 'underground' illustrator Robert Crumb's exuberant picture of 'The Intercontinental Fuck-in and Orgy Riot', a scabrous fantasia of writhing craze-o flesh, but rather the slogan set above the entrance to Hugh Hefner's Chicago Playboy Mansion, that spiritual HQ of sanitised excess: 'Si Non Oscillas Non Tintinnare', a piece of dog-Latin that loosely translates as 'If You Don't Swing, Don't Ring'.

TED POLHEMUS: What we have is a group of people committed to an alternative lifestyle which includes promiscuous uninhibited sex.

Then we have a broader population that says: I don't want to give up my upwardly mobile aspirations, I don't want to live in a commune, but this free sex sounds really a good idea. This gradually emerges into things like swingers' clubs. This touched the mainstream population both in the States and here: in America you've got swing clubs like Plato's Retreat; here it's suburban parties with keys thrown into the conversation pit.

IAN JACKSON: Swinging was well established in England in the Seventies. It flourished in America too, starting in the late Sixties, and there it was more a lifestyle than a pastime. The English view was very different from the American way of treating it as a philosophy, a way of life. And it's a big industry there – you have lifestyle holidays, conventions, there are magazines, many, many clubs. All dedicated to swinging. For them it's more than a pastime.

There were hardened swingers here too, who were seen as people notching up numbers on the bedpost, but I don't think they were truly representative. For a lot of people it was a phase. The hippie ethos was: don't be possessive in relationships, no jealousy allowed. The swinging movement was very different. It was a suburban thing. Quite extraordinary the number of people who come from Essex. There's a major enclave down there, a significant enclave.

ADAM COLE: It's all rather twee, English, and Mickey Mouse. It is like trainspotting – a common interest that brings them together, like joining a cycling club. A sense of belonging somewhere.

IAN JACKSON: I think swingers do keep their activity fairly quiet. It's not like naturism, where you can involve the whole family. (Though I would say most involved do have children – finding babysitters seems to be the biggest deterrent to coming down to the club.) A lot of the women on the swinging scene are looking for action with other women, the AC/DCs. More than I realised. At one time I had a suspicion, viewing it as an outsider, that this was to please men. The idea was a woman would make it with another woman for the benefit of the guys. In fact there seems to be a genuine desire there. You often see a guy standing at the bar drumming his fingers while his wife dances with another woman, and he has to go up and unglue them. A lot of women seem to be very much in charge of the situation. The reasons behind swinging are as varied as the people themselves. A lot of them are fairly confident in their relationships and are fairly happy. Been adventurous, tried quite a few things. And it's the women who
74

go for exhibitionism. Go round with no underwear, very short skirts. Then there's dogging; it goes on in carparks. People drive up in their cars and watch other people screwing. There's an etiquette about covering your car light with a certain colour – things like that.

***

INDIA BATTENBURG: In 1975 I met Heinz. I'd been told he was the kingpin of the whole swinging scene and indeed he was. He had two address books, one for ordinary life, and the other for swinging life. One for England, the other for the rest of the world. He'd started going to nudist clubs in the Fifties because he wanted to be free and easy. He was a real charmer, one of the most charming people I've ever met, incredible sense of humour. He used to go upstairs and say: 'Do you fuck?' Some said no they didn't, but he got quite a lot of yesses too. 'Would you like to fuck?' was the phrase, I think. He was well known for his parties, which he'd been having for years. He was also well known in Ile de la Vent, in the South of France, which was a rather strange nudist island, half owned by the French military, half privately owned by a German nudist colony. Over the years it had become less puritanical and a home for the swinging scene – they'd come there from all over the world. This is where we went for a holiday. His wife went too with her boyfriend. He was forty-seven when I met him. He had very little family left. He'd been sent over from Vienna in 1930. Most of his family ended up in Auschwitz. Anyway, on the island I met all kinds of people from all over the world. They'd been going there for years, parties all the time, incredible amounts of screwing going on. Heinz used to take two or three girls with him, and I was told I was very privileged, when I went I was the only one. I became obsessed by him. I knew him for two or three years. But things started changing then, in the mid-Seventies. However much fun I was having, there was no future with him. He had his own life and family. I used to screw his son as well. Heinz always had a dark room laid out with mattresses, for gay encounters. Then people were embarrassed having bisexual encounters when they were supposedly straight. Very tactful. A lot went in there who otherwise wouldn't have. I went in once, and there were hands, everything going everywhere. Quite exhausting.

SARA DALE: Heinz was the king of the swingers and I was one of his protégés. I knew this photographer and one day he asked if I'd like to go to a swing party. I said: 'I don't have any Sixties clothing.' 'It's not that kind of party.' He explained what a swing party was. 'Give me a raincheck, call me next time,' I said. 'Let me just absorb this whole idea.' And then I did go to a party, dressed like a Jewish friar – long skirt, very old-fashioned – and met two people who I spent a lot of time with. One was a man with a confectionery business. He spent two hours talking to me then made love very gently and beautifully. The other person was Heinz. After this other guy made love to me, I said I wanted to be left alone for a while to draw in this new way of thinking, and I was watching somebody else on another bed – an amazing lady who had five men on the bed with her, and she handled them with such verve. I thought: 'That's how I'd like to be. Just as I was putting on my clothes Heinz came and said: 'Don't get dressed, I want to spend time with you.' I was very shy. I'd just got my bra and pants on and he undid it and took over. I was blown by that. I said, 'I'm going home now.' After two totally new experiences for me. He said he was leaving too, lived in Stanmore and that he'd lead the way to his place. I spent the night there, and his wife was there. I don't think I got home till about seven-thirty the next morning. Heinz took me under his wing after that and I went to nine parties in seven weeks.

***

England boasted a number of swinging clubs, of which two – Candy Club and Nightshift – were the most popular. Until the police shut him down – a raid that led to a £3,000 fine – Ian Jackson ran Nightshift.

IAN JACKSON: I was running the club quite openly. I didn't make much money because it couldn't run for long on a continuous basis. It was either moving venues as clubs were bought and sold, or you'd have police harassment – they'd lean on the club owners: We'll have your licence revoked, etc. – so over the seven years it never ran continuously. Perhaps at best six months at a time, then three months, nine months. It didn't make me a rich man. I went into it rather idealistically: wouldn't it be nice to meet and have a drink with like-minded people? Something like that didn't exist. Didn't like the idea of writing to box numbers, people you didn't know, you weren't sure if they'd received your letter as they often didn't reply, photographs could be ten years old – you'd walk in the door and think: Oh, this must be the parents – that sort of thing. All that's probably still true. It's pot luck for a lot of people.

We operated once a week and were very, very successful. We had rented a club in Kensington on a night on which it would otherwise have been closed. So they had little to lose. Within about three months we were pulling about 150-200 people, all couples. That was a very strict rule. That's what made us different from the rest. We were the first in this country to my knowledge. There are others in Europe and America, but they tend to allow singles at a premium rate, or partition them off into certain areas – they'll put them in a room and say: You can come out to play for five minutes, then go back in there. We felt a policy of couples only was the best in the long term, and most people who did join went along with that.

Couples generally mix within their own class. There's the Epsom/Ascot set, the Kensington/Mayfair set, then the Billericay/Basildon set and they don't mix. But at Nightshift they did, which was part of the appeal – a true cross-section of the community. And quite a large racial mix as well. We had a lot of Asians – more than their national percentage. And quite a few blacks, but mainly in mixed couples, black man/white woman or vice versa. Not a significant proportion though. And every car outside from a Porsche to an old banger.

***

If British swinging retains an element of amateurism, of being one more hobby, best reserved for the occasional weekend, its American counterpart is staunchly professional. Nowhere more so than at Plato's Retreat, a New York club that styled itself quite straight-facedly 'a clothes-optional recreational centre for couples'. For those who believed in the lifestyle, Plato's was Swing Central.

MATTHEW RUSSELL: One night, living in New York, I had some friends over on their honeymoon; they were staying with us. We'd done the usual route of discos and drinks and whatever and we were well oiled. We were in this cab and the cabbie said, 'Do you want to go to this place called Plato's Retreat?' I knew about it: a swinging club. You could only get in as a couple, and while there were (and still are) a number of hardcore couples who liked swinging there was also a large number of single men who would like to go to Plato's Retreat in order to be able to fuck lots of other people, to watch it and so on. But these men can't persuade their wife/girlfriend, so they get a hooker to go with them. And in fact, unbeknownst to them, end up swinging not with amateurs, but with other hookers, because that's exactly what half the other blokes had done. Which was rather sad. The deal was that you checked in for $50 per couple, no singles allowed, and they issued you with a towel that is carefully designed so that when you try to put it round you it doesn't quite meet so you can't actually wear it, you have to carry it. So in you go and there's this big open swimming pool, a bar, whatever. So we did that and it was quite nice, two a.m., smashed, going for a swim in a club. Then one noticed this doorway out of which is coming a faint glow and people are going in and out. So we decided to check it out. One goes through the door and the light is such that it takes a few seconds to adapt to the internal scene, which, when you can see, is revealed as being a couple of hundred people in this large, hall-like room with red velvet cushions, a couple of hundred people fucking. Various things were going on. There was this black guy with the most enormous cock one had ever seen surrounded by at least six girls, all of whom were doing various things to him and he to them. Then there was this middle-aged businessman with a paunch lying on his back with his eyes closed and a girl obviously a good fifteen to twenty years younger than him giving his semi-flaccid cock a blow-job. And looking desperately bored while she does it. Then this rather good-looking young bloke comes up on all fours behind the girl who's doing the blow-job, who herself was on all fours. He taps her on the shoulder, she looks round and gives him the nod and he starts to fuck her from behind and the blow-job suddenly became rather more exciting. While all this is going on my friend and I left our wives and went into this large jacuzzi wherein there were a variety of things happening. But when we allowed our feet to participate in one of the things that was happening this was definitely not welcome and this very heavy guy looked up, 'Butt out, buddy.' So we did. It was clearly not a place where you just went and fucked anyone you took a fancy to. Which of course was the rather childish fantasy that one had. There was definitely a form of etiquette, just as at a dinner party you have to use your knife and fork in a particular way. It was clear that in Plato's Retreat the same sort of rules applied. Us two English boys didn't know the rules, although clearly there were many who did.

LYN PROCTOR: It was a remarkably cheap evening out, all things considered. You take yourself in, you sign your disclaimer. As you go in the first thing you have to do is sign a little piece of paper that says you are an adult, that you are fully aware of what you are doing and what you are letting yourself in for and you are doing this completely of your own free will. Then you take your ticket, $35 a night for a couple. You had to go as a couple – although there were a lot of men who would take a prostitute. Then you'd take yourself into the changing rooms, take most of your clothes off, not all of course, and out you come again and then you realise, 'Oh this is silly, what am I going to do with this pair of knickers when I go swimming?' So you go back into the changing rooms and take off all the rest of your clothes. And you wrap your towel around yourself and stroll on out feeling that everybody's looking at you, but of course everybody isn't and where do you go now and where is everything? So first of all you look for the familiar. Head for the food and drink. You can always sit down and have a drink of something – there you are with your glass of fruit juice, Caribbean punch, whatever – because they weren't allowed to serve alcohol. You didn't have to have a licence to be a sex club but you did have to have a licence to serve alcohol and you did have to have a licence to have a swimming pool. So at this point the pool was full of mattresses and you couldn't drink alcohol. So here were all these people screwing in the swimming pool. The wonderful irony was that what the city was trying to do was stop the sex club existing, but all that happened was that where there could have been swimming and no sex, there was sex and no swimming. So there you are, sipping your punch, eating your Jello and your pizza slice, and these couples would wander up and say, 'My name's James and this is Doris and we're from Idaho and I'm in ceramics and would you like to join us in the mattress room?' You'd either say, 'Yes,' or 'No,' or 'Actually we're eating at the moment, why don't you join us?' 'Gee, you're from England...' This wonderful American politeness. After having sexual intercourse with complete strangers they would leap up and start shaking hands with you. Formal introductions, but after the event.

The most interesting thing was meeting and talking with people for whom these swinging clubs were a way of life. I met one couple there who had been part of the swinging scene ever since it started. They would go to the clubs three nights a week and have on average intercourse with something like five or ten other couples on a night. Whether they've cut down since, I don't know. If they've survived I imagine they have, but at that stage AIDS hadn't had any impact at all. The awareness in the heterosexual community was nil.

The irony, of course, was that few if any of the participants in the swing clubs felt the least sympathy for the 'alternative' theories that had spawned this relatively new and utterly liberal attitude to sex. Far from seeing their orgies as the first stage on the road to political revolution, the average swinger was as committed to the status quo as the most repressed conservative. Life could be compartmentalised and sex, however apparently sensational, was simply confined in one more compartment. Whatever happened after hours, the corporate lifestyle and its enthusiasts were under no threat.

79

IAN JACKSON: Some like to meet on their home territory, or on neutral ground, or they prefer to come to you. So you get ads that say: 'Cannot accommodate', or 'Will travel', etc. They've generally got children. More hardened ones will say: 'No time-wasters' – they can't waste an evening just meeting people and not getting down to business. But a lot of people would meet and say:'Well, we're not that compatible either sexually or otherwise,' and would call it a night there. Others are less discriminating. The hardened swingers will say: 'Let's get down to it, we're here to fuck.' But others have a slightly romantic approach, which is where I am I think. Wouldn't it be nice to sit around with nice people, listen to some music, have a few drinks *and* you fuck as well? An ideal world. And after sex, well there's a special bond there that you don't normally have with people who come round for a drink. When that works, it works very well and there is a special something about it.

DAVID MISSEN: The thing about swinging is the difference between coming from need, which was the old wife-swapping syndrome, and coming from plenty. When you're coming from plenty the other relationships are really an extension of the fundamental relationship rather than a substitute for it. In wife swapping it's a substitution. Your partner's not giving you what you want. I have relationships like this too. Chronologically I've been involved much longer than Sara [Dale]. I started modestly in this area in my very first marriage, which was a very long time ago, in the Sixties. Then it was a bit wife-swappy and we didn't much care for that, and didn't do much of it. There were magazines then as now which told you where to go for it. Occasionally they happened spontaneously. One of my earliest experiences was at the end of an evening in which my then wife and I had gone to a reception with a friend of ours, gone to dinner afterwards, gone back home, got into a fascinating conversation about erotica, which ended up in an alcoholic series of claims about who could do the best strip. We all competed and it led on to a beautiful threesome. So sometimes things happen that way. Sometimes more from planning and advertising.

SARA DALE: Before I went to a party I always masturbated, because I wanted to come from plenty. Therefore if I had intercourse with somebody, it was a summation of what had gone before, rather than because I wasn't getting enough. I was making love to myself. I'd start long before going out. I'd make myself beautiful for myself, then caress myself and I'd talk to myself. My hands would be the lover and
80

my skin would then feel excited. I'd do it with my eyes closed. I didn't use toys to start off with. Toys desensitise, I think. I don't see them as a replacement for a man, they're different. Just like lesbian sex is different. Masturbation is just a different type of sexuality. Masturbation before a party is getting rid of any possible need, so that by the time I went I was coming from plenty.

The scene is many different things. Some groups are Forum Society groups, quite closed. You can't go unless you're introduced by somebody. Single men have greater difficulty getting in than single women. Some of them are very bizarre. They play sexual games. One group I went to, they put coins all over the body and men had to hunt to find them. At others you swap partners. The better ones, you developed a rapport with an individual. You might have intercourse or you might not. I met a number of people I've become very close to, who are friends of ours. One in particular. His business was going through a bad time and he found me a very receptive person to talk to, and I was very positive for him, a good luck coin. He'd talk over his ideas with me, and we also had a very good relationship. We didn't have sex the first time. We cuddled, stroked and talked. Very beautiful. We developed a relationship. The people I have intercourse with are people I have a good relationship with. They are lovers. They all know David [Missen]. They couldn't possibly have intercourse with me unless they accepted that they were an integral part of our relationship and not excluding David. That doesn't mean threesomes. They're just part of my relationship with David. I don't build up something with them that's breaking down something with David. When I come home, David won't say: 'What happened?' I might say, 'It didn't get off the ground tonight, he was upset so I gave him a massage.' If it's got to intercourse he won't need to ask. He'll say, 'You obviously had a very good time.'

TED POLHEMUS: You have a law of diminishing returns here. You're working yourself to death to keep up the score. If AIDS hadn't come along, and herpes before it, we would have had to have invented some other way out of this frenzied cul-de-sac. It was clearly driving people completely bananas. I have to let those involved in it speak for themselves, but it seems to me that there's no logic or conclusion to this line of behaviour. There is a direct but perverse line between this sort of activity and the media focus on the sexual revolution of the Sixties. Everything else that for the hippies themselves had originally surrounded and nourished it – concerns with communal living, with spiritual values above material values, things like that – all these things had been stripped away, and we were left with the simple fact

81

that I do it therefore I am, and I do it a lot, thousands and thousands of times.

RONA AND BARRY

'Philosophers In The Boudoir'

They live in a large converted cottage on the outskirts of an East Anglian town. A sign warns of grass seeds recently scattered on a bare patch of lawn, a Jaguar and a BMW stand in the drive, another Jag, an E-type, is in the garage, a polythene-wrapped, as yet unplumbed jacuzzi visible through the conservatory window. Inside, the sitting-room is neat: nondescript pictures, units for the stereo, the TV, the video, portraits of teenage children. Only a pair of photographs and a magazine indicate a certain ... eccentricity. The magazine is devoted to body piercing; inside, among the pictures of studded penises and metal-laden labia is an informative letter, signed with their names. The portraits, both of Rona, show her tank top pulled taut between her breasts; they spill out to either side, the golden ring that adorns each nipple prominent in the blown-up print.

BARRY: I'm fifty-four, which means I grew up in the Fifties. Sex was important to me in the Sixties, but I didn't make a special study of it. I was training to be a scientist and sex was just a part of my life. I certainly wasn't a hippie, I wasn't a Teddy Boy either. If sex came my way, well fine. But in the Sixties things certainly were swinging. Everywhere you looked. There was dress: the miniskirts, which went right up to the micro-minis, and even topless came in for a while. All of which were part of the sexual aspects of the period. And people were far more free then. Then there was the Pill. That made a big difference. The Pill was obviously a huge change, it made people a lot freer, gave them much more opportunity to do what they wanted to do. That was obviously one of the biggest influences. But generally the times just seemed freer. You could express yourself more, you could dress how you wanted to. Also the governments have changed. They were much freer in their attitudes then – you had a Labour government. Now you've got Conservatives and they always clamp down – we can do it but no one else is going to, that's their attitude.

RONA: I'm forty, just. I was a teenager in the Sixties. And of course that's when I started having sex. But before that I can remember

82

vividly sitting on my father's lap when I was about six and feeling very uncomfortable because I knew he had a penis. Six years old. I couldn't feel comfortable, whereas I've got a twin sister and she sat on my dad's lap happily, and I looked at her and I thought, How can she do that? – because I was very sexually aware, very sexually aware. I just thought that my sister can't be sexually aware, because if she was she wouldn't sit on my dad's lap like that. That was all within me, of course; my dad had no sexual tendencies towards me, it was me. The first flash of sexuality I remember was even earlier. Or somewhere around that time I used to enjoy, how can I put it, holding on to my back passage, right. I used to get very sexually stimulated by that. Though I didn't really know that – I just knew that it was a good feeling, so obviously I done it more. When I was at junior school I had three different girlfriends. Margaret, Doreen and Valerie. I love big women with big boobs, absolutely adore them, and my friend Valerie was big and I was in the bath with her, we were both about ten, and her mother was in the kitchen, they had this bungalow, and I was fingering her and exploring her body, exploring her boobs. They weren't that developed of course, but still. And there was another girl I did the same with, and I remember lying on this playing field with these two boys and this girl Margaret and really getting turned on by her lying next to me. And I started to get a bit of a complex about it: What's going on here? The others, my friends, were experimenting like I was, but we never actually talked about it. It was a bit taboo: we done it, but never actually talked about it. There was no sex education, not at junior school. My mother was very prudish, you couldn't talk to her about anything. So I was really groping in the dark.

BARRY: Literally. I didn't get sex education either. I went to a grammar school and we learnt in the playground. When you're around thirteen you start talking about it and really you pick it up as you go along, from your friends. I didn't have any very early sex experiences. I suppose I started at about fifteen. Not intercourse, just the hoping and groping. I remember in those days I went out with a friend and two girls. The big night out was to go down the local park. We sat on the park bench and I think I spent four hours to get round to feeling her boobs, and that was only over the top of her bra! Those were the days.

RONA: So I was a teenager in the Sixties and I remember experimenting with clothes and shoes. And I really captured all the sexy stuff off television, any form of lust or sex. Pan's People, Hot Gossip later. I was definitely turned on by these girls, I really, definitely enjoyed it. I didn't feel disgusted with myself, I really did enjoy the feeling I got from it. They supplied my fantasies. I remember masturbating with a hairbrush – they didn't have dildos then! So they provided lots of fantasies, and thinking about big boobs, women with big boobs.

Boys came into my sex life when I was about fifteen. Though unfortunately when I did have sex and was eventually broken in, I just wondered what all the fuss was about. Quite honestly. I expected more. I was very lustful – actually I think I nearly killed him – I wanted it every night, I wanted sex every night. To have that orgasm every night. When I did it for the first time we were both lying in this barn, really exposed to the elements, and I suppose I was a little bit frightened. I was having my period and I was educated in the fact that maybe I could get pregnant – he didn't use a condom or anything. We weren't worried about the morals or anything, just that I might get pregnant. So what happened was that he withdrew and obviously that's not the ideal thing to happen, it's a bit of a letdown when a man has to withdraw and ejaculate somewhere else.

From then on I was really lustful, I wanted sex every night. He brought along some photographs and there was this woman on this sofa sitting on this man's penis, all these people round them, and I got so excited about this picture, it was so horny, I just wanted to have sex there and then. He got really frightened. We were just driving along and we could have gone off into a lay-by and had it there and then if I had my way, but he couldn't. What frightened him, because the pictures turned him on as much as me, was that he might get carried away. I think he was nervous as well that they turned me on so much. Then I moved on. I had several cocks after that, sorry, several relationships. But after that first one I did view them just as cocks – a bit naughty really. And then I got married – I was three months pregnant but that wasn't the real reason: he was just a smashing guy. And I think he rather calmed me down. I was going off the rails a little bit; I wanted to do so much.

BARRY: I've always been a sexual 'experimenter' ever since I was a teenager really. I got married at twenty-one. I'd done a little bit of experimenting before that – not much, not serious swinging, but I was trying to get into that scene. At that time it was very small, it was all undercover. I got into the scene after I got married. The way you did it in those days – it was very much undercover – there were magazines like *QT*, the Harrison Marks type things and some of the photographic magazines, and one or two of them had personal ads in the back. So this was a method of contact. I don't know how I found that out – through the grapevine I suppose. All it would say was something like 'Couple interested in photography would like to meet others'. Nothing blatant like you get today. You knew that was the invitation. It was couples only, wife-swapping as it was called in those days. So my wife and I got into this swinging, and she had one or two bits on the side which I knew about and allowed to go on. As it happens I didn't. What I enjoyed was the couple scene, and that was with her. So that went on through our twenties and on to our thirties and then she got a bit bored and things just fizzled out. So eventually, eight years ago, we split up. I met up with another girl, adventurous, liked a bit of fun, a giggle – the big thing was that she was fun. That went on for a while, but that fizzled out too and I went off to live by myself in a mobile home.

RONA: I was happily married for fourteen years, got two lovely children, both at university now, but I suddenly felt very bored with my relationship and knew that I needed more. I started to have affairs but my husband didn't agree, he didn't want to have affairs, although I encouraged him. Obviously I had terrible guilt feelings because we couldn't express ourselves sexually. Anyway, I couldn't live with the guilt and we did actually split up and then I had three years apart on my own to think what I really wanted, which was very good for me. And then I met Barry.

BARRY: The way we met was that I knew this girl, Trish, and she asked me: 'Will you be my boyfriend?' It was a strange request – she was a bit of a strange girl. She was bisexual but didn't really know what to do with that side of it. Anyway, when I met her I was just off on holiday, to get away from it all, and I said, 'I'll see you when I get back.' So a week later I came back, absolutely knackered – I'd missed my flight, been travelling twenty-four hours – and I arranged to meet her. She phoned me up and said,'I've got this friend, is it all right if I bring her along?' This friend happened to be Rona. So I turned up and there was Rona standing demurely in the corner and I thought, 'Cor, she's pretty.' Now up to now I hadn't had any relationship with Trish, so I still wasn't sure what the scene was. I gathered that she probably wanted to have sex with Rona, or at least have someone else there to help her through the situation with me.

RONA: I'd been friends with her, we lived on the same estate, our children knew each other and she was into birth signs and we were

85

both Capricorns, and I think that she would have liked to experiment with me, she knew she could trust me. We'd talked about it a lot already, lesbianism. So that was in the background, though we'd never actually done anything about it.

BARRY: So we met, eight years ago, and this first meeting was a real bang, in all sorts of ways. It developed into a sex scene between all three of us. Trish very quickly got bored with it – she went off to bed and told me,' You can take my friend home.' I did take her home and had sex with her six or seven times, all over the house.

RONA: What happened was that I was immediately taken by Barry – he had a nice tanned body and he looked smart. I just sat and listened to him and he showed us some photographs of his holiday and when he was telling us about them it came over really well. He wasn't just some moron who didn't talk to you 'proper'. I knew his background, I knew he was quite wealthy [He runs three companies, involved in making specialist paints and inks] but mainly I just liked him immediately. Then Barry brought out these really dirty, sexy books. I hadn't seen them before: *Colour Climax, Private*, Scandinavian stuff. Really sexual books. And that was how we got worked up, and then we started stripping each other. And I felt Trish and she was really wet, so she was obviously very sexual and she wanted it. But she in the end she couldn't handle it. [Laughs]

BARRY: I thought something was going on; when she'd phoned me that afternoon I wondered, could this be a two-girl, one-man scene? I'm not madly worried about that, actually, a lot of men go absolutely potty about two girls at the same time, but I didn't really bother. Still I thought that could be the situation. Though I didn't really know what to expect.

RONA: I certainly didn't plan anything. Trish asked me, and she said there was this nice guy, would you like to come round? So I said, 'Well, you better phone him up and ask him first. I'm not just going to call by and intrude.' And Barry said that would be all right. But I was interested to see what would happen too. I literally hadn't had a sexual relationship with a woman at that time, apart from when I was about seventeen when I was in a pub and I was immediately attracted to this other young girl there. She had blonde hair, very sexual, and for some reason we both started giggling. I never really knew her but I went up to her and started talking, then we started kissing

86

passionately in the pub, really enjoyed it. But that was the only thing I recall with another woman, and then obviously I got married and nothing developed there. But with Trisha I would have liked to have got into the relationship and together we could have got something going. I didn't want to stop going with men, but this was something extra.

BARRY: I think if you're sexy you're sexy and that goes for men and women, and the really open people will try anything. Though when I started swinging I didn't get together with the men in the couples. I was still full of the old phobias – keep away – but later on you learn that it's not that bad. Though I must admit they're always there, very difficult to get rid of. But on the whole the men in swinging situations don't get together, not normally. It's not normal. In the couples scene we see virtually no homosexual activity at all, not ever.

RONA: A really laid-back person who hasn't got any worries, any hang-ups, would do it but...

BARRY: You get a swinging party going and there's plenty of women get into each other but not men. I've never seen it.

RONA: The thing is that when two men get together they are actually classed as gay. Because they've got female tendencies. But two women together seem to be seen as more acceptable, more natural. That's the way most people see it.

BARRY: I've only had one guiding light as regards a relationship, and that is honesty. Because you don't need bits of paper, you don't need anything else, if you're honest that's all you need. You tell each other all your needs, whatever they are. But an awful lot of people find it hard, I think most people find it hard. Honesty hurts, after all. You've got to be honest to yourself first and most people find that's too painful. But that's the way I've always been, ever since I was thirteen. I didn't like the values that were being given me and I wanted to work out my own, so I said, right, I'll do what I want to do as long as it doesn't harm other people. As long as I wasn't being nasty and damaging other people, I was going to do what I wanted to do in life. Ever since then I've done the same thing.

RONA: I do feel we're fortunate to have found each other. I was going through a very, very bad patch when I met Barry. Although I'd made

87

the decision to leave my ex-husband, I didn't feel complete. I actually invented a lover, who didn't really exist. But that softened the blow: it wasn't reality but it did help me. This imaginary lover. Some guy whom I knew about vaguely but had never met. A totally fantasy relationship, although for a while I really did believe it. But I've found that it happens to a lot of women.

BARRY: When I met Rona I just carried on as I had been doing in the swinging scene, and Rona joined me. We went on from there. It's not just swinging and sex. It's much wider. If you've got the mind and approach that we have, it is true that we get on better with people from the piercing scene, the tattoo scene, nudists, these scenes where people are much freer in their thinking, they're more honest people. I always say that what sums it up is the old tattoo expression: 'The only difference between us and non-tattooed people is that we don't give a fuck if you're not tattooed.' That sums it up, that attitude. Ordinary people get uptight if you're tattooed or you've got punk hair or your tits are showing; these people just say do your own thing, be yourself, express yourself. It's a matter of being what you are, of expressing yourself. When you have a tattoo or a piercing, you're making a statement about yourself. We're both very much like that and a lot of our experimentation comes from that.

RONA: When me and Barry started to get together and started to sexually explore each other we began with threesomes. One other man. We tried to get another woman but we weren't very successful until we actually invited another couple. That was fine. With couples though there's always something that goes not quite right. Doesn't quite gel. Jealousy can come into it.

BARRY: It's difficult enough for a relationship between two people, getting that right; when you add one more, another male, that's usually all right too, but when it's four, it gets more difficult.

RONA: That's why the party scene is better. Several couples. There's no compulsion like there is when there's only four of you. You can go up to someone and if they don't want you they can just say so. And if you do you can just join in. Anything from half a dozen to twenty, thirty, forty.

BARRY: What matters, what's important is that there are no pressures. You can get yourself lost at a party. You can have sex with
88

any one particular person or one particular couple. Whereas if you've only got two or three couples you're almost under an obligation; you can't just stand there, you've got to join in. So the pressures are much greater. But the open party scene is very much more relaxed. We tend to get invited to other people's parties, we don't have a lot of our own. We do advertise in contact magazines but the number of good couples you get that way you can count on the fingers of one hand. Very few indeed. But we do have various friends, I've known some of these people for a number of years who are always having parties, and things seem to work out better that way. There are groups within groups really. Sometimes you go to a party and you see all the same people there and suddenly you'll get invited to someone else's and there's a whole other little ring. Most of them are held in London.

RONA: It's a long time now since I can reflect back to one-to-one sex. When you first meet up, a one-to-one situation is absolutely explosive, it's really great, but then after a little while, three years whatever – maybe that's just me, another woman might sit here and say I don't agree with you – it gets a little bit boring. As I say, it's just me. If I'd dressed up or whatever for my ex-husband it would probably have been a lot better, but I didn't do it, it wasn't expected so I didn't have that drive. Barry expects me, if I go out, to wear high heels, stockings, suspenders, short skirts. He would absolutely not go out with me in trousers.

BARRY: Trousers are definitely not allowed. Usually knickers aren't allowed nor bras either. That's my expectation, that's how we started off. Rona tends to be more submissive than dominant. Not just in the S/M scene, but generally. After that first night which was a real wham bam scene, we planned to meet a few days later, and she asked me, 'What do you want me to wear, how do you want my hair done?' All this sort of thing. I thought, Well this is great. I like a woman who'll play up to you like that, and at the same time I respect her, because I wouldn't get her to do something she doesn't want to do. But if you find a woman that's very willing to please, all the better.

RONA: I can be very strong in some ways. I have a tattoo on my leg, at the top of the thigh, which I like, and Barry has one on his arm.

BARRY: It's basically a slave girl with her foot chained to her arm. She's kneeling. And there's my name, 'Barry's', and there are flames coming out of the top as if the name has been burned into her thigh.

89

I have the same tattoo, only saying 'Rona's ' on my arm. This was almost like our marriage symbol.

RONA: So I agreed with this because I really liked it. Barry also wanted me to have another tattoo design, on my pubic hairline. But there's no way I would have done it. Because I can see that a symbol there would not be neat, and Alex Binney, who does tattoos, agreed with me: down there you're moving about all the time, you're creased, you're not flat – I'd be lucky if I was, I'd love it – and he said that the actual symbol would be untidy.

BARRY: So we didn't have it done, though Rona is having more work done on a boob. What I wanted was a whip, a curled whip and some initials entwined. But we could never get it quite to fit in that area properly so we gave up that idea.

BARRY: We're into S/M but it's not hard S/M, really. We like a bit of bondage, a bit of light whipping and things like that, but nothing heavy.

RONA: Yeah, but you're not very good at it. You only do it when you're pissed.

BARRY: The thing is I don't really enjoy inflicting pain on Rona, but I don't mind watching someone else do it, that's a better turn-on. And she'll play up to that. She's not a very good performer for me, but if she's got an audience, then she plays up to that. It's interesting to see how much pain she will actually take.

RONA: I rebel against Barry when he disciplines me, I really do. But I'm an actress, and I play up to it. I like being displayed.

BARRY: I think the only way you find out what it is that excites you is by experimenting. If you don't try it you don't know. It's like piercings: people look at our piercings and most of them go, 'Ouch!' like that and they cringe. 'Isn't that painful?' But you say, 'No, it's not particularly painful, it's no different to an earring. You accept having pierced ears, but having a nipple pierced...' But there's no way of convincing them unless they actually have it done themselves. It's the same as being afraid of homosexuality. It actually isn't really painful.

RONA: I can honestly say that piercing does enhance sex.
90

BARRY: It's not simply the physical thing – having a bolt through your penis, rings through your vagina and so on. I've got a ring and a stud in my penis. I don't think it gives me any extra physical pleasure, but there is a lot of mental pleasure. I'm enhancing my body. Rona's rings really turn me on, she's got five down there, it looks nice to me and there is a sexual aspect to it. I suppose between us the sort of S/M relationship would come into it as well.

RONA: I believe that if you want to experiment, to do things in life, then you have to have an open mind. It doesn't matter what background you come from, if you're willing to learn about certain things and you want to learn about certain things, then you're going to. And that goes for sex as much as anything else.

   I've been in some Wildcat videos, which are about the piercing scene. 'Another fantastic insight into the wonderful world of stainless steel: Ravishing Rona and Barry – filmed down in our dungeon.' Are we stars? I don't know. Lots of film and TV people have wanted to talk to me, but I've usually said no. There was one producer wanted me to go on as part of a panel: a *News of the World* reporter, Christine Keeler and a well-known celebrity. I just said, 'On your bike.' No way. I don't want to be under that sort of pressure, and I don't need it for my ego. I know what I know and I do what I do. I've met some really beautiful people and it just doesn't really matter. Maybe in the end I'm quite shy. I would go on these shows if there were something concrete to say, but I can't see any point in spending the time defending myself as some kind of freak. I've been in *Tit Bits*, and the rubber magazines, *PA UK, Body Art*. Barry did send some pictures in to one of the magazines but in the end he thought they were probably too professional. I enjoy pornography. I like the Sarah Young videos, they're really superb. Very erotically, tastefully done. The difference for me between erotic and pornographic is the difference between something tasteful like a Sarah Young video, and something like *Animal Farm*. Bestiality. You get the feminists after someone like Linzi Drew and let's face it, it's envy. They're not very attractive women and they're jealous. But you've got so many conflicting ideas. It's a good job we're not all the same.

BARRY: I think there is a slight analogy with the people who say that with drugs the soft ones lead to the harder, cannabis leads to heroin and so on. It isn't simply a matter of everything being equal and us wandering around sampling as much as possible. I think you do need more kicks, so to speak, you need to do something different, otherwise it does get boring. There's thousands of things we haven't tried. There's far more extreme people than us in the scene in various ways. Let's take S/M: we went to one party, no sex allowed, pure S/M, all the dominatrixes with their whips, flailing guys until the blood flies. Now that to us is extreme and it's a turn-off. It depends on which area you look at it. We try a bit of everything but people who specialise do get more extreme. But we have done a fair few things. Water sports, we've done that. Rona will take it all ways, she'll give and receive. Our interest in water sports started very early on in our relationship. The first time I took Rona to be screwed in a threesome, in this caravan, couple of weeks after we met. Rona said, 'I'm sure you've got some friend that would screw me,' so I said, 'Well there's this guy and he just happened to have asked me if I know someone who fancied a threesome.' So I took her round there and we had a really horny sex session. Then I took her back home. We were still in a high state of sexual excitement and I up-ended Rona and she started peeing everywhere, in pure excitement. And that was how it started. We liked it, it turned us on, and we went on from there. At first Rona would just pee when she felt like it, then you get into other games, having someone pee on you, drinking it ... it just goes on.

We do find that we have particularly widespread interests in all the scenes we go to. Most people are into something – they're into S/M, and all they want to do is whip the hell out of each other and that's all that gives them pleasure, or they're into rubber and they only dress in rubber – but we do everything. Rubber, leather, PVC, erotic stuff, piercing, tattoos, S/M – we cover the whole scene. I think it's coupled with the way our minds work in general. We don't just look into sex whatever the variety; it's all linked to a myriad of other things: philosophy, meditation, yoga, all sorts of experiments. And you do find they're all linked up in a way. I myself am trying to write a book about the interface of science, religion and philosophy – because they're all saying the same thing in different ways.

RONA: The way we got into piercing was that we were looking at a book of nudes by John Hedgecoe and saw this picture of a couple, who turned out to be Henry Ferguson and his girlfriend then, Jo, who had some piercings. We'd never seen anything like it before. And we both said, 'Wow, how amazing. That is absolutely beautiful!' We both agreed. No promoting whatever, we just said it right at the same time.

BARRY: At that time we were both getting into nudism, going to the local nudist beach, things like that, and we thought it would make a lovely bit of body decoration, to walk along with nothing else on but a couple of bits of gold jewelry.

RONA: I said, 'Wouldn't it be lovely to be able to be pierced?' So about a month later we found out there was this thing called the Sex Maniacs' Ball. It was the second one they'd had. We were reading about it – in the *Sunday Sport* or somewhere like that – and I said, 'I'd really like to go to that,' and Barry said it's quite expensive, but we got tickets and we went. And when we arrived Henry Ferguson happened to be there with a little stall. It was so strange. So we booked an appointment with him and had our piercings done. We've been to all the balls since then. We're great friends of Tuppy [Owens]. At the last one we were under the table, providing 'under the table services'.

BARRY: The first time we went to any sort of fetish-dressing do, that was a mind-blowing event. Fetish Fetish, it was held in this wine bar. We were just fringing on the scene, we'd never been to a club like that but heard about it somehow. So we went to this wine bar and went down the steps and we just couldn't believe it. There were about 150 people, couples, singles, you name it, dressed up in anything you could imagine. Five years later, it all seems quite normal, but then: there was leather, rubber, PVC, exotic stuff. It took us about three weeks to get over it. Really unbelievable.

RONA: There was men dressed up in really tight rubber leading these other men round on dog collars; women dressed up as really hard mistresses; and then there was this big-busted lady, absolutely delicious, sort of looked at me and sort of devoured me with her eyes and I really loved that. That was when I did submit to a woman. She spanked me. I was actually sucking cock and I was forbidden. Several cocks. It wasn't really the done thing there. This guy said he'd like to let it go on, but he couldn't. They didn't want the police in.

BARRY: We didn't go to Nightshift. We went to the other one, Candy Club. But I think someone in the police really wanted to get him [Ian Jackson]. Maybe there was someone undercover, a bug. They really wanted him. All the clubs are getting done over now, one at a time. The police can't have anything better to do; what I can't make out is where the orders come from. There's nothing illegal about these activities but these clubs are so harassed. I don't see us as political revolutionaries, no, but there is an element of revolution in

93

the way we're thinking and the way we're going. This is the thing though, it's always been this way – society is always afraid of people it doesn't understand. It used to be the punks, hippies, teddy boys, anybody you don't understand was anti-social, against society. It's utter crap. You should be able to express yourselves freely – as long as it doesn't hurt other people. What's an earring or a nipple ring or a ring through your cock? It's not harming other people. Obviously the way sex came a bit more out into the open has helped the contact side of things, but that's about it. It would be nice if everyone were free and open, but we're not about to start any world revolutions, no.

***

BARRY: When we moved in here it had an old cellar. Running with water, with a coal hole, and a copper boiler they'd used to do the washing. So we thought: this would be a nice place to convert. We were just beginning to get into S/M. So we had it built. The builder must have guessed what it was for, but he's discreet. I designed it, and he built it to my specifications. I'm sure he guessed that something was going on. There's a stocks, a lot of whips, chains, clips, handcuffs from the ceiling, all sorts of things. We have this bed, an old Victorian bed, we got it from a dominatrix, it's got the mattress covered in black.

BARRY: I think our children have some idea of our sexual experimentation, but I don't think they realise how deep it goes. I was quite surprised the first time I went to Rona's, before we lived together: she used to walk round the house totally nude, never hid anything from the kids. It was only a two-bedroom flat. One day we were screwing and Simon, Rona's son, walked in and we were screwing on his sister's bed and he asked, 'Where's my shirt?' Rona told him to go away, but he wouldn't, 'Mum, I want my shirt!' We weren't blatant, but they knew certain things. They used to be intrigued but they don't enquire any more.

RONA: About a year ago my daughter, she's at art school, went through a terrible stage. She went to see her tutor and he had this nude above his desk. And she was really complaining that she had to sit talking to him with this picture over his head. She was quite offended. She was going through this feminist stage, complaining about sexism and so on. 'How dare the tutors have these nude pictures,' all that kind of thing.

94

BARRY: My own theories on AIDS are not the same as those of most people we know in the swinging scene. We've been brainwashed about this AIDS thing. I mean that. If you look at the facts and figures they don't support what the media is saying. I'm a scientist and I look at things from a factual, scientific perspective and I said from the word go, there's something wrong here. When AIDS first appeared the outcry was, 'The whole world is going to be decimated, ninety per cent of the population will have it in ten years', and so on. I just thought: From a scientific point of view it's total nonsense. I still believe that, and my opinion is further and further supported by a lot of eminent people. They all agree that AIDS is non-transmittable provided that your immune system is working properly. The reason they gave for the way it does spread is that in the homosexual community there's drug use, poppers and so on and your immune system does get weaker; then in the Third World, of course, with all the malnutrition and so on, people's immune systems are not working properly there either. So I've altered my sexual habits a little bit, but not a lot.

RONA: I'm very concerned about AIDS, I really am. I think maybe Barry is being a bit too scientific. I have altered my sexual habits. Mentally and physically. When I first met Barry I'd screw without condoms. No way I'd do it now. I will do it in our private scenes but nowhere else. There's too much risk. I might not mind with a couple who we know well, but not at a party. Or I just play safe: I get into the women. I know it's cheating, but it's safe. I get involved sexually but it's less risk. And I think nine times out of ten men do wear condoms. Last night for instance, we had this gangbang scene. There were three guys here and they all wore condoms. So I'm having safer sex than I used to.

BARRY: I think Rona takes the viewpoint of the average swinger: she's frightened by AIDS, and quite rightly so. That's because it's put out as a frightening, deadly thing. But there was this headline in the papers: you're twenty-seven times more likely to die of falling off a ladder than of AIDS. That's the statistics. At the same time, if AIDS was booming in the heterosexual community, so would the other STDs, but this isn't happening. Certainly in the swinging scene we've never come across anyone with a sexually transmitted disease. But AIDS is a great stick for moralists to beat people with. Sexual diseases have always been used in that way.

95

RONA: I don't have that many gangbangs: the last one was in this club in Paris. There were thirty-eight different men in two and a half hours. A lot were in my mouth. They did all wear condoms. It's an open club and it would be very dangerous otherwise. I must admit that I don't think I could do it again. I was absolutely knackered, absolutely knackered. Two and a half hours non-stop.

BARRY: There's this club, La Cheminée, that's well known for gangbangs. They have these Sunday afternoon sessions. It has couples and swinging scenes too, but on Sunday afternoon they specialise in gangbangs – fifty or sixty males and two or three girls.

RONA: At the very beginning I was fine, but after that my mind was really blown. I was absolutely shattered. They all spunked off, though – I would have been really angry if they hadn't. One man actually spunked off five times – though we only count him as one out of the thirty-eight. I suppose it had been something we had been talking about for a long time; I do have a friend who had thirty-three men, including a father and son, so I saw this as a bit of a challenge. So we went round to the club this Sunday. I walked in the door and I must admit, I wanted to run out again. I thought, 'Jesus, all these men.' Afterwards I just thought, 'Well, that's something else I've done,' but really I felt numb, totally. Mentally numb.

We went to another club in Paris, Adam's, an S/M club. There was this top dominatrix there and she actually gave me a real going over. That was really, really superb, she done it really tastefully and it was nice to see someone doing the real thing. It was really good. I didn't even notice the crowd that was gathering round us. She was so good and what gave it this finishing touch was she had her girlfriend kissing me and caressing me. She just knew exactly what I needed.

I do enjoy pain if it's done in a controlled way. If a man just comes up to me and swipes me really nastily, then I will kick back. But if it's done in a controlled way, professionally, then it's different. Proper S/M isn't just swiping across the face, though we do know people who really, really, really whack to hit, and open up their skin, and there's blood and they just go on and on and on. I don't understand it and I don't even like watching it.

I do find I have to suspend my sense of humour with some of the fantasies and I am a bit bad with that. I have played the role of being dominant to men, these little wimps and slaves, but the trouble is I'm

96

not really dominant. Though a year ago I was quite dominant, really dominant, and Barry didn't like it. I was really getting into the swing of being dominant, but then a year has gone by and I'm really submissive again.

I quite enjoyed it but I can't quite understand these wimps. We have a friend who's really bizarre. He has his head used as a toilet seat. And he has this pipe up his rectum and these worms crawling up his bum. Live worms. I asked him, 'How do you feel?' and he said, 'It was excruciatingly painful.' He's a very, very, very intelligent person. A very feeling person and a wonderful cook. But he's basically fed up with straight sex. We've got another friend who's so fed up with normal sex that he really did do something bizarre. He did the ultimate.

BARRY: Yes. He actually chopped his cock off. He'd tried all these various things and decided that this was the ultimate. He was using some kind of black box, a device that you plug into your veins and gives you the ultimate feelings. He did it on video, apparently. But that level of pursuit is not our scene.

★★★

BARRY: The essential thing in life is to keep the mind going, to keep learning. That's why we go to philosophy classes. The Essex School of Philosophy, it's part of the LSE. It's a great mind-opening thing and it's not at odds with our way of life, though if we got into religion it might be. All that 'Thou shalt not...' I always have the premise that you make your own life and your own world, your own heaven, your own hell. It's all here. It depends how you look at things and think about things. I suppose you could say that sex is our religion, it certainly takes up a large part of my life.

RONA: It's certainly very important to me. It does rule my life, I can't deny it. Life's never ending and expanding and that's why I just can't go down one single alleyway. I have to keep trying different things. I take sex light-heartedly, I don't take sex serious; once you start taking sex serious it's over. If sex drives people to commit suicide or do bad things, have a lot of bad stress because they feel guilty, then there's something really wrong. But if you can look at sex with an open mind, light-heartedly, then sex can be a joy.

BARRY: It's like we never go to the same place on holiday twice. But looking for the ultimate? The ultimate sexual experience? There is no ultimate other than to become a wise man. You learn your whole life and you never stop learning. Sex is part of life and it should be as normal as eating a meal. Sometimes you have a good meal, sometimes a bad. It took me until I was about twenty-five to realise there was nothing sordid about sex, you didn't have to do it round corners – it's as normal as eating. I keep saying to people, 'You don't stick to the same food every day, you change it because you like variety – so what's wrong with doing that for sex?' We have all the wrong values in our society. If we didn't have sex we wouldn't be here, yet we're so screwed up about the whole bloody thing. Sex is a joy for us and I trust it will continue to be. We may have mellowed, you wouldn't want to stay the same, but one thing goes and something new comes in to replace it. What we do works for us. I'm not advocating it for everyone, but it does work for us.

FEMINISM: Shattering the Myths

The sexual revolution, Sixties-style, offered, as has been pointed out, more style than substance and certainly more quantity, if one was male and heterosexual, than quality, if one was a woman or what Gore Vidal termed an 'other sexer'. Yet by the turn of the decade the mode of the music, as the hippies liked to parenthesise Plato, had changed and sexually, perhaps more than in any other sphere, the walls of the city shook.

No more than had sexual intercourse 'begun' in Larkin's annus mirabilis of 1963, than had feminism emerged, fully-fledged, in the last few years of the 1960s. The litany of feminist foremothers – Mary Wollestonecraft, sundry Pankhursts, Virginia Woolf, even, in tribute to the newly computerate age, Ada Lovelace, Byron's daughter and the first and most enthusiastic proselytizer of Babbage's pioneering Analytical Engine – was well established. Nonetheless the feminist bandwagon gathered quite unprecedented pace from the mid-Sixties on. Like the gay liberation movement that followed close on its heels, 'Women's Lib' appeared at first as one more strand of the great counter-cultural debate, enthusing more and more women, though men, as yet, paid only lip service. The modern classics began appearing: Kate Millett's Sexual Politics, Susan Brownmiller's Off Our Backs. Severely academic, the product of middle-class intellectuals for the most part, such volumes were noted, but limited mainly to an audience of the converted. In 1970 that changed. Germaine Greer, ex-pat member of Australian Bohemia, lecturer at Warwick University and regular contributor to both OZ and Suck magazines (in which latter she had displayed, albeit somewhat distorted, a close-up shot of her pudendum) published her contribution to the genre: The Female Eunuch.

CLARE CAMPBELL: My brother's girlfriend gave me *The Female Eunuch*. I couldn't put it down, I was riveted. I'd been brought up in an Irish house where all the women waited on the men. This girl saw this going on and so lent me the book. It showed me there were things I could do, that I was freer than I thought I was. It really did change my life. Germaine's attitude is fairly masculine: you take sex where and when you want it, neither of you owing an emotional commitment. I couldn't take that on board then, I was too romantic and young people want to be romantic.

ISOBEL KAPROWSKI: I read *The Female Eunuch, The Feminine Mystique*. They were books my mother brought home. They didn't seem to have a lot to do with me and my sex life. Lots of irrelevant slogans being bandied around. I did go to a feminist meeting with my younger sister – and that just gave me a hatred of big organised people with one aim. Now I'm part of Feminists against Censorship, but I still don't want to be part of a huge movement. I had a horror of organised things. Anyway, we went to this meeting. Perhaps it was my imagination but I felt the women stared at me in a disapproving way, because I was wearing a skirt, had a bit of makeup on. That was the last time I went to a so-called feminist meeting. They were very much lesbian separatists. Orwell's junior anti-sex league if you like. My sister was interested in the political fight, but many women there felt you had to have sex with women to be politically correct. It didn't ring a bell with me.

The Female Eunuch *was a worldwide best-seller, analysing the condoned inquities of male-female relations, denouncing the clichés of romantic love and promoting female autonomy in tones that none of its predecessors had achieved. Enormously popular, it spoke loud and clear to a whole constituency of women whose own idea of a revolution had long since been evolving in a direction quite different to that of their men.*

JANE MILLS: Anyway, here I am at university, monogamous relationship, a Trotskyist. Then the women's movement came along in the second year. It's always to my chagrin that feminism came to me via two men. One was my literature professor and the other was Ibsen. I was asked to write an essay on *The Doll's House*. Literally like scales falling from my eyes. I wasn't a member of International Socialists but orientated towards it. I certainly thought of myself as a Marxist. Then suddenly realised, like so many others, that the left was male-dominated, we were still Norahs and nothing much had changed since *The Doll's House*, which was 1886. That's why I felt I could never join the party, because of their attitude towards women. But nor did I come across any Marxist feminist women's group. Politics with a big P was a man's world. Inside I.S. a women's magazine was 'permitted'.

A big discovery for me was a reaction against what I saw as liberation when I, with other feminists, thought: This isn't so very liberated. Before we were being good little girls and not doing something because our daddies / husbands / lovers told us. Now we're doing something, but who's liberated? Rather than closing our legs, we're now opening our legs. Sexual liberation is not personal liberation. That took me some time to realise.

I think a lot of us suffered from it. After I split up from the lover-of-my-life, I didn't have a sole lover, I was promiscuous and I didn't take sex very seriously. No different from an After Eight mint – that was the image I used. You have it after dinner. I devalued sex, as a lot of us did, and didn't see it could be very, very good indeed. For us this 'Have you come, have you come?' bit was very tedious. Just get on with it. But quality was important, you could and did ask for what you wanted. What I couldn't understand was why I would sleep with a guy and he'd act like I'd given myself to him, that this was some major event. What are you talking about? I don't want to see you again. Actually, I've only had one one-night stand. The fear was waking up next to this bozo, and having nothing to say to him. So for me it had to be some sort of relationship, with someone I liked and perhaps trusted. But I couldn't understand why men thought women were giving them more than a good time if they slept with them. They started talking about faithfulness, etc. I thought: Excuse me? I just fucked you, and I'm fucking several others.

For men, who had never had it so good for so long, the new world of the Seventies posited new and less palatable demands. More sophisticated positions would be adopted as the decade proceeded, and more brutish ones too, but stripped of the ideology that was a by-product of so inherently intellectual a movement, what in short the women's movement was saying was: it's our turn now. There was far more than sex, indeed sex would take something of a back seat for a while, as the purists of some real-life Junior Anti-Sex

League impressed male iniquities on the sisterhood, but initially, as women grabbed for what had once been male prerogatives, the old rules began to crumble. At least on paper. Political correctness was a term for the future, but it was certainly not PC, for instance, to kowtow to that old green-eyed monster.

JANE MILLS: Not being allowed to be jealous was a political position. If you were jealous, it meant you thought you owned someone. That I found extremely tricky. I felt sexual jealousy. Rather than saying anything to my partner, I blamed myself for having such feelings. Sexual jealousy is the most unpleasant feeling of all. It's awful, you hate yourself for it. It clearly punishes the one feeling it more than anyone else involved. I chopped that out, and with it a bit of my emotions and feelings. I felt it was politically unacceptable for a feminist to feel sexual jealousy. The position was if one's partner is having an extra-mural affair, that had to be negotiated. Before, that didn't happen so much. You had a contract, decided whether the relationship would be open or closed. What I was quite proud of was my feeling that if my partner was doing it, he was the one I had to be angry with, not the other woman. That was a relief. Taking it out on the woman was not acceptable. That way women can still be divided and ruled. Sexual jealousy might be a bad thing, but you can't get rid of it intellectually – it's there.

JOHN MICHAEL: By '72-74, there was certainly an idea that you shouldn't be uptight about sex, that you ought to do it, if you fancied each other – get on with it. There was one wonderful girl, Sue Armstrong. Once when we had a meeting planned, she never turned up. I spoke to her the next day and she said: 'Oh yes, really sorry, I was on the tube and when I got my money stuck in the chocolate machine this guy helped me get it out. I rather fancied him and we went off and did it at his place.' I said: 'Oh, well okay.' It was the idea that this was the right thing to do. In the same way you would wear certain clothes, keep your hair long, support certain groups. So if a group of you were together and all fancied each other, it was all right to do it. The fact you had a main girlfriend wasn't relevant.

But when bisexual chic came along, I didn't get into men. There were a couple of orgy situations where one might clasp a neighbouring dick, but not much more than that. It was something the women got into much more. Again underpinned by ideology – it was to do with sisterhood, women coming together, etc. Men were shits, women ought to stick together. The irony of it was that while it was a right-on

101

thing to do for women, it also fitted in well with traditional male fantasies, coming true in front of your eyes. When there were threesomes, it was usually me with a girl I wanted and my girlfriend being brought in on it. Occasionally those worked, but very often didn't. And the business of having it with other people – there were always extenuating circumstances. In theory, yes, if you fancy somebody go off and do it. But on that particular occasion I was feeling a bit upset; or I'd already said I wanted to go home. There was always some reason why that particular case was an exception.

The theory was that we loved and cared for each other but we also fancied other people. This should be fine and we wouldn't be jealous. In fact it didn't work like that at all, and it was a source of constant arguments and fights. My girlfriend was tempestuous anyway and she was always marching off, or locking herself in rooms and refusing to come out. There were other occasions where she went off with somebody. There was one time when I came back from somewhere and she came to the door looking sheepish and embarrassed. She said: 'Hello, there's someone I want you to meet,' and this guy came out of the bedroom, also looking sheepish and embarrassed. Then she said she thought we should have a threesome. I got frightfully huffy and marched off and sat in the bath. She was standing there saying: 'Come on, you expect me to, why shouldn't you?' And this other guy was hovering around looking deeply embarrassed. There was a brief period when it did work. When she was working with her band, there was a girl who fancied her and didn't mind me. So we had several threesomes with her. Those were fine, didn't cause a lot of emotional problems. Some of the others did. We both had quite a few affairs with other people, but it was a source of constant problems and tensions. For instance there'd be a girl I fancied and I'd expect her to join in, but perhaps she didn't fancy the girl, or she might fancy a girl and the girl didn't fancy me.

AVEDON CARROLL: There's different kinds of jealousy. The trouble is when you're really into somebody you stop being able to think about anything else. So you do nasty things without realising it. You're being thoughtless. It's not that you're fucking her that I mind, it's that you'd said you were going to be here at six, didn't show up till nine and you didn't even call. I was waiting for you, there were other things I could be doing. I have pretty much said to my partner: 'Tough shit, that's the way it is.' It works in practical terms though. He has lovers, but not regular ones. His women are in America or somewhere.

ARAMINTA LOCKHEAD: I'm very jealous. Always tried to fight against it. I've learnt to go for people who don't make me jealous. I've learnt to keep it to myself, try and rationalise it. I went through one unrequited relationship where I spent eighteen months being jealous. Sent me completely nuts. I have flashbacks of jealousy, and think: I don't know if I want to get into this again. It's an emotion I'm scared of – it can distort so many things. I'm good at talking others out of it but I can't get rid of it myself.

DUNCAN FALLOWELL: I tried hard to go along with the ideas of the Seventies' sexual revolution: no jealousy and so on, and I did manage. But I'm acutely possessive and I must have everybody but they must only have me. I accept that. But this of course produces drama and tension in one's encounters – you don't want them to be merely gymnastic exercises do you? There must be some kind of human or emotional ballast being exchanged too. Jealousy is a very important factor in sexual relationships and it can be a wonderfully thrilling one. I've actually used it deliberately in that way and it sort of fires you up. The point is that the game of love, the game of sex, has to include all these things. They understood all this very well in the eighteenth century. It's an art as well as an inclination. It reduces the excitement if you try not to be possessive. You should be possessive – the whole thing about having somebody is *having* somebody.

JEFFREY WEEKS: There was a positive ideology in the gay move-ment not to be possessive or jealous. The problem was it constantly conflicted with the reality of people's feelings. Angus and I met in 1970 and were partners throughout the Seventies, monogamously, whilst we were expected to live out a life of polygamy, non-jealousy, open relationships, etc. Many people had similar conflicts. Some tried to live this free life in communes, others set up home together.

MARIA CONCEPT: I did believe that jealousy was bad and all that. I had two relationships before I met my husband where there was a main woman they'd been living with. The first one I met just after he'd split up and moved out. He had a drink problem. I lived with him for three months. I knew he would see his wife as well. Didn't bother me. I saw her as the current relationship, not me. They were keen on us all living together.

   I had left home when I was eighteen and started living in this house with a band – the only girl. No affairs with any of them. Then I met this guy. He was an old hippie – lovely. White reggae mandolin

103

player. One of a string of many musician boyfriends. Anyway, he and his wife wanted us all to set up house. I knew I wasn't going to do that. Despite my philosophy on this, I wouldn't be able to handle it under the same roof. You know: 'Tonight I feel like going to bed with Emily.' A rota or something? That household scene does not appeal to me at all. The harem. She was older, very domineering, Virgo. I'm a Cancer with five planets in Leo. They had a child too, so no way. But it was fine with me if he went off and saw her – no big deal. I might have felt a bit lonely if he did, but he was a nightmare and the breaks were welcome. The second time I felt jealousy was a similar situation – another musician, just split up, but living in his house, the wife had moved out. I was monogamous for five months with him – a lifetime at that time. Then she moved back in. But he still wanted to see me. So when I moved to LA it became a ring twice and hang up job. He could speak to me whenever he wanted, but she didn't know about me. I felt very angry about that. So there was jealousy there. And no child involved. I said to him it wasn't good enough, this situation, so he worked me into being a friend of the family somehow. I became friends with her – another Virgo. But it was all too elaborate. In the end she buggered off anyway. I was then his best friend. He was on the road a lot, a girlfriend in every town – I was the girlfriend in the town he lived in, that's all.

JANE MILLS: You can be sexually jealous without being possessive. 'Why not me?' is what sexual jealousy is about. My take was: just don't lie to me. I cannot stand sexually jealous or possessive men. No way. A relationship need not be monogamous – it's a choice. I've always chosen monogamy. If someone feels it must be monogamy or nothing, it's up to me to decide if I want that relationship. On the whole I find it better if both are monogamous – less messy.

KATE HEATH: Not being jealous is fine on an ideological level, but it's different in real life. Having sex is only a physical act, so having sex with someone else is far less damaging to a relationship than emotional involvement would be. There is a difference between sex and love in this context. I know it's the old male excuse, but women can use it too. It's not a matter of right or wrong, it's to do with this community that you are trying to create, the feeling that you want to be the most important person in that other person's life and that will only work within a certain degree of trust. On another level you also want your freedom, you don't want to be restricted by another person.

104

Fuck knows how you resolve it. I don't know and I don't think anyone's come up with the answer.

ALEX KERSHAW: The Sixties' credo of no jealousy, no possessiveness has always been a myth. Men can switch off, lying to themselves, but they regret it later on. This girlfriend is the first one I've been faithful to. Prior to her, my attitude was: sex is available, I'll take it. It didn't seem to undermine the current relationship, although in retrospect they weren't that healthy anyway. But I didn't tell my partner I'd done it. You don't come in and say: 'By the way darling, I had sex with someone else last night.' But is it ever just one person's fault – the dynamic is created by two people in a relationship. Infidelity has to be seen in that light. There are reasons for male and female infidelity and that goes for both sexes, not just one.

***

JEFFREY WEEKS: The new social movements of the Sixties and Seventies were in a part a product of changes going on in the Sixties and Seventies, partly riding on the back of the new affluence, on demographic changes, etc. But partly a reaction against the worst features of the Sixties as well, like feminism was a reaction against sexual liberation for men, and the gay movement was against the limited changes that the Sixties had given a promise of.

AVEDON CARROLL: To me, feminism was the second phase of the sexual revolution. All the stuff I know now was always there, it was being spoken of. Women were doing things then, being more in contact with their bodies, knowing what they want, what they don't want, that there's more to sex than fucking. But it didn't ripple out into the culture. At the time the most radical thing was saying that women can fuck. They still stamped 'illegitimate' on birth certificates. You had to be locked up for life because you were insane, because you lost your virginity. The situation was really dire. Permissiveness was necessary because it was deadly the way it was. Now it's no big deal if your parents aren't married, but then it was a deadly secret you couldn't tell anyone. That's a really important change.

At first we weren't on the attack – we were just asking questions. Then we started to say: 'Actually, I've never liked doing it this way.' By '71, you couldn't get two people to agree on anything. There was a tendency to bring up these ludicrous arguments and the more you heard them, the more you started to realise how dumb they were. I

105

mean, why can't men do housework? It was natural then for us to be questioning these roles – that's what the Sixties were about. Men were saying: You don't have to go to war/to have short hair/to wear a tie. And we were saying: And we don't have to do the dishes. All of a sudden it was a big problem. Instead of: If you loved me, you'd fuck me, it was: If you love me, how about you do some of the work around here?

By '71, it was legitimate for a woman to question what was happening in bed. That was becoming a general thing. What didn't really come out until the Eighties was the idea that fucking wasn't sex. Feminists were saying fucking shouldn't be central, shouldn't be the goal. But it wasn't until the safe sex stuff you got the idea you didn't have to fuck at all, that all that other stuff is sex, we have a different sexuality. It took fifteen, twenty years for that to come out.

> *Central to the aims of feminism was the overturning of the sexual status quo. In this it succeeded, quite disturbingly well. And few suffered as did the men whose own sexual revolution had been so rewarding. The larger world might ridicule, backing off into easy cliché, but the ideologically pure, devoted to the rights of the black, the Vietnamese or the otherwise disenfranchised had little choice but, however unwillingly, to lend an ear to this more immediate pressure group. What they heard they did not, on the whole, like. The earliest 'New Men' did emerge, but for all their earnestness they were no more popular among feminists – who had no desire to see their movement snatched up and suborned by yet another group of males, however supposedly sympathetic – than their less self-abasing brethren.*
> *The result was a separation. If men could not adapt, then they had best be jettisoned. If sex was necessary, then better find its pleasures in the arms of another woman, far more likely to understand the subtleties of the female body, than in those of an insensitive male. Parties were studded with groups of wretched men, chatting dully in the corners, bemoaning their once omnipotent lot and topping each other not with tales of conquest, but with confessional outpourings of sexism overturned; meanwhile, across the room, their erstwhile consorts made a new style of running. Now there were new couples locked in public pleasure: as the old Frank Zappa groupie team had called themselves – Girls Together Only.*

HAZEL SLAVIN: In the late Fifties/early Sixties what you did was you wanked the bloke you were with and didn't get anything in return. That was having sex. When you got on the Pill, you fucked. But you

106

may not have got anything in return. So it wasn't until people started talking about women's sexuality that women felt that they could ask to be touched themselves, to demand the orgasm. Then we get the whole thing of the emasculation of men, and the demands on men becoming so great because women have become so powerful. And then there were women who said: I can do better with another woman, I don't want to have patriarchy in my life in any respect, and certainly not under the duvet.

JANE MILLS: I've had several relationships with women. It was politically correct for a while. I always was a bit suspicious of women who thought a lesbian relationship was ideologically correct, something they had to do for their politics. That was not in keeping with my form of feminism. Everything depended on the individual. I suspect we're all bisexual. That thesis was so crucial then. It's interesting that men are scared of homosexuality and women aren't. A man is feminised by homosexuality, a woman is made at some level even more feminine by being lesbian. Plus in a patriarchal society, lesbianism can be a huge turn-on. So it's more acceptable. I idealised lesbian relationships. I thought a relationship without the male ego would be bliss. I do idealise women. But it always disappointed me when one of my female lovers turned out as possessive, as controlling as a man. I like women more than men, but always fall in love with men – that's my misfortune. Increasingly as I get older I don't enjoy having sex with someone I don't love. If I'm not in a relationship, I'm not interested.

JANET GLOVER

'The most exciting movement around'

A leather jacket, jeans, cropped hair – it's hard to stand back from the stereotype, but a dress hangs on the back of the door. Fashion, like sexuality, is a matter of taste and timing. Her lover pops in and out. Unlike most interviewees they cuddle ostentatiously. Some kind of test for the visitor?

I was born in 1949. My father was a carpenter, one of the first members of the Communist party involved in trade unions. My mother went to Oxford; she was on the first NUS delegation to Czechoslovakia in about 1927. She went to Africa on her own, worked as T. S. Eliot's secretary. It was when she joined the Communist party that she met my father.

I was aware of sexuality from a very early age. Didn't know exactly what it was, but I was aware of being quite a sexual person. My body was important to me. And I was aware of other people being attractive. My mother talked to me about sex from the very beginning, talked about men having seeds in a little bag that they put into women, then they made babies. I asked: 'Is it a paper bag?' She looked rather embarrassed and replied: 'No, it's skin.' I looked a bit puzzled. But I was about two then. She did believe in saying things right from the beginning.

I went to what was thought of as a progressive school in Golders Green. Not half as nice as you'd think. Didn't have caning, but girls were very much meant to play with dolls and not be involved in sport. Boys were encouraged to be aggressive, tough, uncaring. It was very strange. I went there when I was four, and didn't like it very much.

I didn't like the structure of the sex roles as they were when I was growing up. Repressed, very definite male and female roles, a choice of getting married or the sort of involvement that would be a bit sleazy. Boys eyeing girls up, trying to get one. None of that appealed to me. The problem for me was when I got to adolescence and everything went into these rigid roles. Girls were expected to wear miniskirts and nylons with seams then. I have no objection to those kind of clothes whatsoever, as long as people who wear them feel in control of them. But then it was what you had to wear. Making yourself look stupid was how it seemed to me. It was sexy for other people, not for yourself. It took me a very long time before I could wear dresses and skirts, when I was much older, more in control. I could enjoy wearing them then. That's what the issue with clothes is, whether or not people feel in control of what they're wearing, whether it's something they're projecting for themselves, their lovers, their friends, or something they feel they have to do, either for the opposite sex, or to fit in with society.

I couldn't be a dolly bird. I just didn't look like that and I didn't feel like that. So I sort of rejected all that. But those seemed to be the only options: dolly bird or career woman. I didn't see myself going to university and being a career woman either. So there was a void, what else could you be? There were Beatniks about, but I didn't know how to become one. And Mods and Rockers too. I couldn't have fitted into that either. I didn't feel confident enough. But I was wishing I could be part of it, reading about drugs, listening to underground music, buying it. I was living in London, but couldn't seem to meet the right people to get into it. My clothes were wrong, I was a little bit shy. I felt really in tune with it all – politics, music, the whole thing, the idea of freer sexual mores – but I just didn't know how to meet people.

108

At the same time I was very attracted to boys and really quite interested in sex. I didn't do anything about it. I just thought I'd quite enjoy being fucked. But it wasn't on the cards because I couldn't get round all the game-playing, dating, pretending to be stupid, having to be feminine. I couldn't really do it successfully, and anyway I didn't want to. I wanted to get something out of it. So I'd rather have nothing than have something that was going to be horrible. It was terribly frustrating and I channelled that frustration into politics. I got involved in youth CND, went on Vietnam demos.

Then various things happened. I ended up selling records in a department store, started listening to underground records, and into 'The Perfumed Garden', John Peel's programme. I really enjoyed the music and listened to the words. I thought how much nicer it would be if things could be sexually freer, one could be somehow part of all that. It wasn't to do with marriage and the family and all the other roles. I'd picked up on *The Female Eunuch* theories before the book came out. Partly because of my background. Partly through the underground press. Magazines like *OZ* were pretty sexist in many ways, but nevertheless they did make you think about sex and the role of sex. It may have been male-identified, but it did ask questions, produced new ideas. A lot of young women picked up on that.

What changed my life was that I had a friend called John who eventually told me he was gay. He had never told anyone else. We talked a lot about sexuality and sexual liberation. So we went to a Gay Liberation Front meeting in about April '71, fairly near its beginnings. I thought it was the most wonderful meeting I'd ever been to. It seemed so free, with everyone relating to one another. It seemed to be about really trying to change things, having a revolution that included everyone. That seemed very exciting. Although it was a gay thing, it was to do with everyone being valuable, with gays being as free as everyone else, and trying to show people who weren't gay that you could have a different type of relationship, one based on communication, love, fancying each other, not on other things. The people seemed so nice and so free. That was the first impression. I thought it was absolutely amazing. I felt a fraud because I wasn't gay. It was the most exciting time to be involved, and the gay movement was more appealing to me than women's lib, which I was slightly part of. I've been in various women's groups, but none was as exciting as Gay Lib. It seemed the most imaginative, the people were so together. I remember in demos how the police couldn't pick people off, nobody would allow it. That was such an exciting feeling. It was all very idealistic, and one knew it wasn't going to last. I knew the world wasn't going to change that much.

Anyway, I went to this GLF meeting, then started getting involved in it. I didn't actually lie, they just assumed I must be lesbian since I was there. Your own proclivities weren't important though, nobody asked, and that's what was so very nice. I loved the demos, and particularly the groups. I was in the counter-psychiatry group – I particularly hate psychiatrists – and in the action group, and later on the gay women's group. I was a bit nervous about that one. I was on the young side, but the other women weren't that much older.

I was still definitely attracted to men then, very much indeed. No question about it. I hated being a virgin, really didn't like it. I was very pessimistic and assumed it would never happen. Partly perhaps I didn't present myself in the right way, partly I didn't meet the right people. I can't think of loads of school mates I wanted to go to bed with. When I was at the Arts Council, there was an older man there. We didn't have intercourse but did do bits and pieces together. He was fifty-eight, really nice. I didn't want anything to happen, I was too scared of getting pregnant. Then I met a man on the *OZ* appeal demo. He was a hippie civil servant. Twenty-two, long hair, heterosexual, quite nice. We went to the Miss World demo together with some other GLF people in the Albert Hall. Because I was wearing a GLF badge he thought I was a lesbian. He invited me back, so I went and he asked me to spend the night. He was quite nice, I wasn't wildly attracted, but I quite enjoyed having sex with him in a mild sort of way. There were two other women in the room. They weren't having sex, they weren't lesbians. It was funny that the first time I did it was in front of other people. But I didn't take any notice of them. It was all very laid back. It was funny because he thought I was lesbian, and that I'd also had lots of men. I never told him. He was really pleasant, but that's all there was to it. I couldn't be bothered to keep up with him. That was mutual.

I was really pleased to be part of the most exciting movement around at the time, and it didn't matter too much that I wasn't gay. I started going to the women's group, and I liked talking to them, they were nice, so much more my kind of people than others I met. Then I had a dream, not a sex dream, but about two women I knew, and all to do with changing trains. I looked at both of them and thought: They're very attractive. I woke up and thought: Good heavens, it's happened! I can be attracted to women! I had thought I could never be like that. Everyone has a sexual orientation, and mine was towards men. It was an incredible sense of release and liberation to realise I could be attracted to women. I still never thought anything would happen. But I didn't think I wasn't attracted to men any more. I was just amazed I could be attracted to women, because I was one of the
110

least bisexual people. Looking back I didn't have crushes on women or girls before that. Lesbianism wasn't really talked about. But after that dream, everything was easy. I felt much more comfortable going to these meetings. Eventually I met somebody, funnily who thought I was an experienced lesbian and I had sex with her. It was really nice, really easy, I really enjoyed it.

Before that dream, I just didn't find women attractive in a specifically sexual way. I don't feel I'm a particularly sexually repressed person, but it just didn't happen. Why, I don't know. I was very attracted to men then. Had constant sexual fantasies about men, having conventional sex with men. All the things young women aren't meant to like that much, such as fucking. That was really what I wanted. Many women preferred petting. Probably because of the men's inexperience. But a lot of women prefer non-penetrative sex. To what extent that's because they don't experiment enough I don't know. It depends on your partners as well as yourself.

It was about October '71 when I had sex with Paul. And then in January '72 I had my first woman. I lived with her for a couple of years. There was no fear that first time, it was just really great fun, really enjoyable, really good sex. It was wonderful – sex at last! And really nice sex. It was wonderful. There were other problems in that relationship, but I didn't have any problems having sex at all. I never did, never would have. It was all the outside things. It was society that screwed me up. So many people as teenagers feel all these anxieties and terrible problems about sex itself, and I didn't have that. It wasn't the sex, it was all the other rubbish I just could not get through.

Lesbians come out in the same way as gays. It isn't just one moment. I came out gradually. My mother said she found the idea of lesbian sex rather revolting, which was sad. I don't think she had a brilliant sex life, though she was very good in her attitudes towards it generally. She was really very honest with me, but didn't try to stop me. My mother still hoped I might have children. She died when I was thirty-two, still thinking that. It wasn't an idea I'd totally rejected anyhow. My father thought all this was rather good, he was quite pleased, had quite a kinky interest in it, which I didn't really mind, it was quite harmless. My mother was a bit worried, a bit distressed about it. She very much believed in equal rights for gays, but was a bit worried about me. But she said: 'You're different enough anyhow, you've been vegetarian, left wing and things like that. There are lots of ways you don't fit in, do you really need to do this?' I had to say: 'This is something I really feel confident about. It's not something that's going to undermine it, it will make things better.' Anyway I came out before I was gay. I started wearing GLF badges because I

111

thought it was very important. If people are going to hate you for that reason, too bad. It was also an act of solidarity with John, who was almost suicidal because he had never been able to tell people he was gay. And who told me. I just felt I owed it to him to put my energy into changing the horribly repressive sexual society we had. I used to wear the badge at all times, only taking it off just before I walked into work. I did half come out at work too, but I didn't wear the badge there. So it was really pretty easy because everyone thought I was gay before I was. So there was nothing to come out about. Everyone thought I already was, including the man I slept with.

It would be totally untrue to say I didn't appreciate heterosexual sex. I've enjoyed hetero sex since then. I've had quite a lot of it, had some last year. With heterosexual men. I had a great time. I've always enjoyed hetero sex. I enjoy lesbian sex more, but I still enjoy hetero sex. I loathe categories, but it is women I generally relate to. If someone is discriminating I think it's important to say, yes I'm lesbian. I'm not so attracted to men, but I have quite a free-ranging sex life. I was definitely one of the people Section 28 was designed for. Because if I hadn't been exposed to all this filth, I might be a nice housewife these days, instead of this rotten pervert.

I don't really think body parts are that important regarding sex. It's a myth that lesbians have better sex. A lot don't have much sex at all. There's what is called the political lesbian, in the women's movement, with the idea that men are the enemy, that they should separate themselves from men because it's politically incorrect to have much to do with them, and certainly to have sex with them was just promoting phallocentric sex and encouraging men in their worst habits. Their answer is to be with women. A spiritual and sexual commune. And that did mean not having male-identified sex. Sex would be non-penetrative, or there wouldn't be much sex at all. Unless you're really attracted to women you don't want to have sex with them anyhow. You probably do want to hold hands and kiss – the more romantic and esoteric kind of communication. And there were those who said that was the only kind of sex women should have with one another. That everything else was male-identified. I think penetrative sex is great. And I think that's a complete red herring. I thought lesbians didn't use dildos. They don't need them, but it can be quite fun. You can't say, well then you should be having sex with a man, because it's women you're attracted to. It's something that if you enjoy it, you should enjoy. People should explore their sexuality, find out what they want and then do it with themselves and with other people who want to do it too. What's significant is your personal
112

relationships, not what kind of sex you have. It's not equal sex we want to be looking for, but equal relationships.

It's important to have an equal relationship and to be socially equal in society. If people want to play roles or games within their relationship, that's a completely different issue. That's where I very much part company with the radical feminist analysis. They take all sides of sexuality and say they're all symptoms, they're all problems: pornography's the problem, penetrative sex is the problem, all this kind of thing.

I haven't been without a sex life for any length of time since the dream. I've been with my partner for the last eighteen years, but it's a non-monogamous relationship, and she's having a relationship with a man at the moment. I'm having a relationship with another woman. And we're both happy with that.

Of course the idea of no jealousy, no possessiveness is easier said than done, but I'm not really one who's ever believed in monogamy. I didn't have a monogamous relationship with my first woman lover either, partly because she was in love with someone else. It was all very complicated. When I was with her I had sex with two men and not properly with any other woman except Anita, who is my lover now. But by then she was involved with another woman. So we never had a monogamous relationship at any time. Lesbian relationships vary so enormously you can't generalise. I don't think of myself as in any way typical. I think most people don't have very long term non-monogamous relationships which last though. It's fairly unusual. But we're both fairly unusual. I've never been really frenziedly promiscuous. The last eighteen months is when I've had most sex with other people. Which is funny as I'm forty-two now.

Lesbians attract a different type of reaction and hostility than gay men. Any women who appear to be independent of men attract hostility. A very assertive heterosexual who doesn't take any nonsense, has lots of boyfriends or doesn't have any at all, will also attract that hostility. It's a sex role thing. And that's far more true for women than men. Fairly feminine hetero men don't have that much problem. Only if they're actually taken as being gay is it a real problem. Whereas masculine type women will get a great deal of hostility from men. My troubles have come far more from being unconventional: a pro-sex, anti-censorship type lesbian. That's when you get some hostility, or can do. People thinking your lifestyle is immoral. People have said that to me. They think having sex with more than one person is immoral to start with, irrespective of gender. Then there's also the hassle you get if you have sex with men. You get that from women.

113

Obviously that upsets a lot of lesbians. You should keep yourself only for women. It's selling out.

I have had a great time. I really enjoy it. It was great having six different people who were all great in the last year. It was also very funny. Back in the Sixties, you were finished when you were thirty. Never trust anyone over thirty as they said. But particularly at forty. Now it's not like that. We are the people who were young then, and we realise you don't have to give up at forty.

GAY LIBERATION: Coming Out Loud

Gay Liberation and all that followed was born in July 1969 when the Stonewall, a gay bar in New York's Greenwich Village, was raided by the police. A common enough occurrence, but for a single momentous reversal: the customers, usually resigned to such regular rousts, fought back. The ripples from the Stonewall clash took time to cross the Atlantic, but cross they did. In October 1970 Aubrey Walter and Bob Mellors, two lecturers at the LSE, launched Britain's Gay Liberation Front. It was, in a way, the next logical area of society to join the rush to liberation, the latest domino to fall to an increasingly liberal status quo. There had been legislation; the Homosexual Law Reform Act of 1967 had been a direct result of the Wolfenden Report of a decade earlier, but the law was cautious, and its proponents, however determined, were grateful rather than demanding. With its restriction of legal gay sex to a pair of consenting males over twenty-one – some five years older than the heterosexual age of consent – whose activities were to be conducted strictly behind closed doors, the law was hardly a leap into a new world. Like the newly uncensored Lady Chatterley's Lover *ten years before, one could, as it were, buy the product, but its natural habitat, in the eyes of many shopkeepers, remained definitely beneath the counter.*

The Gay Liberation movement, spawned in America, child not of genteel middle-class protest but of street-level confrontation, was a very different story. The Campaigners for Homosexual Equality (CHE) of the Fifties and Sixties had blended seamlessly with a raft of similar pressure groups, the GLF did not. They were 'glad to be gay', they 'said it out loud', they proclaimed their otherness, like the feminists and the blacks they set out to break the mould.

114

JEFFREY WEEKS: The emergence of gay liberation was a catching-up on the part of gays with the counter-culture of the Sixties. It was the last part of the population to get influenced by the counter-culture. The last part of those going to be influenced, that is. Feminism in Britain pre-dated gay liberation by about a year. There were a number of complex things going on, but certainly people like Germaine Greer who'd emerged that first year, did support the early GLF – financially to some extent. The other thing was the many women who'd been alienated from feminism because of its lack of interest in lesbianism. Once gay liberation started they came through from feminism to us. I know several women who are now very prominent feminists who first became activists in the GLF, then went back through to feminism. So it was an intensely exciting moment because it brought together the traditional homosexual reformers, the counter-culture, burgeoning feminism, to some extent early black activism in this country as well. It also touched the traditional gay subculture, what became known as the 'ghetto' which hadn't been very political or interested in law reform. But throughout the Seventies and into the Eighties they became increasingly energetic in the gay movement.

By the time Gay Lib came along in '70 I already had a group of friends who joined me in GLF. It was not a new world in that I was already aware of my sexuality, so that wasn't a change. But what was new was the complete transformation of my attitude towards it – a more positive acceptance of it. Because however integrated you were into the gay scene in the Sixties, you always had a sense of guilt, of queerness. GLF transformed all that into a sense of collective identity. That was critical in shifting the whole attitude. It made something positive out of what had seemed at worst negative and at best dubious and marginal. GLF was a grassroots movement, and those who gained most from it were very much those whose lives were transformed by GLF's activities. For me, the basic thing was I met Angus and we started living together within three months and still share a house. I met a whole new circle of friends, who are still my closest friends. It made me politically active for the first time.

Tony Whitehead runs Streetwise, a centre for young gay prostitutes – 'rent boys'. In 1969 he was living in provincial Yorkshire.

TONY WHITEHEAD: When the gay movement first started up I was desperately trying to lose my virginity and was still at school. I was in Harrogate where there wasn't any suggestion at all about the gay movement, we didn't know anything about things like that.

I'd been aware of homosexual feelings since before puberty, long

115

before, and after puberty I was trying to do something about it rather more forcefully. I was lucky. My parents moved away, so I was alone up there in digs from the age of fifteen. I'd travel home to my parents in the holidays, and one holiday in about 1968 I met this guy on a train and one thing led incredibly to another, and that's where I lost my virginity.

I hated the single sex school where I was, didn't like the atmosphere at all. It was all about playing games and cold showers, things like that. But the sex play there was fun, nice. I had no abstract concept of being gay, or of sexuality. I just had a recognition of my feelings, and an understanding picked up by reading that there were gay people, there was gay sex, but I thought it was one person in a million. I never seemed to meet any. Not many years ago I met my French teacher in a London pub, he didn't remember me. He was mortally embarrassed. It was a gay bar, so he knew why I was there as well. But I remember feeling that I wished the teachers had been able to at least acknowledge their sexuality. It would have been such a help to have had some role models, to have something to compare yourself with.

Harrogate was terribly isolated and apart from the guy I met when I was fifteen or so and had one weekend with, the next two years were completely sterile. I had no idea how you met gay people. I knew nothing except what you'd pick up in the papers. But that was always about London, and when you're fifteen, seventeen and in Yorkshire, London could have been on the other side of the world – impossibly far, impossibly exotic – and the developing sexual revolution in the Sixties could have been happening on the other side of the world with it. It didn't mean anything, except that I knew as soon as I was able to, I was getting away.

I went to Durham University and by then I was reasonably optimistic because there was now much more information about what was going on and I knew there'd be plenty of opportunities for sex at university. And indeed that's what happened. I went to Durham and found plenty of opportunities.

I did feel a sense of liberation, completely. Coming out was absolutely wonderful. A marvellous experience. I'm glad I did it so quickly. It was immensely liberating and also, apart from sexually, politically and emotionally liberating. You'd make that break, you'd cast off all that tat that had oppressed you as a teenager. In getting rid of the concept of norms within human sexual behaviour, you also get rid of the norms in other forms of behaviour. Not in the sense that you became anarchists, but you became questioning, in a way that even other students weren't necessarily doing. In Durham there were many interested in issues around sexual politics, and the Students' Union

116

was very supportive of the Gay Soc, but a hell of a lot didn't give a damn about it – the traditional beer-drinking, sports-playing, girl-shagging students.

When I was there I formed the Gay Society. I was motivated, I suppose, seventy-five per cent by self-interest – it was a great way to meet other gay men – and twenty-five per cent by political convictions. We decided the only way to make Gay Soc work was politically rather than socially. Gays had been meeting socially for years, but would never dare to identify themselves, or give themselves a label. So we decided you had to be public about it, put your face forward, stand up and be counted. So after a week of planning, the four of us put our names on a piece of paper. And we put out the leaflet advertising the first public meeting of Gay Soc. The tradition there was that you had to have at least one meal in college, with a formal meal a couple of times a week. All the people from various societies would be going round putting leaflets on tables. So while waiting for high table to come in, you'd flick through all this. So that night I sat there watching the entire college looking at the leaflet, and then in a few minutes all staring at me which at the time was quite amusing. Though it could be unpleasant. There was prejudice, being jostled, called names. But I'd always felt an outsider and I'd always been called names at school, always felt different, so that didn't bother me at all. Although small in stature I was large on conviction and well able to take them on. I did use it as an excuse to get out of college quickly. I didn't like living in college and Durham was full of beautiful houses with dirt cheap rents. We were supposed to spend at least a year in college, but I got out by saying: 'It's intolerable living here, I'm being harassed terribly.' Wasn't really true, but it helped me get out.

I was highly active, but I had no great vision of a gay political Utopia. I've always been more part of the politics of reaction. I was reacting to injustice, to prejudice, to my feeling of sexuality and alienation from my peers. I always worked against what I thought was wrong and by a set of moral principles about people's responsibilities to each other. I didn't think they were being very fair to gay people.

After Durham I moved down south and stayed with my grandmother, with whom I'd always been close and who knew I was gay long before my parents did. She was a bit upset about it but had lived long enough to have most of life's assumptions overturned. Anyway, I'd gone to stay with her, near Brighton, which seemed a pleasurable place to live.

The first job I took was with British Home Stores, as a trainee. And at the same time we made a programme for STV about the gay scene in Brighton and I made sure I was on it. I thought it would make a

117

great scene for the opening to see me and my lover kissing at Brighton railway station. It was a bit of fun, a touch of *Brief Encounter*, and the TV people loved it. That was shown the first week I was working at BHS and I was immediately suspended. I was called in by the manager – I hadn't been there many minutes – 'Did you take part in this programme?' 'Yes, so what?' 'Are you aware of your responsibilities as someone who will be a representative of this family store?' He said there'd been a complaint from somebody who'd seen the programme. I was to go home and do nothing until he'd talked to head office. So I went home and immediately contacted the other guys in the group, and NCCL and the media – and because it was as a result of being on a TV programme, the media took it up. That was Friday, and by Monday the whole thing had changed. There'd been angry phone calls to BHS, there'd been a small item on the local news. They put me on a long suspension. By this time demonstrations had occurred outside BHS in Worthing, so it made the BBC Six o'clock news. Then demonstrations started happening all over the country. It just snowballed. That was the power of the media. I wasn't surprised at BHS' reaction – I half expected it. But I didn't do it to provoke them, the reasons were completely different. I didn't do it to get sacked, although I didn't give a damn about the job. But the opportunity presented itself to make a big fuss, and that's what we did. I resigned in the end. I was brought up before the board at head office and they wouldn't allow in my NCCL representative. I was there for four hours, being grilled. All about my responsibilities as an employee to abide by the contract. It didn't have a morals clause, but there was one about not bringing the company into disrepute. And also a clause about the company being able to move me where they liked. They wanted to move me to Scunthorpe. It was a joke. I was not to become publicly involved again. And it was either accept that or resign. If I'd been better briefed I would have said: 'No, either you accept me or sack me.' Anyway, they didn't stop the campaign. It got to a shareholders' meeting and people like Angus Wilson bought shares specifically so they could go in and complain about this outrageous treatment. It was a most exciting time.

The result was that I came up to London. I was coming up anyway, addressing various meetings – student Gay Socs, CHE, etc. – and leading marches. I came up as a major celebrity on the gay scene with my picture already in *Gay News* and gay London at my feet. So of course I moved up to town. Wonderful for my sex life – absolutely wonderful: all the benefits of fame. Groupies and so on.

So there I was in London having fun, very much at the heart of the gay movement. I went to London University to do a post-graduate

118

teaching degree and went into teaching. I wanted to teach because I loved biology – plants, animals, etc. – and I also thought it was a great way to extend my belief in the importance of variation in nature for evolution. But I also saw it in sociological terms and the value within a culture of minorities. Some people might say I was a proselytising homosexual. But I was not trying to turn people gay. I believe that nature takes care of that. What I was trying to do was inform people about acceptance of differences. So it enabled me to do a subject I loved; I was very happy all day fishing around with tadpoles in class, and also just to get across that there is no norm in nature – well, there's a norm, but no norm-al.

I was just very open. I've got pictures done by kids in my class – a comprehensive in Clapham, a girls' school – who'd developed a pash for me. It would be a picture of Mr Whitehead with his punk hair, carrying a copy of *Gay News* in childish writing. The rest of the staff hated me. I was only there for a year. I liked the job, but the staff were appalling. They voted no confidence in the Head who was ousted, along with his friends – it was the most awful atmosphere to work in. It was nothing to do with me at all. There were fifty-fifty white and non-white kids. Some would give me aggro but on the whole it was amazing. 'Well we'll say one thing, sir, you're honest' – this type of thing. Boys would have been much nastier.

When the *Gay News* trial came along in 1977, I was a vociferous campaigner, leafletting, bannering outside the court. I knew all the people, of course. I remember sitting in the public gallery during one day's hearings masturbating with the guy next to me who was in drag. We thought this was a very radical act. Done partly for fun, partly as a radical gesture – oh great. It was easier, coming out then in the Seventies than it would have been in the Eighties. Politics and sex bowled along quite gloriously then. There weren't as many commercial gay venues as there are now, but it was good and the counter-culture was very lively and very productive. Perhaps it's age that makes you look at counter-cultures these days and think they're a bit self-indulgent, anarchist, whatever. But then they seemed exciting, aspiring to great things.

After I stopped teaching I moved into a flat with a guy who was earning huge sums of money working for an escort agency. In the end it was prostitution, but quite different from my idea of what prostitution was all about. He was a middle-class guy, aspiring to be a writer and has done quite well since then. I thought that looked quite interesting. I'd often slept with people and then wished I hadn't, but it didn't seem to be that hard, so I said: 'Well, I could do with a bit of money.' I'd always put much more effort into community work rather

119

than career-type work. I worked much harder at London Gay Switchboard, which I'd been involved with ever since '76, than any job, for example. I was on all the leading committees of Switchboard. So this seemed to be a perfect way of making a bit of money to subsidise what seemed to me much more important, which was caring for other gay people, my community.

So I went into prostitution and found it a most interesting experience. It wasn't hanging round street corners. It was getting into a suit and going to the Dorchester or the Savoy – and it was absolutely fascinating. I could make a great deal of money. I've come from a working-class background, but because of a good education and elocution lessons, no one would know and I was able to pass myself off as a fair-haired English public-schoolboy, which was extremely highly paid with some client groups. So I could make a good deal of money when the going was good. Two hundred pounds one night, I remember – an enormous amount of money. This was in '78. I'd never do it for less than £50. And I was meeting people that way. It would include dinner as well, and some of the people were really interesting – some were absolutely awful of course. Sometimes it was more like being a courtesan. One Arab sheikh would have guards with guns in the dining room, and there'd be a couple of male clients, and he'd fill the rest of the table with high class pulls, men and women, two or three of each – stunning, gorgeous women, beautifully dressed, real diamonds, etc. I was quite impressed by this, although politically it was off. But these people were fascinating to talk to, and our job was to make witty conversation and be extremely nice to them and if they wanted sex, they could have whatever they wanted. So it was fascinating and I earned money. My straight friend had always said, 'Put one third into an untouchable bank account, blow two-thirds, 'cos you've got to have fun, because it is a bit sick after all,' and that's what I did. So I got the money, and then in '78 I left Britain and travelled.

I didn't find prostitution a politically difficult thing to do. I felt the worst sin of all would be to prostitute your intellect – selling cigarettes, making weapons (that's the view of politics I had then) – so selling your body to people who can afford to pay for it, to give pleasure and no harm seemed to be a perfectly honourable thing to do. And still does. I have no time for society's hypocrisy about this. I had something, they wanted it, were prepared to pay for it. They were getting their money's worth and I was good at it. Sometimes they saw me as a piece of meat, but growing up as a gay if I judged myself as other people thought of me, I'd never have come out. Coming out was all about a belief in yourself that transcends what other people try to
120

label you with. The same thing working as a whore. Didn't matter what they thought of me, I knew what I was, was hoping to be. I had a sense of identity.

Of course the very positive things I've said about prostitution are in terms of my own involvement in it. Most of these kids [the rent boys who come to Streetwise] are very much more victims. They've been sexually abused and their reaction is: 'They did it to me, and I'm going to make them pay for it'. That's a very different thing from the way I went into prostitution. They hang around stations and get used and abused for a fiver. Nothing like what I was doing. You can say that prostitution can be morally neutral, that there's nothing wrong with selling physical pleasure, but this is not like that, it's not an exchange of equals between punter and the boys. It's a powerful and submissive thing. It's people with power versus people without, people with money versus people without. They have no choice. I was in prostitution to go to South America, they're doing it to live. It's so different. And it's wrong, the situation they're in, and most of them don't want to do it.

The position of street boys is awful. They come from backgrounds where they're deeply alienated from love and support. They've been in care, been victims of sexual abuse – about two thirds of them. Some come from middle-class homes. That doesn't make any difference in terms of sexual abuse, but matters from the economic point of view. They've been booted out because of the most appalling attitudes from their parents. Most of them come from backgrounds where they don't have any money as well. And to some extent they're alienated now from the gay community. Essentially this is a class issue, and there's no place for these boys, apart from as sex objects. They have no place in the sense that I do within the community and that makes me angry. These are great kids, but they're in a mess and need help and the gay community doesn't do a lot to help them either. The boys' attitude is: 'Fuck it, make it pay.'

I saw myself then as I do now, a free spirit, moral to his friends, who believes strongly in responsibilities to people you care about, ignoring how society says you should behave, finding yourself. As long as it doesn't hurt others. It would have been harder to get into the scene if I hadn't gone through the political process. I'm highly sexed, like sex a lot, wouldn't find it difficult to have sex with clients – as long as they weren't repulsive – but I wouldn't have had quite the confidence in my own identity to be able to go ahead and do these things without the sexual politics angle. I wouldn't have been able to do it. It was self-awareness which gave me the strength to do things. I always took things seriously and believed that the purpose of life was living. I'm an atheist, have always been. It was very much a personal political agenda, about personal development, about support for those I cared for, about fighting oppression, be that racism or homophobia.

Then off I went to South America. I just transferred my beliefs there, and became part of a gay group in Rio where I was working, I had gay activist friends there. I've got a copy of the paper *Lampiel*, the Lamp, the Light, with a picture of me in it wearing very little – it was an advert for the paper, about taking out subscriptions: Look what you get if you take out a subscription. I travelled around, taught English. I revelled in the sexuality of Brazil. I was having enormous fun. I was in Argentina during the dirty war which further politically enlightened me. It was terrifying. People were frightened to be seen talking to you. I met this boy in a little country town, miles away from God knows where, and he'd talk for a minute furtively, then walk on and I'd have to walk a certain distance behind. I was arrested one time and thrown into an Argentinian jail, left there for a day. Most interesting. I knew eventually I'd get out. I was never a legal resident in Brazil and I got tipped off they were coming to get us, and two days later they did, but I'd just left. I had no money, asked a friend in London to help me out. The ticket came through, and then there was a roundabout journey via Peru, Ecuador, the States, all over the place and eventually home safe and sound in '79, and I became involved again straight away with Gay Switchboard and whatever else was going on then. I hadn't finished with wanderlust though, so a year later I took a job in Spain, the Canary Islands. Absolutely no gay political culture of any kind there. Plenty of gay sex, though, and I had a nice time, but I couldn't stand it, so after a year I came back to London, in '81, worked for the Switchboard again.

By this time politics had become much more urgent because the whole climate had become really cold by then. It was an age of anger that had not been there before. The Thatcher era. The tabloid press were much more outrageous in their anti-gay stance. You felt the implicit threat was going to become real any minute. There seemed to be more attacks on gay men, more discussions about tightening up laws. More customs seizures of magazines, more threatened legal actions. But I'm not sure that actually happened. Generally we were also aligned with the anti-racist cause. The feeling in the counter-culture was no longer that of having a good time, but alliances were still made across the different groups.

But my circle and myself, we're still products of that early golden age and unless they lock us up, nothing will change that. We're out, we live our lives as gay men and most of us don't come in for too much hassle. I work in the heart of Earl's Court, live in West Kensington –
122

we're in the majority around there. It's a very charmed life in a sense. You could say it's a ghetto of a sort, and I make few efforts to step outside it. I confront outside hostility through my work, but in situations where I won't get a fist in the face.

★★★

For a country that sustains its own nervous equanimity by the devoted adoration of a menu of stereotypes, the emergence of gay liberation caused real problems. The feminists were easily categorised – dungaree-clad, hairy-legged, crop-haired dykes, whose supposed predilection for discarding their brassieres caused a reaction very different to that occasioned by similar habits among their sisters on Page Three. But gays were different. Like the idiot Irishman, the money-grubbing Jew, and the singing, dancing, sporting darkie, the lisping faggot was easily assimilable. The 'strong gay man' was something else. In time the gay clone scene, with its self-consciously 'masculine' styles – epitomised in the disco band Village People – would descend into tacky self-parody, but when the 'poofs' starting strutting their stuff, certain visceral fears were unleashed. The 'queer-bashers' reacted as might be expected, and by their side, scriptures on high, came the bible-bashers too.

GRAHAM WEBSTER-GARDNER: I don't believe repealing the homosexual laws would stop homosexuality. Personally I'd like to stop homosexuality altogether. What the law does do is say: we think these things are preferable, it's more desirable for you to do this, better for society as a whole. I wish they'd never passed the '67 Act and that people continued to do what they wanted in private. We have the stew ponds here in Epsom, where children used to go fishing, horse-riding and walking; the police have had so many complaints from locals about homosexual activity that they now have to have a permanent watch there. The homosexuals come there from all over South-East England and they want to do it in public. Then they get up in court and say: We're allowed to do this in public now, which is wrong. What the Act said was that it's meant to be in private, no one will bash the door down, and we're giving you *some* leeway. But they have twisted that to mean: We can now do what we want, in public if we want. I think the law should say: We don't like it, it's not natural, desirable, you can do it, but we don't approve. I wouldn't want heterosexuals to carry on that way – I don't want to see copulation of any description in a public place. And my attitude to lesbians is the same as for

123

homosexuality. I don't distinguish. I know they're not as promiscuous, not as interested in sex with children, but it's still sinful, unnatural. Because of their physical structure they can't do as many unpleasant things as homosexuals, but otherwise there's no difference. But going back to homosexuals, in the States they're demanding even more rights now: special political rights, being classed as disabled – going far beyond what was intended in the '67 Act.

RICHARD WHITFIELD: Homosexuality does not go with the grain of nature. We don't fully understand how it originates. From what we can see, it has a long historical standing and I'm not wishing to be uncompassionate towards gays or lesbians. It's only when they wish to assert that their lifestyle does go with the grain of nature, is 'normal', that I get a little anxious, and when they wish to influence young people. Particularly through times when young people's sexuality is at a delicate stage of its emergence i.e. in the latency period and adolescence. Homosexuality is abnormal. It's a minority activity, just like having ginger hair is abnormal. Gays shouldn't proselytise and try to influence others at a vulnerable stage in their development. Any responsible sex education has to examine the phenomenon of homosexuality. I'm not saying we should exclude it, it's part of the general education of all of us. The more we know about the causes of different forms of sexual behaviour/proclivity, fine. But in your book I hope you won't give proportionally undue attention to homosexuals.
  Some of these people, I'd call them 'damaged activists'. Why that term? When groups of people devote a lot of practical and psychological energy to a particular sexual cause and in many cases, invest their own money in it, real money, and feel motivated to stand at street corners pushing certain ideas – I'm talking about the more extreme wings of gay lib, as one of their heterosexual counterparts – I wish to say: Okay, we're in a democracy, we're not going to stop them doing it. But you have to ask, why have they got this crusade, what's happened to them earlier in their lives that has made them become almost like religious fanatics? Why is it that in the expression of their views there seems to be such anger, almost violence? A couple of years ago there was an international congress on the family held in Brighton, at which I was the concluding speaker, with Angela Rumbold. I attended the congress for three days. Princess Di opened it and there was a lot of media attention because some gays came on stage and made their point – that this was a homophobic meeting. Anyway, for three hours a rent-a-crowd of about a hundred gays and lesbians were outside the hall, being extremely insulting to speakers, very aggressive – without police restraint there might have been
124

physical scuffles. They were even rude and intrusive to young mums and dads with their children going in. I found that slightly disturbing. Why did a group like that feel that must be their cause in life? Hurt. Damaged. Some horrific things must have happened in their lives, for such aggression to become one of the external consequences.

CHRIS ESMOND: Homosexuality is a regressed state, which perhaps people can't give up. Some can move on, and I know some who have. My father never mentioned homosexuality to me, but perhaps unconsciously I could have absorbed his attitudes – he was an army man after all. You can imagine the prejudices there. He was a very authoritarian character. I don't like promiscuous homosexuality. When I was working on Hampstead Heath ten or eleven years ago I came across that a lot. I was working at West Heath Park where the homosexuals gather. I had a seasonal job as a park-keeper for six months and used to walk round there. They created a very sinister atmosphere there, hanging around behind bushes, sitting on benches, eyeing you up as you walked by. Very peculiar, and I didn't like it. You can say they're driven to do it, but I feel threatened by that homosexual promiscuity. I don't think it's jealousy. Of course all men would like lots of sex without responsibility, lots of orgasms. That may be the epitome of male sexuality but it completely denies anything to do with depth and commitment. Momentary excitement doesn't lead anywhere. What do you get? AIDS probably. And if you behave like that now with men or women, you're almost certain to get AIDS. I've had casual sex to some extent. Not very much, but I've had some. Now I don't even want it.

HUGH PRATT: Regarding homosexuality, I wish people could become complete people. This misnomer 'gay' – I've come across a lot of homosexuals and they're the most miserable bunch of buggers, literally. That's the most sick way of looking at it but it's the truth. They have lots and lots of problems. I'm not saying this from a judgmental point of view, but that's what seems to have happened in their lives. They've found a relationship which provides some physical satisfaction, emotional satisfaction, but it seems to me there's always something lacking. Now Erich Fromm labels the different stages of love, from mother love/self love/love of the same sex/love of the opposite. Simplistic, but accurate. Homosexuality got stuck on one stage, hasn't developed fully. Before I gained my belief in Jesus, I felt that so long as they weren't hurting anyone, weren't buggering children, that is, were acting as consenting adults, it was okay. But

125

now I think: God made us in his own image and gave us a set of rules he wished us to live by. If you accept God exists then we can't change what his rules are by sitting here and voting in something else.

The point is that children do not change the father. What God is saying is this is how you should live, not as the Canaanites lived when they offered their children as sacrifices (as the satanists do now). God doesn't want you to consort with animals, sleep with your mother/daughter, nor should the same sex sleep together. And if that's what God wishes, I'll go along with that. Not because I'm bright or stupid, but because that's how He set up His creation. It's quite simple: if you look in Genesis, woman is taken out of man. To a certain extent the sexual act is reunion – 'flesh of my flesh' – a joining together of what was once separated. So I see a heterosexual relationship as a reunion. Homosexuals are living outside the grace of God and in His wrath. That's a theological position I would support. God is the judge. I love homosexuals. I hate homosexuality. Love the sinner, hate the sin. That's the Christian perspective.

I know many homosexuals, I know many people with other lifestyles. I love them because Jesus loved them. He didn't sit in a pious church and say: 'Terrible lot outside, but we're awfully nice.' He was down with the tax collector, down with Mary the prostitute, he touched the leper. So as a Christian I say, okay. There's a group near here counselling homos, some gay Christians, who wish to be free of bondage. They're wishing to be free and Jesus does set them free. That does happen. But they must wish to do so. If you meet someone who's developed out of that phase, and see what they've become, you then say, that's good, but wouldn't it be great if others took that choice. But they don't. Either they haven't been told the good news that they can be free from it, or else they decide to stay like that. Same as with pornography. One has to accept that.

★★★

Chris Turner came out in the mid-Eighties. He was 25.

CHRIS TURNER: I suddenly stopped having girlfriends. I was about twelve. Which was strange because from the age of seven I'd always had them, I was even called a bit of a ladies' man. So I was very embarrassed about that. I was sexually curious and I felt unattractive. At that point people began to call me a poof. It seems as if other people knew before I did. But then in those days if you were interested in intellectual pursuits rather than sport, you were a poof. I was
126

mortified by that idea. Although it didn't mean anything to do with sleeping with men. I knew there were real poofs at school. But I wasn't the same as them. The question of sexual acts was not on the surface. I'm not sure why. It wasn't ignorance. We called them bum boys, we knew the mechanics of it. But I never seriously entertained the idea I was gay.

At college I felt I'd missed out on an essential part of my education in terms of having sex – everyone else had been doing it for years – that I'd been living in a backwater. When I moved to the university environment, expecting to find more people like me, I found it wasn't that clear-cut. Through my lecturers I moved into the dangerous lefty sphere, complete questioning of accepted world views and so on. By Christmas I'd rejected Catholicism. By Easter I'd lost my virginity. She was another student, somewhat experienced, but we didn't talk about sex, about what we were doing. So lots of fumblings and gropings. I went and bought condoms before this happened. I remember thinking: this is ridiculous. You're nineteen, this should have happened years ago. I was very obsessed with that. My final year in Cardiff I felt very claustrophobic. I shared a flat with a couple and I started to feel physically ill. Once I thought it was a gas leak in my room. And the political arguments were becoming so intractable that in the end I just wanted to get out of Cardiff. I applied for a scholarship to a college in America and so did my girlfriend. We discussed it fairly coolly and said: if we both get it, we go together; if one of us gets it, they go and we'll accept that. We both got it and went together. If I'd been able to confront it, I wasn't just running away from the political mess – the miners' strike at that time – I knew something had to be sorted out. All my energies were being poured into a fairly abstract political series of problems. I was beginning to react against it, feeling trapped.

When we got to the States, there was a very visible gay community, even in Illinois where we were. Champaign-Urbana – a very big university. I developed a huge crush in the German department where I was teaching. I passed him in the corridor – in this situation it's to do with what you do with information, with sensations, how you make sense of them – and something clicked. But he was straight. That week there was a departmental barbecue. My girlfriend came with me and pointed this guy out to me: 'He's really good-looking.' That was a key moment for me. And ironical, that she dropped the piece into place. Then there was a German girl I got friendly with in the office, and she was told by a guy who all the gay people in the department were. I got very angry about that – it was a kind of outing if you like.

She said, 'There's three.' I said, 'You'd better tell them there's four.' That was when I came out.

I told my girlfriend when I went home. We'd been talking abstractly about bisexuality, which made it easier to tell her. She didn't say, 'Great,' she said, 'Why did you say that? It's ridiculous. Do you want people to think that?' My line was: 'Does it matter what people think?' But she became very uneasy. We still slept together, but there was no sex. Very soon afterwards we broke up, not just about the homosexuality – it would have been more difficult if it had been – but the relationship had run its course. After that I tried to make something happen with this guy. I invited him out for a drink. I'd not been with a man yet. I'd become more comfortable with all things sexual, but I found it difficult to imagine having sex with a man. At this point though I was obsessively in love with this guy. I'd thought everything through so thoroughly. The way I thought it through: Okay, you've been having these heterosexual relationships, you're obviously fascinated by the idea of homosexuality, but you've done nothing about it. I envisaged it as being on a shelf. So I decided to take it off the shelf and put heterosexuality up there instead.

Then, that Christmas, I took a trip to Mexico and the night before going to Mexico I jerked off with a guy in a sauna – in the gym at college. Not a particularly attractive man. My feeling was: You're doing to do this, get it over with. We were sitting in the sauna, just the two of us, he being in his mid-fifties, and I suddenly realised he was looking. I didn't look shocked so he said, 'Do you mess about?' I said, 'Yes.' He went out of the sauna. I thought: Oh, there must be a place where this goes on. I followed and he was gone. Of course he'd gone to the toilets. The special place. It was just a hand-job, jerking each other off. He wanted more and I said no. I mentioned safe sex but really it was nothing to do with that, it was: what am I doing in a toilet with a fifty-five-year-old man? Afterwards I thought: You've done that now, doesn't matter who you do it with. I wasn't going to go down the romantic road I'd travelled as a heterosexual – waiting for the perfect partner bit.

In Mexico I picked someone up on the underground. He was a bit older but not by much. A meeting of eyes across the track, we met at the top and he took me back to his place. Not unpleasant, but not worth much. He was all over me, babying me. I couldn't take that. And he wanted to fuck me, and I didn't want that. And he didn't speak much English. I was hitchhiking some of the trip and got picked up by three men, obviously gay, going to a beach party, and I went with them and shared a room with one of them. A desert island romance for three days. My heart wasn't in it, but I enjoyed it, because it was new.

128

When I came back there was a period of a few months when I didn't have sex with anyone. It wasn't until I came back to London that I had a relationship where I felt completely at ease, wasn't conscious of a male body. He and I were together for two or three months. After about two months, I woke up in the middle of the night thinking: What are you doing? You're in bed with a man. The relationship didn't last very long after that – there was a repulsion there. But I was still getting used to the idea then. One friend, a gay activist who'd given me a number of addresses to visit in Mexico, said that he'd never met someone who'd come out intellectually as much as I had before physically getting involved. A lot of gay people, hearing stories of my heterosexual past, think I'm not really gay. For some, you haven't suffered enough. For others, you're likely to turn back again. I find it hard to imagine that.

I was very keen to have anal sex. I'd bought a book in Berlin, written by a New Man, most of which I disagreed with, but it was really challenging. It was about men's relationship with their body, their ignorance about it. It mentioned stimulation of the anus, and I really did get into that idea, with fingers. And I was aware I really did want to be fucked, something really enlightening. It didn't happen for quite a while. The last guy I had in the States, I fucked him once, in the shower. And I didn't come. That was a conscious decision. But even that's not safe. I've never been fucked without a condom. For some time I didn't have someone come in my mouth. I did eventually. There's conflicting reports about what's safe. For me the bottom line is: not without a condom.

People say gay men are in couples more because of AIDS. Perhaps, but for me a one-to-one relationship was something I was looking for. Within two or three years of coming out, I knew I wanted that. I would pick up people casually in bars. But quite often I'd come home alone. Among gays, sex without emotional commitment is more likely to be comfortable than between heterosexuals. But I think most gays are like me; even while having numerous partners, I was looking for someone to have a relationship with. I had lots of false alarms – falling deeply in love in impossible situations. A series of them. That's something that's mythologised in gay culture and has its pleasures and its pains. It's more complicated than having easy sex and getting on and enjoying it. There are all kinds of scripts to be played out. I ran the gamut of trying out the different things.

I came out to an old childhood friend when I got back from the States. When I told him, he said: 'I'm gay as well.' He'd moved to Birmingham and got married a year before I went to the States. He had two children and had been trying to stave off gay affairs. We slept together then, almost a symbolic act, not one of great passion. My sister says this is a ridiculous way to look at it, but I felt because of the way we were brought up, something that should have happened years ago but didn't happen. I felt I was making up for that. He was divorced this year. I told my younger brother and my sister within the first year of coming out. Their reaction was: 'Are you sure?' The reason I told them was that I was testing out the ground for telling my parents. We argued about it, because all they said was, 'Never tell them.'

I came out to my parents in January 1991, so it took quite a while. My boyfriend and I had been living together for about eighteen months and we went up to my parents for New Year before I'd told them, then went back a few weeks later to spill the beans. I expected it all to be very difficult and distressing, but it wasn't. They took it incredibly well. I expected my father would take it badly, with my mother putting things in perspective. If anything, it was the reverse. For an ex-policeman, my mother a Catholic, both strong Conservatives, the reaction was remarkable. My mother was upset, but it was a confirmation, not a complete surprise. They'd just clung to hope right to the very last minute. Since then they've been very good. They've stayed here. We slept in here, they slept in our bedroom. My father brought us tea in bed. The only person I haven't told in my immediate family is my older brother, who's about five years older, and lives in a village close to my parents. We don't see each other very often, he works in a bank. He left home to get married, didn't go to university. I thought I'd tell him at the same time as my parents. It's just circumstances why I haven't told him yet. Now it's very odd. We're probably going to stay with my parents at Christmas and my brother will be there. I felt I should tell them all as quickly as possible, together, so that they didn't have this sense that one half of the family knew something and the others didn't.

I'm definitely a beneficiary of the Seventies' Gay Liberation movement. The world in which I came out had been transformed by Gay Liberation, and that made it relatively easy. I didn't have to explain to my parents what a gay lifestyle was, for example. They would prefer a sanitised version of my lifestyle and I don't wish to enlighten them further. They've only known me as a gay man in a relationship. And one of the telling questions they asked was: 'What if Robert goes back to the States, what would you do?' I said, 'You wouldn't ask my sister that, what do you mean?' Dad said, 'Would you start going to places, deliberately trying to meet other gay people?' I could have said, 'Of course, I've been doing that for the last five years and there's nothing wrong with that.' I chose not to.

130

***

Nick Partridge is director of the Terrence Higgins Trust, the country's foremost centre for AIDS and HIV information, counselling and activism.

NICK PARTRIDGE: I remember the first person I fell in love with, I was eleven, a gorgeous man called Nigel, he was the same age as me and we were both in the church choir. I couldn't put any sense to it, any framework to it, and I certainly didn't know the word 'gay', or the word 'homosexual'. All I knew was that I thought he was gorgeous and I wanted to see him with no clothes on. Nothing ever developed. I didn't have any school sexual experiences, or choir sexual experiences. When my heterosexual friends started going out with girls, so did I. But there were enough markers at each point. I remember cuddling up to Nigel and getting a rejection, a very polite but a very firm rejection – and as I went through my early teens the rejections became clearer and the risks associated became greater. I could see that you did not step out of line, you had to be interested in girls and if you weren't then there were the taunts. Though they weren't aimed at me. I was quite tall. I wasn't a sissy. I wasn't somebody who was identifiable as gay. One boy was and he had a really rough time. I saw that and said, 'No way is that going to happen to me.'

When I was fifteen my parents moved from where we lived just outside London to Minehead in Devon, which was very rural. It changed an awful lot for me. By this time I had put my gayness into a locked box at the back of my mind. I had an affair which was very pleasant with a girl in the year above me. We had that first groping sex on the sofa downstairs in her parents' house. It seemed fine. I didn't feel there was anything wrong, that this wasn't what I wanted. The attractions of men are very easily discountable in such a heterosexual world. It's very difficult to go against the sexual norm, especially in somewhere like that. That does seem to be a division between people like me, who lock those feelings away, and the other group who get a hand on their knee in the movies when they're in their teens, and carry on from there. I don't know how it works, whether it's confidence, or circumstances. It's partly to do with how you approach sex in the first place. Certainly the way I lost my virginity was a classic fumble. It wasn't particularly enjoyable, but I don't think that was anything to do with my being gay, it was actually that both of us were playing really. I was seventeen, she was eighteen, that's quite late for a lot of people these days, but not then. And at that time I got a lot of cachet being able to talk about it.

I went to Keele from 1974-78 and experienced that thing that happens to a lot of gay men who haven't yet come out to themselves – a first major step in itself – which is having fantasies about many of the men who one knew. But then not being able to progress from the fantasy level, and instead having occasional and not particularly satisfactory or happy relationships with women. I knew I wasn't enjoying the situation, I didn't enjoy the sex, I knew that I had these fantasies about men. But I dealt with this by working very hard and being extremely social. So there was this combination of working and socialising to the point where I could convince myself and partially convince other people that in fact I didn't have time for things like relationships. It seemed like a good way out. I certainly made no effort to make myself attractive to other people. Very much the greatcoat, the slightly straggly hair...

There was a Gay Society, I think. There was also a warden in one of the campus halls who was openly gay and who a lot of people spoke to about being gay. But I had neither courage nor the motivation to go along to a Gay Soc meeting. I just blocked it out. But I wasn't tortured about it in any way. I was leading a very full and very energetic life, I got my 2-1 and then I moved down to London.

It was only then that I finally began to do something about being gay. I moved in with people who had been at LSE and were very much in the straight left camp, informed by feminism, anti-racism, living in a small flat in West Hampstead, high-turnover bedsit land. Involved with Rock Against Racism, the Legalise Cannabis Campaign, that milieu. None of them were gay, however, and gradually that became a problem. I met up with a guy who I had been at school with when we lived near London and whom I fell in love with. We began having a sort of affair and it was at that point that I came out. It was very timid, but it met a need in both of us. They were very different needs; one was about shyness, and the other was about trying to be gay without upsetting anything or anybody, and actually without having to do anything or change anything very much. My friends were very supportive: they certainly weren't going to be anti-gay, but that didn't go as far as saying, 'Okay, we'll come along to gay bars with you.'

Again I created an active social life, and I was working, for Rank Xerox. But the problem now was getting to know other gay men without my straight friends feeling that I had let them down or that I was ignoring them. By this point, 1979, I was twenty-four, well-educated, in work, and yet I remember deciding one day, this is enough, I'm going to go to a gay bar. I went to the King William in

132

Hampstead. I'd found out about it in *Gay News*, which I was buying by now because at this point I had intellectually accepted that I was gay and I'd had this affair, but I hadn't entered the gay lifestyle. I wasn't in the gay world by any means at all. So I went to the pub, and walked up and down outside a couple of times before I actually went in. Then going in very nervously and bumping straight into a six-foot drag queen which frightened the life out of me! Then nervously going to the bar.

Once I'd been to a bar for the first time, I did start going to a number of gay pubs. The most important thing, however, was meeting the younger brother of one of my flatmates. He had come out during a trip abroad and he was far more confident than I was and said, 'Look, this is ridiculous, you've just got to start meeting people.' So I did start doing that, although I did find it very difficult. My group of straight friends were not at all antagonistic – in some ways I was another little cause for them to support – but I did find it very difficult to find the time and space for what I wanted. I'd keep on saying, 'Why don't we go down to Heaven?' and they'd say, 'No.' So we wouldn't go.

It was also quite strange working at Rank Xerox. I don't think there were many other gay men. By 1981 I had started doing things like leaving *Gay News* on my desk at work. This did not go down well. It was being made quite clear that if I wanted to get on the fast track then I had to have a girlfriend, who would become a wife, who could be paraded at company dos and so on. Then on top of this we'd just had the Falklands War and I'd been involved in actively opposing that – which didn't sit well with my employers. So at that point I had become very frustrated. I was frustrated that I wasn't meeting other men, that I seemed to be running around supporting a fair number of causes that didn't seem to be getting anywhere and I wanted a break. So rather than doing the round-the-world trip I decided to go to Amsterdam.

The gay life in Amsterdam was very different to that in London. In the first place it was closer, in walking distance, and the bars were much cheaper. There was a lot more sex going on than I involved myself with – I was still rather serious at that point, I wanted relationships rather than fast-track sex. So I didn't do the sauna scene, for instance. In England there's only a very limited saunas/bath-house scene. The laws permit consenting sex between two men over twenty-one and in private. That can even extend to saying that you can't have more than one gay couple in a house. Really very restrictive. There were a lot of people who were very sexually active, but I was not that involved. I dipped my toe in it, but not much more. The

133

saunas are almost describable as a brothel where your only charge is your entry charge. A lot of sex is going on inside the sauna, but in practice a lot of what you experience relies on luck, on who else happens to be there at the time. It's a wonderful learning experience in terms of who finds whom attractive. It certainly knocks out any preconceptions you might have had as regards any lack of diversity in sexual affairs, it's incredibly diverse, couplings that you would never imagine.

Once I'd come out gay sex was definitely better than straight sex for me. It was very much a case of a light coming on: this was comfortable, this was nice, this is lovely, this what two people being together should be like. I had been very happy with the girls with whom I had had affairs, but I had never felt like that. I'd never really got used to straight sex, I was never very good at it. I'm much better at gay sex, much better.

***

JEFFREY WEEKS: When I was young a sense of difference was clearly there, but it wasn't necessarily in my own mind tied up with sexual difference – that was much later. Working-class family, differentiation through grammar school – I went to the top grammar school and that marks you out from those who didn't go there with you. So you had a sense of difference that way. Then you're in this rugby-playing grammar school and you realise you don't play rugby, you're regarded as a bit of a swot, a bit of a sissy. So you get labelled as different and that feeds into your own sense of difference. But I wasn't yet really very clear about my gayness. By the Sixth form I had a sense of my difference being associated with sexual difference. There was no gay community in the village I was brought up in. There were sexual games with schoolmates, but that happens with everyone. It didn't mark me out as different. By the time I was sixteen/seventeen, there was one schoolfriend in particular. But there was no name for it, it wasn't labelled, didn't constitute a distinctive identity at that stage. I didn't experiment with girls until I went to university. But by that time – I came to London for university – I'd begun exploring the 'scene', such as it was. More at least than I could find in South Wales. And I began to pick up men. Through initial contacts I got involved in circles, got to know where people met. So by the time the law changed in '67, I was fully aware of the queer subculture as it then existed.

Of course it was dangerous. I think when you do it, you're not really aware of the danger, because the imperative to do it is so strong. And
134

I wasn't arrested. I don't know what I would have done if I had been. I don't think the university would have minded, it was more my ability to cope with it emotionally. I think I would have fallen apart. But who knows? One had a sense that one was different, that one's life path was going to be different, without a positive attitude towards it. Though I was attempting, even before gay liberation, to be positive about it. I was reading James Baldwin, and other gay writers, and developing more positive attitudes through that. And I found out that people like W. H. Auden were queer. So there were some positive images. I did feel guilty about it, but felt it was an individual quirk, that all of us had individual quirks and we had to live with them.

I've worked for most of the gay press during my time and I was one of the editors of a little journal called *Gay Left*, a theoretical journal, published in the late Seventies. Being gay also changed my academic career, because I'd been trained as a political theorist, but I decided to start writing about sexual history. So after I finished my thesis in the Seventies I shifted to doing sexology, then did a history of the gay movement, *Coming Out*, then I got into much wider sexual history. So it fundamentally turned my career, changed me into a sexual historian rather than a political historian. When I started it seemed *the* most dangerous thing to do, really suicidal, everyone said it would ruin my career. And it did to some extent in that I was on a research contract at LSE and once that came to an end I found it very difficult to get another immediately. The job market was drying up anyway. But my first book on the gay movement was well received. It was an academic book. It's been very influential in the States especially. Nevertheless, it made me unemployable in a straight history department. I've never had a job in a history department. Instead I shifted to sociology and became employable as a sociologist. And now prominent historians, older than me, like Lawrence Stone, write about sexuality. By the Eighties, partly because of AIDS, there was a new interest in sexual history and theory, and publishers became interested in commissioning books on it, and suddenly I was seen as a pioneer. So ten years of labouring in the vineyards produced that effect, and I'm now a professor of sociology at Bristol. I couldn't have contemplated that ten years ago, when I seemed destined to be on the margins of academic life.

***

For the average heterosexual, and by no means necessarily the homophobics among them, the popular image of gay sex —
especially as apostrophised in such enthusiastic works as the diaries

of Joe Orton or the novels of the American John Rechy or as
peddled in the tabloid press – is a catalogue of sexual voracity.
Multiple couplings, orgasm upon orgasm, at best mindless,
hedonistic and emotionless, at worst the obscene ruttings of probably
diseased perverts. Irresponsible, solipsistic, uncommitted. Quite the
opposite of the much-touted responsible world of male-female
relations, the cosy fantasies of 'family' life. But some, and not only
gays, would suggest otherwise. In the first place, long-term
one-to-one gay couples are far from infrequent. But perhaps more
subversively, there is the suggestion that gay sex, in style if not
sexual preference, is surely the epitome of what men want. If women
want lengthy foreplay, subtlety and sensitivity, isn't this wham-bam
orgy of immediate gratification right up the masculine street?
Especially in its lack of offspring. It's a stereotype, of course, but
fast-track gay sex, according to its proselytisers, is the logical
conclusion of male desire.

TONY WHITEHEAD: Gay men have a lot of sex because (a) they're
men and (b) they can. Why do dogs lick their genitals? The same
reason: because they can.

NICK PARTRIDGE: Fast-track gay sex is primarily to do with gender.
Firstly, of course, there's no risk of pregnancy. There is a greater
equality between two men who don't know each other meeting up
than there is in the assumed equalities between a man and a woman.
Apart from anything else there's the equality of your equipment. I
don't agree with those who see this sort of sex as the logical conclusion
of all male sexuality. It's only a part. A lot of gay men will try it, but
only a few stick with it as a long-term option. Most people will want
a primary relationship, although maybe with other sex outside that
relationship too. The dynamics for gay men are different – you can
find those other sexual affairs for free, in effect, whereas a lot of
straight men would have to use the sex industry, would buy their
relationships outside the primary one. But people who say that gay
promiscuity is sad and that all gays really want is their own version of
happy marriages are wrong. The situation isn't sad at all. There is a
lot of experimenting with relationships. Some found experiments that
worked and found people who were able to enjoy a core central
relationship plus a number of other relationships around that core;
others could never find that central relationship and had a number of
one-night, even twenty-minute affairs. Of course it's these latter that

are outside the heterosexual world, and yes, there is something that is deeply attractive about it; it does allow for a lot of sexual fun.

DUNCAN FALLOWELL: At the end of the Seventies all my hopes in London crashed. That was just after my thirtieth birthday. April Ashley, the transsexual, was a friend of mine and had been asking me for ages to write her life story and I'd never wanted to. She was living in Hay-on-Wye and asked me down there to write the story – which eventually I did. So on my last night in London before going to hide in the country for two years, I thought: I'd better do something. I went out and got incredibly drunk – by myself – and ended up in a squalid dive, the Gate in Notting Hill, above Rymans, a gay club. I could just focus enough to turn down a request from the then head chef at the Hilton to go back with him. But there was a nice black boy leaning against the bar, making smirky, sniggery eyes at me, and I thought he would do nicely as my farewell to London. So we got in a cab and went back to the mews in Lancaster Gate where I was living. We managed to have slurpy sex and then comatose sleep. I woke up very late next morning. My car was packed up, and I had to jump in and drive all the way to Hay that morning. But there was this boy asleep in my bed. And he'd written a note saying, 'I'll have white coffee, please, with two sugars.' He was lying there snoring grossly. So I made the coffee, and nudged him to wake him up. When he did he made the most peculiar noise. I suddenly realised he was deaf and dumb. I'd been too drunk to notice the night before. I was rather freaked about this. But then I thought: Well you may be deaf and dumb, but you've still got to go – I've got my life to lead. I told him this on paper, and he started throwing a fit and pissed into the mattress. Then he started getting violent and I thought he was having an epileptic fit and phoned 999 for an ambulance. When I came back he'd locked himself in the loo. Ten minutes later the police arrived. They knocked on the bathroom door, the naked black boy opened it and started making these funny noises. The police sprang back and said, 'Oh, it is rather frightening, isn't it?' But the violent behaviour had stopped with the police around – he'd been trying something on before. Then he wrote down: 'You should give me some money.' So I gave him a tenner and some cigarettes. (I never mind paying if I have to.) He left, the police left, telling me to be careful who I picked up in future. They were very nice, not at all heavy. Anyway, they'd all gone, I was getting ready to leave, when the ambulance arrived, so I had to explain it all to them. Next day in Hay, taking off my clothes I noticed a very green spot on my underpants – he'd given me the clap. I had to go to the clap clinic

137

in Hereford. If you had clap in Hereford it was through Rosie at the station.

AVEDON CARROLL: When it came to perversion, doing the unacceptable things, it wasn't the straight part of the gay movement, the respectable gays, and it wasn't straight men who opened it up. It was the radical gay men and women, and quietly a few straight women, who admitted they didn't get too excited with hand-holding sex. Everybody recognised, whether they admitted it or not, that a lot of pictures that were being painted about this nice friendly egalitarian erotic picture were actually pretty boring. A little kissing, hugging and holding hands is not great sex. It's friendly, it's nice, it's good if you can do that too, but it's not the bottom line.

GUY SALMON

'The Shame That All Men Fear'

Two o'clock in the afternoon near Clapham Common. Just out of bed – clubbing till dawn – he's still in a dressing-gown, bare legs flashing as he leans forward for yet another cigarette. Newly redundant from an advertising agency, he plans to become a barrister. She would hate the idea, but this, indisputably, is one of Thatcher's deviant children.

It was fairly gradual but I realised from the age of ten or twelve when I was becoming sexual, beginning to have erections that it was always boys. Thinking about boys. I never thought about girls sexually. I never thought about girls at all until I was about sixteen and they were rather superimposed on what was already there. Sex started when I was thirteen with a boy at school, who's probably now horribly respectably married and a chartered accountant or something. We were jerking each other off. This was a public school, Ardingley. I saw it as being a bit of fun; I didn't see it as the fulfilment of my sexuality. I didn't find him particularly attractive, we didn't kiss or anything like that. And there were a couple of others. But then when I was sixteen there was a boy called Miles and we did have what I suppose was a proper sexual relationship in that we had sex quite a lot. That was different. It was beyond experimentation. He's also gay. I quite liked him but basically it was just sex. I used to have crushes on boys – I had a terrible crush on one boy, who I was absolutely besotted with, but I never had sex with him. I don't think he even knew. That was an emotional thing, but the thing with Miles was not emotional at all.
138

By the time I was sixteen I definitely saw myself as gay, very much so. I felt very strange about it, very odd. That dreadful feeling that I think most gay people must have: Oh God, I'm the only one in the world. Until someone else actually comes out to you as gay and you realise that maybe there are at least two, there is that awful feeling of isolation. There's this whole straight world and you're not part of it and you're excluded from it. And that's when I started to have girlfriends. Two girlfriends. But nothing very much happened. I didn't find it unpleasant, though I did find them inept. They were very young and virginal and innocent and so was I and very little happened. The motivation for getting a girlfriend was entirely peer pressure – everybody was, it was the thing to do. You entered the Lower Sixth, you started your A levels and you got a girlfriend. Like you got driving lessons for your seventeenth birthday present.

Durham University, where I went, was quite an education – sexually. I was socially aware, good at my work, but sexually I was really a baby. I was at University College but one of the colleges, St Chad's, had been a theological college and it was still very Anglo-Catholic. It was a very queeny college. There were lots of gays there. I was plunged into a very different world: high camp, high church. Very old-fashioned. Queeny tea parties. Sex was talked about and it was done. There were also lots and lots of straight boys and because it was collegiate and all the colleges were single-sex it was very easy to find sex with so-called straight boys. My friend Anthony, who was at St Chad's, had a sort of affair, just sex really, with someone who fought the last general election for the Conservatives. He's married now, which is very funny since at Durham he literally could not get enough gay sex. But people decide what they want. It's not that they change but if what you really want is to be a Tory MP, then you have to have a wife. Some people have the style and the charismatic personality to get away with it. Thatcher was very funny about gays. She realised the political value of the moral majority and she used them. She didn't give a fuck about Mary Whitehouse but she gave her legitimacy. She used that moral right bit because she realised that electorally it could be effective.

I met my first proper lover, Stephen, at a party during a Christmas vacation. He was a very dashing Etonian, very bright, Trinity Cambridge, didn't work, had a private income. He took me out to a different restaurant every night, he took me to Heaven, bought me clothes, gave me a very good time. I really liked that, being treated like a girlfriend. He was older – twenty-four – my first proper boyfriend, the first man I kissed and spent a night with. It was all so glamorous to me – this protected country bumpkin child.

139

I came out to my parents when I was eighteen. I didn't tell my father but I did tell my mother and she got really upset. There was this year of silence. I was seeing Stephen in London and lying and saying I was staying with my friend Catherine but I wasn't, I was staying with this boy. So I was lying to my mother and I didn't like doing that. I'm very Catholic and you don't lie. It was extraordinarily difficult. It was just a nightmare, and I thought it was easier to be honest. But after I came out I thought, God, lying about seeing Stephen was far easier than this. We got an afternoon of tearful hysteria and then a year's silence, it was a complete non-subject. Yet here were these *Guardian* readers who would doubtless have signed petitions against attacks on gays and so on. And when my mother did her degree – she did it late – one of her tutors was an out lesbian, living with another woman. Then, after a year, my mother just started to talk about it. Since then she's just fine. Now she says she had always known, since I was three. I have this theory that mothers always know, they always do – no one knows you like your mother. But she didn't want to face up to it. It's not so much that you're gay or what they think you do, it's society's reaction, society's attitudes, this horrific heterosexual conspiracy to conform. As she said, 'I was not brought up to have a sexuality. I was brought up to get married and have babies.' That was it. There was no choice for that generation. She was brought up to believe that sex was something she had to endure for her husband: 'It isn't terribly nice darling, but you have to get on with it'.

I do think possibly that all men would like gay sex. The style of it. But the thing is that what men most like about women – it's what I like about women – is this delicacy and softness and beauty. That sort of classic, romantic, beautiful, soft lights sort of passion. That is something I think that men do want, both straight and gay, and that is something that the gay one-night-stand scene does not give you. There's no real romance or poetry or beauty to it. I think men want both. You can't really say men would just want no-holds-barred sex. Men do want that but they also want something more as well. That's irrespective of whether you're gay or straight.

I've had some very, very good sex on one-night stands but the thing about most gay people is that there's this slight dishonesty. People do tend to be performing, because gay men get into this thing of sex as performance. And there is this unwritten understanding that you won't see them again. Most of them have boyfriends and most gay men are having their cake and eating it. They have a relationship and yet they still go out. There's a fair amount of dishonesty. I see gay couples who go out cruising around on different nights, separately, but they don't admit it to each other.

140

My brother's first girlfriend lasted seven years; he started going out with her when they were both virgins and once they started they had a very wild time. And because she was the only girl he had ever been with he thought that all girls were like that but when that broke up and he started sleeping with other girls he realised that they weren't. He realised that women just won't do things. Gay sex isn't like that. For me the idea of going to bed with someone and them not sucking my dick: it's so absurd. Gay men just can't imagine that. You don't have to say to someone... It's just understood that it happens. Some comedian was on Channel 4 and he was saying, 'Why is it that every time my girlfriend sucks my cock, after three minutes she comes up and says, "I think you've had enough"?' I was thinking, if I get less than twenty minutes with someone I picked up, well I'd just think they were very odd. And I'll reciprocate. Of course.

I'm in a rather funny position myself, in a bizarre love triangle. My best friend Anthony I am extraordinarily close to. It's more than a friendship. We phone each other every day. I've seen him every day for nine years since I met him during my first term at university and I've seen him ever since and we're really, really close. We're both gay. We've never slept together. We've slept in the same bed hundreds of times but we've never slept together. I started going out with this boy Edward and because Anthony was so much in my life he got to know Edward really well too. Then he slept with Edward: my best friend and my lover. Edward's reaction was, 'What's all the fuss about?' I was doing my high camp, 'I'm leaving you...' He said, 'You can't leave me, I need you.' So we agreed that the three of us would all go out together. Though we've never had sex together, the three of us. We couldn't – there's such a barrier, a real sexual barrier between Anthony and me. So this went on for three months and then I told them both to fuck off. I just couldn't stand it. I couldn't stand the whole thing. Then Anthony and Edward broke up and I went back out with Edward and now we're two years down the line and none of us have sex together; we often all three sleep in the same bed with Edward always in the middle and as I said to my mother the other day they're just like family.

Edward and I got into having threesomes. We'd go out on a Saturday night and we'd pick someone else up and have a threesome. One night we picked up four men and brought them back here and had this orgy which was wild, very wild. That was great fun, very liberating, very uplifting. I like spontaneous sex. I was at a dinner party in Clapham and I was bored and it was around one-thirty a.m. and I thought well, I can respectably leave now, so I ordered a cab to take me home. Then I thought no, I feel horny, I'll go off to the

141

Market Tavern in Vauxhall, I'll pick someone up. So I get there at about a quarter to two and by five past I'm back in a cab, going home, with someone I've picked up. I just walked in, saw them, went up to them and said, 'Do you want to come back to my flat?' So we came back here, had very, very good sex and he left at four in the morning. That sort of thing doesn't happen to straight men. And they would like to do it. They can only do it with a hooker, to a girl they would describe as a tart, a slag, a girl they would not want to sleep with. And there aren't many of those. Whereas for gays nice boys are available, nice boys are on for it. I'm a nice boy and I'm on for it.

The good thing about the gay scene is the social mix, the class mix. You get everyone from the highest to the lowest. But essentially the people I was at college with, the friends I have now, they're essentially middle class. No one I know has ever had any hassle with the police, no one has ever been discriminated against for being homosexual, no one I know has ever suffered in any way because of their sexuality, but one is constantly reading and hearing about people who do suffer in that way. But we're protected by our education and our background and our parents' money and so on. It's different for working-class gays.

Middle-class boys are better at detail, they're better at S&M. They have better imaginations, they're more creative. Most of the working-class boys I've had simply want to fuck or they want to be fucked. That's the limit of their sexual imagination and they don't go beyond that. They're not into over-elaborate stylised foreplay. But then again middle-class queens are often so unsexy. Whenever I sleep with middle-class boys you'll have sex but then you'll be talking. And the talking takes over: 'You went to Durham...Oh yes my friends went to Durham. I went to Bristol, I went to Oxford. What did you do? Have you read? Did you see...?'

Middle-class people have all these things in common, all these bases they can touch. You always end up talking and not having sex. Particularly on E. I picked up this boy and we were both on E and both really off our heads and we both rolled around my bed for an hour and a half trying to find each other's dicks and trying to co-ordinate and the sexual thing kept being interrupted by conversation. After about an hour and a half we just abandoned it. Working-class boys aren't like that at all. They just want to bonk. Although they often want to be screwed too. Straight men I've slept with only want to be fucked. This guy Terry from Essex, he's a security guard with a girlfriend, it's just a nightmare scenario, and he is just so funny. He's so straight-acting and he just loves being fucked. That's all he wants. He's not into foreplay. He does a bit because I
142

demand it, but if I said we'll scrap it altogether, he'd be perfectly happy. He's a big butch security guard and I'd like him to screw me, but that's not on the agenda. He's such a typical neurotic closet case.

I think every gay person should come out, and come out as much as they can – with their family, and at work, and with their GP and so on – because I believe that things will only change by example. It's only by example that you'll change attitudes. I would credit the GLF era with some gains, but I'm not really aware of it. In the end you're not aware of battles you didn't have to fight. These pressure groups like OutRage and Act Up do possibly have a role to fulfil – it's quite healthy in a democracy to have all these groups going on, just as its healthy in a way to have the National Front – it sounds perverse, but that's a symbol of a strong democracy if they can take these extremes. But I do believe that anyone involved in any extreme form of politics is a loser. They're not getting enough sex, they're not getting enough out of life, and they turn to extreme politics.

What I love is French boys. French gay men are the best. They're just so obscene and so relaxed. I went to Ibiza for a holiday last year. I'd been there for two hours and this French guy was sucking me off in a gay bar. It was a perfect start to my holiday. I've been here two hours, I've had two lines of coke, I've had two gin and tonics, and now I'm being sucked off. My plane landed at midnight and two hours later...

My great theory about sex is this: Protestants in this country talk about Catholic guilt and how repressed Catholics are. It's absolute bollocks. The northern Europeans – Lutherans, Calvinists, the Swedes, the Germans and the English – are the most repressed, fucked-up people in the world, have no doubt about it whatsoever. The Mediterranean countries are looser. And Irish boys too. The northern European states may be more liberal about sex, but the people are more uptight, and they're not as good in bed. I know the Dutch, the Swedes and so on are very laid back about sex, but they're crap in bed. Just awful. I don't want to know, all that awful blond hair. Catholic Irish boys are really good in bed. Are they riddled with guilt? I don't know. Spanish, Italian and Irish boys are the best.

English men are very, very uptight about sex in general and they're very uptight about being gay. When and if they can let themselves go they can be very, very good in bed, but they then can't handle the emotions afterwards. The way I see it, sex is like leaping off a cliff. Once they've actually taken their clothes off in front of another man, they've done the dreadful thing, the 'shame that all men fear' (as the *News of the World* put it once) has been committed, and they can then go for it, and they can be very good. But afterwards their inclination

143

is often to run away, not to be able to accept that they've had a good time, they almost don't want to admit that they've enjoyed themselves. So yes, English gay men are pretty fucked up. I'm English too, but what makes me different is that I don't have any guilt. I've never had it. From the moment that I first started doing things with boys it just felt right. I arrogantly assume that if it feels right, then it must be right. I seem to have missed out on this guilt thing. I enjoy being a masochist, yes, but that's just a game. I don't do it because I feel I'm an unworthy homosexual and I should be beaten up by a real man. Hot candlewax on my nipples can be fun.

So I'm certainly gay but I'm also very aware that I've got a dick and that I am male. I do feel very male. When I'm with straight men I don't feel very different to them. I certainly don't feel I'm in the wrong body. I would not like to be a woman, I like being a man. I do feel very strongly that I don't want to be like the John Inman stereotype on television. The mincing queen. I'm not going to be stereotyped by heterosexuals, I'm not going to be put in a box: this is how gay men are, they work in retail. I mean, fuck off! I have a very masculine haircut [it's very cropped]. That very aggressive masculination of gay men which you'd see twenty years ago was a conscious reaction against stereotyping, and it has toned down now, but I'm not going to run around in a dress because that's how heterosexual men want to see me. And I think they do. I think heterosexual men do like to think of gay men as running round in dresses and being terribly girly. I can be very girly sometimes but sometimes I don't want to be. Gay men have spent so long trying to please heterosexual people and be acceptable. One thing I do like about OutRage and Act Up is that they are standing there saying: Fuck you! I don't know how much they achieve and I do think things will only change by example, but still, I do quite like that Fuck off! position sometimes.

I like sex in public. One day I was in Amsterdam and I gave this German skinhead a blow-job in a crowded bar and he came all over my face and I had come in my hair and I loved that. A gay Nazi skinhead. Nazism itself is revolting but the aesthetic appeal is there for a lot of gay men. Jackboots and treat me rough. Of course it's dodgy – but so much of one's sexuality is dodgy.

I think gay sex can suffer because both parties are determined to give a bravura performance. There is this terrible pressure on you on the gay scene. There's one night only and the last thing one wants is to walk into a gay bar and someone you've slept with the week before is standing with a group of their friends and they look over and say, 'Oh I had him – he was crap.' That is the male nightmare. The worst thing you can say about a man is that they've got a small dick and
144

they're bad in bed. I do feel very strongly about that. There's such an emphasis on the gay scene about has he got a big cock? And if you haven't got a big dick then it must be a bit awful. Women are more tolerant and understanding. I'm a total size queen. I can't see the point with small willies, you can't do anything with them, they're also not as aesthetically pleasing. My friend Anthony has a very, very big dick and he's always berating me for caring about size, but then in his case it's some kind of inverted snobbery. But I'm sure he's just as snobbish too, really. All gay men are size queens. Of course, in the end there's no point. You've got to make the best you can. After all it's all you're going to get. They can't extend it. It's not like your face – if you really hate your face you can have plastic surgery, but your willy is your willy and you've got it for life. Learn to love it, that's what I say.

***

Undoubtedly, gay liberation, a raised gay consciousness, an overall desire to escape the closet and reject society's prejudiced disdain has typified the revised public image that the homosexual community has endeavoured to establish over the past two decades. But the militancy, the obsessive public honesty is not to everyone's taste. The concept of 'outing', of dragging individuals willy-nilly from the closet is, like so many aspects of the movement, originally an American phenomenon. Not everyone approves.

CHRIS TURNER: Outing is counter-productive. It's based upon a very limiting view of sexuality – either/or – you're in or you're out. Outing is playing the tabloids game, while claiming it's a tactic that will help us. Coming out was our own institution in gay liberation, we've created it. Outing shits on it. Coming out is something you do yourself, with the help of others. Outing people is a betrayal. Coming out isn't one moment in the past when you make a decision, have an experience. It's something you're engaged in the whole of your life.

MARCUS RIGGS: I'm not in favour of outing by and large. There are some cases where I'm tempted to do it. I don't, because it seems to me to be infringing the freedom of individuals to share themselves with others. I feel I want to out people when they're saying things that are very destructive for people whose experience of life doesn't conform with the norm – whether sexuality or whatever. For example closet gays being anti-black. I've never outed anyone, but I feel I want to sometimes. Nobody's ever outed me that I'm aware of. Nobody

145

made me admit I was gay till I was twenty-four. I'd have been very hurt if they had. I would have been more negative about myself than I already am. So I'm pleased that didn't happen.

JEFFREY WEEKS: I find it oppressive. Coming out has always been about encouraging people to be open about their sexuality, but providing them with a supportive context. It's always been seen as an act of individual affirmation within a wider context. To use it as a punishment for people suspected of being gay in high places turns it into a terrorist activity. It has no positive effect. Those who are gay, who for a variety of reasons personal or political may not wish to come out, are being dragged out, and those who are not gay are having this label attached to them slanderously by the very community which is supposed to be affirming gay rights. I don't see any merits in it at all. If Ronald Reagan had been known within a limited circle to have a secret gay life but presided over a government hostile to gays, didn't fund AIDS research, etc., then it would have been legitimate to out him. The trouble is, people like that are never outed. They haven't got the nerve. It tends to be rather obscure actors and actresses who no one actually gives a damn about. It's this belief that because you've found the truth, you must assert it for everyone else. You must pull the truth out of everyone else. I don't accept that.

And outing aside, not everything has changed. For some homosexuals, and by no means simply the veterans of an older era, the advances have not really meant that much. For some, the ghetto, not the barricades, still offers a more alluring prospect. And the barricades, in those eyes, are only one more ghetto in themselves.

TOMMY McLEOD
'A Wife on the Ocean Wave'

His basement flat near Finsbury Park is a shrine to high camp, the candles, religious icons, lavish bric-à-brac that peaks in the bathroom is in sharp contrast to the squalor of the North London street outside. In spirit at least, Kenneth Williams is not dead.

I'm working-class Scots. Upper working class if you get such a thing. My father was a miner, my mother was a nurse. My father drank heavily and was quite violent, mainly towards my mum; what I would do was get in the way. I wore nail varnish to school. I was about seven. It was blood-red, my mother's, and the teacher saw it and went bananas and made me stand at the front of the class with my hands up to show that I had this nail varnish. I made up this excuse that I'd been building Airfix kits. I always liked pretty things.

I used to think that everybody felt the same as me. I didn't understand why boys wanted to go and play football; I preferred being with the girls and playing skipping. I had this dreadful fight with a teacher when I was about seven because she wouldn't let me play with a doll's house in the classroom. I had this temper tantrum. The other kids didn't mind, it didn't register with them. One Christmas I asked my parents for a doll's house. I always had dolls at home. But my father had a big castle built for me and they gave me this. I was very disappointed but I overcame that by swapping the soldiers for the girl across the road's doll's house furniture. So I was the first person with a designer castle with all this doll's furniture in it. This caused a lot of trouble and my father took it away. Eventually I smashed it up since I couldn't have it.

I remember having girlfriends, but only because everyone else was doing it. I thought I'd better start. I was always hanging about with girls anyway so I was always the one who got the girlfriends, much to the envy of all the boys. I was the prettiest. We didn't do anything physically, not at all. But I was never ever short of girlfriends and boys used to get extremely jealous.

The boys did start to give me a hard time when I was at secondary school, they used to call me names. Poof, things like that. But I never really understood what that was. I knew it was a nasty name but I never actually understood what it was. Someone told me: it's two men that go together. I thought, a lot of men go together – I didn't understand what they meant. I ended up having my own little court. These other effeminate boys who were equally as bewildered as what I was and never knew that sex happened or anything like that. Some of the rougher boys did get at me. There was this kid who jabbed me in the arm with a compass. I had a complete temper tantrum and grabbed this boy and hit him over the head and said, 'Don't ever do that to me again!' I always had a good mouth when I was at school. That was my defence. I never got into physical violence – I'd always come off second best – so the best protection for me was my mouth. One boy was giving me a hard time, I told him, 'You'd better shut your face or I'll tell everybody that your dad crawled up the road drunk.' It was very effective. I was a very acidic little child and they left me alone for the most part. But the teachers could be very brutal, making remarks.

When I was fifteen I decided that I wanted to join the Merchant Navy. And one of the PE teachers told me, 'You'll have to be careful there,' and I thought what the hell is he on about? It's perfectly safe, they have life-jackets, lifeboats – what the hell is he on about? And basically I didn't understand what anyone was on about, because up to then I had had no sexual experience. I didn't masturbate, I didn't have fantasies. I did have wet dreams, and I didn't know what they were about – although it did feel wonderful when I was having them. I didn't understand – maybe I'd wet the bed? When I was fourteen one of the rough boys told me, 'I'll take you up the woods and shag you.' What was he on about? I still didn't understand. I don't think the others were so innocent, but I just used to switch off when they were talking about sex – I wasn't interested.

So off I go at the age of sixteen to the Merchant Navy. I chose that because when my mum and dad got divorced eventually my mum would take me on these wonderful holidays, on cruises and I thought: This is great fun. I would love to work on a boat. This is what I want to do when I grow up. So eventually I joined. Even at the age sixteen going on to a ship where there were all these queens, these drag queens, it still didn't occur to me. They were very protective of me. I was very pretty. They clucked around me; one or two of them didn't like me, hated me for some reason, but the majority wouldn't let me get into trouble, looked after me, kept what they called the chickenhawks off. They managed to do that for nearly a year, but by this time I was perhaps beginning to think: Maybe there's something more to life. And this stewardette had the hots for me. I thought: I really cannot cope with her trying to seduce me. She was quite forceful. But that still didn't mean it had occurred to me that I was gay. I didn't relate to the drag queens either.

But then I had my first sexual experience – with this engineer. He said to me one day, 'I wish you wouldn't wear these tight trousers.' I thought: What's he on about? I don't understand. So I went into his cabin. He said, 'Sit down,' and I sat down. 'Lie down.' I didn't want to lie down. Then he said, 'I know something about you.' I didn't know what. Eventually he said, 'Look, I am bisexual and I find you really attractive.' But he never really did anything; just kiss me and fondle me; he touched my cock, but I didn't touch him at all, and I did find it very exciting. But then I felt quite guilty, I felt maybe I'm sick, maybe there's something the matter, because by this time I had realised that this was not the norm. People were supposed to have girlfriends and get married and have babies – and here was me and I wasn't going to have babies with an engineer. Then there was: What would my parents say? What would my friends say? I never told anyone about it, not even the drag queens on the boat.

Still, after my first experience of sex I wanted more, though not with

148

that engineer. I was still quite innocent; I wasn't openly gay or anything like that. The first thing was that I thought about that stewardette who'd been coming on pretty heavy and I thought how come when she was doing the same thing to me, cornering me in my cabin, touching me up whatever, all I felt was terrified? But with this engineer I'd actually felt pleasure. I couldn't understand what was happening here. He never came near me again. The drag queens did find out and they closed ranks around me and homed in quite tightly on me.

Then on my next voyage – these were passenger ships, Royal Mail ships to South Africa, I was a page boy – I got a crush on an officer, another engineer. He was gorgeous. I had this dreadful crush on him. He was older than me, early twenties. He didn't respond, but he blushed quite a lot. It was quite obvious to him, I was dripping over him. Later I found out that he was caught with another page boy, in the sack. After this crush I went home and I told this friend of mine: 'There's this guy on the ship and he did this and there was this guy I had a crush on...' 'Oh,' he said, 'you're gay.' 'Gay?' I said, 'happy?' 'No,' he said, 'you're gay. And so am I.' I thought: Oh well, at least we've got something in common. By this time he had discovered the gay scene in Edinburgh – there was one gay bar – and he took me there and introduced me to it. This is about 1975. I felt happy in that gay world. It was totally: I'm not strange, I'm not odd, I'm not the only one. Though this was not gay liberation like it was going on down in London. This was one gay bar and once a month they had a disco in a dancehall they would rent. It was the only gay bar so anybody who was gay went there: drag queens, old men, chickens, rent boys, everything.

By now I was getting quite camp. I'd wear makeup – this was the role model of gay men I saw at sea – they wore makeup so I wore makeup. I didn't really need to do it – most people knew what I was. There was an awful lot of queer-bashing – being gay was still illegal in Scotland. I was queer-bashed a lot of times. They would attack you on the way to the bar, and get you when you left and sometimes they'd actually come in and beat people up.

I was still relatively virginal when I was going to the gay bar but it was then that I first managed to have penetrative sex. By now I was seventeen. There was this guy, a big pop manager, and he employed this guy Miriam, I don't know what his real name was but he was Jewish and we called him Miriam, and he lived in the suburbs and he had a bungalow and he drove a Rolls Royce. I don't know exactly what his job was but what he did was come into this gay bar and round up these young boys and take them home and have these parties. So I went one time and I ended up going off with Miriam's boyfriend and having penetrative sex with him. When it started I thought: I know you're very attractive but I don't know whether I want to go through with this. But it was wonderful. It was very painful, and I remember thinking, I wish he'd hurry up because I'm going to be sick. But it was very nice to feel I was that close to somebody. He was very affectionate. That was the first time. I didn't tell him, but he probably would have known from the way I was squealing.

By the time I went back on my next voyage I was openly gay. I'd come out within my own circle. I'd still go home and they'd be saying, 'When are you getting married, when are you going to get a girlfriend?' I said,'Oh I don't like women,' and my mum said, 'Oh you'll change, you'll change, it's just a phase.' One time I was at home and my mum unpacked my case and found some makeup and ran screaming and crying to one of my sisters. But she never mentioned it to me. I only found out from my sister. Since then I have tried to come out with my mother. I have actually said I'm gay, but she's chosen not to listen. At times I wish I could have talked to her about how I felt, like for instance later when my greatest lover left me, but I couldn't, although at the same time I knew she knew how I felt. She knows what I am, but she's chosen not to. One of my sisters deals with it fine, and I did talk to her, but not now. Her husband came on to me not that long ago. That makes it difficult. I felt his attitude was he's had the sister now he's going to have the brother. He said to me, 'Well we've all mucked about,' but I said, 'No, we haven't all mucked about.' Anyway I think he'd already done some experimenting. It was like: I've read the book, now I want the T-shirt.

Then I got into trouble with the police. This other seventeen-year-old had run off from school and gone to stay with this gay friend of mine whose parents were on holiday. One day they went shoplifting. They were caught and the policeman looked at them and said, 'What're you walking like that for, are you a fucking queer?' And this mouthy little queen said, 'Yeah, I am, what's it to you?' So the next thing, since it was still illegal at the time, the CID was brought in and took this seventeen-year-old and basically terrorised him. So much so that he gave out a whole load of names, mine was fourth on the list. So I was sitting at home – my mum was out – these two men pushed their way in and said, 'We're CID and we're here to ask you some questions. Where's your mum, where's your dad?' – I was all alone. I told them I was on leave from the Merchant Navy. Basically they pushed me about, went upstairs, stripped off my bed, went into my mother's room and emptied out her wardrobe: 'What are all these dresses?' 'They're my mum's clothes. This is her house, I live here.' But they were convinced that these dresses were mine. They made me strip off my underwear, they stripped off all the beds, put them in plastic bags, dragged me into a police car and took me to the police station. That was eleven a.m. I was finally released at eleven-thirty that night. They questioned me and questioned me, they wanted to know if I was homosexual, who I had slept with, who else I knew was homosexual, where did I go, who did I meet. I was totally freaked out, and eventually I confessed. Yes, I was homosexual, but I said I had only slept with people when I was away at sea, and there was nothing they could do. I wouldn't give them names – basically I didn't know that many people anyway. They took a statement and gave me a whole list of charges that I could be prosecuted under. The one that really worried me was under-aged drinking – the rest, I felt I'd not done anything. They released me but dragged my friend off to the sheriff's court the next day. Then he was taken off to Barlinnie prison in Glasgow and he was panicking because he'd painted his toenails. I was terrified. After that whenever I went out the police would follow me. I wasn't angry. I felt I was a freak, and there was this awful feeling that they might be right. And they said, 'What would your parents say if we told them?'

By the time I'd made a few voyages I'd become an out and out drag queen on board. We used to make up our own frocks. I was on this passenger liner by now and there must have been two or three hundred drag queens – nearly all the other ships had been scrapped. So there was this concentration of queens. And when we docked somewhere we'd just take over the whole town, running about screaming and laughing and going into shops and so on. We'd be trying on these dresses in all the shops and it would be so funny. We had such a laugh. I was drinking quite a lot. Gin, which was what we all drank – £1.50 a bottle. Though I didn't like doing drag shows on the boats – I never really felt comfortable. I didn't mind the makeup but I didn't really like drag, I always felt it wasn't really me. I'd look at some of the queens and think, how sad you have to wear a dress.

After the passenger ships I moved onto cargo boats. Basically there weren't any passenger boats left. Though at first I thought: Oh my God, how am I going to survive on a cargo boat with no other gays? The first cargo boat was an iron ore ship with a Highland crew, all Gaelic-speaking. I had such a laugh with them – they couldn't cope with me. They'd sit in the corner, talking Gaelic and looking at me. But we got on okay, I never had problems with them. The first time on a ship I did have problems was on a Blue Star Line from Liverpool. There was this other queen I'd known already. We were both First Class waiters and he didn't want to work with the crew. 'I'm a First

Class waiter, a First Class steward and I'm not working with crew. If I have to serve any crew, I'll only serve officers.' Her name was Shirley. I was known as Mary. You know: the Queen of Scots. I told her, 'This is a cargo ship, there aren't any passengers, but you do the officers and I'll do the crew.' There was no air conditioning, the run to South Africa and it was very hot. We were used to passenger ships where there was air conditioning. My makeup started melting in the heat. Elizabeth Arden – only the best – and I was heartbroken because even then it was £30 for a pot of foundation. And in that heat it was just a puddle in the bottom of the drawer. So I was serving the crew and wearing just this giant T-shirt, like a mini dress, and I had such a laugh with the crew. Meanwhile Shirley was getting such a hard time with the officers, with starched whites in 100 degrees. The crew were all coming on to me and I could never make up my mind which one to go with – which meant that in the end I never went with any of them.

It wasn't a boy in every port, but it was on every ship, on every watch. Mainly seamen. Usually they claimed to be straight: 'Don't tell any of my friends.' This was a very old-fashioned gay world in many ways. There was no gay liberation. In the Merchant Navy queens were actually treated with quite a lot of respect. The crew never ever messed you about, never ever threatened you, never ever gave you a hard time about your sexuality. Though this was basically because of the reputation the queens had, that if you did go on at them they would always get you back. Less tolerance than fear. So it was a good place if you were gay because we were very much empowered in that situation. We were performers, basically. Their stereotype was that homosexuals were effeminate, they wore makeup, all that. So you took that on board, you wore makeup, you camped it up, and you were so effeminate – and they didn't feel threatened so they didn't threaten you and you had quite a good relationship. And they could sleep with you without feeling unmasculine, because as far as they were concerned you were almost like a woman. And you'd feed into that. On the one hand it was sex, which you wanted, and I would feel, well, I'm almost like a woman, because I'd always wanted to be like a woman. I did think of getting an operation to change sex but I don't think it works.

My experience on the ships was that people would leave you alone to do your own thing. It was very, very safe and the straight guys were very respectful and very protective. You almost became a mascot. One time in South Africa I went ashore to this bar – a straight bar – and there were soldiers who'd been fighting in Namibia. We were sitting there, my friend Shirley and me, and we were very drunk, really camping it up. Of course we'd been used to passenger liners where

152

maybe 200 of us would go out and you could camp it up, but this was slightly different – it was just Shirley and me. So this table went over, someone had been dancing on it, and the bouncers came over to me: 'You'll have to pay, you smashed the glasses.' I said, 'Hang on a minute, it was him, I never jumped on the table,' but with that the bouncers started laying into me. Shirley jumped in and they started laying into her and so the two of us got beaten up. Basically they kicked the shit out of us, and when we got back to the ship the crew and the officers said, 'What happened to you?' and we told them. The following night the crew said, 'Right, we're going to show them.' I said, 'There's no way I'm going back to that bar, the bouncers'll kill me again.' But this hairy-arsed seaman just said, 'You're going back,' and he dragged us back. So there we were in the bar and once again some glasses got broken – deliberately this time – and the bouncers came back: 'Did you not have enough last night?' I thought: Here we go, but with that bedlam broke loose. All these guys from the ship jumped up and there was this huge brawl and this time it was the bouncers who got beaten up.

We would have steady relationships on board. For the first couple of weeks we'd suss out who we wanted. The first week they've just left their girlfriends and their wives and they're still quite healthy. The second week they're feeling frustrated. The third week they're fed up with masturbating and the fourth week that's when you move in for the kill. Then you've got maybe another five or six months together.

The longest I spent with the same guy was about two years; I was about nineteen, it was up in the North Sea. He had left his pregnant girlfriend to live with me. I didn't seduce him, quite the opposite: when I first met him I thought what a horrible little nyaff, silly little idiot, because there I was holding court and he was butting in, trying to crack jokes and upstage it. But then we had this stormy relationship, love-hate really. It was another typical sea romance: he has a girlfriend, but she's ashore. I don't think about the shore, just what happens on the ship. But we'd meet on shore as well and got quite into each other. We were having sex on shore too. I would have done anything for him. Then he came and dropped this bombshell: his girlfriend was pregnant. I thought: This is going to do my head in, I don't think I can deal with this. I was jealous, I couldn't stand it. So I gave him an ultimatum: you have to make a choice. Surprisingly enough he turned up on my doorstep: 'I've chosen and I've come to you.' I was so pleased. He'd left his girlfriend, she was eight months pregnant, for me, but at the same time alarm bells were going off – if this person can do that he's a bit of a rat. Even so I was glad that he

153

had done it. And we started living together. It was very intense, lots of sex, and we were both very jealous of each other. Eventually it broke up. He went and never came back. I was quite distraught. Eventually I got a letter and called him up and got this history lesson from his father about Hadrian's Wall and how it should have been ten miles high to keep the Scots out, and he called me a dirty old man – which to his eyes I suppose I was. Though I was only twenty-one myself. It took the fun out of life and I became very depressed. I blamed myself: I must be a really horrible person for someone to finish with me. I internalised it all. Which started me on a road of self-destruction. Drugs, valium in a big way. Drinking heavily. And it hasn't really gone away.

My days in the Merchant Navy were the fun days, and those days stopped when finally I got into that relationship. Every voyage had a different aspect but basically we were camping it up and having fun and there aren't many days now when I don't miss it. I wish I could bring back the old days, though what it's like now with AIDS I don't know. The thing about camping around wasn't so much the sex as having fun. Being totally rebellious. These straight people turn up on the ship and lo and behold the first thing they meet is me. They could be very hostile. One time this guy asks me for an omelette. Very nasty guy. So I went to the chef and ordered the omelette and I put a plate on the hotplate. I left it there. I went out, had a cigarette, and there's this guy screaming: 'Where's that queer with my omelette!?' I thought: Keep it going, you're going to get it. Eventually the omelette was ready. I put it on the plate, grabbed it with a cloth, ran in and said, 'Mind the plate, it's very hot,' camping it up. This big hairy guy, very tough, just says, 'Give me it.' And I did. He took it and I could see the pain on his face and he was trying to be so macho and not scream or drop it. He walks back to his table and I stood and thought: This is killing you, and he walked faster and faster and his hands were burning and I thought: Don't ever, ever muck about with me again. He never ever did. Must have stopped him masturbating for a while too. Another time this guy threw an ice-cream at me and I was so embarrassed and annoyed that I picked up this jug and smashed it over his head. He couldn't believe that the queer had bashed him. I just thought: Don't come near me or I'll kill you. In those days I'd always take this kind of thing as a challenge and I'd rise to it. Now I don't.

I was in the Gulf when the Iranian revolution broke out and the Revolutionary Guard came on board. I knew they were stoning prostitutes and I thought, this is totally not the best place to be for me at the moment. But they left me alone. I think they took one look and

154

felt that I just reaffirmed everything they knew about Western decadence: this man running around covered in makeup.

I was still there during the Iran-Iraq war, the tanker war. That was so camp. I had this unbelievable crew which fed into my campness and I rose to the bait. I just got more and more camp. This was the Irano-British shipping company. These Iranian ships started firing at us and I became hysterical. Also I was running out of valium, which I was taking by the handful by now. There was Diarrhoea Doris, he was the chief steward and he was quite camp too, and I was second steward. So I threatened all the other stewards: 'If you don't do something for me I'll give you such a fucking hard time, my dears...' So we're going to have something called Operation Valium. There were all these different 'operations' at that time, this was ours. By now I was known as Daisy. The chief said, 'Daisy, you shouldn't really do that, you shouldn't really do that.' 'Shut up, Diarrhoea.' I was a real nasty piece of work. Doris was always whinging, complaining and he wore these clogs. One time I got so fed up I superglued his clogs to the bulkhead. He couldn't find them for days. 'Have you seen my clogs?' 'Why would you ask me?' Eventually when he was lying in bed one night he looked at his ceiling and there were his clogs! He screamed into the kitchen the next day: 'I know it was you who superglued my clogs...' I said, 'Yeah, and the next time you might be wearing them.'

So we had Operation Valium which consisted of me placing the stewards along the corridor with mops and buckets to look out. 'If anybody comes rattle your mops and buckets.' Then I stole the keys from the medical officer's cabinet and got into the medical locker, which was like Aladdin's cave. I ransacked it, filled up the buckets with all these potions and pills, ran back down to my cabin and emptied them out – and basically this saw me through the Tanker War.

One day I just went to the Captain and told him: 'I want to go home now, I've had enough of this. It's no longer fun. I don't want be here, they've opened fire.' The Captain said, 'Don't be stupid, pull yourself together.' I went back to my cabin, and I had this turban, and I put rollers in my hair, coming out under the turban, and I had a skirt on with stockings rolled down to my ankles – it was like Corporal Klinger in M*A*S*H – and I grabbed this mop and bucket and went back to the Captain: 'I'm sorry I want to go off.' It still didn't work though.

I was in the Falklands too, during the war. I was very heavily sedated most of the time. I was on a supply ship, the *British Avon*, which was taking oil. I didn't volunteer, just found myself there. This was as much a giggle as the Tanker War. I was sleeping with this guy, an able-bodied seaman, he'd been married three months before we

155

sailed, and we spent five months together. That was good. But it ended very badly. When we came to the end, the last night, I asked if he was coming to my cabin. He said, 'No I'm not,' and told me, 'Fuck off, you fucking queer!' He had to get his mind ready for going home to his girlfriend.

I think everybody was quite frightened during the Falklands; I wasn't – I was probably too stoned – until we'd left Ascension Island going south. Then I'd heard that they were actually shooting and sinking boats. Nobody had told us. All I'd heard was that people were getting irritated. But I entertained everybody. So it was five months of sheer hell. It would have been five months of sheer boredom too but I had my able-bodied seaman – who was quite able. So he kept me entertained for the trip and I kept everybody else entertained.

I was still drinking very heavily – we actually ran out of vodka because I was drinking so much, and with this CPO we finished off supplies. There may have been firing, but I didn't really notice. Enemy aircraft flew over one day and I said to someone, 'Isn't it lucky that they're ours?' The next thing was that all the alarms went off. I thought: What the fuck use is that? We were sitting on an oil tanker and one match... Who's going to have time to get in a lifeboat? And even if you got in a lifeboat there'd be so much fuel all over the bloody place you wouldn't stand a chance. We were sitting ducks. No guns. There were three SAS guys on board and that was it. I just had more to drink. There were drugs on board – grass and stuff – and I had my valium. So one day this artillery ship came alongside and I had been starved of vodka for about three weeks. I couldn't drink anything else. Not gin, nothing. So I went on board and camped it up and entertained them. They gave us six bottles of vodka to bring back. And while I'd been there I'd drunk about three quarters of a bottle already, and I went back to my cabin and on top of the valium I felt quite ill. I was also taking anti-depressants, and I wasn't sure whether I'd had any that day – so I took some more. There was this party going on in my cabin, all smoking joints and drinking and I staggered in and someone gave me a joint. I went off to the toilet, still holding the joint and passed out. After that I was violently sick. I realised I had to get off valium. When we got back to England I left the Merchant Navy. I was made redundant, but anyway I felt that all this camping around couldn't go on for ever, the world of the passenger ships was over really, I was getting older...

After I left the Merchant Navy I came to London and made the gay scene there. But although I had a couple of one-night stands, they weren't very satisfactory and more important I didn't relate to the gay world in London. It wasn't at all what I'd been used to. I didn't understand that the gays only went with other gays. That they stayed inside their own culture. We had been gay, but we'd been with straight men. I came from this queen culture, which was not the same as the London gay culture, the clone culture. We had our own language, parlyaree, which we used on a daily basis. 'Varda the omi-palone': Look at the gay man. 'Varda the cod eek': Look at fishface. That stuff. Coming to London where nobody understood it, that was difficult. It was that world of the Fifties and Sixties, and it had been a very insular, self-contained life. But London was just as insular in strange, different ways which I didn't understand. People weren't hostile, but they didn't understand me and I didn't understand them. I looked at them as second-class queens who didn't know what they were doing. These people, they all go about in checked shirts – what are they trying to prove?

I couldn't comprehend it all. In a way it was like those rent boys who say, 'I'm a real man, I'm not queer, I just happen to go with men.' I couldn't deal with them. They were totally alien to what I was used to. I didn't like the scene and I still don't like it that much. I preferred our scene which had been good fun and nobody felt threatened by us and so they didn't threaten us. They claimed that we lived in a ghetto and they didn't want to live in a ghetto, but what do they do? Set up a ghetto – Earl's Court. They ghettoise themselves and they're so aggressive and hostile. We were ghettoised, of course we were, but at least we're not hypocrites about it. They are. Saying [camp voice]: We're gonna be butch, we're gonna be butch. Who gives a fuck? I'm not saying that to be truly gay you can't be butch, but I am saying, Who cares? Why rub it in somebody else's face? Just to irritate people. Likewise you get these left-wing councils who spend so much money on lesbian and gay centres which is basically they're jumping on the liberation bandwagon for political reasons. It's still jobs for the boys or girls. They're on about equality but they're still so hostile to women. I just can't deal with them at all.

I've had lots of arguments with gay liberation people. I've probably taken on more of their attitudes since I left the Merchant Navy but things like total equality – nobody gets total equality. What I want is tolerance. For straight people not to impose themselves on me. Gay liberation doesn't relate to the camp world. I didn't understand what they were making all the fuss about. I didn't understand what all this oppression they were talking about was. I never felt oppressed. Only by the guy I was going out with.

The political gays claim they have a right to go into toilets and have sex. They don't. It's a public place. Animals, dogs, do it in the street, we're not animals. People who do that belittle that so-called love that

157

they have so much esteem for politically. A toilet isn't a place for doing sex. The reason it started up was because there was nowhere else to go, no clubs, but now there are these places so why don't they go there? You go up to Hampstead Heath tonight and the bushes are moving. People enjoy it, because it's, I don't want to use the word 'perverse', but it becomes a sexual act in itself, just going to that sort of place. It's not like having sex in a bed, it's having sex in a toilet and I think that says a lot about their attitude to what we, as gays are. If sex is beautiful why do they do it in a public lavatory?

For a while I worked for an agency doing prostitution. I didn't need the money but it was during a period of deep self-loathing and quite honestly it was about how low can I get. At the time I thought: Why don't you go and get paid for it? You'll get lots of sex and you'll get paid for it. I thought that sounds like a good idea but in retrospect it was how low can I get.

So I phoned up an agency, went along for an interview, took a photo which they put in their files and paid a fee, I think it was £50, and after that, when people come in or they phone up, they pay an introduction fee and they pay you when you meet. Basically you were dealing with businessmen who are in town but don't want to go into the gay scene, nor look around for rent boys, but want to meet someone. They sit in their posh hotel and buy their company from these agencies. It's purely for sex. There's not much escorting – just hanging around at dinner parties or parties as adornment. I was hired by Prince Faisal of Saudi Arabia just to sit around and hand out drinks or whatever. No sex there. The amount of money depended on how many times you went out in an evening, I'd only go out once. The most I earned was £300 and the least was £50.

The £300 was for an hour and a half at this place in Sloane Square. It was my first job. I arrived at this big house and there was this Irish prostitute who opened the door looking like something out of *The Rocky Horror Show*, high heels up to here, stockings, the lot. I thought: What the fuck have I let myself in for? I told her it was my first time, she said, 'Oh, hell.' Anyway she said that basically we had this client and he was into being a slave. He was filthy rich, had a house just off Sloane Square with a big glass dome over the staircase and I was thinking: Shit, does he own all this? She'd been there all night, I was only for an hour. She explained that all I had to do was treat him like a slave. So we went in and there was this old bald-headed man with no clothes on. I was in a suit. He asks me, 'Does Master want a drink?' I thought: Let's milk this to the hilt, so I said, 'Master insists on having champagne.' So he brought me some champagne; I thought: This is quite good fun, I could get into this. Meanwhile she was there with a
158

whip and she'd be giving him a tap every so often and I had to keep telling him to do things – clean this up, do that, whatever – and she'd whip him some more and then I'd go out have a cigarette and a glass of champagne and she'd go in with the whip and then we'd swap over – this went on for around an hour. Then she came out and said, 'He wants to get fucked, can you do that?' I thought: I don't think I can. She said, 'There's an extra hundred for you.' So I thought: Okay. I went back in. I said, 'The Mistress will have to leave, and you, bend over the bed.' But still I thought: There's no way I can do this, but... an extra hundred, *improvise.* I turned round and there was this bottle of wine which I grabbed and stuck up his arse. He was screaming, but I thought: I suppose he likes this, so I kept on. Then I was supposed to urinate on him, and I couldn't do that either, so I poured the wine on him, and that was that. I thought: I've got to get out of here, and I left. I got £250 and £50 for a cab.

You don't always want sex. You don't always get turned on. I had these friends of mine round, and they brought this guy who was really cute, really handsome with chiselled features, and this one friend of mine was like a dog in heat, just drooling over him. I never sleep with people at once; I have to grow to like them, but this guy I rather liked, so I said, 'Do you want to stay the night here?' – he lived down in south London – and he said, 'Okay'. This friend of mine was so uptight, but he stayed with me. So he came into my bedroom and he took off his clothes and he was covered in hair – which I don't like. He looked like a gorilla, so hirsute – hair from the neck to the soles of his feet, I'm sure they were furry too. I thought: Oh my God how do I get out of this without offending him? I thought I could pretend I'd had too much to drink, that I'm too tired, so that's what I did. I went to bed and it was like sleeping next to a shagpile rug. So I get away with it that night but when I woke up in the morning he was still there. The hair was still there. So I tried to sneak out of bed and get dressed. He woke up. He wanted sex. I just thought: Let's hurry up and get this over with. So I gave him a hand-job.

One-night stands are difficult. A couple of years ago, I'd been drinking, I was very drunk, and feeling a bit down. I'd hit the vodka quite heavily. I was just going home, I was clinging to the front gate, when this guy came by. He looked like Quasimodo. He said to me, 'Good evening to you and how are you this evening?' I was so drunk. I started camping it up. I said, 'I'm fine and I'm looking for fun, why don't you come in for a drink?' He was drunk too. An Irish Catholic labourer. I think I tried to give him a blow-job but I'd drunk so much I nearly threw up. So it was just a hand-job. I ended up having to throw him out at three in the morning; the only way I did that was saying that my boyfriend would be back soon and he was very jealous. I felt so guilty and dirty. It was two days in the bath with TCP. Every time I have a one-night stand these days I feel so guilty, I have to clean myself, have a bath. I spend the day in a bath with TCP trying to get myself clean. Strip the bed so I won't have to smell anything, wash the sheets, all that. It's not the sex that's dirty, it's having sex without any emotion. That's what I feel terrible about. I have to have some emotional feeling. Which in the AIDS era has become a good thing. Before it was seen as freaky, but now it's sensible. I'm a romantic, a relationship is more important than sex; sex has to be part of it, but only a part. I think that more and more gay people are coming round to this – except perhaps for people who are still in the back rooms of clubs – at least I hope they are.

I first knew about AIDS in 1983. I didn't believe it was true: they don't know what they're talking about. This was the 'gay plague', this mysterious disease that had killed a few homosexuals in America. I couldn't relate to that. I thought: It's American, it's got nothing to do with me. It wasn't till there was a case in London that I began to think about it again. At the agency we were told it was Americans who were bringing it over and so we stopped going with Americans. We thought that would be safe. I turned down a couple – I told them why – and they were horrified, they were quite aggressive. 'I'm sorry: I don't go with Americans.' 'Why?' 'Because you have your own problems over there and we don't want to get them over here.' But it still wasn't real for me. I didn't know anybody directly involved. But all of a sudden, like lots of people, I thought, no I can't take that risk. So I stopped the agency work. Now I only know two or three people who've died. At the time I panicked – I had these night sweats, which I believed was AIDS but what it probably was, since I don't have it, was fear. I developed a hatred for clones – I associated AIDS with them, they'd been going round the bath houses and in the back rooms, not us. They had brought this thing to us. That put me off gay liberation too.

In many ways I'm glad AIDS exists because I no longer have to get fucked. There's safe sex and I can say, 'No, I don't want to do that because I'm practising safe sex.' I think it's given people who want to be celibate an excuse. Before you were a freak, now you're a sensible person. So on the whole I am celibate. It's not so much something I've chosen but it does seem to have happened. I have been more or less celibate for the last five years.

I do have a number of friends with HIV now. My reaction was, well, I won't panic, I'll be a good person, a supportive person, but when I first came across somebody with AIDS I did panic. A friend of mine

160

worked for the National AIDS Helpline and his lover was HIV positive and now he has AIDS. I went round to their house and there was this guy who already had AIDS and he was very sweaty and covered in red blotches, and all I could think of was survival things: God, I hope these glasses are clean. The guy was coughing, I felt: What am I going to do? I can't cope with this. I could get it just from being in this room. I knew perfectly well that this was nonsense, that you couldn't get it that way, that you have to have sex with someone. Still, my gut reaction was to get the hell out of that room – I didn't want to be in the same room. But I was so drunk that I couldn't drive and I had to stay the night and I slept in the same bed as this person and he was wheezing and coughing and I couldn't bear it. What if I got it by lying next to him? Some people react the same way to any illness. When I came back I just had these totally irrational fears: I bet I've got it, I know I've got it. The most frightening thing was that I knew I was being irrational. But my emotions were just running amok.

This hysteria went on for some time. Every time I got a cold I thought that was it – AIDS. I was going to get tested but I didn't. If I did go and find out that I had AIDS I don't think I would suffer well. I'd just lie down and die, I'd bring it on. But if you can go ten years without sex and nothing happens, then you haven't got it, and I've done five and I've only got five to go. People say I'm wasting the prime of my life, but I say that my prime was when I was twenty or so. But still I am frightened and this silly bloody disease is robbing me of something.

I think that less people are absolutely straight than pretend to be. I think people tend to be too frightened by bigotry to experiment. So they say, 'Well, I'm able to do it with a woman, so let's stick to that. It's what people call normal and that's what I want to be'. These are often the people who when you question their sexuality they become very aggressive. Sometimes I've felt that I'm abnormal, but not these days. If I do suffer from guilt it's not because of my own sexuality, but because I can't deal with casual sex. I'll stand before God or anybody else and say there's nothing wrong with what I do, that it's perfectly normal and perfectly natural and if you feel emotion for anybody or anything you should follow it through. Of course there are limitations – I would never condone anyone who had sex with children, that's exploiting someone who's vulnerable and helpless – but I'm not helpless. I may be vulnerable at times but I'm not helpless.

PORN: One Man's Meat

Obscenity, it has been suggested, is anything that gives an elderly judge an erection. And not only elderly judges. Pornography, literally the 'writing of whores' (whether literary or otherwise), has a specific, if often unstated aim: the facilitation of, usually male, masturbation. In magazines, in books, in videos, in films and these days, down the telephone wires to one's desktop computer screen, porn is probably the most focused of all the media's productions. The stroke book and its higher tech analogues are very big business indeed, and the Hugh Hefners, the Paul Raymonds, the David Sullivans, all the myriad merchandisers of solo stimulation are very rich men.

And for all the pious cant that has ever surrounded the topic, what truly irks those who oppose porn is that cash. Like cannabis, whose defenders set it among the softest of drugs, it's the profits that excite the sternest antagonism.

The topic bows beneath its weight of subtexts – the alleged links to rape and sexual violence, the alleged exploitation of the sex workers, usually women, the threat to men, the threat to women, threat above all to children – but perhaps the real subtext, and the truly potent threat, is the threat to the status quo. Sex, as Gore Vidal has pointed out, builds no bridges, writes no books. Sex is. Tout court. Plain and simple. In a puritanical world such unashamed hedonism can never find an easy passage; that such hedonism goes even further, and makes money, appears the last straw. The least that 'society' can do is hedge the topic around with penalties – emotional guilt, legal constraints, psychic dirt.

But as the currently popular term 'sex industry' denotes, what we have here is not some evil octopus, its spreading tentacles ensnaring the innocent. What we have is a business, like many others if more profitable than most, a business that the disinterested observer can credit with quite remarkable survival given the efforts made to drive it underground, and a business that above all, underlines that ethic so beloved of those same right-wingers who use porn as a convenient scapegoat: the undeniable primacy of market forces.

GEORGE HARRISON MARKS

'I have a clientele out there who need me.'

An unassuming terrace in North London. Inside the walls are covered with 'showbiz' pictures, the proud homeowner and a variety

162

of stars. Only a pile of spanking magazines – Kane at £10 a shot
– breaks the respectability of the sitting room. And the front door
mat: two cartooned female bottoms, poised for the slipper or strap,
and like the particularly British pleasure they enshrine, more like
Mabel Lucie Atwell than anything appealing to the Marquis de
Sade.

George Harrison Marks, perhaps the best-known and certainly the
oldest name in British porn, started shooting still pictures for
London's variety theatres in the years that followed World War II.
Showgirls, dancers, 'leggy lovelies' in all sort of poses and not too
many clothes. A career spanning the best part of half a century was
born.

There was no sex industry at the time – I started it, opened the floodgates. My pictures started to appear in various magazines. All very arty-crafty stuff. Publishers got in touch asking to use them. It snowballed from there. It started with magazine publishers asking for my work, then the overseas ones came. They'd never seen nudes like it. I was photographing as I saw people, but it revolutionised the set-up of sex photography. And by this time I was booking models and photographing nudes. I started a market I didn't know existed. The girls were mostly showgirls. One day a publisher from Denmark – at that time Denmark was very straitlaced – came to England and wanted to buy a lot of pictures from me.Anyway, this chap bought a lot of pictures and as he was leaving he said, 'We'd like to use your name on the cover, we'll pay you another £100.' I couldn't believe this. That was a lot of money. I'd have given him the money to have my name on the cover. Then I thought: If my name is worth £100 just to be on his cover, it's worth a lot more to me. So I went into publishing. Three years later I was a millionaire.

My first magazine was *Kamera*. It was going to be a one-off. I decided to put a collection of forty-eight pictures together. I wanted to do something that was marketable to the ordinary public. Up to that time there were a few arty-crafty books, which were very expensive – £2.00, £2.50 each, a lot of money then – coffee-table type books. Very beautiful nudes, but very soft focus, terribly misty stuff. I thought: I'm going to give the public what they want at a price they can afford.

I decided to do a cheap pocket-sized book, in a run of 15,000. I found a printer who would do it – I must have gone to nine printers: 'My God, we can't print *that*!' – and then I found a distributor. Again having to hunt around because nearly every distributor said, 'Oh no, this is a bit too naughty.' And these were very arty-crafty classic nudes. So I found a distributor, but he said, '15,000 is a lot.' I said, 'If it takes six months to sell, I don't mind.' So we printed 15,000, went into the distributor. Three days later he was on the phone: 'For Christ's sake get the machines going again!' Eventually we printed 85,000 of that issue. He said, 'When's the next one coming out?' I said, 'There's not a next one.' But of course there was. The cover price was 2/6d, pocket-sized. Anyway, that started it off and it ran for 180/190 issues. It was a monthly.

I got knocked over and over again, went to court three or four times. I was charged under the Obscene Publications Act. I got away with every one. No, maybe there was one I didn't. By that time the magazine had taken off, distributed all over the country. My print run was 280,000 a month. My printer became a very rich man on it – so did I, thank God. Soon other magazines started up. *Spic 'n' Span*, stuff like that. Mine was *Kamera*, and it raked in the big money. I spent it on women and me, having a bloody good time.

This is all in the Fifties. There was an Obscene Publications squad then. I was in Gerrard Street at the time. There were dozens of heavy porn bookshops and a very big porn industry, which doesn't exist now, strangely enough. Proper hardcore stuff. The Old Bill were paid off regularly.The stuff came from abroad, not home-grown. Soho was flooded with porn. I got knocked on a calendar. I was the first to produce a nude calendar, with twelve nudes. I got pinched under the Post Office Act, a nothing Act. Fifty pound fine or something. That can still happen today. If you sent the *Sun* through the post and someone took offence, they could knock you. That was a joke. The judge was a character. He took one look at the pictures: 'This is grossly indecent' – the girl had a big bust – so I got fined fifty pounds.

I got leaned on by villains many many times. Heavy people. But I didn't pay up. Two doors along from me was a club, owned by Billy Hill – he was the top. The club was run by his ex-missus, and Billy came along regularly to make sure no one was bothering her. So I got to know him very well. He'd say: 'Anybody bother you, George, any trouble, let me know.' One day two characters walked into my studio and tried to put the squeeze on me for protection money. What am I going to do? I wasn't doing hard stuff, but because I was in the business, obviously I'm doing other things too. I said, 'I'd better speak to my partner, come back tomorrow.' 'We'll be back tomorrow.' Shit, what am I going to do? They turned up the following day. I said, 'I've spoken to my partner and he said, "Tell them to fuck off or they won't see tomorrow morning."' 'Oh yes, who's your partner?' 'Billy Hill.' They just turned round and walked out and that was the last I saw of
164

them. I hadn't even spoken to Billy, I just had to mention his name. I was never troubled again.

From there I went into making feature films. I made the first film that ever showed a nude on the British screen, *Naked as Nature Intended*. Nudey type film. It took me six months of arguing with the censors to get away with it, and eventually I did. That was 1961. I got certificates for the films. I can't remember if there were X-rated films then. I think it was U, A, and H for Horror. X came later. I think mine went through as an A, played all over the country in straight cinemas. The plot for that first film was totally innocuous – wrote it on the back of a fag packet. It was about five girls going on holiday – more like a glamorised travelogue. In the end they meet up in a nudist camp, and then it was: bang, nudes on the screen, my God. No sex whatsoever. Same as the magazines – they were just poses. In all the films I've made there really hasn't been any sex. It was always Harrison Marks and birds, but very little sex – more comedy than anything. Sex and comedy work in England – worked for me anyway. Like a Carry On film. Look at Benny Hill – everyone knocked him but everyone loved his stuff. Typical seaside postcard. That's what I did with glamour.

I made a film for America, *Pattern of Evil*, which if you saw it today you'd think: What's wrong with that? But when I made it, it was quite raunchy. Had a bit of everything, but nothing over the mark – no explicit sex. Raunchy for its time – it would never have received a certificate here. There was an awful lot of money in it, but there was such a to-do in America about it – a case went on for nine months, through this film, and the people who put the money up eventually won the day, and it opened simultaneously in nine cinemas in New York – made a fortune for them. But they were too terrified to have another go, so that was it. That was about 1966.

The sexual revolution didn't affect my business much. It was the average bloke in the street who's always bought my stuff. They're great, given me a good living. Anyway, what was the sexual revolution? Fucking everybody without worrying. That's about it. People were suddenly freer, I suppose attitudes were more relaxed. But that's about it.

By that time the market was flooded with magazines. *Kane* is the mag I produce now. It's not bondage, purely a spanking mag. I've had no trouble over it. You go by guidelines, don't go over the top. Don't make them vicious. Happily they leave us alone. It was pure chance I did *Kane*. I was doing some work for the people who had the original spanking magazine, *Janus*, which had been going for over twenty years and their editor snuffed it and they were in schtuck. They asked me to help out. I thought: Spanking? Got to be a bit of a joke. Who buys this stuff? But I helped them put the next issue together and realised that there was a very big market for it. The people who are into this are so serious about it, it's like a religion. People volunteer for posing, and it's amazing the numbers who are into spanking. I don't laugh when I see the cheques come in. It's very, very serious. I don't go in for schoolgirls at all. They're not mentioned. You're getting near the mark with schoolgirls and I won't touch that. Also there's a line between what I do and S&M. I don't have leather, rubber, chains and whips. I'd never use any of that.

I couldn't care less about hardcore. I'm totally against the weirdo type films. Straight ordinary screwing videos – who cares? Nothing wrong in that. But nothing more than that. Utterly against that. I don't know what the market is for that. I don't get asked for it. My clientele is into spanking. They know this is what we do. The type of videos I produce go so far but not over the top. If they went over the top I'd lose my market. They don't want to see girls getting the shit knocked out of them. I know my market, know exactly what they want. They want pleasure. Obviously they're jerking off. In my videos they get a good storyline – we script our stuff very carefully – and it's very well rehearsed, so the dialogue is good; the acting is reasonably good, and the girl – it's always a pleasurable experience for her, not a hard one. The sex has to seem pleasurable.

I'm not contemptuous of my customers. I don't secretly think: What a load of idiots. I listen to what people want and don't want. I've met a lot of my customers and I take notice of what gets them. I meet them all over the place. Go out of my way to do it. They're not embarrassed, they open up. I take serious note of what they want and don't want. That's unusual I suppose.I have club get-togethers, I have a private members' club for *Kane*. About four times a year we have a big get-together, a big lunch, the whole bit. Eighty, ninety people turn up. We go to a top restaurant. They know me personally. To them I'm George. I think I'm unique in the business, always have been.

Mary Whitehouse probably thinks I'm the one that started it all. But I don't feel I'm dirty. I'm marketing something people want. And will continue to do so. You don't retire in this business, you die. What on earth would I want to retire for? I'm sixty-five. I'm into showbiz now, putting on variety shows. Top line stars. I hope to have variety shows all around the country. But I won't give up *Kane*. I have a clientele out there who need me.

***

166

NETTIE POLLARD: So much depends on what you call porn. Some people would say a magazine like *Penthouse* isn't porn because it's not hardcore. I'd say it is because people find it sexy. But anything can be. I don't think porn exists. If you look at *Penthouse* from a doctor's point of view, it isn't porn. If it doesn't turn you on, it's not porn. If you read something ordinary, not meant to be porn, that you find sexually exciting – say pictures of shoes: you find a shoe catalogue very exciting – that is pornography. If you want to masturbate over those pictures, that's definitely pornography. Yet it may not have been designed that way. In the end porn is anything people find sexually exciting. And it depends on how you react. And you can react differently at different times to the same material.

It's not about pictures, it's not about whether people want to look at pictures, it's about how people behave to one another. That's the only important thing. If you want to masturbate to torture reports put out by Amnesty – a lot of people are very horrified at that idea, but it doesn't do anyone any harm at all. What's wrong is the torture, not whether you want to masturbate over the idea of it. Torture is what's wrong. That's what ought to be banned. The worrying thing is that so many people are wanting to ban things like that. Anything can be used for sexual excitement – news items, reports of rape. Sometimes it can be done deliberately. I don't think Amnesty puts out its reports with that in mind, but perhaps someone working there finds them exciting. Does that really matter? What does matter is that Amnesty is working towards stopping torture.

I don't see porn as only something for men. It can have many roles for many people. Basically it's about sex. I think a lot of people don't masturbate over porn mags, just enjoy reading them. They find it sexy without doing anything. But you can't generalise. There's been almost no research done on it. Couples looking at porn together is becoming more common, particularly in America. Forty per cent of porn videos are taken out by women.

KENT BOLTON: Pornography isn't important. It's almost irrelevant. By porn I mean anything which normal people do legally between themselves being portrayed on film. I'm not talking about kiddie porn which should be covered by entirely separate laws. My films were just fucking. Hardcore is perceived as anything that involves erect penises, genitalia, fucking. There are refinements if one's talking about perversions, special interests, fetishes, etc. But the dividing line is between things which simply portray the body without any sexual involvement, and things which go beyond that. That's softcore and hardcore. How I think about pornography is incidental. I'm entirely

167

against violence. Gratuitous violence would be pornographic to me. My films are definitely to wank over.

TUPPY OWENS: As many married men wank as unmarried, and women as well probably. If people haven't got porn to jerk off with, they're going to use their fantasies, and if they haven't got a good imagination, they'll have a miserable wank. Pornography's just a tool. It's sad that there isn't a closer link between the model and the magazine, a situation in which the model acknowledges she's exposing herself as a favour for the man, and the man respects her for that. But in fact it's all done in a very furtive way.

AVEDON CARROLL: Men seem to like stuff that's unreservedly about sex more than women do. I think Mills & Boon is pornography, people just won't admit it. A lot of women like S/M stuff. I know women who like just to see people fucking but I know a lot more men who find that enough. Most women I know want something more. Men seem able to get excited by very simple stuff like that, just pictures or movies about fucking, come shots, etc. Funnily enough, women don't like softcore. A lot of women do find gay porn interesting.

ISOBEL KAPROWSKI: I saw my first gay male porn in '81 in Soho and it was stunning, because both were very beautiful. It made me realise why men like lesbian porn so much. I'd never understood it before. You can imagine yourself in either position, active or passive. It was somehow more satisfying. I still like that very much.

KIM WEST: I had a porn party one night, girls only, twelve to fourteen of us, specifically to talk about men and sex and just to have a laugh. I had porn films going. The girls were all going 'Uggh!' It was gay porn. That's all I watch. They've all got big cocks, good looking. In straight porn the men have big moustaches, beards, completely different. Gays are really beautiful, usually keep their boots on. Better quality of men. The night I showed all the porn films to the girls, out of the lot of us, only two liked anal sex. That surprised me. All these sexually liberated women. And another thing they gagged at was the blow-jobs on the video. 'Oh, I could never do that. Only if I really had to. A special treat.' It's something I've always enjoyed doing, never a chore.

TIM WOODWARD: Gay porn sells a lot to women. A photographer called Trevor Watson invented the concept of pictures of beautiful
168

men, sold in British high streets through Athena shops to secretaries and typists everywhere. When he first went to Portfolio Galleries, his publishers, they said, 'They're lovely pictures of handsome guys. They will sell well in the gay community. But women don't respond to this.' Trevor said, 'No, no, I think they will.' So they tried a few, and they sold really well. And now every typist in every suburb has a Trevor Watson picture. They're not terribly rude, just soft and erotic. Women buy them by the ton.

SUZANNE MOORE: Women like gay porn because it gives them a space where they can be active when they're looking at it, it lets them objectify men, which they can't do in straight porn. The attempts to make porn for women – *Playgirl*, things like that – were just rubbish.

ALEX KERSHAW: A guy will wank over a porn magazine. A woman will not want to wank over *Playgirl*. She might masturbate, but it'll be her head that's doing the visualising, a fictionalisation of what she'd like to happen to her. Whereas for a man it's Page 3, penetratively based.

GUY SALMON: There's a great deal of difference between straight porn and gay porn. Gay porn tends to be pretty Californian beach boys who are just doing it for a laugh and thinking of the pay cheque. Whereas the straight porn I've seen is very disturbing, horrible, rape scenarios and all this crap. What I do love about gay pornography is that here are these beach boys with these wonderful plastic smiles thinking about the $500 or whatever they get and they're just doing it all. And I'm constantly aware that in front of them, behind the camera, you've got some queen director, you've got two or three cameramen, technicians, makeup artists and this whole team – it's so professional. One of the best thing I've ever seen is a tape of out-takes from a Jeff Stryker movie. Jeff Stryker is a very big gay porn star. 'It'll Be Alright On The Night', but from gay porn. They are just hilarious. There's Jeff Stryker fucking this boy and he won't acknowledge him. He won't address any of his remarks to this boy. He just turns to the director, 'Tell him to tighten his ass, I can't fuck him like this, he's too loose,' and he just pushes this boy aside and he's standing there with a hard-on, saying, 'What the hell is going on here? You've given me this wanker to fuck. Get me someone else.' Then the director's saying, 'Jeffy, Jeffy, we'll redo it, okay.' And they do it again. Then Jeff Stryker is fucking this guy across a dustbin, this prop. Halfway through, the

169

dustbin slips away, the boy falls over, Jeffy, Mr God, falls on top of him. Just hilarious.

ALEX KERSHAW: I am a porn fan. I feel a bit embarrassed talking about this. Pictures, not prose. Men tend to need the aid of visualising images more than women. Books don't go far enough. Pornography has a role to play, but hasn't been properly discussed and democratised as yet. It's an easy target for a lot of women. For me, porn is interesting because of the male/female fantasy, and how it fits in there. Whatever people say, it creates an attitude in porn users of women being sex objects. My argument is that women are sex objects anyway. Men will see a scantily-clad woman in real life and want to have sex with her. If they could be a peeping Tom, they'd have a wank over it.

ARTHUR BANNER

'The Flesh Is Weak'

Pseudonymous here, but you've seen him on television, or your teenage children have: a popular member of the latest combo in the long line of witty Oxbridge graduates that stretches back via 'Monty Python' to 'Beyond the Fringe'.

I'm twenty-nine, born in 1964. My first memories of sex are very much linked to childish, prepubescent voyeurism. Mainly daughters of friends of my parents who would come round and expose themselves to me. Though I never did as much of that as I wanted to because my brother, who was a year above me at primary school, indulged in it to excess. I think one of the deep psychological motivations for me in my sexuality is that I felt I'd missed out on that. I never got enough.

At the age of about nine or ten I discovered this very hardcore Swedish/Danish pornography in my father's drawer and thrived on that sexually for a couple of years. That was my main stimulus. I don't think I was jerking off, I wasn't able to jerk off until I was about twelve and a half, but I was getting such pleasure as is possible for a prepubescent of that age. I was obsessively keen on it. How did I interpret it at that age? There were certain things that I didn't understand – oral sex, and I don't think I really understood sperm, in the pictures. I just didn't know what it was; the first thing I thought was, why is he pissing on her? That seemed a bit horrible. The fact that I have absolutely no sexual inhibitions is a lot to do with being very inured to sex at an early age. I do believe that if you have this
170

experience, discovering the parental pornography at an early age, it does determine what comes later. I never talked to my father about his pornography collection. I think my elder brother might have, but I never did. But both my brother and I have this golden idealisation of that porn stash, but it disappeared around 1979, it just vanished. We were both really upset and spent a lot of time searching the house for it. I think my brother asked where it went and he said he'd thrown it out. We had to buy our own after that.

I came of age as regards sex at a time when there was a short period, 1968-74, when among the results of the sexual revolution was the idea that pornography was purely liberating and part of the whole freeing of the shackles of Victorian morality. Before feminists came down on it and it became unacceptable again. In this period where there was a kind of naivety around pornography. Though I personally think that those are simply new moral reasons dressed up in political terms. The Mary Whitehouses were still there, of course, but for a while the liberal middle classes did embrace pornography as part of the whole counter-culture, *OZ* and all that stuff. Then they stopped, around the mid-Seventies. Feminism attacked it and the left disowned it. But that interlude period was very much the time that I was starting to become interested in sex and I think for people of my generation it did have an influence.

This taste for pornography has got me into enormous ideological hot water. There was an article about a phenomenon called the 'New Lads', a very journalistically hyped phenomenon, which was created around me and my writing partner, and the idea was that we represented a kind of cross between the New Man and the Old Lad. In so much as we really knew the requirements of being sensitive and anti-sexist and stuff like that but at the same time we were into football and drinking and shagging.

I was quoted by someone as having said that men can view women as sex objects without viewing them as sex objects. Now of course I didn't say that. What I said was: men can view women as sex objects without being sexist. One can be interested in a woman's body and not necessarily be sexist. What I meant by that was that there is a real problem in not being able to say I really fancy her or even she's got lovely tits, because you can say those things and not necessarily mean that I therefore think she should have a second-rate job. You can be utterly obsessed and utterly excited by the female body without necessarily, and this is what feminists assume, meaning that you cut that person off in any other respect. Nor do I wish to rape her. The idea that porn leads to abuse is absolute nonsense; there's no evidence. What there is evidence for is that people who abuse have

171

read porn. Though that doesn't show that porn leads to abuse or rape or whatever. It simply suggests that people who do these things have high sex drives and maybe they read pornography too. But that's not to say that the one leads to the other. After all there's no evidence that countries that have much less restricted pornography than we do have any higher rapes or abuse.

Any kind of expression of pleasure in a woman's body is now taken as being sexist. I don't think it is. The big problem with the standard feminist attitude is that it goes back to a nineteenth-century attitude about women's sexuality which is that it is somehow less dark, more ethereal and less aggressive than men's sexuality. But if you read any of Nancy Friday's books you'll find that's simply not the case. The idea that pornography is simply a male domain – outside of the basic financial and marketing terms – is more to do with the way women are taught to restrain desire than it is to do with anything natural to men or women.

I'm very aware of all the feminist arguments. I was a feminist. I was never breast-beating, but I was a feminist. When I was at university I was probably as right-on as I've ever been, but even then I never completely gave up pornography – I just read less of it. The most irritating thing about dealing with feminists is their assumption that you don't know the arguments, that because you say you like porn that makes you into a *Sun* reader. I've been through that whole argument and I now feel that I've come out the other side of it and have thought quite deeply about it.

I don't just see women as objects. I do consume pornography, but the idea that that makes me see women only as objects implies an attitude towards women that is summed up by the desire to fuck them. I don't think I have that attitude. This may sound crass but I would actually say that I am one of the least sexist men that I know, despite the fact I read a lot of pornography and that often when I meet a woman my first thought is, 'Can I sleep with this woman?' Because I divorce those things from what I think of the woman as a person. I'm sure that lots of men do this. There are men who only want to fuck the women they meet, but that is never the case with me. I've never understood men who sleep with someone and then leave that night. I would never do that – mainly because I would think that I could fuck them again in the morning for a start, but also, what's the point, why leave? If I do just want to fuck someone, and I do have a low opinion of them, that one thing has nothing to do with the other. You can like sleeping with someone but still not like being with them that much. Some people will say that the two things are interlinked, that I have less respect for the woman as a person because I see her as a sexual
172

object – that is bollocks. The fact of fucking implies nothing about whether or not you respect someone as a person. I see other men in operation, coming on to women: I change my personality not one iota when I talk to women. I don't put on a particular act, I don't chat them up, I've never in my whole life 'chatted a woman up'. I relate to them as I relate to men and judge them as I judge men – it's just that I want to sleep with them as well. And I don't want to sleep with men.

There are things I hate about pornography. I actually agree with an awful lot of Andrea Dworkin's readings of pornography. I agree with her reading of the semiotics of it, the way it is designed to humiliate the women. I just think that those processes of humiliation and things like that are part of sex and women have them as well. Power is involved in sex and there's no point in trying to get rid of it. The other thing I hate about pornography is that it is an incredibly spiralling thing. I now get bored with pornography magazines after one reading of them. I do have some videos, hardcore from Europe and America. What I very much like are shots of a woman being fucked when she's on top of the man and the camera is behind, I like that very much, I always think there should be more of those shots in pornographic videos. I'm very keen on the female buttocks. It's not that I'm that interested in spanking: in the end it's too ridiculous. I'd just start laughing. I don't really know how people get into certain fetishes. I can understand things like golden showers – it's to do with domination and power and degradation and so on – but I've never understood the process whereby things that are basically not sexual are created into sexual objects. Basically what I'm interested in is the female genital area.

I think what has shaped my voyeuristic instincts is the porn I came across very early. Also this feeling that I didn't have enough of the 'You show me yours and I'll show you mine stuff' that I wanted to have and always felt that I missed out on. All of which has created this obsessional interest in looking. I'm very anti-Freudian most of the time, I don't even believe a lot of the time that what happens in your formative childhood does shape your adult consciousness, but sexually I am possibly prepared to accept that it does.

Of course I masturbate over pornography. Good Lord! What do people mean by 'reading' pornography ? Of course you're wanking! I don't just flick through it on the train. I stand around in newsagents looking at the porn magazines and trying to choose the best one and there's always that terrible moment when the newsagent comes up to you and says, 'This isn't a public library.' Once in ten times that happens. I don't like the 'Readers' Wives' thing at all. I always skip those pages. But I have a friend who's really into it, and he gets English amateur videos, proper hardcore stuff, and he really loves it because it has this real cottage industry, secretive, under the tablecloth feel to it. That's what he likes, and I suppose that's why some people like Readers' Wives – that sense of ugliness being an index of reality. These are real people revealing themselves to you like models who're just doing it for money. And for some people that's exciting; but for me it's the models doing it for money that's exciting. For myself, of *Penthouse* and *Escort* I would prefer *Escort*, without any doubt, but of any magazine I'd prefer *Colour Climax*, proper Swedish hardcore. The thing about *Escort, Razzle, Cheap Thrills*, all those magazines, is that while they're pretty softcore, basically they're builders' magazines. But they're not just for builders – though they do have lots of shots that are taken on building sites. It's the downmarket, lower-classness of it that's part of its appeal. Middle-class fantasies of working-class bimbos.

When you have been brought up on pornography and are very obsessed by sex then sex can often be very difficult. I have had what I consider to be great sex, but it's often not quite how you imagined it would be. It's like flying through a cloud. It's not quite how you imagined it would be when you're lying on your back. When you look at the clouds and you've never flown through them you imagine them as this substantial thing; when you fly through them it's not quite like that. Sex is like that, it's often not quite like you'd imagine it is or would like it to be. Which may be because porn itself deals in idealised images. For instance you imagine sex as being a total loss of self, but it very rarely is.

I've got a very high sex drive. I'm very obsessed by sex. Someone asked me about condoms, and I said I'm not too bothered about wearing condoms because for me the seat of pleasure is in the testicles and condoms don't cover them. This could be why I have an abnormally high sex drive. A lot of men talk about their penis and stuff, and obviously my penis is incredibly important to me, but I have this kind of itch in my testicle lower groin area which is at times almost unbearable, and at times I have masochistic fantasies which are not to do with pleasure, but just getting rid of that constant sexual background noise, that itch in my groin. I spoke to the editor of *Skin Two* about those guys in Manchester who were sentenced for self-mutilation, and I put it to him, though he very much wasn't having this, that the sandpapering of the testicles that went on there was to do with an actual rubbing away of that appalling sexual itch. When it's there it means you can't do anything else, you can't read a book, you can't just get on with your life. I have it all the time. At times it's not so bad but I never go through a whole day without at some point

174

being beset by the desire to have sex. It's not just the way the average guy is supposed to walk down the street and think about sex every fifteen seconds, it's more than that. I can't imagine that every single male has this terrible almost torturing impulse. It's a more physiological thing, it can come on while I'm on my own in the flat making a cup of tea, watching football, whatever. So I masturbate, but it's terribly unsatisfactory from that point of view.

Masturbating is fine, I like masturbating, but I must say that in terms of getting rid of this itch, only sex will really do that for a long period of time. Good sex will get rid of it straight away. Masturbation only irritates it. And I honestly do think it's physiological and not psychological. It's a definite burn – and it's been there since I was a teenager. Since the first time I came. Though it's possibly brought on by masturbation, it's a sort of vicious circle – the more you masturbate the more you want to. If I was abstinent for a very long period perhaps it would go away – I don't know, and I've never tried. The longest I've ever gone is about a week without some kind of orgasm and that must have been under some extraordinary circumstances. I still masturbate about twice a day now. You can always find the time.

I don't know how interesting this is, but since I am now 'a celebrity' the last person but one I fucked was shagging me because I was a celebrity. From about July of last year till then I had been actively getting cancer from not shagging the hundreds of young girls who wanted to sleep with me because I wanted to keep my relationship together. Then finally I got into a situation whereby I was in a club and there were just loads and loads who obviously wanted to sleep with me, and I just cracked. I thought: This is ridiculous, I've been fantasising about this kind of thing for ages, ever since I was four... So I had this epiphanic moment: the next woman who came up to me and spoke to me, I was back at the hotel with her fifteen minutes later. She didn't quite say, 'You're really wonderful, I want to fuck you.' She said, 'Oh I really like your show and I think you're funny,' but ten to fifteen per cent of the women who do write to me do say, 'I want to fuck you', or 'I'd like to sleep with you' or 'You're really horny, you really turn me on'. I get some very strange letters. It is like a pornographic fantasy.

When it all started happening it was absolutely brilliant. Then it became incredibly frustrating. For months there was all this sexual possibility and I wasn't exploiting it. It wasn't just to do with my relationship; it was all to do with the fact that it can be very difficult: after gigs there are say fifty girls crowding round for autographs. I can't imagine how to transform that into an actual sexual situation half the time. Unless I was an extremely unpleasant bloke who was

175

able to cut someone dead when they were idealising me and just say, 'Forget the chat, I want to fuck you.' Interestingly enough another well-known comedian said he'd been told by someone who'd been in show business for longer than him that the thing to do with groupies is not allow them to talk to you at all, just immediately they come backstage just ask, 'Do you want to fuck me then?' When he said that to me I thought how absolutely right that was, because the minute you start talking to them you get filled with doubts, you start to think, 'Can I last the whole night with this person?' Beyond the sex you have to talk and you realise how artificial the human relationship between you and this person is and doubts begin to fill your head – and there is a side of you that doesn't want their idealism to fade, that doesn't want you to become no longer a demigod but a man with his trousers round his ankles.

Having sex with this groupie I met in this club represented quite a big step for me. I suddenly just decided: Fuck it, I'm going to shag this woman. It was the first time I'd ever picked someone up in a club and just fucked them there and then, that night. It wasn't great sex, but it was all right, it was pleasurable, entirely pleasurable but just not great sex, which may have been because she was eighteen. It may be exciting on a psychological level, but not in the actual sex. She had only slept with one other person, and I felt sometimes that she wasn't really behaving naturally, but just doing what she thought you were supposed to do while you were having sex. The way she moved was a little bit self-conscious. Not just going through the motions, because I think she was enjoying it, but kind of sex in the head rather than like behaving in a natural way. She wasn't really uninhibited. I suggested we use the mirrors near the bed but I got the impression she wasn't entirely happy with that.

I am completely uninhibited in bed. There's nothing I wouldn't do, although I've never been interested in being gay, so I would be inhibited with a man. There is no sexual practice with a woman that I would feel at all worried about. I'm always much happier having sex with the light on. I sometimes feel that I'm not really having sex, but directing some vaudeville show. I do a joke in my set: I was once asked which sort of film I'd most like to be in. On reflection the film I'd most like to be in is a film I once saw in Soho called *Spunky Birthday*. It's a joke, but it does have a certain truth: there is a side of me that longs to be in porno films. But I've not done it, nor have I made any amateur videos. You have to take sex so seriously to do that, and I don't take sex very seriously.

I don't take sex that seriously, I'm not trying to deal with sex like a train-spotter, notching off each new experiment, but there are things
176

that it pisses me off that I haven't done. I've never had anal intercourse – I did almost manage the other day but she insisted on stopping. It's quite painful. Nor have I done golden showers. I wouldn't balk at it, but I haven't found a woman who's into it.

None of which means that all my sexual partners have been equally uninhibited; in fact none of them have. Coming in the mouth is not always an option; I'd like to use more mirrors and not everyone's that keen on that. I would very much like to sleep with more than one woman. I wouldn't be bothered if there was another man round – group sex is something I could do – but I'd be more into sleeping with multiple women. Though from the pornographic point of view there's something I'd quite like about shagging someone over here and watching someone else shagging over there. Once again from what I hear the reality isn't like the image – too much like a conveyor belt when you actually do it. The point to me would be the gymnastic triangle. The problem for me now, and perhaps it's going to be the problem with my sex life, comes from the pornographer within me: I always want to see myself having sex. My writing partner said, and it's to do with having a pornographic imagination, that when you're fucking someone you really want them to have another vagina that you can look at at the same time. On the head or somewhere. I agree with that because sex for me is only sixty per cent feeling; forty per cent, at least forty per cent is visual. Though when I'm having sex I'm not fantasising about other things. I think what I am is a participatory voyeur – my basic sexual interest is somehow to be both a participant and a voyeur.

***

NETTIE POLLARD: There's been the most enormous change in porn since the Sixties and certainly since the Seventies. It was all spanking lesbians, and these appalling films with the two women pawing one another ineffectually and the man comes in, throws off his bath robe and shows them what it's all about. I see quite a lot of porn and there has been a big change. *Penthouse*, generally considered a sexist soft porn mag, had a lead letter from a man who thought it would be fun to get in another woman with his wife, which he did, and then there was a description of them all having sex together. But the end of the letter was: 'I'm pretty miserable now because she won't ever have sex with me except when the other woman's present and they exclude me.' That was the lead letter of the month. In videos I've seen, they have the two women doing things together, then you have a man coming

177

in, having sex with them, they're sucking him off, then the phone goes, he goes away and they just carry on. It's much more equal than it was. Male power has declined in a lot of porn now. Some of the old stuff was pretty offensive. Unrealistic. It is stronger now, except the laws mean you can't get most of this stuff legally.

KENT BOLTON: Originally I was putting on pub/club acts. Not just strippers – comedians, singers, etc. It seemed easy and led on to published work, then films. It was explicit erotic dancing. I got to know people in the pornographic publishing field. I got to know David Sullivan quite well. He's very successful, I envy him enormously. If I'd have been as ruthlessly singleminded as him, with that degree of business acumen, I'd have made vast amounts of money. I provided the girls for his film starring Mary Millington some time ago. I told him: 'That film was really shit, let's face it.' 'Yes,' he said, 'it was. I cried all the way to the bank.' But he just laughs at people like me. Knows where he's going, got there long ago.

So I started with the pub/club acts, putting ads in the *Morning Advertiser*. You get in touch then with the photographers etc., and a network builds up, one gets known. Mike Freeman of Videx Video Films responded to an ad of mine. I thought he was a bit fishy to start with, but he's the most up-front honest guy, recklessly so. Everything was grist to his mill. If it moved, he'd shoot it. Quality suffered inevitably. He's in Amsterdam now. He was on licence at the time, and pursued all over the place. He's the ultimate punters' surrogate – he'd look at everything from their point of view. In fact too much so. He was paying everyone huge sums, getting people doing things he thought the punters wanted. No compromise. He was very successful, for a short time, in the Eighties. Then he stood all manner of trials. I stood with him as well.

I did some scripting for my films, and acted in them. Some of the titles: *Knacker of the Yard, Police Corruption*. I was very good at playing corrupt police officers. Some people say I look like one. *Flat Sharing Shaggers* was a seminal work. Marvellous title. *Glass Table Orgy*. In that I played Sir Jack Buchanan-Smythe, with a large-busted lady. We'd hire very palatial places along Green Street. In the film we were trying to suborn young schoolgirls. My trial was over the films we were making together. The only charge brought against me was for acting in them. I wasn't part of the company that made them – therefore not living off the profits; and there was no charge of procuring because no girl would give evidence against me. But just by taking part I had conspired to deprave and corrupt. I was found not guilty, the other three were and got sent down – because they were part of the
178

company. If you were procuring you could be leading girls on to prostitution. The only way to avoid that would be to prove they were prostitutes already. The law is an ass. The trial took place at the end of June. The problem was that at the same time I was still working as a lecturer. Modern languages. The LEA were having end-of-term administrative meetings. I was mysteriously away for a week, and I honestly believed nobody knew about it. And as I was found not guilty, my barrister didn't have to detail my antecedents in mitigation. The Maxwell papers felt cheated when I was found not guilty. They followed it up though, and as I can't resist a pretty face, in this case their agent provocateur, I was entrapped.

Gangster pressure must exist although I didn't come up against it. The only people I came across that really scared me were some of the police types. Any evidence that exists, exists on tape. I've seen people convicted of having illegal heterosexual intercourse, a man and wife, purely because the evidence was there. Buggery I'm talking about. They'd try and browbeat girls into saving their own skin, if they'd give a bit on the evidence they were put up to give. I was naive about the law, didn't think I'd broken it. If there was no victim, no fraud operating. As I discovered, that was a total fallacy.

There are two aspects to what I was doing. One, I was leading a humdrum life and wanted some spice. And I thought what I did in my own time was my business. During the Eighties we were the only group making hardcore movies. Involved actual sexual intercourse. The problem was we made them, publicised them and sold them in this country. And the other aspect, which might sound a bit false, is that I believe that if you're going to make explicit films, make them. No cop-outs. We were prepared to take anything and we did. Suddenly the whole world descended upon us, not just the press but the police, who brought charges against all of us. At the beginning I sat down and thought – and I'm not making a moral issue out of this, it's amoral if anything – what I could do that would afford the maximum possible enjoyment, with maximum demands on my creativity for writing and acting which might bring in some money.

We advertised for the girls we used, and names were passed round. There is a network, almost a co-operative in a way. If anybody is mistreated you all get to know about it. I can't see this thing of forcing people to take part in porn – what do you get out of that? How does a bored or terrified girl come over? It would be a perverted mind that would go for that. Most of our girls are amateurs. I would never use a prostitute in my films. Their attitude towards sex is wrong. For a day's work the money would be into three figures. Even for *Penthouse* they'll only get £250-300.

Yes, the photographers do fuck the models. We're talking about a commodity, human bodies. A currency. It's no accident that photographers are usually middle-aged. If Tracy from Basildon has her head screwed on, she'll titillate people, make sure she's available. She can say fuck off if she wants to, however. But the word will get around. That's not a plus. A girl can make herself more in demand if she puts it about apart from the filming. To me that's not a quid pro quo, more of an understanding. If a girl likes doing it, can take it in her stride, then no feminist should take up the cudgels. I'm fed up having feminists dictate terms to me. The idea that men are always wrong.

The general attitude to the punter: they're despised, somebody from whom money can be sucked. That's what it's all about. They set themselves up to be ripped off. Someone in the business, say a photographer, must consider he has some aesthetic judgment, therefore must be able to put himself in the punter's place, must know what the punter wants. He decides to what extent artistry or eroticism comes into it. I see things from the punters' point of view. The only difference is that for me the sex doesn't have to be secondhand. I am a voyeur, I am a punter. For the person that buys the material, it might be the closest they can get to it. That's why others despise them, get money out of them. But the punter may also genuinely enjoy it. Who's to deny them that? The only proviso for me is that in the making of it, nobody is exploited.

The people who control the market are very mercenary. They want to know how many girls are in it, how many come shots and so on. They create the conditions in which you exist. But I don't buy all that. I don't believe for example that black girls are not commercial. A friend of mine ran a publication called *Dark*, on subscription, and ninety-five per cent of the subscribers were white. Asians and Chinese are different – they are in demand.

As a producer I'd like to know what is illegal and what isn't. I went to the Obscene Publications people at Scotland Yard and I saw a real yob from whom I tried to find out what is allowed and what isn't – how naive can you get? Is it permissible to shoot material in this country for sale abroad? I wanted it from the horse's mouth. Couldn't get a thing out of him. Nor from the BBFC. They say: 'We wouldn't want to interfere with your artistic integrity' – ha-ha – 'by imposing what you can do pro facto. We'll either censor it or take it to court.' Well I don't want to do that, when there's a prison sentence in the offing. The cop just regarded me as a time-waster. I suggested he come along to a Campaign Against Censorship meeting and offered to give him the details. He said, 'If I need to know where it is, I can find it out myself. I got my contacts.' Yobs like that are dictating what people should be allowed to do and see.

SUZANNE MOORE: Sex does require a bit of 'dirtyness'. There's this feminist erotica, supposed to be anti-pornography, which is all sort of nice and cosy and warm and it just takes the sexiness out of sex. Sex isn't about that for most people. People like to think what they're doing's illicit even if it isn't. That's all part of it. This Candida Royale stuff, in the end it is crap. Trying to draw a line between pornography and erotica is completely false; erotica to some people is porn to others. How do you classify half the stuff in the British Museum, the Private Case? I've seen one of the Candida Royale things and I'd like to say that here's a woman doing this stuff and it's really good, but it isn't. But I don't have a big relationship to pornography. I don't find a lot of it that offensive. Other things are far more offensive. Some advertising really offends me. I know all the objections to porn: the kind of women that are used... That kind of porn that's just very fantasised images of women – *Penthouse, Playboy*, very glamorous. Then there's the Readers' Wives. They're a far more accessible fantasy. They do look like people a man might know. I find it quite sad. These horrible bedspreads...

ADAM COLE: The British porn market tends to be a bit beer-and-skittles. You can't sell upmarket men's mags in this country for instance. Something like *Lui* in France, or *New Look* or something like that. Over here you have *Fiesta* and *Cheap Thrills*. That's the difference. *Escort* too. It's the difference between *Playboy* centrefolds and 'Nude Wives'. In this country there's a major attraction for Nude Wives, the girl next door, what's going on behind lace curtains – suburban fantasies. Nothing to do with style.

The *Electric Blue* videos, which I run, offer a mix of all these things. We offer the *Playboy* centrefold but also the Nude Wives. Rather than a feature story with a beginning, middle and end, it's something people can dip into and view frequently. It's topical, just like a magazine. There are celebrities, stories – more of a lifestyle type thing, an *Electric Blue* lifestyle. We don't have a philosophy as such, but there is an idea of what *Electric Blue* is about. There's one film, *A Day at Electric Blue*: it entails enormous hordes of women fighting for my attention, climbing all over me and distracting me with enormous pairs of tits that they ram into my face. We project this tongue-in-cheek idea of the continual casting session up here, fighting women off left right and centre. Trying to dictate a letter but – again a Benny

181

Hill kind of thing. Then we have *Electric Blue* parties. We're projecting a Martini lifestyle. They're supposed to be envious. I've never researched whether people wank while watching *Electric Blue*. It's just my idea of what they do, but I have no real idea. They will seek relief – I imagine.

The limitations are that this stuff is what it is, and whatever you do, however much you spend, it's still going to be a skin flick, people will have the same attitudes towards it. You're basically dealing with the amorphous mass of grey man. He's just as happy to live out his sexual fantasies with Beryl from Neasden as he is with a Helmut Newton-esque extravaganza. In this country it comes down to the lowest common denominator. These mags and tapes are just like food. People don't say: 'My goodness, I had a meal last week, why would I want to have another one?' It is an appetite. I can believe it could be addictive. Very lonely people who feel inadequate can become quite self-destructive.

I've often done chat shows with the Clare Shorts and Dawn Primarolos of this world. They usually talk about the exploitation of women, and from my point of view they have a complete misunderstanding of this business and the meaning of feminism. The simple fact is, this business is not about the exploitation of women, it's about the exploitation of men. It's men that're putting their hands in their pockets, forking out countless millions of pounds every year to devour this stuff. Women in this country control the sexual favours. Men control economic assets. Men take the sexual favours and turn it into money. Men are addicted, enslaved, tugged by their dicks into this arena. It's women who are in control, not the men. Feminists think the girls are exploited, not paid enough, not getting a fair deal and that it's debasing to women. That's more a reflection of men's attitudes than it is of women's. I'm sympathetic to the feminist view to a certain degree, but I feel these things can't be legislated out of existence, people have to be free to explore the limits. It's only through freedom of choice that people find their own truth.

The girls that want to do it find you easily enough. They have to be exhibitionists to do it. The feminist idea that we're exploiting these poor girls – this Dickensian exploitation of hapless, innocent creatures – is absolute rubbish. They're doing it because they really enjoy doing it, and because they want the money. They're far less likely to get led astray in this business than they would in the fashion or commercial world. Getting involved in drugs, fast-lane living. They come up from Basildon, drop their knickers, go home to Mum and Dad. They're mainly working-class girls. Middle-class girls will fuck anything that moves, but won't take their clothes off in front of a
182

camera. They don't like to be seen to be doing it. They're far more amoral than the working-class girls. The latter usually have one steady boyfriend, have maybe slept with two or three people and they see nothing wrong in what they do – 'I'm proud of my body, I don't mind people seeing it'. It's far more straightforward, a nuts-and-bolts approach, rather than the middle-class girls, who present themselves as nice convent girls at home, but will slip out to all-night parties, gangbangs, etc., doing unmentionable things behind closed doors.

The girls we use generally come from a close supportive family, happy family backgrounds. We've had a couple of girls offering to pose with their mothers. The length of time they stay around varies. You have a handful of stalwarts who've been around for a while. A lot stay in for two or three years and then drift off. A lot of them are strippers as well. I think they enjoy the attention – they are exhibitionists, Page 3 types, although some of the real Page 3s are a bit more precious. Though you do get Page 3 girls that have fallen on hard times, need the cash, or ones that want to be Page 3 girls. It's all the same sort of girl: Essex girl, really. I like some of them. Some have a really straightforward honest simplicity about them. They're not pretentious, no airs and graces, not hypocritical. A lot of them are very lively and vivacious. Generally a good bunch.

ISOBEL KAPROWSKI: I went to university late, when I was twenty-six. I read classics. A job came up on *Forum* and Tuppy Owens, who is a friend, rang up and said, 'You've got to go for it.' I said, 'No, I can't.' I was just about to do my part-time Ph.D. She said, 'You're the only person I know who can do it.' So I went for an interview, told them I had very little editorial experience. It was wonderful for me. I felt privileged that anybody would want to give me this job. I felt responsible. I felt the philosophy of *Forum* was right – people should be able to write in in confidence about any fantasy they liked, as long as it was legal, and they shouldn't be judged. I edited *Forum* for eighteen months, then they wanted me to edit *Penthouse* as well. So I did both. I'd read men's magazines before – finding the stories more a turn-on than the pictures. *Penthouse* was only slightly different from *Forum*. Letters are the selling point for *Forum* – people get turned on by them. This is one sort of fantasy. *Forum* has two sorts of letters, the advice letters that go into quite a lot of depth about their problems, and then the readers' letters which are the sexy ones. We try to filter out those we think are fantasies. With *Penthouse* we're less bothered – it's more of a fantasy thing anyway.

The girls love doing it. All right, they get paid, but they enjoy being the centre of attention. A fantastic experience. When I was younger I

183

used to look at magazines like *Penthouse* and wish I was attractive enough to pose. They know all the guys are out there wanking. Linzi Drew used to be our editor for four years, and said she'd never received a letter anything less than admiring.

Penthouse and *Sunday Sport* are both masturbatory, but *Penthouse* is an aesthetic product as well. As a straight woman I prefer working with an aesthetic product. I like looking at beautiful people. I wouldn't like to work on *Sunday Sport* or *Razzle* – a horrible magazine – but I wouldn't have an ethical problem about it. The difference is the aesthetics. *Fiesta* has a jokey way about sex, it doesn't denigrate anyone who buys it.

LYN PROCTOR: I was always very fond of *Fiesta*, for which I used to write in the Seventies. We had Readers' Wives. I used to talk to my editor, who liked his readers. He had a lot of female readers. This was very interesting and the reason why I enjoyed working for the magazine. Their attitude was that sex is not just the prerogative of busty nineteen-year-old girls, that sex and sexuality is the prerogative of everybody. We'd get these letters which would say 'I'm seventy-nine and I really like your magazine. I like Doris on page whatever because she's a mature woman, a real handful. I can't look at these pictures of nineteen-year-olds, because, well, they're like my granddaughter. It's not decent.' What *Fiesta* does is not just have the very attractive, very young, one style of body women. They have the Readers' Wives, the glamorous grandmothers, all kinds. And they do have Sharon from Basildon too. But if you have a waist of more than twenty-two inches, fine, why not, why not be in *Fiesta*? So it's a much broader spread of sexuality, and it does have this edge of Carry On. The ultimate in that is *Splosh*: the magazine of messy sex. If you want jelly, cream, mud, it's in *Splosh*. Though it's not in general newsagent circulation.

The men's magazine industry has an enormous honesty. Most of the people involved have no illusions about what they're doing. Though some of the advice has been wrong. For instance they'd have a piece on 101 Things to Stick Up Your Bum by Dr So-and-so, where the author was definitely not a doctor and a lot of the things he recommended were in fact highly dangerous and some poor chap who tried them had ended up in hospital. The great thing about *Fiesta*, when I worked on it, was that it was very honest. You might have wonderful aliases – I used to write under the name Dardanella Jones, I wanted to be Dardanella Straits, but they said, 'No, no, people would realise it was a piece of water between Turkey and Greece.' Very often men's magazines are perceived as being dishonest as compared to, say, women's magazines, but I don't think so at all. In
184

the end they're all peddling different kinds of fantasies and the men's magazines are totally honest about that. Sometimes they do believe the fantasies about themselves. For instance when I worked for *Penthouse* it was carefully positioning itself as an upmarket magazine, aimed at AB readers, but in fact its main readers were C3s. Plumbers, albeit plumbers who aspired to Porsches. The glossy lifestyle and the glossy birds that go with it. But *Fiesta* never pretended to be glossy, it never pretended to be upper class or sophisticated or anything silly like that.

Fiesta really understands what people enjoy: Readers' Wives, pies in the face, Barbara Windsor tripping over the picnic table and her breasts fall into the trifle. There's also the fact that they show women not just as observed objects, but as people who enjoy sex themselves. None of those awful little glossy write-ups that most of the magazines use for captions. I really really disliked them. The ability of many men seriously and honestly to believe in those things because they wanted to do so is absolutely mind-boggling.

LINDSAY HONEY

'I've died and gone to heaven'

In four words: a Rod Stewart lookalike. We sit in the small cottage he shares with Linzi Drew, shelves covered in model sports cars, red ones like his own. It's all devoid of flash, a few hardcore magazines in the rack, nothing exceptional. A far cry from the monster of depravity due to stand in the dock a couple of weeks later, charged with breaching the Obscene Publications Act. He ends up with nine months inside, though today he seems relatively optimistic.

I was expelled from school when I was seventeen and I'd already been playing in bands as a drummer. Semi-pro. This is 1973-74. So I applied for this job out of the *Melody Maker* and did a summer season down in Newquay with a pop dance band. That was kind of fun. Then when we came back to London we'd do the winter season in a strip club in Soho. I was seventeen, I'm thirty-six now. It was great. There was all these girls, I thought they were older women – they were about twenty-two, twenty-three, twenty-four – and they all took a bit of a shine to me and of course I was constantly surrounded by all these beautiful women with no clothes on. So I was opened up to all this and they took a shine to me 'cos I was so young and pretty. I ended up bonking all these strippers. Then the next summer I did another

185

summer season – tons of sex there as well, all these young girls on holiday.

Then I joined another band, the Ian Mitchell band, it was an offshoot from the Bay City Rollers when they split up. We were really successful for about two years, we had some hits and all that stuff. We're talking 1977-78. This was mainly in Japan and Europe and touring quite heavily, but when we came back to England we lost our record deal, there was this shake-up in the record company, and basically it all gone wrong. We'd gone from being successful to absolutely nothing, and I didn't know what to do.

Because we'd been in a band we'd done loads of straight pictures for pop magazines and I just saw this ad in the *Stage*: 'Models Wanted'. So I went along to this like really major seedy room right at the top of some building in Brewer Street. Met this guy, funny old boy, and he was running this agency. He said, 'I've got this bloke coming down in a minute, he's got this video company called Videx. Do you fancy the gig?' I said, 'What is it, then?' He said, 'Oh, it's making dirty movies.' Then this chick turned up, she was about 17. She was there to see this guy as well. So the guy turned up, looks like an old hippie, and said, 'I do these films and all that.' Very nice bloke. So, cool. I'd spent my entire life bonking anyway. That's the only reason I'd got into rock 'n' roll in the first place – I realised that everyone who played in a band, no matter how ugly you were or whatever, if you played in a band you got your dick sucked on a fairly regular basis. So I thought, sounds pretty good. I couldn't believe it. He said, 'I'm gonna pay you if you want to make these films. Shagging.' I said, 'How much?' He said, '£150 a day.' I thought: Fucking hell this is it, I've died and gone to heaven. I'm getting paid for something I was doing for nothing. That was the only equation that I drew. The fact that there was cameras there didn't matter: I'd been on stage. This was an ego thing. Brilliant.

There was nothing like an audition. In fact before I did my first video he already got me a lot of work for these magazines that David Sullivan had. *Raider*, stuff like that. Posing. Then I started doing the hardcore magazines for Sweden and Germany. I was really good at it. Which meant simply that I could keep it up. You basically do about eight or nine different positions for a set. I could do a whole photographic set in about two hours. So I got a lot of work because doing it all in two hours is very good. I work as a photographer now and I went to Sweden last year to work and we took fourteen hours to do one set! I could stay erect for two hours, but most people couldn't. I only found that out when I started working on the other side of the camera. Not everyone was like me. You really need people who get off on the bizarre situation, the fact that there are people around, that you're really performing to, and you want to do a good job. I actually found that situation quite exciting. Doing it for the camera, people watching. The naughtiness of it turned me on.

But most normal people, the fact that there's loads of other people there and lighting, cameras, it puts them off. Most men find it very difficult to get an erection in those circumstances. So what you have to do is wait ages and ages and ages. You can get the girl to go down on him, but I don't like doing that: it tires her out and then she doesn't look good for the pictures. The problem is there's the girl sucking him off to get him hard, and then she's got to go and do her makeup before we start taking the pictures, and while she's doing that the guy's dick goes down again. This is the eternal problem you get. So I assume, given how much work I got, they had the same problem then and when they found a guy who was just like up for it, could do the whole thing in a couple of hours without it going down, it was really useful to them. So that's the porn business: you just have to fuck all these women.

At a later stage, when I got a reputation for doing all these pictures and so on, me and a friend of mine used to get invited to these, like, swingers' parties and all that. We'd get like handed out as presents to all these women, the young studs to give them a good shagging when their husband was like fifty and past it. He'd watch and so on. It was funny, there were these couples and he'd ring me up and get me to go round and fuck the missus and all that. He'd sit there watching, and asking the wife questions about what it felt like when I was doing it. It was kind of bizarre, but you don't think about it. You just think: Yeah, I'm getting all this free sex. That was all that was on my mind. Just an ego thing. Now you do think: This is a bit bizarre, but not then. When you're young you don't think about that kind of thing.

So I did some hardcore and then I did some movies for this guy. We shot them in England, this was 1979-81, before there was any legislation, video was still such a new thing, it didn't come under the auspices of the Film Classification, you didn't need a certificate. It was simply a case of someone's opinion. The Obscene Publications Act isn't black and white, it's down to individual opinion, and we didn't think any of this was going to deprave or corrupt anyone. Straight hardcore. Someone else did a bit of gay stuff, some light S/M. I did do some spanking stuff. I can't get into S/M, but spanking's different, it's just sort of frivolous really. Harrison Marks does it, he does some good stuff, but it is very much a genre, spanking. Mainly I did straight bonking films.

Then the authorities started to look at this stuff and they had to
187

make some kind of stand, 'cos they didn't really know what was happening. And we were the only company that was producing this stuff at the time. So in 1982 we got a real heavy bust, a big long trial and the Old Bailey and that was that, closed the business down. After that, I'd already met Linzi [Drew] by then, I went back to the music business. We got another band together, did a record, did some touring. And then I took up photography and started working as a photographer and video cameraman. Which is what I still do. Though I mainly do video these days – photography's so over-subscribed what with the recession and so on. So many advertising and fashion photographers coming into the glamour business. There are only two major magazine companies now: Paul Raymond and Galaxy.

People always say this is just a seedy business full of perverts and girls who are too thick to know any better – and unfortunately at the moment, generally speaking, they're right. I'd like to turn round and say, 'No, it isn't.' Ten years ago it was a business. A photography business. But that's all changed. There's more magazines, more photographers. When I started there were maybe ten people, the same people doing all the pictures. Now there's about 150; you see sets in magazines from people I've never even heard of. In 1982 it was an easy way to make a living, because glamour photography is not that difficult. The lighting's easy, basically flat lighting, you just want to see the girl. So it was the easier end of the market. It was good money: you were getting £1,000 a set and a set was costing you all in probably £300-350 to shoot. The girl got £100-150. They're still paying them the same now. A roll of film was a fiver, the girl got £150 and all the other expenses were less – it was ten years ago – and you were making money. Now, because there's so many photographers, and there's so many magazines, and there's so many models, you're getting £400-600 a set and the set is actually costing £450 to shoot. So it's just not worth it.

It's all gone downhill in the last ten years. Just like I realised when I was seventeen that everyone who plays in a rock band gets laid, now a lot of people realise that being a glamour photographer means that you get a lot of sex. Another thing is that most of the girls really are your typical stereotype bimbos. I'm sorry to say that, at the moment, it's very much the truth that if a girl wants to get into the glamour business, she has to sleep with people. Photographers give them all this bullshit and take sexual advantage of them, really badly. There's loads of these photographers now got no interest in the photography at all, they're just doing it so they can take advantage of all the models. Give them all this bullshit: I'll get you on Page 3, I'll do this, I'll do that, and unfortunately, because of the tabloid myth about these Page

3 girls they think: Great, I can marry a secondhand car dealer from Essex and be on telly and do pantomime and all that – and that's as far as a lot of girls' aspirations go. They think that's being a celebrity and their aspirations go no further than that. So all these photographers, all they have to say is, 'Right, I'll get you on Page 3, but suck my dick first,' and the girls go, 'Oh yeah, great.' And they just do it, straight away.

It's a shame, because the only way this business is going to survive against all the flak we get from the puritans is to make it like a proper business. Okay, if you do a photo session and the girl fancies you and you end up fucking her, well so what? But there's so many people in the business, who are there for one thing only, what I'd call mental abuse of women. They don't even pretend. They just say, 'Come round my house,' and when they do they come straight out with it: 'If you want me to put you in the papers you've got to fuck me. I'll be back in five minutes, get your clothes off.' You look at these blokes and think, bloody hell, but they get away with it. Fifty-year-old men, big fat fifty-year-old men. I know this model who had a terrible scene in Paris. They booked her and her mate to go over there and the pictures were secondary. It was for them to get laid. The guy's fifty-two or something, big fat gut, just gross. She had a real problem, she almost got raped. There are so many instances of girls being forced into sex – they're away on a trip or something and they've got no choice. The photographer engineers it some way and in the end the girl thinks: Well, here I am for two weeks, what can I do? The trouble is a lot of the girls go into the business knowing what they've heard but still believing that it's not going to be like everyone's told them it is. Unfortunately sometimes they find out that's exactly what it's like. That said, is it worse than a lot of other ways of making a living? And a lot of the girls do like it, they love it, getting shagged, left right and centre. I haven't heard any of them complain. Well, a few do complain when it gets a bit heavy and they're with someone they don't like, but not many. They still keep going back for more.

I'd like to get the girls to be more streetwise. There's one photographer, we really don't like each other, but he's a great photographer and he shoots a lot of stuff for *Penthouse*. Now he tells every single girl that goes to see him that he's going to shoot them for American *Penthouse*. They believe him. He fucks all of them. I just think that's wrong. If you want to shag the woman, fine, but do it on your own merits, not by dangling all these stupid carrots in front of them all the time. There's so many girls I've seen come into the business for two weeks and they've met three or four photographers, they've all tried to fuck them, they've all given them all this bullshit and girls have realised that the business was just as bad as their parents or whoever told them it was.

If you want a stereotype it's the northern girl, no money, it's grim up North and all that and down she comes, tries to be a celebrity, makes her into a big fish in a small pond in Darlington or somewhere. Trying to get on Page 3 rather than work in a factory. That's all they're interested in – do that and they think they'll be famous in the town where they come from. And they'll meet some bloke who runs a Y-reg Jag or something and they'll be set up for life. What happens to them afterwards? Not much. They usually end up having kids or going back to the factory or getting married to a scaffolder or whatever. But they don't get deeply corrupted. That said, a lot of models do go on the game. A good twenty, well-known girls, who I could name now. They'll all do this dodgy stuff at night, what the euphemism calls 'escort' work, or they meet this bloke, he runs a few magazines, and they'll all troll down to his house and fuck him, and that's being on the game as well. There's no difference. Just that they think if they do it they'll be able to bask in the reflected glory. Because he's got £82 million in the bank, if they shag him they'll end up with some of it. It's grabbing at anything just to get on in life. 'Here's this bloke, he's got all this dosh, all these books, therefore I'll give him a blow-job, it might lead to something. I might get in the *Sun*, then he might take me down to Stringfellows and I might meet a West Ham footballer and then I can fuck him and sell my story to the *Sun*, and then p'raps I can go on *Blind Date* or something and then I'll be really famous.' The *Blind Date* mentality, I call it. Tabloid fame. I've met models who've been proud of showing me how they've been in the *News of the World* in these scandals: 'I Shagged West Ham Centre Forward'. They're in the paper and they think they're famous.

All these girls. They're all doing it privately. But I'll give them a grand to do it in front of a camera, they won't do it. When you suggest it, it's all, 'Oh no, what kind of a girl do you think ... dear, dear, no. The mere suggestion.' As if you'd just asked Mother Teresa to get fucked by a pair of scaffolders. Ludicrous this attitude. 'Sorry,' you say, 'I thought you'd been to see Mr So-and-so..' 'Yes I have. But what's that to do with it?' 'So if you went to see him you must have fucked him, what's the difference?' 'Oh no.' 'Hang on, I've been in this business twelve years and you're trying to give me this bullshit. Just be straight: you fuck for money, you fuck to get in the papers, why won't you do it in front of the camera?' If they then turn round and say, 'Yes I fuck for money, yes I fuck to get in the papers, but I'm still not going to do this', then at least we know where we stand. All this bullshit really annoys me.

190

You can be quite successful in this business. It's not just posing for magazines and that's the end of your career. Linzi's done more than that. But that's what I call the old school: back in '82 there were a few models around and you could use them again and again and again, you'd shoot a set for *Club*, say, then three months later, book them again and shoot a set for *Men Only*. But now, because of the competition, because the money's so much less, someone like Joanie Allum, the photographer, she'll book them for two days. She pays £200 a day, so the girl gets £400 and she thinks: that's good for a week's work. But she'll shoot four sets a day, so at the end of the two days she's got eight sets – the standard ten rolls of film per set – and that eight sets will possibly last all the magazines in the country for ever, or anyway a couple of years down the line when they've used them all up. So now, rather than ringing up the magazine and saying, I've got a set of Susan Whateverhernameis, and they'd say bring it in, now they'll say no. They want to see twenty sets at a time. So Joanie Allum goes in with eight sets of the same girl and that's it, that's her career finished. She's just been sucked dry. So if I take in a set of that girl they don't want to know. They've seen her.

I used to be a male stripper and I still do a bit of work – circumstances being what they are, you take work wherever you can. That's another industry that's changed. It started in the early Seventies but then it was very much a burlesque thing, mainly one male stripper and a load of drag acts. Now it's a male strip show so you get three strippers and just one drag act. That's all changed since the Chippendales. All the male strippers now, they're twenty-two, body-builders ... I can't compete with that. But I still get booked when there's no one else free, or it's a weekend and everyone else is booked up. Though I am pretty much fed up with it. You get £75 a show. You just take your clothes off for fifteen minutes. Turn up, take your clothes off, that's it. You can do two a night. Hen nights, football clubs, social clubs, that sort of thing. Guys come up afterwards: '£75, that's half my wages.' I say, 'Fine, you do it.' 'No, I could never do that! I could never go out in front of all those people and take my clothes off!' I said, 'There you go, that's why I get £75 for fifteen minutes and you get £150 a week. That's the gig.' It's like playing football – if you can do it you earn four grand a week, if you can't you don't.

There's no magic formula, no union card, you don't need twenty O levels to be a male stripper. I thought you had to have a big dick, but you don't even have to have a big dick, though fortunately I do have a big dick – which is probably why I'm still working even though I'm ten years older than everybody else. All you need is a bit of an act – a theme – I do a Rod Stewart number. Took me about three seconds

191

to think of that idea. A lot of people do the clone stuff – cowboys, policemen, whatever. Eighty per cent of the male strippers are gay anyway. They all get into it via the drag acts and they're usually one of the drag acts' boyfriends who start going along to the shows with the boyfriend and then he says, 'Oooh, why don't you be a male stripper?' and there they go. So all those Chippendale fantasy clone-type things – biker, cop, all that Village People stuff – they're all gay clones. They're going out in front of women as their fantasies but they're really doing it as gays. Half the Chippendales, they're woofters – I can't quite work out how women go for it.

Gays used to come on to me, when I was young and pretty. I went to this orgy once, with a friend of mine who'd just joined the band, a guitar player, and we took him to this party and there was all this sex going on and he couldn't believe it and he was laid out on the bed in the middle of all this and there was this guy sucking his dick and he didn't even realise. I've never tried it. I can't handle all that. Though it's a shame, because in a way I wish I was gay, because there's so much more scope in any field of the entertainment industry nowadays if you're gay. Even back then. I remember getting propositioned by this very well-known disc-jockey, he was a big name at the time and he had a record deal lined up for me, and who knows, I could have been quite a star in my own right. He made it fairly clear to me what I had to do. I was about nineteen, I went round to his house in Bayswater and there he was in his dressing-gown and I thought: Hang on, this is a bit strange. But I just took it for what it was. He wanted to do something with me and made it clear that we were only going to get together musically, he was only going to make me a star, if I let him suck my dick and all that. I was thinking about it: if that was all he wanted I might have been wiser to go for it, but at that time I was young and idealistic and I also thought if I did that it would turn me into a raving homosexual and I'd never be able to live it down. Now I'd think: Fuck it, it's only a mouth, who cares.

These days I'm putting together my own productions, directing, cameraman. I'm working for a Swedish magazine called *Private*. That's how Sullivan started, putting out a magazine which was called *Private*, though it wasn't the Swedish one. But he's cornered the market – his is the only magazine you can get where there's close-up pussy shots. The closest you're going to get to hardcore – so that's how he gets away with it.

The stories I could tell you about people in this business. There's this bloke, a publisher, his classic thing was he put this ad in the magazines: 'Magazine featuring women and horses.' So that all these real pervies, wanting all these animal magazines were sending their
192

money in. He sent them a copy of *Horse and Hound*. Brilliant. He made a fortune out of that. But you don't have to rip people off: people will pay for sexually orientated material, but he just gets off on ripping people off, that's his kick. I'd rather make four million out of giving people what they want than six million out of ripping people off. The top guys in the business are worth so much now they could really be doing something to push forward the frontiers, they could be putting a lot of effort in trying to change the law, to repeal the Obscene Publications Act. But they won't do it – they'd rather rip people off. They stick these editorials in the magazines – 'We're up for this, you must write to your MP and so on' – but they never do anything about it. They just want to make as much money as possible and they think the punters are all thick as shit and if they get ripped off, then they deserve it.

If you carry on like that you're only one up from the bloke in Soho with a bunch of cloakroom tickets who's telling people, 'Live show, live show' and you give him a fiver and he says, 'Straight up the stairs, live show.' So up you go, knock on the door and some bloke answers, 'Yeah? What live show?' You go down the stairs, the guy's fucked off. Their favourite scam was to advertise hardcore magazines, hardcore films, all that. They could get away with it because there's no definition of 'hardcore'. To Mary Whitehouse, Page 3 is hardcore. We all know what 'hardcore' means, it means shots of actual fucking, basically, but they can send you a picture of a girl topless, nothing else, and if you write back and say, 'I sent off for hardcore material,' they write back and say, 'Well, I call this hardcore.' What can you do?

Another bloke, he'd put in this ad for hardcore pornography. He'd get 2,000 replies. He cashes all the cheques, the replies go straight in the bin. So out of that 2,000 maybe 200 complain. 'I sent off ten pounds, I never received anything.' They go in the bin. And most people accept it. They're just too embarrased to go anywhere – Trading Standards, whatever – and say, 'I've tried to buy this hardcore film and I got nothing.' Instead they just forget. But out of the 200 there are a few who'll write in again. And gradually it gets whittled down and he's left with five people who are major pissed off: 'I sent for this fucking film and where is it!' And these he can't get rid of. They won't give up, they threaten to sue. So what he did then was he got this letter printed up on really official looking solicitor-y type paper and sent it out. 'Dear Mr So and So, I understand that you have been conducting a correspondence with my client. Apparently you asked him to supply you with hardcore pornography. You may or may not be aware that it is an offence for him to supply hardcore pornography under the laws of this land and as such I am afraid that if you insist on continuing to request material such as this we will be forced to hand your name to the Obscene Publications Squad at Scotland Yard, whereupon you will probably be receiving a visit from several officers ...' That was it. End of story.

All right, on one level you've got to admire it – it's so fucking clever to play on people's weaknesses and emotions, at the same time it is absolutely despicable. With the amount of money he made he could have just given them what they wanted and they would have been happy and come back time after time. But his argument was: Well they come back time after time anyway. Because every time they send in they believe that this really is the point where I'll finally get something back.

It's that cloakroom ticket thing again. I used to work as projectionist in a Soho cinema club and we had a bloke who used to do just that. Sammy. One day this bloke Dougie, who had the club, he said, 'Look Sammy, sod all this up and down stairs, these tickets, come and work for me. I'll pay you six pound a shift.' Would have made about £100 a week then, quite good money. So he tried. He did about a week, then he said, 'I can't carry on doing this, you gotta be joking, I can earn four times this with the tickets.' I said, 'Sammy, you stand at the same stairs, three different sets of stairs, every day, don't anyone ever come back and bop you on the nose? You've been at it for ten years. People must be wise to this by now.' And he says, 'No. They come back time after time; I get the same people come back. If they do complain I tell them, "I'm sorry sir, I realise that when you got to the top of the stairs actually there wasn't a live show but what happened is this: ten minutes before the police had come round so we had to clean everything up. But this time, I promise, there's this great show round the corner. I can't take you, but what you do is give me a fiver, I'll give you this ticket and there's this bloke Bob, in the Corniche Cinema Club. Go and see Bob and he'll take you to this really dirty show."' He goes on and on like this. So the bloke gives him another fiver. Goes round to the Corniche, 'Can I speak to Bob?' 'Bob? No one called Bob works here.' 'But Sammy told me to see Bob about a live show ...' 'Sorry mate, don't know what you're talking about.' So he'd go back to Sammy. 'Oh well, that's because Bob doesn't know you, you'll have to go somewhere else. Give us another fiver ...' People will pay, people want sex, they want this elusive material and they want it so badly that they will keep on paying and paying ...

Maybe porn is addictive but so what? People do get addicted. I'm addicted to fast cars. I just love fast cars. I'm addicted to TV, I watch so much TV it's ludicrous. I'm addicted to rock music. But I can't see anything wrong with it. Addiction I see really as drugs or alcohol,

194

whereby if you give it up you do yourself physical damage or you go through some sort of emotional or physical state of withdrawal. But I think that with sex they're more addicted to the whole Soho thing. I used to see it all the time. The seediness, the underground-ness of it. You can take all this a bit too seriously. If they are addicted it's because they can never get it. They pay a fiver for a magazine – they don't get it – what am I going to do, I'll try another one. It's frustration; if this stuff were freely available there wouldn't be this addiction. Some people are addicted to fox-hunting or gun clubs. Given the choice I'd rather have someone addicted to sitting in front of his telly wanking over videos all day. If that's an addiction then so what, it's not doing anyone any harm. I can't see the problem.

Pornography is a very useful stick to beat everyone with. The thing about pornography is that it lays itself open. Last year we were at the porn convention in America, and the FBI are trying to close the business down. They can't, because of the First Amendment, but they're trying to do it in other ways. This bloke from the Adult Video Association of America, they have this campaign 'Freedom Isn't Free', got up and made this speech. 'The FBI are trying to close the business down; the FBI don't need to close the business down – two or three years and we're doing the fucking job for them.' And I think we're doing the same thing over here, we're giving them all the ammunition if we carry on in this sleazy fashion. They don't need to attack us, because when they do attack us we've got no argument. We can't say this is a perfectly respectable business because at the moment it isn't.

I think the change for the worse came around '85. I'm not really sure why. I think Thatcher had a lot to do with it. She reinforced people's visions of what the industry was like – bimbos being taken advantage of and all the rest of it, which is perfectly true. Then there was the classification of videos – people started to expect a lot less when they bought something. So it was Thatcher and the people around her and Mary Whitehouse and the media in general: they all have very high profiles, a lot of credibility and people believe what they say about the industry. I've spoken to countless people who think Mary Whitehouse is government appointed. They think she's got some job. They pushed all this family, moral values stuff and a lot of people took it on board in the Thatcher era. So they could use pornography as an excuse for all sorts of things. Porn leads to riots, whatever. So porn gets a very bad press, and some of it unfortunately is justified.

If we could clean the industry up we'd have a lot better chance of defending it in the way that I want to. Though I guess I'm exceptional in feeling that – because most of the business is inhabited by people

195

who just want to get laid. There's nothing inherently wrong with that, just the way they go about it. And I don't see why you have to be a misogynist to be in the business. People accuse me of it too, because I'm in the business, but that's like black people saying all white people are racist by definition. People say I must be anti-women, but it's not true, I have the greatest respect for women. The fact that I find them attractive has got nothing to do with it. I still like to have intelligent conversations with them, but having said that, my argument falls down, because most of the women in this business – you can't have an intelligent conversation with them. So when we are allowed to go on air and justify the business, which anyway is not often – generally speaking you just get the anti mob – you get a couple of models and ask them what they mean by pornography and they don't even understand the question. So that's just more ammunition: here's some other dumb girl who's been exploited.

If you're talking about exploitation, everything's exploitation. People who work in Tesco's filling shelves at night for £80 a week, they're being exploited, people who work the tills at Sainsbury's when John Sainsbury's on £2m a year, they're being exploited, but no one ever goes on about them. Just because people take their clothes off and get quite well paid for it – are they being exploited worse than anyone else?

If we were in France, Germany, let alone somewhere like Thailand, there wouldn't be all this fuss about porn. But this country is still very deeply rooted in religion. That's the problem. When we were on trial in 1982, in one of the films there was this girl getting fucked and I did a close-up of her face and she had this crucifix on her necklace. It was swinging backwards and forwards. Then when she was sucking this guy's dick her head was bobbing up and down and the cross was banging against his dick. The judge was going on and on: 'The juxtaposition of the religious symbol hitting against his genitalia ...' I never even thought about it. She just turned up on set and she just happened to have it on. There was nothing deliberate. Then I thought, hang on a sec, he's thinking about this more than anyone else is, so what's his kick then? They read so much into it. These people go on and on about all the evils of pornography and all the rest of it – it's a case of the lady doth protest too much. You start to think: Hang on, this is the kind of thing they must be into – they're so anti it. The anti-pornographic rhetoric is so extreme that I sometimes wonder where they're coming from. They just want to enjoy it on their own and they don't want anyone to know what perves they are.

When the whole video thing started there was a lot of amateur stuff. Which meant people were saying it can't possibly be art, it's too amateur. Two women sitting on a sofa and there's a knock on the door, 'Oh you must be the plumber, oh why don't you come in, oh what a lovely bit of hose you've got there ...' Just like the old stag films. These people like Clare Short, they've obviously never seen anything modern, because they still think it's like that. But in the Eighties there was a surge of incredibly high quality, incredibly made films, especially from the French. Massive production values, gorgeous women, cars, locations, all the rest of it. But now the whole thing's turned full circle. People are fed up with the classy stuff, now Americans love Readers' Wives. They're fed up with seeing these glamorous women they know they're never going to meet; they want to see someone who looks like the woman who lives next door or their mate's wife getting fucked. The upmarket magazines – *OUI*, *Lui*, *Penthouse*, stuff like that – are too good for the British. What they want is *Escort*, *Razzle* – the biggest selling magazines in the country. Full of birds smiling at the camera. From Doncaster, Barnsley, places like that: 'This is Sue, she works in Tesco's. "I've always wanted to be a model, 'cos my boyfriend works in the garage ..."' All this very working-class stuff.

I know lots of guys, they can't stand these stylised sets; it's straight to the Readers' Wives.: 'Look at her, she looks right dirty ...' There's always like the archetypal council flat, incredibly bad wallpaper with a gas fire stuck on it, all you need is ducks on the wall and you'd have the whole thing. I have actually done sets for videos that have been styled to look as if it's going on in one of these council flats. On purpose. When I started, you'd go round to someone's house to shoot them for *Escort* and you'd look at this and you'd think, 'Jesus Christ, what am I going to do with this?'

The problem is whether art can be erotic. You look at these upmarket sets and you ask, 'Is it horny?' And I just don't think it is. Do you think sex is dirty? No? Then you're obviously not doing it right. You've got one of these pictures with some gorgeous girl dressed in some Renaissance uniform and it's all very beautiful, and then you look at *Escort* with some little nineteen-year-old flashing her arse up the stairs of a bus or something with her knickers pulled right up into her pussy, and you think, 'Cor, fuckin' hell.' It's just instant turn-on. The other stuff is too far removed. The one might happen, the other never would. It's more real. It can be brilliant technically – as a photographer I'll look at it and see how brilliant it is, the lighting, the costumes whatever – but you're not getting a hard-on. And that's the bottom line: what you're producing is stuff to wank over.

That argument that porn leads to rape – it doesn't hold up. People say that pornography leads to sexual violence; as we all know what pornography leads to is a good wank, half of lager, a sandwich and a good night's kip. If someone's sitting there watching a video, maybe they'll have a wank over the video, but they're not going to get dressed and think: Oh yeah, I'll go out and rape somebody. Anyway rape has fuck all to do with sex anyway, it's to do with violence. And of course they're always bracketed together. Sex-and-violence – it's almost become one word. It annoys me: I'd rather be fucked than killed. Look at *Terminator 2*, stuff like that. I can't see any justification for pumping this stuff out in video shops when you're not allowed to watch two people making love. If they're talking about family values, and violence in society, I don't see how they manage to put it all down to pornography. The funny thing is that in all the countries where it's legal they have much less rape than we do over here. But people believe it's all linked. A girl kills herself, they find out that her father reads some porno magazines. So that means that he abused her and she killed herself. No proof, but that's what they say. You can't argue against people like that. They just believe. That's it, the end of the story. They don't want to hear any arguments.

All the stuff I do is hardcore. All these other arty-farty photographers, they all want to shoot for *Men Only* and *Club*. I work for *Private*. They've just started a video company and I'm shooting all this stuff for them. I go over to Sweden and do it, I go to America, I go to Germany, I do some here. Shooting hardcore is no big thrill. Horrible. It is a pain in the arse. It is the most bizarre situation, almost enough to put you off sex. This new set I did for *Private*. I was using the other photographer as a close-up, because he was the only guy who could get a stiff dick. You can never, ever find guys who can do it. That's the problem at the moment. Fourteen hours we took to do one set. The guy takes half an hour to get a hard-on and he stays hard for like thirty seconds. I don't know why they bother to take the work. I did this video shoot for *Private* the other week. Three guys, one girl. One guy never even turned up. The other two just couldn't perform at all. Cost me a grand. Just a complete waste of fucking time. They think it's all going to be a big thrill, and it doesn't happen. There's only me and my assistant, it's not as if there's a massive crew with people sitting round, eating sandwiches, making phone-calls or whatever. I had this lovely little girl, beautiful little body, shaved pussy and all that, right horny little bitch. She's sitting there on the couch, starkers, just waiting; they're sitting in the chair over in the corner, wanking over a magazine. I'm thinking: Hang on, they've got a horny little nineteen-year-old bird there, that they can both fuck and do what they want with, talking dirty – she was really good, I was really pleased to get her – and they're sitting wanking over magazines. Just a complete paradox.

Ideally I want them just to get on with it, but in the end I usually do give them some kind of chance to get to know each other. We just fuck off for half an hour. Sometimes you do have to take an attitude though, because in the end, you have to cover your arse. I did some shoot in Sweden with a girl who'd been sent over by an agent and lines had crossed. Now in *Private* we always do come shots in the mouth. I think it's the horniest shot, what they call the money shot. It's the sexiest, the ultimate thing a girl can do to show how turned on she is, I think, anyway. But some of the girls come over and they don't want to do it. 'I never done that, I don't even do that with my boyfriend,' and they really start kicking up. In the end you have to say 'Look, either you do it or you don't get paid, simple as that.' I really don't like putting people under pressure but sometimes you do have to treat them not particularly well. But if you do give in, if you say, 'All right love, you don't have to do that,' word gets back, which it does. A friend of mine does that, he's a director, he'll say, 'All right love, you don't have to do that.' I've heard girls talking in the dressing-room, 'He's great,' she said, 'you can get away with anything. Just say you don't want to do it.' They take advantage. Treat them too nicely they take advantage. Then again I've had girls in tears and I don't like it. But at the end of the day I've got a job to do and I've got to cover my arse. In the end I tell them, 'Look, darling, that's the gig.'

These guys, they should just be able to come and do it. But sometimes, you give them like half an hour with this chick on their own and they'll be fucking her rotten while the camera's not going and I'm thinking: She's not getting paid for that. She's not getting paid to have sex with you per se, she's getting paid to do a job of work in front of the camera as, not art, but as a job, to create a sex product for people to use as a sex aid. But you leave them alone, she's getting fucked rotten by this guy she's never met before, he's getting off on it, and as soon as I go up there to start taking pictures his fucking dick goes down. He's having a great old time, he's thinking, 'I'm getting all this sex and getting paid for it,' and as soon as I get the camera out his dick goes down, and this girl's got to perform to try and get his dick hard for another half hour. It's not on and I don't like it. Again, I feel sorry for the girls. They've been doing it for half an hour, they're knackered, their makeup's all over the place and they've got to try to look good for the camera.

Americans are brilliant. That's why their stuff's all so fucking clinical. You can do a whole set, five positions, in forty minutes. He's there, looking at his watch – five minutes doggy, five minutes sucking, so on. There's no intensity to it, it's just clinical. But it's great. French guys are the same. Walk in, take their trousers off, you just look at their dick and it goes hard. But what's wrong with the English? I've no idea at all. It's very worrying. Loads of people ring up: 'I can do it, I can do it.' But of course they can't.

I've seen some of those films by Candida Royale, porn for women made by a woman, they're all crap. It's all foreplay. It's supposed to be sex films for couples, or for women, but it's just a gimmick. That said, I'd love to do it. Another argument for the anti mob is that it's all for men. This girl asks me: 'Why don't you ever do anything for women?' I'd love to do porn for women. But as far as magazines go, Smith's and Menzies' won't take it. But if you want pictures of guys, you can go to a Pakistani shop and buy them, you can go to a gay shop in Camden Town and buy them. It's the same shit: pictures of guys sitting there with a hard-on. Women have this problem. Women's pornography, apart from the text or the way the magazine is laid out, is exactly the same as gay porn, it has to be: good-looking guys in sexy poses with erections. And women have a bit of a problem with that.

Gay men are very sexual, but gay women aren't. This fantasy of young good-looking lesbians, it's all bullshit. All the lesbians you ever see are big fat old tarts with crewcuts. Most lesbians are more into it as a political thing than a sex thing. I've only met one lesbian who's really into lesbian sex. Let's put it this way: real lesbians generally speaking don't look like the lesbians I pretend are lesbians for two-girl sex on film. Real lesbians, you wouldn't want to see them having sex. On the other hand, gay sex is all Adonis type men, Chippendales, guys like that and they're appealing to guys and women. So when women are looking at those guys and masturbating or what, in the back of their mind they're thinking, this is the stuff them pervy gay blokes wank over as well and I think that puts them off. But the main reason there's no porn for women is that you can't get it in the shops. Smith's and Menzies' won't have naked men because of the gay connotation. Funnily enough though there's a lot of videos coming out supposedly aimed at a female audience: the Page 7 Men, the Dream Boys... But the daft thing is that all the ads for them are in the gay magazines.

The main anti-porn argument from feminists is that it's always men dominating women. But it isn't. Mostly it's just good hard sex. There isn't one person in control or another person in control. A lot of the stuff is women in control. So I would assume that if there were pornography for women made by women, it would be exactly the same as the pornography we've got now, but it would just be women in the leading role. But I can't really see that there would be a difference. Perhaps there'd be a lot less cock-sucking, maybe women don't particularly want to see that, but I know loads of women who just love sucking dick. Perhaps it just means women taking the lead more. So when they change positions which is usually the guy moving the woman around, maybe this time the women would be taking the lead, telling the men what they wanted. That's what you get in the Candida Royale stuff. And you never see any come shot. Though I don't know why not seeing a come shot automatically makes it more suitable for women. Women like seeing guys come: it means they've turned the guy on enough to make him orgasm.

One of the fundamental problems with porno films, is that there isn't anything particularly satisfying about pulling your dick out and coming over someone's tits. Arguably, apart from coming in someone's mouth, which is just so dirty, so ... nice, just great – because for a woman to do that is the ultimate thing she can do for you, the ultimate gift of herself – the best thing is coming inside. It's like a together thing. So pulling your dick out just before you're about to come, then coming over her tits is a bit unsatisfying really. I used to think that when I was performing in the films, but that's what you always have to do. Perhaps that's why you don't get the come shot in women's pornography, perhaps women see it as a man's thing, coming over the woman is a symbol of domination maybe ...

I've never really made the film I'd like. I can be pretty perverse, well not perverse but I'd like to run the gamut of every sort of sexual variation, every sort of extravagance. The stuff I'm doing at the moment, for *Private*, is incredibly formularised. Ninety minutes. Eight sex scenes, one lesbian, same every time. When I'm working for producers in the States, they don't even look at the film. All they do is check the sex scenes. Sometimes they don't even look at anything. 'What did you get buddy?' That's all they ask. And they don't count the lesbian scene. That's extra. They look at it. 'You promised eight sex scenes, there's only six.' 'But there's a couple of lesbian scenes.' 'We don't count that, that's just a couple of dykes. And one of these girls, she gets fucked twice by the same guy – we've seen it once, why see it again? We need somebody else.' So there's been an incredible backlash. People aren't buying it: it's crap, it's all crap.

I've always believed that porn, it's a luxury. People should have to save up to pay for it, it's like going out for a special meal. If you could go to Maxim's and eat for a fiver a head, you wouldn't appreciate it. But now, in porn, you can walk into a shop in New York and you can buy properly packaged tapes for $11, six quid. People can't appreciate that, they just treat it like it's nothing. Then you get Soho and they overdo it, £80 or whatever. But there's a reasonable price: a good quality porno film should be £40-50. Some of the stuff that comes out of Germany is £200 each. But there you get a broadcast quality, incredibly high standard, gorgeous women, fantastic locations. Though I don't think the punters care. They don't. I can see in a way why people treat punters like shit – because they are the most annoying people in the world. They don't care about quality. If I sold a film for £50 and said this was the most incredible quality, brilliant film you will ever see, and then underneath it I put: this film is fourth-generation video copy, but it's just £5.50, I'd sell two copies of the £50 and 150 of the £5.50. They don't care as long as it's cheap. They just don't care. That's why the industry in America has completely fucked itself because people have got so used to paying for cheap films. If you want to do a film now you get a budget of $8000, four and a half grand. I can't make a film for that. You're cutting corners everywhere and it ends up looking like shit. I need twenty grand for a decent film. They just won't pay it. Five or six years ago they would, but not now. The amateur market's the biggest thing now. No porn stars. New girls, they last two or three weeks and then they're out again.

How do you become a porn star? People like Traci Lords, Amber Lynn, Savannah. You have to be gorgeous, stunning looking, and give great performances. In the end it's the power of the punter. It's like how do you become a pop star? People buy your records. It's how many units you sell. Also they all have these big fan clubs, so you can see their popularity from that. And they do personal appearances in clubs, tabletop dance clubs in the various states. Traci Lords became a big star because she was incredibly good-looking and because she was a nymphomaniac. She'd just give an incredible performance. Amber Lynn's another one: she can suck the chrome off a '57 Chevy. But most of them aren't nymphomaniacs, most of them are after the money to feed a coke habit. All the ones I've met, almost without exception are doing it to feed a coke habit or to feed a boyfriend, some thick American prat who sits on its arse all day and has its mates round to drink beer while she goes out fucking to bring the money home. And the girls go along with it. I said to one girl, Christiana or something, absolutely gorgeous, a really nice girl, and she's got this boyfriend who's just the biggest wanker you'd ever meet. I said to her, 'What are you doing with this guy?' We were on set once, it was her car, this Ford Mustang – she'd always wanted a Ford Mustang, which was one of the reasons she'd got into the business – and he dropped her on the set and then fucked off for the day in her car. She asked me when we'd be finished so she could tell him when to pick her up. I didn't know. So we finish the shoot, she rang him up and he was round at his mate's house, got a bit drunk, and tells her he can't really make

202

it, she'll have to make her own arrangements. He was being really off. I thought: Hang on, it's her car, all he's been doing is sitting on his arse all day while she's been out earning a living and he wouldn't even come to pick her up from the gig. What can you say? And at the end of the day a lot of people take the attitude, well, if she's that fucking stupid then I might as well take advantage of her as well.

As to the future, the industry is up against it and it's not going to get any better. Nor are the people who are in it. I think 1993, going into Europe, is just going to make it worse. They'll use this morals clause in the Treaty of Rome, it lets any country use its own moral standards if it wants to ban things. The English are always the last bastion, like the troops up against the wall with the Zulus coming at them. 'Don't worry chaps, we're British dammit.' It's like the opening titles of *Dad's Army*, all the arrows moving towards us and England standing alone against them. The more the rest of Europe has access to pornography and the more people see this and say if they can have it why can't we, the more they'll close ranks and try harder to keep it out. I was listening to this guy on the radio. He was saying, 'We're having discussions with other European governments about pornography, to bring them round to our way of thinking.' No thought of, Hang on, perhaps they're right and we're wrong. We're British so we must be right, and now we're trying to convince everyone else to do what we want.

I did hear through some people in contact with the BBFC – the C not for 'censorship', but for 'classification', I love that – that what's going to happen is this. They won't be able to stop it at the borders any more. And they can't stop anyone exporting or you're interfering with their right to trade. So it will be exported from Germany or wherever. So the Customs aren't going to try to stop it – they'll just pass it over to the police to decide whether to take action. It doesn't matter to me, the fact that it's not legal, because I can still make the stuff in this country, sell it abroad with no problem. And if it is made legal here there's going to be every farmer and his cow pumping stuff out. At the moment I'm like a big fish in a little pond, because no one else is doing this shit. If it's made legal we're going to get swamped with it.

It's frustrating, this business. The punters won't pay good money for a good quality film, which means we can't improve the industry; it's frustrating that there's all these peasants who treat the girls like shit; it's frustrating that there's all these girls who are so thick that they'll get treated like shit. It's all very frustrating. But on the whole it's the nature of the business – these are the people who are attracted to it. It's just the nature of the beast and there's nothing you can do

203

about it. In the end, they say we get the politicians we deserve, well, we get the pornography, and the pornographers we deserve too.

***

SUZANNE MOORE: One of the big issues for feminists here and in the States for the last five years has been this whole debate about pornography. I am completely anti-censorship; it's not that I love pornography, but I certainly don't think it's the worst thing in the world. There are far worse things. If I had a choice between getting rid of pornography and providing child care, I know which one would make most women's lives a lot easier. But for some feminists it's become the cause rather than a symptom of what's wrong.

JANE MILLS: I do find pornography very tacky. I'm very ambivalent on the subject of censorship. I used not to be. I used to be secretary of Defence of Literature & the Arts Society and was really opposed to all forms of censorship. But when I made a film about rape and its representation in Hollywood movies, watching ten to fifteen rape movies a day – about 300 altogether – at the end of the day I'd think: censorship is too good for them. At the very least kneecapping and probably more. I was absolutely disgusted at what I saw – the misogyny and the hatred.

KATE HEATH: I have quite ambivalent feelings towards porn. I'm very anti-censorship and I don't think it's ever an answer – there's so many links with right-wing arguments and once you've made that link, you can't reverse it. I don't think there's ever going to be a satisfactory resolution of the arguments. It would be great if you could distinguish between porn and erotica. I'm not anti all porn. I find Page 3 much more offensive than a sex film. I think it has a far greater effect. It's difficult to start saying whether pornography does have a direct link with sexual violence. Though I believe there is a direct link, because porn creates an atmosphere where men see women as being accessible, as being somehow not real people, and because it's so inbuilt with the power structure that men feel, somehow it gives them power over women. I don't believe the argument that porn, by offering masturbation fantasies, actually helps men who would otherwise rape. The two things haven't got much in common: rape isn't about men's uncontrollable sexual urges, it's got very little to do with sex and a fuck of a lot to do with hatred towards women. It's not about lust. There's this whole mythology. The second-wave feminists didn't believe it,
204

they were among the first to explain that this was what rape is all about: hatred of women, not lust for them. Before that people did believe that rapists were men who were so driven by lust that they couldn't control themselves.

ISOBEL KAPROWSKI: Clare Short has been trying for years to get rid of Page 3. Then Dawn Primarolo came up with her Bill. She was saying *Penthouse*-type magazines should only be sold in sex shops which have to be licensed, and the licence is discretionary – i.e. get rid of all the stuff. Arguing against all that has been very good for us. If people know *Penthouse* and *Forum* are run by women who are not stupid – and someone like Linzi Drew has been very good, because she actually takes her clothes off and says: I love it – it will make people realise that what's regarded as pornography – and we talk about 'pornography' now, it used to be 'glamour magazines', or 'men's magazines' – has become the great scapegoat of our society: any problems, very simple: blame it on pornography. Most people are hypocrites – they all enjoy erotic material of some sort. They may call it Mills & Boon, *Gone With the Wind*, the Happy Mondays rather than pornography – but they get sexually turned on by it. But if it's only available to adults, on the top shelf, it's pornography. Ridiculous.

Avedon Carroll and Nettie Pollard are founder members of Feminists Against Censorship.

AVEDON CARROLL: The big fear about pornography is that guys are going to be wanking off after it. Nobody says: So what? Who cares? What's the trauma? So they're having a sexual fantasy and getting off on it. What's the problem? We've been raised to react against that idea. If they're having sex that's not connected to how wonderful we as women personally are, it's a mass insult. It's a sin, a personal insult. Every single woman in the country is being insulted.

With extreme feminists like Andrea Dworkin it's not just an insult, it's far more profound. As far as she's concerned, when you look at that picture in *Playboy* and it turns you on, you're thinking about raping, possibly killing her. No middle ground. In her thinking, intercourse is men oppressing women. Even if you're just thinking of fucking, you're thinking of doing something terrible to a woman. For them it's just a shading between the real rapists, wife-beaters etc. and the ordinary male. No real difference, just a matter of degree.

The idea that there's some difference between fantasy and fact, that there's male desire that isn't violent is beyond her. Okay, society encourages stupid behaviour between men and women and okay

205

some men *do* beat and kill their wives, but that doesn't mean there's a direct line between every man who wants to have sex with the woman he's in love with and every rapist who beats and kills his wife. They see that as a direct connection, a logical progression. There's no evidence to support it, but they still claim that men progress from *Penthouse* to the most perverted hardcore porn.

The Dworkin view is to a large extent what we're reacting against. Most of those a bit older know we couldn't have got anywhere without freedom of speech. The Civil Rights movement, the anti-war movement and the feminist movement would have been impossible in the States without the First Amendment which guarantees it. England makes me crazy, you don't have any rights here. Not one. In the US the First Amendment is an absolute right. But censorship, either in law or de facto, is always there. Feminists against Censorship is against all censorship, but we focus on specifically sexual censorship. We lend our support to others. We formed in 1989, because of a specific incident when Catherine Itzin and her friends came into NCCL. They cried about rape, child pornography, child abuse and so on and by a narrow margin got NCCL support for an anti-porn campaign. We said, 'This is ridiculous,' and we went in the next year as FAC and made some speeches. Our resolution didn't get passed. But last year we went in and were really good. We had one official FAC resolution, which I wrote, which was passed overwhelmingly. It said we were opposed to sexual censorship.

NETTIE POLLARD: The feminist position on porn was that it ought to be censored, that women were all sexual victims or potential sexual victims. That's really sad and very much not what the women's movement was meant to be about. It was meant to be about women being a bit more assertive and getting what they wanted.

DUNCAN FALLOWELL: Look at Clare Short – she's completely round the bend. What is degrading about naked women? In that sense women should be degraded. Having sex is not about making it with the Virgin Mary. It is about degrading yourself to an erotic, animal level and there is nothing wrong with that. The Greeks well understood it: you've got to get down there and enjoy it and stop being afraid of your animality. And only then will you be free of it. If you want to get beyond something, and not be totally trapped in a cul-de-sac of sexual obsession, which I suppose is what a sexual neurosis is, then you've got to start by accepting it, not by trying totally to eliminate it from your nature. Yeah..let's all be sex objects, let's all
206

be degraded, let's all have a wonderful time. Then when we've come and cleaned up, we get on to the next thing and do something else.

AVEDON CARROLL: We now have the spectre of Clare Short and Andrea Dworkin who *know* what men are thinking. Now we don't *know* what a man is thinking. He may not know a lot about sex at all. We don't *know* that because a guy is looking at a woman and thinking: Boy, I'd like some of that, that the thoughts he's having are violent or offensive. Ken Livingstone has said that when men look at porn they're thinking of rape. The boys at school snickered over porn and *they* were thinking of rape. He said that. The fashion of intellectual thought towards sex is to see male sexuality as being mostly negative and it has to be beaten into shape.

TUPPY OWENS: I've had nothing but hostility from the women's movement. They think the *Sex Maniac's Diary* is sexist. In fact it's aimed at both men and women. You could call it sexist for listing more brothels for men than women, but the fact is that there are many more, and that's not my fault. It's with the Outsiders, the club I run dealing with sexuality and the disabled, that I've had the most terrible trouble, still do. That's feminists thinking I'm encouraging disabled men to have their evil way with poor vulnerable disabled women. They've absolutely no sympathy for disabled men at all. It's quite tragic, because disabled men have a harder time finding partners than the women do. So obviously I give them some attention. But the women's movement have no sympathy with the problems of men, any men, disabled or otherwise. That's why I'm hated by the movement – because I sympathise with men. Any sort of debates or discussions with them have ended so terribly I've stopped doing it. It seems to inflame their hatred of me, they set out to get me.

The thing is that they're the sort of women who've got so little innate sexuality, so little confidence in their own sexuality, that they can't cope with the sort of sex men like. Whereas I'm quite masculine in my sexuality in that I'm very aggressive, get on with it as much as the man does. That's not catering to what men want, it's what I want out of sex – which is a lot of very active sex. If I wanted to be turned on by porn I'd look at gay porn because two men together is my ideal. Very heavy stuff, very hot stuff. What most women like is gentle stroking – most boring porn in the world.

ISOBEL KAPROWSKI: I debated with Mary Whitehouse at the Cambridge Union, and won. We had dinner with her and I said, 'You won't bring in anything about children will you?' – the remit was strictly adult – and she said, 'No.' Then when she got up that's all she did talk about, children having their genitals manipulated – as if that's anything to do with pornography. It is an act of violence. It's mutilation not manipulation. Whitehouse is a megalomaniac. She told me at the dinner she'd been speaking to, say, 500 million people on the World Service and it had given her a real kick. She's very self-seeking. Sincere in her beliefs – but so was Hitler. I asked her how much pornography she'd seen and how much had it damaged her. Her answer was that she hadn't seen any for years, but she knew what it was about.

AVEDON CARROLL: The safety valve argument is rubbish. Okay, porn does reduce the incidence of voyeurism. But it's not the point: those men are not thinking about rape. If you're having S/M fantasies of dominance, that's a game, it's not the same as attacking, terrifying somebody. Those people are not likely to rape anyone. I don't think it's reasonable to assume real rape has anything to do with it. And a lot of men have passive masochistic fantasies. From the rapist point of view, there's no joy in raping a photograph. Rape is about getting on people, ripping them off. You can't get that effect from a picture of a nude woman. And forty per cent of rapists are wife rapers. Marriage is more dangerous than pornography. I go by the one third rule. One third hate pornography, one third love it and one third are indifferent. That's the way it is with a lot of things. It's that one third in the middle, that neither hate nor love. They're all your bad examples. The husband that rapes the wife, the accepting wife, thinking of England.

DUNCAN FALLOWELL: The British have a problem with sex, there's no doubt about it, but this in itself can be incredibly sexy. The problems are in a sense what gives sex its refulgent excitement. But there are some practical problems: for example the whole law-making paraphernalia which the British feel necessary to bring into action the moment the subject of sex is raised strikes me as unbelievably foolish. And basically neurotic and therefore unhealthy and a symptom of the very things they are trying to stop. You do not stop child sex abuse, you do not stop rape either of women or men, you do not stop what we call sex crimes by basically enlarging to a ludicrous point those human activities that are legally defined as sex crimes. And a society that is so pruriently obsessed with the desire to eliminate all public manifestations of the sex instinct seems to me bound to be on a losing wicket. Now you can't even make a pass at a girl in the office without being accused of sexual harassment – it's just childish. What's happened to the great human drama, the great human story? Aren't you allowed to flirt any more? It's been rendered beyond the pale. Either you have a label that says I am a faggot, or I am straight – we're supposed to fulfil rigidly defined functions and never go outside them. I find that absolutely appalling. It's more highly evolved here than any other country except America. It comes from puritanism. Mediterranean society is in many ways very repressed but in this particular area it is not. Maybe it's the climate, I don't know, but the body is not by and large a source of terror to them, whereas it is to us.

GRAHAM WEBSTER-GARDNER: The majority of those who read pornography don't all go out and rape someone. But certain of them *are* influenced by it and do dreadful things. So at the very least pornography makes that outcome more likely. Therefore if we bombard ourselves with bad language, blasphemy, derision of marriage, acceptance of homosexuality, divorce, and illegitimacy through the media, and that's what drama puts across, let alone the news, over time that will influence social mores, particularly of young people.

HUGH PRATT

'Hate the sin and love the sinner.'

His office, on a canalside in Bristol, is a mix of the Cross and the tensile steel bolt, witness to his professional role as an engineer and his evangelical calling in the fight against filth. Charming, equable, absolutely unswerving in his belief, he exudes unshakeable conviction. Our conversation is what would happen if one let the Jehovah's Witness stay on the doorstep. As I leave he presses a Gideon Bible on me: 'Don't forget: Jesus was a Jew, just like you, and he saw the light.'

Men Against Pornography is against all forms of porn, whether it be straight or gay, animal porn, child porn, etc. Our basic premise is it puts people in bondage and stops them from becoming complete people. Men Against Pornography is not boys against porn, it's not wimps against porn, it comprises men who are involved in activities, and groups of men and women who support the aims of the organisation. The organisation has a narrow focus in order to effect some changes. One aim is to help people who are addicted to porn, men and women, to counsel them should they wish to. The second thing is to create awareness in people about the truth about porn. We speak at schools, colleges, universities, often in debates against people who are for the illusory freedoms supplied by porn. This lets people make their own minds up. At the moment society is not provided with an alternative view, there's just a media view about the correctness of porn. It's important that children and adults make up their own minds. We also provide councillors and politicians with a more detailed brief, so they can frame the environment in which people live in order to reflect the wishes of the people, so they can make effective laws to protect children and the vulnerable – especially women who are raped as a result of pornography, and children who are sexually abused – there's a direct link between the two.

An addict is one who has a 'life control problem' as they call it now. They're unable to do certain things unless they're stimulated by that substance. With drink and drugs it's quite obvious. It's also obvious with porn. If a man or woman is able to dispense with either visual stimulation from photos or videos, or is able to reject them totally when they're involved in their own sexual activities, then they're not addicts. Many people can't get through without their daily fix, or are unable to perform sexually unless they superimpose pornographic images in their own minds. This reduces their sexual abilities and has many side-effects: depression, feelings of inadequacy. Many people are drawn into porn addiction with the illusion that it will increase and improve their sex life. They can be drawn in for many different reasons: inadequacy, curiosity, everyone else is doing it, so why not me? They're curious at first, but what happens is the same as with drugs, people become dependent.

Porn addiction results in a very disappointing sex life. You can't get out of the bondage, can't perform without it, are unable to break away from something which controls your life. As with an alcoholic, you can't help them until they realise they have an addiction problem. With an alcoholic in decline, you can only offer them another drink, they won't listen to sense. Same with a porn addict. But they're harder to counsel. Like a cancer ward, we're dealing with the people who are dying.

At the moment, most people think porn's okay, and there's a mega industry. In a few years' time people will realise the effect that porn is having on their lives, but still people, and those who are selling porn, will not accept the direct evidence between porn and child abuse, porn and rape. That's been clinically proven.

About nine years ago the Northern Publishing Corporation, which runs *Penthouse* and *Forum*, did a survey that found the sales of
210

Penthouse were dipping fast. They had sociologists, sexologists, psychologists in to tell them how to boost sales. They found people were becoming desensitised by the material available – seeing bums and tits was not providing sales. The psychologist said, 'What you need to do is go for taboo areas.' *Forum* then set out to go closer to the edge of acceptability. One of the main taboos is incest, so *Forum* started a section called 'Home Sex' (which is just another term for incest) and people wrote in – really ghostwriters – on how they'd had sex with their children. At the same time *Penthouse* started using pictures of younger girls, or older ones wearing gym slips, with pubic hair shaved to make them seem younger. And sales improved. So now they're promoting areas society has always considered wrong. They've achieved their sales aims, but it has resulted in lots of children being abused. The people reading these magazines think: If they can abuse their children, so can I. They show these pictures of children being abused to their own children: 'Look, let's do this too.' I have proof of this.

This is an affidavit written by Dr Elizabeth Holland, who served as chairman of the Memphis & Shelby County Child Abuse Community, chairman of paediatrics at St Joseph's Hospital for ten years. She says: 'I treated a young boy in my office who was four years old. His family was divorced, he lived with his mother. He visited his father on weekends. From the time when he was two, when the child returned home to his mother after visiting his father, he would cry and be irritable and none of us could figure out why. At age four we learned the father of this two-year-old-boy had been systematically raping this child in his home, many times every weekend for two years. The father bought pornographic magazines. He shared them with his two-year-old child and then forced the child into anal intercourse. This child's rectum looked like hamburger meat.'

Apart from the perpetrator of these acts, those around him are damaged. A drunken driver is considered by society to be at fault because the people he runs over have not been drinking. I would suggest that the abused child is an unwilling partner. As is the woman who is raped. Society is rather lenient on the abuser, say the drunk driver. Some people can see the worst porn and be unaffected by it, but it would be wrong, we believe, to make certain things available. You can buy undercover Nazi hate magazines, where people are systematically mutilated. Society has decided these are unacceptable. So we're quite happy to choose *some* visual and written material as being unacceptable. Even the mildest form of racism for example. But to have fifty per cent (the women) and eighty per cent (the children) existing as a risk zone just to cater to a small section of society – we've

211

got our priorities wrong. We are not here to coerce people, that's important. We're here to help people to free themselves from addiction, to be free of this pollution. It's a form of slavery. Being such big business it's able to effect political change for its own ends. So you'll always get vast lobbying on the pro-porn side.

We deal primarily with addicts. They ring up, often abusive to start with: 'Why are you doing this?' I run through many of the things we've discussed today, clarify a few things they probably knew inside themselves but wished to have affirmed. And at the end I say, 'If you're still depressed, still want an improved sex life, come and see us. Or when you realise you've got a problem. But go away until then. This is the problem, this is the solution, this is the cause. When you're sufficiently hurting come to us.' We're not so much a talking shop. When they do come they say: 'I can't stop looking at these magazines, I can't go into a newsagent without wanting to buy some. I can't pass posters without looking at them.' When we've finished with them, hopefully they can control their life and free themselves. Most then think they're free of it, but many aren't.

What is pornography? Pornography comes from 'Pornae', which was a Greek slave girl captured in war, kept in a cage for sexual gratification of the soldiers. It was violence, sex, unwillingness of the partner. That's pornography's root. The actual pictures sold in the porn shops, with pictures of men and women in various sexual positions – the women are paid for their services, and they're not married to the men they're pictured with. So we're seeing pictures of prostitutes. So when you buy porn material, you're buying pictures of male or female prostitutes. You have to ask yourself, is it normal for a man or woman to look at pictures of prostitutes engaged in sexual activities? Does a man want to look at a picture of another man screwing a child? So what is a man? People have the impression that if you're a man it's quite okay to do various things – drink, drive around – and it's also okay to have pictures on your wall or look at magazines. That's a manly thing to do?

Little children in a playground examine each other's genitals to see the differences, and I would suggest that no man would partake of porn or derive enjoyment from porn – that's what boys do. Psychologists now show that when men are under pressure, they revert to childish behaviour. That's what's happening. Looking at porn is a childish thing, something an underdeveloped person does. So it's boyish behaviour. That's why we call ourselves *Men* Against Porn. 'When I was a boy I did childish things, when I was a man I put away the things of childhood'. So we're saying, if you're a man you don't need to look at this stuff. If you're a boy, you've got a problem.

You need to sort out what a girl's genitals look like, or find out what to do when you get into bed. But *men* don't do that. A man behaves in a different way towards a woman.

A man has a different view of women, of his own self; he wishes people to be fulfilled, to have a proper sexual relationship, and not substitute a counterfeit one. People who've been counselled find their sex lives improved, or their marriages. They've broken away from the bondage that held them down, the illusory enhancement was just rubbish. That's what we want, people to be developed fully, not be held in childhood. Women are people. So are men. But there's more to us than just a collection of bones. We can think. Men and women are different and thank God for that. Let's fulfil what we started off with, not putting anything counterfeit in its place.

A good analogy: if you're really thirsty and I give you a picture of a beautiful glass of water, would it quench your thirst? No it wouldn't. It would make you even more thirsty. If you were needing a sexual relationship, and I gave you pictures of one, would that in itself fulfil your need? No, it will make it worse. So porn makes a situation worse. And that's what happens to a porn addict. It starts off as just an interest, then it escalates to desensitisation when nothing affects them, then they must live out what they see. That's where your rapists and killers arise. Everyone is positioned somewhere along that line.

Lots and lots of children are abused in this country, and that's not new. The Obscene Publications Act is wet as water, you can drive a coach and horses through it. That's why we give advice to those wishing to effect changes. 'The tendency to deprave and corrupt', the basis of the Obscene Publications Act, is almost impossible to prove. As is 'causing gross offence to a reasonable person'.

If you go to Amsterdam, you'll see how we're going to be harmonised in 1993. What they sell there, they'll be allowed to sell here. What will happen, unless people react fast, is that we will by default become like Amsterdam where everything is available. After a few years people will wring their hands, 'Oh, isn't it terrible, rape's gone up as in Holland, child incest has gone up as in Holland. Oh dear, we had the figures, why didn't someone do something about it?'

Statistics from the States prove that for every two per cent increase of availability of porn there's a one per cent increase in rape. So with tight porn laws there's less rape. Which proves that there's a direct correlation between availability of porn and rape. I'm an engineer by profession, and if you've got cause and effect you take note of it. If in Denmark and Sweden they have an increase in rape, in child abuse after the freeing of porn, one should take note. Many now non-offences are no longer recorded there. So they don't show in the

213

statistics. But of rape and child abuse there is an increase. I'm not anti-gay, or anti anyone. That's important. I'm not against porn addicts, I'm against pornography. Not against drug-users but the drugs.

The media's full of porn. Look at the *Radio Times* and see how often it mentions sex. It goes into so many households. And so much of it is not suitable for children. But it's readily available for them to read, and they're not ready for that, they don't have the critical facilities. There are articles about multiple relationships, different styles of sexuality or lifestyle without any critical judgment. There's no warning that this is just some TV producer's view of life. So a child wouldn't know if that's how the majority behave, or people want us to behave. No guidance at all. And then newspapers. They dwell on doom and gloom and you're constantly reinforced with murder, rape, child abuse, salacious details about private people. A child could think: If my family doesn't do this, there's something wrong with us, everyone seems to be doing it. The media normalises the abnormal. Every day in a paper you can see a topless girl. Given a few years they'll be copulating. People will then think it's normal. Are they married, is there a long-term loving relationship there, or are they paid to do it? The impressionable child will think it's quite normal. If you're not doing that, there's something wrong with you.

We're not here to change the world. But if during the life of our organisation one child is saved from parent abuse, one woman escapes rape, my lifetime's work is fulfilled. I'm one up.

I'm forty-two. I've been reasonably successful in a worldly sense. Before I was thirty I thought no man was better than me. He may have more, know more, but not better. I was successful academically, in business. I built my own yacht, sailed round the world for seven years with my wife and kids. First yacht into China since the Cultural Revolution, went up the Bering Sea. The driving force being curiosity. I was born at a good time, just after the last war. But while I was travelling I met many people, had time to think.

I was baptised as a baby, but it wasn't till I was travelling that I realised Jesus is alive and well. Religion was a force in my childhood but I wasn't aware of it. I'm an engineer. It's very simple for me, it either switches on or off – either there is a God or there isn't. Can't be a Sundays-only God. If God exists, he's pretty important and it would be worth finding out about him. Seek and you shall find. I decided to find out, and I did. That was when I was in my thirties.

There was no blinding vision. More like the road to Emmaus, with two people wandering along after Good Friday, saying: 'Oh terrible, Jesus was crucified.' A stranger joined them and they were bewailing the crucifixion. Then Jesus went through Isaiah, the suffering servant, and pointed out that Christ fulfilled all the Old Testament prophecies. Then they had a meal together, during which Jesus broke the bread. Then they recognised him and at that moment he disappeared. They rushed back to Jerusalem: 'He's alive!' That was more as it was for me. Talking to many people about Jesus. The light went on.

I started reorganising my life then. You don't just sit around saying: 'Oh what a nice intellectual concept. Jesus says go out, serve the poor, wash the feet of even Judas.' A biblical call to service. My wife was a Christian who'd never left the faith as I had. My children have made the faith their own. My daughter's going to be a missionary. As a child I didn't have strict guidance. But I knew right and wrong and was protected by that. And now by my prayer life. I can look back at my childhood now and see where I was protected. Christ is the perfect man. He wishes to set people free and people are captive to many things – drugs, alcohol, TV, porn.

If you pimp on a street corner it's an offence. But if you pimp pictures of prostitutes, it's not an offence. People like [George Harrison] Marks can say they're satisfying a need. But to a certain extent they create that need. And it's pandering to an illusory need. It's a market that exploits people's weaknesses and stops them becoming rounded people. If you wish to provide that 'need' and make money from it, you'll find a million ways to justify it. But the people we see are those that have been abused, have suffered.

Most of the time we're fighting with our arm tied behind our back. When I go to a school I can't say the things I know. It would be obscene for me to talk about them, legally. I can't talk about what pornographers are selling or doing – that would corrupt the children and it would be obscene. Some things I know about pornography I haven't even said here, because they will affect the other person. Our group has decided not to act as disseminators of such information. It's bad enough it's got as far as us. We're like a mop absorbing evil – we don't want it wrung out on other people. I don't mean that I'm better and stronger than the people I'm talking to, just that I don't wish them to be damaged by it until they've put their own foundations in. If there's been an accident for example, you say just that: there's been an accident. Not go into all the gory details.

There's a faction that believes women like to be raped, for example. We provide councillors with data that shows in fact women don't like to be raped. People say: 'In Denmark and Sweden rape totals have gone down.' Disinformation. In truth, the figures have gone up. The

215

politician can say, not having too many pages to read: 'It has been shown ... it has been shown ... it has been shown...'

The biggest mistake people make is in thinking the devil goes around with cloven hooves and little horns. In fact he goes round in a smart suit smelling of aftershave, and sometimes he wears a dog collar. People are seduced by the devil's image. They don't realise what's going on. One has to be careful. I'm an evangelical, and an evangelical is one who tells the good news.

***

ISOBEL KAPROWSKI: Most women and some men are exhibitionists when it comes to walking down the street – dressing well, etc. Magazines like *Penthouse*, people say, 'Oh it's exploitation of women,' but most women like being looked at, most women would like to be on a photo shoot all day, where all the attention's focused on them, they're made to feel attractive – absolutely the ultimate in femininity. And most people are like that in their everyday lives in a lesser way. Women dress or undress for effect. Women who wear short skirts don't want to be raped or sexually harassed, but at some level, conscious or unconscious, they want to be admired. To be admired in a way that's not threatening, which isn't trying to force a woman into a sexual situation she doesn't want to be in, is fine.

LINZI DREW

'I don't like being called a bimbo.'

For a body that's more usually displayed in near-gynaecological detail, she seems paradoxically overdressed in the ripped jeans and décolletage. Well-recommended by her peers in the business, the articulacy comes as no surprise; the soft West Country accent, for some reason, does.

I started modelling when I was twenty. That's quite late really. I worked in an office when I left school, weighing out cigarette vouchers for W.D. and H.O. Wills. Then I started working as a barmaid for Bristol City Football Club. That was when we were in the First Division, and they decided to have some cheerleaders: the Rockin' Robins. So, being behind the bar and looking reasonably attractive, they roped me in. We got a lot of national press through that; we were on the credits of *Match of the Day* for a few years. I'd never had that
216

many boyfriends, I wasn't one of those promiscuous schoolgirls at thirteen or fourteen or anything. I wasn't ugly, but I wasn't terribly confident. When I started behind the bar my Mum really had to persuade me to go, because I didn't like it, I felt embarrassed, I was reasonably shy and Mum just said, 'Go and do it.' So I did. But by the time I was eighteen and I started doing the promotion work and going out on the pitch, it changed. Bristol City vs Liverpool, and there's 30,000 people there and you go out on the pitch and they're cheering – it's a buzz.

Then the *Star* came down and the *Sun* came down and the *Mirror* and these photographers said, 'Why don't you try modelling?' So I thought: Why not? I did some pictures for a photographer at the *Bristol Evening Post* and I posted them off to London, to some picture agents. I already had a boyfriend in London, I'd come up to see him or see rock concerts, so I thought I'd move up. Which I did – working in a recording studio as a receptionist. Gradually I started to get some work.

When I started I said, 'I'm only going to do topless.' Models think that's acceptable: 'I'll show this part of my body, but not this part.' As if a man wanking over you for showing one bit or another is any different. Though at the time I didn't think that it would be that – people wanking over the pictures. No, I didn't. I just thought: Would I be comfortable doing more than topless? and I thought I wouldn't. Now I'm a real exhibitionist, but I wasn't then. I think you do need to be an exhibitionist to do well as a model. I've got on well because I'm game. None of that, 'I'm not doing this, I don't think I want to do that...' Photographers don't want to work with models if you turn up and you won't stay a bit longer, or you whinge about the cold or whatever. People want you to do a good job, and whatever I do, I do try to do a good job. When I started modelling I was thinking I could be a fashion model. But I couldn't. I didn't look like a fashion model, I never did do. There are different qualities for a glamour model and a fashion model. They've got cheek-bones, great hair ... but if you're a glamour model, if you've got a sexy body and you enjoy doing it, then it really shows in the pictures.

When I first arrived in London and joined this model agency, there was a French photographer who wanted girls for a trip abroad. At that stage I was strictly into topless modelling. I'd done some tests for the *Sun* and so on. I hadn't been in yet, but I did some test shots. So the topless work hadn't bothered me. I'd done a bit in Bristol already. So I got offered this trip to Senegal. This was nude, but it was on a beach and when you do nude shots on a beach they're not as rude as if the set is in a studio. It was a beautiful country and we stayed in this Club

217

Med hotel – and I'd only been in Benidorm at that stage of my life. But everyone else was French and they're not the most overfriendly race in the world. There's seven of them and there's you. But I enjoyed the work and it did pay well. Five hundred pounds or so, after I'd been in an office getting fifty for a week.

I don't think the models do screw the photographers very often. In all the time I've been modelling I think I've only had scenes with three photographers. On trips abroad it does happen – you're on a beach, it's nice, you all go out... But not a quick bash on the floor at *Fiesta*. After a while it's too much. All this sex, especially the letters people write in, it's making your head explode, it's just too much. I write about sex all the time and sometimes it does make me feel very horny, but other times you just can't be bothered with it – it's just work, and you have to force yourself into throbbing this and pulsating that.

Of course, there are photographers who try it on. Girls start their modelling career working for them, they do ten sets in a week, get paid with a bounced cheque and then the girl thinks, 'It's such a horrible business, I'm getting out of it.' So that one photographer has ten sets of a brand new model who's lovely, makes a lot of money, but that girl gets out of the business because he treated her so badly. But people are like that, real sharks, in lots of businesses; I don't think it's more so in this business. Of course there's photographers who promise you this and promise you that and take you on a trip abroad and all they want to do is get in your knickers, but that sort of thing isn't more so than any other business. But you have to have the right mentality, because it can be disappointing, but you have to carry on. People do get exploited: they get booked for topless shots and when they turn up it's, 'No, I did say some nude shots too, and some explicit open-leg shots too,' and the girls get coaxed and talked into it.Yes, that does happen. But the girls who aren't that bright, or at least not wised up, they don't stay in the business that long anyway.

The end product of all this modelling is guys wanking over the pictures. I know that, and I quite like it, I quite like the idea that people think of me as a sex object, it doesn't bother me at all. You meet people and they tell you I've been a fan of yours and you think, I hope I can live up to your expectations, I hope they don't go home and think: God, I've spent years wanking over this woman, what a pain in the arse she is, or, she's a bit rough, or whatever. People masturbate, that's part of their sexuality. I don't know why people call other people 'wankers' to put them down. It's something we all do. There's nothing wrong with it. But sex is like everything else – for weeks you can be really horny and then for weeks you can't be bothered with it. It is flattering to have all these men wanking. It certainly doesn't bother me.

The men who buy the magazines aren't being ripped off. Not really. They talk about exploiting men as much as women, but this is a product, do you want to buy it, this is the cover price, the choice is yours. They're not really being ripped off. If they buy a magazine and it turns out to be rubbish, then they can always stop buying it. In the end it's just a business designed to make money. Like fruit and veg, but people don't get criticised for selling fruit and veg. Maybe with the 0898 phone lines men are being ripped off, but not magazines. I did the phone lines for a while too, but I did try to give some kind of value. Lots of Page 3 girls did them, but all they'd say was 'Me and my boyfriend were decorating this weekend ... ' I bet they really wanted to hear about that.

People do get ripped off in Soho. We had an American guy, an ex porn star now a director called John Stagliano. He came over here last year and made some films. So we found him some girls, found some locations and so on. One night we were out at dinner in Soho and we went into this sex shop and there were a couple of his films on sale – *American Buttman, American Buttman in London* – all these hardcore US films with lots of anal sex. They also had some slave sex films, very, very heavy German bondage films. The sort you don't really want to watch. I said to the guy in the shop, 'Is this for real?' He said, 'Of course it is.' So I said, 'You shouldn't be selling this because this is John Stagliano and you're bootlegging his films.' But the bloke didn't believe me. I didn't buy one, they were about £80. But if it is a rip-off the police don't want to know. They won't do anything, and anyway the punters are too embarrassed to complain. If they're selling something that isn't hardcore they should be done by the Fraud Squad and if it is, then they're going to get tried by the Obscene Publications Act. I don't know. It's the same in every business, people do get ripped off.

But British porn is really a slightly raunchier Benny Hill Show. America is very different. The amateur video scene is very much up and coming over there. They look at these amateurs and they know the one reason they do it is because they just love sex, rather than for money. What the girl looks like isn't so important. People like this voyeur stuff. We printed one voyeur letter in *Penthouse* and we were just flooded with them. Watching the wife get fucked is such a popular fantasy. How many of them fulfil it, how many actually watch their wife getting fucked by two of their mates, I don't know, but the idea that they'd like to remains a constant fantasy.

There's people who started writing to me nine years ago when I

219

started working for *Club* and they're still writing to me. Lots of people in prison. I'm very big in prisons – probably one of the biggest names in prison – because that's what guys do in prison, read these magazines. People in the forces, separated people, lots of lonely people who haven't got a girlfriend. Or people who just enjoy the magazines as an added bit to their sex life. I've never had hate mail; occasionally I do get criticism – I didn't like that set you did in so and so – but no hate. Though I did have a religious organisation write to me with some film about Ted Bundy, the gay serial killer, claiming he was influenced by pornography, and I sent them back a book written by someone who knew him for fifteen years who said it wasn't the pornography, it was him. A 600-odd-page book and there's one mention of pornography. But Bundy's always the one that gets thrown at you – it's all down to pornography – so I reckoned I'd better find out something about it. Most of the letters are fantasies they had about me, or things they did with their wife or whatever. I had one disgusting one – 'Dear Linzi can you send me a used tampon ...' I've never had something really insulting. But that was the only one that made me cringe.

Sometimes you do meet the readers. At conventions, things like that. *Penthouse* do one. And people know you're going to be there and they turn up and introduce themselves and you know the name because they've written to you for ages. I met this one guy – I was doing the Jonathan Ross show and walking through the West End for lunch and suddenly this bloke came up behind me and tapped me on the shoulder. Made me jump a bit. He said, 'You're Linzi Drew aren't you?' I said, 'Yes.' He said, 'I'm...' –he was one of these blokes who write to me three times a week and I recognised his name. He was all excited and I had to go because I had this appointment and off I went. So when I went on the Ross show I told this story and the next day I got this letter: 'You mentioned me on the Jonathan Ross Show!' He was ecstatic. Okay, he was in awe, but I've been in awe when I've met people I admire. But people in that situation are in awe. They don't know you, they've never met you, all they've done is see you being very sexy in a magazine for years.

I don't do much modelling these days. It's a young girl's career really, though you can do things with lighting. I've just taken over Northern and Shell's magazine *Men's Letters* as editor. I did some sets for that. I have this column every month – 2,000 words with pictures. But the photographer took more time lighting me than he would an eighteen-year-old girl. I told the photographer, 'We'll have to be careful with the lighting – I'm thirty-three years old.' It's very different
220

from the days we used to work together when I was twenty. But he knows that and it's all right.

People always ask you if the letters in magazines are real and they are real but they do have to be tidied up a lot. When a man writes in he gets so excited – 'then I did this and then I did this and then I did that' – and you have to slow them down, tidy them up. When women write in – and one in every ten is from a woman – they're much better written. Women have a much slower build-up. When you edit a man's letter you have to slow it down a bit so it builds up to a climax. Women's letters can usually be left alone. But the men get so over-excited they have to be edited to make sense. 'I put my leg here and she ... ' So how many legs have you got?!

I was modelling for about six or seven years and I knew this editor who worked for *Fiesta* magazine and he started working at *Club International*. We had quite a good rapport. The thing about modelling is that quite a lot of the people in it don't take it very seriously: they've met some bloke so they don't turn up or if they do turn up they don't bring the right clothes or whatever. So if you're a little bit reliable and take the job seriously, and think of it as a career, you can go a bit further.

So when this chap took over *Club International* he wanted to relaunch the Fiona Richmond type of piece: the sexy scenes a model gets up to every month. So he called it 'Life with Linzi' and asked me to do it. They sent me round to see a writer called Brian O'Hanlon and he interviewed me and he wrote the first one, but it just didn't work. 'I live with my boyfriend, I've got two dogs...' I thought: They don't want to know this, what they want to hear about is going on a trip to Barbados and the photographer shagged me senseless over the rail of the boat. They want some smut. They might want to know how I did a kissagram and it was funny but in the end they always want a raunchy bit. I think Brian was a bit too embarrassed to write this kind of stuff about someone he knew: 'Linzi spread her legs and played with herself ... ' stuff like that. So I got it back and I sort of edited it, made it much raunchier. And the second one, I said to the editor, 'Can I write it myself?'.

The week before I'd done an interview for *Knave*, an anonymous model talking about her sex life. So I looked at it, worked out the formula, and sat down for about three hours before I got the first paragraph, but after that, off it went. I'd never done it before, though I quite liked English at school, though I'm not that good at punctuation ... Within six months, because it was a real person writing, not just 'Fiona likes windsurfing and men with big dicks ... ', but 'Linzi went out and did this kissagram and this happened and then she met some guy at a party who fucked her senseless in a lift ...' So there was as a sexy story and a few bits about what did happen when you worked as a model. Every month there'd be a few things to write about. I did kissagrams and striptease and strange jobs where you'd meet famous people and so on. Of the 2,000 words a quarter was this sexy story and the rest was what I'd been up to. It was all true, at least in the sense that if I didn't have anything particularly brilliant to write about, then I'd use something that happened to one of my girlfriends. Often you have to draw on things that happened a while ago. I was writing a piece about good cars to screw in and I got to the Ford Fiesta and I realised: God I haven't screwed in a Ford Fiesta for ages.

Making love to your wife and thinking of some other woman, that's what sex is about. If you're making love to your boyfriend and you've been together for ten years or whatever, if you actually think of someone else as you're building up to orgasm, or just about to come, I don't think there's anything wrong with that. As long as you don't insult the other person by discussing it at length. When someone doesn't know what we do to have a good time, if it doesn't hurt anybody else, I don't think that there's anything wrong with that. In magazines you do see women who look unbelievable, and perhaps that's not fair on real life wives, but they've had an hour and a half with a hairdresser and the lights are right and the set is expensive and you're in this great lingerie ... but it's a bit like advertising on television: you see someone in a Diablo and we'd all like one, but we haven't all got £160 grand to buy one. That doesn't mean that people who do have the cash should be stopped from buying one. There's a lot of fantasy things – sex, or living in a castle or having a very posh car – and we can't have them all. But that doesn't mean we can't have the fantasy and with sex, that fantasy just adds a bit of spice.

People don't get 'addicted to porn'. I've never known it. There are people, lonely people I suppose, who write to me and I write back, and they'll be writing three times a week, but I don't see that as being like a drug that's doing them any harm. I don't think if you masturbate fifteen times a week or you masturbate twice a week that it's going to make much difference. I did meet a guy from one of the campaigns against pornography and what he said was that if you read porn it stops you having relationships with women. He's blaming his own inadequacy on something else. He's blaming the fact that he can't get a girlfriend on the fact that there are sexually explicit magazines on the market. He's just looking for someone to blame. It's like saying that some film, *Terminator*, whatever, could send someone over the edge, but anything can send someone who's already slightly unbalanced over the edge. You can watch the news and go over the
222

edge. But we can't censor everything for the crazies. Something will always set them off – a traffic light, red to green, stop to go.

There has been a new puritanism since the Eighties. People who want to buy magazines, or want to watch sex films on the TV, they're not making a fuss, they just want to do it and get on with their life. But the people who are anti everything always seem more vociferous, always up there on their soap boxes. The problem is that very few people are prepared to stand up and argue with them. It's hard to stand up in this country and say what you believe when it comes to sex because sex is such a problem here. It's difficult. I find myself up against politicians, which is difficult. I left school at sixteen.

Is there a difference between erotica and porn? One person's erotica is another person's pornography. In the same way what some people see as disgusting and immoral and so on doesn't have the same effect on someone else. Down here in the country there's a newsagent who won't sell men's magazines, but will sell hunting magazines. So they'll sell some magazine with a fox being torn to pieces on the front cover, but they won't allow a picture of a woman spreading her legs and showing what is an attractive part of her body.

I did striptease to get my Equity card and actually I quite enjoyed it. The problem was men and alcohol. I love men dearly but when they get pissed they can be a right bunch of cunts. They really can be a pain. You do some stag night and when you start the person is completely sober and you do that first spot and it's fine, but when you come on for the second spot his mates have fed him some concoction and it's all different. They can be right lairy – you get your bum bitten, all sorts of things. But if it's a good stage, good lights, it can be fine. I always liked it when there were mirrors everywhere – you could see what you were doing. But sometimes it was awful: the lighting was more like Tesco's and all you wanted was to do your ten minutes and get off. I did it for about five years, I stopped about three years ago. You'd work a show with maybe a comedian, a ventriloquist, whatever. This was private parties, functions, Round Tables, cricket clubs, rugby clubs, stag nights. Sometimes you'd do somewhere smart, the Dorchester, some big hotel, and there'd be a thousand people and it was fine. But then you'd do these rough places and it's like the pits. We did Crystal Palace Football Club, we had to climb out the window, there was fights breaking out, terrible. Another time someone slashed my tyres and we were chased by these men ... You do put yourself in some difficult situations. So girls would come with their boyfriends. Or you'd get someone to drive you.

Kissagrams I did on and off for a year. I didn't like doing them. Turning up in East End pubs and taking half your clothes off was a bit dodgy. A bit dangerous. One friend of mine got punched on the nose, people get stabbed, whatever. Stripping's fine, people know what to expect, but with kissagrams you're imposing yourself on other people and they don't always like it. They're out for dinner and they don't want to have you come in and show your tits over in that corner. If they don't want it they shouldn't have to have it. So I tended only to do the ones which were in private rooms. At least everyone knew what was going to happen. A lot you didn't even take your clothes off, just turn up in stockings and suspenders or dressed up as a police lady or whatever. But I don't think I was much of a policewoman – for a start you'd always turn up with tons of makeup on – the police don't have all that red lipstick. Most of the time, say you had four in an evening, you'd be driving round London, I'd have my mac on, with my underwear on underneath, you've got to get your clothes afterwards, find your contact, get the money and then you do it, and they'd want you to stay for a drink but you have to rush to do the next one ...

I did quite a few movies. I did the Ken Russell segment of *Aria*. I did some stuff for a South Bank Show he did. He just felt I was a game girl. I did a sex film in Paris last year for this big German porn producer. It cost £200,000; we did it in this château in Paris. I was the second lead, doing a lesbian role. But actually it was a load of rubbish. It was so complicated. There was French people, Italian, German and it was all in English. We worked so hard, seven in the morning till two or three the following morning. Eleven days in a row. The actors had time off but the technicians never stopped. People were almost coming to blows. We were all just so tired.

I've never screwed anybody on screen. Though I did some shots like that for a magazine about ten years ago. It's still around in Amsterdam. I'd always said, I wouldn't do it but I did and I did enjoy it. I turned up with my friend Marie Harpur and we'd always said we wouldn't do it but one day we got booked to do this job and off we went. We got there and it was one boy, two girls, hardcore. So we said, 'All right.' I can't remember now why we did. There wasn't very much money. We were just in one of those moods and we just did it. It was quite fun in the end, quite a turn-on. I bumped into him a while later. My PR sent me off to see this guy and they told me who he was. 'Don't you remember him?' he said. I thought: Oh yeah, I remember him, but I shan't tell you why. I hadn't seen him for about eight years and the last time he was ejaculating on my face.

Later I did another one with a different guy; funnily enough he was the stills photographer on the film I did last year in Paris. That one was awful, I didn't enjoy it at all. He showed me a photo of the boy I
224

was going to do it with, very nice-looking boy, I okayed it and all that, but it wasn't a turn-on. Just do this, do that, this position, that position, you couldn't get into the sex. You spent half the day fucking in a normal position so you could almost do it hanging on the chandeliers so he could stay hard in that position. If something's terribly uncomfortable, his dick's going to go soft. It took seven hours in the end. He was great, he never came, but in the end I didn't enjoy it. Too much being ordered about. The thing is when you do sex shots, especially films, you are treated like a machine. 'Lick here, lick there.' The girl I did this lesbian film with was a very pretty girl and I thought it would be a turn-on, but it wasn't. Knew her too well, whatever. But I'd been offered quite a lot of money so I did it, even if afterwards I wished I hadn't.

The difference between doing sex films or sex sets and straight prostitution is that in this case both participants are getting paid. You're selling sex, which is the same, but the person you're having the sex with is also getting paid. Though if you can handle prostitution – it may seem sleazy but people do it, and I know very high-class callgirls who make a living, travel all round the world. They're saying, 'I need a winter coat and all he's given me is £3,000!' I think, all I spend is £300. But I make my living in a different way. If you can be happy as a callgirl, like I'm happy doing what I've done, then it's entirely up to the individual. But if it makes you feel bad, and you still go and do it again, then you are silly. The saddest thing is people who get hooked on drugs and are working as a prostitute to pay for it.

I don't like being called a bimbo. If you've got blonde hair and large breasts and people call you a bimbo it puts you into this category of being nothing else but a dumb blonde. And these days it's also someone on the make. They should have just put in the dictionary: 'Bimbo: Fiona Wright' and that would have summed it up. I don't kiss and tell. I had these tax problems so I did this piece for the *Sunday Sport*, well paid. But I didn't give him any names. I'm not stupid. I don't admire people who start telling all these names. There may be reasons – a friend of mine did a piece for the *News Of The World* about Robert Kilroy Silk, she'd just had a baby and she really needed the money – but I don't think it's an admirable thing to do.

I've appeared in all sorts of magazines, from *Penthouse* to *Fiesta* and I don't really fit into any category. I'm just someone who has made a career out of being a model. Most of these girls don't do that. They do a few sets, make a bit of money, meet a guy and quit. My appeal when I did a lot of modelling and writing in the magazines was that I was the first girl to be a real person who was talking back: 'Yes, I like to be fucked, this is my favourite sexual position,' talking back instead

225

of just being there with my legs spread and saying I like windsurfing. But some of these magazines, you'd get these US porn stars and the caption would read, 'This is Suzie from Surrey.' And I'd say, 'That's not Suzie, it's Sandra Scream, she's a really big porn star.' One of the punters is going to know that, so why don't we say her real name? But the caption writer probably didn't know her real name either. But I think the punters ought to get some realism and I think that realism was what appealed to them about me.

The Eighties

While the easy segregation of sociological developments into decades remains invidious, there's still an argument for seeing the start of the 1980s as a major turning point as regards the status of sex. The first and most obvious change came in the resurgence of right- wing, conservative attitudes. The decade had begun with the elections of Margaret Thatcher in Britain and Ronald Reagan in the United States, both pledged to reject the relative liberalism that preceded them. Both politicians brandished the flag of 'family values' and for all that each of their Cabinets would see a succession of scandals that pointed up the essential hypocrisy of such empty pieties, the theme would stay at the forefront of their speechifying for the next decade. And with it came the scapegoating of a number of advances, notably in the sexual arena, which were quickly bracketed together, and duly condemned under the blanket title of the 'permissive Sixties'.

The Sixties, it now turned out, were the root cause of every evil, and nowhere more so than in what was perceived as at best the moral laxity and at worst the downright perversion of a period that condoned abortion, accepted pre- and extra-marital sex, and, worst of all, gave the green light to that most threatening of sexual orientations – male homosexuality. As the decade proceeded, the moral right, with the verbal, if not always the statutory backing of the authorities, sought to overturn two decades of retreat. Ridiculed by the permissive Sixties, ignored by the sexual politicians of the Seventies, the traditionalists, born again beneath the aegis of their right-wing governments, gathered to stage a counter-attack.

Given the new moral tone, their efforts would have doubtless borne some fruit come what may, but in 1982 they received an unprecedented boost to their cause. A new sexually transmitted disease, known first, from its apparent target sector, as GRID

227

(Gay-Related Immune Deficiency) and then as AIDS (Acquired Immune Deficiency Syndrome) had emerged. It was seemingly incurable, it appeared almost invariably to prove fatal, and as far as the advanced nations of the West were concerned, it focused its depredations predominantly upon male homosexuals and intravenous drug users. Tempers have calmed a little since, but looking back a decade, it is impossible to ignore the relish with which the moralists greeted the onset of a disease that they interpreted as the greatest piece of divine justice since the deity smote the sinful Cities of the Plain. The lip-smacking prurience of the tabloid press, who promptly categorised an illness that, in Africa at least, was equally predatory upon heterosexual lives, as 'the gay plague', was rivalled only by the smug sermonising of the morally sound. Blessed indeed were the pure in heart.

For those for whom AIDS was a hellish threat, rather than a heavenly redemption, the illness required an immediate and infinitely more positive response. The concept of 'safe sex' developed – it was essentially non-penetrative, and participants attempted not to swap bodily fluids, be they semen, blood or spittle. Condoms, largely discarded twenty years earlier as the contraceptive pill took over, returned to favour, now chosen less for their prevention of pregnancy than of transmittable disease. Grudgingly at first, but in due course with commendably greater enthusiasm, governments acknowledged the need not merely to admonish the sufferers, 'I told you so', but to issue advice as well. Warnings – of variable efficacy – appeared in the media, AIDS counselling centres were funded, condom advertising, so long a pariah, was permitted on television.

For those, the heterosexual majority, who foolishly or otherwise did not see themselves as in the front line of vulnerability, the onset of the disease still made for some changes. Cynics pointed to the blindness of youthful lust and derided such declarations as short-term lip-service, but heterosexuals too opted for safer sex, notably in the wider use of condoms, which would now be carried by women as well as men. Whether such admirable intentions counted for much in the boozy passions of the pub or disco, or in the sun-drenched delights of package-tour couplings, was at best debatable, but the principle was certainly there. The dread acronym had come to stay and sex, once a source of unalloyed pleasure, had taken on a grimmer, more minatory edge.

Nonetheless the moralists were far from wholly victorious. They could point, with pious hand-wringing, to the inexorably mounting death toll, and trumpet the virtues of chastity outside marriage and fidelity within, but those of less fundamentalist beliefs preferred rather than to break beneath the threat of the disease, to bend with the new, chillier wind. The old sexual revolution of the Sixties might have been vanquished – its once-happy abandon leading seemingly to disaster – but new problems spawned a new revolution. The Sixties' revolution had set out to see off the moralists, proclaiming cheerfully that a negation of what would later be termed 'Victorian values' did not lead helter-skelter to the Pit. It had been, if anything, a revolution of quantity. In a world still emerging from the substantially greater repression of the Fifties, simply enjoying as much sex as possible was revolution enough. Twenty years on, with new challenges, far more concrete than the mouthings of the puritanical and the repressed, there developed a new revolution: one of quality.

If one could no longer enjoy the delights of random, casual sex, then the stated aim was to perfect what one had. This did not mean a rush to the altar, nor did heterosexual partners opt for nothing but the missionary position. Refinements took over. Variations on the theme. Sexual experimentation gained a new fascination: bondage, sado-masochism, rubber, leather and PVC, golden showers and 'scat', body piercings and tattoos. Once taboo practices came into the open; S/M in particular gained a wider following, moving outside the fetishistic few into the fashionable mainstream. Underpinning it all was the idea of non-penetration, of safe, if sometimes painful sex. The polymorphous perverse, much-lauded but less often attempted during the relatively 'straight' Sixties, had now moved centre-stage.

OSCAR MOORE

'God save me from being a pensioner.'

We sit in his cluttered flat close to the Angel, Islington, which he shares with two straight friends. For all his intimacy with the gay scene, he objects to abandoning himself to the ghetto, to be trapped within one's sexuality, defined by the people one sleeps with. As well as editing Screen International he's written 'A Matter of Love and Death', a novel that appeared originally under a pseudonym, but has his own name on the cover now. A cool appraisal of twenty

I'm thirty-one, born in 1960. It was 1974 when I became sexually active. I was fourteen.

I grew up in a fairly ordinary middle-class home in a polite suburb of London. My parents were not participants in the Sixties. Just a nice middle-class, liberal, decent background. I went to a fairly macho school, Haberdashers. The guy who was the first to claim he'd fucked a girl, I ended up in final term fucking in the lunchtimes. He was something of a straight icon at school. He got married immediately after school. I've heard he has a very miserable wife – she never sees him, he spends all his time in bars. But it wasn't until the Sixth form that you had the confidence and prestige to stop denying things. All that mattered was how clever you were. I was quite conspicuous. I think most had guessed about me from a very early stage, but they lacked the vocabulary or sexual experience to point the finger. A name like Oscar traps you in stereotypes anyway. I was born in Sweden of a Dutch mother – she didn't realise the connotations of Oscar. I had to fight my corner very hard. I had a smart mouth, got punched a lot, but for being a smart arse, not for sexual reasons.

I never had any doubt of my homosexuality. I was a mixture of complete awareness and total ignorance. I knew what I was after but didn't know how to get it. I didn't even know how to masturbate at thirteen. I didn't go to a boarding school, so I couldn't learn that way. My father certainly wouldn't tell me – he's embarrassed if you mention the word 'buttock'. I did everything to try and discover what to do with a hard-on, stretching the limits of imagination to work out what I was meant to do with this thing.

When boys started getting off with girls I played along. I went to parties, but I'd take along a lot of drugs and just opt out. That was a viable alternative. I couldn't stand up and say: 'I don't want to grope a girl in the corner.' But I could say: 'I don't want to sleep with a girl because I'm off my face with Julian's father's sleeping pills.' There were a few gay masters, none of them overt. When Mary Whitehouse came to address us, I found myself on my feet and shouting without any idea what I was saying or how I got there. The deputy head said I had to write an apologetic letter, which I refused to do. But various other masters, some I now know are gay, some straight, were very supportive. Intellectually they disagreed with her. But it was a liberal school, and if you fought your own corner articulately enough, you were all right, nothing mattered.

There's an element of ambiguity that you have as an adolescent.

People don't know enough about you to pigeonhole you. Your contemporaries are immature, confused, don't know what the labels mean. So I wasn't labelled, and I can't even remember much abuse. I might have been called a poof occasionally, but then so were a lot of others. Common currency of abuse. In the year below me there were some gays. I stayed on an extra term to sit for Oxbridge and I spent some time with that group. Even then I felt more a visitor than a participant. Being submerged in a gay herd is as bad as being submerged in any other team.

I used to go on long cycle rides. One day it started to rain, and I took shelter in a loo on the roadside and I walked into a full-scale one hundred and fifty per cent active cottage. And that's how I stumbled into homosexuality on a practical level. I joined in without much encouragement. It was like the door of the sweetshop opening. Thereafter I sought cottages everywhere, from Hertfordshire to Leicester Square; I became a very keen cyclist as a result.

Cottaging has a long and – with the advent of the superloo – probably dying tradition. The male toilet was the last bastion of male privilege. Cottaging is a hangover from the past. What wasn't was the emergence of gay discos like Heaven. That was the new world. From the small gay bars of the early Seventies, upstairs in Soho, with a combination of queens and rent boys – sleazy self-indulgent gin-soaked atmosphere – to the big powerhouse discos where people dressed up, unafraid – different set of icons. It had moved from the theatreland gay, effete and skinny, to a very aggressive thing.

My family have known I was gay since I was sixteen – my mother read my diary. Big family scandal. Obviously she was disappointed – every mum wants her son to be a real man and also to produce grandchildren, but she does have two daughters to do that. She was more worried about the danger I was putting myself into at sixteen. Also it was clear I was meeting people they would consider unsavoury – whom probably anyone would consider unsavoury. Interestingly they didn't take any action. My mother's a very strong person and she could have interrogated me about the names and addresses of my regular contacts, who would if prosecuted have gone down for substantial periods of time. But she didn't. I know someone who got eight years for being with a seventeen-year-old, and I was only fourteen or fifteen. Two years on they realised this wasn't just a phase I was going through, and there's never been a problem.

After Haberdashers I went to Cambridge, which was much less sexually sophisticated than I expected – full of people emerging from monastic seclusion and discovering girls and alcohol for the first time. I had the idea I'd arrive there and find my dream person – a

231

combination of intellect and physique. Instead I found a bunch of naive schoolboys from boarding school. So I'd come down to London for weekends, go to the Subway club in Leicester Square, take a lot of acid, go back on Sunday night feeling pretty bruised. But you had to do that. There was only a Monday night disco in the one gay bar in Cambridge. Real provincial scenario. Very butch dykes and some old-style queens. All very conservative, gay or not.

Punk had been very useful for me. I was sixteen in '76. It was a gift from heaven. I couldn't have wished for a more timely eruption of a new youth culture. The Seventies musically were very boring up to then, and socially I hadn't had any experience. So punk arrived and it was brilliant. Sexually it was irrelevant. Punk was fairly heterosexual. Even if it was skinny macho with beer and acne. And it wasn't comfortable sex either. Obviously not romantic, but also unappealing. Humping drunkenly in a corner, waking up in a pool of somebody else's vomit – not particularly appealing. But at that time the gay world had moved into the current American icons – the muscle man, the cowboy, the GI – as far from the skinny white-faced punk as you could get. If I went to punk clubs I'd go with a group from school and it'd be very much a straight experience. If I wanted to get laid, it had to be in a completely different environment – I'd have to go home and get changed first. You couldn't attract the right people in a punk outfit.

I never had trouble attracting people. I was a desirable object and could say yes or no depending on who I fancied. I was tall, young, good-looking. I was aware of being a rarity when I was young. People are endlessly searching for an available fourteen or fifteen year old, one who won't panic, is bright, sexually attuned, with an insatiable sexual appetite. I was God's gift to North London.

But this wasn't the fringes of paedophilia. That's something completely different. The age of consent is now twelve in Holland. But I don't think you can legislate for what is right, everyone grows up differently, matures at different rates. Child abuse is one of the most horrible red herrings in the British sexual pantheon. Specially the media handling of it. Some friends in France have a son of twelve and I took him to Brighton one sunny day, and all the time I was thinking: I wonder what his parents are thinking, do they think I'll molest him; are people on the street thinking: is that his brother, or is this a dirty old man? I told his parents about it afterwards and asked them what they thought. Being French, they thought this was an astonishing thing to say. They were delighted I'd taken their son out. But that shows the degree to which the tabloids can poison our minds. I had no sexual desire for this child. He was just a very nice kid I got

232

on well with. But that poison was there in my mind. The ghastly prudery and prurience of the British. How shy they are talking about sex, except when it's really sordid. I have a couple of friends who only find attractive prepubescent boys. That for them is a real cross to bear – anything they find attractive is illegal. It's not their fault. They didn't choose to be that way. They have no option, other than celibacy.

I'd passed puberty, so it wasn't paedophilia. Paedophilia has a ring of exploitation about it and I was the one doing the exploiting. I had a limited awareness of the dangers I was putting others into, but they had to follow me. It's strange that I was sexually so sophisticated, having started with no knowledge whatsoever, not knowing how to masturbate. Also I was incredibly horny the whole time. You learn quickly the ritual and the venues. I was very good at playing the games, giving the signals. I was good at sniffing out the right places in foreign cities too. But a lot of it was bullshit, me pretending to know what I was doing. There was only one occasion where I got into deep water. This man tried to rape me in a wood in Hadleigh. It didn't have a profound effect on me, partly because it was unsuccessful. I made such a noise he lost his erection and couldn't carry on. Then he drove me back home. But I wasn't really frightened. If I was ever frightened, it was a situation where I wasn't sure who was a policeman and who wasn't.

When finally I did get caught, I was arrested at Piccadilly Circus and I went to court the next day and got a £50 fine. The police kept apologising all the time. What I should have done was get in touch with a proper lawyer. Their whole case is based on the idea that you'll be panic-stricken the news will get out – people will find out you're gay. So the spiel was: 'If you plead guilty, we'll get you off, you'll get a suspended sentence, no fine, nobody need know.' I said, 'It doesn't matter, everybody already knows.' I was twenty-two, just left Cambridge. And I wasn't famous, had nothing to lose, wasn't going into the civil service or anything. But I played along with this line, and ended up with a short-tempered bigoted magistrate who slapped on the maximum fine. That made me very angry. At the time I was working for an escort agency to make money, so that was the way I paid the fine. More illegal than what I'd been caught for. So they got £50 worth of immoral earnings.

The escort agency thing was okay, but had a bad effect on me in terms of sexual habits. It's difficult having sex for money with people you're not attracted to. You have to get excited somehow. So you turn in on yourself and do your act; getting undressed becomes very erotic. But only if you think you look erotic. So you start fancying yourself, or treating yourself as something special. You present yourself to

233

them as a fabulous object. If you can't believe you're a turn-on, you'll never get it up. You're looking at somebody not in the least attractive, who'd never normally turn you on. I only did it for about nine months. Then I realised that every time I had a bill to pay I'd think: I'll just do another job. It could have gone on forever. Money like that is easy come, easy go, and you blow it very quickly. Two hours was £40. A whole night was about £100. It was an escort agency in the loosest sense. The euphemism was 'massage'. Sometimes you'd get there, and they'd have the oils lined up, lying on their belly and you'd think, Oh, you *do* want a massage, how weird. The problem was when it came to sleeping with someone you did fancy, you became very passive, you'd got used to not doing anything, just existing as a desirable object. So sexually you were completely boring, and people began to complain. The effect was insidious. It took a while before I realised it and snapped out of it.

My mother is Dutch and I spent a lot of time in Amsterdam where my grandparents lived, and Amsterdam was probably the European equivalent of New York. Much more open than London. When I was about sixteen or seventeen I met someone there, from Paris, and I was startled that he held my hand as we walked down the street. I wasn't comfortable with it because I'm not into public displays of affection – typically British – but I still got a thrill out of it, just from the sheer novelty of being able to do it. That was the first inkling I had that these things were possible. But they didn't feel possible in London. Later, in the West Village in New York you saw it too, but there it was more aggressive, less affectionate.

The first time I went to New York was just before I went up to Cambridge, in my year off. New York was mind-blowing. Going to New York for the first time is like losing your virginity anyway. Driving over the bridge and hitting the skyline, arriving in Manhattan. When you're nineteen and your immediate destiny is completely secure – you know you're going to university in a few months' time, you've worked for some money in your pocket, you're staying with friends – I just ran amok. I'd slip off into the bowels of the Village and sate myself, then go off with this girl friend to Studio 54 and the other clubs. To be nineteen at that time was great. There was something about New York that left one in a state of constant sexual anticipation. It's a bit different now, rather sad, but then it was the one place where anything you wanted you could get.

I'm a great starer, and I just walked round New York staring. I never felt part of it there though. The bars and clubs have such a high level of aggression – if you don't strike your pose you're done for. Standing at the bar, every muscle has to be tensed and ready. Very intimidating
234

and exhausting. Nobody speaks to anybody and you can spend hours watching beer going up and down, then you leave. They have this male icon thing, and build up the muscle to suit but have none of the actual resemblance. Things as obvious as voices, manners, characteristics. They're not lumberjacks, they're accountants. But New York being Attitude City it was gay attitude versus every other attitude. San Francisco, where I didn't go till years later, was different. The scene's been decimated now, but then it was more about having fun, and also wielding some political power. In New York there was less feeling of a concerted political lobby, or of people enjoying what they were doing. People turned their back on the effete type, the drag scene, the theatre and club scene, and invented another little prison for themselves, the strict bar scene, within which they had to live.

The crucial change, which made New York a kind of sexual inferno, was the passage from the old gay bars to the clubs and then to the bath houses. I remember those emerging. I went there first in '79 and went back every year for four years, and each year there were more and more places, more crowded, the drug-taking was harder, heavier; they stayed open longer, were full twelve hours a day. Then it suddenly stopped. I don't think bath houses were around in '74. An American I knew in '78 said, 'There's this new place in New York you should go to, Men's Country,' and I think it was one of the first. That trend peaked about '81-82, then disaster began seeping in.

There were two S/M clubs, the Mineshaft and the Anvil. The Mineshaft I went to once, but if you weren't into rendering yourself semi-comatose and being fist fucked in a hammock, forget it. It wasn't for the casual bystander. You really had to need it. This is hardcore, the piss-shit-and-fist brigade. You can tell them, they have a dazed look in their eyes – Bambi who's just been shot. Nobody would get that far without knowing what they were doing. The Anvil was quite fascinating. Late-night bar, got going at three or four a.m. and finished at eight or nine a.m. It was a wonderful combination of real lowlife in all its range – the real hard nut hustlers, the docklands types (or those pretending to be), then the very elaborate transsexuals/ transvestites who'd dance on the bar with glorious fans. And downstairs there was a rudimentary screening room with a dirty sheet hung on the wall, projecting Super 8 porn movies, moisture running down the walls. But it was a very peculiar place. You'd come out at eight a.m., stumbling out of a dark gloomy place into the bright light, seeing skinned cattle passing before your eyes.

The Sixties were crucial to all of this, from the then sexual liberation to the present sexual panic. I may be over-romantic about the Sixties – maybe I'm just looking at a media version of it – but I feel that being

235

born when I was I missed an era of self-discovery and emancipation. Maybe it's been over written up, but it seems a unique period with its sudden dissolving of taboos. Punk was full of taboos for example. Its position was established by so many antis. The Sixties were the moment when people had got their affluence sorted out, teenagers had been invented, sex and gay lib were coming in. So by the Seventies it was as if the old rules – none of which I'd experienced – had disappeared. There were enough people older than me to pave the way – so there were gay clubs, pubs, bath houses – and nobody could see a reason why it should stop. It therefore became more and more intense. And by then people had become sophisticated at using drugs as recreational drugs – mood-enhancers for the evening, sex-enhancers for coupling – and it was no longer mythologised the way it was in the Sixties. People had become more cynical but also more adept. By late Seventies/early Eighties you'd reached either a peak or a trough, depending on your perspective. Certainly an intensity that probably can't happen again because of AIDS.

I learnt about AIDS first through the newspapers, although it didn't take long before it hit people I knew. There were people who disappeared mysteriously, and with hindsight you realise it was because of AIDS. For a while they were only friends of friends. The last year I was in New York was '83, and I didn't go back again till '89, and by then it was very much on the agenda. Everyone I knew, knew someone who'd died. Then about two years later it came one step closer, when it was happening to friends of mine. Everyone was inventing their own theory, and suddenly everybody wasn't sure what to do, whether to believe the hysteria that you could get it from somebody else's toilet seat, or believe it didn't exist at all.

My feeling was, it was the worst thing that could ever have happened but it was no surprise. We were doing things to our bodies with a combination of drugs and sexual indulgence which pushed those bodies to an extreme which was likely to have an effect. Everyone knew how bad they felt when they woke up next day. Some people were drug dependent. No one was saying, 'That was visited upon him, it's not his fault.' One thing caused the other.

AIDS was the by-product of self-abuse. And expecting it to happen doesn't mean you want it to happen. Anybody who's educated, taken drugs, seen their friends die of it, doesn't have illusions about what you're playing with. You know you're playing with fire. Drugs lowered people's resistance, made them more unhealthy. That was added to the brew. Most of those I know who've died have been in the age group thirty-five to forty. So they had three or four years more of it than I did. And being that bit older, their resistance was probably
236

lower anyway. There must be a link between people's health and their susceptibility. Not to the virus, which you get or don't get depending on bad luck, but to whether it develops to stages two and three. If you were very healthy you'd probably survive at stage one much longer. The people we really need to feel sorry for are the thousands of Ethiopians who've been exploited, who need to do this to make money. Not New York gays who went at it hammer and tongs because they wanted to. They didn't need to earn a living that way, they weren't abused or exploited by others. They did it to themselves.

There's a persistent measure of self-disgust under the surface, you see it in things like the *Guardian* piece that Rupert Hazelden wrote. The *Guardian* got very nervous because they were suddenly picketed by gay action groups, very disconcerted. The piece raises the issue of can you talk openly and honestly about gays, death and AIDS without being shot at by the propagandists of the gay action groups, who in a sense have manipulated the disease politically. Okay, they needed to do that, but they're denying some of the basic causes and effects, in a desperate attempt not to be blamed for their own deaths. I can understand that, but there's a basic dishonesty there.

It's hard to behave reasonably when you're in the throes of sexual impulse. If you've spent your nights having sex with five or six people in a drugged stupor you have to have been more at risk. Who's fooling who? Also that you can say one thing and behave another way. The inevitability of it is no help to anybody in terms of curing it or even raising funds for it, but it's foolish to refuse to acknowledge the real cause just because it's politically dangerous to do so. That's only telling lies to protect oneself against hostility. It's fighting from a dishonest position. It's better to say, 'Yes, we know its cause and effect, but that has nothing to do with it.'

Safe sex means to me – if you're going to fuck or be fucked, use a condom. I was never a hardcore sexual person. It depends on what you like. But I'm HIV positive, so I was clearly at risk. Sex now is a lot safer. But penetration was not always the be-all and end-all for everyone. And coming in each other's mouths was not everyone's cup of tea. It was always possible to have inventive sex without putting yourself at major risk. It's to do with exchange of body fluids, not the number of people you're touching. How, not how many.

I don't really know what it's like for fifteen- to sixteen-year-old gays now. I don't know how they feel about the whole scene. It must be different. It must be sad to be coming out at sixteen now, with AIDS putting the lid on sexual freedom. What's sinister now, the young gays have a great suspicion of anyone my age and older – we're the dirty generation, the besmirched generation.

237

Initially AIDS was the worst thing you could dream of for the gay lib movement. Every reactionary bigot jumped on the bandwagon. Now it seems that because the tragedy has been disseminated through films, literature, plays, journalism, people's personal experiences, people are a lot more educated about AIDS and not so reactive against gays. Maybe after being reviled for unleashing this foul illness, we're now being pitied because we're the most conspicuous sufferers.

***

One of the key aspects of homosexual promiscuity is that sex involves much less effort. If you think of the physical and emotional sacrifices a girl has to make, apart from the moral taboos – it's much worse to be called a slut than a stud for example – and also, I've not had a female orgasm, but one feels it's harder to get, and when you get it, it's more worthwhile. Sexual appetite is a factor too. If sex for men is therefore slightly less fulfilling, you want more of it. Not so for women. Especially among teenagers. It was much harder for boys in my year at school to get beyond first base with a girl. Specially with girls your own age. But at that time I was dealing with people quite a lot older, ten or fifteen years older, and where there were no taboos. Although, of course, you were in a taboo area anyway.

I don't think straight men see themselves so much as desirable objects. Women always complain that men don't keep themselves in shape. In the gay world there's constant pressure. Certainly initially all gay men choose their partners by physical characteristics. Women don't, they look more at personality, at intellect. Because of that, there's less pressure on straight men to keep themselves in good shape. The gay world is vicious, cruel, narcissistic. There's nowhere to hide if you don't measure up physically. That's why gyms are full of gay men.

In the old days if you didn't want to come out you could hide behind the manly image – even if you were married it wasn't macho to spend time with your wife and family. So you could create an illusion just by having children. Like Oscar Wilde. But then you get gay liberation, and you end up with no focus but yourself. I've just come out of a six-year relationship. One of the problems is the inherent competitiveness of two men. There's a lack of complementary characteristics, a lot of conflicting ones. We were both aggressive, ambitious, intelligent, articulate people who wanted our own space, wanted people to notice us. We fought like cat and dog, really heavy. But neither of us were involved in the gay world.

238

***

When I was first diagnosed they said, what are you going to do? I said, 'I'm going to go away, get on a boat, travel the world for five years and die abroad.' Well what happens if after five years you're still alive? There's no point in thinking: I may be dead in ten years. Everyone can think that. So I have no position really, except I've joined my company pension plan, so obviously I think everything will be all right. That had never occurred to me before. I just felt: what's the point? Part of a self-reinforcing attitude rather than a strongly-held belief. If you say you're not going to get AIDS, you probably won't. If you believe you will, you might get it.

I'm suspicious of all the acronyms. PWA [People With AIDS], things like that. I understand the need for it. But it's entering into the political arena. 'Victim' is a loaded word in every way for me. I refuse to be a victim. I believe confidence wins. Optimism breeds opportunities. I don't dwell on being HIV positive. It doesn't mean anything in the short term, and I've no idea what it means in the long term. I'm more afraid of growing old in this country than I am of having AIDS. God save me from being a pensioner.

AIDS: The Light That Failed

JOHN MICHAEL: We did have diseases before AIDS. There was NSU, very widespread; there was a bit of gonorrhoea, but that was rare. Then herpes emerged, which fulfilled the AIDS role a bit. All the fuss about it looks rather pathetic now. I wrote a piece for *Honey* about what it was like having herpes – all about my knob looking like a stick of broccoli, because I was all swollen up with pustules and blisters. I remember being at a fireworks party, standing in the toilet peering at this thing. I thought: My God! The only thing I knew about was syphilis, but it didn't seem quite like that. I'm holding this thing looking at it with fireworks whizzing and banging outside. My God, what have I done?

JOHN LANKIEWICZ: New Puritanism was worldwide and I remember seeing TV programmes in the Eighties about herpes, dealing with it in the way they were going to treat HIV. Objectively, though, it was never more than a nuisance, any more than cold sores are. It was curious how they hyped it up, as they've done with HIV – hyped it up and then forgot about it. But HIV should be hyped, it is a mortal danger.

239

HAZEL SLAVIN: The quality of danger is different today. It's not moral danger any more, it's physical, medicalised danger. But always for others, never for us. This is one of the real problems for health education over HIV. It's never a problem for me or for you, it's always a problem for them. It's either gays or crazed druggies. For people who live a bizarre, bohemian, edge-of-society life. Not us, living here in nice streets, with ordinary jobs. I talk to fifteen- to twenty-year-olds and they say: We do know there's the odd person who's had lots and lots of sexual partners. Of course *we* only have one at a time, one for six months, one for two months. There's the notion of faithfulness, you're not sleeping around. Sleeping around is one-night stands as often as you can, and then there's the notion of serial monogamy, which in HIV terms is just as dangerous. More so, because if you have sex with somebody once you might not get the virus.

KAYE WELLINGS: We use deviants to reinforce the moral order. You always need deviancy to ensure a ninety-nine per cent regular society. Up to a point, AIDS was fine for this. This is where the need for moral panic comes in. Herpes was a moral panic. After that we were left with a hiatus. There was no getting pregnant, getting syphilis, gonorrhoea, because medicine had removed the deterrent to unorthodox sexual behaviour. At one time promiscuous sex was managed by disease, precocious sex by fear of pregnancy and the Pill; now the magic bullets have removed those deterrents.

AIDS came on the coat-tails of herpes. Suddenly in the early Eighties the press came out with: 'Love bug crosses the Atlantic.' This was herpes and the parallel with AIDS is very clear: 'Sex bug will wipe us out; Threat to infants' – I've got a wonderful file of clippings like this. The clinic figures did start to rise, but the papers were paying great attention to the promise of a cure. Suddenly it was called the sins of the fathers, it would affect offspring. In fact it affects very few women in childbirth. You've got to have a herpetic lesion there at the time when you're giving birth, and then they do a Caesarian. So it's not so serious. Irritating but not life-threatening. But it was being called a plague. Therefore people who had coped with it as an irritant till then, started going to the clinics. The newspaper coverage predates the rise in clinic figures. I think it was a moral panic, media-induced. With the advent of AIDS, I think there was a pent-up moral repression that needed expression. The AIDS scare was almost deliberately fanned. Every social institution was involved – the press, the Law, even the Church.

240

MICHAEL VERMEULEN: I wrote the first magazine story in America on AIDS, in 1981, for *New York* magazine. They rather stupidly called it 'The Gay Plague'. It got a lot of attention because nobody had written about it. The gay community was totally unaware of it at that time. It had received no news coverage. I found out about it because I was in Atlanta on another story at the time. And Atlanta has the Centre for International Disease Control. I was in the airport and somebody had left a newsletter on the seat next to me. I picked it up and there was this chart. In those days AIDS was called GRID – Gay Related Immune Deficiency. All in scientific language, just like a government flyer, with this amazing graph, which had caught my attention. The chart showed GRID cases in New York City. It looked like a cliff face. I read it again as I flew back to New York, then said to my editor: 'I got a story for you. Deadly disease, no solution, get it – you're dead. Sexual transmission, guys dying like flies, etc.' I also said, 'I don't believe this is only homosexual.' So what I did in my story, I found the first female victims, prostitutes in New York, and I suggested that since we know women can get it too, with it having nothing whatsoever to do with homosexual sex, perhaps we should change the name from GRID to AIDS – Acquired Immune Deficiency Syndrome. Who knows, maybe a scientist thought of that at the same time, but it got a lot of attention.

So it was a great story. I talked to a lot of doctors who were treating these cases. I talked to the doctors, to sufferers, who were dying, and I found heterosexual cases. At the same time I had a subversive aim: to give dignity to gays. Which is why 'Gay Plague' got on my nerves. The article focused on the horrible tragedy, the almost metaphorical thing, the notion that gays who in a sense feel damned should in fact be damned.

ARNOLD LINCOLN: I remember going down Christopher Street, and these young kids were trying to distribute Gay Plague leaflets. Prophets of doom. That was at the beginning of AIDS. Then one saw people dying and it became a gay problem. Gay sexuality was at its height in the Sixties and Seventies, very depersonalised. Sex for immediate satisfaction. No feelings of love. It's one way of doing things. Nothing is wrong, it's just that things are in fashion. America did things beautifully. They organised their AIDS services very quickly. And we took our cue from them.

AVEDON CARROLL: I saw a TV programme interviewing young people about how they deal with AIDS and they said the same things

241

we said when we were younger. One of the most common things I used to hear, and I certainly felt it myself, was that birth control felt planned, not spontaneous. If you were a woman you couldn't be 'out for sex'. If you're carrying birth control, you can see what that means. You were *planning* to have sex.

KAYE WELLINGS: My job at the Health Education Authority was to evaluate the campaigns, whether they worked. There was a lot of simple ideology, totally predictable reactions. We ran, with the British Market Research Bureau, a survey of gay bars and we used that to monitor the effectiveness of the gay public education work. What that study showed was that initially, when the AIDS epidemic first broke, gay men reduced the number of partners. Then as more information became available, they reverted to their original number of partners, but practising safer sex.

TONY WHITEHEAD: The first reports of AIDS started coming through in '81 – I was on the Gay Switchboard then and we knew what was happening. We organised a conference on it around '82-83. The health authority paid for that. There were only ten cases of AIDS in Britain then. A couple of doctors spoke. Terrence Higgins had just died. I went in as Switchboard's rep to give them some support, because I'd become pretty adept at knowing how organisations worked by this time – on a micro-level I was politically astute, I knew how to get things done. My involvement with the Trust developed very rapidly because I was doing things others didn't want to do, like forming and organising meetings, getting people along, taking minutes, writing them up. So I took over very quickly and I'm still doing it. I was director and ran it for the first four years. I'm still president of the Terrence Higgins Trust, though I left the Trust in '88 when my lover became sick.

So I was very aware of AIDS and very much at the spearhead of the gay community reaction to AIDS and was meeting with medical officers, government ministers from about '84 onwards. I had a perhaps unique view of what was happening over AIDS. There were rumours, fears. Education was available from the word go, when Switchboard knew about it. But it wasn't real to people, so that while everyone else was running around either not knowing or frightened and confused, I was as informed as anybody could be. I sat on the Department of Health committees, had regular meetings with the Government Chief Medical Officer, sat on various medical boards.

The bureacracy was infuriating. As time went on and the situation grew, less things seemed to get done. But I remember Sir Donald Atcheson (the Chief Medical Health Officer) with immense respect. He did listen and we worked together as equals in terms of respect, interest. There was a genuine concern on his part to do something about it. This country has him to thank above all others for any response at all to AIDS.

There was a period of great shock as people started to die, as news reports became both grimmer and much closer to home. The Trust dominated the media for a period. It still gets a lot of attention, but then you couldn't turn on the TV without seeing stuff about AIDS. It was a great shock. Bars closed, a lot of people went into a huddle, and then confidence was regained through safer sex. Though you still get that sort of self-blame. I'm thinking of a *Guardian* article, quite recently, which says the life of a gay is just death-by-AIDS, that because we don't have children, we live for self-indulgence. That's totally wrong. That's the sort of thing that was around at the beginning, when self-blame was paramount – gay people became very questioning about their sexual activity and the peak it was reaching. It was a case of: We brought this on ourselves. There was a strong element of that.

NICK PARTRIDGE: I'd been living in Amsterdam and in 1984 I came back to London. I knew a guy who was working in the STD Foundation in Amsterdam and one of the joys of being there had been that the central library held all the American gay magazines and *Gay News* on public display and you could go in and read them there. So I knew what AIDS was by that point; I had read through some of the early material, one early piece called 'How to have Sex in an Epidemic'. That appeared in late 1983, early 1984. This kind of knowledge certainly put me well ahead of most people in London. So when I came back to London the first thing I did was join Gay Switchboard as a volunteer. In 1983 Switchboard had run the first AIDS conference in the UK. It got very little response in the mainstream media. The first major piece, 'A Killer in the Village' – about Greenwich Village – was on *Horizon*. That was '83. It had a major effect, certainly on gay men. The [Terrence Higgins] Trust had been set up by that point, following the Switchboard conference. Terrence Higgins was one of the first people to die of AIDS in the UK and he had also been one of the first people who had recognised that something had to be done about it. In 1985 I became the THT office administrator. We had maybe 300 volunteers, based in tiny offices in Mount Pleasant. It was gradually getting better known, both in the medical world and in the general population. We started producing

243

information leaflets: *Safe Sex for Gay Men* and *AIDS: What you need to know*, which was for the general public. At that time the Trust was the only organisation putting out this sort of information. It was an extraordinary atmosphere to go into. Very overstretched, very over-crowded, and very well aware that this was a major job, especially in the face of Thatcherism.

TONY WHITEHEAD: My lover's death from AIDS didn't change anything at all. I did drop out of all activities for a while, not because I didn't believe in them but because I was just emotionally and physically exhausted, and was sick myself. I had HIV and knew it by then. But it didn't change my values at all, his death didn't make it any better or worse. I knew for a long time he was going to die, and other friends had died and are dying, and that's life. I also have a philosophy of life that underlies political ideas, and that's: we come from dust, we go to dust. The only self-doubt that crept in was whether I had the energy to continue living. I don't mean to kill myself, but to find any pleasure in life. There was always meaning and purpose and duty, responsibility and politics, but I lost sight of the pleasure in life for a while. That was the only change.

GUY SALMON: The first thing I ever read about AIDS was in the *Guardian* in 1981, before it was called AIDS. It was about the first three deaths from this mysterious illness. So I've always been rather aware of it. I was only sixteen. I thought it was very odd and I thought: 'How worrying, how strange.' Then in 1983 it really began to take off – the virus was identified and the disease was named and everything took off. I remember feeling a complete paranoia about it then. But now I think that gay people, we're not blasé about it but we're very relaxed about it. My active sex life has after all been lived out in the AIDS era. I've always had safe-ish sex and now I have very safe sex. I use condoms, and I don't let people come inside me and I don't come inside people. I didn't really go in for fucking very much until about three years ago. Being fucked, that is. Before that I was into oral sex and lots of extended foreplay. Which is what a lot of gay sex is. You come once and you fuck once, if that. That's what I don't like about one-night stands. Unless they're some god I will not be screwed on a one-night stand. I just have a problem about it. I feel that to allow someone to do that on a one-night stand is quite a lot. I have done it. There was one boy last year, I'd seen him four or five times, and I knew that I'd only have him once, this would be the one chance. So I wanted him to fuck me. He was surprised that I did. He asked. He

244

didn't assume that he could fuck me. And if anyone assumes that they're going to fuck me, they don't. However nice they are. Because I don't like that assumption. At all. I really don't. I find it easier to screw someone. I love rough trade: they might want to be screwed, they might want to screw you. That depends on how things work out.

DUNCAN FALLOWELL: AIDS has changed everything in this area. No doubt about it. I know very little about gay politics, but I know lots about gay clubs and gay bars and gay beaches and gay forests all over the world. And what is happening in these gay clubs and gay forests is that they are all packed to the rafters boogieing along very nicely. People are very circumspect about what they do. That doesn't mean it's all non-penetrative, but it should be unless there's a condom around. I certainly don't do what I used to, but I do other things instead. I won't go into the details – any gay sex manual lays out what you can and cannot do – but when I occasionally get sucked off by strangers, I do think: You bloody fool. But I enjoy it all the same. And in fact I know I'm not giving them anything because I've had AIDS tests and I keep myself clear. Also I have a regular relationship with this boy and if you've got a relationship you don't want to poison your lover.

AIDS is a double-edged sword. Certain things you cannot do, but certain things you can. For casual sex, it's facilitated it, because it has defined what people can and cannot do. In the old days when you picked someone up they'd come out with this awful phrase: 'What do you like doing then?' Well, we now all know what we can and cannot do. This question of who's going to fuck whom was often a big problem, if anal sex or something like that was on the cards. Now that has basically been removed, certainly on the first encounter. Most people, even if they have condoms, won't get into a full-blown fucking thing unless they really get to know somebody. But that's actually facilitated casual encounters, because now there's not the same sense of uncertainty. And of course if you stick to safe sex guidelines you can't pick up anything.

In a sense the fact that I wasn't fist-fucking in New York bars by the age of twenty-five meant that I didn't get AIDS. And that's only luck. It's a lottery. Those who get AIDS – they haven't *done* anything. They just drew the marked card, that's all. I think I actually had a relationship because of AIDS. I grew up in the sort of free love, promiscuous world in which any form of restriction rankled, except that of life and death, of survival. So when I actually found someone who fell in love with me, I returned to him more and more in a way in which the relationship started, if you like, folding back into itself.

245

Energies or attentions which, before AIDS, would have been constantly dispersed, were actually reinvested in the original partnership. That resulted in my first full-blown affair. This was already in my thirties. Not that I've abandoned short-term affairs. The person with whom I have this relationship, which has gone on for six years now, doesn't live in England, which may also be why it has survived. But it's survived because there is a genuine bonding of the soul at a very, very basic level – which is the same for anybody regardless of your label. When you really need somebody to form that connection it has a momentum which is independent of both parties. And it cannot be destroyed very easily. But that I continued to reinvest the self in this one other person, instead of just going off to another country for a few more raunchy experiences, I think AIDS played an enormous part in it and I'm thankful to AIDS for that.

AVEDON CARROLL: I do think safe sex rhetoric is creating a different approach to sexuality. There's a broader acknowledgement of different kinds of sex, and less centralised a focus on intercourse as the be-all and end-all. What's wrong with the sexual revolution as it affected most people was that people did only think about fucking, with maybe a little fellatio. Even in the Fifties people recognised that the most important erogenous zone is your brain, but it's much more understood now than even in the Sixties/early Seventies. It's the same way that you hear a lot less of people putting guys down for jerking off. You now never hear crude remarks about hand-jobs. It used to be an insult if all you could get was a hand-job. Now it's done on purpose, it's part of safe sex And that is now trickling into the heterosexual community.

MARCUS RIGGS: In the broadest terms there's no such thing as safe sex. Sex involves risk, emotionally if not physically. For me anyway. If you approach sex as: it's a good screw, all that matters is whether I'm enjoying it or not, maybe there's a limited risk. In terms of condoms, yes, I suppose it's safe. Providing you have no cuts. Mutual masturbation is safe sex. Nobody would argue with that. I don't think we live in a safe world though. When I'm driving there are two rules: one, I may drink and drive, and two, I always wear a seatbelt. I could still kill myself or somebody else, but I've reduced the risks to an acceptable level. Same approach for safer sex. Use a condom. It could break. Life is a risk, we just reduce it to acceptable levels.

246

ALEX KERSHAW: I have a very good friend, a guy, who I talk to about sex, and he's met someone recently, in the last couple of months, and he's not using a condom. I said, 'But the affair might end tomorrow.' He said, 'But when you have an intense relationship, when you're in love with someone, you don't think it is going to end.' And in that relationship can you really have sex two, three, four times a day or a week, always using a condom? It's an impossible concept. I don't think there is such a thing as safe sex, but the concept is accepted by a lot of people. This friend of mine will say, 'If I had a one-night stand, I'd always use a condom.' But for many, using condoms in a longer term relationship doesn't arise. I lived with a girl for two years and I used a condom for a long time. But you do other things. If people don't use a condom for missionary position sex, they won't use it for anal sex.

KITTY GADDING: I met this German woman of about sixty at a party. I brought this guy I was having an affair with, and it was basically a gay party. So she asked me, 'Is he gay?' I said, 'No.' So she said, 'Oh thank God, thank God! I'm just so fed up with gay men, and he's gorgeous.' So I said, 'Yes, I'm involved with him,' and she said, 'Yes I knew, I could tell,' and I said, 'Oh, but I have a boyfriend in England and what shall I do?' She said, 'Well, I don't see what the problem is, I've always had affairs' – she'd been married twice, has no children, can't stand children. Then she said, 'AIDS has just ruined my sex life. I can't stand to use condoms, I'm terrified of having it, and it's so boring because I have to sleep with my husband all the time.'

RICHARD WHITFIELD: We're only devoting resources at the moment to advocating safer sex, not safe sex. You could argue we're encouraging more promiscuity by saying everybody is doing it/ought to be doing it, and if you're not, why not – here are the condoms to do it this way rather than some other way. The fact is, condoms have a failure rate, resulting in about fifteen per cent of pregnancies. A woman can only get pregnant over a small number of days in a month, but could receive/transmit the HIV virus any day of the month. That virus is a quarter of the size of a sperm. Condoms provide significant protection, but looking at whole populations, it's not really all that safe. Condoms should be shown as second class options, the first class option being either a combination of fidelity in marriage, or abstinence outside it. Abstinence from penetration as a serious option must be presented to all young people.

247

JOHN LANKIEWICZ: AIDS has had much more of an impact on the practice of gay men than it's had on heterosexuals. Heterosexuals talk an awful lot about it, and in their talk they're not necessarily discounting the link between AIDS and themselves. They might agree, yes it would be a good thing to be careful, but they go on screwing away without being careful. Maybe the fact that venereal diseases have been treatable since perhaps the late Forties/early Fifties with the introduction of antibiotics was a factor. So diseases that had been dread diseases – much in the way AIDS now is – became trivial; it was known they could be treated. So that was maybe a factor. And also perhaps the fact that young people had more money than previously. My observations are not scientifically valid, but it seems to me that a lot of young people, heterosexuals, know about HIV, know what they 'ought to be doing' and then don't do it. Like everyone *knows* about smoking, or drinking, or seatbelts in cars. The relationship between knowing and taking these things into account in practice is a loose one.

IAN JACKSON: In '85 very little had been said about AIDS. In one of our very first Nightshift newsletters we made this very clear, that there was the possibility of an AIDS thing, and the only source of information then was the Terrence Higgins Trust. We ran pieces in several newsletters. In subsequent years my view was that people were suffering more from fear than from AIDS itself, and that the case was overstated. We'd had the God Squad moralising on too. And having spoken to quite a few medical people their argument was: if you were healthy and heterosexual there's very little chance of contracting AIDS. The government campaign suggests we are all equally at risk, rather an overstatement. The probem is that these days we tend to treat everything as having a risk factor of seven or four or three, whether it's smoking, drinking, eating, whatever. We're assaulted by these threats to our immortality. I felt the AIDS scare was just one more. I thought it would be awful if the young had to go through this whole routine all over again; it seemed to be setting us back thirty years, before the Pill, all the way back to the guilt-ridden Fifties. Instead of fear of pregnancy, it would be fear of disease. There's a danger now of equating sex with death.

ARTHUR BANNER: I have a lot of opinions about AIDS which will no doubt come to haunt me when I get it. There's a huge celebrity bandwagon surrounding AIDS now. AIDS is something that celebrities have decided to cotton on to and blow out of proportion.
248

It has modernity, celebrities, death and sex, just like a little American mini-series. Most importantly it allowed famous people to establish their credibility by coming out in support of AIDS and showing they have no prejudice about it. But the fact is that it's an extremely difficult illness to catch compared to most others. It's a very weak virus. There is absolutely no doubt that heterosexual intercourse is much less likely to give it to you than homosexual intercourse. It's transmission of bodily fluids, and for men not that much transmission of bodily fluids goes on during heterosexual intercourse. My own concern, because I am fairly uninhibited, is that AIDS may come to me not because I don't wear a condom, but because I'm very into cunnilingus and stuff like that. That I suppose is a worry. But not through straight heterosexual sex. The situation in Africa is where my argument does come unstuck, I presume that it's spread there because their sexual culture is completely different to ours.

RICHARD WHITFIELD: The bottom line in the light of AIDS (although there are other risks too) is if, as now looks very likely, we're seeing the low part of the exponential curve of heterosexual transmission, then we have to ensure somehow that significant numbers of young people are kept totally safe. Not just perhaps, but for sure. And that's because of the virus transmitting through to the next generation. Smoking and one's own health is one thing. The issue of permanently disabling, reducing the lifespan of one's progeny is a rather different matter. Young people will, I hope, believe and reflect: 'I don't have to take account just of my own health, but the health of the little baby I helped to conceive and whom I love.' We don't know yet how responsible the young are going to be. There's little to suggest yet that large numbers of the population have changed their sexual behaviour. Although much of the gay population, the section of society that isn't so concerned with procreation, has done.

KATE HEATH: I don't think heterosexuals are really taking that much notice of AIDS, certainly not to the extent to which they should be. I did a round table discussion on condoms and what I found was that there's this great difference between knowing what's right and sensible and actually being about to have sex with someone, when it's very difficult to be rational and say hang on a minute, because you don't. Lust overtakes you, and you stick AIDS at the back of your mind. I don't particularly like condoms and I think most women would say the same. There was this idea of making the condom part

249

of the whole sexual experience but it didn't work, people weren't convinced. But people's awareness has changed. *EastEnders* covers it, and other soaps do too. There's various debates on TV. And it's still a happening debate largely because of the gay movement. Though a lot of the gay guys I know, I don't believe they've let up their sexual activity. They're still regularly going out having lots of partners but they have tests and they all practise safe sex. They've definitely adapted, but they haven't restricted their activities.

MICHAEL VERMEULEN: My strategy regarding AIDS is simply not to get it. You're reasonably selective about who you sleep with. You take a gamble. Reasonably selective implies a risk. On the other hand I'm probably more of a risk for the women I sleep with than they are for me. So I'm not going to get real weird about it. Also I've been tested a bunch of times, with certificates to prove it. Writing the first article on AIDS didn't do a lot for me professionally. It didn't change my behaviour either, and that still hasn't changed. I'm a big believer in contraception. I was then and I've always found nothing wrong with condoms. Condoms and me go back a long way. The thing that makes condoms do-able for me is I use these lambskin jobs, made in America. They're not inner tubes like you sell over here. British condoms break, and that's worse than useless. So when I go to New York I always buy a bunch of lambskin jobs.

STUART MORRISON-WALSH: I don't worry about AIDS. No. Not at all. I just don't like getting worried about things like that. I'm eighteen and I don't think I'll live for ever but I can't worry all the time. If I let myself become so aware of it, all the time, the way some people who get fanatical about it are, then I'm never going to have a good time. I just accept that these days it's a part of what goes on. I realise it's serious, I realise it's there, it's been there ever since I've been having sex. But every time I've had sex it's been with someone I wanted to have sex with, and they've wanted to have sex with me, and I've never wanted just to go round having casual sex, so I don't feel AIDS is a problem. I did know one heterosexual guy who died of AIDS. A barman in Belfast. He was twenty-five, twenty-six. I don't know where he got it. I think it was just a cut or something, something ridiculous, he was fucking and he ripped his foreskin. Something like that. He wasn't aware that he had HIV. He never thought that he'd need to think about it; he was confident that he didn't have it and that was enough for him. But he found out otherwise. That was tragic. But it still doesn't make me worry. There's just not enough good times to
250

start worrying and spoil them. Anyway, I do think that after the sex life I've had, then if I had AIDS I would have already known about it. Which gives me all the more motivation to carry on the way I am. In the end it's as simple as this: I don't care, I literally don't care. If I am supposed to die of AIDS then I will. That's the way I think. Whichever way my fate lies, then that's it. AIDS or whatever. As far as women are concerned, all I want is to have a good time. Have some fun with different girls until one day I meet someone with whom I can keep on having fun every day.

ALEX KERSHAW: I went to university after the comprehensive – the only one to go to Oxford. I fucked around a bit, and then AIDS appeared. I remember distinctly when the first articles and TV ads came out. Almost like a chill wind. It was a very big factor, and truncated the Eighties in terms of people's attitudes. Friends were saying: 'God, I'm going to have to be monogamous for the rest of my life, it's the only way to avoid AIDS. Why haven't I screwed around more already?' People felt this was the end, that it was unfair that we were the generation that would never get our rocks off whenever we wanted.

AIDS has had a repressive effect, limiting people's ability to feel unashamed about their fantasies and to live those out. The climate my generation grew up with, which includes AIDS, has prevented fantasies and the kinks that others have had. They've been limited in experience, there hasn't been that lack of repression. It was a gradual thing. There are a lot who carry on as normal, for whom nothing's changed, but among the more sensitive, thinking, chattering classes in my generation it's had a definite effect. And a lot of them have a very unsatisfactory sex life because of it. They're not into serial monogamy, they're searching for fulfilled sex lives, but don't know what that is because of their lack of experience.

With some people a fatalism has developed. 'I've had sex with eight, ten, five, ten people, didn't use a condom. If I've got it already, so what.' That's a more widespread attitude now, perhaps in a different socio- economic group. It's still a part of heterosexual young people's attitudes towards AIDS. I could be HIV positive now. I haven't been tested and I don't want to be. I'm more unlikely than many others to be vulnerable. My assumption is that I haven't been with a risk case, but I don't want to know if I have. That attitude is widespread in my age group.

CLARE CAMPBELL: AIDS hasn't impinged on young people at all.

251

It's still: It won't happen to me. Which is why it's increasing so dramatically. I haven't met gays who practise safe sex. All the young gays I know say it hasn't made any difference, they're carrying on in the same way. They have more oral sex than before, but that's still a way of passing on AIDS. If it's digested, you're all right, it passes through you. But if you have a stomach ulcer or something in your mouth where it could enter the bloodstream, you could get it. Our children won't take it a step further on. And they won't listen to us saying they shouldn't have unprotected sex. I find it difficult with my two girls, who are thirteen. They don't want to talk to me about it. Any more than we did to our parents. They get biology lessons, and I noticed some stuff about AIDS, how it's transmitted. But I don't think they're taking it in. They'll reproduce it for an exam, but I don't think it affects their behaviour. I haven't come across any myths relating to AIDS. Except, like pregnancy, you don't get it the first time, if you've never had sex before. What they see on adverts has nothing to do with them, nothing to do with the guy they're meeting tonight.

KIM WEST: What really hits home is when someone like Freddie Mercury dies. But he was gay. There was a huge rumour that Madonna is HIV positive. If she comes out with that, we'd all start thinking: 'My God, how terrible.' And with Magic Johnson it's a real double standard: they keep saying he's slept with 10,000 girls – oh great – they don't say he's infected them. I'd like to know what the truth about AIDS really is, how many people are HIV positive, how many women – they say women are twelve times more likely to get it than men. Women have become more liberated than men, but AIDS is changing that. When AIDS started I was with this boyfriend, Kevin. Three years ago we split up, I went to Thailand and slept with two boys, but I made them both wear a condom. I was really worried. Kevin had had an affair, but he said he'd used condoms, though I knew she'd had a lot of men. The question didn't arise until we split up. I went straight from him to this other guy and we used a condom twice and didn't after that. I'm not on the pill, I've got a coil. We didn't like using condoms and decided to take the risk. And it is a huge risk. You only have to sleep with one person to get it. It could be the one person before him, and I don't know him, who he's been with. I definitely think AIDS will change my attitude. A lot of people now stay in relationships they would have drifted out of before. After Kevin's affair I felt: I can't bear the thought of meeting someone else and having to use condoms etc., and that affected my thoughts, definitely. I'm not saying I'm not interested in sex at the moment because of AIDS. I just feel if I want sex I'm going to have to use a condom, and that's fine. In theory, every single person I meet, I'll be using a condom. But if it turns into a relationship, I'll say let's have an AIDS test, then go for it, don't use a condom. But I know in my heart that's not going to happen. Every time I'll take the risk.

CAROLINE STANDISH: I don't think I've got AIDS. Various boy-friends of mine have been tested or are regular donors and they're all right. If I'd been passing it round, somebody would have got it by now. I haven't been for a test because it shows up on mortgage applications, and I'm trying to get a new one. You can go to a private clinic and use a false name, but generally they ask for your GP's name, and they send the result to him, so it's on your medical records. And at our age, if you get an endowment mortgage, they ask for a medical. And there is a line in mortgage applications: 'Have you ever had an HIV test?'

JEFFREY WEEKS: You can see positive sides to disasters – the AIDS crisis for example. What I want to assert is that things have not necessarily deteriorated disastrously since the Sixties or even the Seventies. Because what it ignores is the real gains that are continuing to go on underneath the noses of the morally righteous and the New Right and Thatcher and all that. That is a grassroots achievement. The gay community and popular attitudes generally have continued to liberalise, despite everything. Of course AIDS has been a terrible setback to all that. Yet paradoxically even within the AIDS crisis we've seen what Dennis Ordman has called 'a legitimisation through disaster'. Because it's involved lesbian and gay people being involved in policy making for instance. A certain acceptance on the part of the government that they have to consult with the gay community, a recognition that the only way to combat the spread of HIV is by talking openly about sexual practices. There's been a greater openness about talking about what people do in bed and behind closed doors than ever before, and it's been caused by the disaster itself. Another side of it is that academic research on sexuality is expanding as a result of AIDS. It used to be virtually impossible to get any funding for research on sexuality. It's still not easy, but as a result of AIDS it became possible. And because AIDS is not just a disaster for small groups of a population it will constantly come back to the forefront.

GRAHAM WEBSTER-GARDNER: I give credit to homosexual lobby groups over AIDS. Worldwide they have done a remarkable job in taking away from a disease which is primarily caused through sodomy

253

or drug abuse in the Western world a lot of the sting from themselves, through very, very astute lobbying. As a political scientist and as a rival I salute that. It's remarkable that the Terrence Higgins Trust gets £450,000 of government money and it puts out what many people would regard as homosexual propaganda. At the same time, the National Family Trust, an innocuous secular body headed by a professor, other distinguished worthies, wanted £90,000 to do a parenthood project for schools but didn't get a penny farthing. I don't like the homosexual lobby, I don't agree with it, but I admire their skills. On the other hand, given our limited resources, we've done rather well. For instance, we've spoilt them on the Isle of Man. They're keeping their sodomy laws.

RICHARD WHITFIELD: In terms of investment in forms of human relations education, we don't at the moment have a free market. We have a very biased market, in which people with a blinkered biological view of human interaction seem to have the clout. Family dimensions are markedly lacking. The ethics of gay and lesbian activists, and those who indirectly or covertly support them outside that collective – many entertainers, and some key figures in quangos – seem to dictate a lot of the investment. There is an establishment surrounding these matters which in practice is very little to do with party politics, but yet is drawn out of party political connections in some shape or form. Other people who are no less capable, who don't have quite the right connections or haven't written in an appropriate 'politically correct' style, or have been pigeonholed in some other box, don't get a look in.

The FPA, HEA, National Aids Trust, Terrence Higgins Trust, there's a wide range of organisations receiving AIDS-related government health money. There's a network there, whose workings I don't fully understand – I'm not an insider. But that sense of exclusion, felt by many other responsible practitioners, over something so fundamental as sexuality, education and the development of reliable intimacy, is improper when it comes to the disbursement of taxpayers' money. Mention monogamy or marriage and one becomes a moralistic outsider. Sadly, some of the clerical establishment, in trying to be compassionate about sexual proclivities have indirectly downgraded the cultural importance of marriage.

GRAHAM WEBSTER-GARDNER: People who get AIDS by sexual means I feel very sad for. They should be looked after with all the medical care that's available, realising they can't be cured. The best thing that could happen to them would be if some Christians got

254

hold of them and saved them. And I mean save their lives here. Through faith. I believe there are some instances of people being healed through faith. One of the things we wanted years ago was a growth in the hospice movement for AIDS victims. We still do. What we find sad is that homosexuals are running the hospices, some of them. There are Christian hospices where they can go. Victims would receive medical care, nursing care in both. But the homosexually run hospice can only be friendly, understanding. The Christian ones offer hope. Dying is a difficult thing without a faith. And being able to offer hope at that stage is very valuable. We can say we think how you got this was wrong but that can be forgiven. Personally I couldn't forgive, but I'm not a priest. A leading libertarian Conservative died recently, about my age, homosexual with AIDS. In the last two years of his life he became a Christian and was cared for in a Christian hospice. He asked forgiveness for his previous life, which he got, and I think he died at peace. It was a tragedy. But at least in his case, this man changed his whole pattern of belief in his last two years and repented his previous life. And people with AIDS have to recognise that what they did was wrong. If you don't recognise that, there's no hope.

RICHARD WHITFIELD: I'm a Utopian, but also a realist. Psychological pain and lack of real fulfilment trouble me. Things have to be transformed so much in terms of a whole range of our social policies to get us there, that I suppose I have to say it's not likely to happen. A new order might eventually have to be imposed, but the popular call for that could only come after some pretty devastating turmoils in society – the collapse of the school system, with more domestic and other violence related to people's unmet emotional needs with a lot of sexual blackmail. The more people become infected with AIDS the more it distorts relationships. So it's quite a fearful time, to be looking forward into the next century. Cures for AIDS are a long way off, we have this long dormant period in which the virus doesn't show itself. So while I've got a Utopian view about people being nurtured reliably in family and community contexts over the life course – and I need to have that to sustain my work as an educationist, or as a father and possibly later a grandfather – so fundamental is this sexual and reproductive agenda that we now have, involving a crisis of commitment and attachment. I fear for some kind of real and widespread social holocaust.

255

RELIGION: Those Without Sin

DUNCAN FALLOWELL: The Church has played an unnatural, perverse, perverted role in its relations with one what might call a healthy
sexual psyche. People tend not to go to church any more, and in the
UK we've generally escaped the tyranny of priests but the mindset has
not retreated, we've inherited the shellac coating and have to cope
with it. You go to a working-class suburb of Liverpool, say, where
there are a lot of Irish Catholics, and see the extraordinary, twisted
sexuality. Try picking up someone in Ireland, or Poland. Neither
country has the advantage of a pagan Mediterranean sanity on these
matters to leaven the weight of the Catholic teaching. I went to this
sauna in Ireland and all the men are going round with hunched
shoulders, cupping their genitalia in their hands. The most sickening
display of shame. I don't know whether Catholics are the worst in their
attitude to sex, but they certainly try to be. At least in Puritan cultures
there is the tradition of individualism. All extremely defined
organisations of either type – left or right – are anti-sex and pro-
family. You can't organise society around sex, you can around the
family. Someone comes along and says, 'We want to go to gay clubs
till four a.m.,' and they say, 'Oh you won't be fit and ready for the
factory. That can't go on.'

JEFFREY WEEKS: The real battle is between, on the one hand,
various sorts of absolutisms, which say this is right, this is wrong –
which could be fundamentalist religion or physical absolutism, like
some of the radical feminists, against what I call radical pluralism,
acceptance of diversity, acceptance of freedom of choice. My
fundamental argument is that over the last twenty years we've come
to accept a degree of factual diversity – we now accept there are a
range of different sexualities. What we find difficult to accept is the
normality of diversity. We still want to search all the time for new
absolutes.

GRAHAM WEBSTER-GARDNER

'Christianity is not all compassion'

*On the front door a childish illustration has been tacked beneath the
bell. 'Suffer the little children' reads its inscription. The same
children play in the sunny garden, far from London's snares, one of
many among the manicured cod-countryside of Home Counties'
suburbia. Like most fundamentalists, he is reasonable, charming*

256

and utterly convinced of his own impenetrable rectitude. But then for true believers, of whatever hue, the end is always justification enough.

I'm a marketing director of a printing company, one of three directors. But I do two jobs. The other is as Chairman of the Conservative Family Planning organisation. We launched it in March 1986. There were four founders, of which I was one. Another used to work for the Responsible Society. He was deeply concerned about the issues of family life. He thought they lacked two aspects in their organisation: (1) they weren't political enough, shying away from party politics, (2) they were too secular, not spiritual enough. He thought you needed both those elements to be truly effective. So he looked around for others of like mind: Conservative, Christian. There was a lady who worked for the Society for the Protection of Unborn Children, the pro-life organisation. She worked on their political side, but saw a need for a pro-life campaign that was tied to a particular party, the Conservatives. She was also a Christian. And a doctor in the West Country, very active in the Tory party, who'd become deeply unhappy about trends in family life. At one stage he was the official adviser to the local health authority on young people. He was against contraception and abortion for under-sixteens who were in care.

I'd not met any of these people before, but we were put in touch. I had no contact with any of the above organisations, hadn't been active in the Tory party since '71. I'm forty-four now. When I was a teenager and at university, I was very active in the Tory party. Everyone thought I'd become an MP, I read politics, President of the Union etc. In those days I didn't hold the views on these issues that I now hold. I'm really a child of the Sixties. I was in favour of the Abortion Act in '67, in favour of the Sexual Offences Act, of abolition of capital punishment. Typical Sixties' moral permissive issues. I lined up with them.

There's no question that there was a sexual revolution in the Sixties. My parents' generation certainly did not do the things we did in the Sixties. Some people did, of course, but knowing it was wrong, that society and family disapproved. It was not the norm to have sex before marriage, to sleep around on your first date. But when we popped up in the Sixties we took advantage of the revolution, me included. Now I reckon I was conned. I had no church input whatsoever. That was my parents' decision, which in turn was the church's failure to attract them. They did attract my mother at the end of her life, but not my father. I blame the Church for that vacuum. At the time I enjoyed myself, but I regret a lot of things now, and not only sexual things. I

257

would get blindingly drunk again and again. Go through the list in the bar, twenty-one cocktails, then go and get your stomach pumped out. Now I'm giving my children the opportunity to decide not to do that. When they reach eighteen or twenty, they'll do whatever they wish, but at least by exposing them to church and at home to Christian values, they'll have the background. But they'll go their own way of course. I just hope they'll have a better life than I did through the swinging Sixties.

Now I can look back on the Sixties and tell you why it went wrong, why I was taken in by it. It's my thesis that people were taken in. There were a number of influences: the Church, the media, the Law.

The Church gave up the fight in the nineteenth century. Liberal theology (I think it's appalling) took root – and that was the first weakness. It allowed the state to have a much bigger say in education. Shaftesbury said at the time we'd rue the day we allowed that to happen. The first fatal error. Secondly, the Church decided not to take on Darwinism and to allow humanism in. And that began undermining the basis of Christianity. Because free will is not a good thing. The only free will you have is to choose God or not. What's important is what you do when you've made that choice. And the influence of those who choose God on others. I hadn't done that in the Sixties. I was brought up an atheist, nothing Christian in the house at all. When I began going out with my wife we went to church and I was petrified. Didn't know what to do.

On the question of the media, it's had an enormous role to play. Reith appreciated the power of the media even in the early days. I don't like the news, I don't accept it. I've been involved with TV programmes, seen how things are edited, the sort of people who are involved. A researcher rings up from a leading BBC programme and she's never heard of a whole string of organisations which are pro-family, Christian and so on, and she's meant to be putting together a balanced panel, a balanced audience. One girl said to me, 'I don't know any Christians and there's nobody in the office knows any – can you help us?' They're starting from a different perspective. Even Religious Broadcasting at the BBC, not many of them are believers and the ones that are, are liberals. You wouldn't find them in my local evangelical or pentecostal church. My church is what you'd call a house church – that means independent, non-conformist, a New Covenant church. It's called the Epsom Christian Fellowship. We're evangelical now, previously we were Anglican.

So the media has had an enormous influence. I watch my own children, and they're strictly controlled over what they're allowed to watch or read. We have video because it gives us better control.

Fortunately there's lots of wildlife programmes and knights in armour stuff. We let them watch some trash, we don't filter it all out, but we notice even with the seven- and ten-year-olds it creates a change in their behavioural pattern even around the house. Amongst the boys it takes the form of fighting – emulating the violence. But the girls are now teenagers and we occasionally let them watch more adult programmes, and they raise a lot of questions in their minds. I see the way they devour literature, pulp literature – Mills & Boon – and that must condition their viewpoint. They go to a Christian school and their friends are drawn from there or the church and so the values of each will be similar. Other households where there are less controls, with working parents, etc., there you have them watching almost anything. So I think the media has been fundamental in changing people's attitudes to illegitimacy, homosexuality etc.

The third thing has been the Law. Nobody can control what colour or sex they are, but sexuality is a matter of choice. The equality of opportunity for blacks or women is a completely different issue from equality of opportunity for homosexuals. I do believe there are areas where they shouldn't be employed – teaching for example. Too many of them are paedophiles. One of my contemporaries at university told me he was going into teaching because he couldn't keep his hands off the boys.

I don't approve personally of two men living together as man and wife, but it's nothing to do with the State. But neither is it anything to do with the Church, and they shouldn't bless them. We want them all to go back underground. That wouldn't be persecution. They shouldn't be in the security services or the Armed Forces. There are plenty of other employment opportunities for them – the media being one. We should be more cautious in employing people like that.

The single-parent situation is very sad and there are so many of them now. We have some in our own congregation. Their children have greater problems socially and academically. I have no position on two adults breaking up, can't be bothered with it. But when there are kids involved it's very different. Research now shows that for the sake of the children, parents should stay together. Okay, it might not then be a perfect marriage, but who says you should have a perfect marriage? My parents divorced when not too many did. But their children individually decided their marriages would be for life. We went through the trauma of the divorce and it's not good.

The reason my youthful views changed was firstly because I met my wife and got married in '72. I changed my views rapidly on abortion, for example, when I became a father. The wonder of the first baby, all that sort of thing. I found I couldn't countenance abortion any more.

259

I changed my views on all the other things when I met God, which was ten years ago. Although I've never been a liberal on divorce because of my own experience. Becoming a Christian has certainly made me more conservative on all these moral issues.

I didn't become a Christian through any wonderful spiritual experience, it was intellectual. Once a week for a year I went to the vicar of the church where my wife worshipped, and I said to him, 'I've seen in my wife and members of her family a joy, a life I don't have. I know it comes from their faith. I'm not coming for confirmation, I just want to talk.' He suggested I read a few things, which I did. One of them was by Colin Urquhart, *In Christ Jesus*, and at about page seventy-eight, I knew I couldn't intellectually resist the arguments any more. Ten years on, although I still espouse the intellectual arguments, faith is much more than that. It's a personal, individual thing – I can't give it to my children for example. That is what's helped me to carve out my present beliefs. No one could stop a believing homosexual proselytising. This is a democracy. There's no such thing as neutrality, you take one position or the other. So if we don't work against, say, public homosexuality, then the reverse position dominates. Things like pornography, divorce, homosexuality would still exist even if legislated against, but it would be more restricted, affect less people and those who did it would know they were going against the disapproval of the majority.

I've set myself up as a moral arbiter because in '85 I was asked to do that by the Lord. And in those circumstances you do what you're told. Some words of prophecy came to me at a meeting in Dartmoor, a Christian conference. My two little sons were then four and two and both in hospital with asthma, which delayed our arrival at the conference. When we got there, we asked if the conference would pray for our boys to be healed. During that a pastor had a word of prophecy, a word from God – i.e. God spoke through him – and there was a lot of it that had nothing to do with asthma or healing, everything to do with righteousness, putting up a standard, standing before kings and princes, things like that. Afterwards I was talking to the pastor, and he said, 'What was that all about? I didn't understand it at all.' I explained my background to him, and also discussed it with my own pastor, and we reached a conclusion within a few days that it was a message for me, that I was meant to be doing something, and that's when I set about contacting people. I felt I was given liberty by God to campaign on these issues for righteousness. Most of what was prophesied has come to fruition. And both the boys have been healed of asthma. I never thought the presented before princes and kings bit would come about. But three years ago we were presented to the King of the Belgians and his brother in the palace in Brussels. That's because of the pro-life movement.

If I didn't have such a firm faith, I don't know that I could do this work. Those who do it without that faith must answer for themselves how they do it. I don't know. Without absolutes it's very difficult, because then everything is relative. There are groups who've been campaigning longer than we have who have not been very successful, and in part that's because their movement wasn't based on faith. Admittedly with the new government, without Mrs T., we haven't been so successful. We had the Sex Education Act in '86, which we were very pleased about. We've played a role throughout in keeping Sunday special, we work very closely with those people. We were instrumental in the 1988 Religious Education changes in schools. We and one other organisation, the Freedom Association, got the '88 Act that stopped local authorities proselytising on homosexuals. And we had some success in the Child Support Agency. It wasn't our original idea – we don't claim to have original ideas. We take up other people's ideas and push them. We're not a think-tank, we're a pressure group, lobbyists. It's not a case of let the best man win.

Christianity is not all compassion. This is a fundamental misunderstanding. Righteousness is the basis of Christianity, and love (which is what charity is) which is fundamental to my faith, requires truth. You can't love somebody unless you're truthful with them. We've had homosexuals come to our church and been saved, or divorced people, criminals. But in love we have to make sure they understand that we forgive their sin, provided they've given it up. Go away and sin no more. We're working in a democratic liberal framework, fighting extremely hard against tremendous odds, trying to preserve our own families and point others to a better way. We have as much right to change the law back to what we want as others had to change it the other way.

The big issue is between rights and responsibilities. I believe responsibility must win out. I have a responsibility to my children before I have any rights as a parent. That doesn't mean you don't have rights, but responsibility must always come first. I couldn't stop you, for example, bringing up your children another way, and wouldn't want to. I would try to filter the media that goes into your home, I admit. I'd like the church to take more fundamental stands – over women in the church for example. I'm very fundamentalist and think the only way to God is through Christ. Therefore I can't be happy with the Jewish religion. They are still in the old covenant and they should come into the new life, the new covenant. At least they have a faith. Muslims I'm less happy with, because I don't believe they have the same God. At least the Jewish God is the same as ours. Muslims have been seriously misled. But they still have more absolute values, than say atheists. There is a lack in people without a spiritual side and I'm very sad for them.

The Tory party wasn't right wing until Mrs T. came along. It was more centrist up till then. And it's less right wing now. Mrs T. knew something had to be done, and she surrounded herself with people like Brian Griffiths to implement it. But it never got onto the agenda. She made some very sterling speeches and began a few things – stopping proselytising of homosexuality by local authorities for example. In the end Mrs T. didn't do what she promised. Though if she'd another term, I've no doubt she would have done.

Although Mrs T. was a disappointment to moral pro-family campaigners, she was so much better than what we've got now. We moaned about her inadequacies regarding pro-life, embryo experimentation, taxation. But now we have a man who has not yet in a speech mentioned the word family, we have a woman, Sarah Hogg, heading the Policy Review Unit, who is a militant feminist, not interested in the family, who doesn't want to see groups like us. We used to regularly meet with Griffith and others in No.10. Central Office used to welcome us – they officially invited us to write the family section in the manifesto. Now, we're not persona non grata, but the channels have been squeezed. Quite simply the family is no longer on the political agenda. That stopped when Mrs T. left.

I'm against feminism not because I don't approve of women having responsible jobs but because of positive discrimination, the quota system. It has some unnatural features, lesbianism for example, and there's an anti-male aspect which is a little unpleasant. The attitude of, 'I'll use a man to have a baby, but I don't want the marriage'. That's not feminine. And it also undermines a role some women want at some time, motherhood. I don't believe you *have* to get married, and if married that you *have* to have children. I'm not a Catholic so I'm not opposed to contraception. But the role of the mother in marriage is a responsibility where she must give priority to the children while they need her. That doesn't mean we're against women having careers. Not true. But I do believe in career breaks while bringing up children. Ten to fifteen years even. I find it distressing to see women trying to combine an executive career and bringing up kids. They won't do either job properly. It could just about work if they're rich enough to afford a full-time nanny. Crèches are an abomination. The thought of carting a two-year-old up on the train every day, and dumping it in a crèche, that's Victorian. That's child abuse in my view.

When we set ourselves up we did look at the Moral Majority in

America, and decided we didn't want to be like that. But we did want to do what has been done successfully in the States – you cannot be a presidential candidate for the Republican party unless you're pro-life. You wouldn't be nominated. We had in the back of our minds that we could get ourselves in such a position as to control the Tory party so that they would not put up a leader who was not pro-family. Well, we haven't succeeded. Yet. But it took the Republicans twenty years to get to that stage. We're only five or six years down the road.

The Moral Majority doesn't represent the whole silent majority in America, but it does represent a very large group. Say forty per cent. Here of course it's very much less. We've discussed the problem with many leaders: how do we turn our constituency into political power? We probably represent two to three million at present. Because of the differences in electoral systems between here and the States, we believe that with the right sort of campaign it's possible to influence the outcome of the election. We weren't all that organised in '87, but in Hindburn in Lancashire and in Basildon – not natural Tory territory – there were two Tory candidates who'd in '83 won on the Thatcher bulldozer, with very small majorities. Both increased their majorities to over 2,000. They took extreme pro-life positions and they won because of the pro-life vote, coming from Catholic and evangelical voters. So it can be done.

People talk about cycles in society – a conservative period followed by a liberal period, and so on – but now I definitely believe we are in what theologians describe as the end time, the millennium. I'd accept that the pattern of the last 2,000 years has been cyclical, but I think it's different now. There's a school of Christian evangelical thought which says the recent events in Russia and Eastern Europe are to do with the beginning of what we call the end time. This time we're not going to see the reaction, there is not going to be a change. So what is required for Biblical end time is a lot of what we're now getting, the immorality. I don't see us changing back. We're in for a pretty rough ride the way things are going, a complete moral breakdown.

***

RICHARD WHITFIELD: I have my own religious view. I'm a rather uncomfortable Anglican – in the sense that I was brought up as an Anglican and see no reason to change. I'm uncomfortable because I feel the Church is fiddling while Rome burns. On the subject of sexuality the Church of England appears pretty wet. But I feel that a

263

greater sense of preciousness in sexual encounters can stand separate from religious belief. That is, the sociological-psychological-medical evidence gives other reasons, which are good enough in their own right yet reinforce religious tradition. I'd want to say, 'The scientific evidence on human nature is this, and the studies of sexual behaviour seem to be showing that, therefore this seems to be the right kind of advice to give people, and to practise oneself.' I'm not saying the Sixties were an unwise period just because I'm a Christian; I'm an academic, a social scientist and an educator, and that is my view.

I believe very strongly that the challenge is to articulate a really caring morality. An unsophisticated form of morality is to say you just obey the rules of the Good Book, or what the Church might say. But the only form of morality that's likely to hold in the heat of emotion is the kind where there's been reasoning going on in the individual's head, and therefore a basis of discourse between the man and the woman, instead of them just being carried away by emotion and sexual desire.

Personal morality cannot be enforced, either by Church or State. People wear seat belts in cars because it's the law, not because each time they get in there, they think: 'Consideration for myself, for others, etc.' One's talking about shifting norms, and the imposition of a morality by Church or State is not on any more. But it's a proper part of a democratic evolution for us to shift norms and attitudes of outlook and if that's to happen it will be the result of investing resources in the promulgation of certain ideas over others.

JEFFREY WEEKS: What we're seeing is border disputes: clashes occur over censorship; the anxiety about the break-up of families, divorce and all that; illegitimacy. All these represent anxieties about changes in sexual mores which have been going on on the ground. In a major way they're irreversible, I believe. Thatcher's anxiety about the family in the Eighties, which she did absolutely nothing about, was an indication of the family as we've known it being changed beyond recognition. There's no longer a single family form. That shift in the pattern of the domestic life is related to a shift in sexual moralities. The language hasn't changed dramatically. The increase in visiblity of any community, black and Muslim as well as gay, causes backlashes. You don't have a backlash when there's no threat. And the openness of gay people since the early Seventies has caused a backlash. The *Sun,* with its racism, homophobia and sexism, plays on anxieties aroused by the shift in the social geography of the nation. But that's not confined to sexuality, it goes right across.

264

JOHN LANKIEWICZ: Every time something vaguely to do with sex occurs, everybody gets rather twitchy about it. Although that doesn't necessarily reflect in a deep way what people feel, it does create an influence. So all this stuff now about poofters in the Church of England, it moves two ways. On the one hand one could see that gay people will find more of a place in the Church – or could – but on the other hand there's a lot of publicity that scandalises gays around those debates. It may be too early to say where that will settle down, whether in the future this will be seen as part of a sexual revolution or a sexual repression. You can't really make predictions. Back in the early part of this century when doctors were publishing books warning about the grave dangers to health and to morality of masturbation and surgical catalogues were being published that promoted devices designed to prevent 'the evil of masturbation', it would have been hard to predict what sort of reaction this would cause. Whether masturbation would be entirely liberated or whether society would agree with these doctors and attempt to prohibit it completely. Now we know it enhanced the prohibitive attitude to masturbation. But you couldn't tell at the time.

MARCUS RIGGS

'The glorious liberty of the children of God'

A small terraced house in the Kemp Town area of Brighton, maybe one hundred yards up from the seafront, chilly and devoid of tourists this winter's morning, although the arcades and the candy-floss merchants still gaze hopefully at the passer-by. The door opens directly onto a crowded room, men, women, young, old, all touched by AIDS. I ask for Father Riggs, a thin boy, a nascent crusty, shouts for 'Marcus', and turns: 'We're all first names here, mate.' Upstairs the Father's room is an oasis of quiet. On one wall a large crucifix is flanked by two Herb Ritts hunks, bare-chested like the Saviour, posing in a rough-trade fantasy.

I'm thirty-seven. Too young for the Sixties. Apart from the fact it was all disgusting and filthy, according to my parents. I was born in 1955. I remember the Sixties through television, the flower-power hippie days. My parents thought it deeply disgusting and kept talking about it. That makes it very fascinating. The sexual revolution didn't impinge on me directly until I left home. I lived in a little village in Wiltshire where such things didn't happen. If somebody got divorced it was shocking.

I had no sex education at home; sex wasn't talked about then or now. At school we did things about monkeys. They seemed to have a good time, but there was no connection made between what they did and what human beings do.

I was about nine when I realised I was gay. That's about an average age, but it was centuries later before I did something about it. I had such real guilt about being gay, and what I thought God thought of it. I can see a lot of connections between my perception of my father and God. They were both fairly angry people who didn't approve of me.

My father died in 1975, before I met my first lover. I did tell my mother and stepfather. Oh gosh, they're still dealing with it three years later. I've just been there for a family New Year – absolute disaster. Mother's all right, she's come to terms with the idea that Frank's here to stay for a while. I don't like family gatherings because they're so dishonest in our family. But she coerced me into this one. She said, 'If Frank's in England, bring him too.' I felt at least she's prepared to be honest at that level. Frank wasn't here as it happens, but I went anyway. I would have taken him if he'd been here. I wouldn't have gone without him if he'd been in England. And would not have played pretend games with the family about who he was either.

I have two brothers – one of whom is married with two kids. We don't get on. Very right wing. I swore at him quite extensively this time, told him to fuck off out of my life. He'd wound me up all evening and I hadn't responded. My youngest brother is gay. He's not told Mother. She knows though. I'm the oldest of the three. So I have done some of the groundwork for him. Mum invited his boyfriend for New Year as well – but he's never articulated it as such. He was in England from Italy for the holidays, but didn't want to come down. Don't blame him.

Frank is very much: 'The world is going to accept that we're a couple.' We're not going to go out waving banners or having a gay wedding, but each is going to be involved in the other's life. I've met lots of his friends. Not his family, he doesn't communicate with them. Apart from his brother who's really into everything the Pope says. He had a real go at Frank recently. So Frank told him then that his boyfriend was a priest, which caused a bit of a stir.

The changes in sexuality hit me when I came to college in Brighton. Everyone seemed to be having quite a good time – anything goes, mid-Seventies. I kept detached from all that. But what I encountered of the sexual revolution was very heterosexually oriented, which I didn't identify with. And because of a strong religious upbringing I had a lot of hang-ups about being gay. It took a long time to work through those. Church of England. High Church background, going

266

to confession, etc. I had wonderful sin lists that told you what you might have done that you should confess. Catholics have the same. Instead of saying what you'd really done, you could just use these general categories of what you'd got up to. But sex with someone to whom you were not married was definitely on the list, and so was masturbation. There was a lot of guilt about masturbation.

I wasn't really aware of gay lib in my teens. Until I came to college. But then I had so many negative feelings about myself and my sexuality that I wouldn't have wanted to explore that anyway. It was when I went to London I was confronted by a person I found attractive. I felt guilty about that, but he found me attractive as well. In Brighton I was well aware there were lots of gays about, but I gave them a very wide berth. It was very lonely, although I had two or three very good friends at college with whom I'm still friends. One lives in Brighton and she and I still meet up at least once a week. One I shared a flat with, I don't see so often now – he got married about four years ago and moved to Hong Kong. But we still write to each other, and they visit me when they're here.

The first time I allowed myself to express anything sexual was after my three years' college in Brighton. I didn't sort things out in Brighton, which is absurd considering the large gay population there. I had to go to London. I guess it was the only place I could ever meet someone, the only place where I could fall in love; and the only place where I felt I could confront all the stupid things about religion and sexuality was in church. I met the first man in my life in church, on a Thursday evening at a six-thirty mass. We said hello, got talking, went for a drink and got to know each other over a period of months. He was my first boyfriend. It was 1980; I was twenty-four.

That first relationship was monogamous. The following year I went to train for the priesthood and things were very different. In the year before I went to college I began to start thinking things out, and thought maybe the Church is wrong. Then I went to theological college and discovered there were a lot of gays there. But everything was in compartments and the fairly traditional line was presented on Christianity and sexuality. People seemed not to tie it in with all these gays there, having relationships and casual sex. I never sorted it out in my mind.

I was ordained in 1982 and went to my first parish. I decided all I could do was be celibate – that was the only thing that gave me personal integrity. That continued until I came back to Brighton in 1986 and started meeting people with HIV. Then life started to change. A host of things happened. I thought: Christianity must make some sense out of these people's experience of sex or sexuality. It must make some sort of sense out of their experience of living with HIV. The other thing that really hit me – I'd been living my life like: well, it will all be better next time, not thinking maybe I should be living life for now and being who I am now. And when people started dying, I started thinking: It could be me fairly soon, and all of my life I'll have ducked the issue of sexuality. Partly because of my religious background, and partly because of the negative view of myself – which is quite common among gays, a very negative self-image. Which I suspect accounts for the higher incidence of alcohol and drug dependency.

I don't think the gay community reinforced positive images at all. It might have been the party line, but that's not my experience of the gay community. They're reinforced by negative self-images. The sort of images I see in the gay community at the moment – which is surprising, given we've had HIV in Brighton for nearly ten years – is a lot of people who seem to think that what life's about is the thrill of the moment, rather than finding any sort of fulfilment in commitment, in working at things. My attitude is dictated very little by religion; it comes from my experience of living. The things that are really fulfilling are the things you commit yourself to and work at. I'd apply that to other areas too. For instance Open Door here, which with my previous bishop I've worked very hard to set up and has now been running for five years, and which I and a lot of others get a lot of fulfilment from. But only because we've committed ourselves to it, worked at it, rather than just saying: Oh, this is an exciting thing for the moment, then we'll move on to something else.

From my experience of living, the things you actually see as opportunities which, even if they're going to present difficulties are worth tackling and working through, are the things that bring fulfilment. For me anyway. For a long time I've hoped I'll meet a partner who would be prepared to make a commitment and work at our relationship. It's taking me an awful long time to do that. The last relationship I had failed after two years, principally because we had different views. I wanted to work at the things that weren't working, make things grow, and my partner didn't. If it didn't work, tough, move on to something else. That's common amongst gays.

I spend a lot of my time listening to gays telling their tales of woe, and a lot seem to be spending their time thinking of something more thrilling, more exciting. I hear a lot of people saying that gays have really woken up to AIDS and they've changed their behaviour and lifestyle. I can't see it. There was a young man here last week in a terrible state because he had sex with someone who's HIV and hadn't used a condom. I delved a bit deeper and found out I knew the other
268

person, who *is* HIV positive. But delving a bit deeper still, I discovered this chap had never used a condom and his approach was that provided he didn't sleep with someone with HIV, there was no problem. He'd slept with hundreds. But if he turns up positive, he wants to blame it on the one person he knows who's HIV. People have their heads buried in the sand.

One of the drawbacks of being gay is that the great liberation thing has become a stereotype and people feel that if you're gay that's the way you must live. If, like me, you don't think like that and it's not borne out in other experiences of life, you've got a real problem. The chances of meeting someone who you get on with, have something in common with, you find sexually interesting, wants to work in a relationship with you are pretty slim. Personally I've actually met such a one, but I had to go all the way to Germany. He still lives there at the moment. But it can be very difficult. The gay lifestyle looks very glitzy and exciting – flashy nightclubs with live music, everyone dressing up, wandering around apparently enjoying themselves. But if you go there, the chances of meeting someone who isn't very drunk or high on Ecstasy are pretty slim. I'd rather meet someone with whom I could sit down, have a meal and a bottle of wine and communicate with.

The other thing that's happened is that we live in a world where everything is about getting what you want here and now. The credit culture. Learning to meditate to achieve tranquillity is too much hard work – having a smoke is much easier, or having a drink. And people come in here, they want their problem solved now. I might be doing ten other things, but they want a solution now or it doesn't matter. That's a Western approach to life nowadays, and it's affected what we expect from and what we put into the experience of being sexual beings. I've been there, done that, tried it, and never felt so lonely and desperate.

I've had to work out what I need to do in life and what gifts I have to use. One of the reasons I'm grateful I'm gay is because it's made me think through a lot of things, rather than conforming to a stereotypical behaviour pattern. There's a whole world of difference between being able to make your own informed decisions, knowing what the consequences are, what the cost is for other people, than just doing what the fuck you want. To do what you want is just anarchy, it's exploiting and using other people. I don't think that's okay. One thing gays, or some of us, have learnt in the light of HIV, is consequences, there can be consequences, and it's not good enough to just say: 'Well I enjoyed it, he enjoyed it, who's hurt at the end of the day?' One of

269

the people hurt at the end of the day is me, because of what I feel afterwards. Probably the other person too.

If you accept my thesis that our approach to sexuality is like our approach to life, those who are saying we need to go back to more traditional family values may be saying that about sex and sexuality but certainly not about the rest of life. They still want the thrill of their fast car, they still want to live on credit because they want it now. The hedonist view – sex is there, take it when you want – was at least consistent with other aspects of their lives. But now Western society seems to be saying: Carry on living like this, blow the consequences to the environment, blow the increased cost of everything because of the interest we have to pay on borrowed money; if we want it now, we're going to have it. But we'd better put the sex bit in a different compartment. That's a response of fear. AIDS is obviously a contributory factor. We're frightened of what the cost of sexuality might be.

The Sixties was the beginning of something that's continued ever since. When I was a child my father bought me a box of Meccano and when I opened the box it was terribly exciting – there were all sorts of wonderful things I could play about with. Maybe the Sixties/ Seventies is like that a bit. Then one day, screwing things together, I jabbed a screwdriver in my hand, had to have stitches. Maybe that's what AIDS was. Maybe now, having finally learnt how to use the tools, having discovered the pieces I never knew were there before, I can now begin to make constructive things with them. In the Sixties we discovered a whole host of new things about sexuality that we'd either never admitted or never discovered before. Our task now is to find constructive creative ways of using that knowledge. I think we're making slow progress – no major revolution. The revolution was freedom from the stereotype. But to what extent have we just created new stereotypes? If I try and discuss with others my relationship with Frank and where we're going, people look at me as if I've got two heads – I'm not conforming to stereotype. Gay men don't do that. Not the ones that come here anyway.

I'd want to say as a Christian that the whole sexual revolution thing could challenge the Church to look very closely at its whole approach to the way we relate as human beings. Instead, as far as homosexuality is concerned, the bishops have just produced a report that I see as a sort of lid on Pandora's box. Keeping it shut tight. They see the sexual revolution as having got out of hand and the only way to tackle that is to push it back in its box. But we need to be open about what's come out of Pandora's box and say there are a lot of things in here which are
270

really exciting and interesting, that can help us live more fulfilled, rewarding lives.

It's very difficult being a gay vicar. Everyone wants you to be the person they want you to be, and that isn't somebody gay. For me it's easy, I'm running a house for people with HIV. A lot of gay priests say, 'It's all right for you.' My response is, 'Yes, but only because I've worked bloody hard to make it that way. You have to decide what you want to do with your lives.' I don't have a parish of my own, but I'm working in a parish at the moment whilst we're waiting for a new priest to come. Fine. We get on fine, no problem. By and large people don't ask, but I think a high percentage know I'm gay. Probably through my sermons. But a lot of people don't want to know, and those that don't shut the knowledge out. That's their choice. What is not people's choice is to take away from me the right to be myself, the person God created me to be. One of the things I find difficult about the Church and homosexuality is that – and this report is a classical example – when people are trying to explore an area of human life – for instance, if you wanted to bake bread, you'd ask a baker; if you wanted to know how to put an electrical circuit in, you'd ask an electrician – but if you want to know what the experiences of gay people are like, they're the last ones to be asked. 'They would say that wouldn't they, they're gay.' The underlying thing that gays are irresponsible, self-centred, immoral, do what they want. The assumption in that report is that if you sat and talked to me, I'd give you a biased viewpoint. But what I'd say is, 'I'm a Christian and I'm gay and it's caused me a lot of heartache to work through what all this means and come to some sort of way of living my life that has personal integrity. And that also enriches my relationship with God and the people around me. That I have worked very hard on.'

Open Door is just that, an open door. It's open to anybody infected with HIV or AIDS. We sit and listen, encourage people to support each other, try and help people work on their own attitudes, to get them to be more positive. A lot are frightened, think they'll die tomorrow. But quite a lot come because there's a free lunch and you start from there. People from the parish come in a lot, two or three a day, to help with ironing, typing, etc. That's good for breaking down barriers. We also throw things back at people, encourage them to do things for themselves. Few people who come here have transport. We were given a minibus, so they can drive it, take people places. We provide complementary therapies free – acupuncture, aromatherapy, reflexology, homeopathy. They're not normally accessible to those who come here because they cost a lot. It's a very open family really. There are four staff including me, and we've all got totally different

271

skills. One's a mother of four, an auxiliary nurse. One's a chef, another's a builder. I'm a priest. Those skills come in useful quite often. But it's not a place for people to come to be counselled, to have their problems sorted out. It's a space where people can find out how to do things for themselves and each other. That works in the community in Brighton.

Ninety per cent of those with HIV in Brighton are gay. But we're seeing a slow increase in heterosexuals now. There are two straight men, neither drug users, who are here every day. We have a mother with a little baby, about six weeks old. Recently a maternity hospital was randomly tested, and thirty per cent of the mothers were HIV positive. We don't know what the detailed figures are yet. If it's only ten per cent it's a huge number of people. The people we know about are those who've felt at risk and been tested. The vast majority of heterosexuals don't feel they're at risk and don't get a test. It's not their problem. So how do we find out? The majority who get tests are still gay men and drug users.

If you've been exposed to HIV you don't necessarily contract it, and it seems the state of your immune system will dramatically affect how likely you are to contract it. It so happens that in England, as a trend, gay men's immune systems are not as strong as straights'. Which may have something to do with self-image. That feeling that we've laid ourselves open to AIDS is a lot about how you feel about yourself. Around here if you open a gay bar, it's popular in seconds, if you open a gay restaurant nobody uses it. Gay scene people aren't into sitting down for a meal. It's a beer and a smoke. It's possible in Africa that with their lifestyles, poor nutrition, bad medicine, their immune systems are more susceptible.

I know a lot of gays in Brighton, nearly all through working here. My personal friends by and large are heterosexual. So my perception of gays is limited to a small group. The reason gay people like me live in Brighton is it's such a big liberation – being able to go to the supermarket together without being looked at: 'Why are those two men shopping together?' I notice it if I visit my brother in Devizes and we go shopping together. 'Oh, that's strange.' That just pisses you off. You could say we have a ghetto in Brighton. But what I love about it is that I can live here with a boyfriend and I'm accepted as a normal person with a valid relationship. Not just by gays, but by the old ducks in the street: 'Oh, how's Frank, has he rung lately?' This old lady is eighty-odd. And we can go in the straight pub up the street and it's: 'Oh, hello you two.' The word 'normal' is horrible, but we can just be normal people. You're not freaks. I like that.

My position on celibacy changed when I came to Brighton attached to a parish where there were a lot of gays. The majority of the congregation seemed to think gays were fine, it was the Church's problem not theirs. I didn't make a thing of saying I'm gay, but people began to realise and it wasn't a problem. One of the congregation is downstairs doing the ironing at the moment. So that problem disappeared on coming here. The same could be said of a host of churches. The Catholic church here welcomes gays. The Pope condemns homosexuality completely, but the parish people just say: 'Well, the Pope's wrong.' Though I wouldn't say that happens in many other Catholic parishes. We're very much an exception. This parish is in Kemp Town, a place with more gays in the population than anywhere in the country probably. Interestingly, they don't go to Anglican churches, only the Catholic one. Catholics take their commitment more seriously and want to work through the issue. People brought up Church of England say: 'The Church hasn't got room for me, I'll fuck off.' The only other Catholic parish I've found which is similar is the Church of the Holy Redeemer in San Francisco, round the back of the Castro, the gay centre. Same approach. They're running a lot of support groups, provide a house for the local AIDS hospice, etc. When I asked them how they reconciled all this with the Pope's pronouncements, they just said it was simple: the Pope was wrong.

I was in San Francisco in 1987. The diocese paid the air-fare for a sabbatical for me to do a four-week study of support for HIV people in San Francisco. They do deal with things differently there. What I've found with HIV services in England is that they try to do what they do in the States, not recognising how different the two cultures are. It's very much more militant and political there. I wonder what they achieve. In the Church, if you're militant or political about sexual issues, all you achieve is stupid reports produced by bishops which just make everything more difficult. As an Englishman I'm not very militant – political but not militant – and my approach to getting people to change attitudes is at grassroots level. But in England we're not very good at revolutions. Never had a major success with them.

The big word in the States is confidentiality, and the big word here is the same. Cobblers. The more you deprive people of knowing things about people you already know, the less you break barriers down. We encourage people here to be open and honest and we find that more and more people are realising they know people with HIV, that's okay, and they can talk to other people about it. So no problem. Anybody can come off the street for a coffee, and they do. It's not necessary to be political in an activist way. What we need to do is break down the barriers. The barriers are people's fear. So if you can build a trusting relationship the problem's going away already.

Going back to that report, the bishops are fairly liberal but they can't alienate the extremes. The great mass of middle-class Sunday churchgoers are fairly liberal. But in terms of religious expression, they're fairly conservative, principally because no one's encouraged them to think things out for themselves. If you go to some of the posh Sussex villages, you meet very intelligent people, degrees, high-powered jobs, but when it comes to what they believe, they're like five-year-olds. Reason is suspended. What this report is all about is the vicar staying a nice little man instead of being a human being, able to love. The parish here is waiting for a priest at the moment. Parishes are always asked what sort of priest they want. They said they wanted someone in his thirties with a wife and two children. I asked them why. Because some people had said they'd like me to be their vicar. I said, 'I'm not married with two children and I never will be married.' They said, 'But that's okay.' I said, 'So what are you playing at?' People want a cushy life somehow, want things to be as they should be.

The day the bishops' report was produced I went to an induction of a new priest in Brighton, and there were a lot of people in the congregation that I knew. I talked to about twenty or thirty of them in little groups about the report and what they thought of it. They'd come from all over Sussex, from little villages, small towns. They thought the report was absolutely disgusting. The report is called *Issues in Human Sexuality: A Statement by the House of Bishops*. What it basically says is that marriage and the family are God's ultimate will for man – which I find very dodgy, since in one of the gospels Jesus makes it clear that in the kingdom of God there's no place for marriage. The story of the woman who marries the seven brothers – whose wife is she in heaven? None of them. The report is about power and control. It goes on to say if you're a member of a congregation and you're gay and you have a relationship, provided it's just like a marriage then we will have to accept that. They have to accept that, otherwise people will vote with their feet.

I'm not saying I want to see stereotypical marriage. I'm saying that for a lot of gays, relationships, if they happen, are for the time they happen. The idea of working at it is peripheral. My relationship with Frank is not a stereotypical marriage whatsoever. The Church would therefore say because it's not (if I weren't a priest), then we can't be quite sure about it. The Church would be happier if one of us wore a dress all the time. They want these very clear dominant/passive roles. If you're two old queens living in a rose-covered cottage, then that's okay – provided one of you isn't a priest. They're prepared to tolerate
274

gay couples in congregations, but certainly not prepared to tolerate gay priests having relationships.

I was very fortunate with my last bishop. He and I felt the Church should respond to the HIV thing, and personal things I said about myself he agreed with, and this place started. When I leave here I guess I'll go to a parish, but not to one where they don't want a gay priest. If nobody wants a gay priest I'll get some other job. Perhaps even outside the Church. That won't stop me believing what I believe.

In fairness, I've never had problems with the Church, because they never ask questions they don't want to hear the answers to. And I only answer questions I'm asked. So there's a conspiracy of silence. Terribly English. Bishops are wonderfully English. In terms of the clergy it's very definite that you can't have a gay relationship. Some of the reasons they give are mind-boggling.

The Church is very clever, especially with pious emotional blackmail. The one good thing is they don't use the word homosexual by and large. They use the word 'homophile' which is rather better, because it's not just what you do with your bits, it's about your loving. It says: 'Of Christian homophiles, some are clear that the way they must follow in fulfilling this call is to witness to God's general will for human sexuality by a love of abstinence', and goes on to say: 'In the power of the holy spirit and out of love for Christ they embrace the self-denial involved gladly and trustfully, opening themselves to the power of God's grace to order and fulfil their personalities in this way of life. This is a path of great faithfulness, travelled under the weight of a very heavy cross. It is deserving of all praise and support of Church members through prayer, understanding and active friendship.' All those things are true of a celibate, but the language about great faithfulness and the heavy cross and all that, when it comes to people that are having gay relationships, it's very much, 'Well, you know, if they must be so self-centred, perhaps we have to tolerate it.' Though they do examine a lot of the biblical stuff and debunk it. That's quite constructive.

I've seen seventy or eighty people die of AIDS. For some, it's the conclusion of their life. It feels quite good for them. A friend of mine died three months ago, and his death was the conclusion of his life. That was fine. For others it's a struggle and a fizzle-out, very negative. You can feel by the way people are dying that they have different approaches to death. Most of the people I see don't believe in Heaven. My approach is, if I'm lying dying tomorrow I won't be thinking: This is terrible, I should have lived for another forty years, there's all these things I should have done. Because there are always going to be things you should have done or want to do.

275

Safe sex is important, but what's more important is what we're exposing ourselves to on an emotional level by not thinking out what the sex means, whether it means anything, or whether it's just a cheap thrill. A lot of people get a lot out of constant casual sex. I wonder if that's consistent with their self-image. They feel they might be a good fuck but as human beings they're not too good. Do I feel worthwhile as a human being, am I worth relating to? A lot of the gay scene is about image. People are very fashion conscious, is their hair the right length, what do they look like, what the image is. I'm not saying anything I haven't been through. I did the multiple partner/casual sex bit years ago. It was fun while doing it, until I got home afterwards. Fun for thirty minutes after it finished. One of the most lonely periods of my life. Half the people I had sex with I could have made good friends with, but they were sexual encounters so it wasn't on the agenda. I'm not saying I've stopped doing all that, but I'm moving away from finding satisfaction in that.

I've always sat back from my sexual experience – it hasn't been the centre of my life. There are a lot of other things in life for me to look at to see what works and what doesn't, and I can apply what I've learnt in terms of commitment, tackling problems and working at them to my experience of sexuality.

The motto I would put above my door would be what seems to be the crunch of the gospel: 'Love one another as I have loved you.' I can only love with the gifts I've got, not the ones you'd like me to have. I find with people who take fundamentalist views that after talking to them for a while it becomes very clear that some of the things they're very dogmatic about correspond with things they're frightened of. A lot of people's religious beliefs are a response to fear. The gospel is about tackling those fears, learning to trust, grow, mature.

St Paul has a lovely phrase: 'The glorious liberty of the children of God.' I find it difficult to find much glorious liberty in the children of God who take a fundamentalist stance. There seems to be little liberty and certainly nothing glorious about it at all. It's about fear and what things look like rather than what they are.

I'd be happy to have a discussion with any fundamentalist but I couldn't because 'discussion' presupposes that one person listens to and tries to understand the other. That wouldn't be the case, so I wouldn't be prepared to enter into dialogue – it wouldn't be dialogue, it would be a polemic. I'm trying to become a good Christian and I hope they are too.

Everyone uses religion as escapism in one way or another. There's a world of difference between people that know that and those that don't. People who realise that tend to grow quicker, become more

276

open. St Paul has a list of fruits of the spirit – love, peace, joy, kindness, gentleness, patience, etc. – and people who are aware of the way they use religion as a prop by and large overcome that. Whereas those that see religion as the solution to everything in their lives seem not to address the issues in their lives that should be addressed. And therefore become more extreme in one direction or another. There's little difference between biblical fundamentalism and papal fundamentalism. 'The Bible is true' or 'The Pope is true' are both responses to the same thing. I don't fall into either of those categories. I think the gospels are true. As it speaks to me, the gospel is true for me.

FRINGE BENEFITS: Years of Living Dangerously

'He that is without sin amongst you, let him cast the first stone.' But most, after all, are not, and while the Church, in whatever guise, may ponder just what qualifies as acceptable or unacceptable sexuality, the great majority remain ungodly. Sex hardly emerged fresh-minted in the 1980s, but the onset of AIDS and the accompanying calls for safer sex, continues to generate an ever-broadening compendium of alternatives to 'straight' pursuits. God, for some, is in the details.

ARAMINTA LOCKHEAD: I was tour-managing a band once and got stuck in LA with no money to get home. I saw this ad, went along, and met a really nice girl. It was working for this phone sex company, Phone Sex International: $36 for a regular call, $42 for a dominant mistress, $50 for three at once, and so on. To start with I was taking calls, checking credit cards. We had speakers in the office, and I'd tape some of the calls. Then I got bored and decided to do some calls myself. They'd ring up asking for eighteen-year-old Vietnamese girls, and I'd go: 'Hello, this Lim Ten Ping.' Very entertaining. The first one I had to do was a crucifixion, the guy wanted to be crucified. I ended up giggling hysterically and had to pass it on to somebody else. I couldn't remember what I'd done with him, where I'd put the nails. All this is on the phone. To start with I was going red, sitting there saying: 'I'm driving in the first nail...' The girls were great there. It was quite funny watching them. They would sit there for ten minutes, and while they're looking at their watch they're saying: 'I want you to come NOW!'

Phone sex wasn't disturbing, but what was was working in a topless hostess bar, the Director's Lodge in Jermyn Street. I thought it was a

277

waitress job to start with. I was about nineteen and I got completely into the psychology of it. They'd walk in, you'd chat to them and you had to work out who was going to spend money – because we weren't paid a wage. If you persuaded them to go downstairs to the restaurant, they had to buy you dinner and ten bottles of champagne, you could charge a hostess fee. The first week I didn't make any money at all. You had to work out if they were going to spend money, and also work out what type they were looking for: the girl-next-door or a complete slut. We wore stockings, suspenders, a skirt or a scarf tied round your waist. Nothing else. The girls were so bizarre. The ones who were really good at it were totally straight – worked at Selfridges, would never dream of telling anyone what they did. Sometimes their boyfriends would find out and come storming in and drag the girl out. But I told everybody what I was doing, I found it so interesting. These were people I'd never mix with normally. I'd get the night bus home at four a.m., the other girls would get cabs.

It was illegal to have sex with the customers. But lots of girls did. They'd meet them later. I decided one night I wanted to do that – I wanted to see what it would be like. So I arranged to meet this pretty ghastly Arab, and with another girl we went out to dinner. He passed me a note: 'How much will it cost?' I wrote on the napkin: £250. He was horrified. I found out later the going rate was £100. But he came back to where I was staying and I did it with him. Took about four minutes. I was completely disgusted by it, and after he left I took three baths one after the other. Before I went to sleep, I laid all the money out round my pillow, so it would be there when I woke up. I thought I'd never get his face out of my mind. But I forgot it quite quickly. I've never done it again. But I was interested in those feelings. I was trying to decide whether I'd like it. The girls in the club seemed to be addicted to it. They seemed much more dishonest than I was, because they seemed so straight, so different in the daytime. They were really good actresses, and I wasn't.

PAULA LEWIS

'It's tough to be in business.'

Anonymous, potent purveyor of myriad telephonic fantasies she sits in the few square feet available in a room packed to walls and ceiling with erotica. It's her brother's flat, from which he supplies mail-order erotica – both modern and antiquarian – to a vast database of collectors. A five year veteran of credit-card sex – you pay, I'll say – she's reached, one might say, the end of the line.

278

I run a telephone sex business where people phone in and pay by credit card for a telephone sex call. The ads say they're uncensored but they are censored to a certain degree – we do stick within the law, and we don't talk about children and things like that. We advertise in all the top shelf magazines, *Fiesta*, Forum, Penthouse – we used to advertise in *Private Eye* too until they realised what it was and kicked us out. We did very well out of them, almost as well as out of the sleaze magazines. A lot of our customers are doctors, psychiatrists, professors, reverends. A lot of celebrities too.

Phone sex is still pretty new. There's no one group of people that phone us. There's so many different types. One guy who's disabled, his mother found out what he was doing and stopped him doing it, which I think is tragic really. He still needed sexual release. The disabled, the ugly the virgins, everybody needs it. It's a shame that there can't actually be a telephone line that can actually be monitored for quality and legality. I think in fact there is a line you can call, voice activated, and you answer various questions and there's a qualified therapist who gives an answer. But it's not really very personal.

We don't get women ringing up. I don't think there'd be any money in doing a lesbian fantasy line. It seems that there's a great difference between the sex drive of men and women and the emotional content of men and women. Men seem to be all sex and no emotion, and women seem to be the other way round. Sometimes you get a guy who's got his wife or girlfriend there and they want to do a call together, and she listens while you chastise him or spank him or whatever, but I don't know whether the woman is really a willing party or not. I don't know: can women cut off sex from emotion? I don't think they can – because I certainly can't. When you're young you can – you go out screwing around and finding out what sex is all about and that – there's not much emotion involved there, but now I think if someone's going to penetrate you they need to penetrate your soul first. When I was in search of sex I always thought that love would be at the end of sex, and mistakenly took sex for love. But not now. I don't think I'd even consider a one-night lay now. I couldn't just screw around. I've got more self-worth now.

It's tough to be in business anyway. To be a woman in business in a man's world is even tougher, and to be a woman in business in a man's world where men seem to abuse women – the sex industry – is tougher still. That's partly the reason I've got to get out of it. People want blood in that industry. I've met no one that I like, not in my end, the sleaze end – which is what it is really.

When we first started, in 1986, it was £37.95 a time and the phone did not stop ringing. The first year we turned over three quarters of a

279

million – which left us gobsmacked, absolutely gobsmacked. I was in a partnership with another girl then, and we ended that partnership in October '87, since when we've been in competition. Which is good for business – it makes you work hard. The calls have gone down now – people haven't got the money – and they're anything from fifteen quid to £37.95. The difference is with the specialist lines – S/M, rubber, watersports, transvestites and just normal – though what is normal? Straight sex, anyway. Straight fantasy.

What happens is this: the customer sees the advert, which usually says something like 'Call Naughty Nina for a live sex call – instant call backs.' So he phones up, our receptionist answers the phone and says 'Hello this is Naughty Nina, would you like to book a telephone call?' He then enquires about the service and we tell him how much it is. Then he gives a credit-card number. We take his details and authorise the card. Then there will be a girl at home, waiting for information, and you phone her and say, 'Right, can you ring Jonathon Green on 071 whatever,' and she'll ring, introduce herself and then give him the telephone call which goes on until he orgasms or a half hour is up. Half an hour is actually a long time, and that's why we made so much money in the beginning, because we got so good at our job that the guys were coming in about five to ten minutes and still paying for half an hour!

We have a very good system of detecting fraud. We check with BT that the customer does live at the address he gives. If people say they're ex-directory, we check with BT that they are, and we take that as gospel. Occasionally we do get burnt, but it's mostly by people who book a call and then they regret it and they think: God, I spent £37.95, had a wank and I don't want to pay for that. So they start complaining. We do sort some out though some we just forget.

Me and my friend both started off working for a guy in Soho, Mark something or other, who had a recording studio. One night we did seventeen calls in a four-hour shift and we thought: God, this is a licence to print money – so we started doing it ourselves. I suppose there's about ten or twenty people doing it now. A lot of girls who have worked for me have thought what I thought when I worked for Mark: 'Oh, Paula's making lots of money, we'll go off and do it for ourselves.' But it's not that easy. You've got to know the industry a little bit. I learned the hard way and they're gonna learn the hard way. What they do is go off and advertise in magazines and take out little three by one boxes. I take half pages, which means my advertising bill is £5,000 a month. We turn over about half a million a year now. There are advertising bills and then we pay the girls per call; they're self-employed so they have their own phone bills to pay. When I
280

started with Mark I used to get £15 per call. Now it's down to about £3. It's the recession, people just can't afford so much.

I was about thirty when I started doing the calls. Though I've been anything you like: a Pakistani, a West Indian, French – you just tell the customer what he wants to hear – after all, it's his fantasy – and it works. We try all the accents – though they may not be perfect. It's their fantasy. It is similar to masturbating over a magazine or a book but more senses are heightened because you're actually coming with a person. If the man can believe that the woman is enjoying it too, I suppose that must make it more intense. Self-inflicted orgasms, as it were, can be more intense than orgasms between two people. It used to be odd, listening to someone masturbating down the phone, but it's become a part of my life now, I don't find it odd any more – which is quite dangerous. I've become very blasé about sex and when I'm talking to people they can be quite shocked about the things I'm saying. And I suddenly realise that I shouldn't be talking so openly about sex. But it doesn't embarrass me any more.

We give value for money. Not like the 0898 numbers. Lots of what I'd call porn barons have got into it because they know how much money it makes. One guy employs girls for only a year, he gets rid of them quickly so he doesn't pay PAYE or anything like that – gets them in, gets them out, that's it. But our regulars say that they don't give a very good service. A lot of the girls that work for me really get into it. I started off using friends and then it was friends of friends and so on. It just escalated. When they start I just say, 'You've all had sex, all you have to do is talk about it.' Obviously they haven't all done everything, but that can work for you – some of the guys quite like that virginal aspect. They like to introduce them to new things. You soon pick it up, it's like any job really, you learn as you go along. You do literally get thrown in at the deep end. You get a call and you're off. That's it. Some girls do ask for training and they'll go to one of the other more experienced callers and listen to a couple of calls, or we get some books – *The Handbook for Slaves* we use quite often. We don't have scripts because everyone's an individual.

The first time you take a call is nerve-racking. None of the girls ever forget their first call. Never. But after you've put the phone down you think: Christ, that was so easy. I mean everyone's screwed, all you have to do is talk about it. The customer leads you through it, anyway. You introduce yourself and say, 'What type of girl do you like?' and he'll say, 'Well, I like tall girls that are red-headed and big boobs...' and you say, 'Well, it's your lucky day because you've just rung me and I'm extremely tall with red hair and big boobs!' Ha! That's how you do it. Then you say, 'What are you into?' and he'll start to tell you and they

281

sort of lead you through – it's almost like counselling really. I think I'm relieving male sexual neurosis, which is a pleasure for them, but it's only short-term relief – which is why they keep coming back. You ask him what he wants all the time. Meanwhile he's jerking off and I'm painting my nails, reading the paper.

The way I feel towards the guys varies. When I first started I thought it was a great laugh and then as I was listening to more and more bizarre fantasies I was beginning to get a bit worried and thinking I was in quite a dangerous position doing this job and a lot of guilt came into it, that I was encouraging these people. Then after that I realised that it was a good service because it was available for anyone, ugly ones, virgins, people in isolated buildings; there's no AIDS risk, no pregnancy risk, you don't need condoms, no one's getting hurt...and I convinced myself then that it was okay. I've since found out that it *is* okay and it does have the potential to reduce sexual violence when people can jerk off over the telephone. It's definitely better if he jerks off than goes off and fulfils some violent fantasy.

It is pornography I suppose. But if you stick within the laws, you don't talk about children, then it's okay. And if someone does ring up and when you ask them what they're into and they say eight-year-old girls, we just say, 'I'm sorry, we can't talk about that.' People who want younger girls usually have a sort of code. They ring up and ask 'How old are you?' and you say, 'I'm eighteen,' and they say, 'Well, you sound a lot younger than that,' and you know instantly what they're into and you just very firmly say, 'No, I'm not younger than that, I am actually eighteen,' and they push and push and push but we don't do it.

I don't know what is going to shock me now. I've just started a course to train as a sex therapist, because there are a lot of questions left unanswered for me. After reading this book by Robert Stoller, *Perversion: The Erotic Form of Hatred,* it's given me a greater understanding of what perversion is all about: perversion being unresolved childhood conflict. But I've developed an empathy for 'perverts', whatever a 'pervert' is. S/M certainly doesn't shock me. It's not really violence, is it? It has come out of the closet in the last two or three years but it's still very misunderstood.

I knew nothing about S/M when I first started the telephone business and it was only through what customers wanted – to be spanked and things like that – that I thought: Christ this is really weird. Why are they getting turned on by pain? How we first learned about it was these guys were ringing up wanting to be spanked and things and we didn't know anything about it. So we started buying books and reading up about it and we thought: There's a gap in the market here, you know. So we invented an S/M phone line – we called it Domina – and we couldn't believe the calls we had. People wanted to eat shit and be pissed on and used as human toilets and spanked and pierced and things shoved up their arse and they were into animals. It was all such a laugh to start with, all such a giggle; we thought: This is going to be so easy, just shit in this guy's mouth and he comes. What could be easier: you don't even have to talk about fucking.

I found it quite easy to be dominant. My idea of men had gone down and down and down. After a couple of years in this business I thought men were shit, I thought men were absolute shit and I hated them and I just thought that the small percentage that phoned me accounted for the whole of the male population. I really got to hate men. I was almost turning into a feminist, but I never got that far, thank God, thank God for that! I even thought about lesbianism: I got to the stage where I was hating men so much I thought well maybe I should be a lesbian. But I'm not. I'm convinced I'm not. It was only thoughts.

When I started the domination line I really did live the part, I got very stroppy and bossy and I didn't understand the whole act. I thought they were paying for my time and I was in charge and it was my business and I did feel very superior. But now I've learnt that the dominant one really is the inferior. The point is that they're paying for your time and the one who pays has to be the dominant one. You are giving your time to be whatever they want you to be, so if they want you to be dominant you're submitting to their whims and wishes. And it's not just on the phone; the relationship is the same in the club or in the bedroom. I've got a friend who had a dungeon and she's still under the illusion that she's the dominant one because she's taking the money. I'd like to be there to pick up the pieces when she finally realises that she's not in charge, that it's the men that come to see her who are in control. And they are, most definitely.

I'm sure there's a big link between religion and sado-masochism. Definitely. There's lots of symbolism in sado-masochism – the purging of the soul, down on your knees, begging for forgiveness, confession, beating, birching, whipping. These guys are ashamed, yes, bowing down to the mistress. I'd like to know what sort of lives they have or have had.

I did once meet one of the people who call. It was quite freaky. He had made a lot of calls to us. We do get addicts, there's a lot of phone sex addicts that we've got – one guy spent all his redundancy money with us. His wife was out working and he was making calls all the time. Literally thousands and thousands of pounds. If they are regulars we still check them every few months, just to check they are who they say

283

they are, just in case we've missed something. So with this guy we were doing the checkup and BT said, 'Oh would that be the Reverend Joe Bloggs?' That shocked us quite a bit, this was after he'd had about six months' worth of calls. So we said, 'Yes, it is.' We all hooted around after that, giggling and laughing: a vicar was phoning us up. He would only speak to me, and I charged him a bit extra because I'm the boss: £45 a go.

This guy was really into death. Not necrophilia, but death. He liked to be in a Roman amphitheatre and he liked to fight for his mistress's approval. He liked to fight to the death, until either he died or the other person died. How he killed was by biting the other person's jugular – at which point he would come. After he'd come, after he'd bitten the jugular, you had to brand your initials on his backside so he was permanently your property. Anyway, he would only speak to me, and I'd really got into this fantasy. Though it's one of the fantasies that has really freaked me out – this connection between sex and death. So, there's a pal of mine who runs a bed and breakfast place in London. And I was staying in his place and he happened to say, 'Mr Bloggs is staying here tonight' – the thing was he actually had a rather strange surname. So I said, 'That's not Mr J. Bloggs is it?' and he said, 'Yes,' and I said, 'J for Joe?' and he said, 'Yes.' I went, 'God, that's one of my best customers, can I check his credit card number?' I called the office. It was him. I said, 'I've got to see this guy.' It was the first customer I'd ever met after five years in the business.

He went out that night to this new club that had opened up. A Gothic S/M scene. Next morning I went down to breakfast and there was this guy who looked like Death himself. He had a white, waxy skin, these really dark hollow eyes, the typical Reverend's blue boat-necked sweater that they all wear. About forty-five. So I sat down at the next table and got chatting away, and the guy who owns the B&B said, 'Oh this is a friend of mine, he's just been to the S/M party.' He was really open about it, and started talking about this Roman amphitheatre stuff. It totally freaked me out. I thought: I know so much about you that you don't know about me. I know your deepest, darkest fantasies and you know nothing, you just don't even know I'm here. I sat and chatted away to him and it did leave me with a chill in my spine, it really did. He said that he went to a lot of the clubs, he's 'on the scene' as they say, and people take advantage of him, because he's so much into pain. If anyone's going to take a beating it's always him. The dominatrixes like to see who can give him the best beating.

The thing I'm trying to investigate is just how close fantasy comes to reality and do they cross over? This thing with sex and death, that's really fucked my head up. Loads of people are really into sex and

284

death. They want to kill. I'd like to know where they're coming from, I really would. This business has left a lot of questions unanswered for me, which has led me to this course in sexuality. I couldn't go through my life not knowing the answers. Was it Freud who said that fantasy and reality are the same thing? If someone comes to you with a fantasy, for them that is their reality.

The last fantasy I did was with this guy. I said, 'Hello, my name's Paula, what're you doing at the moment?' 'Oh,' he said, 'I like flashing I do.' I said, 'Flashing, eh. Have you been out flashing today?' He said, 'I went out flashing last night.' I said 'Oh yeah, what's your kick then, when someone screams and runs away?' 'No,' he said, 'I flash. I just want to fuck 'em. I wait till I've got a good hard-on, I flash my prick and I just want to fuck 'em. Last night there was this woman of sixty, I flashed at her, she lay down on the ground, pulled up her skirt, she had stockings and suspenders on, no knickers, and I fucked her! I fucked her good and hard and she loved it, she absolutely loved it!' I said, 'Is that a fantasy or is that reality?' He said, 'No it really happened. It's true, happened last night.' And I said again, 'Is that a fantasy or reality?' He said, 'No, it happened last night.' Then he orgasmed and put the phone down. That really flipped my mind. I thought: God what am I doing here? Am I encouraging this guy to do this sort of thing, or I have satisfied him so he won't do it again? What was the weather like last night, would a woman of sixty be lying around on the ground waiting to be fucked? Had he raped her? I've got his name, address and telephone number, shall I phone the police and say did a woman of sixty get raped last night because I've got the information and I know who done it? And that's when I realised that it had to be the end – I couldn't cope with it any more. I didn't call the police but a week after I went to see a doctor and went to hospital for two months. I had a breakdown.

I do feel ashamed of the things I've helped people indulge in. Straight sex, fucking's the easy part. Domination, defecation, urination, piercing, blood – that's all pretty disgusting. I know this girl, a dominatrix, who nails a guy's testicles to the floor once a week. He loves it. Forty per cent of the business is weirdos. But then what's crazy, what's weird? I sold my shit once, for £25. That was the most disgusting thing I've ever done, I was absolutely disgusted with myself. It was a laugh at the time: £35 for the call, £25 for the shit, that's sixty quid and then he phones back again when he's got the shit to talk to me about it. He wanted it in a pair of knickers, which is how I sent it. And when he received it he phoned me up with it in his hand and he talked to me and while he talked to me he ate it and told me

285

what colour my hair was. I was just so disgusted and repulsed. That was the lowest of the low.

TIM WOODWARD

'These people are not undesirables.'

Fetish Central is a modern brick warehouse at the north end of Ladbroke Grove. Downstairs the shoppers browse the racks of rubber, leather, PVC, and allied impedimenta. Upstairs all is efficiency, Apple Macs and DTP. The magazine Skin Two, *where sado-masochism meets fashion's cutting edges, is produced here. Tim Woodward publishes and edits it. Despite the stock downstairs, he's dressed conservatively: a blazer, shirt and tie. His conversation is as quotidian as his outfit. Sado-masochism may have its dark and dirty side, but Mr Woodward is at pains to present its most acceptable face.*

Up until 1982 if you were interested in anything like rubber fetishism, S/M, bondage, submission and domination, transvestism – a whole load of aspects of human sexuality across a broad spectrum – you were completely consigned to the world of porno books and dirty old men in macs. There's nothing intrinsically wrong with either of those, but it isn't a pleasant milieu in which to find yourself. So if you were into this area you probably thought you were the only one, there was something wrong with you, and that you could only buy mucky books. People are harassed if they're into this. It's like being gay or black twenty years ago. If you were a teacher, you'd lose your job, portrayed as a child-molesting criminal. I'm a sado-masochist and I know thousands of them. We have 850 people come to our parties, 200-300 to the smaller clubs, 25,000 read our magazine. These people are not undesirables, not criminals in any sense. So what you see in the Sunday papers is a load of crap – very cynical.

Skin Two, the club, opened in '82. I started going a month or two after it started up. It was a group of people involved in pop music, fashion, photography, the arts generally, who were into this sort of thing. And they included middle-class suburban people. Although there were a lot of trendies involved, you were made to feel welcome even if you were fat, bald, fifty and horrible. People were dressed up in leather, it was fun, non-exclusive, not very sexist. That caught the mood. Women as well as men. Not a Stringfellows scene where if you're in a miniskirt eighty-nine guys with sports cars want to take you out. More relaxed than that. Originally, it was just word of mouth.
286

Fewer than 200 people at first. So it was friends of friends of friends. Then *Time Out* picked it up, it was on the front cover. That drew more people in. The men and women who started the club hadn't realised how many people were interested. They just started it for fun, there was no money in it. And still isn't, I can tell you that. But the popularity was a great surprise.

That mixture really took off. The trendies liked a place they could relax in – lots of pop stars went there – but it wasn't precious, and what worked was that suburban middle-aged people found somewhere they could feel fine. On the whole it was more of a fashion statement for the trendies, and a sexual thing for the bourgeoisie. But the mixture worked. Everyone was very tolerant. It was a really nice space. It was a club in a basement in Soho. I saw it in the Ad Lib column in the *Evening Standard.* I went with a friend, neither of us wanting to go on our own. She wore a catsuit, six-inch heels. It was just thrilling, terrific fun. It was completely different from anything that had gone on before. I'd looked at the Mackintosh Society for rubber fetishists – charming people as I've come to know them – but this was different because it was fun. A nice quality to it. And a lot of rudery went on.

Then one evening at the bar, Grace Lau, a feminist erotic photographer, was moaning there was nowhere for her to publish her pictures. She didn't want them in top-shelf magazines. Quite a lot of feminists are in favour of censorship – the Clare Short argument – but there are loads who take a more intelligent view. As Grace would put it: 'Women like sex as well, why would they want to censor anything?' We then decided to have our own magazine. Publishing is my background, and just over a casual beer I said, 'I'll be the publisher.' We printed 1,000 copies of sixteen pages each – just a fanzine really. We sold it to our friends at the club, didn't go to newsagents or anything, and that was it.

People loved it. They'd tell us, 'We've been into this for years and we got a couple of porno magazines and they're a bit naff, not very satisfactory. Then we got a copy of *Skin Two* – and it's nothing like that at all. It really is nothing like a top shelf mag. We're stunned, it's changed our lives. Now we realise there are tons of people into this who are not sleazy at all.' After that we thought: Suppose we'd better do another one.

People involved in the club were quite creative and lots of them came forward to help: I'm a writer, I'm a photographer, I'm this, I'm that. There was this generosity of spirit – a bit like the camaraderie of the gay world. Peter Ashworth, who'd done album covers for Annie Lennox, Phil Collins – a major star photographer, works for *ID, The*

287

Face, etc. – said he'd take some cover pictures for issue No. 2. All for free, and he paid for processing the film. So he took the pictures. Daniel James was then inventing rubber haute couture. Jerry Hall has a Daniel James dress, absolutely beautiful. He's taken rubber away from old men in welly boots and given it class. Others have now come along, like Kim West and Marion Verne, Gaultier, Pam Hogg, Thierry Mugler etc. But at that time Daniel James was inventing it. Around the time of our second issue. So the magazine had photos by Ashworth, clothes by Daniel James – not that we realised they were becoming stars, we were just all friends and pitched in. Then Tony Mitchell said, 'Do you want a proper journalist? Have you heard of sub-editing, do you know what captions are, can you write a headline?' 'No, what are those things?' So he came on board. We ended up running the club and the magazine. It got bigger and bigger, and I gave up my other work.

People ask, 'How come the S/M scene flourishes in England?' We have the biggest scene here, the biggest magazine, we've just published our first book – it's all happening. But why in England, which everybody knows is so repressive? It's really strange. I don't know the answer, and haven't met anyone who does. Why am I heterosexual and not gay? – I don't bloody know. You're into these things or not. The fetish scene in England's a bit like the music scene. Nobody knows why it's so healthy and vital. It's strange. You go to a society that's more democratic, more prosperous, has a better health and education system, such as Germany, you find their pop music is absolute crap. Their fetish scene isn't, but it's still more or less a copy of ours. There seems to be one thing that works fairly well in Britain – and I'm speaking as rather a critic of the current bleak, grey generation we're living through, someone who preferred the old Sixties thing – we do seem to be creative people. Not just sexually, but in every sense. We have the best pop music, very healthy literary scene, healthy theatre scene. Now we're putting our sexual energy into those things. We are repressed though. We still have this hypocrisy which we haven't dealt with. The English vice is not being spanked or caned, it's hypocrisy. After all, loads of famous people are into S/M – pop stars, politicians, TV announcers. Frank Bough the only one? You must be joking.

But being English we pretend we're not into it. Nobody knows why we do this. The only thing that's different about the S/M and fetish scene now is we're all doing this openly. If you pick up *Skin Two* it says: Editor, Tim Woodward – that's my real name, here I am, I really am a sado-masochist. That's new. Jean Paul Gaultier really does come
288

here, really does subscribe to the magazine. That's different, not how it was before.

I came to it fairly late in life. People often ask us, 'What do you personally do in bed with your partner?' I don't want to get bogged down in that. Whether I'm a rubber fetishist, she's a bondage freak, or he's gay, or she's into having custard poured over her head doesn't actually matter. We don't go into details. Some people find it hard to come out. And some people ring up asking which club to go to to get into the scene. But it doesn't work like that. You meet people in the ordinary way then find out what their sexual tastes are, then come to the club or the magazine. You can't be an S/M without being open and discussing it all with your partner. You wouldn't know what to do with each other. The tabloids promote the 'evil beasts' bit, but they don't really believe it – it just sells papers.

I've heard all sorts of theories about the scene and why people enjoy it: the most popular is that English upper-middle-class men like to be caned because of going to public schools. Absolute bollocks! I went to a public school, went through the caning and so on and it was bloody awful. If you'd told me that as a middle-aged man I'd be into whips and chains I would have thought you were raving mad. Anyway, many have not been to a public school, are not English, are not boys. This kind of theorising belongs to a generation ago when it was thought only men were into this stuff. Cynthia Payne said women only agree to do this to get a new three-piece suite, or keep their husband happy. That may be true for many people but for many others it isn't.

I'd always thought women looked pretty in black stockings, suspenders, high heels. Then I fell for someone very seriously who was into all this stuff and she wanted to go much further than just that. I'd had a leaning that way, but the opportunity had never arisen. I thought this woman was the cat's pyjamas, I was absolutely barmy about her. She wanted to do all this and I thought: Well, I'm game. I would have done anything that she said she wanted to do. Then I realised, over a period: Oh yes, this is really it. A lot of people discover it that way. They have an inclination, then meet someone else who feels the same. In particular a romantic partner. After that it may lead to something or not. One friend of mine, a committed feminist, tells boyfriends that she's keen to be spanked, but she always goes out with responsible New Men, pro-feminists. And they say: 'Well fine, women have a right to choose. What would you like me to do?' Which is not what she wants. 'No, no, I want to just *do* it!' Others I know started off at an early age. One of my friends, in her early thirties, when she was a little girl she would spank her little playmates. And by the time

289

she was twelve, she knew she was different. Some people involved say: 'I was into this sort of thing when I was three or four.' One of my friends says, 'I remember punishing my dolls for fun. I didn't know I was a sado-masochist.' I wouldn't proselytise. I'd never say people should get into this, it's brilliant, try it. Rather the reverse. I'd like a situation where S/Ms, all types of fetishists are ignored. People who are into this should know we're here, but if you're not, that's fine, we won't get in your way.

There's a lot of humour in this too, it's not all serious. If you're doing an S/M scene with your wife or husband, it's all very black leather and ritualistic. That's the thrill of it. So you probably won't fall about laughing at that point. But there's a tremendous amount of humour in the whole thing. The anecdotes flow. At least once or twice a year there's a barbecue in the summer, for people interested in pony-racing – where the submissive man or woman pulls a little chariot with the dominant one sitting on their back, saying, 'Get up there!' That's erotic if you're into that sort of thing. If you're not, it's not. I don't personally find pony-racing erotic, but these people do and it's great fun, they enjoy it. There was a race between three people – a male submissive/woman dominant, a male dominant/woman submissive and two lesbians. One gets beaten for coming last, the one who came second got beaten for cutting a corner, and the one who won got beaten for winning. One argument against S/M is that it's demeaning to women, because it makes them parade in thigh boots while you should be looking at the inner person. I agree with that, but some people *like* thigh boots and the rest as a theatrical prop, or they *like* rubbing themselves in baby oil or whatever it is. If you're into whips and chains, of course you still love your partner – these are just props you use to achieve a sensual intensity. You do need a sense of humour, but if you're into it, it is bloody thrilling. It operates on different levels. There's a kind of Beryl Cook end-of-the-pier strand of British humour in it. A bald fat man in a little tutu who's a transvestite is going to look a bit funny. There used to be dos at the Porchester Hall where you'd get six-foot-tall blokes, blue stubbly chins, in fishnet suspenders, with beards, moustaches, wigs. When you're actually doing it you don't laugh. You're doing it in private. We have parties, and you will see little scenes on a more frivolous level. But serious S/M takes place between people who know each very, very well – usually married to each other. When you're doing it, you say: 'On Friday night, we'll have a session.' It's not every day of course. And you won't laugh at the time.

There are loads of funny stories. I used to live in the Orthodox Jewish community in Stamford Hill, and when we took all the dungeon equipment out of the house, lots of these very Orthodox people were passing by. We were saying: 'Left a bit with the rack, Joe. Up this end with the whips.' Chains clattering etc. Without wishing to offend these good people, it was pretty funny. How could it not be?

I don't want to be pompous, and I'm definitely not in favour of censorship, but a lot of the top-shelf S/M magazines are a load of crap. They're produced cynically by people who are not into those things. I'm very sympathetic towards books, clubs, magazines – whatever's produced by people who are genuinely interested. I don't mind tacky as such – tacky can be fun. It's the fact that top-shelf mags are very cynical and completely dishonest. I know there is a crossover among purchasers, and I wouldn't turn them away. I wouldn't be offended if someone wanked over a copy of *Skin Two*, that'd be perfectly all right. But it has a much longer life. People don't throw them away, and the early issues are now worth £20-30. There are articles by famous writers – Pat Califia, Terence Sellers (usually known as 'Angel Sterne') – it's sexual, but on a more serious level. You won't be turned on while you're reading it – which is the main point of a porno magazine.

If S/M has boomed because of AIDS it's surely because S/M is safe. It's completely safe. No one injures anybody. Nobody goes out, picks someone up and does S/M with them. It doesn't work like that. You can't go to a pub or club and pick them up for S/M. You need to know what they're into, you need to know what to do. You need to know someone really quite well. If someone says she'd like to be tied up, what does she mean? Restricted for three hours, or just having her wrists tied up? You don't know that if you've just met them. You have to establish trust. You can't do it with someone you've just met a week before. S/M is a deep subject. You don't know how far someone is into it, what rituals they follow. It takes weeks. You can have S/M with your good friend, but if you want to be tied up and beaten, are you going to do that with a stranger? You'd be crazy. You could perhaps be in danger, but it's more the person wouldn't know what you mean by, say, being beaten. You've got to know in what way, on what part of your body, to what extent. That's part of the fun – you meet someone and it develops. There isn't a rush. You're not going to catch AIDS from this. If you're dressing up in rubber, acting out all kinds of fantasies, you're not in danger. It could be dangerous – not as dangerous as cooking or DIY – but it could be. The one time S/M *could* be dangerous is if you don't use common sense. That's why it's a good idea to have things like *Skin Two*, to have clubs where you can exchange information. So you don't get cases of poor sad lonely people who tie each other up and restrict their breathing with hoods or masks. If you've got a cold, you could suffocate.

Occasionally people have died due to ignorance. There was a police officer some years ago. He wasn't in a relationship where he freely exchanged with his partner. You know: live with someone, eat and sleep with them, but don't freely exchange what's in your heart. There's cases – like this one – where the man is into all this, doesn't tell his wife, wife is away, man has a couple of beers (first mistake, you should never have alcohol when you're doing this stuff, your mind should be clear), ties himself up (second mistake, never do that, have your partner on hand in case you get cramps, etc., never do it on your own) – and the poor guy in some way contrived to hang himself. I think he was on a chair. This was due to ignorance. But he should have shared with his partner.

You don't have to browbeat your partner into it. If they're not into it, fine. But at least have them there to keep an eye on you. Or do it with your friends. One of my friends is into all sorts of S/M, her husband isn't. No problem. She goes to the club, gets dropped safely home and he doesn't mind. He's into other things – amateur theatricals, whatever. You can't expect a mirror image in your relationship. If you agree on everything, great, but it's just as healthy if you have slightly converging, slightly diverging interests. It's not the end of the world if you're a sado-masochist and your partner isn't.

I feel reasonably optimistic. The effects of the last ten years won't last for ever, but the effect of the Sixties will last. Stephen Fry was on TV last year behaving in a gay clone fashion. If Sid James had done that twenty years ago, his career would have been over. Kenneth Williams never admitted to being gay. It was all right to be camp, make jokes about gays, but it was safe because the subtext was always 'I'm not really gay.' These days, gay celebrities couldn't give a toss.

For me, getting involved with *Skin Two* was something that just happened in a bar-room conversation – I'd never addressed it or thought about it before that. But when it came to giving up my old business, a personnel agency for the publishing industry, it was then that I thought: If I'm going to be secretive about this, what does that say, and anyway, why be secretive? So I decided I'm either not going to do it, or if I did I'd be completely open about it, because what am I ashamed of exactly? That's proved to be the right decision. Hardly anybody has disowned me as a friend, family member. My sister, brother-in-law, mother – they've heard me interviewed on 'Woman's Hour' about S/M. I don't see myself as being outspoken. And certainly I'm never proselytising. I don't think everybody should try this. People should be as they are.

There are lots of misconceptions. People say: there must be something wrong with you if you can't achieve satisfaction without all that. Such bullshit. Of course you can. What I personally do, and how often doesn't really matter. It could be a week, or a month, twice a week – when I feel like it. There are different levels. You can have an S/M scene, involving lights, music, costume, ritual etc. Or when you're having a cuddle in bed you can spank each other in a larky way. People do both. It's like reading. You can read the *Evening Standard* and Proust. Nothing's mutually exclusive.

NETTIE POLLARD: *Kane* and *Skin Two* are very fashionable. I quite like *Skin Two*, but you've got to be pretty rich – the magazine costs £7-8 and you're expected to buy the most extraordinarily expensive outfits. It isn't like punk where you could just use a plastic bag. I'm glad *Skin Two* exists and it's an interesting magazine, but they're mainly young and beautiful people in it, and they're all rich and you have to be rich to buy it. I don't think S/M clubs are cosy, but they're not threatening either in the way people think they are. I've been to S/M clubs a few times. You meet very nice people there. Which doesn't mean they don't have real S/M sex. And some of the outfits can be quite threatening-looking unless you're in tune with them and realise they're actually to do with sexual fantasy, they're not to do with being beaten up in the street. That's what the general public have a problem with. They see somebody in a leather jacket, handcuffs, spikes round their wrist and see it as aggressive. It's not at all. It's to do with sexual fantasy. People have great difficulty divorcing sexual fantasy from everyday behaviour.

People who are into S/M don't necessarily go round wanting to be bullied all day, persecuted in the office, beating people up in the street. It's not to do with aggression, it's to do with sexuality. It's fantasy, it's sexual conduct, but not connected with cruelty and aggression. Men beating their wives up at home is not S/M. That's wife battering. A lot of people confuse the two – radical feminists most certainly do. They see something like Della Grace's photos as violence against women. And all it is is women looking quite assertive, dressed in leather with whips. They're not really porn. And also these are her friends. They're doing it because they want to, not because they've been told to do it. Being a porn star is just one kind of acting. Being in a Fairy Liquid commercial is another kind. You're still acting in a peculiar way. The *Kane* style of thing doesn't appeal to me, but I don't want to knock anyone else's fantasy. If you have a fantasy about naughty headmasters, naughty schoolgirls, that in itself is not sexist

293

and it's not oppressive to anyone. It's how you treat people, really treat people, not what kind of fantasies you may have.

Some people say role-playing or S/M is wrong because it's a power imbalance. I'd dispute that; I'd say it was people doing what they enjoy and as such it can be a very equal thing. It's just the actual act you're doing that may appear unequal to people who don't understand it.

If you see S/M as a logical extension of power over another, you don't understand what it's about. S/M relationships can be some of the most equal and loving relationships. As a fashion it's like punk. Punk was considered very aggressive, but if you were involved in it there wasn't a great deal of violence there at all. It wasn't like skinhead culture. It just appeared to be aggressive and people were frightened of people with safety pins through their faces. But they didn't put safety pins through other people's faces very much.

The *Skin Two* type of thing has made S/M very fashionable. It's a subculture that's moved out into mainstream culture. S/M can go into mainstream just because you're wearing something. Most people think leather jackets look good. So it has a very, very wide appeal. The S/M look is generally appealing, even to people who aren't the least bit interested in having that kind of dynamic between people in sex. It's just exciting to look like that and it's sexy.

ARNOLD LINCOLN: I believe you've got to educate. You can't say what's going to happen, but you have to put the ambulance service into gear, just in case there are casualties. So leather, S/M may be the next development. There'll be a lot of casualties and the medico-psychiatric services should be on hand. S/M is very English, because it is heavy work. Being bashed by your nanny doesn't come into it. It's working-class S/M attitudes. S/M will percolate through to the happy middle-class couple. Now they have these counselling programmes on radio, which are quite amazing to me. People are now looking into other areas of themselves, to learn about themselves. They might find there's a little bit of S/M in their lives. There's emotional S/M going on all the time. Look at Mrs Thatcher – verbal S/M. She was a bully. With the Cabinet as slaves. The cartoonists saw this. Now it's permeating society in a sexualised way.

IAN JACKSON: The implication with S/M is that it's one step away from paedophilia and rape. But fetish clubs are non-aggressive. It's very chummy, a friendly atmosphere. Most of these things are. They can look formidable in their leather, etc., and when they're seen in a

294

full leather face mask, people start thinking, 'Oh-oh, is that guy snooping in my back garden?'

TED POLHEMUS: S/M clubs are getting bigger and bigger. They now represent *the* main thing happening in London night life. More important is the area of fetish fashion. There's hardly a designer working today – and I'm not just talking about the Kim Wests, Jean Paul Gaultiers – right up to St Laurent, who is not utilising the symbolism of fetishism. There's hardly an advert on TV either. There was one recently for tights, a tiny ad, beautifully shot. We see in close-up this girl in stockings, suspenders, very fine silk lingerie. We see the female hand, leg adjusting the stockings. Then in some very, very rapid shots we are introduced to the completely contrary symbolism of the high chunky leather boots with metal on them, the leather jacket besmeared with studs, sharp pointed hard fetishistic symbolism.

***

TIM WOODWARD: Gay S/M is often thought of by straights as being very much more aggressive, promiscuous, and there is that element in it. Gays would point out though that there are tons who are not like that at all. You see the primping queen with the little moustache and tartan shirt, tight jeans. You think that's all there is. It's the tip of the iceberg. The gay S/M club scene is very hard-edged. But there are plenty of gay S/Ms who are bank managers, wear cardigans, sandals, wash their cars on Sunday.

GUY SALMON: With gay S/M we are talking about real pain. I've been to Der Putsch, which is a straight S/M club and I've been to a Skin Two party and it was all great fun but it does seem to me to be dressing up, dressing up in a lot of leather and rubber. It's essentially suburban. I went to Der Putsch with a group of dykes and some gay boys and we all found it very suburban. The thing I most got off on in a way was the fact that they were probably all bank clerks from Croydon. I found that very exciting, because whatever they were, here they were liberated. I found that quite cheering. I thought: My God, these people are heterosexual, they are probably frightfully net-curtained and uptight in everyday life, but they are able to let go a little bit here. I think heterosexuals do let go within their marriages and relationships but they're just terrified of talking about it with anyone else, of admitting that they like bondage or whatever.

I like S/M. I find it very cleansing and purifying. You feel so wonderful after it. You feel somehow purged. I got into it this way. I had this relationship with Stephen, who was sort of like my mother's dream boyfriend for me. Met him at Durham, nice family, good A levels, he came home a lot. Very sweet and so on. And he just drove me up the fucking wall. But I left Durham and Stephen was still up there finishing his degree. And I had been very good and faithful until one night I went to Heaven and met this guy. He wanted to go home with me, but I wouldn't and he was pissed off and he gave me his number. I agonised over whether I should phone it and eventually I did. So we had dinner. But still I wouldn't sleep with him because of Stephen – this is how moral I was and how virtuous – but then I did see him again and this time I did sleep with him and he was very dominant in bed, very, very dominant in bed and I really liked it. With Stephen I had to be dominant because if I hadn't been nothing would have happened. We'd have just lain there. But with this new guy it was very different. The way he handled me, the way he was in every way. So I found this a complete change. Stephen wanted sex to be like a Laura Ashley catalogue, he wanted it to be really nice and fluffy and lovely and romantic. I liked it, but in the end it's that thing: is sex dirty? Yes, if it's any good. Then along came Peter.

We had sex and it was nice, it was really nice and I wanted it again and Stephen was doing his finals and he was miles away. The next time I had sex with Peter we had a full-scale S/M scene. Hot candlewax on the nipples and the cock. I was tied up. God knows what. It's pain, yes, but it's nice pain. This was the first time I realised that there could be nice pain. Peter just totally opened my eyes to a whole new world. I will qualify this, however. When I was at Durham, I was about twenty, and a friend came back from a holiday in Los Angeles. And he brought back a gay S/M novel. So we all read it and everyone was horrified – it was very extreme, real American Tom of Finland bondage, branding, fist-fucking, all that stuff. They're all saying, 'This is the most disgusting thing I've ever read.' But I read it and was really turned on by it. So I was aware that there possibly was more to sex. So when Peter started doing all these things to me I just loved it. I would see him two or three times a week and we would have these very stylised S/M scenes. Stylised violence, stylised beating up, stylised pain. I liked that side of it. And you are allowed to come – at the end.

I love baroque opera because it's so stylised – it's the same sort of thing with S/M sex: it's dressing up, it's controlled, it's an outlet for fantasy, it's an outlet for pain, but it's within limits and it's safe. I was Peter's slave, all that. Quite a lot of pain. He did beat me quite hard.
296

But you are allowed to say stop and he would stop. There was one hilarious moment when we were drinking red wine and I was blindfolded and tied up, my hands behind my back, standing up, and he just dribbled red wine over me and that was really nice – it was really cold – and he took the blindfold off and he said, 'Oh, it looks like blood. I just said, 'Peter, don't even think about it' and he said, 'It's okay.' But my friend Tom literally wants Sabatier knives, the lot. He's got scars over his nipples, all over him, where his boyfriend – this psychotic skinhead boyfriend – cuts him up. He took his shirt off one day and I just thought: My God. You can get into this sort of thing with pickups, if you go to the right kind of bar, a leather bar like Back Street. Of course you don't know whether you can trust the guy, you really don't, but that in itself has its own frisson. That said, I'd never be tied up with anyone on the first date. Then again I went out with Anthony, who is the love of my life, for two years, and I'd never ever let him tie me up. I knew how mad he was sexually and I wouldn't trust him. One time he was fucking me and it was first thing in the morning which is my worst time for sex – I never feel randy first thing in the morning – and there was no foreplay, he just started screwing me, and it was really hurting. I was saying, 'Get off me, stop, I don't want this, I want a cup of coffee and a cigarette, I do not want this.' He just wouldn't stop. He said, 'Is it hurting?' I said, 'Yes.' 'How much?' 'A lot.' And he said, 'I really like that.' And he was fucking me and saying this, 'I really like the fact that it's hurting you and you're suffering pain because of me fucking you.' And when he stopped I just went mental. I hit him and went completely berserk. I said, 'Don't ever try that again!'

I can be dominant too. One time I met this little boy Martin in The Block, which was in King's Cross, the City Pub in King's Cross. It's closed now, all gone. It was very, very wild there, absolutely fab; this was the summer of '89. I was wearing all my rubber stuff – cycling shorts, rubber vest, rubber jacket, leather jacket over that, boots – standing in this bar one Saturday night. And this boy, little Martin, turns up. Looking so sweet and innocent and I just thought: What on earth is he doing in a place like this? This is a place for hardened sexual deviants and this cute-looking little student – at that stage he was at Imperial College, he's now a civil servant – he came in. He just followed me around all evening and then came and sat next to me. So I said, 'What's a boy like you doing in a place like this? Have you come looking for some wild sexual time?' He said, 'Well, yes. I have.' He'd only had one boyfriend and they'd broken up. So we had an S/M relationship but this time I was dominant, and very sadistic. It was brilliant. He just wanted to do everything, so I did all the things that
297

Peter had done to me – and more – because he was marginally less of a baby than me and could take more pain. I really enjoyed that too. Being sadistic – but in a nice caring, sharing way! It is shocking. It does shock you when you first start doing these things, the fact that you can get off on them. But these days I just think: Accept it. You're not a monster. The fact that you have these things within you, you're not a monster. Everybody has them within them, but we're brought up to believe that we don't. And we're brought up to believe that sex should be this wonderful, spiritual and edifying experience because Christianity has tried to Jesus-ise sex. And you can't. They're completely incompatible and it just doesn't wash. Jesus didn't think it washed and he didn't say anything about it. It's the Church since. St Paul, Augustine, Jerome, Origen, all the Church fathers with their neurotic obsessions – they've tried to make it something that it isn't. That's what we all suffer from still. It's 2,000 years later but we're still suffering from it.

So much of one's sexuality is dodgy. But for most people what happens is that they open up the box and it's all too frightening and it's all too nasty and they just close it back up again as quickly as possible. But I don't think that's a healthy way of dealing with it. People do have these nasty things within them but they're all part of being a human being. When I started my first S/M relationship I felt: What is wrong with me, is there something wrong with me? Why do I want this, why is it turning me on, it's sick, it's dreadful. Then I realised that it wasn't sick, that it was between two consenting adults in private and it was fine. But this isn't the same as saying, 'Go on, do whatever you want, including child abuse.' Because the point about this box of delights is that sex has to be mutually rewarding. It has to be a mutual thing. For me the idea of sex with a child is abhorrent, because the idea of the exploitation of power, of manipulating someone who is weaker and more vulnerable and who doesn't know what is going on is disgusting. When I engage in S/M games, then I've chosen to do it, I know the score, I'm of an age of reason, I am capable of saying that this is what I want. Children who are abused are not. For me the death penalty for child abuse is too kind. If people are paedophiles and their only sexual outlet is children, then they have to be castrated to stop that desire.

MICHAEL VERMEULEN: Just for the hell of it I went to the Hell Fire club in NY. It's the most famous of the American S/M clubs. There's always a gay edge to those clubs. You'd get guys crawling on the floor, being pissed on, having their faces pushed by the heel of a boot. There were stanchions where people would do sex acts with everyone
298

watching them. You'd have sixteen people watching a transsexual giving a blow-job to a guy, some of the observers wanking off. There was very little fucking. But if you're fucking you are watched.

***

TED POLHEMUS: So, for one reason or other, you want to keep excitement going on within your relationship. What are the means by which you could accomplish this? One is dressing up, which always has a role-playing dimension. Even if she's dressing up in French lingerie – a fairly straight thing to be dressing up in – there is the symbolism of the mistress. And if we're talking about leather and rubber and uniforms and PVC, then we're talking about people applying symbolism to their body and to their sexuality. We're also talking about at least some mild versions of S/M, bondage, a whole host of things that can be tried out. These are all things that you don't do in a promiscuous pickup situation. He's dressed up in leather, she in rubber, they've got all the bondage equipment, the dungeon in the spare room, they've got the cat-of-nine-tails etc. The objective is to achieve some sort of experience which is not normally open to them.

In all the years I've been going to these clubs in London, I don't think that I've ever seen anybody pick up anyone else. I don't think it happens. What you have is couples coming together, bringing into a public or semi-public context the kind of game-playing that has probably gone on throughout history in the privacy of people's bedrooms, but there's this exhibitionistic element. You're playing it out in front of other people. There's a voyeuristic element too. So I'm suggesting the second sexual revolution has been about finding ways of maintaining sexual excitement within the context of a stable relationship. It fits fine in terms of a world with the shadow of AIDS falling over it. But I believe it would also fit fine in a world that had come to recognise that the first sexual revolution really wasn't going anywhere.

HAZEL SLAVIN: We don't have a clear notion of how people's sexuality becomes defined. We don't have a clear notion at all. Gail Ruben has written this essay called 'Thinking Sex'. And what she says is that it's time to think about sex: I'm not going to do it, I'm going to think about it. Her theory she calls the charmed circle. On the inner rim of the circle are all the socially accepted mores: people of the same age, straight sex, for love, not for the disabled – all the things we think of as normal. Then there's the outer rim, which is the opposite:

inter-generational, same-sex, cross-race, etc. She looks at each of these. The more I talk about sex to people, the more I realise how various people's experience and needs are. So you won't meet another man in this street who dresses in leather in Epping Forest with his two women, etc. But what you will meet in this street is a variety of male fantasy – not necessarily practice; a variety of practice; a variety of female fantasy and practice and nobody does it like you do it, basically. The edges are the same, the fill-in is different. That's what's so extraordinary.

ARTHUR BANNER: I do have a bit of a penchant for the spanking industry and its magazines. Partly because of its comedy – those magazines are incredibly comic, there is a quality in them of being written, and the photographs taken seem to have been taken as if it were 1950 or even earlier. Not just the dressing up but the dialogue, everything about them. Despite the fact that they represent what most people see as the perverted or harder edge of the pornographic market, in tone they have an incredible softness to them. It may be true that spanking is the British version of real S/M, but if you read the magazines closely they are probably the most into humiliation of the female body of any pornographic magazines. The situations they contrive to put the female body into are much more humiliating than anything you'll see in a hardcore pornographic magazine.

LINZI DREW: There's a big difference between spanking and bondage. Schoolgirlie stuff over the desk, maybe, but not real S/M. The thing is people do like being locked in cupboards for three hours and all that – the feeling of helplessness. I did a little film with Harrison Marks. I was a traffic warden and a taxi driver spanked me. It was the only time when I've been spanked that it went past the pain barrier and it felt quite nice. Something I wouldn't want to do again, though – especially if you're a model, it's no use having a red bottom for three days. Then Harrison Marks asked me if I'd do a film – *Madame Monique* – as a dominatrix. So I said fine. I had to do all the caning and spanking and all the people I had to spank or cane were really into it. I found that quite weird. I quite liked dressing up in all the sexy PVC stuff and strutting around and all this, but actually hitting these people... There was another girl there, she worked in one of these sex clubs – the rip off clubs, 'Give me fifty quid and I'll meet you round the corner and give you a hand-job,' and then you run off with the money. So she was quite a tough cookie and we had to spank this guy. She was hitting hell out of him. I didn't like it at all. 'Haven't you run
300

my bath water properly?' Slap! My boyfriend said it sounds just like me nagging.

JOHN LANKIEWICZ: There are all sorts of theories that connect, let's say, shoe fetishism with early learning. If you talk to someone like Graham Wilson, he's a professor at the Maudsley Institute of Psychiatry, a pyschologist, and he has theories that are interesting but a bit fatuous, I think, about how if a baby is having his nappy changed, having plastic pants put on, or he's got some kind of a rubber sheet underneath his bed sheet, and he has awareness of that while he just happens by chance to be having erections – as babies do have erections – the two become linked. I don't believe it. There are a lot of rubber freaks, but there'd be a lot more terry towel freaks than there are if that was the case. Or cot freaks, or bootee freaks. With the shoe fetishist, it's almost invariably the high heel, stiletto shoe. There are explanations given. One is: Mummy, while doing the housework, might well have been wearing patent-leather six-inch stiletto heels. Little Jimmy is crawling along the floor at the age of eight months, and Mummy walks by with the Hoover and her spiky heels. Then there's a link. So why don't you get Hoover fetishists, rug fetishists, breadcrumb fetishists? Another theory is the triangle shape the shoe makes is somehow reminiscent of the pubic hair region of a woman.

TED POLHEMUS: The history of fashion since the Renaissance has been one of dipping into and out of fetishism. Fetishism is a museum of fashion. The true fetishist finds something that is a fashion in his or her youth and gets stuck on it. And that's probably true for sexual predilections too, though you should talk to a psychiatrist about that. If we look at the true fetishist – which some psychiatrists maintain are only male, but that's another story – it's true there's this museum like quality to it. So all the men in their fifties/sixties who are interested in rubber macs grew up at a time when rubber macs were a fashion item. This group is very small. We're getting to almost homeopathic limits here. The homeopath says the fewer drops in the overall solution the more power in the thing. I think this has become a primary symbolic meaning system, fetishism. There are few things we're capable of expressing without using a fetishist or S/M iconography any more. You could cite lots of reasons for this, but the first one is the failure of the quantitative first sexual revolution. The second is the introduction of herpes then AIDS, suggesting the logic of monogamy. And the third factor is the general spiritual malaise of our society as a whole with the obvious recognition that fetishism is something that,

301

in a world of muzak and symbols stripped of their power by advertising, by media etc, still has some symbolic efficacy. In a way it's the only thing that has power any more. Certainly the only thing that has a sexual power.

We're not just talking about people of my generation who lived through the Sixties' sexual revolution then got bored with it. If you look at *Top of the Pops*, or *Dance Energy*, *The Chart Show*, you'll see that every other video – maybe every video – and every pop performer short of Cliff Richard is out there in some sort of an outfit which has a meaning which is rooted in fetishism.

The young teenagers pick up on that, and it flavours everybody's life. In many ways they pick up on it more than we do, because we have other vocabularies to draw upon. The thirteen-year-old sees Kylie Minogue in a PVC cat suit, sees every single one of their pop performers dressed this way. There seem to be eras of kinkiness and there's no question this is one. There seems to be a cultural intercourse between natural healthiness on one hand and perverse artifice on the other. These cycles have gone on as long as there's been fashion change, basically since the Renaissance. The only difference is that in the last few decades the speed of these cycles has changed incredibly.

***

ELLEN SEVERIN

'Kiss the boots...'

Dressed from head to toe in stygian black she could, for those that way inclined, stand muster as a pretty fair stern mistress. Low on overt leather, and there's no actual whip, but the menace could be exciting. The interviewer, disinclined, edges away along the sofa at tales of such literal carnality. Though, some might suggest, isn't it all less of a blood wedding and rather more a revenger's tragedy?

I'm now a haggard bimbette of twenty-eight, but I used to be considered a most fantastically sexy woman. That was the first thing people used to notice about me. I wasn't in fact having a lot of sex – in college, at work – but I still have this persona of the femme fatale, of being filthy. Which I think is because I swear a lot and I talk about sex. Indeed, although I've never had sex with anyone at my job, I'm still credited with having fucked my way ten times around the boardroom table. Anyone and everyone of importance. I'm not a
302

particularly sexy woman, but that's the image. My ankles have a fetishistic reputation; I've had them measured on many occasions. A gay boy nearly married me on the basis of my ankles.

Once I'd lost my virginity and got rid of the first man I slept with I had various other unsatisfactory experiences with other guys in college; not an immense lot. I went to bed with quite a lot but to be honest I can't remember the ones I fucked, the ones I only sucked off and the ones I just slept with. Just a lot of Ruperty boys. Just experimenting. Most of them were unsatisfactory. But I did think I ought to have a boyfriend – most people at college had paired off. So it was my duty to try it on with various presentable young men of my set. Which I did. I didn't really like any of them. Then, in my third year, I did find one I did like, and I've fucked him on and off ever since. He's a don now. He was very, very good at sex.

Since the first person I went to bed with invested me with a lot of experience I didn't have, I just decided to live up to that. I very quickly picked up the things that boys liked and would do them. Blow-jobs, fancy fingering, various carrying on – as opposed to just lying there and thinking of England. They liked you to do things, a lot of wriggling around. I worked out what passed among undergraduates as being 'good at sex' and quickly learned it; it's not very difficult to learn.

I suddenly went from being this blushing schoolroom violet to being this world-weary woman. So for a while I found myself one of the women whom everyone chased. Which was not that hard. Most of the women were so geeky and awful and wore anoraks and college scarves, so the very small number of women who dressed attractively, flirted and generally knew how to deal with men stood out. I very quickly learnt. It was as much an intellectual exercise as anything else. I constructed this persona – the sexy attractive woman – almost overnight. It took a lot of being pursued by all these Ruperty boys and having a lot of flowery declarations made to me. But once I'd realised that I could do this then it became the best game ever. I started off not believing that these people were attracted to me, but once I accepted that yes, they were, I thought: This is wonderful. The first two years I worked very hard and did very, very well academically but for the third year I was just this total party animal. It was an irresistibly wonderful game. I'd always wanted to be a pretty, popular girl at school and now I was. I did think they were fools to be taken in, but that didn't stop me taking them in. I didn't even fuck a lot of them. The standards were so low, it really wasn't very difficult to be admired by a lot of people you didn't even know.

I liked having sex with this man I picked up in my third year. It was quite S/M-ish actually. This became the leitmotif of my later sexual career. Not so much bondage or whips, but a lot of biting, and quite fiendish sexual violence. Later I became a real vampirette. I like blood immensely but I got my teeth fixed and my canines aren't quite as sharp as they used to be. I used to do very painful things to him all the time, which seemed to be what he liked. Too fiendish to describe but he really did enjoy it. Violence. He liked to be abused, to be made to feel like dirt and to be hurt by me. He wanted a stern mistress and I played the role. Basically beating up and genital torture. I picked him up at a Commemoration Feast in college and it was immediately, 'Hit me, spank me!' spookiness. We were both at High Table and he made eyes at me all evening and then we went off to the Dean's party. At some stage I put my hands into his trouser pockets and started fondling him, at which point his tutor was watching and when he went off to the loo or whatever this tutor leaned over and suggested that if Mr X couldn't oblige me, then he certainly would. He'd won a lot of prizes for academic things and when we were leaving the tutor called after us that he'd get a college prize for this. So he asked, 'Is it for ordeal or effort?' to which the tutor replied, 'Ordeal'. We fell into this scenario whereby I ignored him in public, never introduced him to my friends, then turned up at midnight and was fiendish. This went on for years.

I really enjoyed it. I enjoyed the power very much; I just thought: Fuck you you bastards, now I've got you where I want. There was a problem when he fell in love with me: he thought we were having a relationship whereas I just thought we were having a lot of dirty sex. I'm not really promiscuous by nature. To be quite honest I don't get a lot of physical pleasure out of sex, but I did get a lot of naughty, intellectual pleasure out of this idea of picking up someone, snapping my fingers and being able to have who I liked.

I think I've become almost asexual now. I've had loads of friends I'm very fond of but would never go to bed with. No doubt because I think sex isn't sex unless it's dirty and if it's all cosy and loving it's not sexy. I just can't fancy people in that way. Though I would be too frightened to have sex with absolute strangers who dragged me into an alleyway – I'd be far too scared of being cut to bits. What I like is a situation where you don't know the person socially and they're not part of your daily life, where you go to a party, pick up a good-looking guy, take them home and fuck them. You don't really know him, he isn't part of your circle, but you also know he's not some kind of serial killer.

I've rarely had sex I enjoyed with men. I've only come with one man, and with my one serious woman lover, who I still see. Lesbian sex is better than heterosexual sex. I come with women. Most men haven't the slightest idea of what to do in bed with a woman. At the same time I started having the S/M affair with this boy, I started having an affair with this woman. They were the two best classicists the university had had in about fifty years – I had the pair of them and I thought that was pretty cool. She was adorable and I still adore her. Initially she made a pass at me and I didn't understand what the devil she was on about. She'd had a lesbian relationship, I never had. It always seemed such a waste of time: why get into what's supposed to be a gay thing when all that happens is you act out heterosexual roles? The same thing about dildos: why go to bed with a woman if you want a cock. Tongues and fingers are enough. Otherwise you can always get a man. I can see no point in re-enacting heterosexual rituals with a woman. For me having sex with a woman is another ballgame.

She was easily the cleverest woman in our year, fantastically beautiful. She invited me to supper and we all got very drunk and she said, 'Why don't you stay the night?' I said, 'Where will I sleep?' and she said, 'Why don't you sleep with me?' The penny didn't drop. It hadn't entered my head that this could possibly be on her agenda and I got very embarrassed – 'I couldn't possibly,' etc., etc. 'This is silly, I'll go home.' That was at the end of my second Easter term. Then what happened was something out of a pulp novel. We came back for the summer term and what all the girls talked about was getting their dresses for the end of summer balls. So we were talking about our dresses and she looked at mine and said, 'Oh, what are you going to wear under that?' I showed her this wonderful pink corset I had. She asked to try it on. She took off her clothes and tried it on and then suggested that I should try it on – my breasts were bigger than hers, it didn't fit her properly, and so on – so I took off my clothes and put it on, and then she started kissing me and then we ended up in bed and that was wonderful. We continued going to bed together for the rest of our university careers. As we do now when we meet.

It was physically much more satisfactory than with men. None of that 'do you love me' or jealousy. I think it's physically better because you each understand a woman's body better than a man does. That said I still basically fancy men and I wouldn't want to lead a totally lesbian lifestyle. But what was good was the lack of emotional weight, of jealousy, discussing it afterwards or whatever. No games at all – just a physical diversion that we both enjoyed. It wasn't discussed, it wasn't the main focal point of our friendship and it was all quite lovely. But in the end I've had too straight an upbringing to feel that I want a lesbian relationship for the rest of my life. I think it was only possible, on this absolute physical level, because basically we were both

305

straight. Though it has amused me that the relationship has proved far more durable than those of many supposedly committed lesbian couples. It was just a charming recreation which we've enjoyed whenever we've had the chance.

I haven't done what I'd call anything really weird sexually. I suppose drinking blood was the weirdest thing. What I like to do is make people consent to things which they don't want to consent to. It's not a matter of launching non-consensual assaults on people – that's tedious – it's making them consent to something that they wouldn't otherwise consent to because your power over them is so immense. I had a relationship with one man in Dublin to whom I was just fiendish, he was my total emotional and sexual slave. I treated him abominably. That's when I got a taste for blood, and I used to drink his blood the entire time. He sort of hated it but always went along with it.

I did use to be a great devotee of Sade. I worked as an au pair in Lausanne for a while and terrified the staff of this local bookshop by making my way through the volumes of Sade they had on their shelves and then coming back and asking for more. They were practically handing them to me with tongs by the end. The thing about blood was that I just found it tremendously erotic. I used to draw blood mainly with my teeth, but I also used to make little holes in various boyfriends of mine with scalpels and stitch-cutters. They also made little holes in me. From which we'd both drink the other's blood. I don't know where this all came from, and I don't think I'd want to do it now. I was very depressed, very sick, very wretched at the time. These sexual things seemed to be exciting and interesting at the time but now I've done them I don't want to do them again. But I did have a very twisted sexual upbringing and I was brought up to think of sex as filthy and deviant and unmentionable and dreadful. Also it did occur to me that blood was too AIDS-y, and that was another reason to stop. But I had to get rid of that guy, he was just too wet, too subservient. The whole relationship was sick, I was keeping this dog and doing nothing but beat it. I just thought: This is sick. The fact that he lets me do it is no excuse and this has to stop. So I stopped it. He wrote me a dreadful letter at the end: he thought everything was fine, that it was all totally vanilla, that we were going to be married and that maybe I had slightly unconventional tastes. This was 1988, the last time I drew blood and drank it. But I just gave it up, I decided that this was not a road that should be followed. He went on to become a Senator in the Irish Parliament.

I do tend to despise a lot of the men I fuck. I've felt that way for quite a long time. What I want most out of men is that they are very

306

clever. My don gave me that, but with the others it was power, the idea of being able to reduce people to such a state of thralldom was absolutely intoxicating to me. It was simply wonderful. But this was the idea that counted, rather than any physical sensations of bliss. The idea that I could do whatever the devil I liked and they would accept it. That was quite wonderful for a number of years – but then I did decide it was sick. I thought I was turning into a seriously twisted, sick, weird, sadistic woman. I did hate men very much, I'd had this twisted upbringing, and I just wanted to have power over them.

I use sex as a currency now. Most of the men I've been to bed with, the sex was physically unsatisfactory and boring. This is something I've got from my parents: sex is a currency that women have to trade with men for economic favours. I've never come across a situation with a man that has caused me to feel otherwise. Maybe one or two, but the relationships didn't last. I never let them know how I feel. How I despise them and just use them – maybe they have a nice flat to live in, whatever. Never. I feel sorry for them. I do know that I've fucked up the lives of three or four men quite seriously. I did use to be a tremendously bitter and venomous and vengeful woman. It's revenge. I don't know quite what for – maybe it's just the generic female revenge of women on men for being totally insensitive and not knowing what to do in bed and just proving to be such unsophisticated organisms. Why aren't they better? I've very rarely met anyone that I really felt was my equal. I felt that most of them have been much more stupid than me, in very significant respects. Emotionally less sophisticated, and less aware of what goes on. And I've never met anyone who could outfox me. I've been dumped by two guys, but no others. I've only ever been kicked out of bed once, in a one-night stand. I give them good sex, or at least I act good sex. It's porn, basically that's all it is. It doesn't connect to anything else, you just go through the show.

I love blow-jobs. They do live up to the advertising. They do what it is said they will do. The man will then eat out of your hand, because he'll be so delighted and grateful. There're people I'd suck off whom I wouldn't kiss. It just seems like nothing to me. It doesn't matter at all. Last Christmas I sucked off this unbelievably awful person at work. Not really a celebrity, though most people would know who he is. I thought I was punishing him, but he didn't see it that way at all. It was really annoying me. We were in the bar there and we were quite drunk and he was going on and on and on about his marriage and his divorce and how miserable his sex life was and how his cock was small. I thought: Right I've had enough of this, and if he thinks this is a bluff I won't call he's wrong. So I said, 'Right, honey, show me your cock.

307

I've had enough of this, how small can it fucking be?' So he freaked out: 'No, no, no. I can't possibly, it's too small, you'll burst out laughing.' 'I insist on it, come with me now, into your dressing-room, you're going to show it to me.'

So I bullied him for a long, long time and he was very unhappy, as if he were being dragged to the electric chair. I was just annoyed. I think he thought he was being sexually intimidating, as if this whole line was in some way shocking to me. So I dragged him off into a dressing-room and I just wished that the *News of the World* could have been there. 'I can't, I can't. Oh you'll laugh, it's too small...' I said, 'For heaven's sake, will you get your flies down, how small can it be, for God's sake? If you won't then I'll do it for you.' This whole bickering match went on for ages. Just when I managed to get his trousers off he thought someone had followed us in. So I said, 'Yes, I did see someone come in, I thought it must be some friend of yours.' At which he totally freaked out and pulled up his trousers again and rearranged himself and hunted through this whole dressing-room complex and couldn't find anyone and eventually came back. And eventually I got his trousers off again and eventually produced his cock. I thought it was all right, I couldn't understand why he'd made this bloody song and dance about it. It was fine, quite nice really.

Then somehow or another – and I don't know how I conceived of this – but I decided to put him in his place: 'You think you're embarrassing me, you think this is intimidating to me, okay,' so I sucked him off. At which point we had this second-person mon-ologue, like some kind of pornographic script, while I did it, which was pretty disgusting. Once we'd finished I was tremendously nasty and breezy about the whole thing: 'I always find the aftermath of these things so tedious, I'll just get my bag and go.' And I fucked off. I think he thought this was the beginning of a great romance. I've had ongoing problems with him ever since. Inviting me out to dinner, trying to get me to suck his cock again. Fiendish. I don't know what got into me. I was extremely drunk, maybe fifteen Pernods, but what I was trying to do was show him that I was a cool ballsy woman who could not be intimidated and nothing mattered a damn to me and if he thought he was embarrassing me, then we'd see who was really going to be embarrassed – but of course he thought it was all a great treat.

★★★

GUY SALMON: I've had some very wild sex on acid. With lots of piss and putting bananas up each other's bottoms and all sorts of things.

The first time I experienced piss in sex was with Peter and he just said, 'Kneel down,' and I knelt down and he started pissing on my chest. I actually said, 'What are you doing!?' and he said, 'I'm pissing on you.' Which was rather funny. I just loved it. Golden showers are great. I love pissing on and being pissed on. The first time it was partly because it was with Peter and it was his piss and the humiliation and all that. But now I enjoy it and I do quite enjoy drinking it. I wouldn't have pissed on Peter, that certainly wasn't part of the scenario, but with David it was completely mutual, we just pissed all over each other. Now if I have a sexual encounter and there is no water sports, no piss, then I feel slightly cheated. Though I did make a ghastly mistake recently when I was on E and I just assumed, I was right off my head and I thought well, you're into piss, everyone's into piss, and I said to this guy I picked up, 'Oh, are you into piss then?' in this very casual tone and he was clearly completely mortified. I couldn't believe it. The thought had never crossed his mind and he said, 'Well, I haven't really ever tried it,' and I was thinking, 'Oh God, Guy, what have you done?' Nor did I say, 'Well now's your chance.' He just completely threw me.

I'm not into scat. Shit. Some people are, but I've always termed scat 'the final frontier', the last taboo of one's sexuality. This great wall that maybe one day will be broken down, but I cannot really foresee it. The idea of someone shitting on me is not very pleasant. But that's about the only thing I wouldn't do. That said I like rimming, I like licking men's arseholes. Rimming's like... it's just nice. Rimming's safe. It wasn't for a while. Rimming has been the great reappraisal. It's very funny because in the first safe sex guidelines that came out in 1985 from the Terrence Higgins Trust rimming was high-risk, it was as high-risk as fucking and I can remember Anthony saying, 'Oh, God, it's my favourite thing and it's high-risk,' and being terribly bereft. But it's low-risk now.

I do want to get my nipple pierced. I slept with this guy who had a pierced dick and I was really intrigued by it. He fucked me but you can't feel a thing. It's all round edges. I was thinking, 'Will it break the condom, will I feel it?' Nothing at all. The condom goes over it, it's smooth, you can't feel a thing. He said it intensified his orgasm by about 150 times. Changed his life. He had also had his nipples pierced. He was standing with his shirt off in this club and I could see that he had his nipples pierced and thought: Oh, yes, and then he said that his dick was pierced and immediately I just wanted to see it, to see what it looked like. Though it wasn't a very nice dick, not very nice to look at. The rod goes through the top.

LYN PROCTOR: A lot of current sexual experimentation is trying things out. They're not completely convinced it's for them but with S/M, rubber and things you can do that. Why not go down to Skin Two, buy ourselves a fun outfit, you can be the slave this week...let's go and play. The difference with tattooing and piercing and these other forms of permanent body decoration is, although with the piercings you take them out, it's not something that people can take on lightly. There are the taboos against pain – the possibility of pain is very sensibly one that they shy away from – and it takes a real desire, a real interest in piercing or tattooing in itself. With tattooing it is permanent, there's no turning back. With piercing you have to find someone to do it, which is not easy, and there is for most people the feeling that this is going to hurt.

The various forms of permanent body decoration are not really unusual and if you consider that throughout the world most societies indulge in some form of permanent body decoration – tattooing and body piercing are the norm rather than the exception in certain cultures – so in that context it's not strange, it's not weird and it's not bizarre, as most people in our society originally felt themselves to be.

There are two different elements in piercing. There's the element that people can actually see: which is facial piercing. And the rest of your body which is hidden under clothes. Unlike tattooing, which you do see when people are working or on the beach, in general piercing is done in places that people keep very private. Unless it's facial. And as with tattooing any form of facial decoration is considered to be very anti-social and unacceptable. The reason for this is that your face is your public face and as such is public property. People get very, very outraged if people decorate their faces in unacceptable ways. Even down to the level of elderly ladies who put on very heavy makeup in a messy fashion – this is considered to be very anti-social, very unacceptable. People may say that's unattractive – smeared lipstick, whatever – but how do we define attractive? In general attractive equals natural. So any form of body decoration that is declared to be unnatural is seen as unattractive.

Still, there is a remarkable desire by a lot of people to pierce their bodies. Even when they believed that they were the only person in the world who wanted to do it and were therefore really strange. After all it's not the kind of thing you can talk to people in the pub about. People are squeamish. A friend of mine who has her belly-button pierced told me that the first time she went out in public and people saw it, they would say, 'How could you, oh, how could you?' Then the second time people said, 'How's it going?' and the third time they said, 'Oh, can I get that done.' People start off by thinking: Oh my God,
310

how awful, I couldn't, then they think about it a bit and they say, 'Hang on a minute, what is the difference between doing it to your ear and doing it to your belly-button and then doing it to your nipples or whatever?'

The eroticism of body decoration works in that by decorating a part of the body you draw attention to it. So you ought to choose a part of your body that's attractive. Anyone, for instance, who gets their ankle tattooed and has bad ankles is going about things the wrong way. Someone who has an enormously fat belly is probably better off not getting their belly-button pierced.

Decorating your penis by putting a bolt through the glans is about increased sensation. You feel through skin, and the piercing itself has nerve endings and sensations inside it which develop after it has healed over. Most people are very concerned about the initial pain of the piercing, but of course most piercing is actually done under anaesthetic. So as opposed to tattooing, there's actually a great deal less pain. What a lot of people use is a barbell, a completely, absolutely smooth object which is inserted, and which has nothing even resembling a sharp edge. People do get particularly outraged when they see ones that are notably large, but with a large surface area there's actually much less in the way of pulling. If you have something too thin you get a cheesewire effect.

Most of the people who have genital piercing do so because they find that they increase the level of sensation, and simply by increasing sensation and increasing the possibilities for sensation, combined with the fact that they have done so of their own volition, it's of their own choice, there is this pride in having increased your own sexuality. You've taken it out of the hands of nature, of what you were given, and taken it one bit further. It's like the pride people have when they customise their cars. By customising your body for your own purposes, to enhance your own pleasure, there is that pride of ownership, which is very, very strong in people who enjoy body decoration. But there are big taboos against most forms of permanent body decoration in our society, and what elicits the reactions of shock and horror are those taboos, which extend to people even thinking of doing it, rather than what has actually been done. People do think about the pain, they wonder: What would I feel like if someone did that to me? Yet nobody says that about circumcision. Which is effectively a mutilation and which has no medical justification, yet is enormously widespread. People don't look at a circumcised cock and say, 'Oooh!' You don't look down and think how wicked and dreadful. But in fact with most body modifications, the actual piercing takes a very short time compared with the amount of time that you benefit from what it gives you. And unlike tattoos, if you're not happy, you can just take it out. A piercing will normally heal over quite effectively without any problems.

My husband Henry first thought up our magazine *Body Art* in 1984 and the first issue appeared in 1987. It came in response to realisation that there were people interested in body decoration, very interested; but there was no magazine catering for them. Henry started off as a photographer who had lots of photographs on the subject and he thought that there ought to be a magazine, because he certainly wasn't getting his photographs published in any existing magazine, and since no one else was creating a suitable vehicle, he thought of creating his own. Then he noticed an ad in *Forum*, someone was starting a magazine for people interested in body piercing. He contacted them and it became clear that while the advertiser wanted to start a magazine, what they were really thinking of was more a fanzine for body-piercing fans, dealing mostly with the sexuality and not the glossy and sophisticated magazine that *Body Art* is. What Henry has done is put piercing in the context of body decoration in general.

Young, New Age people are very excited about body piercing. They see it as a cross between the punk and hippie aesthetics. It's also a way of being different and slightly outrageous, and every new alternative culture needs a way of being different, different in a way that their elders will look at it and go, 'Oh my God!' Body piercing works very well like that. Also there aren't very many people who do piercing. Some advertise in *Body Art*, but it's not easy to find someone. So there is this underground flavour. Then they find that as well as the shock factor, it has its own rewards. So you then find that people will not just stick at one body piercing, or one tattoo, but they will continue and have more. There's a definite level of addiction in tattooing. And with some people the same thing goes for piercing. People for whom it hits that chord will continue and have more.

People do wear their body jewelry at the office, wherever. Even if it's invisible. Because the body has remarkable abilities to heal itself and if you don't actually keep your piercing open, then the body will simply heal up. You have to keep your jewelry in all the time, and not take it in and out, particularly while it's healing, which is the best way to introduce infection. You have to keep it in all the time. There are a lot of people wandering around at the office and elsewhere with goodness knows what underneath their clothing. Which is, of course, one of the great attractions.

The complication of body piercing, which is true of tattooing, is that it goes through so many different social groups. It takes in every

312

age. As well as the young New Age people we have a lot of retired people who are very, very interested but who didn't get any form of piercing until after they had retired. I know two classic cases. One gentleman who was an ex-headmaster, another an ex-public-school housemaster. They both felt that before they retired the possibility of being caught in an accident and being zipped off to hospital was too dangerous; it would have ruined them, their social standing, and their family's life as well. This feeling that not only would revelation have been a blow not just to themselves but also to their family made them hold back. But they retire and the feeling changes: 'What am I waiting for and whose life is it anyway?' At that point people really go for it. They say, 'Why not?'

They're also people whose sex lives had become, perhaps, more theory than practice by then. One of them told me that his wife hadn't joined him in the bathroom for maybe twenty years, but after his piercing that changed. Whether it actually revives one's sex life, that's debatable, but on the level of his own auto-eroticism, of his pleasure in his own body, it certainly revived that. He's retired, he's not really expecting a lot of his physical sex life any more but he has found that the pleasure that piercings have given him in his own body has worked. Not so much through masturbation, but simply knowing it's there. The awareness as you walk down the street. Also the sheer physical sensation. Just as some people like wearing certain textures of clothing, sensuality is very important in piercing.

I had no personal interest in piercing or body decoration, although there was a theoretical interest, but Henry did. So because of that I became more interested and I have found that it works, in that the piercings do increase sensual pleasure. It's definitely worth it. I have clitoris and labia piercings; I did have nipple piercings too, but I took them out when my son was born. But piercings have very definitely been an erotic plus; it does work very well from that point of view. It does provide a great increase in sensation. But I don't find the auto-eroticism, the pleasure of simply having the piercings, is enough in and of itself. A lot of people do find that, and that they don't even require any sexual activity.

MATTHEW RUSSELL

'Doctor In Love'

A smart house in a downmarket street near Wandsworth Common. Typical of their class and generation he and his wife – their

sitting-room walls offer pictures of her in schoolgirl strip mixed with
their children's nursery-school daubs – are both veterans of
Narcotics Anonymous. Questioned, his friends divide sharply.
Some approve, taking proxy pleasures in his hands-on past; others
recoil, their hip stance shaken – 'a thoroughly bad lot'. On a single
meeting it's hard to tell. The tale is lurid but the teller is infinitely
charming, attractive and plausible. His bedside manner, now as
doubtless then, remains impeccable.

I'm thirty-nine years old and I trained as a doctor and went to Oxford
from 1970-73; qualified in 1976, practised medicine, went to New
York in 1979 and worked as doctor there doing neurology for three
years. What I am now is a totally, well, relatively respectable con-
sultant psychiatrist, having switched from medicine in 1984.

I suspect that the style of my sexuality was more to do with my
mother than my father. My father was wonderful; he was extremely
warm and a very good Christian chap, quite apart from his exciting
political side. Mother was a product of the English country
upper-middle class, corsetted, regular bowel habits, not horsey but
could have been. Four boys, no girls. Quite castrating of the boys,
idolising my father who was anyway seen as a godlike figure, a saint.
It must have something to do with that.

I left school, which was Eton, in 1969 and did a trip out to India. I
did the hippie trail, though I did it in a slightly different way to most
hippies. My father was involved with this Indian chap who had come
to London and founded the School of Non-Violence and he was going
back. He was an ex-Jain monk who'd walked round the world for
peace and various things like that. So I went back with him on a sort
of Gandhian peace mission and we drove out in a battered Ford
Cortina. It took three months and that's when I first encountered
hippies. By the end of my school career I had been aware of the whole
hippie thing, the way it linked music and sex and drugs. I had met the
music at Eton, I had met limited versions of the sex, though not quite
in the way that the hippies were on about, and I'd met the drugs.

I spent the next nine months in India, and ended up in Nepal. I
lived in a commune on the edge of Kathmandu valley to which we
used to issue passports: 'Loveland passports'. These Californian
chicks would fly in every month with several thousand microdots of
LSD. There were about fifty of us living there and a lot of people
passing through. This was the real hippie, free-love commune, oh
God yes. And this was my heterosexual loss of virginity. In fact it was
with the daughter of the CIA representative in the Nepalese embassy.
She was older, about nineteen, and I was seventeen. She used to hang

314

out with the hippies and the thing was that you had to get a taxi back and if you missed the last taxi you had to stay – there were wild dogs, things like that if you walked – and she missed the last taxi and I quite naively said, 'Oh, you can sleep in my room,' though I didn't mean anything more than that when I said it. So she came back and I began to realise through the clouds of cannabis that I was in the room with a girl! And we dutifully lay down and she took off her one-piece caftan which was all she was wearing and we did it. And it still is one of my most memorable sexual experiences.

I can picture the whole thing, this scene of lying down rather gauchely and suddenly thinking aged seventeen: This is it. I had been in India for nearly a year by then and had had frantic sexual yearnings but nothing had come of it and this was going to be it.All those things like you knew when they were ready by feeling if they were wet or not – I had acquired this information – and dutifully putting one's hand across and noticing wetness and thinking: Right, she's ready, then rolling over and there was this moment of pause before penetration, thinking again: This is it. And the moment of penetration was accompanied by a sort of gasp from the girl – 'Aahh' – and then pulling back for the next thrust, on which thrust I came. So there was the first 'Aaah' of penetration followed by another 'Aahh' then 'Uuhh-oh.' That was it. I'd lost my virginity. Later on we had a talk, and talked about the Pill and was it my first time and yes it was and so on. Then we did it again. Then we got up and started hanging out with everyone else. At which point her father appeared, this crew-cut US Marine CIA man. 'Jay, are you comin' home?' and she did.

Once I'd lost my virginity it was anybody and everybody in the commune for two or three months. There weren't orgies as such, but there were often couples who would be doing it in a rather public place. It was terribly uncool to comment or even notice. 'Yeah, man, they're getting it on, right...'

While I was at Oxford, where I went on my return to England, my sex life was restricted by the fact that I rather quickly linked up with the girl who would become my first wife. But I did have this visitation from three of the hippies who had been in Kathmandu. One was Dutch, one was Australian, and a girl who was Irish. They turned up in my rooms in Magdalen and we had this gangbang. Though this wasn't violent, just the fact that there were three men and one girl fucking consecutively and sometimes simultaneously and she was quite happy to oblige. I very proudly told everybody all about it and it gave me the nickname 'Gangbang'. Which meant that when I finally got married and was standing there in the line-up next to my ghastly

American mother-in-law and one friend came up and said, 'Hello Gangbang, well done.'

I got married in 1974, went to London to start hospital work, and that was how things stayed, albeit with a fair bit of fucking around on the side. Which related very much to the way I saw the sexual revolution as it was in the early 1970s: that I could go off and bonk anyone I liked. But she wasn't into that so what I did get up to was all fairly surreptitious. I do remember agonising over whether I should go down on her when she had her period, because that was what one was supposed to do. But in fact I didn't – which was my choice, all those public-school sensibilities.

Medical school on the whole was very unliberated. Though there were nurses. Oh God, the nurses! There was a *lot* of hospital sex. It is true – all those clichés about looking at horrible things all day and bonking all night. I was at St Stephen's, working two days on, one day off: far more of one's time was spent on call at the hospital than at home. Lots of nubile nurses, the authority of my white coat, the compliance of their uniform, yes doctor, no doctor, can't do anything unless the doctor says so – it's all a total set-up. St Stephen's was quite a lively place, a very good bar and rather classy girls. Radiographers were always good news, and some of the physiotherapists. Aussies. Everybody was doing it and the hospital used to shake. The standard things went on: the vignette of doing it with someone you've been longing to do it with and literally as you're about to come the cardiac arrest beep goes off and there's that terrible decision: a man's life or your orgasm. I regret to say that I felt, well, a few seconds aren't going to make too much difference. The other cliché being running at three a.m. to a cardiac arrest and trying to work out who there had just been on the job: the ice-cool anaesthetist who arrived in a state of considerable déshabillé and so on. It's *Doctor in the House* stuff – with me as Terry-Thomas.

Drugs certainly loosened people up for sex and the two very much went together. As the 1970s went on drugs became more and more common. Whereas Oxford had been for me cannabis, acid and Mandrax, London life led on to cocaine occasionally, to heroin for the first time. Though not through the hospital; it's a myth that it's easy to get hold of hard drugs. My sources were invariably illicit. Heroin by itself is not great for sex, but the mixture of heroin and cocaine was a very nice cocktail. But all I did was flirt with it, just the odd party, whatever.

In 1979 I went to New York, where I worked at the Bellevue Hospital. After about a year in New York our marriage was falling apart. We went for this weekend, Mick Jagger was a guest. He said,

316

'Matthew, you wanna go bus-stopping?' This was basically cruising by the bus-stops in your car and seeing someone you fancied and saying, 'You want a ride? I work in a band.' Which if you're with Mick Jagger is quite a successful line. And there were also this pair of punk sisters, half-American, half-Swiss, quite well off and they were into heroin. This was 1980. Heroin was still not really around; cocaine was there, but heroin was still a black or Puerto Rican drug. Anyway, these two girls pitched up for dinner and they were rather exciting and very beautiful and they took heroin. I then had one of my quickest fucks. One of the sisters, the elder one, and me, our eyes met across the table. There we all were having dinner and after dinner she and I decided to go for a swim, which we did and we did it. That was frightfully exciting, fucking on the lawn of this amazingly rich mansion, a frightfully well-known family. And my wife, who was still at the dinner table, was very possibly going to come down for a swim too. Which made it very exciting. Not that I saw myself as a stud in this situation, hardly a swordsman. My self-image is much more the little boy getting lucky. It's the candy store, and if you happen to be in Mick Jagger's candy store there's a lot that he isn't eating. These girls weren't his groupies, but he was there and this doubtless added to the feelings that might lead people to behave in ways that they mightn't have done normally. Anyway, I started an affair with this girl and very shortly afterwards left my wife to go and live with her in a loft in downtown New York.

So I moved from the upper East Side where I was living with my wife as a respectable married doctor to living in this punk loft on the lower West Side where they tie-dyed T-shirts and lived in squalor with dogs and a bath in the middle of the living room and so on. Meanwhile I'm going to Bellevue Hospital every day being a neurologist. I lasted in that loft a month or two until it became increasingly clear that I needed another apartment. I looked in the *Village Voice*, saw this ad and I rang up and arranged to meet at two o'clock, though somehow I interpreted two o'clock as two a.m. I rolled up to this wonderful, huge loft in the garment district and met Roy. It was still frightfully unfashionable, just off 42nd Street, and quite dangerous. He was an actor, and I asked him what he'd been in – *Godfather Part II* – and I thought, 'Great, this is the place to be, Al Pacino knocking on the door.' So I moved in. But when I got to know him I realised it wasn't quite like that. He *had* been in *Godfather Part II* but on his CV there were all these other titles which seemed quite familiar; I couldn't quite place them until I looked in the paper and of course they were porn flicks.

He was a porno actor and he and his girlfriend did live shows six times a night. Came every time. Just like the movies, the audience had to see the come, the money shot. He was well-known in the business – he could come on demand. The director would say, 'OK, Roy, thirty seconds,' and thirty seconds later he'd come. He was in his late thirties, and around twenty years earlier he'd been living in London with an NHS heroin script. Now he was very healthy, he'd given up drugs, and was into white meat and exercise. Very nice, very intelligent, extremely well-read. Quite un-American. He found me very intriguing. The first time I realised this was not a normal set-up was getting up one morning, going to brush my teeth prior to going to the hospital, and seeing this naked woman lashed to a bar that I had thought was just a pull-up bar. But there she was, stark naked, covered in weals. She was his slave. Just as I was leaving, eighteen months later, he was actually constructing a cage for her in one corner of the loft. The guy was setting iron bars in the concrete. He was seriously into S/M.

At this point drugs come in seriously. I used smack a fair bit, it was the first thing I injected, but really I was interested in cocaine. I never became addicted to opiates, I enjoyed using them and I did inject, but what I did get addicted to, what utterly wiped me out, was intravenous cocaine. The moment I discovered injectable cocaine that was it. This was my drug of choice as they say at Narcotics Anonymous. Basically sex in a liquid form. It was 100 or a 1000 times better than an orgasm when you shot up. Quite similar to freebasing. The nice thing too was that you did everything in clear consciousness, you remembered everything. What it really enables you to do is encapsulate the whole sexual encounter between men and women into about twenty minutes. So what might normally take several weeks – meeting, courtship, seduction – would take twenty minutes. I got heavily into this. I used at times to go completely mad. I'd get these very large quantities of cocaine and just do them continuously until they ran out. One time I did twenty-eight grammes in seventy-two hours. Which was the nearest I got to being dead. I paid for it in various ways: working hard, moonlighting and doing quite a lot of borrowing. I was also selling some – lots of lactose was bought.

This occasion on which I used twenty-eight grammes of cocaine in a weekend: I'd got it on tick and I had this ounce. I remember vividly knocking off work at two o' clock, when the call came through that it was ready, and getting a taxi to where he was, about twelve blocks from where I lived, and about three in the afternoon getting this plastic bag with twenty-eight grammes of fucking good quality cocaine and tremblingly and shiveringly just about making it back to my place. Then I had this lost weekend in which all sorts of things
318

happened: sex with a stranger, sex on the telephone, sex with quite a few friends, watching sex, hallucinating, going up to the seventeenth floor of the building, the top floor and having an encounter with the girl who lived up there and was said to be 'rather strange' – and she was rather strange. Then on Monday morning towards the end, very nearly dead: how am I going to find $2,000 to pay the Mafia and everything, this unbelievable comedown.

So there I was in my apartment. There was this Italian-American girl attached to this department in which I worked, very attractive. And I rang up the secretary to the chief of neurology and told her that I had this very important clinical matter, I needed this girl's home phone number. I called her up and managed to persuade her to come to my flat. There were two or three calls over an hour, gradually revealing, 'Well, I'm in a bit of a bad state, I've been doing this and that...' and the important thing was that this was a totally straight girl. So eventually she arrived, walked into this room with the carpet littered with syringes and me half dead on this filthy bed and we ended up having sex. And that was above all what turned me on, that ability to do that. It was infinitely exciting. The idea of going out into the normal world, travelling on the Clapham omnibus and realising that this hidden sexuality is the truth about lots of people. Perhaps this makes me sexually immature. Certainly this attitude is a long way away from a [US accent] 'mature total relationship' in which sex is an expression of etc., etc., etc. And of course the pathetic nature of a lot of male/female communications is such that with all the sex what I was actually doing is communicating with the woman concerned and maybe even respecting her.

I'd get obsessed with sex on cocaine. In terms of performance, you didn't necessarily perform, but mentally you did; the fuck was a mental fuck. My excitement was to get stoned and then use it to arouse the baser instincts of people who weren't remotely stoned. There was another loft, two floors above ours, up to which there was a set of back stairs without any lights. I don't think the people living there knew about it, but I did. Anyway this girl moved into this loft, two floors up, and she was very attractive. In her mid-twenties. Roy was really into sex, he'd substituted it for smack, and he said to me, 'Don't you touch her.' He liked to be first. But I was on one of my cocaine benders and I went up the back stairs and into this girl's flat. I appeared and she was actually in bed with her boyfriend. I was stark naked. Before that I'd swapped pleasantries on the stairs, that was about it. I said, 'Hi, welcome, I'm your new neighbour...Why don't you come down and say hi.' Then I went back down. Ten minutes later she appeared. Twenty minutes after that we were having sex.

319

Then it turned out that she'd been into coke and fixing it and we started having sex and fixing as we were about to come which means you don't come, and you do it again and so on. All quite exciting.

Anyway I stayed in Roy's flat and got to know more about what he was doing. One of his films was called *The Lewd Olympics*, which was a sort of tribute to the Winter Olympics which were being held in the US that year. There was a sanitised version for *Saturday Night Live* – unfortunately they axed the show the night before it was due to be aired – and a rather wilder version for other distribution. Basically everybody took quaaludes and got on with it.

My theory of sex in New York is all based on the ratio of sexually active women between twenty and thirty and sexually active heterosexual males; also the tall buildings that mean that there is a lot of stagnant air. All these women are emitting their sexual chemicals and instead of being blown away they just sit there between the tower blocks and little innocents like me just pick them up.

I'd go to various clubs with Roy and his girlfriend. He did this show with another bloke and his slave, the three of them. It was a scripted, costumed show. I'd contributed something to it, a bit of English culture, some Latin. It was a full spectacle. So one night he had this big show at a place called Club O at Fantasy Manor. An S/M swing club. I never personally got into S/M, but this was very definitely hardcore. People got hurt and injured. Lots of torture chamber stuff, middle-class New Jersey lawyers who would come in with their wives who would be led around with rings through their clitoris and be chained and whipped and all that. Nothing lavatorial, thank God. Just pain. This evening was particularly important, because there were going to be some Californian producers there. But the night before his partner got ill and clearly he was not going to be able to perform. Roy turned to me and told me I'd just got to help him out. It was one of those moments where time stands still and you look at your situation in life and here I am, young English lad in New York, doctor, blah, blah, blah and I thought: Why not? I said, 'Fine, I'll do it.' I already knew the script and I knew the moves. So there we were, dressed up as Spanish Inquisition monks, and I had this large dildo under my habit and we did the show. Maybe 200 people and us on stage. 'Ladies and gentlemen, tonight for your entertainment we have a live show featuring an S/M theme with live unsimulated sex...'

We had this tape playing, and the lights went down and there we were at the back of the audience, dragging this screaming girl onto the stage, then manacling her to various bits and pieces and she was stripped naked and she was whipped a bit and she was accused of being a harlot and whore, she had to pee in a bucket and drink it, she
320

had burning candles poured on her and clothespegs on her nipples and her clitoris. At one stage I produced the dildo, which wobbled, and all this time Roy's girlfriend was taking pictures. Then some guy was brought up from the audience – a Puerto Rican guy with a cowboy hat – and she had to give him a blow-job while blindfolded and so on. The climax was Roy and me simultaneously fucking her. I genuinely can't remember whether I got the front or the back, but it didn't make any difference because although I ought to have done, I certainly didn't have a hard-on. I had to use my habit to hide this problem. Roy was fine, he was a professional. The audience loved it. I was rather detached. I was fairly heavily influenced by chemicals. Was it sexy? No, it wasn't remotely sexy. I was just watching myself. Then when we went backstage these three pint-sized pinstriped-suited, dandruff-collared, balding Californian producers were saying, 'Boys we loved the show!'

Every few months Roy would get bored and he'd put an ad in the *Village Voice* – just like the one I'd responded to – purely to get thirty or forty girls coming to see a potential room. He'd do it through an answering service and tell them only to send girls. Somehow I'd slipped through. These girls would do anything to get a room in New York, because it was so difficult. Basically he'd end up having sex with at least half a dozen of them. One day when one of these ads had been running, I picked up the phone and started talking to one of these girls. Somehow we hit it off. So she made an appointment to come, but when she did come I was asleep, so I never saw her. She saw Roy and they didn't hit it off and she left. So later on I rang her up and said how sorry I was to miss her and she said, 'Well I have to go out, but I'm back around midnight – give me a call if you're up.' Which I proceeded to do. We then talked until six a.m., while every thirty minutes I was shooting up cocaine. We ended up in this 'total self-revelation' phone call, absolutely open in a way that is perhaps only possible on the phone.

Then over the next week or two I had two or three more calls. It became very sexy, although that wasn't the only thing. It was only words but we definitely had orgasmic sex on the telephone. It was terribly exciting. The upshot was that we decided to meet. We arranged it as a little scenario. The arrangement was for me to call from the phone on her block, two minutes away, and she would put on a blindfold. I went and I called and said, 'Hi Elizabeth, it's me.' I was terribly solicitous, I said, 'Are you sure you want to go through with this?' She said, 'Fine, okay, I'm ready, I'll expect you in two minutes.' In a state of considerable excitement I rang the bell and she said, 'Who is it?' I said, 'It's Matthew.' She said, 'Okay' and opened the

321

door and she was wearing a blindfold and maybe a dressing-gown. And she was beautiful, really beautiful. About twenty-eight, very long black hair, quite lovely. She looked towards me with her blindfold and I looked at her and we kissed. We'd known everything about each other but we'd never met. We went to her bedroom and continued to kiss and I slowly undressed her and she's still blindfolded and we proceeded to make love, which I use advisedly because this was not pure sex, there was something more to it. Literally at the point of orgasm I pulled off the blindfold. It was a very powerfully erotic experience. I stayed the night and then I left. Two days later I left the States for ever. We didn't see each other again after that. We spoke on the phone a couple of times. She's now a rabbi. I found that out because six years later I'm at home with my wife, a child asleep, and the phone rings and I answer it and instantaneously I recognised the voice. I said her name in full and she was blown out that I'd remembered. This time we chatted for twenty minutes and then we said goodbye.

I'd go to after-hours clubs in New York, not for the drinking but because these were the places where you could pick people up at four in the morning. There were orgies. I went off with this Italian guy, some middleman for the mob, to Engelwood, New Jersey, where he had his girl. He said to me, 'Matthew, I want you to fuck her.' And she said, 'Matthew, I want you to fuck me.' So I did. And he watched and then did it afterwards.

It is forbidden fruit that turns me on. Not as in other people's wives, but as in girls who don't particularly want to but then discover that they do. In sex the ritual is all-important. What I believed, possibly by deluding myself heavily, was that I was not remotely like your lager-lout on the make wanting a fuck. Although that was probably exactly what I was. Nor did I see myself as some kind of decadent English gentleman. The whole thing was to sit back and not have any male aggro, but simply to adduce it from the woman. To make the desire for the sexual encounter come totally from her. It is about power, yes, but not in using male power to overwhelm the woman. I always loved the women. There were exceptions, yes, but on the whole, on the majority of occasions there were no bad feelings afterwards. And the twenty minutes encapsulation that came with injecting cocaine did not restrict the relationship to twenty minutes – that was just the lifespan of one hit of cocaine – but could be endlessly repetitive. You could stay with one person over and over again.

I am a sexual experimenter to an extent. I am open to most suggestions. Not real S/M, because I'm a coward when it comes to physical pain, so that's out. But I do like elaborate fantasies. Diceman

322

fantasies. Some people do whole weekends; I did do a mini-diceman, a day. It was fairly tame. This girlfriend and I: you do what I tell you, or what the dice says, then vice versa. Carefully orchestrated so one didn't get arrested. We were in a hotel room and the girl had to go down to the street and the third man she saw had to be invited up to the room and fucked. The condition was that I would watch. The third man she saw happened to be quite a decent young bloke; he was told, 'This is your chance, no strings, you can fuck this girl. But I have to watch.' He did it and that was that. She actually didn't make me do anything exciting, which was slightly disappointing, she just got me to do various things to her which she might not have otherwise got me to do. Various non-vaginal penetrations, various objects and so on. I had a friend who got into it much more heavily, whole weeks with a whole gang of people. Twenty or thirty people went off for a week and spent it all doing diceman stuff, some of which was quite banal and some was quite interesting sexual encounters.

One time in New York there was this doctor who'd just got married. We all had these bleepers. I rang her up on the bleeper and said, 'Dr So-and-so I'm on ward whatever and room such and such and I really need your assistance urgently,' and then arranged myself stark naked on the bed. Then somehow talked her into it. The excitement, aside from the sexual frisson, was in not having what I was doing interpreted as being what it probably actually was – a dirty old English pervert lying there trying to get his rocks off with a rather Christian-looking, no longer virginal but obviously monogamously married woman – but getting her to stay and not only to tolerate the situation but actually to take part in it. It's power. An attempt to impose your own view of the universe on everybody and show them that that's what they think. It's my view of sexuality. The power bit is not the forcing, but in getting them to do things without apparently being seen to be persuading them. I am a seducer, but not as in carving a notch on my bedpost, and not as in then going off and talking to the lads, but as in having made that woman reveal her rampant sexuality and share it with me. The fantasy was that I would lie there in a drug-induced haze and ordinary, totally normal women would get into my clutches. It was not bimbos or sex sirens that I was after, it was a secretary living in the Bronx coming into Manhattan to go to the office from nine to five and then going back home. That was the sort of person that I enjoyed seducing.

On one flight – it might have been the Laker Skytrain or possibly People's Express – I made the Mile High Club. I'd had this classic thing of coming across this unconscious body on the middle of the floor late at night and making the fatal error of saying, 'I am a doctor,' and discovered that it those situations a doctor in fact becomes superior to the captain of the plane. In fact I've had more than one sexual encounter on an aeroplane; there's something about that cigar tube that encapsulates you and you're away from reality and time. This was with a Greek model, flying New York to London. We basically formed a friendship on the plane and we both decided it might be quite fun so we went to the back of the plane and did it. That was it.

By the time I returned to London I knew I was in serious trouble with cocaine. I was staying in a house in Chelsea and one night, around midnight, I burst out into Sloane Street and there were these two girls walking down the street with backpacks and I marched up with some frightfully original line like, 'Excuse me, have you got a match, I've run out,' and quarter of an hour later they were back in my mews house. We ended up all going to bed together – in fact I caught crabs. But obviously I must have been good at chatting people up. But by this time it wasn't so much sexual experimentation as terminal drug addiction. I may have seen myself as being in control, having a good time, but actually I was just a terminal cocaine addict getting into very major trouble. So I decided to go into treatment, which I did.

But before I went into treatment there were lots of scenes. I had this girlfriend and I'd watch her fucking with her boyfriend and then I'd fuck her and then we'd get dressed up – the boys in girls' clothes. I also got buggered just before I went into treatment. Again, a drugs-driven situation. I have this friend, Gavin, who I had known since Oxford. Lovely chap, merchant banker, very macho, he really was the notch on the gunbelt, sling it on the photocopier type. And like all real macho men secretly uncomfortable with his homosexual side. My theory was always that the macho hunks were always terrified of being emotionally close with men. So I would tease him, and he'd never had any homosexual experience in his life. Just a great man for old-fashioned seduction. But he quite fancied me and I knew it. We used to take quite a lot of drugs together and this one time I seduced him as a woman, dressed up. I got a whole lot of clothes from a friend of mine, dressed up as a woman and seduced him. And got him to bugger me. I never was remotely interested in buggery, in either direction. But I enjoyed it. It didn't hurt, we used lots of KY, and while it wasn't a turn-on I enjoyed it. That was it. Just once.

The theory is that that the sexual revolution has changed everything but I believe that there's nothing I've experienced that would be much different at any time over twenty centuries. I don't think I was into seduction for the macho side, the need to claim, 'Hey, I've scored

324

more chicks than you.' But maybe it is the Etonian version of Essex Man. I think that may be very much what I did. There is an enormous banality about sex and what I've been describing is a slightly jazzed up version of the basic stuff, just as I might have been describing a trip to India and Joe Bloggs might have gone to the Taj and I might have gone up the Ganges in a truck. But basically it's the same deal. The whole thing with sex was the little boy let loose in the candy store. I had intelligence, Englishness in New York which was very important, the right accent, I'm quite good-looking, so what I did has the accoutrements to make a better story than some. 'I went bus-stopping in New York with Mick Jagger' is better than 'There we were in the back of the Mini down Dagenham way and I fucked her'. My whole sexual life in New York was infused with drugs, and there was some adventurousness, and I did go to places that might have been slightly incautious compared to what others might have done. But fundamentally, like all sex, it was banal. There is an argument –he was looking for something and all he found was physical gratification, he didn't find spiritual ecstasy – but I wasn't looking for spiritual ecstasy in the first place. It was all hugely narcissistic and egocentric, but for the majority of the time I don't think it was exploitative, though feminists might claim it was. I think on the whole the other person was getting exactly the same deal. A very masturbatory world, yes, except that there were other people watching and helping.

The Nineties

So where are we now? Three years into the Nineties, the so-called caring Nineties, a respite from the Sturm und Drang Eighties, a brief pause before the new millennium, a world of Post-Modernist self-invention, culled from a century's hip artefacts. Sex offers no greater claims, no worked-out position. The permissive society, the great liberation movements, the New Puritanism: the three strands seem, paradoxically, to be sharing one cosy, if uncomfortable bed. Each has had its achievements, each its gains and losses, each has chipped away at the others to greater or lesser extent. But don't they all make too much fuss? In an ideal world one would like to see sex as less important, less central, less public. Relegated to its proper place – pleasurable, yes, problematical, certainly, but hardly the great panjandrum of daily life. Such pious hopes remain mere hopes. The permissive society of the Sixties has, undoubtedly, shifted the common perception of sex a good way from that which preceded it; the legislation of the period, more important by far than the 'love' that underpinned the hippie agenda, has not been repealed. Roy Jenkins, not Richard Neville, remains the most important figure of the era. The gender politics too have altered perceptions. Anomalies remain, but once more perceptions have shifted. Pandora's box has been opened, the truth is out, and the lid cannot be resealed. New Puritanism, the fundamentalist Right, call it what one may, has not lost every battle. AIDS has seen to that. Sex, once pleasurable, has for many become a threat. The mass response can be seen from Clause 28 to the Sun's *front page splash.*

TED POLHEMUS: My theory is that in the Eighties and Nineties we entered into what I call the second sexual revolution. If the first was about promiscuity, and basically a numerical sexuality – quantity not quality, it was clearly reaching its limitations in physical exhaustion

327

and in the fact that human beings really aren't meant to function this way. It's curious that we see the Plato's Retreat thing as being like animals. But there really aren't any higher primate animals that function in this way. If you looked around Plato's Retreat, you had a vast room full of women going down on their males, desperately trying to get them erect. So if the first sexual revolution was about doing it a lot, the second sexual revolution of the Eighties/Nineties seems to have rejected promiscuity and focused instead on how to keep things hot and interesting and sustained within the context of a relationship, a monogamous relationship.

The easy explanation is AIDS, and it's a very real explanation. But if AIDS and herpes hadn't come along, people would have realised they were living a dead-end lifestyle. It would be playing into the hands of the moralists, right up Mary Whitehouse's street, if not for the fact that the alternative dimensions of the second sexual revolution would scare the daylights out of her. What are the alternatives, what are the ways one maintains one's sexual life? Say you're in a stable monogamous relationship. You want to stay that way, you don't want the frisson of sexual excitement to go off. It was always easy in the Sixties. You met somebody, there was that initial frisson of excitement, when that died down you moved on to somebody else. Let us also note, in a fuller discussion of the second sexual revolution, that although once again the media has focused on our age range, because we are the largest chunk of the population, most if not all of what I'm saying I believe to be applicable right down to those in their twenties and late teenagers. They're not recycling the Sixties. They're also faced with this logical problem: how do you keep the excitement in a relationship? You don't want to go out and get AIDS, you don't like condoms, you don't want the meat market pickup joint, waking up in the middle of nowhere the next morning.

The whole context of this has to be considered in terms of the spiritual bankruptcy of modern day Western culture. I think we're trying to use sexual experience as a religion, and that both sexual revolutions share this element of trying to find God, so to speak. Both the first and second sexual revolutions share a motivation of trying to find intense experience in sexuality, to find something that catapults your life into something beyond machine-muzak/shopping-mall existence.

In our society, people don't feel anything any more, don't experience anything. They're cushioned against it in any way possible. In any other society in human history and throughout Western history there has been – usually in the form of some kind of religion – a religious ritual, some means of trying to heighten experience, so that
328

one is plugged into the higher electricity of what might be called spiritual excitement. The two sexual revolutions of the post-war age have been an attempt to say: Okay, we're a secular society, we don't have religious ritual any more as such, how are we going to really experience anything, feel anything? And the answer – ironically following in the path of Eastern Tantric religions – is to try to find nirvana/ecstasy through sexual experience.

AVEDON CARROLL: What has changed is the consequences. I don't have to confess to a past now. I don't think the past rankles. For women a few years older than me, they had to confess they weren't a virgin. For me, it was understood that I wasn't a virgin – even when I still was. You can't say men want virgins any more, even if some still do. If you did say it, people would say: 'Why? What are they afraid of?' It's not a legitimate complaint, that you're not a virgin. I know a lot of guys who are just as happy not to have to go through that. You know: Am I going to expose her to the big disappointment of her life? – which is how it is for a lot of women. If I were a guy, I couldn't bear having sex with a virgin.

In a way the sexual revolution *is* over because of AIDS. Although a lot of the surface rhetoric is anti-sexual revolution because of AIDS, underneath, because of the whole safe-sex thing, and a lot of what the gay community has been doing, there's an extent to which that third part of the sexual revolution that was missing before in the over-culture – the idea that intercourse isn't central, that there are lots of kinds of sexuality – a bit of fire was built under that because of AIDS.

KATE HEATH: Women still have to keep their behaviour under control whereas men are much freer. There are certain choices that women do not have. I live near the river and I'd often like to go out and have a spliff down by the river at two in the morning, but I cannot do that. It's not an option. It would be stupid. As a woman I shouldn't walk around the streets at a certain time of night. You have to impose a curfew on yourself. But it's not my fucking problem, I'm having to restrict my behaviour, not because I choose to, but because of something that men do. There's always been this onus on women to adapt, but these days I seriously think that they've had enough of it. This whole thing about date rape, the Kennedy Smith trial. That woman was still being tried for the clothes she was wearing, the fact that she went back to his flat. The fact that she was wearing 'provocative' clothing gets taken into consideration. If you take that

329

on board then you're saying that men can't control their actions, which is highly dangerous ground – it's total bullshit. I may see this guy in a nice pair of Levi's or a nice shirt and think he's got a nice face or a nice body but I don't go over and abuse him and invade his space. Like that case where a woman was walking down a country lane at one in the morning and she got raped, but the guy got let off because she was wearing black knickers. 'Provocative clothing'.

NICKY SUTHERLAND: I don't see people having that Sixties' casual sex any more. Meeting, going to bed just like that. Not since AIDS. These days people probably know each other first. Courtship does exist these days, but for different reasons. It's not to get someone into bed, you know you'll do that, but to get to know the person you'll be getting into bed with. To find out about their past. My idea of the Sixties is that is was all really casual. Everybody just jumping in and out of bed with each other. You could screw, so you did. Today that's changed. You can't just jump in and out of bed because of what might come with that.

ADAM COLE: I have a feeling that there is a bit of a change. A lot more women are involved in sex and there's a lot more activity from women in the whole arena. They take the initiative more. More of a shared responsibility to make relationships work on a sexual level. Less chauvinistic than the old approach. Man had his preserve, probably slept around a bit without the wife finding out. Women have now done a bit more of that. But AIDS is focusing people more on one-to-one relationships rather than escaping down fantasy alley with a number of different partners. Producing something like *Electric Blue*, we don't actively promote that, we don't take a position on it. We're not telling people how to live their lives. We're just providing a little entertainment. The media, advertising, myself are still promoting the idea that everybody's getting it and I'm not. And they're getting it with gorgeous women with legs up to their ears etc. That permeates music, advertising, everything. There *are* people getting it, but... I'd say we are presenting entertainment, escapist fantasies.

JANE MILLS: What I see among my peer group who are married is that when the relationship is happy, there's a much greater atmosphere in the home of sexual ease, pleasure, happiness. We know people inside relationships are now fucking more than they did, having more orgasms, it's not just on Saturday night. I think there is more sexual pleasure about. I have a twenty-year-old girl friend, who's
330

always been very discreet about her sex life to her parents. That's true for most children. Whereas in our generation, we do talk about sex. 'Oh, not talking about sex again, Mummy.' I think that's healthy though.

JEFFREY WEEKS: Generally since the Sixties, there has been a widening of cultural space for people to experiment with their sexual lives, with relationships, less hidebound by religious or traditional conventions. Part of that expansion has been the development of a visible gay/lesbian community which has made it easier to be openly gay. It's certainly much easier today, AIDS notwithstanding, than in the Sixties. There's been an explosion over the last fifteen years of meeting places, pubs, clubs, discos, dating agencies, journals, books, everything. Accompanying that visible presence have been two major setbacks. One is the impact of AIDS and its concomitant backlash against homosexuality, but even that has had its positive side. The other thing is that homosexuality has become much more of an explicit political issue. So in the Eighties we get prominent Tory politicians doing populist things attacking homosexuals, attacking the lesbian/gay community. Thatcher did, Tebbit did. Culminating in Clause 28 in '88. But that backlash, that willingness to politicise the issue, attacking local authorities who wanted to promote homosexuality, that is actually a tribute to the growth of the gay community rather than a sign of its weakness. Similarly, the increase of police prosecution is another sign of our greater visibility.

New Puritanism didn't go that far. Underneath, what's happening all the time is this increased diversification, pluralisation of culture, which is a reflection of changes going on in the wider world. It's the breakdown of traditional orders, the breakdown of class boundaries, greater freedom of travel, which make it impossible to control people's private lives in a way in which the Church, State, traditional or class moralities once tried to do.

The paradox is that these days people are more liberal in their attitudes than they were in '67 when the law changed. That may not be saying a lot, because they weren't terribly liberal in '67, but it's an interesting paradox that we often forget, that the Sixties was hardly for gay people a paradisical time. All right for David Hockney who's commuting to LA, but not people in London, Glasgow or Cardiff.

And the supreme paradox is that Maggie Thatcher presided over the biggest expansion of the gay community in its history – there's a stronger gay presence in the Nineties than there was in the Sixties. There is a vibrant gay and lesbian identity in a way there wasn't twenty or twenty-five years ago, and that is a real historic breakthrough.

331

NETTIE POLLARD: I'm sure things will continue to change. They'll change as attitudes change. I don't think they'll change back though. That was a movement of the Eighties rather than the Nineties. The idea that women should be sexless, and the fear of AIDS in the Eighties. People are less frightened of it now, even though it's just as much of a threat. But they're thinking of ways round it: How can we enjoy safer sex? It's not: We've got to give up sex. Which is what people were thinking in the Eighties: We don't dare to have sex any more, or we must only have one partner. That's much less true now.

Other things have changed too: There are a lot of working-class lesbians about now. And lesbian relationships generally are now more acceptable. It's easier now for women not to marry. And much easier to have children if you're not married. You hear less about unmarried mothers, more about single-parent families. It might be only words, but it matters. And now thirty per cent of children are born out of wedlock, a staggeringly large number. There's no pressure now to marry if you get someone pregnant. So things have changed. The idea of women bringing up children on their own is more accepted, women having careers. How many housewives, in the old sense, are there now, for example? Most do work outside the home now. Whereas it was generally accepted in the Fifties that women don't work. You worked till you got married and then your husband, if he's a real man, would support you. That's gone out of the window. Women don't earn as much as men, they do have the worst jobs, but there's less stigma attached to having a job, or bringing up children on their own.

LYN PROCTOR: It may be that there have been two revolutions – quantity followed by quality, but it might also be simply that we're all growing up. At the beginning there's the idea of trying absolutely everything, or in the case of the Sixties absolutely everyone. This was based on the idea that sex is only one thing: sex is sexual intercourse, it's a very simple activity, it involves simple, straightforward vaginal intercourse and that's it. But that's a very juvenile view of the world, a sixteen-, seventeen-year-old view of the world – and from that age's point of view that is all that sex ever is. The ultimate. Have you gone all the way? This enormous goal. The idea of having that kind of sex with lots of different people really seems the only possible option. When you get older you begin to realise that that's not all there is to it. There's a great deal more possibilities, many more ways of enjoying things than simple vaginal intercourse. At that point you start to expand out into the whole world of sexuality, as opposed to simple sexual intercourse.

332

What the Sixties' sexual revolution achieved was very, very simple: the idea that it was not necessary to be married to someone in order to have intercourse with them. That sexual revolution happened and it stayed.

We have never stepped back from that point. Look at the statistics for illegitimacy, the fact that people live together rather than get married. There has never been a step back, even at the worst of the Thatcherite Eighties, the return to Victorian values. What's happened now is that those people who were having all that sexual activity at that point are now a lot older than they were then and those same people are no longer having all that sexual activity and most of those people now perceive the sexual revolution as having dissipated and disappeared because they aren't getting the amount of sex that they were. But what has happened is that in the same way as when you're seventeen you want to go to every party that's going, you sit in the corner, you feel bloody miserable, you feel everybody else is having a good time and you go home bloody miserable. But you still want to go to the next party and you feel awful if nobody invites you. By the time you get into your twenties you go to the parties you think will be good. By the time you get into your thirties and forties you're not very interested in parties, you much prefer to sit around with a few good friends and have a chance to talk properly rather than being elbowed into a corner and having foul red wine poured over your feet by some drunk.

NICKY SUTHERLAND: It doesn't just come as a screw these days. You can still get a screw, of course, but it doesn't just come as a screw. It's a screw and a wallet, literally. That's the attitude now. The feminist movement didn't help much on the male side. Back in the Sixties everyone was screwing. Nobody screws about these days. The thing is that these days we're all living under the shadow of the Sixties. Everyone wants to live out this idea of going to parties and living it up and screwing everybody and that doesn't happen at all. All right, there's people kissing and stuff and getting off with each other, but even that's fucking scarce these days. People are becoming fucking fucked up, right? Sex is turning into a god, relationships revolve around sex. You have to perform now. The thing is now that you're either completely into it or not into it at all. And these days most people are so shit-scared of AIDS.

KITTY GADDING

'Material Girl'

One in the morning and one should by rights be drunk. The usual suspects: a couple of publishers, an art critic, she's in television. The jobs are half right, the ages - late twenties - and the geography - W11 - but they're too bright to be yuppies. Anyway there's not a dealer among them. The drink has loosened tongues, a certain candour, born of the early hours, is out. Losses of virginity, compromising situations, small, restrained confessions. She stands out among the old friends, their prize exhibit, a precocious peer pushed forward to captivate the grown-ups.

People always want to talk about sex. Everybody does; they really do. Deep down we all have this extraordinary curiosity.

Women talk about sex much more than they used to. I wonder whether my mother and her friends talked about sex quite so graphically. I don't think my circle is exceptional. It's not just girls from my background. In work situations I find girls from all sorts of situations will just talk very graphically. I have some girlfriends for whom sex is not very high on the agenda, but with most of my women friends, who are very close and very important, we talk very graphically, very openly about most things. What their boyfriends do to them or don't do to them, how they feel...

A few years ago I had an affair while I was away from England, with a Frenchman. He was younger than me. Although he'd slept, or said he'd slept with a lot of women, and had started having sex when he was thirteen, he was surprisingly squeamish. He wanted the lights to be off, he wouldn't go down on me unless I'd had a bath, though he was into buggery and had clearly buggered a lot of women. I found that really extraordinary. I've always gone out with men who are scrupulously clean, though English men are quite smelly really, compared to American men who wash and blow-dry their hair and use perfumes and unguents all day long. But what surprised me about this French boy was that despite all this experience, the first time he was very rough – which may have been following his French girlfriend in Paris, and you do behave in bed with the new partner as you had been doing with the previous one.

The sex we had was nice, but we argued about it a lot. He said that I wasn't very responsive, which astonished me, because no one has ever complained before. I was just very surprised, so I said, well you're not very responsive either – because he just didn't make any noise, and I'm quite used to noisy men. And you could barely tell when he came. He said that he'd slept with women who'd shouted and screamed. So I said, 'Was this on the first time you slept with them?' He said, 'Yes.' I said, 'Perhaps they were faking it.' Which made him very angry. He was only twenty-four and I don't think he'd ever thought of that. He said American women particularly would shout, 'Fuck me! Fuck me!' and go absolutely wild. I then realised that perhaps one of the reasons that I wasn't responding like that was that I didn't feel totally abandoned, totally uninhibited.

Certain other boyfriends made me feel that if I'd farted in their face it couldn't have mattered less. They gloried in every aspect of sex, the fact that you do sweat, you do smell, that people's breath is never perfect and all of those things. And to be made utterly confident about your body, and to feel that your partner loves it and enjoys it and revels in it is amazing.

There was this guy called Simon I used to go out with, we were both in our early twenties, and the thing was that although the relationship deteriorated over the two years we were together, our sex became dirtier and dirtier ... well, not dirtier, but more extreme. It became an act: fucking rather than love-making, and we got very good at it. It was extraordinary. Recently a friend of mine asked me, 'Do you have a vibrator?' and I said 'Yes.' But the odd thing was that I had bought it with this guy Simon and although I have used it perhaps once since, with my current boyfriend, otherwise it's been locked away. It's tied into that relationship and somehow it would be sacrilegious to use it with someone else. Or perhaps it's just not necessary.

With this French guy I sometimes felt under quite extraordinary pressure to come. I've never faked an orgasm and I hope I never would. But he was useless at foreplay. I thought the one thing I would give him, I would teach him was to change that. I told him, 'You're very selfish in bed,' and again he was very, very shocked, and again I think that was his age. He'd never slept with one woman over a period of time. It wasn't that he was perfunctory, he could go on for a long time, but he wasn't good at foreplay, which made him a bad lover. Another thing which made me quite annoyed, which again I think was lack of experience, was that when I had my period the thought of sex obviously made him feel a bit sick, and a bit strange. Before that I've never encountered a man – in a longer relationship anyway – who's had a problem. But when I said, 'Look, if we're going to have sex I'd better go to the loo and remove my tampon,' he found that a bit much, as if he couldn't bear the reality of sex. He actually said, 'But if you do that won't there be blood everywhere?' I just said, 'No, it's not a flood, I'm lying down, there's gravity ... It's all right, I'm not going to gush

335

with blood all over the sheets.' I was really quite annoyed and thought: You are really very childish and you're showing your age. You're inexperienced and ridiculous.

My current boyfriend is a very good lover. I think this may have come from his being initiated into sex when he was about seventeen by a much older woman, and the one thing she taught him – which has obviously stood him in very good stead – was that you just need patience. And obviously some women take longer to respond than others.

That time when I was away I knew I'd be there for three months and if I met someone I'd probably sleep with them, I'd have an affair with them. I did have a boyfriend in England, but I've decided that I'm simply not a very faithful person. So very quickly, very early on this affair happened. He initiated everything, he was very attractive and we just got on fabulously well and I think he was very surprised that he felt as much for me as he did and that it became more serious. At the beginning I just thought: This is very safe – I'm in a long-term relationship, he's terrified of commitment, we get on very well and this is fun. But it became more and more serious and we became more and more involved with each other.

My boyfriend came to visit me and I thought that perhaps I should tell him, that perhaps I wanted him to find out. So I initiated a conversation along the lines of, 'Well, if you were unfaithful to me I wouldn't mind', and he said, 'You've changed your tune.' I thought: Why am I saying this, I don't want this conversation to carry on. He said, 'In my experience people don't say those kind of things unless they've done something.' I backtracked very quickly, I said, 'No no no, I've been talking to all sorts of people, my flatmate's been having this long-term affair....' and so on. He seemed to buy that. But he then said, and I thought this was extremely shrewd and clever, that perhaps this was like a last fling for me, like being a student again and having no responsibilities, and doubtless if he were in my position he would wonder whether it was that thrilling to have a girlfriend back in London. It was almost, 'Look, I know you are tempted or you have been tempted, so just get on with it but I don't want to know.' Then a few months later he came out again and the other boy had just left and I was feeling very iffy about our relationship anyway and I thought: If he asks me I will tell him. But I also realised he never would ask me because he knew that I would tell him the truth. In the end you can't ask those questions unless you're prepared for any answer. Ignorance is bliss.

****

My big revelation came after I had split up from a longish relationship, when I didn't go out with anybody properly for about a year. I thought that casual sex is dangerous, I've got to use condoms from now on, and suddenly I thought I don't want to 'put out' for them, because I'm not going to come the first time we have sex and why should I? I liked being able to say no. So I would go to bed with these people, and I'd stay the night, but what would happen is that I'd just give them a blow-job. I always felt: Well, I suppose I'd better. I used to think I was rather good at it, though now I'm not so sure. A lot of women won't go down on men at all, or don't really like to. I will, and it's one way of gratifying them. It's easier to give a man a blow-job than to jerk them off. They can do that a lot better themselves. We're never taught what to do, and different men like different things, but on a casual level, when you offer them a blow-job, they're often shocked and quite pleased and perhaps it approximates sex more than just using your hand. I wouldn't let anyone go down on me in a casual situation, because I do think that's more intimate than fucking.

I was talking to an old boyfriend who was astonished that I used condoms. He said, 'Aren't you still on the Pill?' and I said, 'Oh no. I haven't been on the Pill since 1987.' So he said, 'Oh do you use a cap?' 'No, condoms.' He was so amazed. But after I ended my last long relationship, which went back pre-AIDS, I did make the decision always to use condoms with anyone I slept with. Although I did make the mistake of sleeping with someone and using this horrible cap. I do hate the cap.

Having a lot of gay friends, I'm terrified of getting AIDS. After this long relationship had ended I had a few rather strange encounters and that's when I decided I was going to use condoms. I also decided, and I think I felt confident for the first time, that I wasn't going to have sex with people unless I really thought it was going to be very good. I discovered that you could say no and it wasn't a problem. I could just go to bed with people and say I'm not going to have sex with you – right from the beginning. All right, you were a bit drunk and you fancied them and they fancied you but you didn't have to have sex. If I was going to have an orgasm, sure, but in my experience I don't have orgasms first time I sleep with someone, it takes me a while.

I'm not sure if there is such a thing as a good lover. Some people fit together well and others don't and sometimes it just doesn't work, however much you might like someone or find them attractive. It's very sad but it doesn't work in those situations and no matter how hard you try, it will never work. And that's that. It's sad that a lot of women don't enjoy sex as much as they should and in fact feel a bit put upon. Why it is, I don't know, but maybe they've never been with the right person, maybe they've never realised their potential. Some men unfortunately can be very clumsy.

Good sex is all to do with feeling utterly confident and being able to communicate. But a lot of people have a problem with the language of sex; it's very hard to communicate and the words that are available are never really right and they are slightly embarrassing. For instance, I would say 'fanny', and I'd never say 'pussy', that would just make me sick. I wouldn't say 'cunt', not during sex. I used to be very bothered by it, I used to think it was the most awful word and I'd never say it, but it doesn't worry me now. Some women are embarrassed to talk about sex to men, though perhaps not to other women. They don't know what words to use, they're embarrassed by admitting that they might have certain fantasies ... Men don't talk about sex in the same way, it's more competition, conquests, boasting. They won't start saying, 'I'm really worried about the size of my cock' – even though they all are. I love the conversations women have about sex. Talking about the encounters they've had, rolling around on the floor laughing and laughing about what men have done or what men have said. I'm sure men would feel very threatened and frightened if they knew the half of it. I remember one friend saying how she hated the way men stuck their fingers inside her. They obviously thought that the more they could get in the better and they were pushing their hand up and down and it wasn't arousing it was just rather uncomfortable and not very nice.

I don't think casual sex is ever that good, having slept with men who are so embarrassed about having sex, who clearly don't know what to do. The worst was an occasion with a soldier, an army captain. I just remember him asking,'Are you all right down there?' and I just thought: Uurrgghh! His just really not knowing. The wonderful power women can have over men. At the end of the day you have the power to crush. I don't believe this thing that some men say that there are women who can't have orgasms. I really don't believe that: they're obviously lousy lovers. I just don't believe that it's physically impossible for a woman to have an orgasm.

As a teenager I had a regular boyfriend, we had nice sex but it was pretty straightforward. I didn't come very often. But I wasn't very bothered about it. But as a woman, as you get older and older, your potential increases. But in the relationship I started at the end of my time at Cambridge, things changed. It was the first time a man had properly gone down on me, and he'd never done it before, but had wanted to very much. And I was nervous because no one had really done it – and I thought: Well, maybe I taste funny or smell strange. I

338

just felt very embarrassed, very vulnerable. So that was when sex became very much an exploratory thing. We used to have a lot of anal sex – it became a kind of staple of our sex life. I liked it very much, but I don't now. I don't understand why I've changed, but no, I don't like it now. I had done it before – I'd done it once with my first lover. I thought: Oh that's all right, and he'd wanted to try it once, but that was it. I didn't feel there was any taboo, I was never problematised by it. Then with this guy, we just did it a lot, and it became a real staple of our sex life. I really liked it, I thought it was absolutely fantastic, and we'd use a vibrator at the same time and even when we split up we continued sleeping with each other maybe once a week and he still buggered me a lot. I thought it was great. The interesting thing now is that I'd like to do it – one's arsehole is very erotic – but it just seems to hurt much more. Whether that's because James has a bigger cock, which I suspect he does, I don't know. I was talking to a friend of mine from New York and she said her boyfriend really liked it, and she was quite happy with the idea, but it did hurt. We both said how awful it is – you don't want to say no, but because it hurts you get tense and the pain is even worse, it brings tears to your eyes. You do have to be very, very relaxed, so unfortunately what has happened is that because of the pain, although James would like to do it, we don't. He doesn't want to hurt me or force me to do anything I don't want. The times we have done it successfully are when we've already had sex once, and I've come, so I'm very relaxed already. It's a shame. Maybe we need more KY jelly.

I don't know whether I'm more highly sexed than other people. I don't masturbate – I can't. I don't know why not. Clearly there are women I know who do masturbate and who don't come with men or don't enjoy very good sex. I think there are a lot of women like that. So the odd thing is that I feel faintly embarrassed about masturbation. Not about touching myself, because obviously I do that, and I have been able to masturbate in front of someone else, although that was only one particular person, so physiologically I must be able to do it. When I was away I did feel pretty sexy most of the time and I felt quite powerful and I felt: God, there is sex everywhere and all you need do is reach out.

I do like the idea of a zipless fuck. Perfect casual sex. When I was abroad I began to feel: Well, perhaps I can never be faithful to anybody. New bodies, after all, are exciting; exploring someone, the first time you kiss them ... you can never recapture that – unless you've spent some time apart and you're having sex again for the first time. My ideal relationship would be to be with someone and to be utterly devoted to each other and you really loved each other and you knew that was where home was, but that you both probably had affairs and you didn't talk about it and you were discreet and you never embarrassed each other. But it doesn't work like that. But we're not naturally monogamous and I think most people do have affairs or at least 'indiscretions' at some point.

There's definitely something sexy about having sex with someone you've never had sex with before. The trouble with me is when I'm pissed I may feel quite randy, but I don't actually ... kissing is enough. I don't object to casual sex morally at all. I just think it's not safe now, after AIDS. And I don't do it any more. I do have women friends who clearly can enjoy casual sex and have a great time in bed and come and I just know that doesn't really happen to me. Perhaps it's because I have been drunk a lot of the times I've got off with people. And if I'm drunk I feel very horny but actually all I want to do is kiss, I want to snog. But I don't really feel much like real sex.

AIDS has changed everything. One ex-boyfriend has not had a girlfriend for eight months. He's very moral and he wouldn't have a quick fling. It's very serious for him. But if you're twenty-eight-plus it's a lot harder to meet people. They're either going out with other people or they're married or they're engaged or they're not quite right in some way, and if you're a woman maybe they're gay – which is definitely a problem for American women in New York or San Francisco. I do think it would be really nice to be able to sleep with people and have unprotected sex and not worry about it.

Women who sleep around have less of a reputation than they used to. It's promiscuous men who get a reputation. I have friends who sleep with more people then I do, and people who sleep with many less, but the overall thing is that these days it's become all right for women to admit to liking sex. If women sleep with a lot of men there's no moral judgement to be made: they just like sex. Though it's not really that simple because those same women, who do sleep with a lot of men, often do it for very negative reasons because of their conditioning. They're unhappy, or they hate themselves. Women always did like sex, but actually saying so is some kind of feminist triumph. I also think that people are realising more and more that we're not really naturally very monogamous and one does want other people. People are in relationships, maybe for two or more years, they're not married, and they're asking themselves, 'Where does this go next?' And the old answer, which is marriage and children, isn't there any more. It's more likely to be serial monogamy.

Sometimes I do feel contempt for men. I have this very good gay friend, Neil, and when we were together in America we went to this wedding in Virginia. We were camping it up and we were both agreeing that all men are jerks. He was saying how he much prefers women – other than sexually. They're cleverer, more fun, more interesting. We went to this wedding where we were very concerned that everyone would be straights from hell. And there would certainly be no one he could flirt with. I knew that there was one person I could flirt with. He was the best-looking guy there, but he seemed slightly asexual, slightly boring, which was rather depressing. So Neil and I eventually decided that the only way to cope with the event was to behave as outrageously as we possibly could and Neil became fixated on this man whom he was convinced was gay, or certainly had potential. He had a very boring looking girlfriend. So Neil, who was very drunk, was going to go up and say 'I want to suck your cock, she doesn't do it for you, does she? I know, I know.' Unfortunately he never did. However I did get off with this other guy, this English guy, and I did end up going to bed with him and having sex with him. The next day Neil and I went back to New York and we both felt rather contemptuous of the whole thing. There we were, this whirlwind of sex descending on Virginia, and aren't these men pathetic and aren't we cruel and so on. So I suddenly felt rather awful about this weekend of excess, but also slightly contemptuous. For the first time in my life I began to feel that if I put my mind to it, I could probably have any man I wanted.

Sometimes I want my body to be a tool, just to lure and entrap men. I suppose what happened was that I suddenly realised that I really did have a good figure, it was in proportion and most men liked my tits and my legs weren't bad and basically I went in and out at the right places. I suddenly thought that it would be wonderful to be a sex object. It was this Madonna attitude of being really, really feminine. One of the guys on my course, he was twenty-two, said that it was really strange the way I dressed because it gave off such conflicting signals – both sexy and demure. I would dress deliberately to look sexy. Though that's a recent thing. I've only recently started wearing miniskirts. I love it. I love being whistled at in the street. That really makes me feel good. As a teenager I didn't see myself as attractive, but I think I've grown into my looks. There was this Italian boy on my course and he obviously saw me as this older woman and I did have this fantasy he was a virgin and that if I had the time and energy I'd initiate him. But of course I didn't and anyway he wasn't. But every day he'd come in and kiss me quite hard on the lips and say something like, 'Ciao bella' and walk off. So right at the end we ended up in this nightclub, kissing away fast and furiously. And it delighted me that as an older woman, aged twenty-eight, I could still turn on someone six years younger. I know that's not a huge gap but I thought: Hey, I'm not that old.

The other terrifying thing is that having gone through this stage of thinking: All right, I'm only twenty-eight, that is young, I am young, I'm not that old and there are all those men out there and I fancy them and I want to have sex with them and they fancy me too and how extraordinary that is. I still feel the ageing process is moving on. But I do like revealing clothing, I like lycra, tight dresses. I do think if you've got it, flaunt it – while it lasts. I think some people, some of my girlfriends, find this slightly surprising. But it is nice to be wearing a short tight skirt and know that you're probably titillating someone and perhaps what feminism has done is that women are now saying, 'Look, we're allowed to wear those clothes and tough, you can't rape us, it doesn't mean we're available, and we can say no.' All of which may be very, very confusing and quite difficult for a lot of men. But why can't you flirt, why can't you wear those sort of clothes? Of course men don't dress like that, they don't wear codpieces, we don't care about their nicely-turned shins. Though there is mounting pressure on men to look better; they're more worried about their weight, they do work out, they are worried about their clothes.

Of course it puts a lot of pressure on women who don't look good in those clothes. There is a problem for middle-class, intelligent, well-educated women who want to dress in a certain way, but realise that if they do then they are going to be treated in a certain way. I have a friend who is very sexy in a sort of dirty way, but she covers herself up from head to toe, although it's all very well tailored and form-fitting and you can see she has good tits and all that sort of stuff and she is very, very open and frank about sex. And she can't understand why that upsets and annoys some people. Men are allowed to behave like that, older men in positions of power especially are allowed to flirt, to pat your bum, but women simply aren't allowed to behave like that. Which is grossly unfair, even if it is the way of the world. I never reversed that, although it might be kind of fun to tease someone who was terribly shy and blushed an awful lot. No one's ever harassed me, no one's ever made me feel uncomfortable. Though there was one guy who was very sweet, he sat diagonally across from me at work. Older than me and married, but so what. I was wearing this very low-cut blouse and he kept staring at me and I kept looking at him and grinning at him and he finally just said, 'I'm so sorry, it's just your cleavage is so marvellous I can't help looking at it.' If he'd been more lecherous and ghastly about it it would have been awful, but I just laughed. It became a huge joke. I didn't feel oppressed or angry or anything.

342

The best part of my body is my tits, and I've always known that. Men always tell me: You've got wonderful breasts. They're quite firm, even though they're quite large. There was this guy, we'd been out and got into this cab, spent the whole way back to his apartment kissing, and he got my top off and then he said, which made me want to laugh and I felt slightly sorry for him, it was awful, cruel, 'You've got such a beautiful chest.' It was the word 'chest'. So I said, 'Your girlfriend has big tits.' 'Yes, but not as sexy as yours.' It was at that point that I suddenly felt, what an extraordinary power one can wield over men. That was a fascinating feeling, an exhilarating feeling, but at the same time slightly frightening.

I would hate to flaunt any power over a man in a sexual situation, because that's so unfair. I'd never say, 'Oh I hate that,' or 'Don't do that,' because I think you could squash someone utterly and completely. When someone can't get it up you always say it doesn't matter, but of course it does matter to them. So it's rather difficult. There was one man I went out with for a short time. He was the most fantastic kisser, a very, very erotic kisser, but he really wasn't very good in bed. He refused to use a condom and I gave in and said, 'Okay we'll use the cap,' and this was something I'd promised myself I wouldn't do. He'd get an erection but he'd lose it very quickly if I moved or did anything out of the ordinary. It was a terrible strain. It's exhausting, because what I'd say is it doesn't matter, that's okay, that's really fine, and try and just talk about something else or just try and relax, but he would just keep on trying and trying until he finally did come. It was dreadful, absolutely dreadful.It happened every single time. I'm not saying he was a lousy lay or he was impotent, but maybe we didn't fit together, maybe it was just us. Maybe I was threatening him in some way. Other times it's men who've not put condoms on quick enough and then they lose their erection. They obviously feel very upset about it. But what can you do? Women don't have pricks and obviously they can technically have sex whether they're turned on or not and for men you're putting your trust into this external part of you, which you just hope won't let you down. Then there's the other frightening thing for men: What if she is faking it? That's an extraordinary power a woman can exert. I'm not letting him have any power over me, or take anything from me.

The problem is this: you don't want people to stop fancying you – it's nice, it's very flattering and that's appealing. So you indulge the flattery, but it still isn't a turn-on. Not at all. There was this guy who I met last summer, the friend of a friend. He's small, not very attractive, but he's quite nice and very, very enthusiastic. Anyway, he'd met me in the summer and I'd heard from lots of people that he'd really fancied me and he'd been obsessed by my tits, because I was wearing a low-cut summer dress. So when I was in New York he came over to run in the New York Marathon and wanted to take me out. He rang up and said, 'Would you like to go to the opera?' He almost appears to be gay, he's so fruity, almost a young fogey in the way he talks and dresses. Despite all this he's clearly very successful with women, though he's not my type. So we went out to the opera. I knew that I'd flirt, but that would be that. He's someone who's very clutching, who touches your arm a lot. I was wearing this black dress and he started off the evening telling me, 'My dear, you look so splendid, absolutely gorgeous.' I thought: This is ridiculous, that's so over the top, he doesn't actually mean anything. But we went to the opera, went out to dinner and got on very well. And he asked whether I was having an affair, and I said, 'Yes.' We left the restaurant together and were saying goodbye and we suddenly started kissing. I wasn't drunk, there wasn't that excuse, but it was almost as if I was paying for dinner. I really felt quite whorish. Paying for dinner, paying for the opera. So we kissed. And I like kissing, though I didn't especially like kissing him. So he said, 'Come back to my flat, come back.' I said, 'Okay, I will but you know what'll happen. You'll want to sleep with me and I don't want to.' But he said, 'Just come back.' So I did. I didn't want the evening to end and I was enjoying his company.

We carried on kissing and of course he took my dress off – I let him – and he went mad about my tits. In a way I found rather laughable: 'If only people knew how magnificent they are ... they are fantastic ...' So he asked me again to stay, and I said again that I didn't want to have sex with him. So he said okay. But the odd thing was that I did stay, which was partly because I was too lazy to call a cab. So we went to bed. But I kept my knickers on and he kept his underpants on and he just had this erection for hours and hours and I guess he expected that gradually he'd wear me down. But I just thought: No, I don't want to. I kissed him and let him touch my tits, but I didn't touch his cock, even through his pants, and certainly didn't let him go near me. So what we ended up with was this awful rubbing and pawing and I just felt exhausted. For a while I thought: Oh God, maybe I'd better give him a blow-job or a hand-job, but then I just felt: No, I really don't want to. Finally he did stop and we did go to sleep, though of course he tried again in the morning. I still said no. It was awful. If it had been a good old grope, a kiss and a cuddle, that would have been absolutely fine, but it really wasn't. I thought: I'm not sure why I'm doing this, it's very, very strange. Then I thought maybe I'm being unfair, maybe I'm leading him on, but then again, it's also my right to say no. The other day I saw him in London. He tried to kiss me again,
344

but this time I wouldn't. This slavish adoration of my body – it just made me feel contemptuous in the end.

Though I've definitely given charity fucks. Oh yes, definitely. At university there was this nice Jewish boy. I don't know why I slept with him. He was very religious and he was fascinated by me because he'd never met anyone who knew quite so much about Judaism as I did who wasn't a Jew. I am obsessed with Jews and things Jewish. He wasn't very attractive, but very clever, very interesting, and he did have another girlfriend. One night, very late, I went to his room to talk, assuming that, well, I'm a shikse, I'm forbidden fruit and anyway I'm not attracted to him. So we were talking and he told me that his girlfriend wouldn't even jerk him off and he was a virgin. Then he said, 'I think it's time for bed.' I said, 'Oh yes, the gates will be closing soon.' He said, 'No, no, no, I mean here, now. I want to make love to you in every way possible. You're much more attractive than I think you realise.' And I felt sorry for him. What was really funny was that he took off his glasses and he took off his yarmulka and carefully placed them by his bed. It wasn't very good and he had to take off his condom because he couldn't come with it on. That was definitely charity, but I did feel that maybe I was doing good for Jewishkind.

With my boyfriend I find that while tension puts me off sex, it seems to excite him. Whenever I get a bit upset or start crying he immediately gets an erection. Maybe he feels very protective, I don't know. But he said to me, 'You know what happens when you cry – you get fucked.' He says I'm unusual in terms of the women he's slept with in that I never say no to sex. Even if I didn't particularly feel like it I was quite happy for him to fuck me, and indeed I quite liked that, the human rubber doll; it's quite nice being 'used' in that way. It feels nice, obviously, someone penetrating you. Usually what happens is I'll say, 'Okay, you can fuck me, but I'm not going to come, I'm not going to do anything,' and he'll say, 'That's fine.' Though what happens is that I do end up coming because I end up getting turned on, so it's a sort of game that we play. A friend of mine said that sometimes her boyfriend is very good at foreplay and sometimes he's not – maybe he wants sex more than she does. So one night they're in bed and she's reading her book, and he asked her, 'Would you like a hot stiff one?' and she said, 'All right, as long as I can carry on reading my book.' He laughed his head off and they did have sex. I don't know whether she managed to carry on reading. But I do enjoy that sort of sex sometimes, it's pleasant, you lie on your back, you're not having to clamber around or make an enormous amount of effort and I don't find it demeaning either to me or to my partner. But we do have a good relationship. I know that for a man to make love to a woman

345

who just lies there and doesn't make any sort of response is very depressing. They might as well have a wank.

I have very sexual dreams. I suppose they're the equivalent of a wet dream in a man. I remember them very vividly in the morning when I wake up. I've definitely had an orgasm in a dream. I reproduce the exact mental feelings. I don't know whether physically I manifest the signs of having an orgasm in my sleep – though I'd love to know, I'd love to attach electrodes to myself. That can happen especially when I'm not having regular sex. More than ten days celibacy. What I would like is more sex in the afternoon; I think a lot of women probably would. It's nice having sex before you go to sleep, it's a lovely way to go to sleep, no doubt about it. Sometimes though you have to make an effort to have sex. The more you have the more you want and the less you have the less you have. Relationships are cyclical. You get bored. What was happening was that before I went away I'd have sex with my boyfriend and I'd be thinking about the other guy with whom I'd had the affair. Even though I had not enjoyed such good sex or such fulfilling sex with him. But it was different.

If I'm sitting at work and I'm bored and I'm surrounded by men I do start thinking about sex and I wonder what their cocks are like. I do that a lot and I know other women who do that a lot and I bet men just don't realise, because they're looking at women's tits and think about them sexually. What makes me laugh about men is the way that sometimes they stare at your tits and they think you don't know, meanwhile you're thinking: God, you're such a fool, I know exactly what you're doing. Women are a lot more subtle. I do like flirting, definitely. I like reading about sex, I like talking about sex and I like doing it.

I don't go to clubs or discos, or at least not straight ones. So I don't get that problem of dressing like a sex object and then having to turn down men who assume that means I'm going to sleep with them. The clubs I go to are gay clubs, which means you can wear whatever you want, and you can flirt outrageously. I was in this gay club in Washington and it was quite wonderful. There were these boys dancing on these small stages and I went over to gaze at them – they all have very good bodies, they work out a lot, they're quite tanned. And because it was so hot and sweaty they started taking their tops off. So I went over, because I love the smell of fresh male sweat and I thought: Why can't I just look at these lovely men, they're gorgeous. And this hand reached down and pulled me up onto the stage and for the next hour I just danced, sandwiched between these four sweating, heaving males and it was brilliant, it was such fun. I was tweaking their nipples, they loved it. It was absolutely safe sex, literally. I've never
346

had sex with a gay man, though I do have a gay friend – he has AIDS now – who I did really fancy. We once snogged, but that was all it ever amounted to. I have been to bed with somebody who's bisexual, a long time ago. There was this gorgeous Jewish gay man in New York who said, 'I'll marry you and you can stay here and get a green card.' I said, 'But you wouldn't sleep with me, would you?' He said 'No, I'm really sorry.' What women and gay men have together which is so nice is being able to cuddle, to sleep in the same bed or for you to be with a man without the slightest question of sexual threat. You can also get together to look at the posturings of straight men.

I can't understand some of my friends who get so angry about men. I have a friend who constantly boasts about how much sex she has with her boyfriend, which is rather tedious, and we were talking about prostitutes and she said that she thought about being one and I said, 'Yes, I wouldn't mind, because you don't have to kiss people.' She said, 'Oh really,' and I said ' No, no, no, prostitutes don't kiss men.' And I said that James used to go to prostitutes. I thought she'd be interested and curious but in fact she said, 'Oh, I think that's absolutely awful.' I said, 'Why?' She said, 'It's just using and abusing women.' I said, 'Is it really? Isn't it actually just a transaction that's mutually beneficial? I know that some women are oppressed and pushed into prostitution but not all of them.' She said, 'Well, you could just pick someone up in a bar if you were going to do that.' So I asked her why she'd been talking about being a prostitute herself and she replied, 'It's because I hate men so much it would be one way of getting back at them. They're so awful, I just hate all men.' So I suggested that her boyfriend was all right.'No. I'm just waiting for him to fuck me over. Every man fucks you over at the end of the day.' But women fuck men over as much as men do women.

It would be nice to be a mistress, a courtesan. But to be a straight prostitute ... It would be awful to have to go to bed with someone who was very unattractive, I don't think I could do that. Though in fact I probably have in the past, in terms of people who I didn't really fancy. It would be very boring to be a kept woman, but it would also be lovely in a way. It would just be lovely to know that somebody was absolutely totally sexually fascinated by you and in your thrall.

Sex is power, because it is an exchange. Some women certainly sleep with their husbands and partners and continue to do so because they want certain things. I want that new bathroom suite, I want that new Hoover, whatever. It's mercenary and depressing perhaps, but in the end on a certain level sex is quite mercenary. Some women don't have as strong a sex drive as their partners do, the men want sex more often than they do, so by doling it out, apportioning it, that gives them

347

a degree of power, of control. For some women sex is one way of getting a man's love.

FEMINISM REVISITED: Actions Speak Loudest

In some ways, for all the impassioned debates of the era, sex – at least as in traditional, heterosexual entanglements – went off the agenda for the feminists of the late Sixties and early Seventies. There were other, more urgent imperatives. The need to change the female image, to deny the bimbo/housewife, whore/Madonna stereotypes, dictated a deliberate diminution of what was seen as traditional feminine sexuality. The noisy chorus of media disapproval, casting the emergent feminists in the new stereotypes of crop-haired, dungareed 'libbers' and 'man-haters', only pointed up the general effect. Twenty years on the women who were growing up in that period, and whose lives have benefited from the vital, but still circumscribed successes of those early struggles, have different priorities. The earlier battles disposed of, they reject the need to desexualise themselves. As writer Suzanne Moore has said, an epitome of the changed style can be seen in the resurgence of the miniskirt, condemned by 1970 as a vehicle of male fantasy:'The Sixties miniskirt was part of the era of "permissiveness". Women who wore those skirts were saying yes to sex. The difference between those miniskirts and ones people wear today is that now women choose to wear it, but now it goes with the right to say yes or no or whatever they wanted to say. Also the way it was worn with padded shoulders and so on – a much more powerful image.' The avatars of the new style, the power-dressing yuppies of the Eighties, did not see themselves as feminists – far from it. Thatcherites, they had imbibed a decade's negative images of bra-burning harridans. The Nineties have ushered in a new style, what might be called a third wave of twentieth-century feminism – perversely labelled 'post-feminism' by the media – with a new agenda that both builds on the old manifestos, and advances into new, contemporary areas. Foremost among them is sex, definitely rehabilitated, but with a new twist: the conflation of what for many men are still incompatible concepts: the genuinely powerful woman and the sexy one.

MICHAEL VERMEULEN: I've tangibly benefited from feminism because, personally, now I've got much cooler girls to go out with. That's a real benefit. They're cooler, more independent, emotionally, intellectually, financially. Everything is great about them. They're stronger. Stronger women are good. We all wish to go out with strong women. It would be totally wrong to say men want soft pliable girls who'll do what they're told. If you do want that, you should seek professional help. Wanting strong women is better in every way – it's better for your head, for your dick, for your pocket. There's nothing bad about it.

KATE HEATH: Sex is a pet subject for me. It grew out of a lot of things, but basically it stems from feminism, which I tie in very much with sexuality. I found the brand of what I'd call second-wave feminism – Germaine Greer, Andrea Dworkin – hard to identify with. That feminism had said: Create your own identity. I understood that, and I identified with it, but it seemed to me amongst the women's groups at college and later, when I worked at *Spare Rib*, that there was a split between the experiences I'd had when I was growing up, and the experiences I'd had with my girlfriends, and what we were told by feminist theory. I'd wear miniskirts and makeup and I'd enjoy that and I'd generally try to be quite flirty and I found that this was somehow not acceptable and that I was having to justify it to myself. It took years to get beyond that. In the feminist context you built up a guilt trip. I saw it as going from one stereotype to another: don't shave your legs, dress down, don't liberate your body or your sexuality. The idea was not to accentuate sexuality but instead to neutralise it so it wasn't threatening. But what I wanted was a celebration – I didn't want to go around feeling guilty. I wanted it to be empowering.

SUZANNE MOORE: That first generation of feminists, *The Female Eunuch* lot, what they were doing was completely outside my experience. When I got to college and read it, it was like a historical document. Interesting, yes, but purely as history. This was 1983, and the book had come out in 1971. I was impressed: when you discover something you always think that no one else has ever thought like this before, so of course to realise in fact that someone else had been writing this stuff for a long time was very satisfying.

When I was young I didn't call myself a feminist. I was wearing lipstick and so on and I always thought that I can't possibly be a feminist because I like these things. The women whom I came across who did describe themselves as feminists didn't like these things and I thought, I'm clearly not one of those. But looking back I realise that I was a feminist without calling myself one. I was always very independent, travelled round on my own and did all that sort of thing. What finally made me identify myself as a feminist was reading Erica Jong's book, *Fear of Flying*. We all read that at school, passed it round when we were about fifteen or sixteen. I don't think so now, but then I thought: This is it. Then, when I was twenty-four, I went to college and did cultural studies which has a lot of Marxist and feminist stuff and I realised then that yes, I was a feminist, and it was silly saying no I'm not. I just thought: I can no longer ignore this, I can no longer pretend that this stuff that I'm reading doesn't apply to me. I can no longer stand to one side. But I did react strongly against what I saw as the puritanical streak in it; what I didn't want was to just swap one set of rules about what being a woman was for another.

KATE HEATH: At a certain level I can identify with the problems that second generation feminism had: the difficulties of communicating with men. A lot of it was very American, dwelling more on the housewife, on women not being able to pursue their own goals in life, on being tied by motherhood and other restrictions. But by the time feminism got round to me, attitudes had changed. You'd had the equality laws and all the rest of it. Though I still very much believe that women still get the raw deal.

Second-wave feminists had to take up a defensive position. Obviously you wanted to shift the agenda and move the debate on, but first of all that early feminism had to justify its own position. A lot of it was very insular, more into separatism and women creating a space for themselves, which they needed to because they needed to recreate their own identities. Like any political movement you try to build up your strengths first and try to get your arguments right, and then you go out and say this is what we want. And it was the legacy of that period that I benefited from. Attitudes had changed, which meant that my experiences were totally different.

By the time my girlfriends and I were growing up we were strong, we had that security, that freedom to choose. We were proud of ourselves, we wanted to be women, but at the same time we weren't going to take shit off guys and we couldn't understand how the scales were still weighted against us. It's not strictly speaking an aggressive form of feminism, but since certain questions have already been answered for you, you try then to move on to a different set of questions. And what happens is that you think it's not enough that women have changed, what you want now is for men to change.

350

My generation of feminists has the opportunity to be more honest and less ideologically bound than the one before us. I don't want to be defensive, to have to spend my time justifying my position. I've spent a lot of time trying to achieve the identity that I have and I enjoy it, I enjoy the freedom I have, I enjoy the opportunities I have, sexually and otherwise. A lot is down to my peer group, seeing what their experiences are. I have quite strong female friends and we talk about sex a lot and joke about it, and we'll trot off to a movie together and talk about wank fantasies. It's all on a jokey level. It is quite laddish in a way, because when you work in a left-wing culture which is supposed to be quite PC, you do need to have a sense of humour. If I got depressed by the objective situation, I wouldn't have the sense of humour I do. I think we're still ideologically sound – we can trot out all the theories but you still don't want the guilt trip, to wear a cross round your neck saying I'm a woman or I'm black or disabled and trying to get that credibility. We don't need that credibility, we've got it already. So let's move it on, let's be more aggressive.

I never grew up thinking I was a second-class citizen. I might have felt victimised in various circumstances, but I didn't identify with being a victim just because I was a woman. It still wasn't really an equal relationship, but you did have the opportunity to please yourself more, you weren't so much expected to go along one chosen path, you actually had freedom. There were various paths to choose from. I suppose that was where you had the beginnings of the Eighties career woman, the power bitch syndrome and all the rest of it.

For feminists of my era there are lots of powerful women role models. There were lots of people to identify with and say, yeah, it's possible. Look at Madonna – she's an incredibly sussed lady and of course she's a major icon. The thing about her is she seems to be in control, she seems to be calling the shots and she's not doing it as a male fantasy. She's directed and she's manipulated her own image and she's created Madonna for herself. Normally female pop stars are told by their agents, by their record companies to behave in a certain way. Madonna is quite the opposite. She's in control, and not only in control but she's redefining things and shocking people into seeing things differently. She's nobody's fool and she's articulate and she's bright and she's successful. What Madonna's about is power; about controlling her own image; the clothes themselves are irrelevant. She's an incredibly astute woman.

SUZANNE MOORE: Do men get Madonna's joke? I don't care. When Madonna came here on tour last time there were all these pieces in the papers saying, 'Oh she's gone too far this time, she doesn't even

351

look sexy ...' as though the whole point of what she does is to look sexy for a particular kind of man. The whole point of Madonna is that she epitomises the girl dancing in front of the bedroom mirror by herself. Auto-eroticism, that whole fantasy. She's not doing it for anyone else. If boys and men don't understand, that's just a part of the problem, because women's understanding of themselves is ten years ahead of most men's understanding. But I don't think that women should have to apologise for that. Women have run out of patience.

I do feel an enormous debt to Sixties' feminism. But I don't feel that any of those people have the right to dictate my attitudes. I'm not accountable to them, though I think they want me to be. Feminism cannot deal with generational differences at all. A lot of people are very, very worried about me because I'm not in academia writing feminist books. They see me as having gone astray. They say I'm not a good enough feminist because I work in the mainstream. After I wrote a piece on advertising I had somebody say to me, 'When I was your age we didn't waste our time on advertising, we used to be writing Utopian novels.' I'm sorry, that's not what I do. I don't know whether I'm doing anything better, but that generation does have to realise that the institutional bases have changed. Those people, a lot of them, got jobs in academia, which gave them a base from which to work. Women now, what do they do? Where do they go to 'do' feminism? It's not so simple any more.

Those women may have won their battle – they did get into the power bases they wanted – but I don't know. A lot of them feel incredibly personally let down. I don't know exactly what they wanted, but a lot of them feel passed by. They feel that no one did ever thank them; I think they wanted to be thanked and they weren't ever thanked. They did all this stuff back then, but young women today don't thank them. It's like the *Feminist Review Collective* – they all think that they own feminism, but they don't. It's an idea, they don't own it. But they were really there, they were there in '68 and you weren't. It's like a hierarchy: you're never going to know what it was really about. I resent that. And that generation has alienated so many people. Something happened that's made it very hard for younger women to come up. There is this generational jealousy and that's what makes it very hard to talk about. If you look at all the latest books that have been coming out – Germaine Greer, Gloria Steinem, Naomi Wolf, Marilyn French – they're all terrible. Awful. I had to review Marilyn French's book and I thought: Who is this book for? And I thought maybe I shouldn't, it was for the *Literary Review* and did I want to bash feminism in Auberon Waugh's magazine? But I couldn't say it was any good when it wasn't. But why is this generation of
352

women producing this complete tosh? Does Germaine Greer or Naomi Wolf represent anyone but herself? Has Germaine Greer ever represented anyone but Germaine Greer?

KATE HEATH: My attitude to feminism is both a development of what happened in the Sixties and a reaction against it. That Sixties generation did do a lot, they set the wheels in motion and we get the benefit of the way they changed attitudes. There was the question of patriarchy, and the emotional side of it and the economic side, and the idea that women could have careers and that they didn't need to be tied to the home and that there were other roles for them as well as having children. So I benefited from all those ideas because I've grown up with that freedom of choice. But, on the other hand, when I talk to my girlfriends and see what their experiences are, the thing is that men aren't as sexist and they're re-evaluating their position too, and while they may not be changing quickly enough, they're definitely changing.

I'm not a post-feminist. Definitely not, because post suggests that something's ended and that's not the case. It's not like one particular strand, it's not one homogenous group. I think a lot of women have changed but there's no such thing as a group of 'post-feminists'. It's all on an individual level rather than a collective one.

SUZANNE MOORE: The whole relationship to the left which feminism has had here, I originally found productive but in the end I've moved away from that. At college there was this thing of the feminists saying, 'Well, Marx is great, but he didn't do this and all we've got to do is add on this extra bit to Marx and the answer will be there.' I never believed that. Anyway I didn't think Marx was the Bible: that if you stared at it long enough it would produce all the answers. I thought it was good and it was useful, but that's what it was. Going to college later than a lot of people, and coming from my background, I just didn't have this reverence – 'Oh my God, this is Marx, this is Germaine Greer' – I always thought you could just have a bit of this, a bit of that.

KATE HEATH: You can't separate socialism and feminism. They are so totally integrated that you just can't divide them. It's that whole argument about post-modernism and post-Fordism. You don't just have one identity or one belief, you have a fluid choice of identities and you can have links with various different groups. So my ideas of racism or sexism or homophobia are so intertwined, because all of them are some form of repression.

Instinctive sexual politics arrived in my life quite early. On the most basic level I noticed the way my brothers got treated differently from my sisters at quite an early age. I always had this sense of injustice; I didn't just accept things. I had this basic perception that something wasn't quite right in the world. Then proper sexual politics arrived when I went to college. I started to learn some theory, which backed up what I already knew from my own experience. I'd read a lot of women-centred books. It did affect my relationships with my boyfriends: basically they thought I was a stroppy cow. The biggest argument was that I didn't always say yes to what they wanted. I'd say, 'Well no, I want to do this' – I'd always argue my own corner. Whether that came from feminism or whether I was just spoiled, the youngest of six, I don't know. It certainly became more of an issue the older I got and the more I got into it.

I'm very anti any essentialist arguments, because I don't see them as really advancing anything. The whole idea that somehow women are inherently good and men are inherently bad always smacked of someone trying to work out a biological reason. Whereas it seemed to me that it was socially constructed. The idea that men were one way and women were another suggested that you couldn't change anything. It's wrong to enforce things, I don't like the idea of coercing people into changing or doing something because they feel they have to. I'm really anti political correctness. If you want to do something you do it, because that's what you believe in. It has to be something you firmly believe in, not acting out something, adopting a position. Everyone should be able to justify what their political beliefs are.

I don't believe that women have to become more masculine to succeed. I think that's something else for which second-wave feminists are responsible. This idea that in order to succeed as a woman you somehow have to become aggressive, beat them at their own game. But using bitterness as a starting point, I don't think that actually worked.

Now women are more aware of their own sexuality. Masturbation wasn't talked about in my mother's day. I don't know whether the second-generation feminists did, but we did. I found that as I got older my women friends would talk readily about sex, and be quite open about their experiences. There weren't any taboo subjects. I find that talking to women now most of them have got vibrators. You don't hear guys talking openly about wanking. My girlfriends all sit down and we'll discuss it and say this was good, this was enjoyable, whatever. I was about fourteen, fifteen when I had my first orgasm;
354

that was through masturbation and I continued doing that. The boys I slept with were all right, there was some pleasure, but it wasn't really good. There was a difference between just having sex and having really good sex. It all tended to be quite mechanical. The boys weren't very sexually experienced. So we were both in the same position. Because a lot of sex is to do with how experienced you are and how good the other person is. It's something you develop as you get older and you get to understand more. But at that age it's quite mechanical and quite quick. In the end it's like most things: sometimes you enjoyed it but most of the time it was just another day.

I quite enjoy wearing stockings, or wearing particular underwear. But the second-wave feminists drilled into you that that was male fantasy, that you couldn't participate in that – and if you did you were just acting to please the male. But I get pleasure out of it and I get pleasure out of seeing my partner pleased. For instance one thing I enjoy and I know my boyfriend enjoys is spanking. Or I'll dress up, wank in front of him or whatever. But for those earlier feminists you weren't supposed to do things like that, things which were traditionally seen as being a male prerogative. Sometimes I'd do it as a surprise element, I thought: Oh yeah. I'll try that one. It's a two-way thing. You don't really talk about it – you just get on and do it.

The thing is we do have fantastic sex, and Nick is my best sexual partner – although that's a lot to do with the emotional side too. We have this level of trust and I can be who I want to be and do what I want to do and I know he'll support it. At the same time it's quite safe for us to play out sexual fantasies. I suppose it's great that he still wants sex as often as he does. It's really nice still to be desired by someone. I think what happens now is that we go for quality rather than quantity. I suppose like most people when you first start going out, all you want to do is fuck the brains out of them most of the time, that's the focal point of the relationship. You go out for a meal and you're thinking: How much longer have I got to wait. We certainly did. But after two and a half years it's different. Maybe we'll do a bit of coke and I'll dress up and we go to bed for the evening and it'll be more an event, rather than just continual lust. But because we've been together for some time, there are no inhibitions now, you trust each other, it's all about experimentation. Sometimes I do expect him to perform. I'll just be really passive, though it's not that I'm deliberately challenging him, I'm just lazy and selfish. I'm knackered from work and I just enjoy what's being done to me.

I held an Ann Summers party recently and that was really interesting. I was quite interested in what it entails. There were about eight women here. Most of them already have vibrators. I showed them the catalogue and it wasn't the underwear that they were so much interested in, as the sexual aids. Someone wanted to get another vibrator and someone wanted some love eggs. I thought perhaps there would be some element of shyness – you can make your orders in secret so that no one else knows what you're organising. I got some underwear, but most of my friends got either love eggs or vibrators. One girl had her boyfriend pick her up from here and she immediately got the love egg and started playing with it – they're quite funny. All these things, they're just acceptable now. I don't think I'm a prude, but I was quite surprised.

SUZANNE MOORE: People are certainly more open about things like vibrators. At one time it was more of a secret, but now it's much more talked about. It's also partly the way they're sold – it's easier for women to go and buy them. All those Ann Summers parties. They are amazing, selling all this really horrible, tacky kind of underwear. 'Lager-flavoured booby drops' that you put on your nipples. Now if you wanted someone to lick lager off your nipples you can just put lager on them. Why buy this little tube of lager-flavoured gel? It's incredible to me. But they do have all these dildos and stuff, though they don't do any sales pitch for that. They just appear and the women pass them round and giggle. If you ask the rep, 'What's this one?' it's funny: that's the one thing they won't talk about. They'll talk about these revolting acrylic nighties but not the vibrator. A lot of women I know will go to a sex shop with another woman, but it's still quite difficult. Not the same as it is for men. But a lot of young women are a lot more open. It's the whole thing of masturbation. We've been told that we can do it and that really has made a difference. You used to read those really sad letters in the women's magazines – 'Will something terrible happen to me if I do this?' – you realise how far, in some ways, we have come.

KATE HEATH: Sex is always a major talking point, wherever I've been working, *City Limits*, even *Spare Rib*. Constantly discussing it, constantly making references, constantly joking about it. Sex is seen as a source of fun; sex wasn't seen as much as a source of fun with second-wave feminism. You were supposed to be guilty, you were supposed to be apologetic. Whereas I like the idea of having fun, of trying to shock, of provoking comment. The girls I work with now are far more crude than the guys. We'll often be sitting there talking, 'Did he come in your mouth?' whatever. I guess it is a deliberate reaction to years of women being barred from saying these things. Now you take a delight in being able to talk about it.

356

I get quite stressed out at work – the deadlines, whatever. So I was talking to my boyfriend and he said, 'Why don't you go and have a wank in the toilets, calm yourself down.' I did think about it, but there's no way I could get turned on in the toilets, or even do it on a release level. I talked about it to a couple of girlfriends: 'Can you imagine it, trying to wank in the toilets at work?' They both said, 'Well, we find it quite useful.' They both work for big magazines. They do it, they go off to the toilets, either because they feel horny or because they want relief. Maybe offices are full of men and women rushing off to the toilets to release tension.

Men have much less of a sense of humour when it comes to sex. They're far more strait-jacketed by what they are supposed to be sexually, far more tied up with performance and having to achieve. Women are more willing to laugh at themselves, to ridicule themselves, it doesn't matter if they show themselves up; when guys discuss sex they don't have that humour. Even if a guy cracks a joke that is derogatory about his sexual performance, often what he's really doing is looking for reassurance. Deep down it's not a joke, but this plea: 'Don't laugh, reassure me.' 'No, that really was perfectly all right, darling.' You do have this great power. You know what's going to hurt the other person, you know what their weak spots are.

There are still huge gaps between men and women, but what has changed is attitudes. It happens on a very basic level, even if it takes time for the Law to catch up. Look at dietary habits: for years white bread was the norm, and now most people choose to eat brown. That hasn't been forced on us, but it's developed naturally and that's far more lasting and far more successful.

ALEX KERSHAW: Men just want to have sex. Women want something more. Their sexuality is different. They want more, expect more. And that's why they're often disappointed by men. Not many women are just looking for a piece of meat, whereas men still are. That's where the superiority of women comes in. Men's sexual fantasies are a lot less developed and healthy than women's. Women have a greater capacity to fantasise about sex, to bring in different elements.

KATE HEATH: Most women would say that emotion is important in bed, not just plain sex, but I also know a lot of women who do like to go out and pick up guys and have sex with them on a purely physical level. Simply because they want sex and they're attracted to someone and it's purely a one-night stand. Though they do tend to have a

357

bigger guilt complex about it afterwards than men, they feel they have to justify it. I'm quite prudish myself, I've only ever had one one-night stand. No casual sex. I've obviously experimented, though, got into being tied up, taken various amounts of drugs while I'm having sex, and some sex aids.

ARAMINTA LOCKHEAD: Women are the initiators more now. Specially when you get older. When you're younger, it seems a bit clinical to ask for what you want. You're afraid they'll go off you if you issue instructions. I've generally had to make the first moves. People expect it of me anyway, because I'm quite bossy. So I get submissive men, which isn't what I want. I'm not interested in the stern mistress bit. The worst thing is when you pick somebody up you think is going to be really cool, tough, all the time you're out they boss you around and you get them home and it's really disappointing. All gone. I don't indulge them, that turns me off completely.

One time I decided my friends were getting too boring, all going with regular boys and so on, and I thought I'd liven things up a bit, and started a gang. The criterion was you had to be single, have a car and a wig. It was all going out and behaving like teenagers again, picking up boys, etc.. We'd go on the Chelsea cruise every month, all dressed in our wigs, in my American car, showing off. We had the Gang Girl Knickers – which you were awarded when you joined the gang. Black rubber knickers with a six-inch dildo and a four-inch dildo. We'd have meetings, go to parties. It was my way of trying to bring fun back into sex. I was really bored with them all living with their boyfriends, thinking of having babies. Their male partners hated it, hated me. They thought I was a subversive influence, and how childish we all were. But we just had a really good time, for about a year. We took the Gang Girl Knickers into the office one day. Everyone had an initiation to join the gang. I can't reveal that. Mine was a cop-out, nothing to do with sex at all, I was to do a parachute jump. Something I'd always wanted to do but was scared of. I did it, but broke my back, so it didn't work out. For one of the other girls, she had to seduce her boss, in a particular situation. That backfired – she's now married to him. It was all things you'd do when you were eighteen, in the backs of cars, etc. We were all in our thirties. It made everything fun for a while.

NICHOLAS CHARLES: I was with a girl once who was really turned on by group sex but had never done it. She fantasised a great deal about it, so I suggested we advertise. So we did. It ran: 'He, thirty years old etc.; she, twenty-four years old, blonde. She wants a birthday to remember. Write with gift suggestions. Send photo.' We got about thirty-six letters. They all sent photos, and some letters were pretty interesting. One was a psycho. Wrote the letter with his dick.

We did actually do it too. Men often want to realise their fantasies, women prefer to fantasise their fantasies. So for her it got a little out of hand. I think she felt a little manipulated – she didn't think I'd really do it. We had two guys. I interviewed them first, over a drink in a pub in Bloomsbury. I'd asked her what kind of guys she wanted to sleep with. Part of her fantasy was for me to pick them. So I picked two of the five. One night they came back here, got my girl stoned, a little drunk, we had a few drinks in the living room, then I sent her off to bed with one of them. The other guy and I sat and chatted, then I sent him up too. I think I watched the news. Then I went up and joined them. We did this for a while, then we all went to a late-night pool hall, put the guys in a cab and sent them off. That was it. We didn't argue about it; she just didn't think it was as great as she'd imagined. The problem might have been that I was too cool about it. I just got the feeling it wasn't great for her. Anyway, she never asked to do it again. We still see each other, too.

ALEX KERSHAW: I've met a few wham-bam women. It's quite a turn-off. It was a one-night stand, me getting my sexual kick, they getting theirs. But they were enjoying it more than me, they were the ones demanding more. It's women being in a situation where they can get what they want sexually. Maybe that's what they've always wanted. You can't separate the social conditioning and expectations women grow up with, from what they feel able to expect in bed. I've found women who were more highly sexed than me, just from the way their bodies worked. You knew they wanted it, needed it, and that was fine by them. I didn't find it threatening or worrying, but I didn't like it. Wasn't something I wanted. Couldn't imagine being in love with them, or caressing them, or it becoming a fulfilling relationship. That's what I didn't like, so I didn't want to repeat it.

NETTIE POLLARD: A lot of men do like assertive women. But male chauvinism has taken a bashing. You can't feel the master the whole time any more. It's not considered unfeminine for women to be assertive. That must be nice for some men, they don't have to perform on the woman any more. And young men today don't know what it was like to be a young man twenty years ago. Some men do feel threatened by assertive females. That's a transitionary thing probably.

359

I don't see it going backwards. Women have more right to sex now. It's not something men do to women, it's something people do together. We're in transition to things becoming more equal. Things may not necessarily get better, but men may get less tense. It is difficult for men at the moment, they're not sure what's expected of them any more. Women's roles have changed and men's haven't. Women are much more assertive than they used to be, much less likely to put up with being bullied. And the whole way women are presented is different now.

SUZANNE MOORE: I really object to this moral thing. Feminism to me is a politics, I don't want it to be a morality that's imposed on me from people who don't really know what they're talking about. That Robert Bly stuff, *Iron John*, it's all so moralising about everything. They're very anti-sex, you can only have this cosy, consensual sex; there's good sex and there's bad sex; I think it's got very little to do with what I consider to be any kind of sexual liberation; it's actually quite repressive. I don't think there is such a thing as good sex or bad sex. There's all kinds of sex I might not want to do. There is bad sex in the sense of sex where force is used, and child abuse and all that, but there's a fair consensus about that. But what people actually do on their own that they want to do ... There are a lot of things I might find quite revolting and I don't understand, but that doesn't mean that people should be imprisoned for it.

KATE HEATH: Women do have men as a sexual fantasy in the same way as men have women. So they'll quite often joke about using some guy on TV or wanting to go to bed with him or wouldn't it be nice for him to have cunnilingus with me one night and you joke about them in the same way as men have always joked about women as sexual objects. Which is me being incredibly sexist. Sometimes I'll say, 'Well, I'd give him one'. On one level I pretend it's ironic, but on another level I do really enjoy it. Sometimes I do use men as pure sexual objects. You want sex, and the prior concern is to get yourself off. That's also part of the fantasy, whether it's because you want to satisfy your own sexual need or whether you want to have that power over someone else. It's also a turn-on to create desire. To see your desire for them reflected in their desire for you.

I like men, oh yeah, I love them. I also think some of them are complete bastards ... anyway, they've got a lot to answer for. Men are expected to behave in a certain way; there's this onus upon them to be seen to be male, and if they are seen in any way to be sensitive it

360

somehow detracts. This mythology that if a man is caring, there is the immediate assumption that he's therefore effeminate. Which is awfully strait-jacketing – at least women can assume different roles. For men, you're either weak or you're powerful, there's no in-between ground. Half of me despises them, half feels sorry for them. My one gripe is that now it's up to men to change. They must know by now where they're going wrong, but they're still really only paying lip-service; they don't actually do anything constructive – they're still unwilling to give up their power positions. There's still this selfishness: They want women to be equal, but on another level. They don't actually want to give up power themselves, they don't actually want to shift the hierarchy.

SUZANNE MOORE: I've become tougher, more demanding. Though it's as much getting older as some political stance. I won't put up with things I used to put up with. The obvious thing is housework. The thing that everybody argues with. It may not be much to do with sex, but it's more important, it's more destructive of a relationship. You can go without sex, but you can't go without someone doing the housework. I suppose I am more demanding sexually. Though I don't think men have to perform for me. I've got two kids, I'm too tired. The reason I don't have a lot of casual sex now is not moral, I don't think it's wrong, but because a lot of casual sex isn't very good sex. How many times do you have a one-night stand that actually isn't that fantastic? If that's demanding, then I'm demanding, yes, but not in terms of pure performance. I do think women verbalise their sexual wants more today. This may have been a hangover from the Sixties, but for myself and my circle of friends, I think we felt that whatever men wanted to do, whatever their fantasy was, you should go along with it. Even if you didn't really want to. If you read something like *Forum*, it's still full of it: try anything, it's all positive. But now I'm more sure of what I like to do and confident enough to say, 'No, I don't have to do such and such.' Not that you don't experiment, but you do it because of what you're into, not to please a man.

It's not a matter of 'what do women want?' That's not it. Women say very clearly what they want. The question is when will people believe that what they say they want is what they want? If you take the basic demands of twenty years ago – none which are so extreme. Should women be able to have abortions, should women be able to walk the streets without fear, should childcare be easier to get, should there be equal pay ...? These are very basic things and that's what I would still argue for. A lot of what I write about is about image and culture, but until you've got those basic things the image and culture

361

aren't going to shift. What is so hard about dealing with what women want? There seems to be this fear that if you give women what they want they're so insatiable that they'll want more and more.

If women are becoming less tolerant, if they're saying enough's enough, well that's great. Maybe we are moving towards separation. Maybe people do have to have that space apart. Maybe that has to happen? But I will not feel sorry and I will not take responsibility for the fact that so many men feel confused. That is entirely their own problem. Men aren't prepared to take responsibility for the things they've done to women, collectively that is, and if they don't know what to do, all this stuff about, 'Oh I don't know, I thought I was just having fun in the office and now you tell me it was sexual harassment ...' actually most people do know what they're doing. People can draw a line between behaviour that's mildly flirtatious and behaviour that's actually offensive, most of us pretty much know what it is. Men have got away with saying, 'Oh, I didn't really know the difference ...' for too long. Tough. Anyway, there's only a few people trying to make this change; most of the media is controlled by men, men who aren't interested in changing anything.

This whole debate about political correctness is interesting – why are these guys so threatened, why are they so worried about it? If people like Michael Ignatieff feel uncertain and threatened, then as far as I'm concerned, I feel very happy about that. If PC is a threat, then it shows the success of some of that lefty feminist stuff. If you say,'Well, language is important and language carries ideology,' the fact that the right is reacting so strongly against PC means that some of that has got through. Some of it is dumb – the extreme, nutty things – but some is important and valid.

NETTIE POLLARD: Things have certainly changed for women to some extent, but a lot of it is pretty tokenistic. The movement has largely been taken over by the mainstream, which is very sad. It's more acceptable now. It is much easier for women to get into the professions now, but the lower-paid women are in the same old position, working in sweatshops, etc. The better-off, more privileged women have been bought off by being allowed to be called Ms now. I try to avoid it, just give my full name, and if pushed I'll say Ms, or occasionally for fun I'll say Mrs. I enjoy a good laugh.

SUZANNE MOORE: In the mid-Eighties feminism had evolved to a point where you could have this kind of cultural feminism, where you could read Virago novels and go to a nice feminist play and that made

362

you a good feminist. But what did they actually mean about your life? As a movement there was no centre, no leaders. There were feminist attitudes everywhere you looked but nowhere you could pin down and say, 'That's what feminism is now.' It was everywhere and at the same time nowhere. The success of this cultural feminism meant that the actual politics, the debate about how you actually changed things got a bit lost. You always have 'I'm not a feminist but ...' coming from people who then proceed to say very, very feminist things. The media have been very successful in portraying feminists as hairy-legged harridans and that has worked. A lot of people feel that.

ALEX KERSHAW: The 'ideal woman' is still associated with gentleness, femininity, caring, the maternal instinct. That's the stereotype that still attracts men. But now women have extra elements – not necessarily masculine – they're more able to be confident, positive. It's the confidence factor really. If it's aggressive confidence, men do feel threatened, feel inadequate. Definitely. And rightly so. It's the man's problem, he has to pull his socks up and progress a little bit. Not the women. I would never say women have gone too far. People can go as far as they want – that's the nature of progress. We should all be progressing.

NETTIE POLLARD: Women do demand more now. All the surveys now show that. It's reflected in women's magazines. There's been a big change in *Cosmo* in the last few years. One issue had in it '101 Uses for Sex'. Very much going away from the idea as women as the potential sexual victims to male aggression. It's much more how to handle your man, how to get what you want, how to get your orgasms. But I'm not a *Cosmo* fan, and I don't like that attitude much either. It's very competitive: if you're not having sex you're a bit of a failure. There's not much in those magazines about problems. You're meant to be having wonderful sex, wonderful orgasms. Which is certainly a long way from the position where women weren't meant to enjoy sex at all – it wasn't 'ladylike'. But there is this pressure to be having a fantastic time, having multiple orgasms and so on. That can be quite oppressive.

SUZANNE MOORE: Sex, on the level of what people do in bed, rather than just gender, has become far too important. I personally feel it's got boring and that there are more interesting things to talk about. People think they're being radical just talking about sex, but a lot of what's done in the name of being radical isn't actually that radical any

363

more. Obviously sex is important in people's personal lives, but what women need to do now is not all this introspection – Is my sex life good enough? whatever – but to look at what's going on outside, outside in the world. The problem for a lot of women is that they live in this emotional world and they should be encouraged not to.

Women are continually being told that the battles have been won and we shouldn't be angry any more, but why shouldn't women be impatient? That whole thing about feminism being some sort of nice thing that will just happen. But it's not just going to happen. It's never going to be a clean fight, it's about power and nobody wants to give up power. I do believe that if the goals of feminism were met a lot of men would actually be happier too.

ALEX KERSHAW: The truth is that men haven't changed much, and women are more intolerant of their attitude. Men do bring things that can be seen to be bad to women, but some women enjoy it. They like the firmness, the traditional male qualities, the risk-taking, the aggression, the need men have to dominate, the element of security that men do and don't provide. All those stereotypes do still work powerfully and still apply. I don't think men will ever catch up, because of the different makeup of men and women. Women are just superior in so many ways. But so far, until men do change, women don't have much option but to sit and twiddle their fingers.

TRACEY MINTO

'I tell them what I want'

In 1976, when she was born, the Sixties were fast receding into history, punk was the happening thing and gender politics rampant. Labour would have three more years in power. In the streets the National Front, waiting for the consolations of Thatcherism, fought bloody encounters with the Anti-Nazi League. She, and her peers and juniors, are the proof of that pudding.

My mum had said to herself: 'When my children are four years old I'm going to tell them what sex is.' So we never needed to ask because we just learnt. My mum and her boyfriend – he's a sort of hippie, long after the real hippies had given up – run a health-food shop. What I've learned from them is the balance you have to achieve in your sex life. But their generation were brought up when all sex was seen as not the done thing and their reaction was to do exactly the reverse. So I can see that what you want's between that.
364

My parents were real Sixties' people. They were very over-sexual. Always talking about it and in some ways pushing it onto me. The effect that had was to put me off for a while. Because what happened was that I connected sex with my parents which meant that if they liked it it wasn't something I wanted to do. It wasn't rebellious to do it any more, it was rebellious not to. I couldn't stop connecting my parents with sex, which just made it off-putting. But I realised that this was stupid, and one of the reasons why I started off having sex quite young was because I thought I've got to get over this, I've got to sort it out. I wanted to have sex but didn't want to have them ruin it.

So at first I thought the whole idea of sex was totally repulsive. But when I started discussing it with friends I did see it was a pleasure, for women as well as men, and not a duty. Anyway I already knew pretty much everything about sex by the time I started doing it. I was fourteen. That's quite average these days. I was looking forward to losing it: I just wanted to get it out of the way and I felt that I should have been doing it. That had started when I was about thirteen and a half. The first time was really shit actually. I didn't know the bloke, really. I'd only met him the Saturday and I lost my virginity on the Monday. But I can't actually remember much, because I was drunk at the time. It wasn't that important. I knew it was going to happen pretty soon, so that's why I did it. He wasn't a good screw and yeah, I would have known if he had been. Even though he was a lot older than me, he was twenty and I was fourteen, he seemed to think that there was a certain way that you should do it, and that's what makes people crap in bed: if they sort of think you should do it that way and it's not because they want to do it that way, just because they think you should do it that way. So all that made him crap in bed. Still, I went out with him for eight months, but after six months of it I just stopped having sex with him, 'cos I thought it was just not worth it, at all.

He was a lot older than me, but he didn't feel as if he was. I actually felt older than him, emotionally and mentally. I basically babied him throughout our relationship. I was like his mother, even though I was so much younger. I've never had a man who didn't see me as his mother. Sometimes that's what I want but it really does vary. When somebody brings out your maternal instinct is when you feel most feminine, and it feels nice to feel feminine, but after a while it can get on your nerves, when someone starts depending on you. It might be nice in the beginning but it just gets too much after a while. And that doesn't make the sex any better. I prefer it when you've just met somebody and you don't know them that well, because it gets boring after you've just done it so many times.

Boys may want me to be their mother, but no way do I want them to be my father. No way, I hate that. Totally. I don't actually want anything from them really. I'd really prefer friendship and staying single. I definitely prefer being rated as a friend by blokes than as a lover. Much more. Most of my friends are male. When you meet somebody you think: Are they attractive or unattractive and if they're attractive are they a friend or sexually attractive? I go for the people I like as friends first. Though there's always an element of sexual attraction, with men and with women as well. I haven't actually had any sexual relationships with women, although with my best friend it's a very sexual friendship, though not physically. Sometimes it's been pretty close and neither of us would worry if it did go further. I'm inquisitive and I don't want to die without having had some sort of lesbian experience. We talk about it all the time, and at the moment we both find it hysterically funny. I do think that she's really attractive. We talk about our boyfriends all the time and maybe it's true, we're living out our own relationship through them.

We're always sitting there together telling each other what we've done with our boyfriends – 'Oh yeah?' 'Oh yeah!' – and we're swapping hints and so on and I think half of the fun of the relationships with the boys is telling her what we've been doing, and vice versa. But it's not boasting, the way boys do. It's, 'I really shouldn't tell you this, you'll be shocked, you'll be shocked.' 'No I won't, no I won't.' Then I tell her and she goes, 'Oooohhhh!!! God. I'm not shocked.' I did French kiss her once. It was an experiment at the time. It wasn't to see whether we could do it with boys; it came way after that. We just wanted to see what each other was like and see if kissing a girl was the same as kissing a boy. We were both very drunk and we both had hysterics afterwards. We did it in public, but I don't think anyone noticed.

The fact that I started having sex at fourteen doesn't make me a slag. It might have done twenty or thirty years ago, but that's not how I see myself. My friends are all doing the same thing. My mate Natasha she didn't give a shit, she had twelve blokes in a year. I've had three long-term relationships – the first for eight months, the next thirteen months and I'm in one now – and I don't see myself as a slag at all, that's the last thing I'd call myself and I'd find it really insulting if someone called me a slag. A slag is somebody that tries to gain respect by shagging. It's not because they want it, but just because they think that people will like them more if they'll have sex with them. Which a lot of people do.

I wish I could just screw and move on but I feel too guilty. It would be degrading myself. I've got this big thing where I need to be respected and I feel if I did that I wouldn't respect myself, let alone anyone else respecting me. So I couldn't do that. Which means I put myself through these long-term relationships that eventually go a bit stale. I don't actually like relationships. I prefer to be single. But I always end up getting into a new one before the first one's ended, so ...

What happens is that people get attached to me too easily, people like me too much, and it gets impossible to get out of a relationship. They get too dependent. I'd just like it if they liked me a bit less. I'm extremely faithful – I've only been unfaithful once. I make a point of being totally monogamous. I wouldn't like someone to do it to me, so I do my best not to do it to other people.

***

I have had an orgasm with a man. But only with his hand, not his cock. It was brilliant. Just being on this total high. Rushes going up and down my body, feelings all through you, everything at once, really overpowering. You just lose your sense of self. It feels like you're taking off, flying. It's always before we actually fuck. And I'm satisfied then and it doesn't matter whether, when we have penetrative sex, whether I come or not. I don't go out for it. Sometimes I'm just thinking, after an orgasm, That's it. Aaagggh, aagghh! and I can't think of anything else. Sometimes I think: Right I know exactly what I need. I need to be fucked now. And that's all that goes through my head. Orgasm means loss of control, but I always feel that I'm in control of the situation. My attitude is if they're not going to finish me off, then I will, and when I do I know that they're getting a kick out of it as well.

I can't be bothered to masturbate – I just get my boyfriend to do it for me. It's really tedious, and I really couldn't be bothered to do it myself. So I've had more orgasms with a boyfriend than on my own. I don't know whether he likes it that way, and I don't really care. Most boys like it: women who know what they want and don't mind asking for it. If I didn't like a bloke that I was getting off with and he tried to make me come, I wouldn't, purposely, I wouldn't want to give him the satisfaction of doing it. Blokes are pretty hung up actually about making girls come and they take it as a big compliment if they manage to succeed. So if I don't like a bloke I just won't let him. I've never pretended. I do feel I've always slept with men who are less attractive as males than I am as a female. But that's fine: I don't want some egotistical bastard who thinks: I'm a stud and I can have anyone that

367

I want. I want to be in control. I always feel that I am the attractive one.

I'm very selfish. Boys have to work hard for me in bed. I tell them what I want and they have to do it. I do go out to please as well, but only if I want to. I'm not doing anything that I don't want to, just for them. If I want to go down on a bloke I will do it, but if he asks me I deliberately won't. The only thing I won't do is anal sex. I can be invaded through one orifice, but I won't be invaded through all of them. My ex-boyfriend hinted for it, but I just thought: Uuugghh, dirty bastard, just fuck off and get away from me! What I don't like is that apart from the physical side, it means that the man isn't happy with what I am prepared to give and that pisses me off. I've never tried S/M either. No way. That's so pointless, just your psychological defects coming through. So fucking pointless, it's pretentious and it's boring.

Men have shat on me. And sometimes I'm getting revenge. Sometimes even when we're fucking I feel really angry and I just feel, stop it, then and there. I cringe. This anger comes mostly from my family, my older brothers. One is twenty-three and the other is twenty and they're both sexist arseholes. I get really angry with them for the way they see women. Women find men attractive for what they are, not because they're good-looking or whatever. If you find someone really attractive in other ways, that can make you see him as good-looking anyway. But men have a stereotype woman – blonde hair, big tits, quite tall, thin, long legs, small waist – and that pisses me off, that they've all got this similar woman in their head. Women are much more open. But women are all under this pressure to be perfect. Men are much more picky – that's not right, that's not right, – and that really fucks me off. I don't succumb to all that. I'm not going to fucking shave my legs. I do the opposite of what men want, I try to be as imperfect as possible when it comes to a sexual ideal. I don't bother to make an effort with myself, I just can't be bothered. And if somebody says, 'I find hairy legs really unattractive on a woman,' I'll make a point of not shaving my legs and flaunting them everywhere. What I want is not to conform to some sexual fantasy, what I want is respect. For who I am and for being female.

Men can be quite pathetic. When I see that sexist attitude I just think: You are so pathetic. I can't be bothered with you – just fuck off! If a bloke starts coming on like a stud, it's just a joke. It really puts me off, when a bloke starts saying I've got such a big cock, all I think is fuck off, *fuck off!* If a bloke seems so sexually frustrated and the only reason why they'd be interested in you is because they haven't had the opportunity to have anybody else, and they don't really give a shit about who you are, that pisses me off as well. What I want is respect. I don't give out charity sex. Anyway, if you're mean, they'll always come back. I'm not looking for love, I'm not looking for sex. What I want is respect.

I don't find men threatening, but they find me threatening. I don't mind that. Some find me over-sexual. They also find me too honest and they don't like that at all. Though every time I've tried to chat someone up I've ended up thinking: What a wanker, and just left them to themselves. Anyone I've ever been interested in I've met through friends. I was in Manchester one time, staying in my brother's flat. I met this bloke, chatted to him and invited him back to my brother's flat. But when he was talking to me I suddenly thought: You stupid bastard!

I'm very manipulative. Deceitful. If I want to gain something I can do it by being cruel, I can do it in a number of ways. I wouldn't whip a man, I wouldn't dress up in black leather, because I don't want to do it. It wouldn't do anything for me so I can't see any point in doing it for someone else. If they're into that well, that's sexual incompatibility for you. I don't want much from a man, I don't expect a lot at all. If I like a bloke I'll let him make me come, but if I don't I won't. If somebody pisses me off up front, I won't get back at them in an obvious tit for tat way, I'll be more cunning. It's the more intelligent way, the more effective way. Basically it means you can be nasty without somebody knowing you're being nasty.

Whenever I do feel that I'm alone in the way I look at the world, I think about women who've been there before and it is quite reassuring. I don't think I'd be able to do what I do and hold the attitudes I do if it hadn't been for the Sixties. Otherwise we'd have to be doing what they did, fighting those battles now. What you're supposed to think about the Sixties is that everybody was pretty promiscuous, but I'm not sure. But it really varied. A lot of people were being brought up in old-fashioned ways and not everyone was prepared to go that far. You're made to think that everyone was promiscuous, they didn't give a shit, they're all on the Pill, everything was into being open, having sex with your mates. It was just another thing that you did: eat, sleep, shag, that's it. I don't think the Nineties is really like the Sixties. What it is is lots of people that want to be like that but basically haven't got the bollocks to get off their arses and do it. It's probably not the way it's depicted to be but it's exciting and a lot of people want to have that experience for themselves.

The way things work now isn't that different to the way it was in the Sixties or Seventies. There'd be one girl that shagged everybody and

369

it's still the same now. She doesn't give a fuck who it is, but she thinks they'll think more of her, so she'll just shag any of them. I don't admire that. It doesn't work anyway: you don't need men to give you confidence.

Interested isn't an appropriate word for what I feel about sex. I do need it to a certain extent. If I get it into my head that I really need it, then until I get it I'll be in that state and totally switch off all other functions. It's very sexual, not mental. A physical thing. And you tell men, but sometimes they feel threatened by it, because they think you want them to perform extra specially. But in fact all you're saying is, 'I want it! I want it now! I don't care what you do or how you do it! Just get on and fuck me!' I can walk around the streets, it goes through phases, when I just feel very sexual, everything centred on sex. Then there are times when I just feel really loving, and times when I just want to talk or whatever. It really varies. It's an itch and sometimes you have to scratch it. And masturbating isn't enough. I wouldn't masturbate when I'm in that state, it's not what I want. I want sex. I don't really masturbate anyway, though I have had an orgasm that way. It wasn't as good as having an orgasm with a man. Fantasising isn't the same. What I fantasise about usually revolves around somebody I know and there's this scenario of us meeting and then going on to have sex. It's always real people.

Sometimes losing my virginity does worry me, because I feel impure. Because men have actually put their dicks inside me and that's made me dirty. That is the place that is totally just for me and if a bloke sticks his cock in me, then they're polluting me with them. I'm letting them pollute me. Especially when there's spunk running out of me afterwards. I always wash after sex, always. I feel dirty afterwards. I stick loads of tissue in my knickers if that's the case. I don't always feel dirty after sex, but most of the time, yes I do. It's all right when I'm still in a euphoric state, still buzzing from it, but after that ... I don't think that I could ever be a tart, a slag, because I don't have sex with people for anything other than pleasure. If you don't have sex for pleasure, for yourself, then I think that does make you a slag. My friend Natasha has sex with people just to get back at her boyfriend, that sort of thing. I'd never do that. And if someone decides to classify me as a slag, they're not worth me bothering about.

I don't use sexuality as a weapon. Never. I might use it as a way of getting back at men, though. Because a lot of them don't respect women. They won't appreciate you being just you, they want something more. When I first meet a bloke often they will think of me as a sex object but through talking to them that changes. In fact the
370

people I attract, and the people I find attractive like me being tough, like me being intelligent. They love it. They love me being a dominating figure. But I do believe that when it comes to what men want from women, I think they really don't know, I don't think they've got a fucking clue. Though I think most men are looking for their mother. And if what happens is that you then end up as nothing but Mummy, and you can't see them as anything but your child, then that's when the relationship ends. But if you have control, if you only pamper them when you want to – and that can be quite nice – then that's okay.

I pity men these days; it is very difficult for them at the moment. A lot of women are getting the same consciousness that I'm getting and that is making it difficult for men. Though men's fears and problems are a stupid state of mind. Women seem to want everything at once, and at the same time not want anything in particular, and men just want anything, but women don't want men that want anything. It is a mirror of the old male attitudes in a way, but what women want isn't along the same lines as men's sexist ideas, it's just women's personal taste, relative to their family or whatever.

I've been ranting and raving about my feminist attitudes for a long time, and it seems that they're finally getting through. I'm much more into feminism than most of my friends. And what they are, basically, is to get respect for being you. My best friend used to think that by flashing her tits and wearing suspenders and stockings and that sort of bollocks she'll be attractive. I told her, 'Fuck that!' Now she's totally the opposite. She's saying, 'I'm not shaving my legs, I'm not wearing this that, I'm not doing that,' because what she wants is to be respected as a person. It's not just a matter of fighting men. Some you do have to push, though. I don't look to men for guidance, not at all. It's up to me and men are just a burden.

I've basically got to look after myself, and any man who thinks he can hitch a ride with me is just going to be a burden. And that includes anyone who's going to have a relationship with me. I don't have this idea of someone out there who has to help me. I do see myself as a strong woman. Powerful and influential. Nobody can fuck me about. Nobody can change me unless I choose to change. I'd have children. Though I don't know what I'd teach them yet.

The way I see the future is that most likely it will just go back to the way it used to be. Women are going to get way ahead, men are going to get more and more fucked up and they're going to start pushing back and on it goes. One fucking great zig-zag. I think women were probably in control before in the past but they've lost it. Things just go from side to side.

THE NEW MAN: Hope Over Experience

The concept of the 'New Man', that corollary of the feminist woman, emerged during the 1970s as a direct response to the burgeoning forces of women's liberation. Since then the 'men's movement' has gained, if not great strength, then certainly a good deal of (usually negative) media exposure, and won a steady of trickle of converts to its ranks. Earnest, self-abasing, riddled with guilt and desperate for self-improvement, the New Man has never won a good press. The 'old', traditional man despises him, which comes as no surprise, given his abandoning of the entire range of patriarchal structures that underpin the 'real' man's way of life. But less palatable has been the response from those he might have viewed as his natural backers. Neither feminists, nor the left – whether orthodox or radical – nor the gay world has seen fit to embrace him. For all that women, in particular, are keen to point out the extent to which they have changed, and sit there, metaphorically tapping their feet, still waiting for men to catch up, they have little truck with those men who proclaim themelves keenest to change their ways. The New Man, often positioning himself as a 'feminist', is seen merely as playing the old male game: subordinating an essentially women's issue to his own self-aggrandising needs. The word that new men seek is 'ally', the one they most constantly hear is 'wimp'.

JERRY BALIN

'You don't need to feel guilty.'

The council flat is on an estate near the centre of Bristol. Rundown, decrepit. He's young, scarcely born in the Sixties but looks very much the old hippie. The flat is cramped, a repository for child's toys, pamphlets, a guitar. His partner is working, their child at a nursery; this afternoon, as is the daily round, he'll be taking over for his stint of daily childcare.

I'm twenty-five years old. I'm involved in the men's movement on a variety of levels: I'm involved in a men's support group, which has met fortnightly for the last two years. I'm also in a fathers' support group, which has met fortnightly since January. That's a closed support group for my own support, looking at my own issues – a form of therapy. I'm one of the main organisers for Bristol Men's Forum, an

372

open group meeting monthly, which runs workshops on a variety of themes relating to masculinity. I've been doing that for the last year or so. I'm editor and compiler of a Bristol-wide newsletter *Man to Man*, which is now on the third issue. That's bimonthly. I was co-organiser of the latest Calston Park Men's Gathering, a national gathering. I'm one of a couple of people trying to revive MOVE, Men Overcoming Violence – offering counselling to men about their violence. I've been with my partner for six years. I look after my son half of my time, and look after homeless people in a day centre as a volunteer for the Cyrenians. I'm just finishing my training as counsellor of alcoholics.

I first got involved in the men's movement in '86. I'd always felt linked to feminism – my partner was discovering feminism – and I wanted to do more than feel guilty. I also felt uncomfortable with the expectations laid on men throughout my childhood. I grew up in Cardiff, where I always tried to fit in with my peer group and never quite did. Girls were something completely apart from us. There was one girl in our class at junior school and we called her 'it'. Anyone who mentioned her name got punished. She was the most attractive girl in the school but nobody would admit they were all madly in love with her, so they put her outside. With another girl, we were in the park, lying on top of her, kissing her. The others said, 'Go on, go on,' but I didn't want to. I felt pressured into it. I was a bit shy around girls. I had no sex education from my parents, or I can't remember any. But I didn't ask. We had films at school when I was about eight. So we had the mechanics. We just giggled hysterically. My mum and dad never did *that*. I once found a condom in my mother's drawer and just couldn't believe it. I knew they must have done it years ago because of me and my brother, but I thought they were just not sexual beings. My dad didn't even like being touched.

In 1986 I was a student at Bristol Polytechnic and about to become a father. I was involved in CND and at one of their conferences there had been a men's anti-sexist workshop. MOVE sent that workshop a mailshot: they were running their own workshop on why men rape. I went along. My first experience of the men's movement was good, almost like a religious experience. Coming from a very competitive homophobic culture, to go into a culture where people openly supported each other, openly shared their feelings, openly touched and hugged each other felt good. I thought: What have I been missing, why couldn't I have done this before?

Then my son was born, and I didn't get involved again till the end of '87 when I was invited to a MOVE meeting. What I wanted was a men's group but I didn't know how to get it. I ended up on the management committee of MOVE and struggled with that for a year. It wasn't what I really wanted: at that time I just wanted to become involved in the men's movement – I discovered the violence in me later. It was very much a political thing: why are men violent? It's to do with their upbringing, that we focus all our physical and emotional needs on one woman and if we don't get it, it's disastrous. That's linked to the rape issue. Then I ran my own workshop for fathers. In 1989 I went to the Calston Park gathering, and that was my first real involvement with the movement. Then the Bristol Men's Forum was set up, which helped me get into a men's support group. Then I started running workshops for Men's Forum, and writing things for movement magazines like *Achilles Heel*.

The last Calston Park gathering attracted about a hundred people. It's growing. For Men's Forum, I've a mailing list of about fifty. Ten or twenty turn up for monthly meetings. People drift in, drift out, go into other things. I've got three social workers in my men's group, out of five of us. Men's Forum is more diverse, people from a variety of backgrounds. Some people just come once, especially those who want to escape traditional political parties. I haven't met any Tories, though. My own position isn't liberal, rather socialist. Most people I know aren't interested in the movement. And I don't push it with them. There's a huge group of men who could be doing more in men's issues. They're the first people I want to work with. Men on the left, in the Greens, Liberals. I'm also hoping to be working with violent men.

There are two wings to the men's anti-sexist movement: what you could call inner change and outer change. The pro-feminist anti-sexist, overtly political wing on one side and the men's liberationists on the other. They're not organised wings but they're mistrustful of the other. 'Mea culpa' versus the 'positive image' if you like. We feel we need both sorts. Then some people don't even like the term 'men's movement' – they would rather have 'the anti-sexist men's network'. There's a quite understandable resistance to a 'movement', because traditionally men have gone for structures, hierarchies – that feel of the traditional Labour Party, which is what we're trying to get away from: male-orientated smoke-filled rooms. We want something more autonomous.

For me, the men's movement has no link with women or with feminism. Men are individually oppressed by the male image, but they're not an oppressed minority. So there's an image problem in calling it a 'movement'. What there is is a loose network of groups around the country who are active on issues relating to masculinity and anti-sexism. And that network, that attitude wouldn't have arisen
374

without feminism. It shouldn't be confused with the 'masculist movement', which is mainly in the States, and which actually is an anti-feminist movement. Not that you'll learn that from the press. Most press articles are ill-informed, opinionated bullshit. Typical middle-class journalistic pseudo-liberality. It's frustrating. I've come across that a lot. There's a lot of intellectual men standing outside feminism, not doing anything themselves except throwing stones. They see it as an irrelevance, an indulgence. I don't think they understand what people like me are about. I think they're scared. When you indulge in politics on a head level, a level of rational argument, writing papers, making speeches, that's not risky. You're talking in generalities. Where I see my political involvement as a man is to do with my personal life, linking that in with structures. It's more scary to say, 'I am a man and as a political statement I want to share my feelings and be close to other men, to be openly affectionate when I feel like it.' People don't understand that, are frightened by it, by what it brings up in themselves. The implication from the tabloids is that we don't exist, rather than that we're not 'real men'. If the *Sun* had come to Calston Park, they'd have said we were a bunch of queers.

I wrote a couple of pieces for papers in and out of the movement. They both set out a lot of what we feel. The first was an attempt to get more people interested in Men's Forum: 'It's high time more of us men did something about the way we act towards each other and to women. Many of us have spent years paying lip-service to the equality of the sexes while continuing to accept the benefits society awards us as men. At the same time many of us suffer from an inability to live up to the expected image of manhood. A group of men are meeting in Bristol in June to look at these and other issues.' And I asked for people to call me. One man has come into the Forum since that.

I had another article, trying to get people to come to Calston Park. 'On June 15th three or four dozen men meet at Calston Park near Bath for the men's gathering. These newest of the new will abandon their childcare rotas and vacuuming for the weekend. But why? Is it the opportunity to indulge in collective navel contemplation, or to have a contest to see who feels guiltiest? According to one of the organisers, the weekend offers an opportunity for real change. "I get really fed up at the way some people view the idea of men getting together to try and change as some kind of namby-pamby irrelevance. I wonder what they're afraid of." The weekend's theme is "Any Change/How to Change" which he describes as "the blending of looking at ourselves, e.g. our sexism, our homophobia, what we've gained and lost through being male, and gaining strength to take new ways of being a man out into society. This involves such measures as

375

challenging traditional ways of dividing household tasks and childcare; refusing to continue putting expectations on our sons to be cold, hard and emotionless; no longer participating in social situations in which men dominate and generally looking towards a more gentle, caring and understanding way of being strong as men.'"

The dominant image of the New Man is of being a fraud. Somebody who doesn't succeed in being a real man, so is doing something to impress certain sorts of women, who don't want men to be big and macho. It's been suggested that New Men just want to sleep with feminists. There's some validity in the thesis that New Man is not happy in Real Man's world, even if it's not the most relevant point. Not being a very good 'man' I have a vested interest in being something different. But Real Man also has a vested interest in changing things. It's not good for people to be bottled up and competing all the time. I don't think that's what they want. I've seen two boys in a playground facing up against each other, and it seems so obvious that neither wants to be there. But they have to be, because of the external pressure.

I came into the movement because I found that I was in the habit of expressing my partner's feminist views rather than my own. I wanted to change that. I didn't actually say, 'I feel guilty,' but I did feel guilty because of ways I'd behaved as a boy and a young man, conforming to the norm: objectifying women, treating them as objects, mothers, whores, treating them pretty badly really. And I also had guilt (though I didn't feel it really belonged to me) which stemmed from the anger of feminist women towards me as a man, and towards all men through the ages. I had to take on board that anger just because I was a man, because of patriarchy. But I didn't want to take that on board, I didn't want to carry on with that tradition. I wanted to be different as a man. And being political, evangelical, I wanted to convince others of that. When I began taking groups myself I told them: you don't need to feel guilty, you need to look at ways of changing, but you're still basically all right.

Pornography makes a lot of men feel guilty. It's oppressive to women. It's against the direction I'm going to support that industry, to use those ways of picturing women to get my sexual gratification. Having said that, I do it anyway in my head, in my own masturbation fantasies. That's something I struggle with, that I'm working on. There's no way for me not to objectify women and get my sexual needs met. Pornography can be addictive and I can see the link between it and sexual violence. But I'm not a fan of censorship. At one of our meetings it was suggested forming a Pornoholics Anonymous – rather than condemning the men who use it. I would like to work

376

towards getting people not to want pornography. It's through pornography that we've learnt to view the opposite sex the way we do. Maybe we can learn not to. I know people who can masturbate without fantasies, without objectifying women – sex literally with yourself if you like. I can't manage that yet, but I'm trying.

There is resistance to us from the gay movement, some are very angry about us. There are some involved in the men's movement as well though. The lesbian groups were angry about an article in the Anti-Sexist Men's newsletter, which chose not to include anything negative about men. They thought we were sexist pigs, complacent, twee, politically irrelevant. That issue attracted a lot of flak. Putting out a newsletter that's openly pro-men, you're going to get comments: You don't care about patriarchy, or feminism. A lot of men don't want to be associated with that because it leaves you vulnerable to attack. They want to cover their backs. What I want is to make the message clear, both the positive image and the anti-sexist messages. I don't think they're opposed positions. Men *are* all right, it's patriarchy that is all wrong. Men themselves aren't patriarchy – that's a way of organising society, a way men oppress women. Men don't have to oppress women. Men can be all right.

For men's movement theorists there's a journey to be travelled. John Rowan, who's a men's movement theorist, talks about the 'three-stage consciousness' – conscious change, unconscious change, spiritual change. I get confused about spiritual change, I'm looking into that at the moment. Conscious change: yes, I'm a man. I've realised it's wrong to oppress women, I want to do something about it. Unconscious change: because I don't know exactly what's making me act like I am as a man, the processes are subtle and deep. That means a lot of looking, a lot of working, using therapeutic techniques on reprogramming myself in a way. Finding out what the patriarchal and sexist patterns are and trying to work on them, change them, build new patterns, new ways of being which are more harmonious with the planet, with other people.

Rowan says we need to see and accept feminism as a wound to men. It's a process of wounding and healing. It's an attack on men today which is a conglomeration of what men have been doing to women for hundreds of years – so it's a necessary wound. We need to accept it, grieve for it and then heal ourselves. He talks of ritualistic ways of doing that. If I was having a relationship with a non-feminist it would be difficult. I'd be trying to make her into one. And that's not my job. Also with a non-feminist it's easy to slip into patriarchal patterns, patterns of dominance. Anything you do starts off as unconscious and becomes part of you.

I know it sounds like I'm a martyr, making myself do these things because I think I ought to, but it's not like that. If you have conviction, you follow it. I don't continually put myself under a microscope. I find the men's group an indulgence. I get a lot of what I need from it. It's not going and whipping myself, but just having a good time – playing games, having laughs. In a way, being allowed to be boys.

I appeared on a Channel 4 programme on sex. They wanted to expound the theory that due to feminism, women were no longer willing to put up with the type of sex and sexual attitudes that men were putting out. They got men and women to write sex diaries, and showed lots of clips to prove that men had changed a little bit but not very much. They showed us as the lunatic fringe of men, very marginal and irrelevant to the wider society. They assumed the only reason men would change would be to please women; that precluded the possibility it was in men's interests to change anyway. They covered the sex for sex / sex for love dichotomy. Women are into sex for love, although some try to be like men and go into it just for sex. And some men are into sex for love now. What irritated me most was their use of the term 'New Man'. So-and-so is a New Man, he does some of the housework, etc. Yet he goes to a prostitute. This was therefore used to prove that New Man has a long way to go and is a bit of a fraud. He may be doing the housework, but is he working on his masculinity? Probably not.

One of the questions Channel 4 asked was: Is masculinity a social prison? The reply was: yes, but New Man is a social prison as well. Having said that, I'd like to embrace the term New Man and turn it to our advantage. Nobody outside our groups is taking change in men seriously. Why should a man want to change? For me, I suffered from having to be separate, competitive, indulge in physical violence. The threat of being sent to war, having to cope, be strong. Everyone is vulnerable, and if you're not allowed to show it ... And not being able to be real. Men mostly cope with life by blocking things off and putting everything into their work, or using lots of crutches – booze, fags, TV and sex.

Cultural change happens on many levels, and people are good at making changes which are in their interests but which aren't fundamental. Most of the changes for men in the last twenty years are because of the women's movement, not the men's. They're positive changes, small but positive. The men's movement has yet to have an impact, other than on those who are involved in it. I believe that in changing myself I'll have a knock-on effect on men around me, on my son and my friends.

Structurally I would like voluntary statutory agencies to be taking on the idea that society creates a strait-jacket for men. Just as feminism has engendered equal-opportunity units, rape-crisis lines, I want public and private money going into working with men on violence, on sexual abuse, sexual harassment, raising the profile of those issues. In some places this is happening, a lot of Safer City money has gone into men's projects. It could come into teacher training, probation-work training, social-work training. The perception is that our movement is the lunatic fringe. I'd like to change that. I have had a full-time job, and things went wrong. I couldn't fulfil my personal responsibilities and my relationship suffered: with my partner, and with my son. If I give less time than my partner to childcare, I'm tapping in to patriarchal structures. That brings up the breadwinner / housewife issues. That's not inevitable in every relationship. Some might decide to play one role for a year and then change round. It's just that it matters to me in my relationship that I'm doing my equal share of parenting. It's different without children.

I think this restructuring has improved my relationship in general with my partner, although we still go through a lot of turmoil and crisis. It has the potential to improve my sexual relationship. It's a long hard struggle, involving not only my patterns as a man but my partner's patterns as a woman and her own experience. There's no simple answer.

If I compare with how I was before I started looking at my sexuality, I feel a lot happier going into a sexual relationship now, a lot clearer about who I am, clear about my sexual boundaries, about what's going on for me. A little bit clearer about what part of my sexual drive is a power thing, and which part is my own sexual needs. More has to be done about getting my sexual needs met – it doesn't happen very often. I feel rejected if my partner doesn't want sex with me. I'm needy and demanding around sex. At the beginning I thought that was just my own inadequacy, but when I joined a group I found out others felt the same. They'd try to push sex with their partners, induce guilt in them if they said no to sex as well. That's how traditionally we've been led to believe our physical needs should be met. I still have that attitude to my partner, but the group has helped me work on it. I look at what my physical needs are now. If I want to be hugged, I can get that in my men's group or with my male friends. Sometimes I need somebody in the group to play my mother, really just for it to be accepted that these things are something I need and can't get. I've learnt to ask for what I need and if I can't get it, be able to deal with the feelings of rejection. Rather than invade my partner's space.

On the other hand it rarely works in reverse. There are not many times I'd reject sex – I'll have it if it's around. But I'm working on that. Our relationship has ceased being monogamous. This was not a mutual decision at first, though it did become mutual subsequently. My partner had an affair with another man. I got through it in a lot of pain, with a lot of support from my men's group, a lot of dialogue with my partner. I do believe that monogamy is not the right thing, which is probably a legacy from the Sixties, but putting it into practice is hard because of my upbringing, and hers. It happened when I was a full-time student, teacher training, when I couldn't put much into the relationship, so she got her needs met elsewhere. For a year I was completely engrossed in this course, (which I failed in the end). It's been painful, but I've learnt a lot, and have lots more to learn.

I'm interested in feelings. If I'm in a monogamous relationship and she has a relationship with somebody else, I have feelings about that – I'm jealous, I need space to express that. I have to choose whether to stay or go. Being in the men's movement helps me decide those things. If I can handle those feelings and stay within the relationship, good. If not, I have to get out. If I need someone outside my relationship, I must do it. My partner will have feelings about it, as will my other partner. All those feelings need to be dealt with. We'd all need to talk about it and I do have an optimistic view of people's capacity to deal with such things. Feelings are real, are there, and pain isn't to be avoided. I'm coming into the men's movement from a personal growth perspective. My work as a man is an aspect of my personal growth.

Personal therapy would have some of the same functions, but on a deeper level. The therapy movement also provides workshops – for people with lots of money to explore being men. People play out on an individual level the struggles between men and women. There are unresolved issues there, which are part of the whole patriarchy thing, and I don't think it's inevitable we will resolve them. For one thing, most humour and popular culture is a reflection of the 'dominant ideology'.

I'm not sure I believe in love any more. There are things which are right for individuals. It might be right for me to stay with one woman for a long time. If I have strong feelings towards her I may or may not choose to call that love. I may also have strong feelings towards another woman, or a man. I may choose to call that love or I may not. There are so many aspects – giving, receiving, being open to somebody, being closed, giving support, sharing time, sharing physical comfort, sharing physical intimacy.

I'd like to be more open, but if I met a woman who just wanted sex and I just wanted sex, I'd try it. I wouldn't feel I was going against my
380

beliefs. If it was what we both wanted, it's okay. At the moment I'm exploring, and broadening intimacy. I have intimacy with my partner and I'd like to have intimacy with some of my close male friends. I'd like to have more of that. And intimacy with women friends.

Sometimes I get hostility from my partner. She thinks I think more of the men's group than I do of her. I haven't experienced much hostility from feminist women although some men have. I get hostility from women who think: Why do you want to do childcare, I hate it, it's awful, we have to do it, why *choose* to do it? I find that a bit weird. The answer is it's not a question of *wanting* to do childcare. I'm a parent, it's my responsibility. That's my answer. The patriarchal slant is that men can choose to do it or not and women can't. Patriarchy is a structure of society in which men have economic, political and other sorts of power over women. It works in different ways too. Rich men over poor, straight over gay, men have power over children, strong men over weak. To me it's irrelevant whether trying to change this is utopian. If I change myself I've achieved my goal. If anything else is achieved in doing that, it's a bonus. I can only change my patriarchal behaviour, not anybody else's.

***

ALEX KERSHAW: We're all fucked up in our way. Obvious, but important to state if we're talking about relationships. We all have our own problems, different perspectives. That will always complicate the argument about progress, about men/women, about feminism. It's not as simplistic as saying the man has to grow up or develop to please a woman. Very often, more often than not, there are problems and attitudes within these women that they've been saddled with by society. And whichever way you look at it, women get a raw deal. If they're assertive, aggressive, careeristic, they're labelled bitches, and men don't like that. If they're the opposite, they're wimps, they're not men, they don't get far enough, they're to blame. How do they win?

DAVID MISSEN: I've been playing round these areas for years. I don't think I'd like the label New Man at all. I don't see myself that way. But I suppose I do have some of the characteristics. I do find it important to explore my own feminine energy, which I find very much more complicated than I would have dreamt at the beginning. I can identify two quite separate female personae within me. One is an archetypal bitch – which was a great and interesting discovery, and coming to terms with it was very interesting. I realised what I'd previously done

381

in almost all my relationships with women was to deny that I had this and project it onto them. If they weren't bitches, I'd pretty soon turn them into bitches. A painful way of proceeding. That side was very dominant. The other side is very soft indeed, very soft, a beautiful persona. I think most men would find something if they explored. Maybe not what I found, but they'd find something.

I was lucky too in that I never had any children until I was forty-two (I'm now fifty). By the time I got there I had a level of awareness that enabled me to be, I suppose, a far more New Man kind of father than I'd otherwise have been. I would have been a conventional, destructive sort of father. That's not to say the tendencies weren't there, but I could see them. So I could say, 'I'm not going to pass this particular habit down to the next generation.' My son's mother and I have both had a definite non-closing-down behaviour with our son. You can see the results of that already. And you could from a very early stage.

I think it's very important if you're going to go through the experiences of a New Man, that, if you're in a heterosexual relationship, you can do this with a woman. There's a lot to be gained by a man doing these explorations at the same time as his female partner is doing similar explorations. There's an assumption that you have to do this as men together, women together. It's a false assumption. Sara [Dale] and I have done it most beautifully together. There were times when there were astonishing interplays between the different parts of us. In any heterosexual relationship there's a capacity for four or five other relationships within that relationship. Between male to male, female to female, male to female, female to male, plus the overall relationship. And there may be a whole lot more, depending on the variations of the contra-sexuality there is in each person. So I discovered my two feminine aspects, and one of the beautiful relationships between us is between Sara's second femina and my second femina. An exquisite relationship when it happens – which is very seldom. I've taken this into men to men relationships too.

SARA DALE: I was present at some of this. With David and another man who wanted to experience male to maleness without it being regarded as bisexuality or gayness, to experience this safely. So we had dinner together and it developed gently and beautifully. It was very beautiful to see. I was sitting on the chair, they were sitting either side. I stroked their heads and then drew their heads closer, they lifted their heads and kissed. The look on their faces – almost disbelief, shy disbelief, and yet an opening. It just developed very gently from there, like boy meets girl. They touched and caressed each other. This was another heterosexual man.

382

The worst thing that happened to the Sixties was the breakaway into the feminist movement. The women had an evolution that made them equal to men in their chauvinism, and they haven't come out of that. The men haven't had the same thing. And the women never did get into their sexuality. I'm a heretic to the feminist women, a traitor to the female cause, because I happen to like men, I don't think men have had their day. I think these women have overshot in the way they've gone about things. They've gone right over into the men's camp without the step through the sensitivity. When women get divorced they're taking up more and more with other women and becoming 'lesbians', in quotes, because they don't want the aggressive approach they see over and over again in men. That's only because men don't know how to bring forward their sensitivity. I seem to draw out of men that I relate to the freedom for them to be anything they like. I'm not shocked by anything. Most women don't give men that chance.

We went to a conference in Findhorn where this showed up enormously. It was a week about chaos, extraordinary. It really showed how the women think men have had their day, and it's time to put men down.

DAVID MISSEN: It was an interesting conference for many reasons. As it was about chaos they tried not to structure it. And that actually worked. I have a horror of unstructured conferences, but it did work. One day was set aside to discuss relationships between the men and women there. This was slightly structured in that in the morning all the men and all the women were to meet separately in their own place and discuss what it was they'd like to tell the other sex at a plenary session that afternoon.

The women apparently had a very feminist meeting. The men spent the entire morning dancing and singing, doing exercises. It was very pleasant and enjoyable. We didn't want to stop doing that and talk. Very New Man stuff. One or two began to get a bit anxious when there was only half an hour left. I said: Let's not worry about it. Let's do our discussion about what we want to say in front of the women. That way we don't have to bother about it. So we went on singing and dancing all morning.

We had difficulty getting this idea accepted at the plenary session, but as we had nothing to say otherwise they had to accept it. And it was really electrifying. We had a good, positive, very fascinating discussion going on. All the men sitting in the middle of the hall, the women round the edges. What we didn't know was that the women were vastly amazed by this. They'd never heard men talking to each

383

other about sensitive subjects. Had no idea we were sensitive. Including people who'd lived at Findhorn for years, highly-evolved beings. They were just mind-blown. So that part went very well. Unfortunately when we got to the second part, where the women did the same thing (with a third part where we all talked to each other) it went into a feminist uproar. Eventually it fell apart in total disarray.

SUZANNE MOORE: The problem with the New Man is that he's crucifying himself for some kind of ideological reason that he doesn't really understand, and also just wanting to get in on the act, show themselves to be more oppressed than anybody. I know quite a few people in academia who've set up gender studies courses, or men's studies courses. I don't think there's actually anything wrong with that in itself but when it's a question of fighting over money, which it is, I really resent it. What is 'men's studies' if it's not everything else that isn't women's studies?

Some things have changed. I wrote this piece about the image of the New Man in advertising. And I said for twenty years women have asked men to become more sensitive, and what you end up with is men with sensitive skin. The image is there, but the reality ... You have these surveys: how much more housework do men do? And they do three seconds more than the year before. But that's not it. What women want is men who do it but don't go on about it. Any man who spends his time going round and saying, 'I'm a New Man,' is extremely dubious. These men who infer that they might be gay but they're not sure – closet heterosexuals.

CLARE CAMPBELL: It's social workers who live with New Man. Or very political women. Either way it seems an emasculated relationship all round. Certainly you don't get the impression it's very sexy. I don't think New Woman wants New Man.

KATE HEATH: The idea of the New Man is basically bullshit. As far as men's attitudes changing, there's a lot of difference between lip-service and reality. But on a certain level things have changed. Men know that they can't get away with the same sort of shit that they used to get away with. They've had to re-examine themselves. There is a certain crisis in masculinity, though I'm not sure what the outcome will be. I know men get confused, I know they want to know what to do, but if they can't work it out, then my attitude is often: Tough shit! We've had to deal with all these problems, and we've said, 'Okay, this is what's wrong, this is what you've got wrong,' but after a
384

while you just feel: Okay, you've got to do it for yourself. Men have learned certain lessons from feminism and they've had a lot of opportunities, but in the end they have to change themselves.

There's very few women who actually welcome the idea of the New Man. In essence it's something that we should want, and it's good that some ideas are changing, but I still find it quite difficult to deal with. On one level you do want men to change, but you also want both sexes to keep what's good about themselves. All they need discard is what's bad. You want men to change, of course, but you don't want them to come to you looking for the answers. I do find it quite difficult to deal with and I'm not sure that I like the idea of the New Man or the New Lad or whatever. I don't like the term and I don't like the image and I think that most women probably have the same response. I find it very difficult to answer exactly why, but it's something I don't feel good about. It's not a matter of wanting to be taken by the hair and dragged into the bedroom, that's not necessarily how I'd see the old man. But one has different sexual fantasies. If you reject that because it's politically correct, then that's another form of censorship. If you can't do something because it might be ideologically impure, that's no good. Because there are things you might want to experiment with. For instance part of me does want to be dominated, but it's difficult.

JANE MILLS: I don't know what one means by 'New Man'. Another word for a wimp. Which is rather a sexist term. It's used of a man because he's seen to be a bit feminine. The word comes from Oxford University, around 1915; 'to go wimping' was to go out looking for sexually available women.

JOHN MICHAEL: The New Man as he appeared five or six years ago was a media creation, a hype. I've been to quite a lot of seminars, group therapy weekend things and almost invariably the men are in the wimpish mode. Not so much that they're pussy-whipped. They're earnest and wet. The latest thing is the warrior idea. The Wild Man. I think there's an area of aggression and dominance, forcefulness which I think of as being part of my masculinity, which doesn't emerge in a typical New Man way. How that element fits into post-New Man, I've no idea. Simone de Beauvoir said in every man there is a heart of darkness, and I think there is a hardness, an aggressiveness that I know I have.

If one takes the elements of the New Man, I think I'm a New Man in terms of actually being interested in women, what they talk about, sharing with them, being as much as possible emotionally open with

385

them. I've never been a man's man. But the traditional Don Juan tends not to be like that anyway. If you look at the stereotypes in the Twenties and Thirties – the cad, rather too smartly dressed, had a lot of women. He wasn't a man's man either. They'd be rather solitary figures – 'the greasy dago'.

So on the one hand I fit into a New Man image, although on the other I fit better the traditional cad. The traditional cad said, 'I love you, you're wonderful, can't live without you, why don't we go away together?' Whenever I meet people like that, I'm amazed at how cynical they are, and how well it works. I lived with this Welsh guy, both in California and in London, all these people were coming and going, and he'd launch into his routine: 'You've got such beautiful eyes, never seen eyes like that before. My heart's really going, I'd like to sing a song.' Some of them would go: 'Ugh!' but the others would be, 'Oh-oh.' Then three days later it would be: 'How's Cathy?' 'Oh, what a slut she is, she's so fucking boring and ugly. But have you seen this Julie? Oh, she's ...' Yet I think with him it wasn't totally cynical. Every time he saw a new one, she really was beautiful and marvellous, then after a couple of times he was bored.

There was a piece in the papers recently about sexaholics. There being certain people for whom sex is an addiction. I don't think I was a full-blown addict in that sense, but certainly one rung below. For a long time I was definitely addicted to the idea of casual sex – meeting someone, getting excited, fucking them. But that was separate from a relationship. That's over now, I think, but I'm aware that the beast has not entirely vanished. That element's still there. But I'm not in the grip of an addiction the way I was before. That lasted about twenty years.

Though, once again, what I did was fall between two stools. One was this cad type, but because I was part of that whole Seventies' ideological movement, one strand was that you treated women as people. So there was an element of that for me, but there was an equally strong element simply to go and fuck them. I would have fucked more people if I'd either pursued the Jim Haynes line: 'Hello darling, why don't we go to bed, I think you're wonderful,' seven women would have thought I was a complete asshole, but three every day would have said yes, and that would have been a huge improvement, and one that made a virtue of the fact that if I had been honest I would have admitted, 'Yes, I'm completely obsessed with sex, all I do want is to sleep with people.' Instead of which I would spend hours or even weeks talking to somebody who basically I wanted to fuck. Which probably made them feel it was more of a relationship than I actually intended it to be. I just wanted to have sex, they saw

386

me as a potential relationship. So I was being dishonest. Which I would call fake New Man-ism.

JEFFREY WEEKS: There's been a breakdown of old hierarchies and men are much more willing to care for children, etc. than they were. I can't imagine my father changing nappies for grandchildren. He was more indulgent to my much younger brother than he was to the two of us older ones. That younger brother has two children and he and his wife both care for them. They both work. He nappy changes, walks the baby, etc., a real co-parent; however, he would not see himself as a New Man. And there is still a material disparity between men and women. Part of the New Man is a marketing device. Men still earn more, are more powerful in politics, industry, etc. So this New Man has not broken down the material basis of inequality between man and woman – it's shifted but just at the edges.

JOHN LANKIEWICZ: One of the major causes of sexual difficulties is the power of socially promoted myths. One of the common myths that us poor fellows are brought up with is: men are active, men are responsible, men are on top, men know what to do, and men's energy for sex is greater than women's, or should be. The reality is that in individual cases none of these things may be true. So when we then meet vociferous women, or women who seem confident in what they say, we feel a bit shaken, which is what women have felt for generations of course. So we're getting a taste of our own medicine, and so, yes, I think some men do feel anxious. They find it hard to cope with women who are clear about what they want. That's across the age range. If a woman says: 'Let's wait' – you see, we're all feeble little creatures, men and women – some men interpret this to mean: she doesn't want me. And that's scary, that assaults the personal sense of self-esteem. Whereas it's simply a matter of the woman's choice. It doesn't mean anything as far as personal self-regard is concerned. Why should it? It just means that that woman has chosen at that time not to do it. Maybe she doesn't like you – who knows? Maybe she doesn't like your nose, your feet, anything about you. That's her choice, it's saying nothing about you. But unfortunately we believe it's saying quite a lot about us. So it's difficult.

NICK DAVIES: Being a New Man is definitely not simple role reversal. I don't see it as trying to be more woman than a woman. It's more about finding out what I am and finding out how that fits. If you're with a 'strong woman' then they're defining their own terms. If

387

you define yourself as a 'New Man' simply by telling women the truth when you seduce them, rather than pretending you weren't anything other than a quick fuck, then that's much easier. You're still in control. Women these days aren't all expecting you to marry them. They're working out what they want. And that can work against you: you meet someone you think is really brilliant and you go to bed with them and you find out that they're only using you for a fuck. It's a bit of a turn around.

The idea that a woman should get pleasure out of sex probably emerged from the media as much as anything else. *Cosmopolitan*. My dad ran a newsagents so I read everything from a really early age. The top shelf, everything. As far as satisfying women goes, I think it was just something that grew, partly from my own pleasure: it's much more satisfying to satisfy the woman too. I went out with a woman for two or three years who just couldn't achieve orgasms – and as far as I know she never has. I used to find that really frustrating: why can't I give this woman an orgasm? So I suppose you start trying to concentrate on your technique. But I don't think that technique is all-satisfying either, there has to be something else. Some kind of emotional side. Technique is something I concentrate less on now. You should be able to find your pleasure for yourself, and help the other person towards theirs. I hate that idea that it's totally my responsibility to make sure that you enjoy yourself. There's things I can do to facilitate your enjoying yourself, but at the end of the day I'm here for me as well.

It's not easy living with a feminist. It is in some ways because I've lived away from home since I was seventeen, so I'm used to looking after myself, but where it becomes difficult is when you end up looking after someone else. There is this thing about personal responsibility. Because I'm supposed not to fulfil a classic male role, and I'm supposed to wash up or whatever, in a sense that absolves my girlfriend from having to do anything. Though I'm not passive, I don't just sit there and let it happen. She has to have a lot of balls to get away with it. Though it's not much to do with being a New Man – the root of it is that she's really lazy. But that combines with the politics, and we do have similar beliefs. And it moves things along, because then you start talking about personal responsibility. One of my arguments is that she should take responsibility for her life, which involves doing the washing, whatever. And I hear myself echoing what women have said to me in the past: you have to take responsibility for your actions as a man.

It seems to me that women have gone a long way further than men in changing the stereotypes, the sexual roles. They have gone an awful
388

long way down the line and they have now turned round and said, 'Okay, this is where we are, what are you going to do?' and they've got twenty years of theories and books being written and so on. In a lot of ways it has isolated men from the process. Men are supposed to respond but they can't. I won't. I'm very, very wary of just saying, 'Right, this is my position on this or on that' – because I haven't had time to work it through properly yet. And this certainly doesn't happen everywhere. As far as England goes it happens in certain circles in London, and not even everywhere in London either. If you live in Chelsea or Fulham the men have enough money to ask for what they want, to get the kind of wife that fits in with their demands, and not have to change them. But being skint gives you a very different view of the world. Definitely.

You're having to deal with women at a level where you don't dominate, where maybe you have to go and borrow money from them. Poor women are much stronger than poor men. They have to be, and feminism makes that even more so, gives them something to hang those attitudes on. Not only can they bring up two children in a shitty flat, but there's an ideology that tells them that's something positive, something they can be proud of. Working-class women are necessarily tougher. I knew a woman who was getting the crap beaten out of her by her husband but she was one of the toughest women I knew. So are you a New Man because you literally can't afford not to be? If you're out at work all day and living in male power circles it's easier to be a male power person. But if you're on and off the dole, living closer to the reality of everyday life, going to Safeway's, cleaning the flat, then it's very different.

I think there are people who try to impose an ideology, but that's dead easy to resist. Feminist lesbian separatists will blame you for various things, because as a man you're part of the patriarchy. But like all radical ideologies they're easy to debunk. But it didn't ever occur to me in my youth that I should be racist or sexist anyway. Now it's fun to play games with that kind of attitude. Tell my girlfriend to get in the kitchen, whatever. And she will – if it's her turn. I'm not sure how much ideology affects our relationship. We do hit flashpoints: 'Is this good, is this bad?' She's much more into going out than I am, she'll get dressed up and go out. That can piss me off. Not because she's a woman and she shouldn't be doing it, it just pisses me off because she's doing it. It's not a matter of her not behaving in the way I think a woman should, but of whether she's paying enough respect to me. How do I deal with it? I sulk, pout ... We have shouting matches, we flail at each other ... there's holes in the wall from throwing plates. But the flaming rows aren't about her going out and getting pissed. I just get a bit disappointed if she's out five nights a week. I don't go with her because she goes to things that I don't like. To an extent it is good old-fashioned male jealousy – I wouldn't be human if I wasn't jealous. She's as jealous as I am. But I have to come to terms with the fact that if she's going to be free to do whatever she wants, that opens her up to all kinds of dangers. She's going to meet other men, in other situations, and at the end of the day I have to accept that – because I can't possibly throw the ropes over her and tie her down.

As far as a fully open relationship goes, I don't think we could – we're probably both too jealous. If I did go off with someone else I wouldn't tell. I'd like to but I don't. I'm still attractive, I'm still capable. I flirt an awful lot. I like to be in a position where I know that I could, but I think that's as far as it really goes, mostly. I always feel that the ultimate moment is the first sort of surrender, the most exciting moment. The sex that comes afterwards can be really brilliant but the really exciting moment is that reaffirmation of everything that you think you are. What you feel you are not just as a man, but as a person. I don't flirt in front of my girlfriend –it would cause more problems than it's worth. She'd be very jealous. She did at a party one time that we both went to when we were having a particularly bad time. This woman came over and started talking to me and she was really leggy, blonde, just finishing her law exams, she had everything going for her, flat in Docklands, everything. She was really coming on strong and I was trying to back her off because I could see my girlfriend at the other side of the room. So in the end, I knew what was going to happen, I had to say to her, 'Look, you're causing me a lot of problems, you're very nice, very attractive, but you're going to have to leave me alone.'

I found the concept of the New Lad was a great relief, because the whole New Man thing was very pathetic. The New Lad was a media invention and not a particularly good one, but it did give us that chance to stop for a little while and go back down the pub and have a chat with your mates. I've always had open discussions with a group of friends about sex. What it means, what our fears are. That's always existed for me, since I was a teenager. Talking about masturbation, about penis size, whatever.

ALEX KERSHAW: Things have changed a lot for women, not very much for men but they are changing. Men have to change because change is natural. And the impulse is fairly positive. That's a reaction to the progression women have made. In theory you can go back, but in fact that's forbidden, and accepted as such, which is the real victory of feminism: men can no longer go back. So inevitably they will have to start stepping forward, coming to terms with it. Women are at the

390

cutting edge, forcing the change, and men are following on behind. Men are so gauche, years behind. Women are light years ahead and always will be. The question is just how far men can catch up. I feel I've progressed, that I'm of a different generation.

Having children is the real crunch. That's when the relationships between men and women become very important. That's when the New Woman issue becomes a crunch issue. The woman's having the baby, what does the guy do? That's when it has to change. And that's where it will be a real issue for me. I feel very loathe to be a househusband. Women are expected to do it naturally. I wouldn't be able to afford a nanny, and wouldn't want it, someone strange bringing up my kids. This goes to the heart of men's and women's roles. This is where the New Man has a possibility of existence. Of course New Lads aren't married.

I wrote the original piece on the New Lad. The New Man was a kind of media invention. A figment of the *Guardian* Women's Page, *Spare Rib's* 'Page 7 Fella' with a birth certificate signed by a copywriter. That was the New Man: essentially a Seventies' product. The New Lad was a media invention too, but what's interesting about him is that he does exist to a certain extent. The characteristics I described are representative of a lot of blokes I know. The New Lad is fairly aware of the social issues, has grown up with the shadow of feminism behind him at every point, can no longer make sexist jokes, is fairly middle class, articulate, well-read and educated, aware of the issues, but hasn't gone as far as re-inventing himself to please women. He still enjoys boozing, football and is proud to be a man. He has the best of both worlds. I concluded my article by saying the New Lad is a distinct improvement over the New Man, who is a bit of a wimp and whom women don't fancy anyway because he's a doormat; and over the Old Lad, who is just a George Best look-alike – get it in, get it out, get back down the pub to tell your mates. Though maybe he's just a sensitive Old Lad, just a bit more cocky, sharp, witty.

JEREMY PATRICK

'Salad Days'

After supper and much wine out comes the hardcore video. A man, two girls – one white, one Asian. Fake smiles, grinding meat, bright red close-ups, lips and labia, monster cock, creamy ejaculation. Watching, the men affect nonchalance, the girls peer from between their fingers. No one admits to excitement. The tape ends. The drink flows again, whisky now, amid expressions of pious

disgust and empty concern for the hapless girls. He rummages for a
second feature: Animal Farm. It's lost. Or perhaps, a former
Cavalry Captain, he prefers to spare the horses embarrassment.

I went to Stowe, then went to South Africa for a year after I left. I certainly learnt more in that year than I have in any other period of my life. Sexually, everything. Before that I'd led an incredibly closeted life. From the age of eight at prep school I'd been in a family-orientated, parentally dominated holiday life. The capacity to explore and learn was pretty small. Then public school till I was eighteen; I left not having much clue about women at all. I got no sex education at all from my parents. On the whole I picked things up as I went along. I was shown masturbation at prep school. There were people talking about it and I didn't know what they were talking about. So there was one particular evening and this boy came into the dormitory and all the lights were on and he had a porn mag, and he stood on a bed, leant back against the wall, whipped out his willie and thrashed himself one. We all thought this tremendously exciting. So we all had to experiment ourselves, which was the most mind-blowing experience, the first orgasm through masturbation was tremendous, very exciting.

The only extent to which I was involved in that public school quasi-gay scene was in the junior dormitory in which you spent the first two years. There was this metal tin in which were kept the safety pins which were used to pin socks together when they went in the wash. And this tin was regularly emptied of its pins, then passed around from boy to boy to see if we could fill it up [with semen].

I lost my virginity aged seventeen at a house dance at Stowe with a girl called Polly. It was 1978. We'd have these dances, a disco, very watered-down punch, and girls would be shipped in from the two or three schools around. It was literally like a cattle market, tremendous fun. You'd all line up at the entrance of the school, and all these girls would arrive and you'd literally go, 'No, no, no, yes.' And then you'd go up, introduce yourself to the girl, and take her for a drink. I'm sure they were just as shy as we were, and the girl you selected you tended to stay with all night. I had a study by that stage and I'd erected a false floor decked out with cushions and mattresses, an Arabian tent, and it all took place up there. I have to say it was extremely quick. Whether or not she was a virgin too I honestly wouldn't know. I can't remember now, and at the time I wouldn't have been able to tell you. Was it fun? A difficult question. Basically it was something I wanted to do, to get over and done with. I had a condom; I'd had them for ages, the sort of thing you had to carry around to pretend to everyone that you did

392

use them. You had to have them, just to keep up. The stories we all used to tell about our sexual antics. You'd have thought we'd all been bonking since we were six. You can't possibly admit that you're still a virgin. So when I did lose my virginity I definitely enjoyed it, but mainly I viewed it as an opportunity to get rid of this stigma and I could genuinely claim that I'd been there and done that. After that I wanted to do it some more and the following holidays I thought: I can go and lay any girl now because I've done it once – but that did not prove to be the case. I didn't have a clue what I was doing, didn't know what to say, how to flirt.

I arrived in South Africa as a young adult, for the first time in my life supporting myself financially and thus for the first time able to spend my money and my time as I saw fit. I started off with a rucksack and £100 in my pocket. I fell in with some other ex-public-schoolboys and gradually we met other people and we all lived in the same doss-house together. We started meeting women in this hotel, almost all of them older than us, and fresh-faced, well-spoken young lads from English public schools appeared to be quite appealing to them. One night I was having a drink at the bar and in came this very large, voluptuous woman, mid-thirties, wearing a long white flowing dress with what seemed to be nothing else underneath it. She came up to the bar and the manager of the place, a Yorkshireman, literally put one arm round her shoulders and the other hand went inside her dress and started playing with her tits. This was mind-blowing in a public place. The evening went on and we all got very drunk and it ended with this woman taking me into the dining-room of this hotel, lying down, pulling me down on top of her and away we went.

Once a month these South Africans we knew would arrange an orgy at the top of the Carlton Hotel in Johannesburg. They'd book a room and anything between eight and sixteen people would turn up. We'd arrive, go into the cocktail bar, have several cocktails, then into this room. The very first time I went I was absolutely petrified: everybody just took all their clothes off and got down to it. Swapping and switching around while I stood there going, 'Ooh, ooh, what do I do.' And again I had to be taken in hand and shown what to do. It was terribly exciting and I really wanted to join in, but I didn't know how to approach any of the women. The other guys were managing all right. In the end I went to five or six of these orgies and did get very proficient.

After I finished with South Africa I went to Germany as a cavalry officer. Life there was very enclosed, a very large, self-contained English-speaking community, and it was very difficult to break out of that. I was in Munster where it's very Catholic, very dour, rather like

393

Yorkshire, and they don't like the Brits. Fraternising is quite difficult. So what you do is go up to Hamburg and Amsterdam. You could get a bonk in the Eros Centre, the state-regulated brothel area of Hamburg, for 40 DM, in those days about £12. It was very good, very clinically clean, very businesslike. But after the first couple of times you realised it's a complete rip-off, because they just want to do you as quickly as possible and kick you out. But there were some gorgeous looking women, absolutely stunning. The Eros Centre is like an underground carpark, very warm, very musty, humid. All these girls are just walking around, you go in, mix with them, and they come up and you light upon one, strike a deal and you go out of the back door upstairs to her room and do it. It was very well done, not tacky or dirty and they were nice to you as well. You didn't feel intimidated as one might have done. The Germans do it very well.

There were also a number of girls who went around, not prostitutes, but who 'kept the boys happy'. Some were German, middle-class girls, mainly found through the horsey fraternity, and being a cavalry regiment we had lots of ponies, so there was that contact. Apart from that there were the English girls who came out to be nannies for the married officers. A lot of them were very keen to keep the boys happy too. Nobody ever thought of marrying them, but they were certainly viewed as being good fun. Not as scrubbers, but very affectionately. If anyone from another regiment tried to muscle in it was 'Hands off, this girl's ours.' Then they'd go off to England and get married there.But the bottom line in that situation is that it doesn't come along very often and when you can get it you do. It's that classic case: I've never been to bed with an ugly woman but I've woken up with a few. Awful line, but it's true. Nurses' parties for instance. They'd have a party for one reason. They're not interested in meeting a troop leader from the Lancers, what they want is to get laid. And the guys don't go because they're interested in meeting a nurse; they go because they want to be laid. It was unspoken, but it was absolutely accepted. You'd go, pick your girl, and as long as you're reasonably nice, don't get too drunk and throw up on her, there's a high chance that you'd be getting it off that night.

Every year in our regiment the Sergeants' Mess holds a big ball to celebrate Balaclava. A mega-ball, and obviously all the officers are invited. It was in '88, my last one. I went along as a single officer, sat at the same table as the Squadron Sergeant-Major and frankly it was pretty dull. But after a while you could get up and talk to other people. So I did that and suddenly I spotted this stunning girl at the other end of the table. So I said to the Sergeant-Major, 'Who's that, you must introduce me.' He said, 'That's my step-daughter.' And he did introduce me. We then spent the whole time dancing together. She was nineteen. So we got on really, really well and got very pissed and ended up snogging in the bar. Which was a very, very foolish thing to do from my point of view, in full view of everybody, who can see that there's the Captain snogging with the Sergeant-Major's daughter. Funnily enough though, some of them were really in favour of it, particularly the wives. They were egging us on: 'Go for it, go for it.' So we did. Eventually her mother came up – she hadn't actually seen us snogging – and said they were going and was she coming? One of these sergeants' wives who'd been egging us on said, 'No, leave her, she's having a good time.'

So that's what happened. We danced away and at about four a.m. I took her back to my flat and got stuck in in a major way. At nine-thirty the next morning, the telephone rang, it was the Sergeant Major, very official, 'Is Sharon there?' Oh my God! 'Yes she is, yes.' She took the phone: 'Come home at once!' Most displeased. So we concocted some cock-and-bull story about going for a walk, having breakfast – a complete lie. I regretted lying, but I did feel that from everybody's point of view it was better to have a lie that everyone could latch on to, even if they didn't believe it. So that's what happened. We then embarked upon a five- or six-month affair – and it was absolutely taboo, to be involved with the daughter of an Other Rank. If I'd have been found out I'd have been in serious shit. It was so exciting, smuggling her in, smuggling her out. Then we got a little more brave and we went to the soldiers' bars down town, and the nightclubs. It was very exciting, and I'm sure it was the fact that it was so taboo that made it so. But no one ever knew. They knew something was going on but they never knew what. The pure fact that I wouldn't tell them was enough, though they don't know to this day and most of them think it was someone's wife. But it's not just that she was a working-class girl. I'd get just the same kick giving one to a duchess or a princess. I haven't, as it happens, but then there are a lot fewer princesses around.

I spent eight and a half years in the army before I came back to England. I was bored so I quit. And when I did come back I was warned by so many people, 'Jeremy, just be careful, you're going to go wild. You've been in Germany all this time, you've never lived in London, you're going to go berserk.' I'd say, 'What are you telling me this for? The whole reason I'm coming is because I want to go berserk.' And indeed I did. I got myself a job with Jardine Matheson but before starting that I had two weeks free. It was high summer 1989, really gorgeous weather, and I had two weeks free before I joined my new job. I went to this barbecue in Fulham with a girl who had been the girlfriend of my best buddy. There were forty or fifty people and it was great fun until at the end there were six of us left, three men, three women. We were very drunk and started playing strip pontoon. So soon everyone got undressed. It was unspoken but we were all on for a bonk. Caroline, the girl who was hosting the party, made that happen by suggesting a game of sardines. So we all went off and hid. But I got it slightly wrong. I was very competitive, I wanted to win and I didn't intend to get caught. So stark bollock naked I sat on her roof in Fulham with the stars out, hearing the search go on inside and people being discovered and then lots of people started shouting my name and I thought: Ah, I'm winning, they can't find me, I'm going to stay here. I spent half an hour on this roof and it was absolutely quiet. So I went back inside and the other five were all lying on Caroline's bed, chatting and drinking. They said, 'Come in, come in.' I said, 'I'll only come in on one condition: we turn the lights off and get stuck in.' So we did. The only trouble was that next morning they all had to go to work, and four of them were work colleagues. Which made for very averted eyes, lots of embarrassment at the office. I then came back here, quite knackered, and I lay on my patio with a towel round my waist and drifted off to sleep. So when I wake up, on the balcony of the next-door house is this old woman, about seventy, looking down at me. I came to. 'Morning dearie.' I said, 'Morning.' 'Don't get sunburned, will you?' I thought, 'Sunburned?' then I looked down and my towel had slipped away and I was lying there completely naked with this old crone feasting her eyes.

I don't think it's strictly true that every relationship starts as a one-night stand. Certainly when I'm on the prowl – as I am at the moment having just finished with a girlfriend – I'm out for two things: I'm basically after another relationship but until that comes along there are also certain needs that have to be satisfied and therefore it is initially a one-nighter. Now that one-nighter may develop into a relationship, but the girl who you actually look at and think, hmmm, I do actually quite like her quite a lot, and I don't just want to take her to bed, with her you play a much more careful game. I don't instantly force myself upon her, try to get her into bed on night one. I play, if you like, a much cleverer game, a more waiting game. I try to get her round to it as well, instead of lunging straight into it. So that's the two-pronged attack, depending on what you're after. It is very calculating, yes.

There is this degree of calculatedness, very definitely. I'll meet a woman, wherever, and think I really want to go to bed with her as soon as possible and after that the whole game plan works along those lines. The flirtation: the mental fuck hopefully followed by the physical fuck. You know what you think and you hope she thinks the same. Then there's the finding out about her and building up enough courage to put the question. The moment when you move from mapping it all out to making the leap in the dark is hugely exciting. I think that's often why one-night stands remain only one-night stands. The build-up is very exciting and that moment when you take the leap and ask her to come home is very exciting. When you actually get her into bed and wake up the next morning and think, 'Oh God, time to go ...'

You could say that male foreplay is the flirtation rather than actual physical foreplay itself, but I don't really agree. Unless it's a purely selfish act, in which case the physical foreplay isn't that important since at the end of the day all you really want to do is get your end away as quickly as possible, then go to sleep.

We all know New Men, and I think they're boring. I find them hugely unexciting people myself but it is simply a different viewpoint to mine and if he gets his kicks that way, then good luck to him. In my own life I know that things have changed. Ten years ago I might have gone about sex in a very different way; over the last few years I've changed, I think I've become more mature, more grown-up, but I don't think that makes me a New Man. It's got nothing to do with the attitude of the Nineties. It's simply me growing up. Although you could say that I grew up quite late – in my mid-to-late twenties. But that's definitely more to do with me than with what other people say or what I read. I'm not influenced at all by what other people say I should be feeling or thinking. Just because someone says 'Men of the Nineties should be more considerate', well, you know, that's what you say. For me it's if I want to be, then I will be, but not because I read it in a magazine. And if I do choose to be it may well be true that being considerate these days is a way of getting a girl to take her knickers off. I think there are men who certainly pose as 'New Men' just for that purpose. They haven't really changed at all, only outwardly, to get what they want. Inside nothing's changed.

I've only had two long-standing relationships. One of eighteen months and one of about a year. Otherwise it's quick flings, which tend to last around two or three months. For a one-night stand I'll go to this mix between a pub and a wine bar, the Pitcher and Piano, in Fulham, on the corner of Fulham and Munster Road. Essentially a pickup joint. Very popular with women, who like the decorations. An awful lot of pretty girls go there, Thursday night is very good. Or there's the Hollywood in Hollywood Road. Apart from that, meeting people at dinner parties, drinks parties.

I think there has been a change in women. There's less of the wishy-washy waiting around for somebody to come and marry me. Girls are saying, 'Yes, I do want to get married, I do want to have a family and babies, but I'm not going to sit around and wait for some guy to come and ask me, I want to go and do something for myself until that happens, or as well as that.' They're more independent, aggressive, single-minded. So many more women have professional careers. But there is the big danger that it's easily possible for women to be too struck on their own careers, too involved in their work, and it does become the number one priority. They've had a taste, they've got the company car, the nice flat, they've been promoted – none of which they'd have had had they been born ten years earlier. But what happens is they end up at thirty-plus and they're still single. A beautiful girl, old friend of my sister, has spent all her life working for BAT, she's been all round the world, she's in a seriously good job, but she hates it. She's done it, she's bored, and she's very, very sad that her friends are all married and have a house and kids. As far as sex is concerned, it means, in my case anyway, that with these girls you're less likely to get between the sheets. Though this isn't always so. A month ago I met this Australian girl, very high-powered securities broker. Stunningly beautiful. I thought I haven't got a chance here, I didn't even try. Here is this stunning bird who is very, very high-powered, seen much more of the world than I have, and there's no way she's going to be interested in me. So I chatted to her without any plays whatsoever. But three weeks later she arranged for me to go to dinner with her and some other people. We went to a nightclub, she invited me back for a nightcap and I ended up spending the whole weekend with her. That lasted three weeks. It did a lot for me, I'd thought she was completely out of my league.

With the new sort of powerful career woman there is definitely a sense in which a man is gaining status from going to bed with them. It was always true that you got status for going to bed with a particularly good-looking girl, but now there's status if she's high-powered as well. Though still, in terms of the way other people view it, the core issue is: Is she beautiful? I don't know whether men sleep with their bosses; I'd like to, I'd find it quite exciting. When I was working for Jardines they had a personnel director, a woman in her late thirties, dressed well, good looking. I certainly fantasised about giving her one but it never happened. I wasn't working in the office, though if I had I'd have definitely made myself available, put it that way. I don't know about lady bosses sexually harassing junior men, but I can't see why not.

Career girls in general have a big hang-up, they over-react to this men / women thing. I don't think there is this big problem. I don't think that men in general want to be in overall charge of every aspect of life out there, including sex. I really don't. I don't think that men necessarily want to defend this stand to the last. Women who claim that men do, and they have to fight them, are over-reacting. I question the whole concept, because I don't think that there is this major issue which we have to fight over. Not at all. I don't believe that things are that bad. I don't know any men who want to be the boss and keep women down as secretaries. I don't know many married male friends who expect or want their wives to stay at home.

I don't take myself seriously in sex. I think sex should be a laugh. You should laugh a lot when you're having sex, it should be a joke. I think of one particular friend – whether it's technique or the size of his penis I don't know – but he falls out a lot. And he has a real hang-up about this, it worries him a lot. He's bonking away and his willy falls out. For me it would be a hell of a good laugh, in fact I'd see it as a good excuse to try another position.

I don't know whether it's times that have changed or whether it's me that has changed, but certainly I genuinely want to give women a good time in bed now, whereas in the past what mattered was that I had a good time; if they came too that was fine but ... Maybe it's more a reflection on the women I go to bed with than anything else, but they don't seem keen to do anything more than – well, lying there and thinking of England is a bit too strong, but definitely it's very much a minority of women who take charge, and will actually ask you to do things or do things to you. They're inhibited in bed. I do like it when women take charge.

Oral sex is something that a lot of women are reluctant to do, or won't do at all. I'll do it; I'm reluctant too, but I will do it. It's not the act, it's the smell. If I can get something down there – Bailey's or something – it's not so bad. Or yoghurt or something I can lick off, that's okay, that I can handle with no problem at all. It's difficult to breathe if they're all bushy or they don't take care of themselves properly, keep themselves trimmed, a nice smooth lawn. There's nothing worse than being confronted with a massive haystack down there.

I find that American women – I've been to bed with four or five American women – they're so much more active in bed, and they all love giving head, they love it. I had a six-month affair with one girl who actually told me American mothers teach their girls to give good head. It's very important. Part of sexual education, teaching your daughter how to give a good blow-job. I know very, very few men who don't like it. It's a really nice feeling, I love watching a woman while she's doing it to me, that head bobbing up and down. Though I really don't

399

see it as power. Power doesn't come into my sexual relations, it's all too frivolous to be thinking in terms of power.

I like experiments. One of the oddest things I tried was using a cucumber for sex. In a relationship I had last year, she was a dental nurse from Birmingham, from a completely different class, thick Brummie accent and so on, and there's no doubt that having a relationship with someone from a different class was very, very exciting indeed. So. I had always wanted to know, for years and years I'd wanted to know, does a bigger penis give a female more satisfaction than a smaller one? And having asked various girls, some I was having relationships with, others were one-night stands, I gathered a number of different answers. So I thought that the only way to get an answer was to go for something that is basically bigger than any penis I'd ever seen. So I bought this cucumber, I didn't tell her, I peeled it before she arrived and thought: Don't put it in the fridge, that would be too cold. So like good red wine I let it come to room temperature. So later on there we were in bed, all the foreplay taking place, all the right sort of moisture arising, all that, and then I said, 'I've got a surprise for you.' I went outside and brought this thing. I didn't tell her what it was, I just said, 'Lie back, close your eyes and tell me if this is not pleasant. And if it's not pleasant then I will stop.' This cucumber went in about twice as far as I thought it was going to, I promise you. I'm talking about at least fourteen inches. I put this cucumber up, slowly, slowly, until I met physical resistance. Then I masturbated her with this cucumber. And this girl was helpless, helpless in ecstasy, absolutely, completely, utterly helpless. She was just in a different world. And that made me feel very, very good indeed. She had the most unbelievable orgasm. I wasn't being naughty, but I was bringing her on, teasing her and teasing her with this thing, fast and slow ... And she had this incredible orgasm and that made me feel so good. I had given her this unbelievable pleasure. And theretofore I had been unable to do that. Now this was a total experiment for me, and after she'd climbed down from the ceiling, I asked her about it. I said, 'Was that good?' 'Of course it was good.' 'So was it the same or different to when I was making love to you? And if it was different, how was it different?' So she said, 'Well, it was different for two reasons.' First of all it was novel, she'd never had a vegetable up her before, something so big, so massive, so there was the thrill of novelty. Then there was also this business of stimulation. Her whole inside was taken up. This feeling of being utterly full was very, very sexually stimulating. And yet, she said, while physically it was stimulating, spiritually, emotionally, however you want to portray it, it was very third party. 'I didn't feel that you were making love to me at all.' I then asked: 'Which
400

do you actually prefer?' And she said she preferred to have a person make love to her.

Breaking sexual taboos is fun. My parents are as right-wing, fascist KKK as you can get. If I brought a black girl home that would be the end, I'd be kicked out. So when I went with a coloured prostitute in Cape Town, which I regretted afterwards but which I did, it was forbidden fruit, absolutely forbidden fruit. Forbidden fruit is one of the great turn-ons. Race, and class. Definitely class. I took my dental nurse home to meet my parents. They were nauseatingly polite, so nice, so polite and they got their point across so well. She hated every minute of it. I didn't sleep with her in the house; I wanted to but I didn't. It would have been difficult. I have corridor-crept at home, but not on this occasion. It is exciting to go out with a girl who is, if you like, taboo. And to have her in London and introduce her to all my yuppie friends, I find highly amusing. I was protective of her, I'd never leave her at a party to fend for herself, but you only need to see a glance from someone to pick up what they feel. She holds her knife differently, says 'toilet' instead of 'loo', or whatever. It makes my blood boil the way people react, seeing the way it affects people I consider to be very good friends. It's very amusing but equally so very alarming. They're saying, 'Surely you can find yourself something better?' They're not judging her as a person, but on her façade. Which is why I find 'Fulham women' so deadly boring. Though I would have approached the Hon. Caroline Somebody-Something with a cucumber too, and probably with even more relish. Knowing that she's even less likely to have encountered one before.

I have these pornographic videos, hardcore stuff. I watch them myself, and I also put them on when I have women here. And I've noticed that the more working class the girl, the less interested she is; it's the yuppies who really love watching them. They all go, 'Oooh, how horrible,' and put their fingers over their eyes, but they're watching through the gaps. Their conditioning tells them they shouldn't enjoy it and they shouldn't find it exciting and they should find it disgusting, but actually they can't help themselves. They do enjoy it. It's a great challenge to turn on girls who are brought up not to admit it. And for all the changes in sexuality there are still plenty of women like that. Women who really badly want it but find it difficult to get it. They put across the wrong signals. Breaking that down, getting it out of them is hugely exciting, definitely. The pearl-necklace Sloane especially. I suppose when I get into those situations there is this cruel streak, because what I'm doing is definitely to do with power, I'm showing off my power over them. What I'm saying is: 'You

401

know you really badly want it, but you're not getting it because you're so uptight.'

I think there is a bit of truth in 'they're all sisters under the skin'. Deep down all women want sex. But I would also maintain my belief that in the end men have a much higher sex drive than women. Sex is fifty:fifty for me – I'm getting pleasure because I'm getting off, but I'm also getting pleasure because she's obviously enjoying herself. That definitely enhances what's going on, if I can see that she's really going for it. When I'm having sex the nearer and nearer the girl gets to having a climax, the nearer that brings me. The more turned on a woman gets the more it turns me on. If she starts moaning and panting and puffing at an early stage, then I have to click into serious self-control. Thinking of Matron at school. Something completely unsexy. But I think if you make your mind wander the girl picks that up so I find it's much better to withdraw and just continue with some petting or just continue stimulating her in a different way, and when I feel that the little chap's quietened down a bit, back we go again. Going out with an American has taught me a lot about controlling the little chap. He used to control me completely and utterly. Then we went through a year of fighting, and now I think I'm in charge.

I've never used sex manuals, they don't interest me. What other people think. I love talking about sex, but you can't discuss things with a book – it's too clinical. I definitely discuss sex with my male friends. I'm not sure what women talk about. I don't think they talk about willy size or whatever, I don't think they get that anatomical. Whereas guys definitely do, they'll talk about the size of her tits or the shape of her fanny or whatever. Not really in a laddish way, but in a fairly sincere way. Women won't reveal all the antics that go on in bed. Whereas I'll say to my friends, 'It was fantastic. She did this, that or the other and it was tremendous.' I don't think women are prepared to reveal that kind of thing. But just because I'd slept with someone I wouldn't rush off and tell my friends, 'What a slut.' Definitely not. I don't shout it from the rooftops. After all we're both there, we're both doing it and I must be a slut if they are. If it's a one-nighter, literally, you've picked her up, taken her home and given her one and you'll never see her again, chances are you won't even know her surname – you'll know her Christian name, or at least the one she's given you. I've certainly given false names. But I still won't slag her off. I love the challenge, I love the chase and if I get what I want I'm certainly not going to slag them off.

It's important not to confuse humour with frivolity. I do take my relationships very, very seriously. I commit myself. However tempted I may be, when I am in a relationship I won't go and sleep around with

402

someone else. So I'm not frivolous, but there should be a huge degree of humour and I hope that when I'm married and sixty I'll still be laughing in bed as much as I do now.

I was talking to a woman, a very old friend, and she expressed very strongly her view that she has no interest in having sex on the first night whatsoever. You meet someone, you get to know them, the relationship builds and so on. I think many women are frightened of having sex too early because they don't want to be called a slag. Yet they have the need for sex. But I see that as an old-fashioned view. I think it's changing and I think that women are far more prepared to have sex earlier on than they were before.

One thing I have never been able to fathom. You see your classic, overtly sexy, airhead bimbo walking down the street looking very sexy, quite deliberately, so you give them the appreciative look, or even a comment, which is what their appearance is demanding, and what you get is two fingers, 'Fuck off, mate.' Yet they have spent hours, and lots of money making themselves look that way, and when they attract the appreciation they're after, they don't want to know.

I find this date rape thing quite alarming, I'm genuinely worried about it. I can see it growing into something bigger and bigger and bigger, that is going to be a problem. Date rape per se – yes, I've definitely done it, there's no question about that, several times. Getting her drunk, blurring her emotions, kissing and cuddling and touching and all the rest of it and then making the lunge and she's saying, 'No, I don't think ...,' and me saying, 'Oh come on, it's only one night, no big deal,' and forcing myself upon her. And reluctantly she comes to bed; she wants to because she's all sexed up, but she doesn't want to because it's the first time we've met – but she does anyway. Then in the morning being terribly regretful when she has. At that point I do try to respect her emotion and not dwell on it and not make her feel any worse than she's already feeling. If she's all down and embarrassed I'll say, 'I know you didn't really want to but only you and I know and unless you tell anyone, I'm certainly not going to.' But whatever I say, you can't get away from the fact that had she been fully *compos mentis* she probably wouldn't have done it. And if that's date rape, then I'm guilty on several counts m'lud, all of which I would like to have taken into consideration. How often these pickups are consensual and how often they're really date rape I can't say – but the more women feel that men are threatening them, then the more of an issue it will become and the more it will become a problem for men. But I think it's just fun and it should be fun and the act of having sex should not have read into it as much meaning as some women do.

I know that some feminists will see me as an appalling figure to hold

403

the attitudes I do, but I don't really understand why they should. I don't know that much about feminism, but as I understand it what they want is to be treated absolutely equally and given the same opportunities that men do and not to be placed under anyone's thumb. Simplistically put, but that's how I understand it. But I don't see how picking up a girl in a bar and taking her home and date-raping her falls into the category of oppressing women, of denying their equality. The initial motivation is definitely selfish. I don't sit here and think I must go to the Pitcher and Piano, pick up a girl and give her a good time. What I'm thinking is I'm going to the Pitcher and Piano, hoping to pick up a girl and I'm going to have a great evening. So the motive is selfish, but hopefully, having achieved my aim, of picking her up and getting her home, then indulging in sex, I get an additional kick out of giving her a good time and I make a big effort to achieve that. A girl who won't respond and who literally just lies there – and the more Sloane-y they are the more likely they are to behave like that – the less exciting it becomes. They aren't necessarily much younger, though I do tend to go for younger girls, but having said that it is very exciting occasionally to have a much older woman. Early forties, I suppose, it depends very much on their physical condition.

I know this fellow who says this, and I agree: women go through the pain of childbirth and all the other problems girls have, but God's way of compensating for that was to give women the ability of multiple orgasm. Most women go through the pain of childbirth twice, maybe three times, so you go through that pain three times but have loads of times of multiple orgasm. I reckon that's a bloody good deal. To my mind, the concept of pleasure in giving a woman an orgasm, or hopefully lots, that may sound on the surface very selfless, but actually it's selfish. Because I actually get a kick out of feeling a woman trembling away and having a wonderful time. It's not simply power. It's exactly the same as watching somebody open your Christmas present and watching the wonderful look of pleasure on their face.

I have achieved some of my sexual ambitions. I'd always wanted to have sex in a wood. I don't know why – the sunlight filtering through the leaves, all that. Who says there are no male romantics? At the time I was going out with Holly, my American girlfriend in Munster. She was terribly open and liberal and if I wanted to do something with her sexually I could just say so. The same went for her. If one of us didn't want to, then no big deal, we didn't do it. So I told her, I want to have sex in a wood. So off we went, had a picnic by the canal, and just off the towpath is a bit of wood. So in we went, got naked and started humping away. We were well into it and suddenly this squadron of mosquitoes attacked my bum. I could feel them like little needles.

Decisions one has faced, the crossroads of one's life: do I continue and get a seriously bitten bum, because this is great fun, or do I forsake the sex and not get bitten? I'm afraid the sex won, but I had a very lumpy bum for the next few days. It was very exciting because anyone could have walked down the towpath. They might not have seen us on the towpath, but one step into the wood ... Sex on a train, yes. Blow-jobs in a car when people can look and do look. You're driving along, the girl has her head in your lap. That's great fun. You're driving along and people look in and there's this girl giving you a blow-job, so they wave or smile or honk the horn or whatever. Usually on a motorway, which is very dangerous, but you have to be in a cruising position, it's no good if you're changing gear or constantly moving the wheel. I think it's tremendous watching a girl masturbate. I've asked girls to do it and some do. Those I've been going out with for a while. I've been out with girls who wanted me to masturbate in front of them, and ejaculate on them. It may not be that unusual but they're not exactly getting a lot out of it.

Girls on holiday are just as keen on sex as men. Definitely. I was in Cyprus, which is very popular with the Swedes. These gorgeous beauties, blonde hair, beautifully suntanned, topless, just wandering around everywhere. At night they're in all the nightclubs in these white clothes. Just gorgeous. I did have three in one night once. Which was quite good going. I was in this club dancing with one of them and her friend. I thought we were getting along fine, but the friend was being the gooseberry. So the friend then dragged her off to their apartment. So I stood there for a minute, thinking, 'Who's next?' then I thought: Hell, I'm going to follow them back, and I shadowed them back to their apartment. I gave them ten minutes then I went in and knocked on their door. She came to the door and I asked her why she'd run off. 'My friend wasn't feeling too well, we had to go.' 'Oh, I thought we were getting on very well, can I see you again?' She said they were going back to Sweden the next day. I was pretty disappointed but she said, 'Hang on,' and with me standing in the doorway she knelt down, undid my zip and gave me a blow-job, there and then. Finished, zip up, 'Enjoy your holiday, see you.' Unbelievable. So I went back to the same club and this time picked up another girl. We went back to her apartment with her and three or four friends who shared it. We stayed in the sitting-room and we slept on this sofa-bed. The next morning she went to have a shower and her friend marched in, all stroppy, 'What are you doing here?' I explained. We chatted away and the next thing she took me into her bedroom and had sex. At which point the other girl finished her shower – where was I? When I appeared from her friend's bedroom she was very upset.

In the area of just what it is that people want from sex, I think there's a big difference for a man anyway about whether you're going to bed with a woman just to get that sexual satisfaction, in which case you're probably not that interested in how much pleasure you give her and probably you're less interested whether you see her the following morning, or ever again. It's purely a case of emptying your pods and getting a bit of pleasure. Despunking. But there is this attitude these days that that kind of pure pleasure, selfish sex is wrong, is ideologically impure. And for the first time I've been subjected to it. I've been on the receiving end. I had a two-week fling with a woman and suddenly she just disappeared. Which left me thinking, hang on, what did I do? What's gone wrong, this was great and whoosh! it's all over. She never did give me a reason, though I heard she'd met a New Man, with a Porsche and a house in the country. And I may not have liked it, but she's only doing to me what I've done to countless women over the years: to have a really good time and then when the grass was greener move on.

Am I a slag, am I a tart? I certainly was, but no more. I don't want to catch the Big A. I was, definitely, I was out there to get whatever I could wherever I could. I might not have succeeded every single time but I've certainly kept myself occupied. I enjoyed it. But it's only been in the last three years that I've actually been honest about it, and said to a girl, when you get to that point, that crucial diplomatic point, back home and in bed, what I'm doing. Now that's fair, because if you've got to that position you haven't got there on your own, you've got there because both of you want to be in that position. So just before you're about to launch, just before Thunderbirds are Go, I will always now say, 'Look, we're about to do this and I want to make it clear that as far as I am concerned this is just for tonight.' At which point some do say, 'Oh.'

Some say 'Oh,' but some say 'Okay, that's great, that's what I want and that's fine.' And a few others say, 'Oh, I was rather expecting something more than that, I was rather hoping that this night might have led to something further. But if you're looking at it like this, then I don't want to play.' At which point you turn over with a raging hard-on, very frustrated. But I wouldn't lie. Not any more. I used to, I used to lie through my teeth to get my end away.

But the point is that it just depends on what the guy is after. If at any one time he's after a bonk, to get rid of the tension, to get despunked, that's one thing. And it makes you seem very callous and an easy lay and a bit of a tart and all the rest of it. And that's what he's doing. The same guy, concurrently with that could actually be looking for a meaningful relationship. I'm a perfect example. I am looking for

406

a meaningful relationship, but at the same time I need certain ... comforts.

★★★

AVEDON CARROLL: I almost feel people shouldn't be allowed to get married if they're sexually attracted to each other. Dating is so much more exciting. Familiarity not necessarily breeding contempt, but more familiarity. New relationships are always much more exciting, no matter how much you love someone.

RICHARD WHITFIELD: We've still got a screwed-up society, which is sad. We have not become liberated and sexual anxiety is far more than a mechanistic or biological problem. We can't express all our needs in the course of normal friendships, or indeed within the intimacies and specialness of marriage and family life. I'm committed to enriching and enhancing family life, although quite clearly – partly because of the way we're socialised and miseducated – even in some stable and committed families people don't know how to ask for something they would like from their partner.

Experimenting implies a range of partners. The notion of experimentation tends not to be associated with one man and one woman over a long period going through adjustment / readjustment. The implication is if you just have one partner, you develop a routine early on and then it becomes more of the same. Life is not like that. This is the crunch issue about commitment, about cohabitation, the trial period. We've got the notion, let's experiment, see if it's all right, then we'll know whether a commitment's worth it or not. Whereas psychologically people can only experience reliable unconditional love if they're surrounded by a commitment first – an act of faith which says I'm going to hold your hand come what may. We've done enough courting to know that something's buzzing chemically, intellectually, emotionally. From now on, we're going to have this adventure together. That doesn't demand a marriage ceremony. The crucial thing is that there is a formal promise, a shared contract, whether it's written down or not. That's the important thing.

The reason there have been marriage ceremonies in societies is that – for something so important about two people having a walk together for life – it's been natural in all sorts of cultures to share that with the tribe. That's how marriages got formalised. So there's a ritual and symbolic significance in getting married which still means a lot to many people, and we shouldn't downgrade its cultural importance.

But the crucial thing is whether the couple have this sense of rapport and have made to each other a psychological and practical commitment. Then within all that, if you've agreed to go on a journey together which you know is unpredictable, you've got the possibility of experimenting in whatever way you mutually decide. The whole notion of trying out a person to see if they fit you is damaging – and how long do you try it out for? Human feelings fluctuate so much and we should never make important decisions on the basis of feelings alone.

In a caring community married people do need other friends of the same and opposite sexes. But sexual partner swapping doesn't seem to me to be wise psychologically or medically. There have to be other ways of extending caring support and friendship. Partner swapping, even in the best-run couples' clubs, can lead to the disruption by a third party of an otherwise reasonable relationship. It's playing with fire and unlikely to promote the integrity of family and friendship bonds. People are not playthings. Now we need to move on to what I have called a new sexual revolution. This demands honesty and commitment within sexual relationships, and greater exclusiveness, which will safeguard health and reproduction, and give back some dignity to human sexuality.

HAZEL SLAVIN: It's extraordinary to you and I that a married man, legally married or not, someone who lives with a woman in a supposedly comfortable, loving, heterosexual relationship has to go somewhere else for a cuddle. I'd imagine that cuddling, kissing, caressing would be part of his sex life. It's remarkable that it isn't. It's when a relationship has become routine, over time, that people start looking for something different. People expect a much more rounded relationship. They get married and there's no feeling that you have to work at the relationship, that you have to negotiate things. And a strange thing, it doesn't matter what else happens in the relationship, everyone feels that the sex ought to be all right.

MICHAEL VERMEULEN: A guy wants to have an affair. You say to him, 'Why?' he says, 'I want something new.' But the fact is he does not want something new. What they want is something old. There is a rite of courtship. The words may be different, the circumstances, the pattern may be different; the gestalt is the same; but, you're married or living with somebody. You've never been with somebody this long before. Every day you're setting a new record. You're in hyper space. You have nothing to hold onto because you're on new ground. When you have an affair with somebody, you're deciding to step back on the game board and go through the moves that you are familiar and comfortable with.

There's all sorts of reasons for marriages staying together. My theory is there's no such thing as a successful relationship without shared projects. Their home, careers, children, whatever. And the way people invite others into their lives is by offering to share projects. There's something very intimate about asking your lover to do your dishes. It's bizarre but true, it's extremely intimate. I'm not opposed to marriage. I say if one out of two marriages fail, my next one's charmed. I also say divorce isn't the end of the world, but you can see it from there.

JOHN MICHAEL: I've always been unfaithful in my relationships. In the early Seventies infidelity had an ideological base, a large part of our dialogue was to do with having affairs with other people, why should we limit ourselves, etc., etc. Later on I carried it on in a traditional way. When I got married, right from the beginning I saw it as a nineteenth-century bourgeois marriage – the wife, the home, with a mistress around. So when I started having an affair with the girl who was working as our nanny, I'd thought I'd been brilliant, I'd pulled it off. I've got the wife and mistress, and under the same roof. It didn't work. I thought I could live a pleasant detached life with my wife. I saw marriage almost as a business. It was to do with having property, children, forming a comfortable unit. But you didn't have to be too close to each other. I'd seen lots of people who'd started off with lots of love and passion who'd settled down into a domestic round. I thought maybe you could start the marriage off at that point, at the practical end of things. You say, 'I've got my job which I find fascinating, which provides intellectual stimulation; I may have some affairs here and there for the frissons and thrills, and I'll have a nice comfortable home which the extra sex won't threaten.' In the end I found it dispiriting and horrible. I felt alienated and cut off and separate. My relationship with my wife was lacking a heart. With my girlfriend, she started off as a fantasy sex figure but turned into somebody I felt very close to emotionally.

It was the closest I got to reproducing the relationships I had in the Seventies. She was into affairs with women as well; she was sexually experimental. Had we been together as a couple, we would have lived out that old ideology. I didn't set out with her to do that. But if we'd been at a party and there was someone we both responded to, for her that could turn into a sexual thing. It was a very intense relationship and part of it was undoubtedly because of the hothouse secret nature
409

of it. But I didn't have a grail of wanting to find the right sort of sex. For me sex could take place in a separate box. The addictive element was that I'm looking for the perfect wave. Finding somebody who wanted to go off and do it in a detached way. So there were two of you, you fancied each other, you went off, you had hot sex and then it was: Might call you in a week, we'll have hot sex again. That was the ideal, to find people who wanted to do that, rather than sex as the core of a relationship. Hookers without paying for it basically.

JOHN LANKIEWICZ: It's very delightful to go out and have an intimate candlelit dinner with a lover. And we do that in a public place, although we pretend it's not public because we sit in little inglenooks, in slightly subdued light, etc. But it's a public place and that's okay. But it's a very private ritual. Also, we have the equivalent, which is like buying a chocolate bar and really looking forward to it, or having a beefburger – we enjoy those things, even children do. We have magnificent banquets. But we don't think: 'Well, the right way of eating is at home with the family or privately in a restaurant in subdued light and that having a great public banquet or having a quick bar of chocolate is wrong.' People do a bit of both nowadays.

THE NEW AGE: Mind Over Matter

We live, as a number of interviewees have remarked, in the shadow of the Sixties. And if New Women and New Men are a product of the period, then the third way, the philosophies that might be termed 'New Age', are very much of that era. Not so much a revolution, more a state of mind. Mind-fucking, as it were, for real.

CHRIS ESMOND

'Have you heard the greatest joke of all time?'

The ad asked 'Are you really interested in sex?' Many wrote, some even called, but few were chosen. He was one who made it. The flat is in a rundown Thirties block, hard-by the Euston tracks, on a street you've driven up a thousand times, wondering occasionally just who lives here. Now you know. The place seems to be in a state of deconstruction – boxes, cases, piles of possessions. His girlfriend has left; now he's moving on as well.

My strong feeling is that women are getting totally sick and tired of
410

men's incapacity to love them. Men have to change. If they don't, there's not much future for the human race. I think it's that important. Women feel men don't know how to love women, haven't a clue. They pretend to, but basically what they're interested in is what's between women's legs.

There's an enormous amount of ignorance around what sex is for and what men and women are doing. Sex is for the creation and expression of love between two human beings. It's not for instantaneous pleasure, not to hop into bed with somebody one night and say goodbye the next morning. That's not satisfying to anybody, and never has been. But people have confused sex and emotion, emotion and love. What passes for love is simple emotion, which comes and goes. People are into excitement only. I've realised all this over the last few years. I have tried to put it into practice. The fundamental need of women is for men to love them. More so than vice versa. The dynamic is: man loves woman, woman responds. It could sound very old-fashioned but I think that's the truth. The fundamental dissatisfaction of women is not economic – education, equal opportunities, equal pay is all part of it – but basically they're discontented because men can't love them. It's partly that men are wham-bam-thank-you-ma'am types, and women want more foreplay, but more than that, sex has been confused with excitement, which has nothing to do with love.

I hate the terms New Age, New Man. It sounds like you're trying desperately hard to fit into an image. New Man doesn't mean you have to become female. The real man has to firstly realise that something is not right here, and they have to listen to women. Not become a woman. People have got the wrong idea. The New Man is all female, does the washing-up every day. That's ridiculous. I don't think women want that at all.

A lot of these men's groups are trying to get into your femininity, I find. I went to one as an experiment last year. Down in Devon. I stayed about six weeks. There were about ten of us. For me it wasn't particularly useful. It seemed pretty childish to be sitting round discussing what fantasies you have while you're masturbating. All that is very adolescent, not liberated at all. Masturbation is impossible to avoid in certain circumstances, but personally I hope I never masturbate again. I think the fantasy that goes along with it is part of the excitement syndrome that takes people away from reality, away from relating to individuals on a day-to-day basis. Masturbation destroys love. I'm disgusted now by the idea of masturbation and wouldn't want to do it. I'd rather live with the discomfort.

I was involved for some years with the Sanyassins, the Rajneesh people. That's the Baghwan sect, the Orange people. They were badly distorted by the media – the Baghwan was crucified in the press. My experience of the movement was that it influenced me greatly. And the Baghwan was quite special. When I first heard his voice on tape, I knew it was for me. Within three months of doing that quite regularly, I changed from a person who couldn't function, depressed, fearful. I was able – which was a miracle then – to get a job as a schoolteacher. I was enjoying my life, high as a kite. That was an amazing liberation. It happened to others in different ways. It was very dramatic for me, but others weren't in such dire straits. But they did feel there was something there that was very true. The Baghwan was offering a vision of freedom based on something very authentic and real that he'd attained himself. He was the embodiment of love.

He preached sex liberation and down with taboos, which didn't work for me because I didn't get into that side of it. I didn't think of it as: Now I'm going to get rid of all my hang-ups. All that was irrelevant to me. That teaching was important, though. It was a climate of exploration, a lot of freedom, and that worked on me. No doubt my attitudes have been influenced by that.

I didn't get involved much with the sexual side. It didn't come my way. The whole idea of the movement is to work through your fears and things that prevent you from being free. He instituted incredible group therapies in Poona, and in the late Seventies God knows what went on. I'm sure there was sex, violence, God knows what. Very frightening at times when you went into it. It happened in England too. There was a lot of pairing off in the groups – which would go on for days – and people would make love in the middle of them. It wasn't uncommon for certain groups – like the tantra group, which investigates your sexuality, your fears, your attitudes – for lovemaking to happen, orgies, group sex. That was fairly common. Women in that movement were abused. There was some truth in the 'sex guru' label. The 'dip in to get rid of blockages' idea was very prevalent in the Sanyas movement. He encouraged people to make love a lot. Get rid of all the taboos. Which was very liberating in a way. He gave everybody total freedom, didn't interfere, and a few went over the top. Appalling. A major tragedy.

Since I left the movement my greatest influence in recent years has been Barry Long. He's taken the teaching a step further. He's an Australian. He's rare – a guru, and an Australian.Not an Easterner with a funny robe and all the works. He's a spiritual teacher. He was living in London in 1984, and friends went to see him and I did too. He comes to London every year now from Australia. He says: 'There's no such thing as a free fuck.' He's talking about sex as a central part
412

of his teaching. I haven't suddenly become a person following rules and tenets laid down by some organisation. Far from it, it's complete freedom. But this has the ring of truth. He doesn't have an organisation. He believes organisation corrupts these movements. He was a journalist, a newspaper editor, and in PR. He's sixty-six now, and he's done all this completely on his own. Amazing person. Very true, a father figure for me. He acknowledges, but won't encourage that dependency. He wants you to stand on your own two feet.

This is one of the things he says: 'Have you heard the greatest joke of all time? A man comes up to a woman and says,"Let's make love. Are you available for love? You should be available. Barry Long says so. So be my lover. Let's make love." Well Barry Long does not say that. That's a misquote by man. Women, never put up with that again. In future this is what you do, if it's the truth for you say this: "Are you joking? Make love? You must be talking about a different love to the love I know. You've got to love me, man. You've got to walk along beside me and show me that you love being with me. You've got to do that day after day. You've got to take me to the pictures and sit there and hold my hand if I allow you to, you've got to stay with me overnight and not even think of making love to me. Am I available? Be my lover? You can forget it. You're not capable of making love to me if you talk like that."

'No man who says that can ever really make love. A man who does that will not make love, he'll make trouble and you will weep. He will never get rid of your unhappiness for you. He will never be responsible enough in love to clear all your past lovers out of you, and your Dad and all your own wicked, wicked ways. How many times have you fallen for it, woman? I'm asking you. Is that the sort of love you want? It's the greatest joke of all times, isn't it, and he's always got away with it, and he's getting away with it in the name of Barry Long. But that is what comes of not hearing what I say. Man must face you. He must never get your body until he shows he has the capacity to love you. It seems to be the popular idea that you just go and make love and dip in anywhere to remove the blockage or something. Great idea, but you know whose idea it is, don't you? Man's idea. A silly master's idea or a silly therapist's idea. Is that what you want, woman? Do you think it will ever take the blockages out of you? My God, it won't. Only love takes the blockages out of you.

'The only thing that man wants from you, woman – and I wish you'd get rid of any other idea – is what's between your legs. I have to be very crude, but that is what he wants. If you want to prove that he doesn't – because he mightn't want that, might he? – you say: "Well then, love me, be with me, walk beside me, just take me out." Then you'll know if he loves you for all of those other reasons – your great intellect, your conversation. Or you'll find out that your presence fits his, you just flow into him as you walk along, he enjoys walking with you, enjoys sitting beside you, wants to get on the phone to talk, not about problems, just to say how good it is to be with you. If you hop into bed with him, you're finished. Love has got to be on your terms, woman. When you meet him, certainly you've got to be available for love, but what love? He's going to bluster at you, he's going to accuse you of being frightened, fearful, emotional, ridiculous, a denial of woman. You've got to be able to handle him. You've got to say: "Fair enough, see you later. Before you have me, you'll love me, and not in the way you think." It takes a lot of guts. You're going to have to lose a lot of men, you could be getting older and feel you haven't many chances and up he comes. You think, "He looks all right, seems all right. If I don't sleep with him, am I going to lose him?" Well, lose him. You're going to have to die for love sooner or later. Haven't you been dying for love long enough?'

I recognise myself in that: all a man wants is what's between a woman's legs. But you can transcend yourself, go beyond that by simply being aware of it. My endeavour is to hear the truth of what he says. Most of what he says does seem true, it seems right. Then to go and live it. Not as a set of rules, but as an awareness that really this seems right to me, and I don't want the old ways.

My experience is that women don't want the old ways. Younger women as well as the ones my age. This has got to come, otherwise we'll be in a dreadful mess. It's passed from generation to generation. My parents were nowhere. They were so repressed, so ignorant, so afraid of the whole area that they passed it on to me, and probably my brother, and the reaction had to come. The promiscuity, etc. But you have to go beyond that. When things settle down, you have to be responsible.

When he says 'There's no such thing as a free fuck', what he means is that what people don't know is that you can't dip in and out without paying a price. Somewhere in your psyche – okay, a man having sex with a woman transmits his psyche into her, his unhappiness, whatever it is. She absorbs it and it doesn't help her if he's not loving, or if it's just for excitement. She absorbs that and becomes more confused. Two people coming together just for a one-night stand, that's going to infect both of them if there's no love. Not going to liberate them. Infect them with unhappiness, emotionality. Lack of emotional satisfaction.

I lived these beliefs in my relationship. It meant working on it, learning. She was very clear what she wanted. She wanted love, not

414

sex. That was our agreed basis. If she felt I was too emotional, then she'd say so. I mean in the act itself she'd say that. Emotional in the sense of going away from her, leaving her. Getting into my own emotion. It's the distinction between feeling and emotion. Feeling being the pure feeling, emotion being anything from anger, sentiment, possessiveness, God knows what – sadness. That would be emotion I think. Possibly not. Emotion being something from the past in a way, feeling being directly of the present. Emotion is somehow the past creeping in, corrupting the present. People don't know the difference between feeling and emotion.

Sex is dangerous, not dirty. Human bodies are created out of it. You can create love from sex, so I gather, but it's also the chief area in which love can be made, generated. By good sex I don't mean technically good. I don't believe in sex aids, reading books about it, that's not important. If you love the person, things happen naturally. If you're both in touch with your own bodies, your own feelings, it will come naturally. Never had any problems technically speaking. It bores me, technique. I think it bores women.

I think sex has been devalued. I've done it myself in the past. The media devalues it. Sex crime – terrible. Then it's there in pin-ups and adverts. I would ban the sex phone lines. I have tried that. A couple of years ago I went through a period of almost compulsively ringing up the prostitutes who leave cards in phone boxes, just for excitement. Occasionally you get the person themselves, mostly you get some other person. It's pretty businesslike. The excitement was delving into the darker areas, which I'm quite fascinated by and drawn towards anyway. The thing in phone boxes lasted a few weeks. I was very curious. I wanted the excitement, the kick. Not a sexual excitement. I was trying to contact that shady world, the exciting underworld. But to get involved in that is playing with fire. Of course it's exciting, even I'd find it exciting. But you pay a hell of a price, a price you don't even know about. People are ignorant of this. You can't get it for nothing.

When you phone up these people, you get involved with their karma, with the psychic area that surrounds them, and God knows where you'd end up. People think they can get away with things, but inner things come up in your life. You do that for excitement, and then a week or two later you can't deal with certain things in your life. For some reason it's going to affect you, make you psychically disturbed or unhappy.

I was leaving this party and this woman came up into the street, a young black woman, and propositioned me. I've never been so astonished in my life. She was pretending to be a hooker – she wanted me to pay her. But she turns out to be someone known to the people

415

giving the party. The wife is a homeopath who's been treating the girl. My reaction was fear. I felt very disturbed. She had a very disturbing presence. I told her I wasn't interested, I was in a relationship. And I wasn't very attracted to her either. A few weeks later I met her coming out of another house up the road. And she propositioned me again. This time I thought I'd go back to her place and try and find out a bit. They'd told me she was a bit peculiar. So I went back to her place and she made a drink, sitting in the kitchen. Then she made a grab for me. I walked out, after talking with her for some time. She wanted money. I didn't like her. She was quite dead, out of touch with her own feelings. Unattractive to me as well. Sex is a very powerful energy. I don't think you can trifle with it as people do. Yes, it's fun, but there comes a point where you've got to realise that it's dynamite. Look how many things are sold through it. I've never bitten off more than I can chew. No crisis situations. But I'm the same as any other man – instant sexual attraction, oh yes. In this case if the girl had been attractive to me, it would have been more tempting. No question. Money would have been a factor too. But the strongest factor would be the threat of disease.

Sex bulks too large in the wrong ways. People are sex-obsessed in the Western world. There's no teaching that takes you beyond sex as excitement, as emotion, rather than feeling and love. The teaching I'm looking at is not just about a loving relationship as we normally see it. Yes, of course. But the depth of that. In ancient days it was seen as a vehicle towards spiritual awareness, higher consciousness. That runs counter to today's demands. The spiritual side is something I'm aspiring to. To me that means really getting into your body, not out of it, not some ethereal thing, getting right into your body. Being out of your body is fantasising. That will make it difficult to find a partner. No matter how attractive I might find somebody, if they're not on that same wavelength or open to it, it will be a waste of time. At present I'm not looking for anyone, I'm in a transition period.

What I see around me is absolute ignorance. I know I'm just the same as everyone else. That includes sex. People aren't aware of the possibilities that are there and of the sacred nature of sex. But maybe people have to go through this period. For me it would be a bit absurd in my mid-forties. It's not that I'm physically incapable, or that part of me wouldn't like to do it, but I don't think I could morally in a way – having absorbed what I feel is the truth, that prevents me from going to a prostitute. I was tempted the other day. An advert on a newsagent's window in Kilburn, advertising massage. I like massage. The ad said something like: 'qualified caring massage' with a little flower on it. I thought, there's more to it than that. I phoned her up

416

and I said, 'How long does this massage take?' 'Half an hour to three quarters of an hour.' Most good massages take an hour/hour and a half. 'And there's hand relief at the end.' 'Oh I see, yes, hand relief at the end.' She said she'd got the ITEC qualification – that's the basic one. I was tempted. But then I thought: No, I don't want that.

Men are lost. Women have to be their teachers.

***

ADAM COLE: In certain respects I have an unlikely attitude towards sex for a pornographer. I see sex as being spiritual, symbolic of unity and liberation. There are two times when people get a glimpse of the fact that they're not totally separate. That's when they fall in love, when the ego barriers fall for a while; and when they have an orgasm, when for a few brief moments they get a glimpse of the fact that they are unlimited, they're not restricted to the rather paltry body they find themselves inhabiting. It's such a powerful, such a motivating experience it's inevitable it's going to get harnessed commercially, and that people are going to want to buy it in many different forms, experience and interpret it in lots of different ways. It's such a powerful motivating force in all our lives. But I don't think very many people have any understanding of it, or think about it very deeply.

There's a school of thought – this is quite complicated – that says there shouldn't be any emotion involved in sex, that the cock and vagina should have their own consciousness and just do the thing, that they should be permitted to engage in sex. That's not to say there shouldn't be love between the two people when it happens. But what happens is, you tend to go into it with all the emotions of every wank you've ever had, every idea of conquest, of notches on the bed-head. Every fantasy you've ever had is then poured into it. I remember when I was young having sex with one woman and thinking of another. That's common with a lot of men. And the amount of emotional fantasy that goes along with it. We've all been conditioned into this desperate trying to get somewhere, to get a conquest, achieve something. We store up all these memories and fantasies in masturbating, orgasms, looking at porn and we take all that hard crystallised energy into what we call lovemaking when we do it. That's what it is for a lot of people.

Far removed from what it really should be, which is just a very simple consciousness, the uniting of two consciousnesses, positive and negative energy flowing together hopefully to create a bit more energy. What happens, there's loads of expectations, lots of fantasies

417

all coming together, probably resulting in less energy being created. A lot of sex is quite unsatisfactory for that reason, because of the amount of bad emotional energy that's associated with it. That energy then gets pumped into the woman on a higher level and they're in a sense a receptacle. In every way they receive. And they're conditioned by this. You find it with prostitutes, they're pumped full of this energy, day in day out, and they take on the mantle of that energy and become quite addicted to it on a power level. It's the ability to manipulate, control. Inevitably they hate men and find it difficult to love. Because they've taken on this male energy which is not love-orientated, is manipulative. As opposed to normal female energy – nurturing, mother earth, etc. The more male attitude women have now is part of all this. Women have been filled up literally and metaphorically with all this male energy. It's inevitable they'll take that on board. Feminists will say female energy must become more male, but what should happen is the ascendancy of female energy, rather than women changing into men, being go-getting and successful in male arenas. It should be the female qualities becoming more powerful.

***

SARA DALE and DAVID MISSEN

Sara Dale and David Missen are authors of Taste of Heaven, *self-described as 'a book about sexual opportunity, which heralds the advent of a new, limitless sexuality.'*

DAVID MISSEN: Sex is very much a spirit or energy function as well as a physical one. That's not to put down the physical side at all though. In the Sixties there was something missing, and it was a level of awareness. The thoughts and ideas were there, but the conscious-ness hadn't caught up with the thoughts. Now consciousness has begun to catch up. But not everybody has worked it out well. It's the hundredth monkey syndrome – a concept that comes from the observation of the eating habits of a breed of monkeys on an island in the Philippines. Whatever root it was they dug up, they had a hell of a time cleaning it before they could eat it. One day one monkey took a root down to the sea and washed it. A heretic. Nobody spoke to him. Eventually some others decided to try it, and what finally happened was that at a certain level,which might or might not have been the hundredth monkey, not only all the monkeys on the island changed their behaviour but all those on neighbouring islands changed their
418

behaviour. It's true they didn't have the media saying they were cranks. I can only talk for me, but I think we see increasing evidence all the time that this is happening.

SARA DALE: *Taste of Heaven* was an attempt to show people how throughout one's life one's conditioned into losing sight of one's sexuality. The do's and don'ts: 'Don't touch yourself, sex is not nice, parts of your body are not nice.' So we have layers and layers of conditioning, views of our external, not of our own inner self. Which we call closing down the doors. So we become ashamed not of our own sexuality but of our very faces. The way women wear makeup to hide behind, for example. The book is about how to become more aware of oneself, what one can do to turn around that situation through self-awareness. We go into relationships – individual, person-to-person – then all the different kind of experiences one can go through. When we first did the book we looked into things like group sex, S/M and so on. But now we've decided to slip that out and do it in another book. The times are different, and this is a book that we started writing in '79.

DAVID MISSEN: The original inspiration was AIDS. We didn't concur with the government's view of safe sex as being condoms. In fact we regard that as potentially unsafe sex. We feel condoms are not a wise thing to do. The failure rate is quite astronomical. Seventeen per cent fail. Anyway they weren't designed to stop diseases, they were designed to stop pregnancy.

When we looked around to see what there was on the subject of play, there was absolutely nothing. So the original idea was to produce a short manual on play as part of an AIDS educational programme. But in the course of doing that so many fascinating questions came up that it spread out into a book on what we really believed sex to be about and what its full potential was. There's still quite a large section on play, but it covers a lot more ground. One of the things we found ourselves doing – not an objective we've stated anywhere, but that we felt strongly about – was bringing sex back into the mainstream of life. De-ghettoising it.

We're very much into the view that we're born with an innate sense of our own physical beauty, our own sexuality, without understanding what it is at the time. So if you don't allow that to be obscured but allow it to be broadened out, that is a very different procedure from the mechanistic approach we have in schools at the moment. Our object is to get people back to knowing what they knew as small children.

419

SARA DALE: If you have a baby on a mat on the floor in the bathroom, they'll play with themselves. They'll play with their toes, their genitalia, their fingers, then go back to whatever part gives them the most pleasure. Sometimes my son would hold his cock when going to sleep, which I found very interesting. And he was not the one who sucked his thumb. The one who sucked his thumb was the eldest one, who was so tightly pinned there was no way he could get his hands down his nappy.

I still regard myself as a flower person, and I haven't changed very much since the Sixties. I've always regarded sexuality as tied in with spirituality. If I'm 'dis-eased' in my inner self, which could be called my spirit, then my sexuality is in some way altered; in the same way my perceptions alter when I'm at ease. It's flowing, free, gentle, loving, an expression of that inner self. That's something that has been lost by putting it on the market, making porn films that women don't wish to watch with men. We've created a split between men and women which has widened over the last seven or eight years particularly. Women are sold pretty things, men are sold hard, rough things like porn films.

There's a lot of hardcore porn available now, through newspapers, magazines. Some outrageous stuff. I was invited to make a massage video in Denmark, where I could then do the extended massage. That's using lips and mouth on all parts of the body. Hands are every bit as erotic as genitalia. Even doing massage on fingers and feet, the producers felt it was almost over the top. That was extraordinary to me. We didn't do genitalia at all; in fact I didn't do a massage on anybody's front. But there was the fear that it won't get through English censorship. So the first film was very soft, very gentle, enticing people who might not feel safe with massage to feel safe with it.

I've done two videos on how to massage your man, and how to massage your woman. With a lot of voice-over. It was interesting to discover that talking to men about massage and how to approach a woman is very different to talking to a woman about how to approach a man in massage. And very different from how women would think they would need to talk to men. Most women assume men are insensitive or raunchy in their sexuality, penile conscious. What I've discovered is how many men feel their bodies when they're getting a general massage, where the genitalia are a very small part of the whole. They'll say this is something they'd always missed but now they've had it, they know they've missed it. Men are as needy of touch as women, if not more so, because they don't get as much as women do. That's what the film was really about. We'd like to give people a chance to stimulate their imaginations. I don't want to tell them what to do, just

420

give them enough for them to use their imaginations and be creative in their expression of touch and sensuality.

Massage is to do with the inner core of the person rather than the genital construction. I'm not attracted by looks, physical disposition as much as I am by that inner core of self-recognition. Even if somebody's very shy or very outgoing. It's inner core, then intelligence, then last of all, the looks. I'm surprised when I look at them afterwards and realise they are pretty or good-looking. Or even size. I have to really think about whether the man has the recommended size or not. None of those things concern me because sexuality to me is soul talk. At its best it's communicating, it's dancing, it's play at a very deep level. You're exchanging fundamental things bit by bit. We open very slowly to one another.

Play is an unfortunate word as well. If I take David's hand and do one thing to him, I'm giving him a message. If I do another thing, it's a different message. Call it play if you like, but really what I'm doing is using a physical way of expressing what I can't put in words without becoming hard, cement-like. We can talk through our senses in a greater depth without misunderstandings than we can through speech. There are times when we get at cross-purposes verbally and there's no way he can understand that what I'm trying to put across is not in opposition to what he's getting at, but that it's different because it's coming from within my female self and he's sticking rigidly to his male self, defending a position. Or vice versa, of course. So the only way to get back to saying: 'Hey, we're one, and I want to tell you what I mean,' is by giving him a massage or a hug.

DAVID MISSEN: In the video we've just done with Virgin, there's a sequence where one of the couples are having a slight row, and this is overcome entirely by touch. That's a message we're very much into delivering by whatever means we can. We've found it very effective.

Dale gained some unwanted prominence when in 1990 her 'sensual massage' services, which involve bringing male clients to orgasm, were plastered across the News of the World. *What excited the press, and hence the public, was that her landlord – who promptly evicted her – was the Chancellor of the Exchequer, Norman Lamont. Re-settled in a new flat, she continues in her career.*

SARA DALE: I think it's a great shame it's covert, that you can't do it openly, that money – such enormous sums of money – can be made out of this. I charge the same fee whether I'm doing fantasy or

421

massage, the special massage. And I gather that I charge far less than anybody else in this field. About half as much.

When I was doing the ad for my massage I wanted to get across that I wasn't a call girl, somebody just making money for the purpose of getting rich. So I thought out the ad very carefully, took about a month over it. And I decided I wanted a surname, because I'd realised that all masseurs, therapeutic or otherwise, only used one name or Miss X, Y, Z. I decided neither were right, so I used Sara Dale. It starts with: 'Affectionate, caring, educated Sara Dale offers massage for discerning clients'. I knew I'd get some people I wouldn't want to see, and if I was asked, 'What size are your tits?' I'd ask: 'Which ad do you think you've answered?' They'd put the phone down, which was fine.

What I didn't realise at the time was that 'educated' is a synonym for submission/domination. But 'affectionate' appeals to the elderly, and 'caring' is the person who isn't sure what they're looking for, who doesn't just want a good wank, but wants something more. They're not getting something at home, but don't want to let their wives down. I give them a combination of massage and talk. The very way I touch gets into that soul self and I can tell things about them. When I'm massaging different parts of the body, the way they respond gives me a clue to where their closing-up started, where their first problem arose. Different parts of the body seem to indicate different areas of their life. For example, people who haven't had enough affection and attention when they were little, I pick it up in the head and shoulders. When you touch the arms in a particular way, it seems to echo where they didn't get that touch as a baby. A lot of mothers don't hold their babies and caress them while feeding them. Which is what the baby needs. So when they grow up there's something missing. The centre of the back is to do with sexuality.

I spend two thirds of the time on people's back, because that's where they're less vulnerable, and when I turn them over on their fronts, at least half of the time is spent on their faces, or above the waist. So only one third is on legs and genitals, and half of that time is on the legs. So only five or ten minutes is on the genitals. Even that is divided into stylised, then particular.

I have a stroke which I call knee to nipple, which goes from the knees across the genitals and up to the nipples. I do it with opposing hands. The genitals are included but they're part of the whole body. When I'm doing the face and arms I do touch the genitals, to let the genitals know they're part of this whole as well, but I don't do more than just touch it, it's not a winding up. What's interesting is that when people are having their back massaged, when I turn them over they've
422

already got an erection. So the feeling of being accepted in all the different areas they've been hiding, keeping from their partners, to have somebody who totally accepts them is – and I use the term in its broadest sense – safety. A man has to feel fairly safe to have an erection on his back.

My customers are passive. They may put their hand on my body, but most know not to put a hand between my legs. I explain that this is about them, not about pleasing me. If they try to please me they break the flow of energy. I explain this before we start the massage.

DAVID MISSEN: You can't massage and be stimulated by the person you're massaging simultaneously. It's just not possible.

SARA DALE: Initially, in the very beginning, I have the power, but during that first ten minutes that power becomes shared. If the power stays with me, it's a lousy massage, because they're not giving me anything, I can't feed on anything to give back. It's literally a figure of eight. The more I pick up from them, the better the massage is. The more they get from me, the more they feed me. So it can be mind-blowingly exquisite, and I will have an orgasm at the same time they do. Sometimes they say: 'I can't see how you get anything out of this.' I say: 'Just put your hand on the centre of my back.' And they can feel the heat, the energy. The lower-back area. And when they have an orgasm, my shoulders are going and the back of my neck burns. The energy just flows out and my nose blocks up.

I avoid wearing titillating clothing. I wear nothing at all. That's not titillating. If anything it's almost a shock, makes them shy. There are a few whom it will turn on, but usually they're very young. Invariably the men ejaculate. It's not necessary, but it happens because they don't know the difference between orgasm and ejaculation. The orgasm is the thing. They can take place from the time of the head massage, while they're on their stomachs still.

By the time somebody's been to me four or five times, we've established a rapport, a warmth and a safety. They feel safe enough to talk about things they're unable to experience, that they feel a loss of, and we may go through that. I had one man who'd been married many years, loved his wife dearly. They sleep in separate beds. Sex is pre-planned, which is very difficult for him. He was finding it more and more difficult to get an erection. As the time was coming up he became unwell or various things happened. And he felt this would endanger the relationship. One of the things he missed greatly was never having a bath with his wife. He knew she would never do that with him but he had a terrific desire to do that, which was getting in the way. So one day he phoned up and I got a bubble bath ready and he went into the bath, with me sitting behind him, massaging his head

423

and shoulders. Then I climbed in with him and massaged his feet from the opposite end. That was such a relief for him. Now he can fantasise that when he's with his wife, she's in the bath with him. But he doesn't have to pressure her into actually doing it.

I don't like to say there's a dysfunction between couples. It's just that we've become entrenched in a maleness, a femaleness. It's interesting that when both are earning, the woman doesn't pay in an equal share to the running of the house. They keep their money for spending on themselves or their children, or holidays, not on improving the home situation. And in a divorce, the division is of the man's money. Her money is regarded as a gift. That affects attitudes. Not many women take men out for dinner, and pay the bill. Traditionally if a woman went to a disco and a man asked for a dance, that's all he was asking you for. It might lead to other things, but that was up to the pair of you. Young girls seem to assume now that if they're asked to dance, they must expect to be bedded. She'll say: 'What do you want?' – very aggressive often. Women tend to go in pairs to discos and they refuse to split up. The guys go singly, so they've got a problem. So both leave unsatisfied because they're not getting dates.

There's also a great loss nowadays between women. I have men bringing their wives on occasions for massage. I have hardly any women clients, because of the fear that as I'm a sensual masseuse I'll do a lesbian type of massage. This attitude is a shame. I say I'm a channel of energy and it's incidental I have female genitalia. I'm just a channel, not a person. Women can experience the massage without having to worry about me. That's why I encourage them to shut their eyes.

My hands feel different to a man's. They're fairly small, very, very soft when doing massage, but they can also feel very large and very firm by alternation. I'm able to repeat the same stroke very differently, so they experience both the female and the male touch. It's quite an eye-opener for them. They're then more able to talk to their husbands about what's missing, why they couldn't get across what they wanted. I like to have the man present. I explain to them it's not a massage for them to get off on, although it's possible if they get into that state of mind. They need to change their mind-set and look at it from an educational point of view, understanding what their wives are feeling, by watching my hands and her responses.

When they first come to me, the men don't realise they have the same depth of sensitivity that I have. Eventually they discover it. They come because they see my ad, feel it's different, more genuine than the others – including my surname is an indicator. Also I gather I have

424

a seductive voice and people find it relaxing, it makes them feel very comfortable, and they get turned on by that. Initially they come because they think it will be a turn-on. When they're here they say it's very different from what they expected. It's everything they ever imagined in their wildest dreams, yet it's very safe. Safety keeps coming up with them. They go away feeling more in love with their wives. I'm not judgmental and they feel they can ask me anything.

Someone will say they want to experience a particular fantasy. I won't talk about it on the phone, nor will I allow them to come in and investigate me. If they want to come and see if I'll do the fantasy I say, 'Don't bother to come. Either you're coming and going to do it, or you're not going to do it.' We may then decide the massage is better for the first one, then the fantasy another time. Fantasies should only be done when you feel safe with an individual. If someone is really paranoid, very closed, they need a massage first so they can build that trust. Then the second time they can either have another massage or the fantasy.

The one thing I don't do is intercourse. They're allowed to touch me, once I know them. Sometimes single men are scared of dating because they simply don't know how the parts fit together. So I'm happy to educate them on that. They don't know how to touch a woman, so they can touch me and I can see if they're getting the touch right. I'm not 'on the game', because all the time I'm monitoring their behaviour, their reactions, interactions and responses. If they're reactive, coming from a conditioned state of mind, then my knowledge of how they'd better serve themselves comes into play. I may stop at that point and say let me show you where you've gone wrong. I'll go through what they've done and show why it's not working.

There are all kinds of fantasies. One man wanted to have a bath and be caught in the bath. He was at a woman's house, she was a cleaner and he'd used the bathroom and all her perfumes were there. And she came in, having been out at a nightclub but come home early, and caught him there, and then did a striptease and bathed him. That was the fantasy. With this sort of fantasy I usually go in and out of character. I only go right through to the end without interruption with somebody who's already okay but just needs to get out of their heads because, perhaps, their jobs get them so into their minds that they don't have a way of getting back into their feelings. Whereas in S/M fantasy – which is often hilarious – I become that person.

With one guy, in his fantasy he had assaulted a young woman and been sent to a remand centre. The prison warder was a woman, i.e. myself, and I was to be very angered by his behaviour. In reality he

425

was a shy, whimpering sort of man, and only when he was approaching women in a fantasy, by attacking them was he then a powerful man. So I should be so angry with him I'd throw him around. He must have weighed 250lbs, six foot two, and I'm five foot four. And trying to throw someone around in high heeled boots. So I had to stand on something. The bed has a dais about six inches higher, so I could stand there. So I had to take him in both hands and throw him to the ground. That created his fantasy. I just burst out laughing. I said, 'Don't you dare laugh, I'm the only one that's allowed.' But he laughed, so then I could spank him. I held him down and said, 'If you move I'll pin you down with my shoes.' Then he started whimpering: 'Don't do that.' That made us both laugh. So I said, 'I'm bored with this fantasy. I want to do something that I want to do.' He's not used to being treated nicely by women. I said, 'I like you too much and I want to caress you, stroke you and I'll show you how much I like you. And if you don't like it, tough shit.' I changed the fantasy round to a different one and gave him the affection that he had no way of getting.

Fantasy is something that I do where somebody wishes to express something they can't talk about and by going through a formalised play – S/M for instance is so beautiful, and formal in itself in the stylised clothing, so you're no longer who you are, you are a fantasy – you can respond. Where someone fails in their responses, I am the controller and can redirect or pinpoint where the problem is. We can talk afterwards about how they didn't get what they wanted. So when we go through a fantasy another time they have a bit more skill and can control me a little bit better. Then I try a little harder and they still can't control me, and eventually it comes to a point when they don't even need to do the play, because they can talk it through and they can then be the powerful person without giving that power to the woman. They can share power, then they don't need me any more.

Mostly I care deeply for the men who come here. One of the things I've learnt to deal with is that I genuinely love some of them, deeply. There's some who, if they weren't my clients, if I met them in the street I would love to have a relationship with. Because they're coming to see me, that little veil of separateness has to remain there. So when they suggest a relationship that's when I fall apart, if you like, and explain it would be inappropriate. My real name is Georgette and the more they see of me the more Georgette and Sara become one. Then sometimes I might say: 'At this moment in time I'm talking as Georgette because I like the real you and I want to talk to you from the real me, not the professional me.' So I talk to them person to person as Georgette.

I then tell them I have an open relationship with David, that it could
426

have been possible to have a relationship with them, and it's something I'd have liked. But because of Sara it would dilute in the public's mind or in their mind later if I were to have a relationship with them. That would make things difficult for Georgette. If they were seen in public with me for example, the public would see them going out with Sara Dale. So what I hope Sara Dale's relationship with them will do is to make it possible to find who they want in somebody else, and even if that person is not totally what they want, open or whatever, through treating them well and giving them the safety they've got from our sessions together, they can create in their partner the ideal woman. After all that's all we're looking for in each other, somebody we can be our full selves with, safely.

ENVOI

'Sex is. There is nothing more to be done about it. Sex builds no roads, writes no novels and sex certainly gives no meaning to anything in life but itself.'
Thus Gore Vidal, writing at the dawn of the chronological Sixties, before, indeed the mythological Sixties, that period between Kennedy's assassination and Nixon's expiation, had even begun. Thirty odd years on and only the date has changed; strip away the long accretion of ideology, of no matter what type, and the sentiment seems infinitely valid. 'Do what I say,' intones the parent, 'don't do what I do.' Sex has been the subject of an endless outpouring of 'what I say' for the past thirty years. No sooner had it emerged from its relatively restricted closet than each and every man and woman lined up to pontificate. In fairness things have changed, though to what extent quantity – that democratisation that typified the original sexual 'revolution' of the Sixties – has moved on to quality – a deeper, philosophical change (with or without ideological purity and political correctness) – remains debatable, even dubious. The Sun and its gorgeous pouting Page 3 girl remains the mass-market newspaper of choice, and the 'top shelf' remains the favoured display down at Mr Patel's; sexual peccadilloes still excite the voters far more than political acumen in our elections, and tedious couplings of even the most marginal 'celebrity' seem guaranteed to thrill the punters. This, however, is not a sermon; no moral diatribe is intended. We make our choices, we live with them. 'Is sex dirty?' asked the unfortunate Woody Allen in happier days. And responded, 'Yes, if it's done right.' For

all the ideologies, for all the sexual revolutionaries, the zealots of secular and spiritual religions, the libertarians and the censors, the New Men and post-feminist women, the whole wondrous pullulating parade, we have to ask once more: has anything really changed? Sex is.

ELINOR STARR

'Get Real'

The flat is above a smart shopping street in the West End. Three floors down and respectable women sip their cappuccino and nibble on Danish pastries. Up here she takes her four p.m. breakfast: smoked salmon and scrambled eggs, a roll-up sprinkled with flakes of crack. The flat is not hers, but it's a long way from the Harrow Road where she was born twenty-eight years ago. In the corner a gentleman caller sprawls, languid, sated.

I am as you see. This is me. What do I do? Nothing. I'm a lady of leisure. My job description: I'm an independent entertainer. Anything from cooking to sex to music to joints. Whatever takes my fancy.

I've never had a job in my life. I went to school in Paddington, I loved it, it was an all-girls' school and I had a great time. I never bunked off, though I was always late. I was bright but I was lazy. So I left, went to Brixton College, did a course. I thought I'd go and work with kids, but the work experience soon changed my mind. Then I did a secretarial course. I was going to Sight and Sound College and I was getting work experience at Thomson Holidays. Just a dogsbody really. And it was that which led me to this life. I thought it would be a good idea – with a bit of encouragement from a boyfriend – to supplement my income by working in a hostess club. So I'm going to Thomson Holidays during the day and a hostess club in Burlington Arcade in the evening. I kept going with energy tablets; I didn't know about cocaine then, otherwise I'd have been sniffing and it would have all been fine. So that's what I'm doing. And after a while one of them had to go – and it's obvious which one got the push.

The hostess club life is just a big game really. Because men are quite pathetic. They just want to entertained. though looking back it was quite a laugh. This was very upmarket, you're talking about £250 a throw. Plus you have to buy drinks in the club before you can leave, yeah? The best bit, the bit I used to enjoy was that there's the Cavendish Hotel round the corner. It's three o'clock in the morning

428

when the club's finished and there's no way, unless you're a resident, that you can get into the hotel. A guest can book you in, but he has to pay a fee. So what we used to do, four girls, five girls at a time, we'd turn up, give the porter a tenner each and we'd go up to the rooms. Nine times out of ten the guy's had too much to drink, can't get it together, etc. etc. You still got your money. Two hundred and fifty quid. How the club made their money was through the drinks. You'd get guys who'd come and spend £300 on drinks, but when it comes round to us, they've got £50. And you ain't going to go for that – so you blag for your hostess fee.

In my experience most females I've met, most females that have been hooking, it's not through necessity. Most of the girls I know as friends, we weren't born from anything more deprived than anybody else, we weren't fucking living in no shoeboxes or whatever. It wasn't through needing to, we weren't any worse off than anybody else.

Most women within the sex industry, if they're being really honest, get into hooking directly or indirectly through a man. Whether they say it was for the kids or whatsoever or whatsoever, directly or indirectly it's basically emotional manipulation. After all if they didn't get fucked by a man they wouldn't have the kids. 'Darling, you know we're under pressure and we need this and we need that and you know there is a way ...' and before you know it you're hooking, you're living the life. And he's living the life a little better than you. And that's what happened to me. Of course. But you need your apprenticeship, whether it's in hooking or whatsoever, you need an apprenticeship so you can come out the other side and say, 'Yeah, I know this.'

What people say about pimps and so on is a total fantasy and fallacy. America's a different ball game, a different story law-wise and all the rest of it. Here, in England, from my personal experience, the ponces or pimps are usually husbands and boyfriends. So there's no situation where you have to work and give over a certain amount. It doesn't work that way. It's a lot more subtle. It's more the emotional blackmail, that's what the pimping is, all this, 'Oh babes, we've got problems, why don't you ...' All done in a very subtle, emotional way. Look it it from another way: you're out of a job, your wife is working, course she's gonna help you. There's a difference because we're hooking? Or because we have the potential to give you five grand as opposed to five pounds? It's all relative. It's all the same sort of thing. So it's a fantasy and fallacy, this idea of the poor girls and the evil pimps.

Working as a hooker is a progression. You go through all the different stages – escorts, hostessing, the windows, whatever – and at the end of the day you find out what's for you. What suits you best.

I've worked for escort agencies, I've worked in flats – you advertise and clients come to see you – I've had stickers in phone booths, adverts in magazines. I worked in a sauna once. That was a private members' club and, how can I describe it – oh my Lord, everybody there was kinky. It was just a total fucking trip. It wasn't a typical sauna – come in and have a wank – there was no sex, everybody was fucking perverse, everybody. It was great. You worked three days a week and you turned over about a grand for those three days.

I worked from windows in Germany. For me it was my apprenticeship, because I believe that if you can make money there, then you can make money anywhere. It was in Bremerhaven, on the coast. It just happened: I heard about it through a friend of a friend and I thought, 'Wow, let's give it a go.' And I tell you, I've never worked so hard in all my fucking life. The majority of girls I met were English, because that's their way of not doing it on their own doorstep. So I got there and met some girls and one of them says, 'Why don't you come in the window.' I said, 'What, me!' But by the end of the day I was in the window, because it was fucking easy – it was a trip, it was an experience. I met characters there – fucking hell, they were just unbelievable. Most of them were in the US army. One character, he was an older guy, he'd served in Vietnam, and he was totally off the wall. It was just great. I did it for about a month. I've got to be honest, I hate Krauts, I swallow my words with one particular girlfriend who's a diamond, but the Germans are the hardest working people I've ever met in my life, apart from blacks. I'll never forget one girl who would be outside from eight in the morning until eight at night; they fucking graft, they really do. And when I was there so did I.

Believe me, it's much safer, sitting in your window, than working in London. They had the system. There's a club, and rooms off the club, and they have these windows. And those rooms are safer than anywhere I have ever been because if ever you have a problem there are bells everywhere – at the foot of the bed, by your elbow, by your tit. And if you ring any of those bells every human being in the club is there, in that room, in a second. Here, in England, there is no safety. Two girls are not allowed to work together – the law says that's a brothel – and that makes you vulnerable.

One day, I don't know why, I tried to explain to my mother what I do. Of course she knows what I do, but it's never discussed, it's never open. So one day she found this travel card of mine which had my alias on it. She said, 'What is that?' I said, 'Oh Mum, put it this way – if ever one day you open the *News of the World* you wouldn't want to read my full name there.' Her attitude was, 'Well, you haven't stolen from anybody, you haven't killed anybody, so fine, cool.' I tried to
430

reiterate that it isn't all about lying on your back and I tried to explain that, 'Mum, you have to understand that a lot of people like to get beaten ...' My mother could no more understand that concept than her walking on the moon. What am I talking about, what is this? It's a shock. So I stopped. And the point is that where sex is concerned, as liberal and advanced as we'd all like to think or believe we are, hey, come on ... we haven't come too far from Stone Age days, darling.

Hooking is addictive. Once you've been paid for sex it is very, very difficult to give it up and not get paid. Maybe I'm a hardened fucking whore, but sometimes you almost begrudge giving it up to your man, if he's not delivering you the goods. I don't mean money, I mean sexual satisfaction to the full. You almost begrudge that, because I think, 'Fuck this! I could be getting some money! And come!' But, a lot of working girls would say it's different, in that it isn't about coming for them. The best sexual experiences I've had, I've got money, I've had the best orgasms of my life, so I'm thinking hang on, why should I give it to you for free – and I ain't gonna *come*.

So for me personally it's not the money, no. For me personally it's the power. The men believe that their money is the power. Yes, the money does turn me on because it means that I can live a certain way, but the bit that I actually enjoy is watching – it's like a game of chess – manipulating people, manipulating the men, seeing how weak they really are. To see how weak they are and how weak they become. Because if you know a man's sex, and you know a man's brain – you've got him. And that's how it really, really is and that's the buzz that I get. Women are socialised; this is your role, this is your position – and it's all underneath. Underneath where? It suits us to make it appear that we're underneath; it suits us to lay back and get fucked. That way you're kind of looking at your watch. But why should we as women be labelled as tough, tough feminists because that's our view? A lot of ordinary women feel that but they won't admit it, they don't want to be labelled as dykes, as feminists, whatever. Women are women! We've all got clits and we can all come if you've got any sense. Sorry, but that's it.

Men use their buying power. Women may not be in a position to buy, but we can sell. And buying and selling go hand in hand. And if you think you can buy me, then I'll sell you back three times. And make a fucking profit. Men feel that if they're paying for it they can do what they want. They delude themselves. Men think that they're buying a hooker but they're not; she's just hiring out a bit of her time. Just hiring that pussy. And at the end of the day you get as much or as little as she's prepared to give.

431

***

What I provide is fantasies. General fantasies. I wouldn't entertain you if I didn't know you. You'd have to come highly recommended, and if I liked you then, well, we'd talk about it. But you could be offering me fifty grand and if for any reason I thought you were a prick or I didn't like the vibes I'd say, 'Thank you, but no thank you.' Purely because I'm my own person. I have to get something from it. Whether it's mental, physical, whatsoever. I choose. In a way I always have chosen, in the respect that I go purely by my vibes and the instincts I've found in life. When I haven't, then things go drastically wrong. So you could be Mr ICI and you could have fifty grand but if for any reason I didn't like you I'd say, 'Thank you darling, but no thank you.' But then they just become more persistent, because they can't believe that you – a prostitute! – are refusing them. Because most men think they can buy anything. Particularly when they're very, very powerful and influential. So in that way you show them that *they* are the true prostitutes and not you.

I won't sell my soul. You cannot buy my soul. Jackie Onassis, people like that: *that* is a lifetime of prostitution. Do you know how corroding it is to sell your soul? That is a twenty-four-hour tart. You cannot clock off. We get our money. When our time's up we go. Our life is ours. No money in the world can buy that. No man is worth that much. Okay, you're a client. You're paying her and she's supposed to be doing what you want her to do. You find out that this hooker's intelligent. Then you find out she likes sex. And a hooker is not supposed to be either of those things. All she's supposed to do is perform for the client. But this hooker happens to enjoy being with you. And none of these things are supposed to happen. So I see the effect my being like that has on men and that's what I use. My three tools. Whereas the priority is supposed to be the money, you're supposed to go with big businessmen because they'll pay a grand as opposed to five hundred, I'm supposed to put my foot through my arse because he's offering an extra five hundred.

But I don't play that game. I play my game. And most men – it freaks them out. Now if I didn't like dick as much, perhaps I could play it the other way, but I like dick, I like men – their strengths their weaknesses, their bodies, their heads, their little fucked-up warped-nesses. I don't respect most of them – they don't respect themselves – but I like them. They're prostitutes. Most men are fucking prostitutes – they sell themselves day in and day out every day of the week, but we get the name for it. The art of prostitution goes on over a million office tables every day of the week. Nothing wrong with it,
432

but they can't admit it. But because we do sex, we're the prostitutes. Or they give you, 'What's a nice girl like you ...' 'I'm looking after you, darling. I'm sucking your cock so good. That's what I'm doing.' So don't spin me that shit!

So it's not even a matter of discussing the fee and what they want and saying whether I'll go for it. Before it even gets to that stage I want to know what kind of a person you are, where you're at; so before we get down to fees or whatever, it's a case of who you are and what you are. As opposed to what you want. Then when you say what you want, I'll decide what you're going to have. So now I have a handful of friends I have known for a very long time, and I do consider them as friends, even though we have a business relationship, they're still friends because I like them, I respect them, for whatever reasons. So when someone new comes along, it's purely a case of whether I like you and whether I choose to entertain you. And most men, I have to be perfectly honest, particularly people of power and influence, they are totally, totally phased, they cannot believe that you, who they are paying, are refusing them. Particularly when it's a lot of money.

There's no fixed fee. I like to play a game where sometimes I do a situation where I don't ask for anything. It's like a restaurant where you go and the menu has no prices on it. With a few specialities for select people. The most expensive things, they don't have prices on them in the windows. Shopping in the South of France, you don't see any prices in Cannes, you get the bill at the end of it. There's times when you think, 'Fuck it, you robbed me!' and there's times when you get a very pleasant surprise, and I've got to be honest, eight times out of ten I get a very pleasant surprise, because I'm myself, I'm genuine, I can't be doing with frauds, the world's full of them, and powerful, influential people, they know that. They're surrounded by it. They go home and they've got frauds, all their friends are frauds ... get real, come on. So what I give is honesty, that's what I do.

Men have better sex with me not because they get turned on by paying, but because with me they're getting what they really want. They're able to say what they really want. There are two types of punter. Some are using the money to buy a power trip. They actually begrudge paying the money, which is why I like taking it because that gives me the power. You need to pay, darling, because if you don't pay me in cold hard cash, than you're going to pay a dearer price, which is in blood and emotion. I'd rather pay in cash, because you can only pay what you have in your pocket. If it isn't there you can't pay it. Emotion is unlimited.

***

The majority of people I see are rich and powerful. I don't see what you might call the average punter, the guys who go to the girls in Soho. What they want is release. I'm more ... elaborate.

Usually people ask for what they think they want, then you play around a little bit and you find out what they actually want. People are scared to ask what they really want, people are scared to be judged. So I play it on my terms to find out who you are, what you are and then we find out what you're going to be fulfilled with most. Somebody might start off by asking for something really straight-forward, but after a while you find out, well, hey, they're into something wayout and kinky that they'd never usually even suggest.

The way you find out about your sexuality is purely trial and error. You press a button and you find out what happens and you either like it or you don't like it. And I guide people. Some things I won't do. I won't be humiliated, you can never humiliate me. There are so many people who want you to be submissive and humiliated and I will never do that. No. Or racist things. People come along, want a whole racist master-slavegirl thing and I just reverse it. That's my buzz. Just reverse it on them, because most people who want somebody to be sub-missive to them, deep down they want to be the submissive one. Equally most people who want to be tied up and abused, they want to be the person who's doing it. But they won't come out and straight off ask for that, because most people are liars. What they get with me is I'm just myself – and most people seem to find that difficult to deal with. I'm different to a lot of professional ladies. I'm straight-up, too straight-up. I say what I think. Take it or leave it.

Other girls think I'm crazy. Their attitude is you pay the cash and you get whatever you want. And if you want a little extra, well fine, but that's extra money. They'll play the game, but I won't play the game because I 've written the rules of the game. If I want to play the game one day, then yes, I'll play, but not every day. No way. Come on. The game's out there. Life is the game, one big game and it's too short. You can't play a game on me, my buzz is that I'll play the game on you, and you'll be so shocked and freaked out that you'll come back, to make sure, to reassure yourself – hang on here, did this actually happen? Okay, they come back to ejaculate again, but that's secondary. It is. The way I play it, the way I do it is to stimulate the brain, whereas most professionals I know stimulate the cock. That's the last thing I'll touch. They can do that themselves. But if you get to the brain, if you know somebody's sex, then you've got the person.

***

At the end of the day most people are afraid of their sex, whatever it is. They're scared to experience, they're scared to experiment, they're scared to let go. But what're you hanging on to it for? To die?

This problem with sex is particularly European. If I look at the sexual things that I have seen or experienced, the things that people want. In my experience, for instance, I have never encountered a non-white person who has wanted anything remotely sado-masochistic. I've never come across a black person who wants to be beaten, whipped. Never. As far as being pure physical beings goes, we haven't come very far from the days of cavemen. So the more sophisticated we are, or anyway we *believe* we are, the more sophisticated life we lead, we're looking for spin-off and diversion and we think it's hip to be into S/M or rubber or leather or whatsoever. But let's stop fooling ourselves, in the end we are just human beings. People really do not change. For myself I always used this expression, describing people as being 'plugged'. Which I see as a very British, white European thing. Plugged being a dildo shoved up their arse. And I refuse to be plugged! That means you have to sit there, grit your teeth and take it. And not flinch. I refuse. If I'm getting fucked I'm going to bawl and the world's going to know about it, if I'm enjoying it or not enjoying it, and white Europeans are not about that. Their thing is endurance – take the fuck and let it be seen that you're not getting off. What for? Isn't sex to be enjoyed? If you're getting fucked and it's good, bawl and scream, shout, let's hear about it. And the innate difference you get with more sophisticated societies and cultures is that they get more diverse, but they forget the basics. But why? Just get your jollies off, lay back and have a good fucking time. I like to experiment, don't we all, but I refuse to be fucking plugged. Keep my mouth shut, lay back and think of Britain. Do me a favour!

Sometimes, when you're doing a fantasy for someone it is very difficult not to laugh, but if you are a good professional, then you are a very good actress and that's basically it. Sometimes, depending on whom I'm working with, say a girlfriend, it's easy. I have one particular girlfriend who's a dominatrix and with her I don't need to ask in advance what the deal is, what the guy's into, whatever. She may give me a quick briefing, but basically, when we're in there, we have such a spontaneity between us that it just flows. And sometimes, because of the way we both know how the other's thinking, it is very difficult not to laugh. And if you have somebody blindfolded or whatever, you really have to keep a hold of yourself. But if you're a good actress, you do your thing – and then you crack up afterwards. But you gotta laugh, darling, because otherwise you die.

435

Most people don't know what they want until they've had it. All men have fantasies, about their egos, the whole trip. But in reality they don't know what they want, which is why they spend so much time going from one woman to another woman in the search for some ultimate. What ultimate?

At the end of the day human beings are like this: they'll try one wine, they like it, then they'll try another. It's the same with sex, people are always trying different things. But I personally believe that at the end of the day a real true human being always reverts back to the basics. And if their basic buzz is getting tied up, then that's what they go back to. And it's up to them – if they like it, good on them. It's a sweetie shop. And how you treat the sweetie shop is an individual thing. Some people have addictive personalities, some people don't. Some people are addicted to certain types of sex and they try to kid themselves, just like with drugs: I don't need it, no, no, no, I can do without it, but really in the back of their mind that's all they're thinking about. And that's why some people will go from this thing to the other, or they want to see a different girl all the time – but it's just their own insecurities. Get real! That's all it is. They're trying to find themselves. In the end most people don't know themselves, and for whatever reason most people don't went to know themselves either.

How do you get people to experience and understand what they really want? You have to tease it out. A guy comes to see you. They're not expecting you to be yourself. They're expecting you to play games. If you turn up and you find a real person who is not playing a game but she's being herself, then they're going to be themselves. A lot of people don't come straight out with what they want because they can't actually believe it of themselves. It's only when they've tasted it enough and realise that is what they want, then they can accept it. A lot of people come to you on one premise – straight sex – and it ends up in a very different scene. They allow themselves to be what they really are. Everybody's frightened of allowing themselves to be themselves, so the question is: do you dare? Who dares to be seen as 'abnormal'? Marriage and the family caters for some things, but it doesn't cater for that side of you. The freak side, the subconscious side, all of it. Everything has compartments and you have to put it all in perspective.

I'm not shocked but I'm surprised sometimes. Surprised in the respect that I'm convinced that every human being is slightly bent – sexually, mentally, whatever. Kinky to me is exciting, try something different; perverse is totally off the wall; sick to me is just an extremity

436

of perverse. All of which bears in mind that everyone has their own values of what that is. Somebody said to me the other day, 'What's the most wayout thing anybody's ever asked you to do?' Putting needles through their cock. Needles. Sewing needles, £10 per needle, all the way through. All the way through and out the other end, through his testicles. And nailing his dick to a table – is that normal, or is it perverse? I did it, though my insides were uurrgghh!!! I was like cringing. All the way through his cock, through the meat. There's no blood, because you heat the needle; you heat the needle and you put it through. He pretended to scream. Just pretended. I could see every filling in his mouth, but it wasn't pain. His dick is perforated, it's a teabag. He just wanted to shock me. And he left with the needles in his dick. I'm talking about maybe twenty needles, I don't know, as many needles as was there. It's a regular thing he does. I personally think that his buzz was to see your reaction, to freak you out. And he did. That's the trip for a lot of people who do that sort of thing. To see your reaction. He used to be a policeman. A sergeant, I think.

People who never suffer anywhere else want to suffer with me. Ninety per cent of the people who want to be slaves – I can imagine what they're like at home with their wives. They must be fucking little bastards, right little cunts. And deep down they fucking know it. At the end of the day they don't respect themselves. So they want to reverse the situation. So reverse it, sure, and pay for it too.

In the end, if you feel horny you feel horny, don't matter if it's man, woman, cat, dog or beast, if that's what you feel like doing, do it. Providing you're not offending anyone, you're in private. If it's your thing, do it. Who cares if you want to get tied up, blindfolded, whipped, suspended, stretched, cooked – I don't care. So long as that releases how you feel. Who cares what you are, gender, bender, race, who really gives a fuck? As long as you're being yourself.

There's no written clause to say: these are the boundaries. Provided for the two people it suits them, then go for it! For me, the weirdest sexual thing I ever had to do was putting in these needles, nailing the guy's balls to the table. A friend of mine had something totally different. I found it rather amusing, though she found it weird. The man comes along, he's the slut. Which I found amusing because I like that role reversal. So he put on his dress, his stockings and that. And he had nine different dildos. And he got her to fuck him with them. Different shapes, different sizes. Carried them in his rucksack. What I liked was that he worked in the City, came along to this girl, and brought all his own tackle. He looks after them, he washes them, he cleans them. Now for one person that's going to be easier to deal with than putting needles through someone's cock and balls. I find the needles weirder, though to some people this guy with the dildos, that would be outside their realm, and to them he would be a total freak and a pervert.

Of course there is simple uncomplicated sex; sure, provided people are being honest with themselves, but a lot of people aren't. Not just with sex but with themselves as people. Provided people are honest with themselves and are free enough to lay back and enjoy it and just be yourself and express yourself in any way you like. Whatever your thing is, do it – provided the other person is into the same thing. But if what turns you on isn't the other person's thing it's an abuse, because then you're taking a liberty, an advantage.

But it is fantasy. A lot of people say they think prostitution's a good thing because it stops people from raping. That's total bullshit, total crap. Because someone comes to you and they want you to behave like a schoolgirl, or call them 'Daddy', in my personal experience they are the last person in the world who will actually go out and molest a child. Somebody who wants a rape scene – they are the last person in the world who will go out and rape somebody. Purely because it is a fantasy. Somebody who'll go out and rape, or molest a child, they don't want the fantasy, they want the reality. And what they want has nothing at all to do with sex. It's the same with gay men. People attack them and say they'll abuse kids and so on: bullshit, total crap. They want other gay men, not children. They're the last people who'll do that. The people who do go out and abuse little boys are the closet faggots, the ones who spend their time putting faggots down, the right wing, acting as the most moral people around.

***

I do believe that all men go to whores. I really do believe it. One way or another. Whether they pay me or they get married – one way or the other you pay, you pay, babes. Blood, spunk, cash – you pay. That is how it is. Men are givers and we receive. We take. We extrapolate. It is our given right.

If you don't realise that everyone uses hookers, everyone uses escort girls, then you have been deluded, you have been smokescreened. If one of your friends goes to see a hooker, pays for sex, he's not going to tell you. Get real! For most men that's taking ten inches off of their two-inch dick! Don't you understand? It's as simple as that! For most men that's what it's about. If they tell their friends they pay for it! Come on. The conception is that people who pay for it need to! Believe me baby, it's a fantasy, it's a fallacy, it's bullshit.
438

Let's look at another theory: that it's only certain types of men who will pay for sex. Or a certain percentage. Not travellers' tales, not sex trips to Thailand. Because that's an acceptable form of paying, where you keep your dick erect and your balls still intact. But the day to day form – why do you think there's so many girls out there working? How do we survive? On each other? Get real! Who are the people who are going through all of these doors? Who are the people who are going to these escort agencies? What makes you think that these men aren't like everyone else. They are like you, like my brother, like my father … It's a misconception. Men who go out there, whether they get a blow-job, whether they get whipped, whether they get fucked, sucked, rimmed, felched, whatsoever – they are *not* going to tell you. It's sex. People do not talk about their bank balance and their sexual hang-ups. The two things that people don't discuss. They talk about what they owe, but they do not talk about what they earn. And they don't talk about their sexual fantasies and hang-ups. They may talk about their sexual experiences, provided they fall within the sphere of the normal world, but not their sex. They'll only tell you what they think that you want to hear. People do not tell you what they consider to be off the wall, unacceptable, or deviant, perverse – unless they want to and they know you're cool.

***

Most women think that a hooker cannot be a feminist, but I think I am. I consider myself a feminist because for me my first and foremost things are that I'm black and I'm a woman and those are things I pride myself on. I will not compromise on my womanliness or my blackness.

If women are supposed to be oppressed and so on, then let's use everything God has given us – our brains, our sexuality, every female power that we have. I don't want to be a man. I don't want to walk around covering up what I've got, which is hot, which looks fucking good – because when I ain't got it I'm going to wish I fucking had it. But I'm using that for me. If men are jacking off in the process, well, darling, so be it. But you're going to pay for the jacking off because you're going to see it, want it, and you cannot have it. I'm using it for me. You dangle that carrot and you use it to the hilt. Hey babes, if you can't handle looking at my nipples, well, darling, close your eyes. And if they hypnotise you when you do look, well I'm going to use that power. It's as simple as that. Women have always had the power. We give birth, we make men, and the hole they come out of is the one they spend their entire lives trying to get back into. We've been bred to lay back and think of Britain. Lay back and think of Britain? You clench your pussy muscles and use them. Use them, that's what it's there for. Not just to get fucking slack and push babies out. Get real. Use it to make sure you're not being used. If feminists think that you're debasing your sex, tough. Use whatever you've got and use it to the hilt.

The world revolves around sex and money. Women are the sex, men are the money, but because money is quite powerful, men think that they're the ones who are running the show. So at the end of the day women, if they're clever, let men believe that they're running the show but at the end of the day, darling, you always have to come back to where you came out from. And this hasn't ever changed – not through feminism, the sexual revolution – no way has it changed. The sexual revolution? Get real! At the end of the day men are men and women are women and the thing behind a lot of feminism is a lack of respect for men. I love men, I couldn't do without them, I think they're wonderful, but most of them are still arseholes because they're led by their dicks. Feminists see the weakness in males and they don't respect them. And men *are* very weak, but so are women and at the end of the day you have to respect people's weaknesses as well as their strengths.

What's happened now, the way women are demanding that men perform, in many ways it's an abuse of power. Some feminists are castrators. They're trying to make men into something else, they're trying to make men into slaves and who wants a slave? I've come to the conclusion that a true man is somebody who can take a fuck. I mean that literally. Women are designed by nature to take a fuck, we can take a fuck. So I believe if a man can take a fuck that's what makes him a man. Because we get fucked all our lives. So if a man can bend over and take a fuck, that's when you're a man. Women are more men than men could ever be. Not gender, but maleness. We're more man than men because we can take that fuck. Men take it in the outside world, but we take it both ways – in the outside world and physically too.

★★★

Being black and female in the Nineties, oh boy what a plus. I wouldn't want to be anything else. People have preconceived conceptions of what to expect, preconceived notions – you're a sex freak, you're blah blah blah. A girlfriend of mine sent me a client who she's known for a very long time: he's number two in a very large financial institution,
440

he even wore his school tie – Eton, of course – and along he came. I don't know what he expected, sure he knew I was black, so he came in, I offered him a drink, he was very shocked: 'That's very, very decent of you.' There was classical music on, Vivaldi's *Four Seasons*, that really shocked him too. He was shocked that I could speak English, he asked me, 'Where did you go to school? Your command of the English language is excellent ...' That gives me a buzz. I'm jacking off on that, purely because the conception they have of me as a 'black prostitute', it isn't like that. So you leave thinking, 'Wow!' because I will not give you what you expect, I will not pander to your preconception. And if someone did want that preconceived fantasy, the dumb black whore, I'd tell them to fuck off. That is just direct blatant, patronising and you cannot patronise me for any money in the world and if you do, darling, you pay dearly. Of course they all start off with those preconceptions. They don't meet black people, they certainly haven't touched one. Get real! Even if it is the Nineties. So being a black female in the Nineties – hey, use it to the hilt!

Being black and female, what power do you have? None. Nothing given. So what do you do? You take it. And that's what I do, that's what's my given right: I take it. And I love to meet people who get totally freaked out that you've got a brain. I love to see their faces. Totally freaked out. They don't think about fucking any more.

A friend of mine turned round to me and said, 'Black women have become more attractive.' I said, 'Bollocks, black women have always been beautiful, but now they're portrayed in a different way.' Before, black women were portrayed as big mamas, now they're portrayed as sophisticated, clever, beautiful. All of a sudden everyone's switched. And it makes a white man's dick look slightly harder, or better still, as hard as a black man's, because now he can keep a black woman, that's why it's good for the white man. Most white men, if they have a black girlfriend, their friends see them as some kind of stud. Before that we were supposed to be running buck naked in the jungle hitting each other over the head with stones, which was also the level of our sexuality. Now we can put on frocks and walk on fucking catwalks, all of a sudden we're sophisticated and sexy. Darling, we've always been like that. The difference is now we're fashionable.

If people give you a label, I say tear the arse out of it. You go through dilemmas where you think you have to play it down and be a certain way – fuck it! They've already given you that fucking label, so *do it to the hilt!* It's all labels. Most people, they look at a black woman and if a black woman is with a white man, she's got to be with him because of his money. Or it's age. If you look at a couple and one's older and the other's younger, then automatically, it has to be because of the money. It's sheer jealousy. So, they've given you the cap – then wear it! And wear it fucking good! Because at the end of the day it is sheer jealousy. The other day I saw this woman, long blonde hair, a big fluffy white fox coat, high-heeled black patent boots to the knees, tight black pants, and she was linked arms with a man who must have been seventy, with a walking stick, hunched over. And I thought: Good on yer! Because everybody would be thinking: What a tart, with that old man, but what they're really thinking is: Lucky fucker, I wish it was me. But who has the bollocks to say it? Okay, she was with him for the money – but who cares?

I don't think the race/sex stereotypes will ever fade away. It's back to dick sizes. Men are totally obsessed with the size of their cocks. Consciously or otherwise. You can compensate, you can buy cars, whatever, but you can never buy a big dick. All the money in the world, you can't buy an extension on your dick. But if you've got money and power, you can control the big dicks. The ones our wives want, and maybe we want too, deep down. So the white man has to keep the blacks down. We all know who's got the big choppers, and there's no way you can have a big chopper and money and power. Get real! Those small white dicks – they'd get extinct. I really believe that in the end that's what racism is about. It's a dick thing.

The majority of the people I see are WASPs, and we all know how WASPs think. I will not give you what you expect on that level. No way. You got that from my forefathers, my parents. But you have to realise that most of them are coming because you're black. So they expect a certain stereotype. And when they don't get that stereotype they are totally freaked and phased. So that makes them come back for more. They realise that you can speak, they realise that you are articulate, and they are totally freaked by it. They don't expect it. So all of what they came for has gone out of the window and you're now giving them something totally different. I give them what I want to give them – and they don't expect it and they love it. What I give them depends on how I feel on the day. Literally. How I feel on the day. On a sex level there are very, very few people that I'll actually have sex with. Penetrative sex. Even if you're paying me it has to do something for me and I have to like you and you've got to be good. He has to perform for me too.

WASPs do things just for the sake of being perverse. Whereas Jews, for instance, can be kinky cunts too, but it's in a more real way. More through sheer curiosity ...'I wonder how that works. Let's try.' With a Jewish man it's more, 'I wonder can I get my cock in that bottle – will it feel good, will it stick in there?' But with a WASP it's not whether or not they get a sensation, but just to be perverse. Doing the done

442

thing. 'I've done ABC, lets do XYZ.' No different to going to Ascot – it's what you're supposed to do. And pleasure? That word don't exist in the WASP vocabulary. Pleasure? Pleasure's getting a good thrashing at school, followed by a cold fucking bath. Which is why they never learn to wash their willies. That starts at age five, when they're sent off to boarding school. Who's going to pull back their cockhead and wash off all that smeg in freezing cold water? It disappears for starters. So they don't, and the rest of their lives they're still not washing and then they wonder why their wife won't fuck them. Smeggy cocks. It's camembert and brie up there.

***

Women who are sexually liberated and like dick, baby, they don't charge. Professional women who have mastered the game charge. And most of the girls that I know as professionals, in their own personal sexual lives they are more prudish than most straight goers. And more private than most straight goers. Because at the end of the day they're in the sex industry. They're giving so much, when it comes to their personal self, anyone cannot just have that. But people always ask you, 'You're in the sex business, how can you enjoy it with anyone else?' You just look at them and you think: Don't you believe that you men are that fucking great. Though if there was no dick tomorrow I'd top myself, I wouldn't know what to do, because I love men and I love dick, okay. But I'm being honest and realistic and men will say, 'But you do it with so many men, how can you still enjoy it?' Don't they understand that women are the best actresses on two feet? *Men* are the ones who cannot act. The only way they can act is in a fucking boardroom, in business. They cannot act in bed. They can't. So the girls who just like sex, they don't charge, they give it away.

I do like men. I honestly do. God, I could never be gay. I mean, women, we are bitches, put twelve cats in a room and they'll scratch each other to death. I love men, because I like sex and I like men to be men. I enjoy the maleness of men, their strengths, their weaknesses. I really do. I couldn't be a lesbian, because I like dick and another woman cannot fuck you. Simple as that. Women who can survive without dick, then good luck to them but at the end of the day men have a use and women have a use.

If you're a woman, be a woman, be true to yourself. If you want the dollars, say you want the dollars. If you just want a good shag because you want a good shag, say you want a good shag and you don't want the dollars. Say what you want otherwise you ain't gonna get it! Stop

443

the game playing. I can jack myself off, I've never met anyone who can jack me off better than myself. That's it.

Men are weaker than women. Women can hold out longer than men. Men get to a point where they have to ejaculate, they have to, they have to let it out, it's physically impossible for them to contain it any more, whereas with women it's a little bit more ... complex. You can take advantage of a man's weakness, sure, but come on, not totally, surely? Not totally – because then you won't have a man any more. It's like a bit of dough: you knead it and you knead it and you knead it, and after a while that dough doesn't have the same consistency. It's the same with a man. If you wear them out and wear them out and knead it and knead it, it will not be the same shape, it won't, you won't have the same man. And you wonder why he's not a man any more, and why his dick can't get up? Bitch, it's because you've worn it out, you've drained it. I know you might enjoy the draining, but you've got to give it time to replenish. It's there for the taking, but you've still got to give it time to repair.

What I've learnt with men is this: men are not driven by emotions, they're driven by money. That is the level where they most have to perform. They can get away with the cock bit. A man can always get away with a substandard fuck. Hump, hump hump, two pricks and a spit, and that's it. Because women are trained to bear it. It's only when we're sick of jacking off and we really want to come – then you've got to perform. But in the outside world a man's first priority is the financial stakes. Emotion is not going to keep him at home – money will. The reality of what it's going to cost him to be what he calls free.

★★★

Men are cannon-fodder. They can't be honest, they can't stand up and say, 'Okay, I was led by the pussy. It was good pussy, but I'm awake now.' They don't want to actually say that. They want to believe that the woman was genuinely in love with their brain ... Come on! What more do you need to pump up your fucking ego? They can't be honest about what they need to massage their egos, what they need to make them feel good, what they need to make them feel like men. So each year they trade in their model. And they add up the costs and ask themselves: Okay, can I afford an Aston this year as opposed to the Bentley Turbo? Deep down they really want the Aston, but they're thinking: Fuck, that Aston's a bitch to get serviced, so I'll go for the Turbo which has the prestige and the crystal decanter in the back ... And that's how they think in terms of women. The Aston is great, it's

444

phallic, pricklike, while the Turbo says more about your stature. So which is it? Which do they want? The phallic bit of cock or the solid role in society? And men want both, they want it all! So what happens is that that they keep the Turbo, the wife, in the garage and every now and then it's the Aston, the girlfriend, for a test drive. What they can't say is that they need both to cater for both aspects of what they want. That they need that rev, that vroom-vroom to get their dick going. And what happens if the wife says: 'I need an Aston too.' They'll tell her, 'You're a greedy bitch.'

I know this guy, he's got this ring through his cock. Through the hole. And when he pees it comes out both sides. So I wonder, how's he going to keep that from his wife? I ask him, and he looks at me like I'm mad. 'Don't be stupid, she doesn't see it.' 'So what happens when she's giving you a blow-job?' He looks at me: 'What blow-job? Don't be pathetic.' His wife doesn't get near him. I'm thinking, when I get married I want to see the deepest part of your fucking colon, mate. I want to see the lot! Because if you want to get anything else, I'm going to give it to you first. If I'm pregnant and he's got to pay for the pussy – Okay, I'll buy you the pussy. I'm sorry, I'm a tart, I've been there. Okay, here's £200 a week for pussy. This is the pussy you're going to get, I'll interview her, this is what I want you to give my husband. Give him a little speciality sometimes, he likes that ... I'm serious. I want to know what I'm buying, I ain't buying no pig in a bag. But then you men are such bastards you'll still go out and get some more on the side. Men have got to have something that [stage whisper] *you don't know about*. They don't even want it, necessarily, but they've got to be doing something that their wives don't know about. To be devious. Put one over her. What I say to women: get a little rent boy, let's see how he reacts to that. S/M, rubber, leather, see how that goes. Look, they're going to go out and get it anyway, so ...

Men always need an excuse. They can't just go, just walk out. They're not man enough to say, 'I've had enough of this.' They have to have a reason. The real reason is because it wasn't right in the beginning, but they can't say that.

Women will lie till they die. 'Oh, oh, oh' [fakes orgasm] – come on – who knows the difference? Women will never stop lying, because they've lied so much they don't even know the difference between a good fuck and a bad one. They are so used to going 'Oh, oh,' he's hitting the mattress and they're 'Oh, oh' ... for fuck's sake, tell him to start fucking and performing! Women are trained to lie. We are trained to serve, we are trained to be almost ... subservient. Then, if you turn round to your husband and say, 'I don't actually like the missionary position. I want you to turn me upside down, fuck me this

445

way, suck me that way,' then woah, you're Germaine Greer. All of a sudden you've burnt your bra, all of a sudden you are a fucking cropped-hair dyke feminist! Why? 'Cos you want a good fuck? Because you are demanding that your man perform? Because you are demanding that you don't want to keep going 'Oh, oh, oh'? So sweat when you're fucking me! Because that's what I want.

***

Blue movies, pornography, it's all geared for men. And that's why every man believes that his dick should be swinging at least to his knees because in the blue movies they all do. So every man thinks his dick is small, because the ones they see on screen are enormous. But in reality they just find these disabled people to put in these movies so everybody else feels bad. So these movies, they say all men have to have these big dicks, and all women want to be fucked perpetually for an hour. They make men think they have to be fucking in and out for at least an hour before a woman is halfway satisfied. Please, don't think about getting on me and doing that for an hour, because that will just cause friction and make the edge of my cunt feel like it's tearing. So please, don't even think about it.

I have this boyfriend out in Chigwell. I try to explain to him that he doesn't need to go on and on. I explain about build-up, about foreplay. I put it this way, I put it that way, every way possible to try to explain to him that it's not the actual fucking in and out, it's in the head. So I get to the stage when I just want to get fucked. But he cannot believe that if he's not going on and on I can get anything out of it. I tell him, 'You don't have to be on me for three days to make me fucking come! I'm coming before you get it in you fool!' But there's nothing I can say to him that makes him understand this. But it's the build-up. My brain is a cesspit. But he don't understand that. I'm in a restaurant, I'm jacking off. But because he watches blue movies and all this shit, he thinks that he's got to be on there for three days before you're even wet. I tell him, my brain's a cesspit, I'm already wet just looking at some cunt crossing the road. He doesn't want to know. I wish I could write him a pamphlet. You can have two hours of build-up and the act can be two seconds and you still come your lot! He won't buy it. I'm saying, 'Just put it in now!' And he's saying, 'No,' and I go, 'If you don't this is going to be a rape scene and you're going to get raped!' Men just can't think that way. They have this fantasy of what they think women want. Okay, they don't all have a loud mouth like me and they ain't saying it, but that's their tough shit. Men have

446

these warped ideas of what they think we should be getting. Just ask! 'Is that boring, is that good?' But most men are afraid to ask, they don't want to hear the answers. They're scared that you're going to say, 'No, it's not good, it's very boring.'

In my experience, and I've seen a lot of dicks, most dicks roughly are the same size. And anyway it ain't the size it's how you fucking swing it. Get real! One girl I know will not go out with a guy who's got less than eight inches. And she's a feminist. Her reason for saying that is that she believes that all men have their own specification for what type of woman they want, so she's decided that she's going to have her specification, and the first thing is an eight-inch dick. But if as a woman you say this, you say, 'Show me, pull it out, let's see if it measures up,' they're gonna say you're a freak, a nymphomaniac! Is there a word for a male nymphomaniac? Yeah. A normal healthy man.

***

I'll never get out of the Life. I like it. I like the power. That is the buzz. If I didn't like cocks so much I'd be rich. But unfortunately I do. The same way men can be pussy-whipped, women can be dick-whipped. You get a good fuck, you have a good come, it makes you weak. You wither. Within the sex industry, most women I know like cock, but most set up certain boundaries. I ain't like that. Hey darling, if you are a good fuck, I'm coming all over your dick. Because you've paid me, £500 whatever, so what? That's not it. I'm sorry girls, I'm really sorry to say this, but if it's a good fuck I'm not going to hold back. I'm going to come. But you're supposed to hold back, when money exchanges hands in this profession you're supposed to hold back.

In some ways I wish I was gay, because if you're gay you can't get weak with the dick and you have more control. So what I have instead that gives me control is my lack of liking for the money. But in hooking the money is supposed to be the whole thing. The dollars. The dick is irrelevant. Secondary. But I reverse that.

If I'm sucking and fucking when I'm ninety-five, and getting paid, I don't care. So long as I'm happy. If I'm with a man or not with a man, if I've got five kids, married, unmarried, attached, detached, single parent, I don't care. I have learned in life, and it's taken me twenty-eight years to realise it, that nobody can make you happy but yourself. What happens when I'm thirty-five, so long as I'm getting a kick in some way, so long as I'm getting my jollies off, I don't care. It might sound very irresponsible, it maybe sounds pathetic, but that is

447

what makes me live, what makes me want to live, the freedom and ability to be who I am and what I want to be.

By the world's standards of normal I've never been normal. So I'm warped? Sure, I'm warped. But, remember this, my warpedness is my strength.

People

A substantial number of these interviewees chose to assume a pseudonym for the purposes of this book, and appear here under those temporary disguises. It should be stressed therefore that in no case do these pseudonyms, chosen at random by the interviewees and the author, have any connection whatsoever to any actual individual who has the same name.

JERRY BALIN is an organiser of the Bristol Men's Forum, an open group meeting monthly which runs workshops on a variety of themes relating to masculinity. He is also involved in the annual Calston Park Men's Gathering and in Move, a campaign against male violence.

ARTHUR BANNER is 28. A Cambridge graduate, he has gone on to to a successful comedy career in radio, television and a number of high-profile sell-out countrywide tours.

INDIA BATTENBERG has been one of *Forum* magazine's regular contributors, writing up a wide variety of hands-on experiences in the sexual arena.

ROGER BOLTON worked as a lecturer in modern languages before his parallel career in the sex industry was splashed across the tabloids. He has worked variously as a scriptwriter, 'film arranger' and actor. He also heads the pressure group Public Eye, campaigning against censorship.

CLARE CAMPBELL has been a widely-read 'agony aunt', dealing with a variety of teenage and adult problems. She currently writes on human interest, often sex-related topics for the *Daily Mail* and *Marie-Claire*.

AVEDON CARROLL was born in America and centrally involved in the political and sexual activism of the late Sixties and early Seventies. Since moving to Britain she is a co-founder, with Nettie Pollard, of the campaigning group Feminists Against Censorship.

449

ADAM COLE is the publisher of *Electric Blue*, Britain's first softcore video magazine and part of the Paul Raymond empire.

MARIA CONCEPT swapped her liberal convent education for immersion in the hippie lifestyle before leaving her native California for life in one of south London's smarter enclaves.

SARA DALE and PETER MISSEN are the joint authors of *The Taste of Heaven*, a guide to safer sex. Dale won a certain notoriety when the Chancellor of the Exchequer Norman Lamont was forced to appeal to the public purse to aid him evict her from a flat he owned and at which she conducted her career as a masseuse.

NICK DAVIES is a mature student. He lives with Kate Heath.

LINZI DREW is one of Britain's best-known glamour models, a much-desired star of Page 3 and a wide variety of men's magazines. As a writer she has edited *Penthouse* and contributes to a number of magazines. A regular spokeswoman for the sex industry, she lives with Lindsay Honey.

CHRIS ESMOND is a teacher. A veteran of a variety of men's groups, and of the Rajneesh movement, he advocates a greater spirituality in male/female sexual relations.

DUNCAN FALLOWELL is a writer and journalist who mixes interviews with travel writing and fiction. He commutes between London and Palermo.

KITTY GADDING works in the media.

FRANKIE GODDARD lives in West London with her two daughters.

KATE HEATH worked on *Spare Rib* and *City Limits* before moving somewhat nearer the mainstream. She describes herself as a second-wave feminist, a position somewhat removed from the founding mothers of the early Seventies. She lives with Nick Davies.

LINDSAY HONEY graduated from rock 'n' roll to glamour photography via a successful career in sex films as a director, performer and cameraman, as well as making occasional personal appearances on the male stripper circuit.

IAN JACKSON ran Nightshift, the country's leading swing club, until the police, spurred by tabloid 'exposés', began targeting his regular get-togethers. He is currently editor of the men's magazine, *Risqué*.

ISABEL KAPROWSKI is responsible for a wide range of magazines –
450

notably *Penthouse* and *Forum* – published by the Northern and Shell group.

ALEX KERSHAW is a journalist and writer, frequently appearing in a number of 'style magazines'. His article on the 'New Lad' gave an original twist to the much debated concept of Nineties' masculinity.

JOHN LANKIEWICZ is a fellow of the London Institute of Human Sexuality.

PAULA LEWIS has spent five years running one of the country's most successful credit-card phone sex lines. She is currently studying to become a sex therapist of a more conventional type.

ARNOLD LINCOLN was one of the country's earliest sex educators, working since the Fifties to penetrate the national reticence as regards such topics.

ARAMINTA LOCKHEAD has been a punk band manager, a serious drug abuser and a writer and journalist.

GEORGE HARRISON MARKS is widely recognised as the creator of the British sex industry. A veteran of forty years of film-making and magazine production, his current projects include *Kane*, the country's best-selling spanking magazine.

TOMMY MCLEOD grew up in Scotland and discovered his sexuality aboard a succession of merchant navy vessels, on voyages that took him variously to the tanker war in the Gulf and thence to the Falklands.

ANNABEL MERLIN married young and well and has since parted from her husband. A creator, for a while, of lunches for City boardrooms, she now prefers simply to consume them.

JOHN MICHAEL was involved widely in the 'underground press' of the Sixties and early Seventies. At the same time he was a dedicated acolyte of the 'free love' philosophies of the era.

JANE MILLS is head of the documentary film department at the University of Sheffield-Hallam. She wrote the controversial, mould-breaking *Make It Happy*, widely accepted as the best teenage sex education guide yet to appear.

TRACEY MINTO was born six years too late for *The Female Eunuch* and just in time to have the Sex Pistols sing lullabies across her cradle.

OSCAR MOORE is the editor of *Screen International* magazine and the author of *A Matter of Love and Death*, a partially autobiographical novel of gay life and death in the age of AIDS.

SUZANNE MOORE is a regular columnist for the *Guardian*.

STUART MORRISON-WALSH was brought up in Belfast, lost his virginity in America and lives in London, working in a fast-food restaurant.

TUPPY OWENS is one of the best-known figures in in the world of British and international sexuality. She is publisher of the *Sex Maniac's Diary* and of the *Sex Maniac's Bible* and runs 'Outsiders', specialising in the sexual needs of the disabled.

JEREMY PATRICK spent ten years as a cavalry officer before quitting the Army for business. He is currently the owner and landlord of a public house in the West Country.

NICK PARTRIDGE quit Rank Xerox to work for the then newly established Terrence Higgins Trust, the country's leading AIDS information/advice centre. He is currently the Trust's head.

TED POLHEMUS is a social anthropologist who has written widely on the subject of clothes and sexuality.

NETTIE POLLARD was involved in the counter-culture of the early 1970s. A longtime researcher into the effects, or otherwise, of pornography on its consumers, she works with Avedon Carroll in the campaigning group Feminists Against Censorship.

HUGH PRATT combines his professional career as an engineer with his role as head of Men Against Pornography, an organisation devoted to counselling 'porn addicts' and campaigning against the dissemination of the material in question.

LYN PROCTOR is the editor, with her husband Henry Ferguson, of the magazine *Body Art*, a specialist journal devoted to body piercing, tattoos and similar human adornments.

MARGARET RAMAGE is a family and marital therapist working within the NHS.

MARCUS RIGGS is a priest and a gay man who runs a hostel for people with AIDS in the Kemp Town district of Brighton.

RONA and BARRY live in East Anglia and pursue an exhaustively all-encompassing sex life, whether in their own well-equipped dungeon or in the clubs of Europe's red-light districts.

MATTHEW RUSSELL moved through Eton, Oxford and medical school

452

before travelling to New York in the early Eighties and abandoning his education for the joys of hardcore self-destruction. A reformed character, he has returned to medicine and lives with his wife and daughters.

GUY SALMON was made redundant from his job in advertising and has begun training to become a barrister.

ELLEN SEVERIN abandoned the unpromising North of England for Ireland, although opting this time for Dublin, rather than the rural Ulster of her birth.

HAZEL SLAVIN works as a sex therapist, concentrating on aiding those of all sexes with their problems. She is also concerned with AIDS counselling and education.

CAROLINE STANDISH is a writer and journalist who combines her role as editor of a leading young women's magazine with regular forays into the world of men's magazine fiction.

ELINOR STARR works as a prostitute, plying her distinctly upmarket trade from a variety of smart flats. The advent of safe sex, she notes, has in no way diminished the appeal of her range of services.

NICK SUTHERLAND is a student.

CHRIS TURNER came out when he was 25, right in the middle of the most hysterical period of the burgeoning AIDS hysteria of the mid-Eighties. A former writer on *Marxism Today*, he currently works for television.

MICHAEL VERMEULEN is the editor of *GQ* magazine.

GRAHAM WEBSTER-GARDNER is the chairman of the Conservative Family Campaign. A power in the land under the Thatcher administrations, the campaign has lost something of its influence under the current government.

JEFFREY WEEKS is an academic, currently a visiting research fellow in the Social Work Studies Department of the University of Southampton. One of Britain's leading authorities on sexual politics, his books include *Sex, Politics and Society* (1981) and *Sexuality and Its Discontents* (1985).

KAYE WELLINGS was one of the primary researchers on last year's nationwide survey of sexual habits. Excluded from government funding it was saved by funding from the Wellcome Foundation.

KIM WEST has established herself as one of the country's most sought-after clothing designers, with a heavy emphasis on those styles more usually allied to the S/M and bondage worlds.

TONY WHITEHEAD is one of the founders of the Terrence Higgins Trust. He is currently working with Streetwise, an organisation dedicated to the needs of London's gay 'rent boys'.

RICHARD WHITFIELD is Professor Emeritus of Education at the University of Aston. He is also Chairman of the National Family Trust, which advocates the need for stable family relationships as the basis of a properly moral, and thus equally stable society.

TIM WOODWARD abandoned mainstream publishing for the more rarified delights of *Skin Two*, the best-selling S/M, bondage and fetishist magazine. He is also involved in the club of the same name and visitors to his Ladbroke Grove offices can browse through the selection of garments and accessories in the downstairs warehouse.